# *Operations Strategy*

## *Quantitative Methods and Applied Statistics Series*

## *ALLYN AND BACON*

*Barry Render, Consulting Editor*
*Roy E. Crummer Graduate School of Business, Rollins College*

*Readings in Production and Operations Management: A Productivity Approach*
Ahmadian, Afifi, and Chandler

*Introduction to Operations Research Techniques, Second Edition*
Daellenbach, George, and McNickle

*Managing Production: The Adventure*
Fulmer

*Business Forecasting, Fourth Edition*
Hanke and Reitsch

*Production and Operations Management: Strategies and Tactics, Third Edition*
Heizer and Render

*Cases in Business Statistics*
Klimberg, Arnold, and Berger

*Cases and Readings in Production and Operations Management*
Latona and Nathan

*Management Science, Fourth Edition*
Moore, Lee, and Taylor

*Micro Management Science: Microcomputer Applications of Management Science, Second Edition*
Lee and Shim

*AB:QM Version 3.0 Software*
Lee

*Service Operations Management*
Murdick, Render, and Russell

*Applied Statistics, Fourth Edition*
Neter, Wasserman, and Whitmore

*Microcomputer Software for Management Science and Operations Management, Second Edition*
Render, Stair, Attaran, and Foeller

*Principles of Operations Management: Building and Managing World Class Operations*
Render and Heizer

*Quantitative Analysis for Management, Fifth Edition*
Render and Stair

*Introduction to Management*
Render and Stair

*Cases and Readings in Management Science, Second Edition*
Render, Stair, and Greenberg

*Production and Operations Management: A Self-Correcting Approach, Third Edition*
Stair and Render

*Operations Strategy: Focusing Competitive Excellence*
Stonebraker and Leong

*Introduction to Management Science, Fourth Edition*
Taylor

*Brief Business Statistics*
Watson, Billingsley, Croft, and Huntsberger

*Statistics for Management and Economics, Fifth Edition*
Watson, Billingsley, Huntsberger, and Croft

*AB:POM Version 3.3 Software*
Weiss

*Production and Operations Management, Second Edition*
Weiss and Gershon

*A User's Guide to Business MYSTAT*
Young

# *Operations Strategy*

*Focusing Competitive Excellence*

**Peter W. Stonebraker**
*Northeastern Illinois University*

**G. Keong Leong**
*The Ohio State University*

**Allyn and Bacon**
*Boston • London • Toronto • Sydney • Tokyo • Singapore*

*Editor-in-Chief, Business and Economics:* Rich Wohl
*Editorial Assistant:* Jennifer Strada
*Cover Administrator:* Linda Knowles
*Manufacturing Buyer:* Megan Cochran
*Editorial-Production Service:* Raeia Maes
*Cover Designer:* Suzanne Harbison


A Division of Paramount Publishing
160 Gould Street
Needham Heights, Massachusetts 02194



**Library of Congress Cataloging-in-Publication Data**

Stonebraker, Peter W.
Operations strategy : focusing competitive excellence / Peter W. Stonebraker, G. Keong Leong.
p. cm.
Includes bibliographical references and index.
ISBN 0-205-14253-2
1. Production management. 2. Production management—Case studies.
I. Leong, G. Keong. II. Title.
TS155.S795 1994
658.5—dc20 93-44540
CIP

Printed in the United States of America

10 9 8 7 6 5 4 3 2 1 99 98 97 96 95 94

# Contents

# *Preface*

*The dogmas of the quiet past will not work in the turbulent future. As our cause is new, so must we think and act anew.*
—Abraham Lincoln

Over the past few decades, the foundations and institutions of American manufacturing and service operations have been terribly shaken. No doubt foreign competition is a contributor to the situation; however, the primary causes are much more complex and closer to home. The post-cold-war conversion of defense-related industries is certainly a contributor. Cultural, political, and educational processes may also be related. But even these factors are not sufficient to explain the downsizing of industrial giants and the changes in the way products are produced and goods and services are delivered.

This text argues that the current state of operations management results primarily because operations managers have not clearly defined and communicated an effective operations strategy. Corporate America has lost sight of the primary contribution of the operations function, that of adding value through the creation of goods and services.

The current situation is troublesome. Major U.S. corporations are extensively restructuring and the international trade balance, particularly in durable goods like automobiles, continues to undermine our economic stability. Financial arbitragers disassemble weak links from otherwise effective operations, only to have the remaining links collapse because of their interdependence. Productivity growth is measured by as little as three to five percent of productive activities, and new products are developed only after competitors have shown the viability of the product—causing the loss of precious months or years of market opportunities and many market-share points. More importantly, we have forgotten why we are in business—to serve the customer. For these and other reasons, operations managers must rethink our values, redirect our energies, and reposition our resources to regenerate our manufacturing, distribution, and service institutions.

Some companies and industries have already started the process; these provide examples of what to do and how to do it. However, others must plan and execute a significant recrafting. Still others must literally rebuild from scratch. This is the task of the operations manager. It is a formidable job, both in terms of magnitude and the associated risks. It is not for the faint-hearted and requires extensive knowledge and a foundation of experience; yet, the potential rewards correspond to the contributions made and the risks taken.

The operations strategies of corporations and the strategic thinking of operations executives provide a road map for this effort. However, initially, the foundation of definitions, conventions, and symbology must be reviewed for adequacy; only then can managers create the map. The goals, the routes, the direction and speed of travel, and the type of vehicle all must be specified. The map provides the structure; users must provide the appropriate strategic processes for the situation—and all situations are different.

*Operations Strategy: Focusing Competitive Excellence* challenges readers, whether practitioners or students, to review a manufacturing, distribution, or service operations environment with which they are familiar and to assess areas of potential improvement. Following the thrust of Skinner, Hayes and Wheelwright, Drucker, Goldratt, and Porter, this text identifies the need for and delineates a tentative map toward a new model, or paradigm, of effective operations strategy. This paradigm provides guidance for practices of the millennium, the year 2000, and beyond.

## *Organization of the Book*

The four parts of the book move from an introduction and definition of the strategic overview perspective to structure, infrastructure, and implementation concerns. The focus of these parts is to build a strategic overview perspective, and then to operationalize it.

Part I defines a strategic overview perspective of operations management. Chapter 1 identifies several reasons why operations management is *the* key competitive weapon in most businesses. Subsequently, the dimensions and processes of operations strategy are elaborated. These core definitions and ideas form a foundation to consider both structure and infrastructure components of operations strategy.

Part II concentrates on the structure considerations of operations strategy. The structure variables, including organization design, evaluation of capacity, facilities strategy, and operations systems design, integrate the longer-range content questions of operations management. These issues are the "hardware" of operations because they are difficult to change, at least in the short and mid-range.

Part III emphasizes the infrastructure considerations of operations strategy. The infrastructure variables, including operations planning, materials management, just-in-time, quality and customer service, and work force productivity are the "software" of operations. Because these variables are so closely intertwined with the structural variables, they all have strategic impacts.

Part IV focuses on continuous improvement and implementation topics. The management of processes to innovate and develop new technology is absolutely necessary to a world-class organization. Implementation guidance follows to provide a policy hierarchy. Finally, the future of operations management is projected as a strategic and continuous improvement process in Chapter 15, Operations Strategy 2000: Toward the Millennium. Each part of the book exemplifies an operations focus and uses a variety of pedagogic features.

## *Operations Focus and Thrust*

This book has been designed to explicitly focus the direction of the current and emerging operations strategy topics in several ways:

**Global Focus.** Each chapter begins with one or several introductory quotations, chapter objectives, an outline, and an introductory case. These features focus the interest of the reader toward key topics of the chapter and their relevance in the dynamic and global operations management environment. Chapter topics are founded in classical theory, yet the analysis is directed toward integrated and global dimensions.

**Integration of Structure and Infrastructure.** Following the introductory overview perspective, chapter materials introduce and then elaborate structure and infrastructure considerations. These foundations are integrated by the implementation- and continuous-improvement-oriented final part.

**Balance of Conceptual and Application Materials.** To ensure flexibility of usage, the text offers a thorough explanation of the conceptual foundations of operations strategy, followed by examples and applications. The approach of the text is to teach by example.

**Putting Together a Jigsaw Puzzle.** Perhaps the best analogy to the strategy definition and implementation process is the jigsaw puzzle. In operations strategy, there are many different sized and shaped pieces. A combination of methods is necessary to identify these pieces and put them together into the complex mosaic of an operations strategy.

### *Pedagogic Features*

This text uses a variety of pedagogic features to achieve its focus toward operations strategy:

**Graphic Presentation of Materials.** The materials are interwoven with more than 150 figures and tables, which supplement definitional and descriptive foundations by depicting and elaborating the ideas discussed. This text operates from the perspective that graphic depictions communicate far more effectively than words alone.

**Dramatic Examples of Materials.** Each chapter contains Applications Boxes of example operations situations and Decision Model Boxes that exemplify the scope and applicability of analytical techniques. In all, there are more than sixty application and decision model boxes.

**End of Chapter Discussion Questions and Strategic Decision Situations.** The end-of-chapter materials for each chapter include some fifteen to twenty broad-ranging and integrative questions. Additionally, some thirty-five strategic decision situations exercise both judgmental and computational aspects of strategic decision making. These questions and situations provide an integrative and judgmental supplement to the instruction process.

**End of Part Cases and Software.** A total of eight end-of-part cases offer either a conceptual overview perspective or a computational decision analysis of the material. The conceptual overview cases consider well-known corporations and are supported by discussion and research topics. The computational cases involve a continuously developing operations strategy situation at one firm and are supported by LOTUS 1-2-3 templates to faciliate case instruction and presentation.

**Detailed Instructor Manual.** The instructor manual contains answers to end-of-chapter and end-of-part materials. Relevant operations cases are referenced with comments on the relationship to this text, and a case-writing format gives a consistent structure for written exercises. Additionally, the instructor manual contains an explanation of the software templates.

## *A Note of Appreciation*

To our families, Eva, Katja, and Eric, and Lin and Michelle, whose love and patience have been the foundation of this effort.

To our faculty colleagues and mentors, who have played an important role in the conceptualization and development of this material. Among them are:

Rasoul Afifi, Northeastern Illinois University
W. C. Benton, The Ohio State University
William L. Berry, The Ohio State University
Kathleen Carlson, Northeastern Illinois University
Mei-Lung Chen, Northeastern Illinois University
David Collier, The Ohio State University
Charles Falk, Northeastern Illinois University
Donald Fogarty, formerly of Southern Illinois University at Edwardsville
Lori Franz, University of Missouri—Columbia
Tom Hoffmann, University of Minnesota
Jim Hutchison, The Ohio State University
Lee Krajewski, The Ohio State University
Robert Markland, University of South Carolina
Larry Ritzman, Boston College

Bill Ruch, Arizona State University
Peter Ward, The Ohio State University
Bill Werther, University of Miami

To our students, who have helped in much of the research and preparation of materials for this text.

Victor Berardi, The Ohio State University
Amrita Bhattacharyya, Northeastern University
Ken Boyer, The Ohio State University
Vic Garcia, Northeastern Illinois University
Dreama Perry, Northeastern Illinois University
Venkatesan Venkataraman, Northeastern Illinois University

To our reviewers:

W. C. Benton, The Ohio State University
Philip Y. Huang, Virginia Polytechnic Institute
Yunis Kathawalla, Eastern Illinois University
T. S. Lee, University of Utah
James R. Pullin, University of Central Florida
Peter Ward, The Ohio State University

To the many others who have offered suggestions and advice along the way. We express our heartfelt appreciation for your trust.

P. W. S.
G. K. L.

# Part I

# *Strategic Overview Perspective*

**Chapter 1**
*Operations Management: The Key Competitive Weapon*

**Chapter 2**
*Dimensions of Operations Strategy*

**Chapter 3**
*Operations Strategy Process*

**Case 1**
*Operations Strategy at Waste Management*

**Case 2**
*Business Planning at Elco Manufacturing*

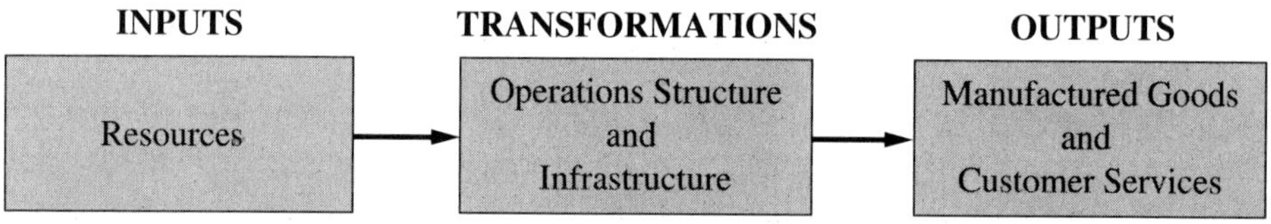
INPUTS
Resources
TRANSFORMATIONS
Operations Structure and Infrastructure
OUTPUTS
Manufactured Goods and Customer Services

# Chapter 1

# Operations Management: The Key Competitive Weapon

*There can no longer be any doubt that the United States faces a real and unrelenting technological threat—a threat that spans both commercial and military concerns. In markets from machine tools to semiconductors, U.S. industry has been battered by foreign competition. Indeed, in some cases, such as consumer electronics, foreign competitors have taken over entire industries that the United States pioneered and once dominated. . .*

*If we are to meet the technology challenges facing the nation, U.S. government officials and private sector leaders must forge new partnerships, accept new priorities and make long-term commitments.*
—John A. Young, Chair of the Executive Committee of the Council on Competitiveness and President of Hewlett-Packard Co.

*The internationalization and globalization of world markets has forever changed the way that companies must conduct business.* —Kon Sera, General Manager, Sumitomo's Communication Development Group

## *Objectives*

After completing this chapter you should be able to:

- Specify the importance and impacts of operations strategy.
- Define key terms pertaining to operations strategy.
- Describe the chain of transformations and apply it to various operations environments.
- Identify the four dimensions of operations management.

- Note the strategic and tactical variables of operations strategy.
- Describe the productivity impacts of operations strategy.

## Outline



## Introductory Case: The John Reed Story*

John Reed joined the First National City Bank in the mid-1960s, after completing a tour in the army and getting a master's degree in management. In 1970, John was selected to head the Operating Group (OPG), also called the bank's "back office," where all banking transactions were processed. At that time, much of the transaction processing involved manual data input and was very labor intense, slow, and error-prone. Costs due to lost availability of cash (not clearing the day's transactions) were 4% of total transactions, and unsolved cases (complaints) were close to 5% of annual transactions. The unsolved cases, however, were only the errors identified by customers; the extent of other errors was not known. Clearly, the OPG was a disaster.

After several months of evaluating his organization and its responsibilities, John received top management approval for a restructuring of Area I, the primary transaction

*Materials drawn from Harvard Business School cases (474–166 and 474–167); "John Reed's Citicorp"; Engardio and Einhorn, 1992; and Levinson, 1992.

processing operation of OPG. As crews repositioned equipment, many documents were found that had been tucked away in accustomed corners. The revised process was laid out like an assembly line. All entering documents came in through one area, where they were date stamped, numbered, and routed to specialized processing sections. When the processing was finished, the completed transactions were checked and dispatched at one "output" location. The quality and timeliness of transaction processing could be managed by comparing these input and output records. The physical reorganization was accompanied by a 30% downsizing of the OPG.

It took several weeks for the new structure to begin to function effectively, and, within several months, error rates and lost availability were dramatically down. This improvement, however, was accompanied by a loss of solidarity of the organization. When asked about the rationale of the reorganization decision, however, Reed stated: "I'm not talking about turning the operating group into a factory. I'm talking about recognizing that it is a factory, and always has been. The function isn't going to change, but the way we look at it and manage it must."

John Reed subsequently succeeded Walter Wriston as the Chairman of Citicorp (the parent organization of Citibank, previously the First National City Bank), where his principal task has been to develop a strategy to lead Citicorp into the twenty-first century. Though Citibank is the largest U.S. bank by a wide margin, it must compete in a global banking environment where the largest banks are Japanese, European, or Middle-Eastern. John devised a strategy he calls "bulletproofing," which includes building reserves from current earnings (rather than selling off valuable, but productive assets) and carefully controlling the cost of operations. In addition, Citibank is growing rapidly in Asia by introducing banking by phone and educating Asians on the use of personal debt.

However, the decade of the 1990s will likely be difficult for Citicorp. Their ranking, based on total capitalization, among the world's largest banks has slipped from the top five in 1986 to the low twenties by the early 1990s. The bank absorbed losses in 1991 and is constrained by the weight of a poorly performing mortgage portfolio. Walter Wriston's vision of making Citicorp the first truly global bank by the 1990s may have to wait. Yet, John Reed's ability to strategically manage the company in this dynamic business has been clearly demonstrated. Citicorp will adjust and prosper in the twenty-first century.

## *Importance of Operations Strategy*

Probably the most important change in business over the past several decades has been the increasing rate of change itself. For those who work in a particular environment every day, the changes may not be apparent; however, for those who experience the environment from time to time over several months or years, these developments are truly remarkable. The rapidity and subtlety of change have emphasized the threats considered by John Young in the introductory quotation and have made the development of an operations strategy an absolutely critical component for a company's survival. Further, John Reed's experiences as an operations manager and executive in Citicorp highlight the importance of operations skills in service activities. Such an operations focus of decisions, though not always popular, is sometimes necessary for the survival of a firm.

The operations environment is becoming more dynamic in many ways. Today, for example, a radio, toy, or computer game may be on the market for only three or four months, the length of one Christmas sales season. Thereafter, advances of product design, the manufacturing process, or customer tastes will result in replacement of the product by a completely new item. Additionally, many small and mid-sized companies are, for the first time, entering the global market. Because their traditional domestic markets are stagnant, these companies are using rapid communications (telephone and fax) to enter more lucrative global markets (Holstein and Kelly, 1992). Similarly, a college education was once regarded as a sufficient knowledge foundation to ensure lifelong relevance and employment. Today, however, most fields are changing so fast that the information of a college degree is now dated after only five to ten years and employees must return to school or participate in less formal education programs. An increasing number of people are changing professional fields two, three, or more times in a career and devoting major portions of their adult lives to personal education.

A few brief examples are offered in Applications Box 1-1 to suggest the scope and impacts of these recent developments in the global operations environment.

These brief examples suggest both the quickening pace and impacts of change on business. Simply, in many businesses, a competitive manufacturing or service operation must produce the highest-quality goods or services at a low cost and rapidly deliver them to global markets. Compared with just a few years ago, entirely new product lines are now widely used. Production, distribution, and service methods have dramatically changed. Companies just cannot produce goods or deliver services using the practices of an earlier era. Those that do are quickly driven out of business. Today, a firm must not only efficiently produce a top-quality good or service, but it must also respond to the rapidly changing global marketplace. The challenge for management is to adapt to the changing roles and requirements of this dynamic new environment (Kim and Miller, 1992).

For the first time in history, manufacturing, distribution, and service businesses are becoming competitors in a global struggle for economic survival. The developing pattern of regional trading blocs and customs zones will require a reevaluation of the opportunities and threats and a redefinition of business and operations strategies (Weihrich, 1990). Interdependence of resources and markets and the rapidly emerging communication technologies have forced industrial giants to restructure, often involving integration or downsizing. Global competitors must rely on several key strategies for success, including: responding to and influencing the environment, time-based competition, closeness to the customer, developing a strategic focus based on core competencies, and maintaining collaborative alliances. These strategic efforts must also encourage an international focus and must strive toward continuous improvement (Albin, 1992).

For example, IBM, Siemens, and Toshiba have formed a one-billion-dollar alliance to build a competitor for the next generation of computer chip. IBM, of course, is the world's largest computer and chip maker; Toshiba is Japan's second-largest chip maker, and Siemens is Europe's third-largest semiconductor house. This global enterprise is expected to invest eight years of research and development to define, by the year 2000, a 256-megabit memory chip. The trilateral team of researchers at an IBM facility in New York, reporting to a Toshiba executive, is expected to define the standard pattern for such emerging global ventures (Port et al., 1992).

## APPLICATIONS BOX 1-1 Snapshots of Global Operations

1. In the mid- and late 1960s, General Motors had more than 50% of the American automobile market and Chevrolet consistently produced the most popular car model each year. Today, GM has slipped to less than one-third of the market and Chevrolet has slipped to third place, behind Ford (first) and Honda (second).
2. Sam Walton built the Wal-Mart and Sam's Club chains from a single store into the largest retail operation in the world, changing the face of retailing management forever. Highly customer-conscious employees operate an inventory distribution system in which goods never stop moving. Wal-Mart demands that its suppliers meet exacting delivery schedules and cost-efficient practices—or it finds suppliers that can.
3. Computer technology was generally understood by the late 1930s, and early vacuum tube models were used in the 1940s. The transistor was invented in 1947; integrated circuits were discovered in the late 1950s; and computer chips were designed in 1971. The first PC was developed in 1975–1976 and marketed by Apple in 1977. Competition from IBM and others developed in 1980–1981 and new generations of equipment have been forthcoming every two years. Today's PC has more power than the mainframe of the early 1980s, and single chips can easily outperform earlier full-sized computers.
4. Throughout much of the twentieth century, most communications devices used copper wire because of its property of efficiently transmitting electric current. However, today fiber optics are used for many applications because the production of optical fiber requires roughly 5% of the energy needed to produce an equivalent amount of copper wire, and fiber optics permit improved ease of installation, higher volume, and efficiency of transmission. By the early 1990s, the impact of vehicle and portable telephone units and satellite communications became significant. Communities that are currently designing and installing telephone systems are invariably selecting a variety of "wireless" telecommunications formats.
5. As recently as the 1970s, mail ordering required a catalog, an order form, and a check or money order. Catalog orders required a week or more of mailing and order processing time before the item was shipped. Today, the use of the computer, telephone, cable television shopping services, and credit cards have made the catalog ordering process virtually instantaneous.
6. Though the postal service was founded in colonial days, competition in the delivery business was not started until the mid-1970s. More recently, overnight delivery of parcels and FAX transmission of printed materials have significantly reduced the required delivery time for many types of products and services. Simultaneously, the range of items that can be transported has been increased.
7. During much of the twentieth century inventory stock levels were calculated by using the "economic" quantity. This method worked acceptably when interest rates were relatively low. However, as interest rates rose dramatically in the 1970s and as efficiencies of process scheduling developed, materials requirement planning, just-in-time, and computer integrated manufacturing replaced the economic methods. In the words of one manufacturing consultant, "There's a whole new mind-set out there today."
8. The opening of the Berlin Wall in 1989 and rapid changes of governmental structure in Eastern Europe and the break-up of the Soviet Union have redefined available resources and strategic markets, both in the East and West. If these Eurasian nations are able to economically integrate, even partially, they will have available tremendous sources of highly skilled labor, extensive capital, and the efficiencies of large, well-organized markets. However, the strategic risks for businesses in this area are also high.

This text is designed to focus and integrate the diverse topics of operations management toward the formulation of a cohesive and globally oriented operations strategy. This chapter establishes a common foundation of definitions and concepts, and the remaining chapters elaborate on both current and emerging operations strategy topics. Particular attention is given to the identification of strategic variables and the interrelationship and management of those variables.

## *State of Operations Management*

The marketplace has changed dramatically in the twentieth century. Following the Great Depression and through the 1960s, the U.S. economy was able to absorb all domestic industrial production as well as many imported goods. But that supply-driven economic environment did not last. The efficiencies of automated production permitted the supply of higher volumes of goods, exceeding demand. By the late 1960s or 1970s a demand-driven environment developed in many industries. The implications of this shift for producers of goods and services are extensive and are being realized today. In the earlier supply-defined market, producers could use large capacities, high inventories, and maximum lot sizes to produce minimum quality items for a guaranteed market. However, success in a demand-driven market requires lower capacity, less inventory, highly flexible production, and high-quality goods to be sold in a very discriminating market (Drucker, 1992, p. A16).

The increased emphasis on service operations has had mixed effects. It has been 25 years since Daniel Bell (1969) optimistically pronounced the advent of the "post industrial" society. Bell envisioned that the dirty, dull, and difficult manufacturing jobs would be sent to other countries and that the more valued service jobs would be retained. Unfortunately, that's exactly what happened. The loss of manufacturing to offshore competitors has dramatically changed entire industries, such as automobiles, banking, consumer electronics, and steel. Recently, we have recognized the illusory nature of gains due to separating manufacturing and service economies (Drucker, 1986). If manufacturing is done primarily in foreign countries, the related support services (that is, financial, design, information systems, transportation, and the like) will also quickly be lost. This would leave only a minor portion of the final-market and after-market services for domestic employment. Such a situation is not acceptable; a healthy national economy requires a balance of domestic manufacturing and service operations, with clear involvement in emerging global markets. For these reasons, manufacturing must be a strong and dynamic part of a national economy.

Growth of American manufacturing and services toward global markets, however, has been sporadic. Measured by the gross national product, national productivity (the total national output adjusted for inflation and divided by the value of input resources) has historically grown between two and three percent per year. But that growth slowed in the 1960s and 1970s, and, in 1979, was actually negative. Since then, GNP increases have been sporadic, but at a lower rate than before 1960. Though labor productivity has more than doubled since 1960, manufacturing productivity increased by less than two percent in the decade of 1977–1986 (U.S. Department of Labor, 1988). These developments, plus the loss of blue- and white-collar jobs and rapid productivity advances of some foreign countries, have combined to suggest the loss of vitality of American manufacturing and service businesses.

Many U.S. corporate giants, among them Sears Roebuck, Eastman Kodak, General Motors, IBM, AT&T, and USX (formerly U.S. Steel), have announced extensive facility closings, corporate downsizings, and layoffs. Joint ventures of American and foreign firms and the outright ownership of American properties and businesses by foreign investors are increasingly widespread. This phenomenon, developed in the mid- and late 1970s, was initially based on petroleum dollars, but today other international consortiums are dominant in world financial markets. As noted by the introductory case, in 1986 Citicorp was the only U.S. bank among the world's five largest banks; but today, Citicorp is the only U.S. representative among the top 30 largest banks, which are increasingly Japanese, European, and Middle Eastern. Even at the level of the individual citizen, Americans have reinvested a much smaller proportion of their income in savings than have citizens of other nations. Low investment and lower productivity of capital have, in combination with other factors, resulted in a slower rate of research and development and slower product and process innovation.

A further, even more troubling, issue is the deterioration in the quality and type of individual knowledge contribution to productivity. John Silber (1989), the president of Boston University, identifies numerous evidences of the decline of American education. Perhaps most telling is that many corporations have found it necessary to create their own literacy and basic skills education programs for newly hired employees. According to one source ("Insights. . . ," 1991), one in five new hires is both illiterate and innumerate. Numerous others, including Marshall and Tucker (1992) and Thurow (1992) suggest that the traditional approach to education effectiveness (workers need to be able to follow simple written and oral instructions and exhibit obedience and discipline), which was the foundation of the mass-production economy of the 1940s through 1980s, is not relevant today. Both workers and teachers must set aside this bureaucratic model and move toward increased professionalism, performance measurement, and quality contributions (Prowse, 1992).

Similarly, investment by firms in new knowledge and research has waned. The issuance of new patents peaked in the early 1970s and by the 1980s, more U.S. patents were granted to foreigners than to Americans. Further, management is spending more time identifying short-range sources of profit than looking for sound bases of long-term growth. This is particularly apparent in the breakup of perfectly sound, but temporarily vulnerable companies through leveraged buyouts and other financial mechanisms. The subsequent gutting of the company's most valuable assets to reduce the financial exposure of the buyout team rarely contributes to anyone's good, except possibly that of the buyout team. Such practices lose jobs, diminish productivity, and create turbulence that slows research and reduces employee commitment; but they do not add real value. Several studies, summarized by Hayes and Wheelwright (1984, p. 13), have shown that such practices contribute little to sales, profitability, or growth. In fact, productivity is often degraded. In these and other ways, the employee knowledge contribution to productivity has deteriorated.

In summary, during the past several decades many American manufacturing and service organizations have lost ground. Loss of productivity, corporate downsizing, lower levels of financial and knowledge investment, and management emphasis on short-term and financial objectives, rather than long-term technological growth, have all contributed to languishing American productivity growth rates. Yet, amidst this gloom, some firms are showing that dramatic improvements are possible. Harley-Davidson, Motorola, Xerox, Hewlett Packard, Allen-Bradley, Cummins Diesel, and others have improved quality and focused on customer requirements. The "value factory," focused on giving greater value with existing products, is seen as a distinct American approach to the factory of the future (Kim and Miller, 1992).

This chapter has initially introduced a global perspective of the business environment and highlighted the importance of operations strategy. Subsequently, some foundational definitions and concepts of operations strategy formulation and contingency management are considered, and transformation management, the central function of an operations manager, is described. Several dimensions of the operations function are then suggested as an analytic framework and key measures of both operations efficiency and effectiveness are identified. Finally, the plan of the book is noted.

NO, it did not

## *Operations Strategy*

This text identifies both a conceptual and a computational framework for evaluation and decision making in global operations. All chapters have conceptual Application Boxes and Discussion Questions, and most chapters have computational Decision Model Boxes and end-of-chapter Strategic Decision Situations which exemplify and apply those concepts. Where used, decision models are conceptually described and computationally developed, but the focus is on the integration of these models as tools of judgmental decision making.

Initially, some common foundations of operations strategy must be established.

**Operations Management.** Operations management is defined as:

> *the effective management of value-adding transformation processes to efficiently integrate resources and achieve specified performance measures toward product/service, process technology, and market goals.*

Several of the terms in this definition are particularly important because they suggest an integrating perspective of the operations management field:

*Effective.* Effectiveness means doing the right job; it involves directing resources toward appropriate operations goals.

*Efficient.* Efficiency means doing the job right; it involves using resources in the best possible manner to reduce waste.

*Value-adding Transformation Processes.* A transformation process is a series of activities that change the state of input resources into product or service outputs and thereby add value.

*Integrate Resources.* Several resources, which are likely to be scarce or costly, must be mixed together in exact proportions or under required conditions to reduce waste or enhance product/service value.

*Achieve Specified Performance Measures.* Performance is evaluated by measures that are generally categorized by criteria of cost, quality, delivery, and flexibility.

*Product/service, Process Technology, and Market Goals.* The operations function makes a vital contribution to organization goals, stated in product/service, process technology, or market terms.

This definition of operations management clearly includes manufacturing, nonmanufacturing production (resource creation activities such as mining or agriculture) and service activities. Additionally, it identifies the linkage between transformation processes and the firm's goals. While manufacturing and nonmanufacturing organizations produce a physical product or good, service organizations provide intangibles, such as information, facilitate production, or add value to goods in many ways, including delivery, storage, exchange, and maintenance. Many service organizations, such as entertainment, financial, or consulting businesses, deliver services that have little, if any, durable content. The production of manufactured and nonmanufactured goods has traditionally been separated from distribution and service operations, because it deals with durable goods and requires "things" skills, whereas service systems are more concerned with people and behavioral skills. However, this differentiation is less important today, as companies create and deliver goods and services through integrated processes, rather than segregated sequential activities.

The operations management function is not new. Most of the great accomplishments and monuments to human civilization, including the Phoenician shipbuilders, the temples of Babylon, the Egyptian pyramids, the Great Wall of China, and Roman roads, as well as many less well-known projects, required an operations manager. So did many early organizations, such as governments, armies, or religious groups. The input resources of labor, knowledge, materials, and tools for these projects and organizations had to be integrated. Of course, the "tools" and environments were less complex then than today; however, the operations function is surprisingly similar.

**Strategy.** The term *strategy* originally derives from the Greek *strategos,* meaning "the art of the general"; however, many specific usages have developed. Skinner (1978) considers strategy to be a philosophy which "relates ends to means." Hayes and Wheelwright (1984) state that strategy must define the domain and allocate resources within that domain. Hill (1989) emphasizes the requirement to link marketing and manufacturing perspectives and to develop an aggregate corporate perspective. And Anderson et al. (1989) consider operations strategy to be a long-range vision consisting of the mission, objectives, policies, and distinctive competence of the firm. As used here, strategy is defined as:

> *the current domain and pattern of resource commitments to transformation processes, and planned improvements, as a means to achieve the distinctive competence and goals of the firm.*

Inherent in this definition are several components that should be noted and briefly amplified.

*Domain and Pattern of Resource Commitment.* The term *domain* describes a static territory or scope of interest of the firm, while the pattern of resource commitments defines activity within the domain.

*Current and Planned.* Strategy involves both the current domain and pattern of resource commitments as well as various types of planned future improvements.

*Transformation Processes.* The organization's activities change input resources to value-added outputs.

*Distinctive Competence and Goals.* A distinctive competence is a unique capability to add value through a transformation and thereby achieve or support organization goals.

The terms *policy* and *tactics* are closely related to strategy. Policy, which is generally defined as a *guide for implementation,* provides for cohesion, consistency, and continuous improvement of the operation, based on the strategy. Policy is more formal and implementation-oriented than strategy (see Chapter 14). Strategy and tactics are also closely interrelated, but tactics, defined as *detailed techniques or procedures applied in specific strategic situations,* can be differentiated from strategy in several ways, as noted in Table 1-1.

The distinction between strategy and tactics is best expressed as a continuum defined by several dimensions. Operations strategy identifies the domain and resources of the organization and addresses its distinctive competence in the long run. It views the environment as a globally interactive system of competitors for resources and subjectively evaluates the effects of changes in the pattern of resource commitments. Strategy actively positions resources within the firm's domain and implements resource transformation processes to achieve distinctive competence in an uncertain environment. Strategy further suggests the need for consistency, both vertically and horizontally, within the firm to achieve effectiveness and efficiency. Alternatively, tactics suggests short-term planning and activities that are more local, specific, certain, and repetitive. This distinction may inaccurately suggest that strategy is applicable only to top management and mid-sized or larger corporations. Though these environments are, and will continue to be, strategic in nature, because of the complexity and dynamism of today's business environment, smaller firms and lower-level operations functions must, for survival, increasingly develop and use a strategic perspective.

**TABLE 1-1 The Continuum of Strategy and Tactics**

| Dimension | Strategy | | Tactics |
|---|---|---|---|
| Time frame | Long-term | ◄──► | Short-term |
| Scope | Focus on global | ◄──► | Focus on local |
| Environment | More uncertain | ◄──► | More certain |
| Value systems | Subjective, judgmental | ◄──► | Mechanical, heuristic |
| Information needs | General, external | ◄──► | Specific, internal |
| Regularity | Continuous, yet irregular | ◄──► | Periodic, repetitive |

**Contingency Management.** This approach to operations strategy follows the theories of contingency management. That school of management thought rejects the universal application of set management principles in favor of situational variables. The manager adjusts the appropriate variables to achieve the best combination for the situation, which is, in essence, a strategy. According to one proponent of contingency management: "The effectiveness of a given management pattern is contingent upon multitudinous factors and their interrelationship in a particular situation" (Shetty, 1974). The interactivity of contingently managed variables is encountered throughout this book.

Several common terms (such as *transformation processes, resources,* and *goals*) are used in the definition of both operations management and strategy. Similarly, contingency management involves an integration of aggregates to achieve an acceptable combination or strategy. For this reason, strategy is considered the sine qua non (without which nothing) of business, and operations is the sine qua non of strategy. Input resources, transformations, and added value are a central part of the strategic domain and distinctive competence of an organization. Because, in most cases, operations manages this process (specifically by producing, for example, high-quality goods at a reasonable cost), the argument may be put forward that operations is *the* key competitive weapon of a business.

## *Chain of Transformations*

The preceding definition of operations management identified a transformation as the change of input resources into value-added outputs. Products and services are created through a series of such transformation activities, ranging from raw material extraction or creation to customer delivery. This series of activities is called a *chain of transformations,* or more simply, a *product chain.* Generalized, it may be described as five types of linked activities: primary resource creation, parts building, assembly, product distribution, and delivery or service to customers. Those firms which extract and create primary resources, such as minerals or chemicals, are classified as *nonmanufacturing goods producers.* Firms involved with parts building and assembly are termed *manufacturers.* Distribution and customer delivery services deal primarily with location and physiological transformations, but also with information, physical maintenance, and installation, and are considered to be *services.* Management of the flow of goods and services on the chain of transformations is central to the operations management function (Tuscano, 1992).

### *Types of Transformations*

Operations management adds value through one or more of seven transformation activities. Those transformations are extraction, physical transformation, location, physiological transformation, information, exchange, and storage. Five transformations (extraction, physical transformation, location, physiological transformation, and information) are directly related to stages of the chain of transformations, although several transformations are likely to be present, to some degree, at each stage of the chain. Two other transformations, exchange and storage, link different stages of the chain of transformations. Location transformation is a specialized stage of the chain (distribution), and it also generally occurs throughout the entire chain. The primary and secondary transformation activities are shown for each link of the chain in Figure 1-1. Additionally, the transformation activities are described in detail.

*Extraction transformation* refers to the creation or gathering of primary resources through various methods, including mining, the extraction of basic elements, cutting

| Types of Operations | | Transformation Activities | | | | |
|---|---|---|---|---|---|---|
| | | Extraction | Physical Transformation | Location | Physiological Transformation | Informational |
| | Raw Materials | | | | | |
| **Nonmanufactured goods** | CHAIN OF TRANSFORMATIONS ↓ | | | | | |
| Primary Resource Creation | | P | | S | | |
| **Manufacturing** | | | | | | |
| Parts Building | | | P | S | | |
| Assembly Operations | | | P | S | | |
| **Services** | | | | | | |
| Product Distribution Operations | | | S | P | | |
| Delivery/services to customers | | | S | S | P | P |
| | Customer | | | | | |

Legend:
P: Primary transformation.
S: Secondary transformation.

*Note:* Exchange and storage transformations may occur at each stage of transformation.

**FIGURE 1-1 Types of Operations and Associated Transformation Activities**

forestry products, harvesting crops, husbandry activities, and fishing or hunting for food.

*Physical transformation* refers to changing the chemical, biological, or physical state of one or several different resources. For example, pulpwood is physically transformed to paper, and iron ore is physically transformed to steel.

*Location transformation* involves transporting a service or good, such as information or defense, from one location to another and, if necessary, accomplishing the appropriate installation and initial servicing. The air-lifting of disaster relief supplies and personnel involves the locational transformation of both goods and services and setting up facilities to distribute those goods and services.

*Physiological transformation* involves a variety of health-related and similar services, including medical service, insurance, exercise, and psychological well-being. A health club or medical doctor offers physiological transformation services.

*Information transformation* changes the state or availability of data to the consumer. Telephone information services reduce the need to buy many phone books, and television adds value for consumers in many ways, ranging from informative and educational information to advertisements, motivational information, and entertainment.

*Exchange transformation* refers to facilitating the payment for and receipt of value. Examples include the exchange rate paid for transforming one currency to another and the cost of facilitating a transaction with either checking services or credit cards.

*Storage transformation* involves a transformation over time which assures that the state of a good or service is retained. Examples are lock-up services and bank vaults.

The transformation process is the "technical core" of a business and a major part of the firm's domain. For example, extracted resources of iron ore, coal, and limestone are mixed with technology, energy, capital, and labor in specific proportions for producing different types of steel. That steel, with the addition of labor and capital, is then machined and assembled into components and finished goods, usually by other firms. Distribution services deliver the product to the customer and often provide installation and maintenance. The process of mixing resources at each stage adds value to the output, such that it is greater than the sum of the inputs. However, a transformation may not add value—it may be destructive. Of course, destructive transformations will not be pursued for long. The amount of added value may be tallied in a number of ways, but, ultimately, value must be recognized by a sufficient number of persons (the market) to make continued operation worthwhile. Thus, at each sequential step of the chain of transformations, the changed product or service state adds value.

## *Vertical Integration*

Although integration of different transformations along the chain is possible, it must be carefully managed to be successful. For example, a major fast food restaurant operator owns a cattle ranch and a potato farm to ensure stable quantities and qualities of input resources. Similarly, a major retailer owns part or all of several durable goods manufacturers, a dessert restaurant chain owns a bakery, and a major hospital runs a nursing school. These linkages along the chain of transformations make good sense because they stabilize supply or ensure standardization and quality of input resources. Vertical integration along the chain of transformations is generally feasible if three conditions are met: the product volumes must be the same and be generally high, the process technologies must be similar, and product quality must be similarly defined. Thus, whereas it is reasonable for an automobile manufacturer to own a tire plant, the auto manufacturer would not likely run a rubber plantation.

The human skills required to create a resource or to build a good are not likely to be those required in the sales or customer servicing of the final product. Although one firm has successfully reorganized its customer service activity and now has the toll-free customer service telephone number ring directly on the factory floor (Chase and Garvin, 1989), this practice may be difficult to implement. Such an innovation would permit operations people, who are likely most aware of product qualities and capabilities, to deal directly with customer suggestions and complaints; however, extensive training in customer relations should be provided.

The greater dynamism and complexity of today's operations require separation of different types of transformations and smooth linkages between the stages of the chain. In an earlier era, a single person, a farmer or crafts worker for example, could perform all activities along the chain of transformations. However, increased specialization of products/services, process technologies, and markets has limited the potential for vertical integration and required that different stages of the chain be accomplished by different persons or organizations.

Thus, the transformation process can be viewed as a sequential series of activities, starting, in many cases, with extraction. Inputs of capital, energy, and knowledge are transformed into an output good, which moves through location, exchange, and storage transformations. The output good becomes a resource input for the next cycle of production activity. The process is repeated through the product chain until the good or service is provided to the final customer. At each stage of the transformation process, or at each link of the chain, value is added by the input of resources. Several sequential transformations may be accomplished by one firm, or by various branches of a firm, and some products or services may bypass parts of the transformation chain. One link of the input–transformation–output cycle is shown in Figure 1-2. Note that Figure 1-2 is a more specific representation of the logo of this book. Figure 1-2 includes a location, exchange, and storage loop to link several processes along the chain of transformations. Alternatively, the logo more generally specifies the transformation activities through operations structure and infrastructure.

There are obvious advantages to integrating parts of the chain; however, there are also difficulties of managing products or processes that are inherently different. For example, the American steel industry has not been able to sustain vertical integration. Similarly, horizontal integration of various steel product markets is limited because of differences in those markets. This creates a tradeoff between the efficiencies of integrating transformation processes or markets and the inefficiencies of managing very different and complex environments. Communications and information technologies facilitate these linkages and encourage integration, within limits.

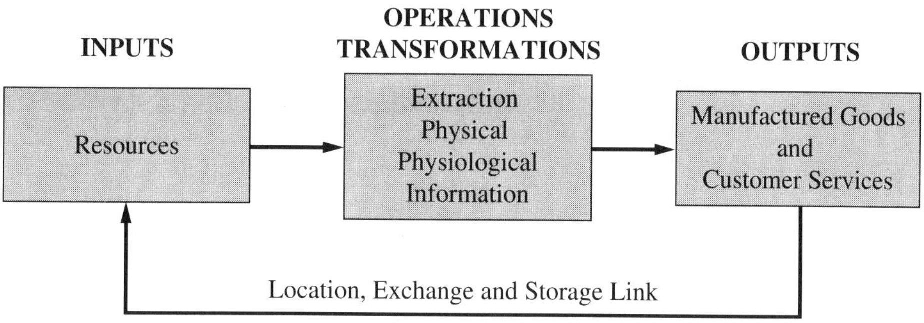


**FIGURE 1-2 The Input–Transformation–Output Cycle**

## *Dimensions of Operations Management*

In response to the complex and unsettling developments of the global environment, operations managers have turned to those things which they can directly control. Many operations managers, even senior executives, protest the very tight constraints on operations decisions, including legal, regulatory, ethical, and situational limits. For example, various federal and state laws define the limits of effluents and pollution, require compliance with safety standards and work rules, and establish guidelines for employment and compensation actions. In addition to constraints set by the government, constraints may be set by the marketplace, employees, the owners of the firm, or other external or internal interests. However, within these constraints, operations managers do set and implement goals, do build and manage production and service delivery processes, and do specify standards of performance, both for their own actions and for their responsible activities. Four dimensions define the sphere of action of operations management: level of interaction, operations management function, critical resource, and focus of operations decisions.

### *Level of Interaction*

Figure 1-3 represents the interactivity of four levels of corporate management with the external environment. Note that the titles and specific functions are likely to change from firm to firm and among business environments, but the basic function of these activities is invariably present, and, when generalized, is often quite similar among various business, not-for-profit, and government environments.

The four general levels of the organization are categorized as top management, general management, specialist staff, and functional activities. These levels are shown as four planes intersecting a cone, each having an interface with the external environment. At the top of the cone, the chief executive officer (CEO) and board of directors (BOD) provide overall strategic direction and leadership of the firm. They are assisted by several general management directors (sometimes called vice presidents) in the sales, finance, human resources, and operations management functional areas. In some organizations, these four general staff functions are subdivided. Those directors supervise a core of

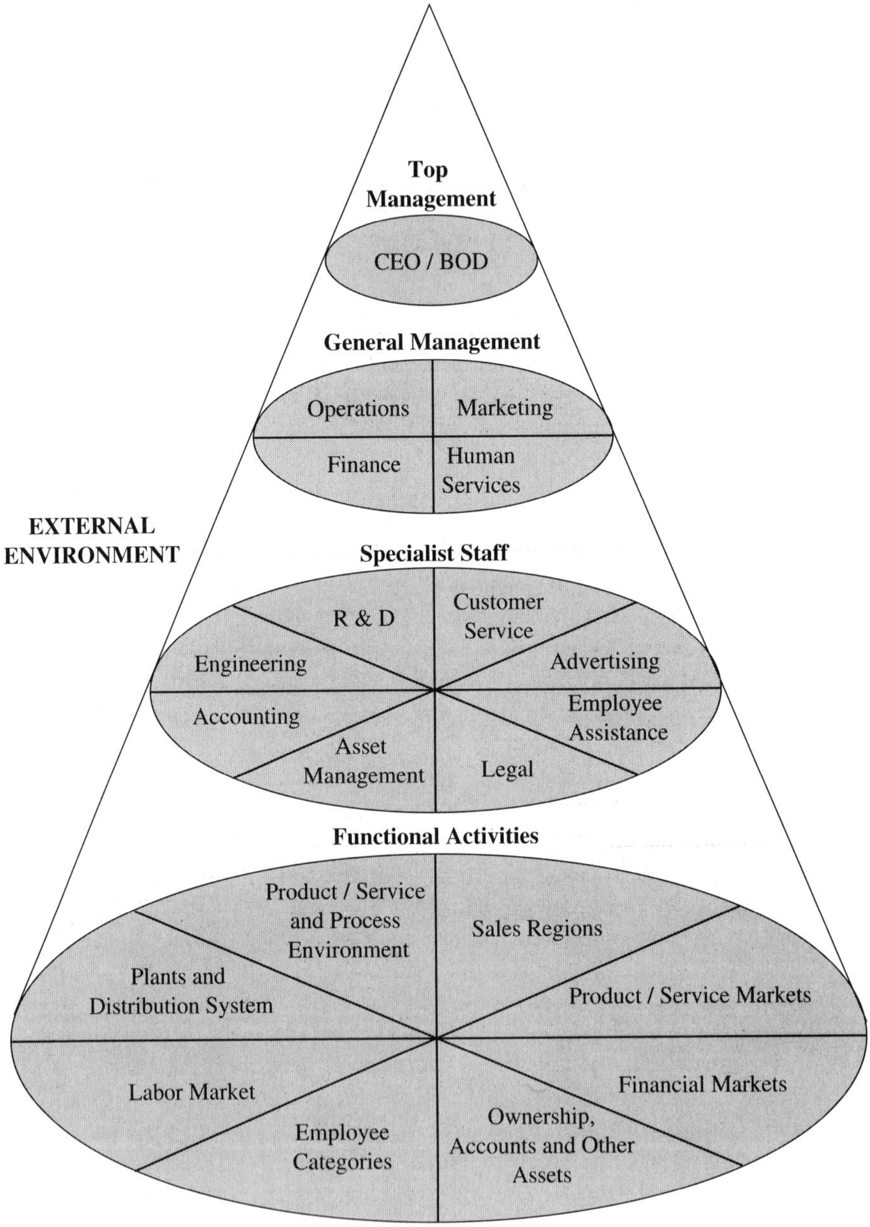


**FIGURE 1-3 The Organization Hierarchy**

specialist staff, including legal, engineering, accounting, advertising, and others. The specialist staffs within the operations area may include engineering, research and development, scheduling, planning, quality control, materials, and maintenance. Though a specialist staff member usually reports to a general staff member, the specialist's duties often require a purview across several different general staff functions. This management and staff organization supervises the functional activities, which is where production occurs. In the operations area, for example, functional activities often include the production plants and distribution system. Smaller organizations may have only three or four supervisory layers while larger organizations may have ten or more layers. Additionally, one supervisor may have several or as many as thirty or more subordinates, resulting in a "tall" or a "flat" organization hierarchy.

The organization hierarchy changes shape and configuration periodically. Through much of the twentieth century, organizations increased in size. However, a greater proportion of the growth during that period resulted from the addition of general management and specialist staff functions. More recently, many organizations have downsized by eliminating middle management and staff functions and by transferring the necessary tasks to the functional activities where they can be more efficiently accomplished. For example, in the mid- to late 1970s, one American automobile manufacturer had more than 20 layers from the CEO to the line employee, though the recent downsizing has significantly reduced the number of layers of that firm.

Figure 1-3 emphasizes the need for vertical and lateral communication among levels of the organization and for interaction with the external environment. The operations manager must establish, utilize, and maintain these linkages with top management, other directors, and, of course, with the operations specialist staff and managers in the operations function. These interactive processes both constrain and empower the operations manager. The level of interaction is the first dimension of operations management.

## *Operations Management Function*

The definitions of operations management and the chain of transformations emphasize three additional dimensions of operations management: the operations management function, the critical resource, and the decision focus. These dimensions of operations, including the level of interaction, are shown in Table 1-2 and are discussed in this section.

Numerous elaborations of the management functions have been published since Fayol first identified (1916, translated to English in 1949) the functions of the manager as planning, organizing, commanding, coordinating, and controlling. Operations managers, however, tend to narrow these five functions to two, which, though sometimes stated in different terms, are capability building and implementation. Capability building functions identify and evaluate (planning) resource commitments and fit those commitments to areas of the organization domain such as skills, knowledge, and tasks (Stalk et al., 1992). The experiences of a growing number of major corporations suggest that capability building may be the most important source of competitive advantage in the coming decades (Ulrich and Lake, 1991). Implementation directs and controls the ongoing transformation process. Thus, capability building and implementation are both distinct and interactive. Capability building activities are separately developed, and then selectively implemented. Simultaneously, implementation of the technical core of the business is continuously managed, but feedback permits further capability-building improvements. Capability building is directly associated with the "effectiveness" part of the management definition and with structural activities, while implementation is more closely related to "efficiency" and with infrastructure activities. In fact, the effort committed to capability

**TABLE 1-2 Four Dimensions of Operations Management**

| Level of Interaction | Operations Management Function | Critical Resource | Decision Focus |
|---|---|---|---|
| Top management<br>General staff<br>Operations specialist staff<br>Operations functional activities | Capability-building<br>Planning<br>Long-range<br>Mid-range<br>Short-range<br>Fitting<br>Implementation<br>Direction<br>Control | Land<br>Topography<br>Water routes and harbors<br>Mineral<br>Energy<br>Capital<br>Money<br>Equipment<br>Facilities<br>Labor<br>Physical<br>Skill<br>Knowledge<br>Data<br>Information<br>Technology | Structure<br>Organization design<br>Capacity evaluation<br>Facilities strategy<br>Operations system design<br><br>Infrastructure<br>Operations planning<br>Materials management<br>Just-in-time<br>Quality and customer service management<br>Productivity and work force management<br>Management of technology |

building, compared with implementation, may vary over time, depending upon the strategic emphasis of the firm (Hamilton and Singh, 1992).

Capability building incorporates planning and fitting to define the domain and distinctive competence of the organization. The domain can be viewed in physical terms (market location or range of products/services) or in knowledge terms (information products/services and process technology), but it must establish a territory, field of action, or area of knowledge. Planning activities gather and evaluate data over various time frames and are primarily used to develop internal capabilities for subsequent implementation. Planning horizons for some operations may be as short as three months or as long as ten or more years. Fitting adjusts the organization, based on a plan, for better congruence within its domain. Implementation involves product or service transformation in the technical core, and ultimately offers a value-added good or service to the external environment. The subfunction, direction, establishes tasks and interactions, while control is used to monitor and evaluate the performance of the transformation process.

The planning process drives fitting, and, ultimately, the implementation process. Planning activities are differentiated by time period. Long-range planning is usually defined by the length of time necessary to develop a new product, commonly two or more years. Short-range planning is the period within which a production schedule cannot be changed without costly disruptions, usually from the present to one to three months in the future. Mid-range planning, roughly those one to three months out to two years in the future, is a period of "soft" commitments. The length of the long-, mid-, and short-range planning periods varies among business environments. Dynamic industries, for example computer software or communications, may have a short-range plan to 30 days and the long-range plan might start at six months. More stable industries would involve a short-range plan to six months and a long-range plan that started at three or more years in the future.

## *Critical Resource*

The third dimension of operations management is the resource that is committed or managed. Resources are generally categorized as land, capital, labor, and knowledge; however, several subcategories shown in Table 1-3 can be further defined. Consistent with the definition of operations management, a single resource will rarely be used alone, because there is little opportunity for the synergy of a value-added transformation. However, the availability of (supply) or requirements for (demand) resources varies over time; thus at a particular time or in a particular situation, some resources are more important than others. These specific resources are critical to the operations function.

For example, in the most general terms, before 1800 land was the critical resource in most parts of the world, because it was central to the primarily agrarian economies. Control of the fertile valley bottoms and the land adjacent to waterways and natural harbors was particularly important. However, during the nineteenth century, as colonial empires developed and colonies provided readily available land, capital became the critical resource, because it was required for commercial insurance and transportation (shipping and railroad) operations. By the late nineteenth century, production processes and assembly-line techniques required large numbers of workers, facilitating the organization of unions. Labor emerged as the critical resource. Finally, during the later part of the twentieth century, the labor contribution to production changed from physical to knowledge input. Today, in many business environments, knowledge or technology is the critical resource used by operations (Drucker, 1992, pp. 95–104).

Within a specific company, for example, a major oil company, various parts of the organization depend on each resource. The exploration for and management of oil reserves involve land and knowledge, while various types of shipping or pipeline operations involve capital and knowledge. The labor contribution is heavy in drilling operations and pipeline construction. Finally, refining is technology- and capital-intense. Note that many oil companies structure their organizations to separate these different resource management environments. However, in many, though not all, areas of the oil business, the greatest risks or uncertainty are associated with knowledge; thus, knowledge would likely be considered to be the most critical overall resource.

In most industry and service areas, knowledge has emerged as the key resource of the operations function. Effective value adding through a transformation process requires the use of specific technologies, often in combination with other resources. Without the knowledge contribution, however, these activities would quickly fail.

## *Focus of Operations Decisions*

A fourth dimension of operations is the decision focus, representing the major operations management decisions. Structure issues include such capability-building concerns as organization design, capacity evaluation, facility strategies, and operations system design. These issues are primarily identifiable in the long- and mid-range planning and fitting functions, though they clearly are also related to implementation. Infrastructure issues of operations management include operations planning, materials management, just-in-time, quality and customer service management, and productivity and work force management. These issues are primarily associated with implementation functions; however, again, they are interrelated with capability building. These structure and infrastructure topics will be further discussed in Chapters 2 and 3, and are the basis for the organization of this book.

Though an argument could be made that structural issues are only strategic and infrastructural issues are only tactical in nature, it would be a mistake to accept that emphasis, because the two areas are extremely interrelated. For example, the scheduled delivery of a product, built to a required quality standard, is clearly an infrastructure issue; yet an extensive capability-building effort, including operations system design, organization design, operations planning, and other structural concerns contributes extensively to a quality control program. As many manufacturing and service firms have recently found, it takes several years or more of capability building to achieve an effective quality control program.

## *Measures of Performance*

Ultimately, the output of the operation must be measured, though the measurement process may be difficult, time consuming, and, in some cases, of arguable relevance and benefit. Productivity measures, defined as outputs divided by inputs, are initially helpful because they directly relate to the added value of the transformation, as shown in Figure 1-2. But, because of the difficulty of measurement, productivity evaluation may not be as helpful as expected. For example, at the highest level, gross national product measures the output of a nation; it is useful in comparing the performance of several nations or in assessing the growth of one nation over time. But GNP may not be as useful today as it once was, because it does not include the value of education or training activities. As noted, knowledge is an increasingly important resource input in most operations.

Similarly, at individual and group or corporate levels, it is easy to measure the amount of labor and machine input, which, coupled with output per period, would give a measure of productivity. But, while such measures are relevant to parts fabrication, they are not readily adaptable to knowledge inputs, for example a computer programming environment. This difficulty prompted Vaughn Beals, CEO of Harley-Davidson, to comment: "Measuring productivity is a total frustration. Any numbers I could quote, the accounting department might choke on. We just have to look at gross measures: we count all the motorcycles that go out the door, then we count all the people working in the plants. . ." (Willis, 1986). Productivity measures should be maintained to evaluate the operations function, but the limits of productivity data should also be recognized.

Because of these limits, more specific performance criteria, associated with the accomplishment of the *competitive priorities,* are used to evaluate the operations manager. Those competitive priorities are cost, quality, flexibility, and delivery. The cost of an operation may be measured in terms of per-unit or per-job total costs, or categorized as direct material, overhead, or labor costs. Quality is often measured by the internal scrap rate or the warranty return rate. Flexibility relates to the responsiveness of the production process to change. For example, flexibility is measured by the time it takes to respond to a customized order or to modify an assembly line to produce a new model. Finally, delivery may be measured by percent on-time, on-specification delivery performance. Classic doctrine (Skinner, 1974) states that it is difficult to focus on more than one, or perhaps two, of these criteria at a time in a particular facility, though recent methods suggest that effective operations management may be able to achieve two or more of the criteria. This topic is discussed in detail in Chapter 2.

Each of these four criteria is reasonably controllable by the operations manager and can be stated in terms of efficiency and effectiveness. Efficiency measures might involve the amount or percent that a particular job was delivered below the bid, the percent scrap, the percent on-time, on-specification delivery rate, or the number of hours of equipment down time due to process changeover. Effectiveness measures consider the level of customer satisfaction and retention due to reasonable costs, responsiveness to customer requirements, convenient delivery (for the customer) schedules, or a product/service that satisfies the customer. Thus, operations performance is measured by the efficiency or effectiveness of the resource transformation process as defined by the competitive priorities of cost, quality, flexibility, or delivery. Such measures may be of one machine or work area or of the entire company. The widespread availability of decision support systems suggests that realistic strategic applications to the value-adding chain are possible (Shapiro et al., 1993).

## *Plan of This Book*

This book is divided into four parts, each of which addresses a major aspect of operations strategy. Part I gives the general and definitional foundations of operations management. Subsequent parts consider structure topics, infrastructure topics, and strategy implementation. The final chapter of the book integrates a conceptual focus with a more general future vision of the operations function. At the end of each chapter, there are Discussion Questions and, as appropriate, Strategic Decision Situations. At the end of each section, there are two cases: a conceptual case and a more computational case.

Part I, entitled "Strategic Overview Perspective," introduces operations management as "The Key Competitive Weapon" (Chapter 1). This chapter has provided the definitional foundations of the book, an overview of the chain of transformations, and the four general dimensions of the operations management function. Chapter 2, "Dimensions of Operations Strategy," further addresses these areas and the concept of managing and reducing the impacts of trade-offs among defined decision variables. Chapter 3, "Operations Strategy Process," offers a nuts and bolts approach to the development of an operations strategy and concludes with the linkage to policy. The end-of-part cases "Operations Strategy at Waste Management" and "Business Planning at Elco Manufacturing" highlight and apply the concepts in Part I.

Part II, entitled "Structure Considerations of Operations Strategy," consists of Chapters 4 through 7. Chapter 4, "Integration of Organization Design," discusses organization design, perhaps the most directly controllable variable for operations managers. Contingencies are identified under which various structural approaches are most effective. Chapters 5 and 6, "Evaluation of Capacity Strategies" and "Facilities Strategy," note the required capacity and plant and equipment assets for capacity assurance, and then identify facility planning and location strategy issues. Chapter 7, "Operations System Design," considers the three classical approaches to process design, and then describes several emerging approaches, interrelating product design and process technology. Chapter 7 also serves as a transition to the infrastructure topics in Part III. The end-of-part cases, "Facilities Strategy at Courtyard by Marriott" and "Capacity Evaluation, Facilities Strategy, and Operations System Design at Elco Manufacturing," apply these materials.

Part III, entitled "Infrastructure Considerations of Operations Strategy," consists of Chapters 8 through 12. These chapters address the implementation topics. Chapter 8, "Operations Planning," integrates the long-, mid-, and short-range scheduling activities. Chapter 9, "Improving Materials Management," discusses strategies of integrating and administering materials management activities, including purchasing, inventory, and distribution management. Chapter 10, "Just-in-Time," discusses the strategies of materials and work scheduling, push and pull systems, and improvement of operations through JIT methods. Chapter 11, "Quality and Customer Service Management," integrates total quality assurance with customer service satisfaction, and Chapter 12, "Productivity and Work Force Management," considers strategies of job structuring and task design. The end-of-part cases "Motorola—In Pursuit of Six Sigma" and "Operations, Inventory, and Quality Planning at Elco Manufacturing" elaborate the concepts and decision models of this part.

Part IV, entitled "Implementing Operations Strategy," consists of Chapters 13 through 15, which serve as a summarization and overview. Chapter 13, "The Management of Technology," describes the methods of encouraging technological development and innovation. Chapter 14, "Policy—The Guide to Implementation," identifies a step-by-step approach to policy implementation. Chapter 15, "Operations Strategy 2000: Toward the Millennium," assesses where operations management is today and where the field is going. While Chapters 13 and 14 are very methodical and structured, Chapter 15 is more speculative and abstract. End-of-part cases entitled "As GM Goes, So Goes the Nation" and "New Product Development at Elco Manufacturing" are designed to apply the materials of this part.

## Summary

The operations function is, perhaps arguably, *the* key competitive resource or weapon of a business. Certainly in many businesses the distinctive competence of the firm is defined by its manufacturing or service operations. The resource selection and value-adding transformation processes are key to the distinctive competence of those firms and often fall within the purview of the operations manager. Performance of the operations function is measured in terms of production/service delivery cost, product/service quality, process flexibility, and customer delivery. Though other functions have gained increased visibility in recent years and the operations function has sometimes languished and been misunderstood, few firms can be successful in today's turbulent environment without an effective operations function and without an insightful and contingently defined operations strategy.

The operations manager is deeply involved in the definition and implementation of that strategy. Those processes involve interaction in various directions, the management functions, the critical resources, and decisions in at least several of the decision focuses. These dimensions serve to identify the purview of the operations manager, and, more importantly, that of operations strategy. Further, they focus the central, if not key, competitive weapon of the firm. As Wassweiler (1991) states:

> *The factories with a future have shifted their traditional focus from finance and marketing to manufacturing and they are regaining their momentum in American industry.*

## *Discussion Questions*

1. Describe several examples of recent changes in a business with which you are familiar that affect the nature of markets, products, or production processes. Describe the operation, why its management is necessary, and how you expect it to continue to change.
2. Briefly note several reasons why operations strategy is of particular importance today.
3. Identify the operations manager who works for your firm, school, or another activity that you are familiar with (if necessary, refer to a recent business magazine article). Elaborate on how that operations manager functions to achieve the specified terms used in the definition of operations management.
4. List and briefly describe in operations terms three activities that used operations management functions before 1900, other than those noted in the text. Support these activities as operations by relating them to the dimensions of operations management.
5. Differentiate and show, with examples, the relationship of strategy and policy, and of strategy and tactics.
6. Show how the concepts of operations management and strategy are interrelated and overlapping.
7. Why is operations management considered to be the "key competitive weapon"? Give an example from your experiences or readings where operations is key to competitiveness and where it is not.
8. Identify seven operations transformations and relate those transformations to the stages of the chain of transformations. Use these terms to describe a business with which you are familiar.
9. What limits the integration of the chain of transformations? Give an example of an integration that would likely be successful, and one that would likely fail.
10. List five specific persons in the organization (by their position title) that the operations manager should communicate with and suggest one specific item of mutual interest or concern with each.

**11.** What are the functions of the operations manager? Give examples of each.

**12.** From your experience or readings, differentiate the time frames of long-, mid-, and short-range planning in two specific operations environments.

**13.** Identify a company or business and describe and support the critical resource for the operation of that business.

**14.** By what criteria may the operations function be evaluated? Give examples of the different evaluative criteria.

## References

Albin, John T. "Competing in a Global Market," *APICS: The Performance Advantage.* January 1992, pp. 29–32.

Anderson, John C., Gary Cleveland, and Roger G. Schroeder. "Operations Strategy: A Literature Review," *Journal of Operations Management.* April 1989, p. 133.

Bell, Daniel (ed). *Towards the Year 2000, Work in Progress.* Boston, Mass.: The Beacon Press, 1969.

Chandler, Alfred D. *Strategy and Structure: Chapters in the History of the American Industrial Enterprise.* Cambridge, Mass: MIT Press, 1962.

Chase, Richard B., and David A. Garvin. "The Service Factory," *Harvard Business Review.* July–August 1989, pp. 61–69.

Drucker, Peter F. "The Changed World Economy," *Foreign Affairs.* Spring 1986, p. 768.

Drucker, Peter F. *The New Realities.* New York: Harper & Row, Publishers, 1990.

Drucker, Peter F. "The Economy's Power Shift," *The Wall Street Journal.* September 24, 1992, p. A16.

Drucker, Peter F. "The New Society of Organizations," *Harvard Business Review.* September–October 1992, pp. 95–104.

Engardio, Pete, and Bruce Einhorn. "For Citibank, There's No Place Like Asia," *Business Week.* March 30, 1992, pp. 66–68.

Fayol, Henri. *General and Industrial Management* (trans. Constance Storrs). London: Isaac Pitman & Sons, 1949.

Fogarty, Donald W., Thomas R. Hoffmann, and Peter W. Stonebraker. *Operations Management.* Cincinnati, Ohio: South-Western Publishing Co., 1989.

Hamilton, William F., and Harbir Singh. "The Evolution of Corporate Capabilities in Emerging Technologies," *Interfaces.* July–August 1992, pp. 13–23.

Hayes, Robert H., and Steven C. Wheelwright. *Restoring Our Competitive Edge.* New York: John Wiley & Sons, 1984.

Hill, Terry J. *Manufacturing Strategy: Text Cases.* Homewood, Ill: Irwin, 1989.

Holstein, William J., and Kevin Kelly. "Little Companies, Big Exports," *Business Week.* April 13, 1992, pp. 70–72.

"Insights—The 21st Century Challenge: Is America Ready for It?" *Focus.* National Center for Manufacturing Sciences, December 1991.

"John Reed's Citicorp," *Business Week.* December 8, 1986, p. 90.

Kim, Jay S., and Jeffrey G. Miller. "Building the Value Factory: A Progress Report for U.S. Manufacturing," Boston University Research Report Series, October 1992.

Levinson, Mark. "Honey, I Shrunk the Bank," *Newsweek.* February 3, 1992, p. 38.

Marshall, Ray, and Marc Tucker. *Thinking for a Living: Education and the Wealth of Nations.* New York: Basic Books, 1992.

Port, Otis, Richard Brandt, Neil Gross, and Jonathan Levine. "Talk about Your Dream Team," *Business Week.* July 27, 1992, pp. 59–60.

Prowse, Michael. "Is America in Decline?" *Harvard Business Review.* July–August 1992, pp. 34–45.

Sera, Kon. "Corporate Globalization: A New Trend," *The Academy of Management Executive.* Vol. 6, No. 1, 1992, pp. 89–95.

Shapiro, Jeremy F., Vijay M. Singhal, and Stephen N. Wagner. "Optimizing the Value Chain," *Interfaces.* March–April 1993, pp. 102–117.

Shetty, Y. K. "Contingency Management: Current Perspectives for Managing Organizations," *Management International Review.* Vol. 14, No. 6, 1974, p. 27.

Silber, John. *Shooting Straight: What's Wrong with America and How to Fix It.* New York: Harper & Row, 1989.

Skinner, Wickham. "The Focussed Factory," *Harvard Business Review.* May–June 1974, pp. 113–121.

Skinner, Wickham. *Manufacturing in the Business Strategy.* New York: John Wiley and Sons, 1978.

Skinner, Wickham. *Manufacturing: The Formidable Competitive Weapon.* New York: John Wiley and Sons, 1985.

Stalk, George, Philip Evans, and Lawrence E. Shulman. "Competing on Capabilities: The New Rules of Corporate Strategy," *Harvard Business Review.* March–April 1992, p. 57–69.

Steiner, George A., and John B. Miner. *Management Policy and Strategy.* New York: Macmillan Publishing Co., 1977.

Thurow, Lester. *Head to Head: The Coming Economic Battle Among Japan, Europe, and America.* New York: William Morrow, 1992.

Tuscano, Diane M. "Manage the Supply Chain," *APICS—The Performance Advantage.* October 1992, pp. 34–38.

Ulrich, Dave, and Dale Lake. "Organization Capability: Creating Competitive Advantage," *The Executive.* Vol. 5, No. 1, 1991, pp. 77–92.

U.S. Department of Labor, Bureau of Labor Statistics. *Monthly Labor Review.* Washington, D.C.: U.S. Government Printing Office, January 1988.

Wassweiler, William. "The Factory with a Future," *APICS—The Performance Advantage.* September 1991, pp. 26–28.

Weihrich, Heinz. "Europe, 1992: What the Future May Hold," *The Academy of Management Executive.* Vol. 4, No. 2, 1990, pp. 7–18.

Willis, Rod. "Harley-Davidson Comes Roaring Back," *Management Review.* March 1986, p. 20.

# *Chapter 2*

# *Dimensions of Operations Strategy*

*An organization can survive so long as it adjusts to its situation; whether the process of adjustment is awkward or nimble becomes important in determining the organization's degree of prosperity.*
—James D. Thompson and William J. McEwen, 1958, p. 25

*The feasible alternatives range in one continuous space, which is often as big as the business environment itself.*
—An Operations Planner

## *Objectives*

After completing this chapter you should be able to:

- State concisely the original basis for strategy.
- Identify the dimensions of the domain and the environment.
- Elaborate the product/service- and process-focused models of strategy formulation.
- Describe the operations strategy development process.
- State the productivity paradox and suggest ways to address that paradox.
- Identify a hierarchy of actions to fit operations strategy.

## *Outline*

## Introductory Case: "There's Something about a Harley!"*

Harley-Davidson can rightfully be called an "American legend." It is the only survivor among numerous domestic motorcycle manufacturers in the 1950s. The company has gone through several crises in its almost 90-year history; however, the crisis of the mid-1980s was perhaps the most difficult. Simultaneously, that crisis is the most significant because of the strength with which the firm recovered. Despite heavy U.S. Government tariffs on foreign competitors, in 1985, Harley-Davidson was only several hours from being required to file for bankruptcy or face court-directed liquidation. Harley's survival was due, in part, to dumb luck, but also because "there's something about a Harley."

Some products, and the Harley-Davidson motorcycle is certainly one, have a mystique, a special relationship with their customers that results from the nature of the product, the production process, or the marketing methods. Corvette automobiles, Apple computers, and L. L. Bean camping and outdoors gear may also have such an identity. However, few products in American history have been able to sustain this powerful, often personal, relationship of the product, its design, and the market as well as Harley-Davidson.

*Materials drawn from Willis, 1986, and Reid, 1990.

The Harley-Davidson Company visibly supports charities, such as the muscular-dystrophy foundation, and has numerous apparel and equipment franchises. However, there is more to the mystique than charities or clothing franchises. As a Harley-Davidson T-shirt articulates: "Harley-Davidson—If I Have to Explain, You Wouldn't Understand." Though such visible activities help, the something about the Harley has more to do with product design (metal—not plastic—fenders, the vibrating "heart," and the throbbing "voice"), the process (a local job shop competing against the high-tech automation of imports), and the after-market services (Harley Owner's Groups—HOGs, tours, identity, and individualism). Though some of these activities may be perceived as marketing gimmicks, the design of the product and the nature of the manufacturing process give substance to the uniquely defined domain of Harley-Davidson.

In the mid-1970s, Harley came under pressure from imports as foreign companies started to build and export to the United States motorcycles in the "heavy" (greater than 750cc) classification. However, the company's difficulties also resulted from other factors, including quality problems, poor inventory management procedures, difficulties with dealership groups, product identity, and design questions. Simply, Harley-Davidson was losing its domain.

The revitalization of Harley-Davidson involved the identification and evaluation of these and other corporate assets, the buy-back of the corporation from a conglomerate by a group of dedicated executives, and support for rather extensive belt-tightening from unions, employees, management, and financiers—even the President of the United States. Harley-Davidson has survived this crisis; it has resecured its domain and its distinctive competence. Harley-Davidson is now expanding production because the company cannot build all of the motorcycles demanded by the market. The Harley is on a roll again.

## *Origin of Strategy*

As the experience of the Harley-Davidson Company suggests, the definition and implementation of operations strategy are extremely complex and subtle processes, which vary extensively between industries and among competitor firms. The environment and the corporate self-definition contribute significantly to these processes. This chapter elaborates the definitional, descriptive, and environmental background of operations management given in Chapter 1. The origins of strategy are described, and several models of strategy are defined. The strategy dilemma is then presented, and a process to address that dilemma is considered. Subsequently, a model of operations strategy to fit the organization with its environment is developed.

### *Principle of Competitive Exclusion*

Though the concept of operations strategy may appear to be a recent development, in fact, as Henderson (1989) comments, the origin of strategy is derived from life itself. In 1934, Professor G. F. Gause, known as the "Father of Mathematical Biology," proposed the principle of competitive exclusion, which states, "No two species can coexist that make their living in the identical way." When two species compete for the same resource, without constraints, one specie will eventually displace the other. Following Darwin's laws of natural selection, some species become extinct, while others adapt to their surroundings and survive. This process has bolstered the tremendous variety of life on earth. Each specie is encouraged to develop a domain or territory and several usable resources, which, taken together, constitute a distinctive competence. Thus, the concepts of the domain and critical resource of an operation, which define distinctive competence, are derived from a biological interpretation of the origins of life.

Though these evolutionary processes may take millions of years, active pursuit of a strategy can hasten the process. Strategy is directed toward identifying and evaluating a situation and developing a plan to create, hasten, or compound a distinctive competence or a competitive advantage. It is the commitment of resources to build the capabilities of the firm or to implement a value-adding transformation. As Thompson and McEwen note in the introductory quote, the nimbleness of the process is the key to assuring the prosperity of the firm. Such efforts would include investment in research and development of a new product or service, the discovery and implementation of a new process technology, or reorganization of sales regions to enter a new market. For example, in the late 1970s, Coors Brewing Company evaluated their regional distribution area (west of the Mississippi River) in view of the increasing threat of companies with powerful national distribution systems. Coors redefined its strategy toward the development of a national market domain.

## *Strategy—Applied Competitive Exclusion*

For success, a strategy must overcome the inherent inertia of the environment and the advantage that naturally accrues to a defender. Military operations, a very measurable environment, suggest that a three-to-one advantage, or some other factor, such as a technological advantage, is necessary to overwhelm a defended position. In most other environments, however, success may depend upon less definable and less measurable cultural or behavioral factors and include, as in the case of Harley-Davidson, the mystique of the product.

Because of the difficulties of overcoming inertia or of gaining control of a hostile domain, the existing strategic relationships will likely continue for years with minor and often unmeasurable variations. Alternatively, if a strategy is either highly successful or a failure, change will likely occur rapidly. For this reason, most competitive environments typically experience long periods of relative stability during which organizations build capabilities (plan and fit) and develop their distinctive competence. For example, Lincoln Electric Company, a maker of transportable electric motors and welding equipment, has a very stable product, process, and market. After a strategic refocusing of the relationship of labor and management in 1934, the firm's strategy has since been relatively stable. Company energies are directed toward internal efficiency and growth through capability-building, including planning and fitting activities.

However, when risks of strategic change are reduced, such as by the emergence of an empty domain due to market or political collapse, a technical discovery, or mismanagement of resources, periods of rapid strategic development occur. Examples of such dynamic change include the emergence of the markets of Eastern Europe and the former

Soviet Union, the North American Free Trade Agreement (NAFTA), the European Community, and the Pacific rim markets. Manufacturing and service delivery examples include the recent precipitous growth of computer technology, the emerging linkage of the communications and entertainment industries, the use of customer data bases, and the tremendous changes in process technology due to automated equipment controls and laser tools. Dramatic shifts in product/service definition, process technologies, or market penetration ensue. This pattern of long periods of stability followed by rapid and dynamic change is found in all areas of competitive interaction, including business, politics, military, and ideology. From a global perspective, Drucker (1992) suggests that business is entering a twenty- or thirty-year cycle of turbulence.

In summary, during periods of stability, capability-building activities predominate. The risks of change in the product/service, process technology, and market domains of the organization are high. However, during periods of turbulence, rapid and proactive implementation of change is necessary. The labor turbulence at the General Motors Lordstown assembly plant in the late 1960s is a classic example. Industrial engineers, using methods developed over the prior 40 years, refined assembly line operations to the point that a worker's task cycle repeated at 30-second intervals. But by the late 1960s and in the Lordstown situation, the needs of the labor force had changed. More educated workers rejected the monotony of a fast-cycle line, leading to a direct confrontation with management over job definition and production process management (Lee, 1974).

Thus, in strategy, the appropriateness of capability-building and implementation activities are, themselves, contingently dependent upon the dynamism and complexity of the environment. In one situation, capability building should be preeminent, whereas in another, implementation should be pursued. Carroll (1982, p. 17) acknowledges the importance of strategic capability-building activities, but concludes that "the cumulative effect of a successful performance (implementation) strategy is devastating, but is rarely accorded its due." More recently, Stalk et al., (1992) emphasize the very significant cumulative effects of capability-building efforts at Wal-Mart.

## *Structure and Process*

A strategy contains elements of both stable structure and dynamic process, either of which, depending on the situation, may take precedence. These elements, in the aggregate, are called the *strategic architecture* of the firm (Kiernan, 1993). This dichotomy is expressed in the terms of the definition of strategy; that is, the stable nature of the "current domain and pattern of resource commitments" to transformation processes, contrasted with the "planned improvements to achieve the distinctive competence and goals of the firm." The organization preserve represents the stable component of strategy, which is often associated with implementation activities, and the planned improvements incorporate the dynamics of strategy, often of a capability-building nature.

### *Organization Preserve*

The structural or stable approach to strategy defines the organization preserve as consisting of organization boundaries, within which are the domain, deployed resources, an area of distinctive competence, and the technical core. These and other parts of the organization preserve are shown in Figure 2-1.

The domain (the area within the organization boundary) is defined as an "environmental field of action" or an area in which the organization is committed. It includes the definition of products/services, process technology, markets, and mechanisms to interface with the external environment. The domain is defined by a boundary consisting of barriers, portals, and buffers. Barriers prohibit entry to or exit from the organization. Portals are designed to facilitate the flow of resources into and out of the organization in a controlled manner. An example would be the labor market portal to acquire appropriate labor resources, which is managed by Human Resources. Buffers are designed to establish a constant interaction with the environment, for example, sales representatives or automated bank teller machines. Boundary-spanning functions regularly interface in various functional areas with the organization environment. Many organizations, for example, are members of trade associations or interest groups to interact both informally and formally with industry and government.

The organization deploys its resources within the domain to protect its implemented transformation processes (the technical core) and its capability-building efforts (its distinctive competencies). Some areas within the domain may not be actively pursued due to constrained resources, and thus are "void." To avoid duplication of effort or failure to accomplish necessary tasks, interactivity and congruence of deployed resources are encouraged. The positioning of deployed resources may be structured or amorphous, but all resources are directed toward enhancing the distinctive competence and the technical

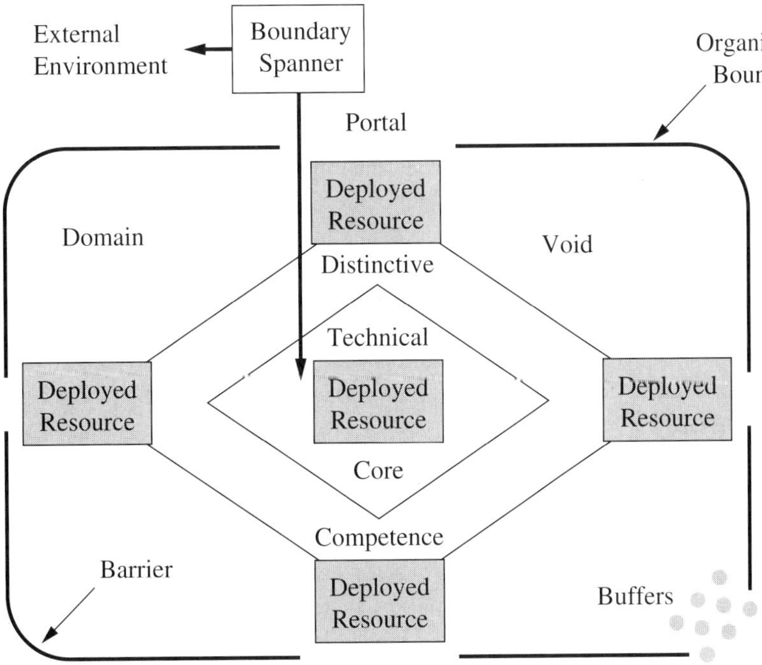


**FIGURE 2-1 The Organization Preserve**

core. Of course, the external environment contains other organizations with similar preserves.

A bank, for example, might define its domain as its services, the processes to provide those services, the market to which it caters, and the capability-building activities (such as investments, market research, design of quality services, and employee skills) that it undertakes. Within the bank, the deployed resources (tellers, and so on) implement the transformation process and various staff functions provide specialized services to this technical core. Distinctive competencies are used to build capabilities, such as the strength of an investment or resource portfolio. Boundaries, barriers, buffers, and portals ensure that interaction with the environment occurs in a controlled manner. Interactions with outside organizations, for example, with the government and banking community, are accomplished by boundary spanners such as lobbyists and information services. This description of the bank is a very physical representation of the organization preserve. However, most organizations, including banks, could use similar techniques to define their domain in terms of knowledge, capital, or specific labor skills.

## *Strategic Processes*

The organization preserve emphasizes the implementation activities of strategy in a stable, unchanging environment. The alternative process approach emphasizes the dynamic capability-building activities of strategy definition and management. According to the process approach, strategy involves a series of congruence-seeking or fitting activities. These processes are addressed at the level of the individual, the group, and the environment.

At the individual level, Henderson (1989) has defined five "elements" of strategy. Those elements are

1. The understanding of competitive behavior as an interacting system
2. The use of this understanding to predict the outcome of a strategic move
3. The identification of resources available for permanent commitment
4. The ability to predict risk with sufficient accuracy to justify resource commitment
5. The willingness to act

These five elements represent the essence of individual strategic thinking skills. They emphasize that an individual must understand the interactive nature of the strategic environment and be able to assess the outcomes of strategic moves by others. Additionally, the individual must have resources available for deployment and must be willing to bear the risks of that deployment. Given the numerous possible individual contributors to a firm's strategy, and the potentially differing capabilities and perspectives of these five elements, the strategy development process in an organization is highly complex. Formal and informal interaction must be developed across organization functions, a process which involves information gathering, mechanical analysis and judgmental evaluation, organization and personal value systems, and intuition. Thus, the corporate strategy will be a composite of contributions from several functional areas, as shown in Figure 2-2.

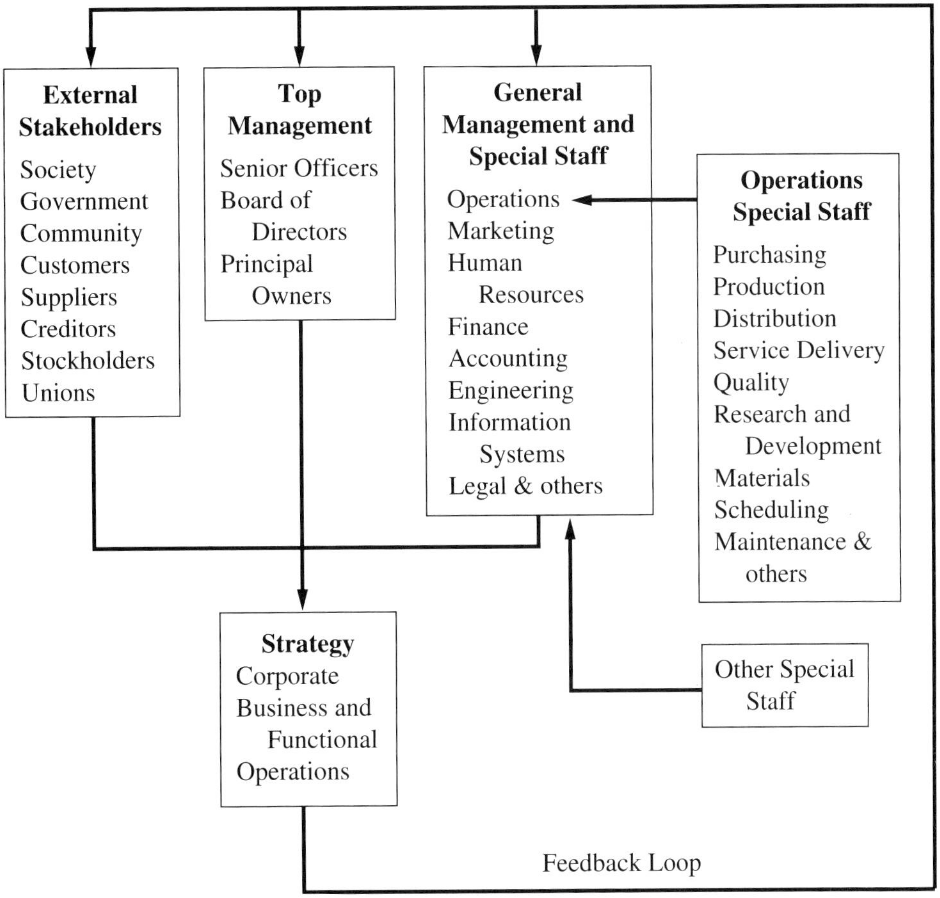


**FIGURE 2-2 Contributors to Corporate Strategy**

Figure 2-2 identifies three primary contributors to corporate strategy: external stakeholders, top management, and, third, general management and special staff. The feedback loop provides interaction among these contributors. As initially suggested by Figure 1-3, this interaction is both horizontal and vertical. The interaction of groups should be viewed as a system to evaluate resource commitments and the associated equilibriums and risks. Of course, contributions will vary from situation to situation, but most groups can be expected to participate extensively in specific parts of the corporate strategy, thus, the notion of "stakeholder."

The Japanese word *keiretsu*, meaning cooperative business groups, suggests a higher-level cooperation between companies. *Keiretsu* integrates customers, suppliers, industry groups, creditors, and other external stakeholders, with an emphasis on mutuality of interest, not individual self-interest or direct competition. Companies in the United States have recently developed their own style of *keiretsu*. For example, with assistance from the government, the big three automakers are jointly working on a new battery for electric cars. Many companies, including Ford, John Deere, IBM, and Digital Equipment are pursuing joint ventures that share technology with suppliers, and, in numerous cases, companies have taken joint equity positions in a supplier or a customer. United States companies are increasingly walking a fine line between effective horizontal and vertical integration of related businesses and illegal trusts designed to restrain or monopolize trade (Kelly et al., 1992).

The involvement of external stakeholders or *keiretsu* groups is of enormous importance in reducing the effects of uncertain environments. Duncan (1972) originally suggested that environmental uncertainty is the most important variable to differentiate the strategic response of organizations. Uncertainty is defined in terms of situational complexity (simple and complex) and the rate of change (stable and unstable). These dimensions may be used to categorize firms according to their markets, products/services, and process technologies, as shown in Figure 2-3.

In the simple-stable environment, there are few competitors, the product has a simple design, and process technology changes slowly. At the opposite end of the uncertainty axis, the complex-unstable environment, there are many competitors with dynamic market

**SITUATIONAL COMPLEXITY**

| RATE OF CHANGE | Simple | | Complex | |
|---|---|---|---|---|
| Stable | **1. Market** | Few competitors, stable | **1. Market** | Many competitors, slow changes |
| | **2. Product/ Service** | Simple design | **2. Product/ Service** | Complex design |
| | **3. Process** | Simple, stable | **3. Process** | Complex, stable |
| | **Examples** | Container manufacturer, commodity processor | **Examples** | Universities, insurance, utilities |
| Unstable | **1. Market** | Few competitors, rapid entry, exit | **1. Market** | Many competitors, rapid entry, exit |
| | **2. Product/ Service** | Simple short-lived design | **2. Product/ Service** | Complex, short-lived design |
| | **3. Process** | Simple, but rapidly changing | **3. Process** | Complex, dynamic technology |
| | **Examples** | Toy manufacturer, retail fashion, housing construction | **Examples** | Telecommunications, information processing, aerospace |

Increased Uncertainty

**FIGURE 2-3 The Effects of Uncertainty in Strategy Formulation**

entry and exit patterns, short-lived and complex products, and rapidly evolving process technologies. The stable-complex and unstable-simple environments may be similarly diagnosed. In this manner, a range of product/service, process technology, and market situations is classified based on the amount of environmental uncertainty. Situational complexity and the industry rate of change contribute directly to this classification. Additionally, the myriad individual and group contributions and evaluations of dynamic equilibrium and risk are focused toward a situational definition, stated in terms of market, product/service, and process technology and market.

This section has defined two general approaches to strategy. First, the stable structural components of a strategic organization were defined and elaborated, emphasizing the current pattern of resource deployment and planned improvements. Then strategy was considered as a dynamic process, initially at the individual level, then at the group level, and finally in environmental interaction. Congruence of individual evaluations of resource deployment and risk assessments with those of the group and organization and contingent on the environment is central to strategy development. A carefully defined and closely fit operations strategy ensures survival in the competitive environment; it involves the use of varying combinations of stable implementing activities and dynamic capability-building processes.

## *Integration of Strategy*

This section starts at the highest level of strategy definition, corporate strategy, and identifies the linkage to business strategy, then to operations strategy. These links may be uncharted and definitionally complex, particularly at the highest levels; but they give a necessary foundation for operations strategy. Unless founded on business strategy, and ultimately in the corporate strategy, operations strategy has little chance for success.

### *Corporate Strategy*

Most businesses are responsive to an underlying corporate strategy, which, though often not clearly stated, links the corporation with its environment at the highest level. Because of the high level and inherent vagueness, the corporate strategy can be described as a mission or philosophy. Corporate strategy must embody the essential elements for corporate survival. The historical evolution of corporate strategy has been described (Steiner and Miner, 1977) in three stages: classical, balanced interest, and socioeconomic. The classical approach, preeminent until the early 1930s, required firms to efficiently use available resources to produce desired goods or services at acceptable prices. The management task was to maximize profits, with little concern for other needs. However, additional requirements were gradually placed on the firm by stockholders, customers, employees, and the general public. The firm's task became that of a trustee to balance or trade off specific interests. More recently, the third stage is gaining prominence. The socioeconomic approach states that the total physical and social environment of the company must be incorporated in management decisions. Though there is no consensus of what the socioeconomic philosophy should include, "safe" products, "fair" employment practices, "reasonable" profits, and "healthy" environments are often identified. The vagueness of the socioeconomic approach makes the management task difficult to define, yet gives management a flexibility and contingent basis for task definition. However defined—and today's corporate strategies are rarely explicit—the management task required for long-term survival is to reasonably respond to these socioeconomic issues.

## *Business Strategy*

Porter (1980) generalizes three generic strategies that a firm can use to competitively distinguish itself: cost leadership, product differentiation, and focus. The focus describes the relationship of the firm with its market and may be further categorized as a cost focus (a cost advantage within a particular niche) or as a product differentiation focus (a product advantage that is directed toward specific characteristics of the targeted market segments). More specifically, the competitive differentiation of a firm must be based on the achievement of:

1. Cost leadership: low-cost, standardized, off-the-shelf products and standardized processes
2. Product differentiation: high-quality products and easily adaptable processes
3. Focus: cost advantage or responsive delivery and customization in response to targeted market segments

These three approaches emphasize that business strategies must be directed toward process technology, product/service, and market objectives. Lacking such emphasis, the firm becomes "stuck in the middle," without a clear business objective. By focusing attention on process technology, product/service, and market terms, the added value of the transformation activity is linked to the distinctive competence of the business.

These three business strategies are directly related to the four operations' competitive priorities. Cost leadership requires that the operations process achieve stable quality at low cost. Product differentiation requires that the operations process achieve high quality with some process flexibility. And market focus requires that the operations process achieve either cost and quality objectives or flexibility and delivery objectives. The definition of a clear linkage between business strategies and operations performance criteria is the key to effective strategy development.

Ultimately, the business strategy must address distinctive competence and the transformation processes whereby value is added to goods or services. It must link the general corporate strategy with the more concisely defined operations strategy. Business strategies may be defined in terms of the extent of vertical or horizontal integration of the transformation processes. Four types of integration, directed toward those value-adding transformations, are considered here:

*Focused System.* Concentration on a single narrow product/service, process technology, and market domain. For example, a building contractor builds houses, but purchases materials from a supplier and sells the finished product through a real estate agency.

*Vertical Integration.* Sequential linkage of the business along the chain of transformations toward either the raw material or the customer domains. For example, an automobile manufacturer owns an electronics assembly plant, a battery maker, and a network of dealerships.

*Horizontal Integration.* Linkage of the business with directly related products/services, process technologies, or markets. For example, a soap maker also manufactures paper towels, both of which involve basic chemical production processes and are distributed through grocery stores. Additionally, a soft drink bottler has a controlling interest in juice and energy-replacement drinks and a sports management business has franchises in several different sports leagues.

*Horizontal Diversification.* Affiliation of the business with unrelated products/services, process technologies, or markets. For example, a major food processor manufactures and distributes leather luggage, lamp fixtures, and a line of apparel.

Note that these four types of integration specifically identify the nature of the transformation relationship of the business, both within itself and with the external environment. Other types of integration describe structural or financial mechanisms but do not directly relate to the technological core, the distinctive competence, or the value-adding process of the organization.

Business strategy requires inputs from various general director functions, which would identify initiatives to reach those goals. Initially, a data-gathering effort, or strategic audit, would develop the foundation data for a thorough evaluation of the threats, opportunities, strengths, and weaknesses of the business. However derived, this evaluation of the corporate product/service, process technology, and market capabilities must be integrated across functions. Commonly, this is done through TOWS analysis (Koontz and Weihrich, 1990) of the external environment (**T**hreats and **O**pportunities) and of the company (**W**eaknesses and **S**trengths). TOWS analysis is called "WOTS-Up" analysis by Steiner and Miner (1977) and "S.W.O.T." by Wheelen and Hunger (1987). This process permits the company to focus on the desired strategic alternatives in terms of cost leadership, product differentiation, and market focus, and links the processes of corporate strategy definition with those of the operations function.

## *Operations Strategy*

Operations strategy must be clearly linked with business and corporate strategies. Companies that develop this linkage tend to be more successful and profitable (Richardson, Taylor, and Gordon, 1985). Thus, a clear distinction between operations and business strategies is often not possible. Of course, operations and business strategies should be mutually consistent, but are often stated with different levels of specification.

**Linkages with Business Strategy.** In defining the linkage of operations strategy with business strategy, top management must decide whether operations strategy drives business strategy, or vice versa. In other terms, should the operations strategy be adjusted to achieve organization-level strategic requirements, or should the business strategy be constrained by operational capabilities?

The traditionally recognized relationship of operations and business strategies describes operations strategy as "richly and deliberately integrated" (Stobaugh and Telesio, 1983), though subordinate to corporate strategy. However, more recently, Hayes (1985) and others suggest that operations should define the distinctive competence and technical core, which is the foundation of business strategy. There is some evidence (Swamidass and Newell, 1987) that as the role of the operations manager in business strategy decision making increases, the economic performance of the company improves. This research substantiates the argument that manufacturing may be *the* key competitive variable, at least in some circumstances.

The distinctive competence of the firm, the nature of resource decisions, and the value-adding transformation process are central to this question. Additionally, the relationship of operations and business strategies is dependent on the product/service-process technology life cycle (operations might be predominant in new product or service development situations, while marketing may be more important as products or services mature) and dependent on the position along the chain of transformations (operations might be predominant in extraction through distribution systems, and marketing management more important in service businesses); however, there are currently no studies to clarify this issue.

The importance of the operations function to the technical core and the distinctive competence of the organization varies depending upon the organization and the specific environment. A fine university, for example, may rightly conclude that its distinctive competence results from recruitment and management of its faculty, not from the administration of the course offerings. Similarly, an importer of fine wines might conclude that its distinctive competence was in marketing (advertising and promotion) of the product, rather than bottling operations or shipping. In these environments the operations function likely is not *the* key contributor to distinctive competence, because the operations activities involve a relatively specialized and limited segment of the chain of transformations.

However, in other businesses, notably automobile manufacturing, air transportation, pharmaceuticals, food products, and furniture, consumers are increasingly cost and quality conscious. They are willing to pay for supplemental marketing differentiation only when there is tangible value added. "No haggle" fixed pricing, enhanced warranties, liberal return policies, and design of functional high-quality products all suggest that customers are increasingly looking beyond marketing or financial competencies to operations, both manufacturing and service, competencies (Power et al., 1991).

The criteria by which to measure the operations function are the performance of the transformation process, which are directly related to the competitive priorities of cost, quality, flexibility, and delivery. The definition of one, or possibly two, of these competitive priorities directs operations efforts to achieve the distinctive competence of the business, stated as cost leadership, product differentiation, or market focus. Operations strategy is more fully defined in Chapter 3.

### *Process- and Product/Service-Focused Strategies*

These concepts, and several further and more general concepts introduced in Chapter 1, suggest a difference between an organization that adopts a process-focused strategy and one that adopts a product/service-focused strategy. The process-focused strategy is applicable to a facility that produces a wide range of customized products or services at low volumes. A production system with a process focus is often called a job shop. Because each product is unique, it requires a different routing through the process and usually involves different processing at each work center. Similarly, in a service system, customers follow different routes. Management of the separate activities is decentralized so that the process may be flexibly responsive to individually supported market demands. This organization is suited to less complex, less capital intense technologies, such as metal fabricators, print shops, and many service providers.

Alternatively, the product/service-focused strategy is applicable to a facility that produces a narrow range of standardized products or services at high volumes. Because the products are standardized, they are most efficiently produced using the same routing through the production process. This type of production system is often called a flow shop because of the linear routing pattern. The product-focused strategy is concerned with the efficient movement of materials or sequencing of value-adding activities through several sequentially integrated work centers. Management is concerned with scheduling, capacity, and inventory management responsibilities. Product-focused strategies generally use technologies that have high capital requirements. Examples of the organizations with a product-focused strategy are petroleum refining, food production and processing, and automobile production.

The distinction between process- and product/service-focused strategies is important because it suggests further categories of strategic concerns that should be considered. At every level of management and in every functional area of operations, these two focuses require different management approaches, employee skills, and resource intensities. Various intermediate strategies may be defined which include aspects of both the process- and product/service-focused strategies. A production system that uses an intermediate strategy requires a combination of resources and methods.

### *Issues in Process- and Product/Service-Focused Strategies*

After the process- or product/service-focused strategy, or an intermediate strategy, has been selected, several further issues must be considered. These concerns are generally applicable to both process- and product/service-focused strategic situations; however, they vary in importance, depending on the specific situation.

The first issue involves selecting the decision focus of the firm. These decision focuses are noted in Table 1-2 and are discussed in many chapters of this book. For example, one situation may necessitate the smoothing of the schedule for the many different jobs so that each work center is permitted to run at or close to capacity. Alternately, other criteria, such as minimizing the cost of inventory, may be the critical strategic factor. In other situations, such as nuclear, space, or aircraft industries, the assurance of quality at each stage of production is of primary importance. Other decision focuses might include the linking of operations system design, just-in-time integration of facilities, or efficiencies of operations planning.

The second issue is the number of products or services a firm wants to produce/deliver and the range represented by the portfolio. A firm may decide to produce/deliver only one or two products/services or a broader or more customized line. Those products/services may be focused on one market, possibly a geographical area, or several markets.

Often the products must be protected through patents, trademarks, and copyrights. Patents held by Xerox, the registered trademark Coca Cola, the copyrighted software used by consulting services, and the widely recognized Kleenex brand name are examples. However, such protections may also limit the market. For example, because it was difficult to copy the "pure" Rocky Mountain water, it was also difficult for Coors to find an acceptable source of water for brewing beer in the eastern United States. Similarly, a "kreuzened" beer (a specific mix of hops and barley) is popular in some parts of the upper midwest of the United States, but that distinction would not likely be the basis for a mass market. Though a product or service may be protected, the protection can also limit market penetration.

Third, the life cycle classification defines development of a product or service from the initial concept (birth), through the product/service design and process technology design stages, to start-up, growth, and stable state, then to decline and renewal. Operations strategy must consider the stage of the life cycle, because an appropriate strategy for one stage might be disastrous for another. Companies that have products or services in stable state or declining stages of the life cycle should start product/service modification or a follow-on product/service which would permit leveling of operations resources, as well as company sales and profits. Table 2-1 lists several strategic concerns of operations managers during the seven stages of a product/service/process technology life cycle. The stages of this life cycle will be discussed in further detail in Chapters 6, 7, and 13.

A fourth strategic issue, the product/service portfolio matrix, defines the dimensions of market share and market growth. Products and services are categorized as question marks, star performers, cash cows, and dogs. This model was originally defined by Tilles (1966) and associated with the Boston Consulting Group; it is still widely used to evaluate product/service growth and market share. The product/service portfolio matrix is shown in Figure 2-4.

The four product/service categories roughly correspond to the final four stages of the product/service life cycle, as shown by the numbers in each box. "Question mark" products or services are those in the start-up and early growth stage. The "star performers," "cash cows," and "dogs" respectively are found primarily in the growth of volume, stable state, and decline and renewal stages. Some products or services may never achieve market growth, but move from "question mark" directly to "dog" status. The arrows in Figure 2-4 note the relationship of product/service life cycle to product/service portfolio. The product/service portfolio strategy should define several different products or services, each at a different stage of the life cycle.

The fifth issue, originally identified by Hayes and Wheelwright (1979), considers market entry and exit timing. Traditionally, a manufacturing or service organization would manage a product or service, or range of products and services, through all phases of the life cycle. Although adjustments were required as the firm moved through the different life-cycle stages, in less turbulent times companies were able to easily adapt. Today, however, with increasing complexity and market dynamism, the adaption is more difficult, particularly with the socioeconomic philosophies of stabilized work forces, broadened community relations, and other constraints. The difficulty is that the management of products/services at different stages of the life cycle requires, as noted in Table 2-1, different strategic considerations and different professional skills. Thus, corporations

**TABLE 2-1 Stages of the Product/Service-Process Technology Life Cycle**

| Stage | Some Strategic Concerns |
|---|---|
| 1—Birth of the Production/Service Delivery System | A. What product/service will be offered?<br>B. What is the design of the product/service?<br>C. What is the expected market for the product/service?<br>D. What is volume and what process capacity is required? |
| 2—Product/Service Design and Process Technology Selection | A. What is the technology of the product/service?<br>B. What are expected product/service costs at various volumes?<br>C. What product/service safety issues should be considered?<br>D. Does the prototype meet market expectations? |
| 3—Design of the Production/Service Delivery System | A. What level of process technology is appropriate?<br>B. What types of equipment and labor force should be selected?<br>C. What organization of the production/service delivery system should be selected?<br>D. What information system should be chosen? |
| 4—Start-up of the Production/Service Delivery System | A. Is the production/service delivery system (training, maintenance) ready?<br>B. Are resources available?<br>C. How will the hand-off from prototype research to production/service delivery be handled?<br>D. How will exceptions (problems) be handled? |
| 5—Growth of Volume | A. What facility and process upgrades are required?<br>B. How will production/service delivery be scheduled?<br>C. How will performance be evaluated?<br>D. How will the distribution system be organized? |
| 6—Stable State | A. What process efficiencies are necessary?<br>B. What product/service features are required?<br>C. What market repositioning is appropriate?<br>D. What follow-on product/service should be considered? |
| 7—Decline and Renewal of the System | A. What is the salvage value of the facility?<br>B. What repair parts stock should be produced?<br>C. How to minimize the effects on employees?<br>D. What are the long-range responsibilities for the product/service, process technology, and production system residues? |

often decide to enter the market at one stage of a product/service life cycle and exit at a later stage. Four generic entry and exit strategies are shown in Figure 2-5.

The traditional strategy, strategy 2, requires a firm to enter when the products/services, process technologies, or markets are new and evolve through stages of growth, stable state, and decline. A company with strategy 1 discovers and develops a process technology, product, or market, and then sells out as growth stabilizes. Recent examples are found in cable television, computer, and airline industries; earlier examples are the automobile and newspaper industries. Strategy 3 is exemplified by IBM, which delayed entering the PC market until the early 1980s, when the tremendous market potential

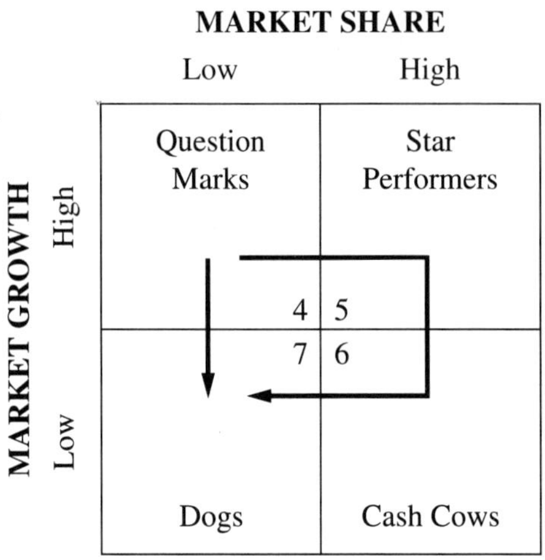


**FIGURE 2-4 Product/Service Portfolio Matrix**

Reprinted with permission from Barry Hedly, "Strategies and the Business Portfolio," *Long-Range Planning,* February 1977.

became apparent. IBM then vigorously entered the market in the growth of volume stage. Strategy 4 is a mistake because entrance during the growth of volume stage incurs high costs, which are difficult to recover in the relatively short time until the stable state market is reached. Strategies 1 and 3 require careful timing and rapid resource commitment. If a

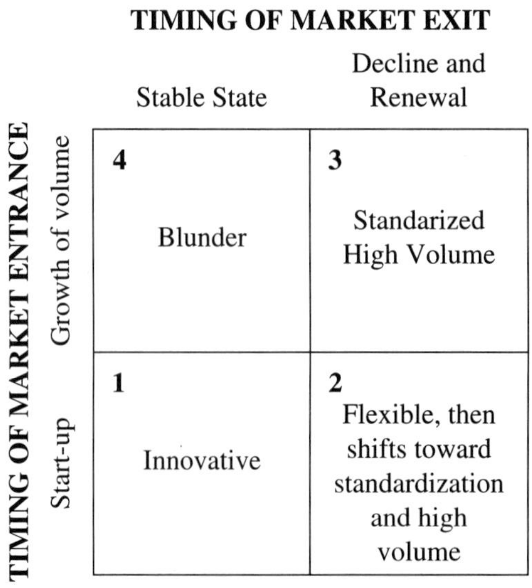

TIMING OF MARKET EXIT
Stable State
Decline and Renewal
TIMING OF MARKET ENTRANCE
Growth of volume
Start-up
4
Blunder
3
Standarized High Volume
1
Innovative
2
Flexible, then shifts toward standardization and high volume


**FIGURE 2-5 Combinations of Entrance and Exit Strategies**

firm with strategy 1 held on too long, it might face a process-driven mass market that it was not prepared for. Alternatively, the difficulty of entering a market late (strategy 3) is that a large investment is required to decisively enter a rapidly changing market, and it may be difficult to "play catch up."

### *Strategy Development Process*

Like all processes, the development of an operations strategy is an ongoing and iterative series of activities. It involves a regular and complex interaction of the operations manager with top management, other general managers, operations specialist staff, and operations activities. Figure 2-6 shows an operations strategy founded in the corporate strategy and

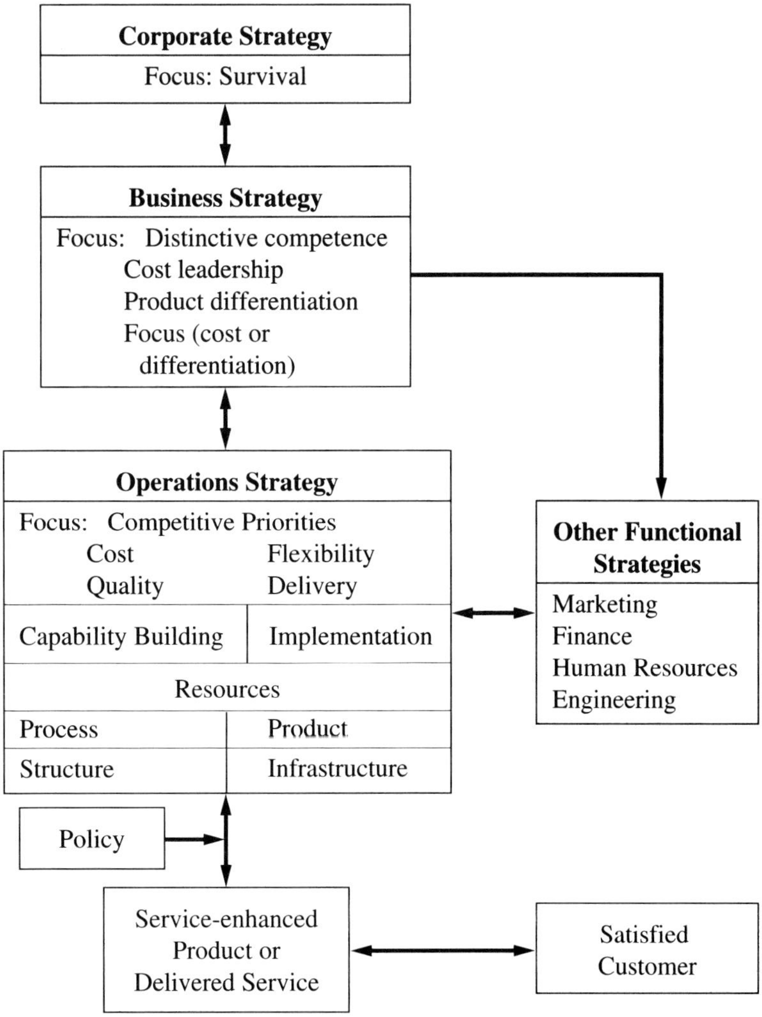


**FIGURE 2-6 Corporate, Business, and Operations Strategies**

on the survival needs of the firm. The operations strategy is further developed through the business strategy and the operations strategy to establish the distinctive competence by TOWS analysis. Figure 2-6 integrates corporate, business, and operations strategies.

The corporate strategy is the highest statement of the corporate philosophy, goals, and mission. If formalized, the corporate strategy will likely appear as a company credo, in platitudes by top management about the firm, or in stockholder materials. At the next level, the business strategy offers a much more detailed perspective of the organization, the formalization of which usually appears in the business plan, a document of some 10 to 15 pages, with more detailed appendices to elaborate on appropriate functional areas. Table 2-2 gives a general outline of a business plan. Of course, depending on the industry, the business plan might include other topics, such as emerging technologies, equal employment opportunity compliance, safety and contingency plans, and others.

To summarize, operations strategy, focused on one or two, or possibly more, of the competitive priorities (cost, quality, flexibility, and delivery), will likely be closely, even inextricably intertwined with the business distinctive competencies (Kim and Arnold, 1991). The operations capability-building (Stalk et al., 1992) and implementation activities use operations resources toward the specified competitive priorities, with emphasis toward either a product- or process-focused strategy. Several resources are integrated through the transformation process that is managed with structure and infrastructure decision focuses. The implementation of strategy is managed through a range of policy directives that specify the timing, actions, and measurement standards of management activities. Ultimately, a service-enhanced product must be delivered to a satisfied customer. Applications Box 2-1 gives an example of these activities. This process is the basis for the strategic focusing and fitting of the organization, the topics of the next two sections of this chapter.

## *"Focusing" Operations Strategy*

The development of operations strategy is definitely an unstructured, dynamically shifting highly interactive process. Though some operations environments are more clearly defined than others and some environments are changing slowly while others are more turbulent, operations strategy is at best a complex process. The function of an operations strategy is to focus (identify, define, and describe) several strategic alternatives, one of which is ultimately selected for fitting to the organization. Fitting is used to adjust the domain in order to achieve a more efficient congruence of activities and resources. Four general techniques of focusing have historically been developed. These are called the overview, trade-off, reductionist, and sequential methods.

The difficulty of focusing the operations strategy is that there are so many possible variables involved. Each of the operations strategy dimensions, originally noted in Figure 1-2 and shown in Figure 2-6, could be used to elaborate subsets of variables. In addition, the competitive priorities (cost, quality, flexibility, and delivery), process or product focus, the stage of the chain of transformations, and the product life cycle all suggest further variables.

**TABLE 2-2 Outline of a Business Plan**

I. Introduction
II. The Firm
  A. Locations
  B. Organization and people
  C. Levels of process technology
  D. The nature of banking and consulting services
  E. Major suppliers
  F. Principal investors
III. Client Base
  A. Location
  B. Growth rates
  C. Changing client needs
IV. Geographic Area (global, regional bloc, national, state, and so on)
  A. Economic considerations
  B. Legal considerations
  C. Business conditions
  D. Major competitors
V. Business Climate
  A. Forecast projections of business growth
  B. Major variables
  C. Impacts of changes in regulatory legislation
  D. Impacts of changes in telecommunications and delivery systems
  E. Other potential changes
VI. Growth Opportunities
  A. Long-range growth in national/international markets
  B. Medium range by business area
  C. Short range by location
VII. Ownership Obligations
  A. Stockholder obligations
  B. Obligations to employees
  C. Long-range fixed obligations
VIII. Conclusions
IX. Appendices
  A. Human resources
  B. Finance
  C. Operations
  D. Marketing
  E. Legal
  F. Engineering
  G. Others

## *Overview Approach*

Though it is not possible to simultaneously evaluate all relevant contributions to operations strategy, the operations manager can identify a small but important subset of decision issues. Hayes and Wheelwright (1984, p. 31) have identified eight such core strategic focuses as: capacity, facilities, technology, vertical integration, work force, quality, production planning/materials control, and organization. This list has been aggregated by

## APPLICATIONS BOX 2-1 Strategy Development at a Defense Contractor

1. *The Environment.* The environment of most defense contractors is somewhat different from that of other businesses. The principal defense contractors commit major portions of their operation (sometimes 80% or more) to one client (the U.S. Government Department of Defense). The standards of product and process design and the criteria for product acceptance often are not evaluated in the open market for reasons of security and proprietary technology. Additionally, the technologies of weapons systems and equipment are constantly changing and the manufacturing and service processes are often very costly and certainly unique in application. Though some products and the process to build them have corresponding or closely related nonmilitary applications, often the costs of conversion from a military to a commercial application are extremely high.
2. *Corporate Strategy.* To survive in such an environment, a contractor must ensure that it is not "blind-sided" by a change in technology or in the market. Redefinition of national defense policy and of technology can happen rapidly, and the contractor must be constantly prepared for such changes. Though contractors are usually bound by socioeconomic constraints of "fairness" in employment matters, historically, they have not been as tightly constrained by safety or environmental concerns. Because this nation, as reflected by political decisions, has traditionally placed a high priority on military preparedness, the costs for research of new technologies and for the development of applications have been accepted.
3. *Business Strategy.* The link of the contractor with the customer is often protected by long-term contracts and a bilateral monopoly relationship; thus, many defense contractors concentrate on production of prototypes of several models in a line of products using similar high-technology processes. Though the product and process development effort is ongoing, contractors must always be prepared to convert to high-volume production of the current prototype. Thus the firm must be able to move quickly from differentiation focus to cost leadership. The TOWS analysis is a particularly important and regular part of the contractor's corporate strategy development process. New technologies for product applications and production process modifications should be quickly evaluated and integrated. The company's strengths and potential weaknesses, in terms of product and process modification, should be carefully assessed in the process. Typically, the strength is in the technology, and the weakness is in the limited applicability of the process or product.
4. *Operations Strategy.* The specific operations strategy and the performance criteria of a contractor will likely vary over time, depending upon the number and intensity of conflicts throughout the world. During times of peace, the single most important goal would likely be flexibility; however, production volumes increase during periods of conflict and delivery would be more important. To achieve these operations and business objectives, many defense contractors maintain large research departments and numerous linkages with the environment through boundary spanners. The market is a niche, with two or three products in different stages of the product life cycle. Knowledge is the key resource. Most defense contractors, particularly those of ships, aircraft, and vehicles, are process-focused because of the necessity to integrate various resources into the product. However, some high-tech items, such as communications and vision equipment, may require a product-focused strategy. In peacetime, efforts are applied to product and process design; in wartime, scheduling issues would become more important.

Anderson et al. (1989) to capacity/facilities; production planning, materials control, and quality; work force and organization; and technology.

Other discussions of strategic operations contain minor variations of this grouping; however, a high level of agreement has been found (Leong et al., 1990) among researchers that these are the important functional topics of an operations strategy. These classifications are particularly convenient, because they may be used as either a formal check list or a memory guide. The rationale of the overview approach is that an operations manager can substantively focus on one, or possibly two, of these issues, and on several important contributing subfactors. This categorization corresponds, with minor variations, to the decision focuses identified in Table 1-2 and to the organization of this book. In that sense, the major issues discussed in each chapter can be used as a check list for evaluation of the operations strategy.

The limitation of the check list approach, however, is that it merely serves as a listing, or a definitional and descriptive assist; it does not show the relationship of these highly interactive variables. Skinner's "Productivity Paradox" (1986) documents the dilemma of identifying one or several variables in an attempt to improve the operation. Manipulation of the particular variable might reduce the cost of that specific variable, but might exacerbate other related conditions, resulting in little, if any, overall improvement and quite possibly an overall deterioration in productivity.

## *Trade-off Approach*

The trade-off approach helps identify which of these variables and contributing factors are more important; and, for a specific situation, what interaction and possible impacts may result from those decisions. For example, a traditional operations approach viewed cost and quality as a trade-off. Higher costs must be incurred to ensure that a good would be of high quality, while lower-cost goods were likely of lower quality. A good, according to traditional operations theory, could be either high quality or low cost, but not both. Further elaboration permits application of this concept to each of the decision focus areas. Support for this approach of evaluating the patterns of priorities and trade-offs among operations managers is provided by St. John and Young (1992). Table 2-3 identifies some twenty-eight such trade-offs, generally categorized in the decision-focus areas.

The limitations of the trade-off approach are that a genuine trade-off may not exist, that the appropriate alternative may not have been identified or selected, and that the decision based on the trade-off may reduce the productivity of other selected variables. Recently many operations managers have found that there is not a trade-off between low cost and high quality. The contemporary approach suggests that, as volumes increase, experience increases and per-unit costs decrease. Because of familiarity, product variances are reduced as well. Thus, as the operations of many firms have shown, low costs are associated with high quality. This topic is further discussed in Chapter 11.

More importantly, with so many possible variables (and other possible trade-offs could be developed), the magnitude of the problem is uncontrollable. When a manager tries to evaluate and manipulate one trade-off, as Skinner (1986) suggests, the other related variables "explode." For example, changing the inventory level would likely affect the process and quality trade-offs, and possibly the facility, personnel, and capacity variables. Several mathematical models could be used to evaluate such a multidimensional problem, but they are not particularly helpful for several reasons. Initially, such algorithms are dependent upon possibly inaccurate and often changing input values. Further, some variables (customer satisfaction or employee safety) are difficult to measure. Third, although the model may be accurate mechanically, senior management may be uncomfortable with such formal computations, preferring intuition. The identification of a strategy to address competitive distinctness or productivity is just too complex and subjective for complete reliance on mechanical processes.

**TABLE 2-3 Common Operations Management Trade-Offs**

| Decision Focus | Variable 1 | Variable 2 | Common Name |
|---|---|---|---|
| Capacity | Fixed costs | Variable costs | Break-even analysis |
| | Build capacity before demand | Build capacity with or after demand | Capacity timing |
| Facilities | Lease facilities | Own facilities | Lease–own analysis |
| | Many facilities | Few facilities | Centralized/diversified |
| | Large plant | Small plant | Plant size decision |
| | General-purpose equipment | Specialized equipment | Choice of equipment |
| Operations System Design/ Operations Planning | Line flow | Process flow | Process strategy |
| | Make-to-order | Make-to-stock | Customization |
| | Carry cost | Set-up cost | Economic lot size |
| | Level production | Chase production | Operations planning |
| | Labor intense | Capital intense | Resource allocation |
| | Preventive maintenance | Equipment failure | Maintenance strategy |
| Materials | Carry cost | Order cost | Economic order quantity |
| | Hold inventory | Backorder/stockout | Safety stock strategy |
| | Build part | Buy part | Make–buy strategy |
| | Direct ship to customer | Warehouse/service distribution centers | Customer service level |
| | Standard product | Custom product | Customer responsiveness |
| Quality | Quality of design | Quality of inspection | Product quality |
| | Reject rate | Warranty rate | Service quality |
| | Proactive quality | Reactive quality | Quality planning |
| Productivity and Work Force | Safety program cost | Accident cost | Safety strategy |
| | Overtime | New hiring | Employment |
| | Specialized labor | Generalist skills | Job specialization |
| | Close/direct | Loose/indirect | Method of supervision |
| | Authoritarian | Permissive | Management style |
| | Functional | Product | Organization design |
| Technology | Rapid production | Long-term process development | Research goals |
| | Develop own technology | Use technology developed elsewhere | Technological risk |

Adapted from Fogarty et al. (1989, p. 645) and Skinner (1985, p. 61).

### *Reductionist Approach*

A third approach, suggested by Skinner (1986), can be used to reduce the effects of such trade-offs. The concept is to address the root causes of the situation and thereby reduce its effect, rather than to trade off one variable against another. By concentrating on the exact "best" trade-off solution the operations manager may ignore the underlying conditions that drive those variables in the first place. The emphasis of the reductionist approach is on management and control of the underlying variables, not on the identification of a particular minimum cost of the variables involved. The use of just-in-time inventory management approaches to address inventory cost trade-offs, as discussed in Chapter 9, is a good example.

### *Sequential Approach*

The fourth approach, labeled the sequential approach by Ferdows and De Meyer (1990), rejects the possibility that a facility can simultaneously focus on multiple competitive priorities and reasserts that a facility should primarily address the priorities one at a time. The selection of the appropriate priority would be contingent upon the external environment and internal factors, such as technology and work-force characteristics. For example, the early Japanese entry to the U.S. automobile market was based on low cost; however, once that competitive priority was met, the subsequent effort was to improve quality. The results of this quality emphasis were felt in the mid-1970s, as costs increased marginally, but quality improved dramatically. By the mid-1980s, Japanese automakers concentrated on production flexibility, and, though quality was still high, costs began to rise. Thus, an operation can successfully concentrate on only one competitive priority at a time, but as the emphasis shifts over time, the residual effects of prior efforts will continue to be felt.

Empirical research (De Meyer and Ferdows, 1988) has found that companies believe that they can improve more than one competitive priority at a time. The predominance of respondents (40%) stated that they improved two of the four priorities simultaneously, though 22% claimed to be able to improve three or four measures simultaneously. The ability to effectively operate on more than one priority may result from what Ferdows and De Meyer (1990) characterize as the sand cone model. The first priority (likely cost or quality) must initially be clearly established, as is the compacted or wet core of a sand cone. This foundation is followed by sequential layers of other priorities. These subsequent efforts have the effect of reinforcing and building upon the foundation priority.

The operations strategist might focus operations strategy by using the overview, trade-off, reductionist, or sequential approaches. Though it is possible to jump directly to the sequential approach, that method requires that the definitional and structural foundations developed by the other methods be in place. The decision issues that most directly affect the particular manufacturing or service situation must be identified. A process of elimination is often helpful to aggregate the grouping to no more than two core variables and several additional contributing factors. Additionally, a manager might consider various trade-offs and compute several minimum values. However, those minimum values should be used only as a baseline for evaluating the effects of contributing variables. The reductionist process is directed toward the root cause of the situation, rather than playing one cost against another. Even so, the dynamism of operations situations is likely to cause the competitive criteria to shift over time. For this reason, effectively defined operations strategies must incorporate the sequentially developed priorities, like the layers of the sand cone. Because of these shifts in competitive priority, the operations manager must regularly address the concept of "fitting" the operations strategy to the organization.

## *"Fitting" Operations Strategy*

Focusing operations strategy is primarily a definitional and conceptual approach to consider the strategic variables. Alternatively, fitting the strategy to the situation dynamically adjusts disjunct parts of the organization and thereby enhances operations congruence, either internally or with the external environment. Thus, focusing is relatively stable, while fitting is more dynamic. Unless there is a reasonably high level of fit among the divergent parts of the organization, inefficiency and waste result (Galbraith, 1986).

A typology of organization change and the mechanisms to adjust organization fit has evolved. The basis for the typology was originally suggested by Leavitt (1964), Steers (1976), Nadler and Tushman (1977), and Galbraith and Nathanson (1978), who, with minor definitional differences, develop four primary organization variables: people, task, design, and technology. Figure 2-7 represents these dimensions.

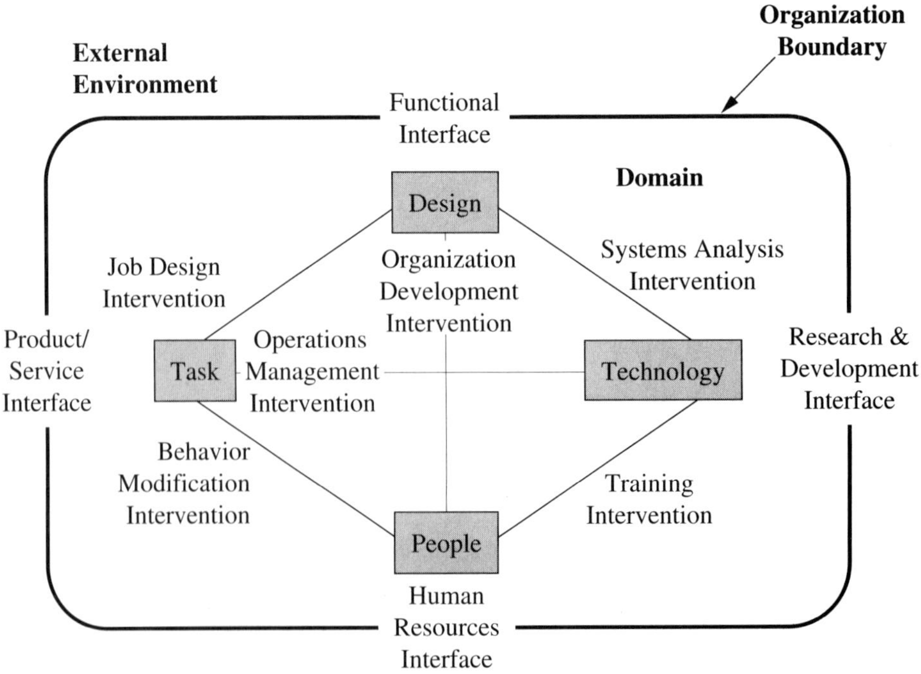


**FIGURE 2-7 The Multilevel Typology of Fit**

This approach is useful because it defines several principal staff activities as components of the external interfaces of the organization and emphasizes the strategic structure and processes of the organization. Additionally, the key organization variables (technology, people, task, and design) are shown. Fitting the organization is accomplished in three ways (Stonebraker, 1986). A manager can *intrude,* or directly change a variable; intrusion is appropriate only in extreme situations because of the potential for serious side effects. Intruding upon the organization design, as did John Reed of Citibank (see Chapter 1), would likely cause serious perturbations to the tasks, the technologies, and the people. *Intervention* is a less direct and more effective method of enhancing the fit of an organization because it simultaneously interacts between two variables to further their congruence. As Figure 2-7 shows, the training intervention enhances the fit between people and technology, and the related behavior modification intervention enhances the fit between people and task. *Interfaces* are used to link key organization variables to the external environment. The product/service interface links the organization task (broadly defined, operations activity) with the consumer; the human resource interface links employment needs with the labor market, and so forth. Interventions and interfaces can be used simultaneously. For example, the contracting with an outside group for a new information system likely would include hardware, software, and training, as well as follow-on consulting.

The multilevel typology of fit provides a framework for diagnosis of the organization; it permits operations managers to adjust their focus either to the organization or to the external environment. Though the notion of fitting is described here in terms of lateral interaction at the general management level of the organization, it can also be applied at higher or lower levels, for example, to the interactions of operations area specialists. Fitting defines three levels of action, intrusion, intervention, and interfacing, which can be contingently used to adjust resource commitments in the domain. Increased congruence within the domain, and, if desired, externally, is an outcome of these focusing and fitting activities, and a requirement for efficient management of both the firm's distinctive competence and technical core.

## Summary

The origin of strategy is best explained by a corresponding concept from biology, the principle of competitive exclusion. This principle provides a foundation for the notions of domain and resources, which, taken together, are the basis for distinctive competence. The principle also suggests the importance of strategy as a means of understanding and potentially hastening evolutionary processes. Strategy was then considered from a stable perspective by describing the technical core, boundaries, deployed resources, and interaction mechanisms with the environment. Strategy can be further considered as a dynamic process, with individual decision-making elements, group interaction, product/service, process technology, and market links of corporate strategy and the environment. Although operations strategy is likely different from corporate strategy and is separately defined, there is increasing support, based on the relationship of competitive priorities and value-added transformations with distinctive competence, that operations, business and corporate strategies are inextricably entwined in many business environments. It is also becoming apparent that operations strategy may, in many businesses, be the key determinant of the business strategy.

Operations goals are measured in terms of productivity, with focus on how well the company has been able to achieve one or more of the four competitive priorities: cost, quality, flexibility, and delivery. The strategies to achieve these competitive priorities, however, involve numerous variables. An interactive process was defined to identify the horizontal and vertical relationships of strategy formulation and the primary variables were briefly elaborated. Because of the complexity, the operations manager must focus those variables, using a strategic overview perspective, followed by the trade-off, reductionist, and sequential approaches. As these underlying factors shift over time, further fitting activities, such as intervention, interfacing, and—rarely—intrusion, should be used to enhance the congruence, and thus efficiency, of the organization. Though these processes are very abstract, they must be thoroughly conceived and carefully managed; if they are not, the viability of the organization will be threatened and certainly the prosperity of the organization will be reduced. To compete in the increasingly global, dynamic, and complex business environments of the 1990s, operations management must develop an effective strategy, as defined by these dimensions.

## *Discussion Questions*

1. Explain, in your own words, the principle of competitive exclusion.
2. How does the principle of competitive exclusion relate to strategy? From your readings or experience, give an example of how strategy uses the principle of exclusion.
3. Describe the parts of the organization preserve. Give an example that exemplifies the various parts.
4. Why is strategy considered both a state and a process?
5. Differentiate the product-focused organization from the process-focused organization. Give an example of each.
6. What is the role of corporate strategy? From your readings or experience, give an example.
7. Why are operations and business strategies inextricably entwined? State and support an example.
8. What factors define business focus and what factors define operations focus?
9. Describe and exemplify the product/service-process technology life cycle approach to strategy definition. How does this approach relate to the product/service portfolio model and to entrance and exit timing?
10. Describe the rationale of the overview, trade-off, reductionist, and sequential approaches to operations strategy. Give an example of a product for which the strategy has shifted.
11. Why is the trade-off approach insufficient as a mechanism to develop operations strategy?

12. Differentiate the "focusing" and the "fitting" processes of operations strategy.

13. What is the difference between intrusion, intervention, and interfacing? When are these fitting activities used? Describe an example.

## Strategic Decision Situations

1. Prepare a business plan for a product that you are familiar with. Consider the outline in Table 2-2 as a general format, and elaborate on appropriate areas. Note that the value of the business plan is that it provides a "formal and specific focus of the company."

2. Prepare an operations appendix to the business plan called for in Strategic Decision Situation 1. Consider, as an organizing basis, the bottom portion of Figure 2-6 and the discussion in the "Operations Strategy" subsection of this chapter.

## References

Anderson, John C., Gary Cleveland, and Roger G. Schroeder. "Operations Strategy: A Literature Review," *Journal of Operations Management.* April 1989, pp. 133–158.

Carroll, Peter J. "The Link between Performance and Strategy," *Journal of Business Strategy.* Spring 1982, pp. 3–20.

De Meyer, A., and K. Ferdows. "Quality Up, Technology Down." INSEAD Working Series No. 88/65, 1988.

Drucker, Peter F. "The New Society of Organizations," *Harvard Business Review.* September–October 1992, pp. 95–104.

Duncan, Robert B. "Characteristics of Perceived Environments and Perceived Environmental Uncertainty," *Administrative Science Quarterly.* Vol. 17, No. 3, 1972, pp. 313–327.

Ferdows, Kasra, and Arnoud De Meyer. "Lasting Improvements in Manufacturing Performance: In Search of a New Theory," *Journal of Operations Management.* April 1990, pp. 168–184.

Fogarty, Donald W., Thomas R. Hoffmann, and Peter W. Stonebraker. *Production and Operations Management.* Cincinnati, Ohio: South-Western Publishing Co., 1989.

Galbraith, J. R., and R. K. Kazanjian. *Strategic Implementation: Structure, Systems, and Processes.* St. Paul, Minn.: West Publishing Co., 1986.

Galbraith, J. R., and Daniel A. Nathanson. *Strategy mplementation: The Role of Structure and Process.* St. Paul, Minn.: West Publishing Co., 1978.

Hayes, Robert H. "Strategic Planning—Forward in Reverse?" *Harvard Business Review.* November–December 1985, pp. 111–119.

Hayes, Robert H., and Roger W. Schmenner. "How Should You Organize Manufacturing?" *Harvard Business Review.* January–February 1978, pp. 105–118.

Hayes, Robert H., and Steven C. Wheelwright. "The Dynamics of Process-Product Life Cycles," *Harvard Business Review.* March–April 1979.

Hayes, Robert H., and Steven C. Wheelwright. *Restoring our Competitive Edge.* New York: John Wiley & Sons, 1984.

Henderson, Bruce D. "The Origins of Strategy," *Harvard Business Review.* November–December 1989, pp. 139–143.

Kelly, Kevin, Otis Port, James Treece, Gail DeGeorge, and Zachary Schiller. "Learning from Japan," *Business Week.* January 27, 1992, pp. 52–60.

Kiernan, Matthew J. "The New Strategic Architecture: Learning to Compete in the Twenty-First Century," *Academy of Management Executive.* Vol. 7, No. 1, 1993, pp. 7–21.

Kim, Jay S. and Peter Arnold. "Competitive Priorities, Manufacturing Objectives, and Action Plans:

Constructs and Linkages." Boston University School of Management Working Paper Series 91–66, 1991.

Koontz, Harold, and Heintz Weihrich. *Essentials of Management.* New York: McGraw-Hill, 1990.

Leavitt, Harold I. "Applied Organization Change in Industry: Structural, Technical and Human Choices," in William L. Cooper, *New Perspectives in Organization Research.* New York: John Wiley & Sons, Inc., 1964.

Lee, Hak-Chong. "Lordstown Plant of General Motors (A) and (B)." State University of New York at Albany, 1974.

Leong, G. K., D. L. Snyder, and P. T. Ward. "Research in the Process and Content of Manufacturing Strategy," *Omega: International Journal of Management Science,* No. 2, 1990, pp. 109–122.

Nadler, David A., and Michael L. Tushman. "A Congruence Model for Diagnosing Organizational Behavior," *Perspectives on Behavior in Organizations.* New York: McGraw-Hill, 1983.

Porter, Michael E. *Competitive Strategy: Techniques for Analyzing Industries and Competitors.* New York: Free Press, 1980.

Power, Christopher, Walecia Konrad, Alice Z. Cuneo, and James B. Treece. "Value Marketing: Quality, Service, and Fair Pricing are the Keys to Selling in the 1990s," *Business Week,* November 11, 1991, pp. 132–140.

Reid, Peter C. *Well Made in America: Lessons from Harley-Davidson on Being the Best.* New York: McGraw-Hill, 1990.

Richardson, P. R., A. J. Taylor, and R. J. M. Gordon. "A Strategic Approach to Evaluating Manufacturing Performance," *Interfaces.* November–December 1985, pp. 15–27.

Skinner, Wickham. *Manufacturing: The Formidable Competitive Weapon.* New York: John Wiley, 1985.

Skinner, Wickham. "The Productivity Paradox," *Management Review.* September 1986.

St. John, Caron H., and Scott T. Young. "An Exploratory Study of Patterns of Priorities and Trade-offs Among Operations Managers," *Production and Operations Management.* Spring 1992, pp. 133–150.

Stalk, George, Philip Evans, and Lawrence E. Shulman. "Competing on Capabilities: The New Rules of Corporate Strategy," *Harvard Business Review.* March–April 1992, pp. 57–69.

Steers, Richard M. "When Is an Organization Effective?" *Organizational Dynamics.* Autumn 1976.

Steiner, George A., and John B. Miner. *Management Policy and Strategy.* New York: Macmillan Publishing Co, Inc., 1977.

Stobaugh, Robert, and Piero Telesio. "Match Manufacturing Policies and Product Strategy," *Harvard Business Review.* March–April 1983, pp. 113–120.

Stonebraker, Peter W. "Managing Organization Fit in Times of Tumult," *The Journal of Management Development.* Vol. 5, No. 4, 1986, p. 24.

Swamidass, Paul M., and William T. Newell. "Manufacturing Strategy, Environmental Uncertainty, and Performance: A Path Analytic Model," *Management Science.* April 1987, pp. 509–524.

Thompson, James D., and William J. McEwen. "Organization Goals and Environment: Goal-Setting as an Interactive Process," *American Sociological Review.* Vol. 23, No. 1, 1958, p. 23.

Tilles, Seymour. "Strategies for Allocating Funds," *Harvard Business Review.* January–February 1966.

Wheelen, Thomas L., and J. David Hunger. *Strategic Management.* Reading, Mass.: Addison-Wesley Publishing Co., 1987.

Willis, Rod. "Harley-Davidson Comes Roaring Back," *Management Review.* March 1986, p. 20.

# Chapter 3

# Operations Strategy Process

*Content focuses on the specifics of what was decided, whereas process addresses how such decisions are reached in an organizational setting. That distinction is useful, in spite of the obvious interaction between the two in organizational life.*
—Liam Fahey and H. Kurt Christensen, 1986

*Flexibility is the key to success —and indecision is the key to flexibility.* —A Cynical Operations Manager

## Objectives

After completing this chapter you should be able to:

- Identify the content and process issues of operations strategy.
- Define operations strategy and show how operations strategy differs from operations planning.
- Describe four elements of the operations strategy process; then, for each element, elaborate several subelements or concepts.
- Use the operations strategy process to evaluate a particular plan and to consider contingently defined alternatives.

## Outline

## *Introductory Case: Operations Strategy at the XYZ Manufacturing Company**

Joan Schouten paused for a moment and looked out the window, reflecting on her seven years with the CRT Division of the XYZ Manufacturing Company. She had joined the firm during her last year at the University and stayed on after graduation. Her first job was as an expediter; then, when she completed her MBA with a major in operations management, she was promoted to Scheduling Manager. Joan was extremely proud of some of the innovations she had introduced, particularly a simple forecasting heuristic to manage returnable packaging for CRTs. Later, she was promoted to her current position as Purchasing Agent, working for Ed Lee, the Production Manager. She was concerned, however, with the lack of an organized planning process.

"Oh, they talk about business planning," she told a friend one day. "Even hired a consultant to give some classes, but then it sort of went away." Joan was then asked to spend more time working with suppliers to ensure effective communication on quality specifications, delivery dates, and lot sizes. The more Joan worked with supplier and customer representatives, the more she recognized the importance of planning, but when she discussed this with Ed Lee, he just shrugged his shoulders and said something about the turbulence of the CRT business.

*Though Joan Schouten is a real person, her employer, who has reviewed this case, requested that the company's identity not be specified.

Ed was right, she thought, because they both could recall many times when a customer canceled an order or changed the quantity, due date, or specification. Other divisions of XYZ seemed to be the most notorious. Possibly they thought that, because they were sister divisions, the cost of changes would be less. In those situations, Ed Lee could be very decisive. "I realized when I came here that this was not a leading edge company—and I sort of accepted that we have few information systems and planning structures. Most people here handle the product on a daily basis, even Ed Lee. We have a low-overhead operation." As Joan again looked out the window, her voice trembled a bit. "I've learned to leave my MBA at home or to use it when I teach at the University. I don't expect anyone to implement computer integrated manufacturing, or even a materials planning system, but I think we should look into some planning and time fence management techniques."

Joan would quickly acknowledge that she was still young. She was gaining experience daily in a business which, though based on traditional CRT-making technologies, had become very dynamic, with global competition, an expanding computer market, and tight cost pressures. "All of this poses several rather interesting questions for me," Joan continued. "Should I shoot for top management or stay a technician? If I choose management, would I still see things the same way that I do now, as a series of simple problems, addressable with some basic planning guidelines, or would I see things as Ed Lee does—from a wider, less definable perspective? Where are this business and plant going to be in five years? If the business thrives, which direction offers more advancement opportunity? If the business fails, which background is more marketable? Should I spend my energies trying to educate my peers and persuade Ed Lee that planning problems are really opportunities to improve efficiency and reduce cost, or should I seek employment at a company that already has state-of-the-art planning techniques?"

"As a professional who thrives on problem resolution, where do the greater challenges lie? I have talked with Ed Lee on several occasions, but he short of shrugs and says something like 'Give yourself time.' You know, sometimes I marvel at the patience of Ed Lee and at other times I worry about his indecisiveness and lack of structure."

## *Evolution of Operations Strategy*

Though strategic management has been applied throughout history in various fields, its impacts have only recently become apparent in operations management. The history of military campaigns involves extensive strategy development followed by implementation through deployment and tactics. Similarly, strategy has played an important role in various political campaigns. However, for several reasons, operations strategy has been ignored in the business environments of the nineteenth and much of the twentieth centuries. Skinner first identified the issue in 1969. Drucker (1988) further explains this situation by his characterization of the organization until the 1960s and 1970s as managed by either owners or by bureaucracies, neither of which necessitated extensive use of strategic management processes. The owner–management structure established sufficient formal and informal power to assure owner control of the organization, while the bureaucracy provided a further, often redundant, control mechanism.

More recently, as Drucker notes, organizations have shifted from a command and control structure to an information-based structure. By its very nature, the information-based structure must achieve a common vision to integrate specialists from diverse professional fields in a highly dynamic, knowledge-oriented, and internationally competitive environment. Operations strategy provides the necessary mechanism to achieve this integrative vision. To paraphrase Joan Schouten in the introductory case, "What is operations strategy and how is it formulated and implemented?"

For organization survival, it is necessary to be effective, or to do the right things, but to prosper, it is necessary to do the right things efficiently. Organizations that use planning activities, as discussed in Chapter 2, generally survive because they are doing the right things, but organizations that prosper often supplement good planning with effective management of their resources and value-adding operations processes. Thus, while the thrust of Chapter 2 was to generally define the dimensions, variables, and content and process issues of operations strategy, this chapter details the process of operations strategy formulation. More specifically, this chapter briefly describes the historical development of operations strategy and elaborates content and process considerations. The four elements of operations strategy: impact evaluation, time dimensions, integrated operations decision-making, and focused operations, are then described.

The characteristics of operations strategy are clearly distinct from those of operations planning. This difference is important because planning positions are technical jobs, defined in support of senior executives whose more generalist functions entail development and management of operations strategy. Operations planning functions are generally characterized by means-oriented efforts, which are analytical, seek an optimal, but often narrow solution, are meticulous in descriptive detail, and are elaborately documented and presented. Alternately, operations strategy functions are characterized by ends-oriented efforts, directed toward a conceptualizing overview to produce satisfactory results through management of the dynamic operating system. Though there are numerous interactions and overlaps between operations planning activities and the operations strategy process, this distinction is useful in that it expresses organizational reality. There is a clear difference in perspective between an operations planning technician, such as Joan Schouten, and a more strategically focused operations manager, such as Ed Lee. As suggested by the introductory case, some technicians mature into operations strategists; some do not. Table 3-1 differentiates the characteristics of operations planning and operations strategy.

**TABLE 3-1 Operations Planning and Operations Strategy**

| Characteristic | Operations Planning | Operations Strategy |
|---|---|---|
| Orientation | Means oriented | Ends oriented |
| Focus | Greater detail | Conceptualizing overview |
| Objectives | Optimal but narrow decisions | Competitive advantage |
| Approach | Variable/Dimension identification | Systems integration |
| Method | Analysis | Action implementation |
| Components | Written plans | Intuitive sensitivity and risk assessment |

This distinction between the planner and the strategist is defined in various different ways. For example, Venkataraman and Prescott (1990) contrast the "reductionist planning approach" with the "holistic management approach." Similarly, Paine and Anderson (1983) emphasize the perspective and process of the strategic manager by differentiating "incremental planning" from "rational comprehensive evaluation." This fundamental dichotomy between the planner analyst and the conceptualizing operations strategist is highlighted by Ward et al. (1990), who suggest that the lack of conceptual synthesis is one reason why U.S. manufacturing capabilities have declined, relative to those of other nations, in the past several years.

Another way of viewing operations strategy is the "configurational" approach, which facilitates the synthesis of reductionist planning and holistic strategic management. Configurations are "commonly occurring clusters of attributes or relationships that are inherently cohesive" (Miller and Friesen, 1984, p. 12) or "tight constellations of naturally supportive elements" (Miller, 1986, p. 236). They are useful because they offer a systems perspective of the important mutually supportive and integrated elements, yet simultaneously give sufficient detail of key elements to permit some understanding of the subsystems and operation. By eliminating or aggregating the less important clusters and by identifying the dynamic interaction within and among the remaining important clusters, configuration theory is able to focus attention on both the content and the underlying processes of an organization.

The configuration approach identifies the few relevant organizational forms and concentrates on the interaction among them. Thus, while organizations undergo the inevitable long periods of relative stability, the focus of the strategic operations perspective is on adaptation of the operation to build capabilities through synergy and consistency. However, when these periods of maintenance give way to periods of intense and multifaceted turbulence, configuration theory captures both the process dynamics and the shifting substance of the organization.

## *Historical Growth of Operations Strategy*

The importance of operations strategy has grown dramatically over the past several decades. This growth has occurred in four general phases, which roughly equate to the four elements of operations strategy. The phases are called *impact evaluation, time dimensions, integrated operations decision-making,* and *focused operations,* as identified in Figure 3-1.

The significance of Figure 3-1 is that it represents simultaneously the general historical development of operations strategy and a typical growth pattern of operations strategy activities in a firm. Additionally, the four phases of this historical evolution may be generalized to represent the growth of an individual from the technical perspective of operations planning to the overview perspective of the operations strategist.

In Phase I, which started in many firms in the 1940s and 1950s, the quarterly or annual budget drives the process. Functional sections bid for program lines; then performance is controlled to meet those lines. Additionally, some static resource allocation and simple forecasting are used. However, by the late 1960s, many firms defined and used time dimensions, growth planning, and advanced forecasting techniques, activities associated with Phase II, in an attempt to better manage uncertainties and project future

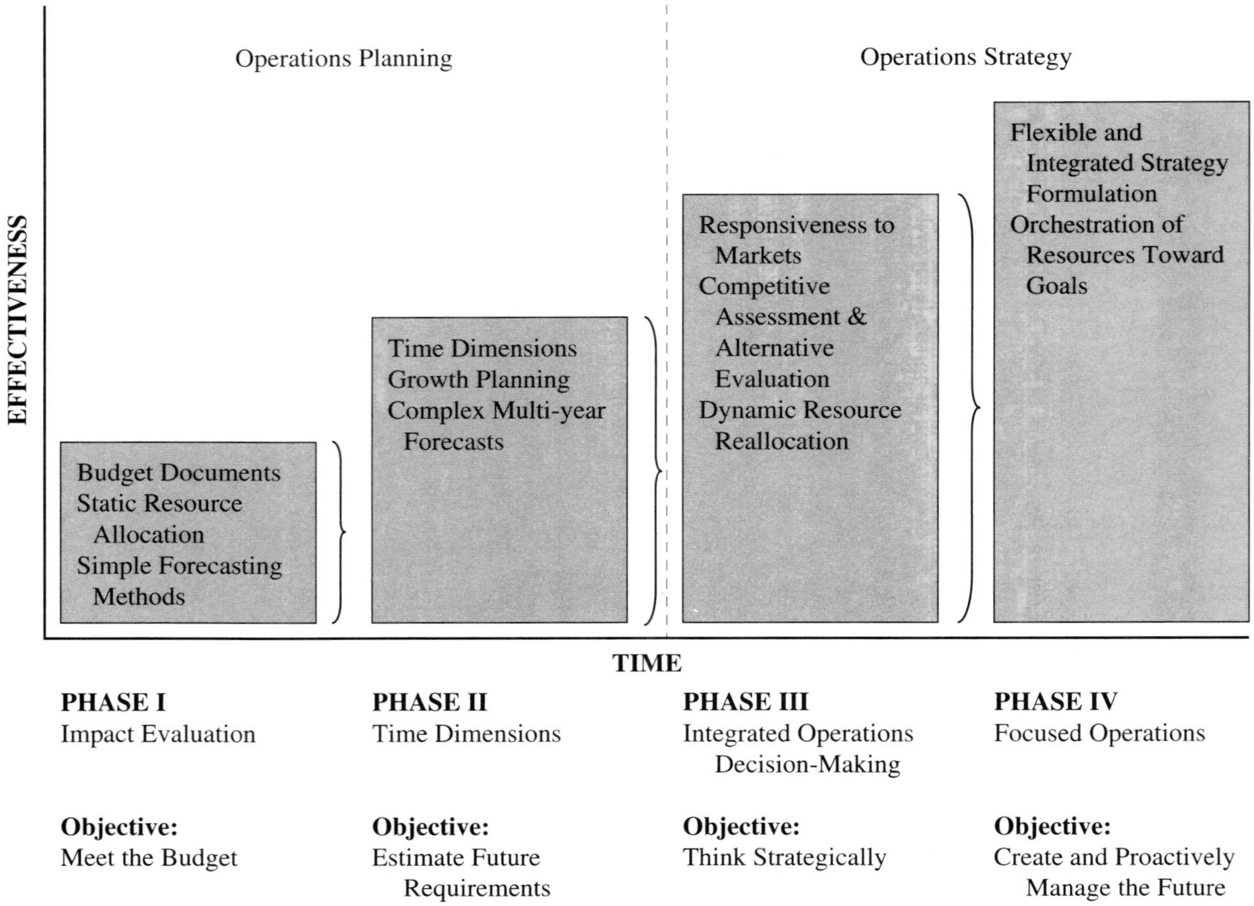
Operations Planning
Operations Strategy
EFFECTIVENESS
Budget Documents
Static Resource Allocation
Simple Forecasting Methods
Time Dimensions
Growth Planning
Complex Multi-year Forecasts
Responsiveness to Markets
Competitive Assessment & Alternative Evaluation
Dynamic Resource Reallocation
Flexible and Integrated Strategy Formulation
Orchestration of Resources Toward Goals
TIME
PHASE I
Impact Evaluation
Objective:
Meet the Budget
PHASE II
Time Dimensions
Objective:
Estimate Future Requirements
PHASE III
Integrated Operations Decision-Making
Objective:
Think Strategically
PHASE IV
Focused Operations
Objective:
Create and Proactively Manage the Future

**FIGURE 3-1 The Evolution of Operations Strategy**

requirements. During the early 1970s, high-cost labor markets, developing technologies, and the dramatic growth of international trade encouraged the development of an integrated decision-making process in order to better respond to markets, to evaluate the competitive situation, and to reallocate resources. During Phase III, those companies which were not able to think strategically found themselves overtaken by competitors, often from other countries. Finally, Phase IV facilitates the further step of proactively creating favorable business conditions and managing those conditions as a strategic system. This is achieved by flexible and integrated strategic planning and orchestration of resources toward building capabilities to achieve competitive advantage. Note that these phases are cumulative and that the activities are both content- and process-oriented.

## *Content of Operations Strategy*

The content approach of operations strategy identifies key variables of operations strategy, which may be further categorized as decision areas and competitive priorities (Leong et al., 1990). Those variables, initially set forth by Skinner, with subsequent elaboration by others, were introduced in Chapter 2 and are summarized in Table 3-2.

Table 3-2 elaborates the important dichotomy between the structural and infrastructural aspects of operations strategy. This distinction, originally defined by Hayes and Wheelwright (1984), is analogous to the distinction between computer hardware and computer software. It differentiates the fixed, long-term and often unrecoverable investments of the firm in durables or facilities from those "software" components that are more controllable by management. As previously noted, structure and infrastructure are central topics of this book.

A second consideration of strategy content is the definition of competitive priority, which includes cost, quality, delivery, and flexibility. Those terms, which were introduced as part of Figure 2-6, are defined as follows:

*Cost*—The production and distribution of a product or delivery of a service with a minimum of expenses or wasted resources such that you have a cost advantage in the market

*Quality*—The manufacture of products or delivery of a service in conformance with specifications or meeting customer needs

*Delivery*—The dependability in meeting requested and promised delivery schedules or speed in responding to customer orders

*Flexibility*—The ability to respond to rapid changes of the product, service, or process, often identified as mix or volume

Thus, content approaches focus on "what is decided" in terms of both decision area and competitive priorities of the firm (Fahey and Christensen, 1986). However, the content approach disregards the processes of integration, interactivity, implementation, and performance measurement. As such, the content approach is a necessary, but not sufficient, contributor to the strategic management process. Companies that use a content approach survive, but they rarely prosper.

**TABLE 3-2 The Content of Operations Strategy**

| | Skinner (1969) | Hayes and Wheelwright (1984) | Buffa (1984) | Fine and Hax (1985) |
|---|---|---|---|---|
| Structure | | • Capacity | • Capacity location | • Capacity |
| | • Plant and equipment | • Facilities | | • Facilities |
| | | • Technology | • Product/ process technology | • Processes and technologies |
| | | • Vertical integration | • Strategy with suppliers, vertical integration | |
| Infrastructure | • Production planning and control | • Production planning and control | • Implications of operating decisions | |
| | | • Quality | | • Product quality |
| | • Organization and management | • Organization | | |
| | • Labor and staffing | • Work force | • Work force and job design | • Human resources |
| | • Product design and engineering | • New product development[a] | • Position of production system | • Scope of new products |
| | | • Performance measurement systems[a] | | |

[a]Addition by Hayes et al. (1988).

Source: Leong et al. 1990.

Many American companies, among them General Motors, American Telephone and Telegraph, International Business Machines, U.S. Steel (now USX Corporation), and Sears, Roebuck, continued to operate through much of the 1980s by refining the methods developed in the 1950s and 1960s. Those companies all survived, in part because of their tremendous size and market dominance. However, though they may have been aware of the changing competitive environment around them, there was little apparent response to those changes until the mid-1980s. In each of these firms, restructuring has resulted in a leaner organization. By implementing an effective operations strategy, these firms have developed the capability to deliver quality goods and services at competitive prices. These firms have repositioned and refined themselves to be significant factors in the global marketplace of the new millennium, just as many smaller, more vulnerable companies have done previously.

## *Process of Operations Strategy*

Operations strategy activities are also a process, or "how operations decisions are reached" in an organizational setting. As might be expected, these processes do incorporate content considerations, but add the further strategic process dimensions of movement and dynamism. Hayes and Wheelwright (1984) identify four elements of an operations strategy formulation effort. Initially, operations strategy requires methods to *evaluate the impacts* of activities and accommodate higher levels of uncertainty. Second, the clear definition of *time dimensions,* including the time horizon and time fences, permits the specification of periods within which actions must be taken. Third, operations strategy must incorporate a *mechanism for integrating decisions.* There must be a change of perspective from a global, long-range, and broadly defined business plan to a focused, specific, and executable operations plan and shop order. Further, the operations strategy must be linked with higher and other functional area strategies. Finally, operations strategy must involve *focused transformation efforts.*

With this introduction, operations strategy is defined as:

> *The content and process of activities, directed toward distinctive operations competence, that* evaluate potential impacts *of situations and alternatives in* structured time dimensions *and* integrate a pattern of decisions *to balance the resource commitments, output requirements, and risks in various* focused transformation efforts.

This definition incorporates the term "directed toward distinctive operations competence and goals," which is drawn from the definitions of operations management and of strategy. Recall from Chapter 1 that those definitions are

> *Operations management* is the effective management of value-adding transformation processes to efficiently integrate resources and achieve specified performance measures toward product/service, process technology, and market goals.
>
> *Strategy* is the current domain and pattern of resource commitments to transformation processes, and planned improvements, as a means to achieve the distinctive competence and goals of the firm.

The definition of *operations strategy* identifies content and process issues, highlights the four elements of operations strategy, and states the dependence of operations strategy on operations planning. These four elements, which correspond closely to the historical growth of operations strategy, are the major topics of this chapter.

As noted in Chapter 2, the content or structure of operations strategy involves the defined and established resource commitments in the domain. These would include definition of work activities and functions and the use of management policies in various areas. Operations strategy as a process involves interaction of the operations position or perspective in business strategy formulation and with the other functional areas. Additionally, the content and position of the primary operations activities, such as facilities management scheduling, inventory management, quality, purchasing, and shipping, should be included both in the development of the operations strategy and in the interaction with business strategy and with the strategies of other functional areas.

Typically, process models establish a hierarchy of plans based on specific time lines, integrated through key decision processes, and evaluated by performance measurement. Invariably, there is a feedback loop to permit interactivity of the model. Unfortunately, as

Leong et al. (1990) point out, these models suggest a structural neatness that does not necessarily exist in reality. Additionally, implementation capabilities do not always follow from operations strategy formulation or plans. Operations planning efforts must balance implementation with an organized process of capability building. The process of operations planning places these analysis- and time-based activities in a dynamic pattern of integrated decision-making, directed toward a focused, executable operation. For clarity of discussion, the next four sections will artificially separate these elements of operations strategy, though they are, in fact, highly interrelated.

## *Impact Evaluation*

Operations strategy must identify the impact that intervening or expected future events or variables will have on the current situation. This process involves the analysis of current changes in competitive forces and the projection of those competitive forces based on one or several intervening events or variables. Of course, the projection of these competitive forces in an uncertain environment is tricky at best and necessarily involves some amount of error. Thus, formalized forecasting and error identification and reduction efforts are used to increase the predictability of future conditions.

### *Analysis of Competitive Forces*

The operations strategy of the firm may be evaluated in terms of three separate competitive forces in a business environment, originally identified by Porter (1980). These three forces are the existing competitive rivalry, the bargaining power of both suppliers and buyers, and the threat of new entrants or substitutes in the product or service market. The importance of each varies among industries and businesses; yet, in sum, these three factors drive and shape strategic management at all levels. For example, competitive rivalry may be changed significantly by advertising methods or sales expenses, which, if effective, can significantly change profits. The bargaining power of buyers and sellers hinges on such things as the number of competitors and the differentiability of products or services in terms of cost, quality, flexibility, and delivery. For example, the emergence of a new competitor or substitute product would likely reduce prices and thus profits. The business environment, including political and social conditions, must be evaluated regularly for the effect on each of these factors. These competitive forces are shown in Figure 3-2.

An intervening event or variable, identified as the organization projects its situation into the future, can take several general forms. These are categorized as:

Random events
Planned for, yet difficult to predict, events
Planned, patterned events

Some business environments may be very stable but are seriously disrupted by a random intervening event. Examples include the effects of weather (tornadoes, hurricanes, and floods) and geologic conditions (earthquakes and volcanic activity), which, although

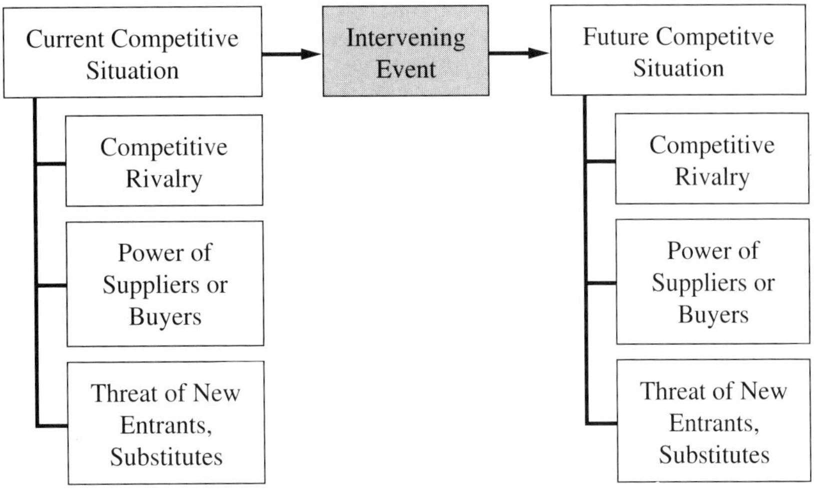


**FIGURE 3-2 The Analysis of Competitive Forces**

they can be generally predicted, appear to strike at random times and locations and often with random effects. These intervening events cause effects that are unanticipated and appear to be random, although some might argue that such events may be better anticipated or that protective measures should be planned. These events clearly change the nature of the competitive rivalry, the relative power of suppliers and purchasers in the marketplace, and the potential for new market entrants or product substitutes. For example, the airline industry suffered from the turbulence of fuel prices and the loss of business from terrorist threats during the Persian Gulf War in the early 1990s.

Planned-for, yet difficult-to-predict, events are involved with many product/service, process technology, or market situations. The introduction of any change in product/service, process technology, or market situation is usually extensively planned; yet such situations, because there is a limited pattern to serve as a baseline for projection, are difficult to predict. Most forecasters would have projected rather good prospects for the personal computer, but few would have anticipated the tremendous growth and impact that it has had. The initial decision by IBM to enter the PC market was a carefully planned and organized decision, but the outcomes of that decision, including changes in the mainframe market, were, at best, hard to predict. The introduction of most new products/services, process technologies to build those products, or the entry into new markets are planned-for, yet difficult-to-predict, events.

The third type of intervening event is based on a pattern which, to a greater or lesser degree, integrates stable and definable plans or events. In many cases, the existing historical pattern will reflect the confluence of several different separately measurable and controllable patterns. For example, most retail goods experience higher sales in the prewinter-holiday period; however, such factors as market growth trends, economic conditions, weather, the number of days between Thanksgiving and Christmas, and the exact day of Christmas also have an effect on holiday retail sales. Similarly, greater volumes of retail sales occur during weekend and three-day holiday periods, and in response to national and international events.

## *Forecast Alternatives and Error Identification*

Forecasting involves capturing, through a model, the inherent pattern or relationships of past observations, and simultaneously recognizing the limits of predictability. Though most managers realize that the "forecast is always in error," most managers also place limits on the amount of error or risk that they are willing to accept in a particular situation. Ultimately, a forecasting system is measured by the accuracy with which it identifies patterns and discovers relationships. However, as a manager repetitively examines a situation, he or she develops a greater understanding of the patterns and an intuition about the relationships. This appreciation goes beyond the forecasting method or tools used in the evaluation. Thus, a forecasting process uses both mechanical techniques to isolate a pattern or relationship and individual sensitivity and intuition to appreciate the effects of related factors. Forecasting is thus both a science and an art.

Quality information and structured process management are prerequisites of an effective forecasting system. Forecast errors directly cause higher inventory costs, schedule adjustments, and lost revenue. Selection of a forecasting method, including incorporation of judgmental processes, error identification, and carefully applied adjustments, are all required for a good forecasting system. General Electric found, for example, that a monthly two-day forecast review process reduced the cost of forecast error by between $80,000 and $150,000 each month. The identifiable quality of a forecast program increases confidence in the system and reduces the temptation among inventory planners to carry excess safety stock (Duncan, 1992).

Most forecasting texts note some twelve to fifteen qualitative and quantitative forecasting methods (ranging in complexity from simple moving averages to exponential, autoregressive and other methods), each with numerous methodological variants and computational factors. Thus, it would be relatively easy to develop three or four hundred different forecasts for a specified situation (for example, sales of product for the next 12 months). The definition and computation of these different forecasting models is the realm of the technician; however, the operations strategist must identify the need for the forecast, evaluate the contributory factors of the future competitive situation, and relate the associated error to the risks involved. Figure 3-3 gives an overview of the forecasting system.

Quantitative methods include time series, regression, and economic methods. Time series methods are designed to address level, trend, and seasonal or cyclic patterns of the data. For example, snowblowers are demanded in the late fall and early winter, and lawnmowers sell well in the spring and early summer. Regressive methods may be used to identify a simple trend relating external data patterns to a variable of concern, or to identify the pattern in a trend or cycle (autoregression). A weather forecast, for example, might be used as an external variable in a regression formulation to project the amount of heating gas (winter) or electricity (summer) demanded by utility customers. Economic multifactor methods, such as national income analyses or international composite models, use regression formats to integrate many factors (upwards of 300). Interested readers can

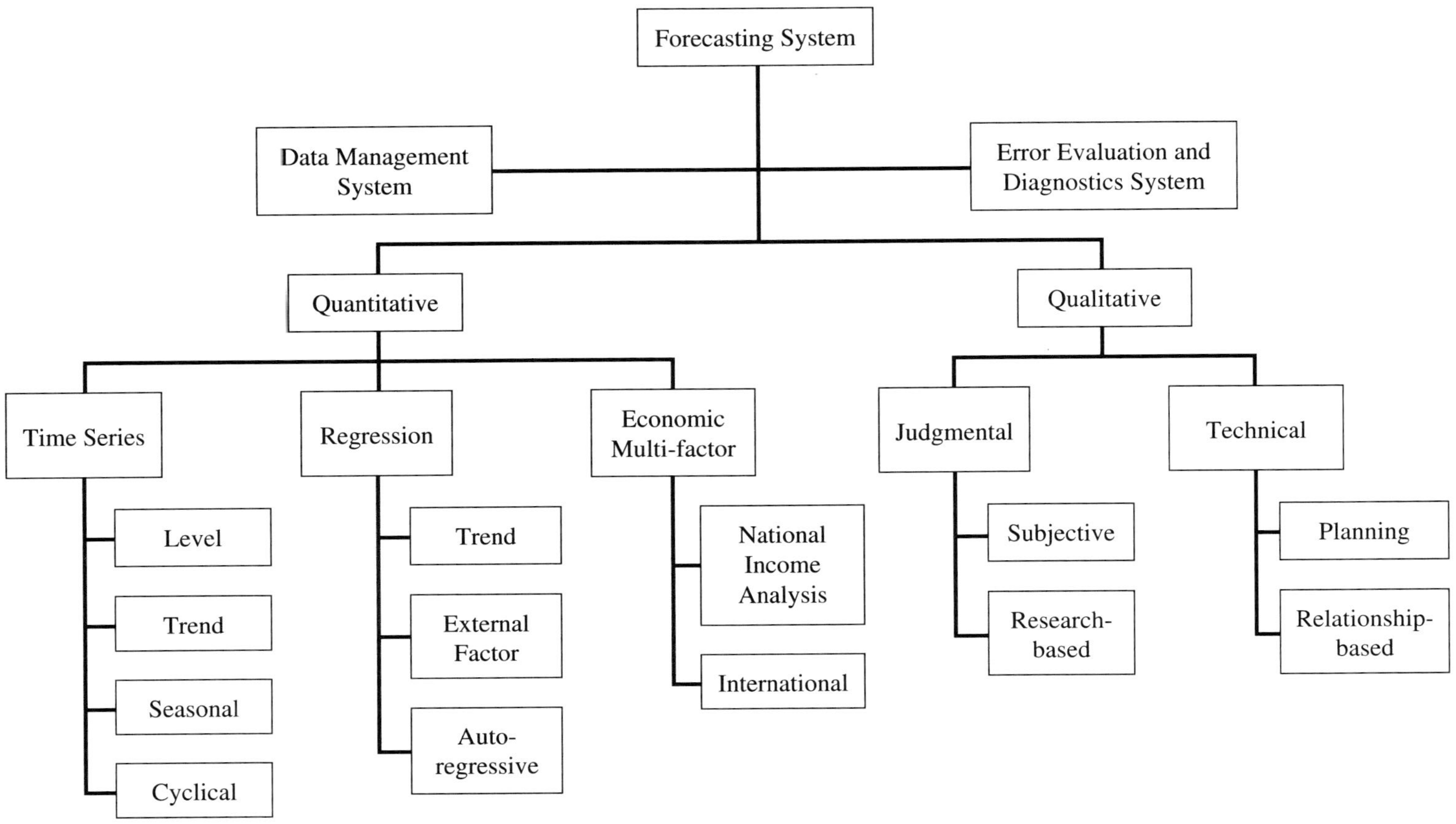


**FIGURE 3-3 An Overview of the Forecasting Process**

pursue these topics in Valentine and Ellis (1991) or other forecasting or econometrics texts. In summary, quantitative models project a series of data by using the inherent pattern of the data or by identifying and using an external relationship.

Qualitative methods of forecasting are generally categorized as judgmental and technical, although there is no clear basis to distinguish these two. Judgmental forecasts include, according to Makridakis and Wheelwright (1989), executive opinions, Delphi methods, sales force composites, anticipatory customer buying surveys, market research-based methods, and a variety of other subjective probability assessments. Judgmental methods may be purely subjective or may incorporate varying degrees of substantiating research. Alternatively, many technical methods, including relevance tree methods, cross impact matrices, and prospective methods, are either planning-oriented methods or relationship-based. Qualitative methods range from purely intuitive judgments to highly structured plans and vary extensively in research- or relationship-based substantiation (Makridakis and Wheelwright, 1989).

The forecast process involves a system for data management and for error evaluation and diagnosis. The data used for the forecast must be stated in terms of the time unit, the entity that is forecast, and the level of detail. For example, a forecast may involve daily, weekly, or monthly time units of sales, profitability, or cost measures that are aggregated by component, item, product group, and product family. The data management system considers these issues.

Additionally, a forecasting system should involve an error evaluation and diagnostic system. A variety of error measurement methods may be used, including the bias, mean absolute deviation, mean square error, percentage error, standard error, correlation coefficient, and tracking signal. Choosing the measure of the error can be as tricky as choosing the forecasting method, because there are numerous different computational processes and each method of error computation has different limitations and advantages. Various of the references describe the computation and interpretation of these different evaluations of forecast error.

## *Methods to Improve Predictability*

One of the limitations of most forecasting methods is that they identify past patterns and relationships, but an accurate explanation of the past may not predict well in the future. Even qualitative methods are based on an intuitive understanding of the past to predict the future. Particularly in dynamic environments, forecasting methods must be able to rapidly identify and adapt to emerging patterns or events. Several approaches can be used to facilitate this process and reduce forecast errors. Among the more widely used techniques are forecast method selection and adjustment, use of multiple forecasting methods (called focus forecasting), rule-based forecasting, proactive monitoring, internalization of the situation and variables, and error cost analysis.

Of course, it is appropriate to select a method that best fits the nature of the data. For example, a forecasting method that captures a level pattern might not be effective with highly seasonal data. The simple moving average method would likely not perform as well with cyclical data as an indexing method. Additionally, the selected method should be adjusted for the data. That is, different smoothing factors should be evaluated for exponential methods; different periods should be evaluated for moving methods; various differencing factors should be evaluated for trend methods; and several periodicity factors should be evaluated for seasonal methods. Often, forecasting results will be improved by combining several methods. The mechanical integration of these methods is a science, but the diagnostic and judgmental process of identifying the most appropriate method or combination of methods is an art.

One approach that has become popular with the advent of low-cost computer programs is called "focus forecasting." This simulation-like technique may involve 15 or more forecasting methods and several different exponents or factors for each method. The logic of focus forecasting is that it identifies the method that gives the least forecasting error with recent observations of a data series. That method is then used to forecast future events, using the rationale that because it was best able to capture some recent (though not necessarily understood) phenomena in the data, it should continue to do so in the near future. Focus forecasting methods are often evaluated and updated quarterly or annually.

A similar approach is used in rule-based forecasting, in which the forecasting process is monitored by a series of rules that are developed for each series. Rules can be defined to evaluate the domain and various features of the series and to adjust for short- and long-range levels, trends, and other patterns. Additionally, rules identify and manage extreme values, specify and vary the number of relevant periods, and manage discontinuities of data and unstable trends. In one study (Collopy and Armstrong, 1992), the use of 99 carefully constructed and validated rules resulted in a reduction of the forecast error of 42% over a comparable baseline method.

Monitoring the forecast for accuracy may involve one or more methods. Some measure of error must be selected; then the process is periodically reviewed. Following the Pareto Principle (which states that there are the critical few and the trivial many), the forecaster may desire to identify the series for which forecast errors are most costly. Those critical few items would be reviewed more regularly than others for which the cost of forecast errors is less critical. Additionally, defined limits of forecast error, however measured, might be used to assess the process periodically and to flag those items for which the forecasting process was getting out of tolerance. Numerous specific control-limit-definition, tracking-signal, and error management systems are described in the references.

Probably the single most critical impact evaluation issue for management is measuring the cost of forecasting error. Of course, if the costs of errors are low, then the selection of the forecasting method may be less important and the periodic review less regular. Ultimately, management will have to assess the risks of forecast error (stated in terms of product stockouts, slow response to product/service, process, or market changes, or inaccuracies in projecting quality or maintenance costs) against the costs of the improved forecasting methods. In today's automated environment, the additional computational costs of very complex forecasting methods are relatively small, compared with the costs of data entry and supervisor training. Though the human variable of forecasting likely is the most costly component, continued work with a data series encourages an internalization and sensitivity toward the factors that drive the series, thus facilitating an intuitive, judgmental, and strategic perception of the environment. Of course, as forecast error is reduced, the improvement is amplified throughout the scheduling, inventory management, quality control, and customer service systems, resulting in lower production costs (Jenkins, 1992).

## *Time Dimensions*

The definition of time dimensions permits the differentiation of planning functions into long-range, mid-range, and short-range planning activities. Time, as well as product/service group categories and geographic areas, can be aggregated and disaggregated through a technique called pyramids of aggregation. Additionally, the long-range, mid-range, and short-range time periods permit the definition of specific time fences which are used to manage the finalization of certain decisions and activities.

### *Defining Time Dimensions*

Initially, the time limit of interest, or time horizon, must be defined as the point of time beyond which it is not necessary for the planning or forecasting system to project. As the forecast projects a greater number of periods into the future, it will generally become less accurate; thus, at some point in the future, further projection becomes pointless. For example, the horizon must be defined at least as far into the future as the maximum order lead time, and it is usually a good idea to have some additional demand visibility beyond that maximum lead time. The time horizon thus is used as a bound for the long-range forecast. Once that time horizon has been specified, the periods of the long-, mid-, and short-range plans can be defined.

The three ranges of planning are described here sequentially from long-range to mid-range to short-range on the rationale, adapted from Plossl (1985), that if long-range planning is good, the mid- and short-range plans will be workable. That is, resources must be well-managed in the long-range aggregate before they can be controlled in detail in the mid and short range.

Long-range plans will rarely cover a period of less than six months and may extend ten or more years; short-range plans will rarely be less than two weeks or more than six months in length. Mid-range plans are in between. By convention, the long-range time frame is often defined as the time necessary to develop a new product and the production process to support it. In automobile building, for example, the long range may be the six or more years necessary for a manufacturer to design an automobile and then build a production process. General Motors took roughly six years to design the Saturn automobile and build the Spring Hill, Tennessee plant. Alternatively, the short-range planning period is often stated as the time within which changes in the production schedule cannot be made without substantial costs. It may correspond to the longest lead time of a procured component or the longest production time for an item that is built in house. Other situations might involve much shorter planning horizons and planning time periods. These relationships are shown in Figure 3-4.

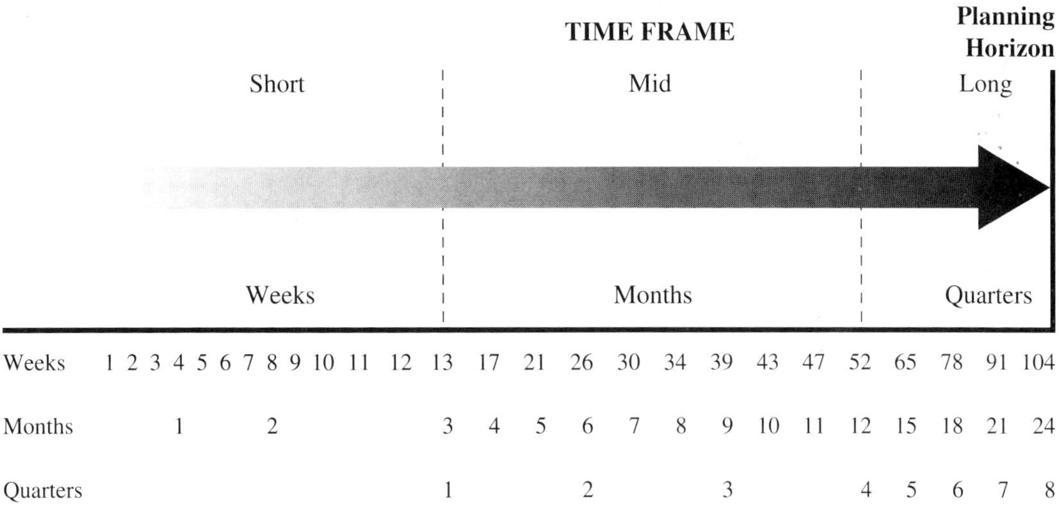


**FIGURE 3-4 The Planning Horizon and Planning Time Frames**

*Note:* The 4–4–5 method of adjusting weekly data to monthly data uses 4 weeks in the first month, 4 weeks in the second month, and 5 weeks in the third month of each quarter. This method permits the accurate identification of 13 weeks in each quarter or 52 weeks per year.

Reprinted by permission, APICS, *Master Planning CPIM Review Course,* 1991, Transparency 1-13.

The planning horizon in Figure 3-4 is set at a relatively short two years, with the long range of one to two years, the mid-range of three to 12 months, and the short range of 13 weeks. The reason for differentiating the long-, mid-, and short-range planning time frames and the planning horizon is that the planning activities in these periods have different characteristics, are used for different types of decisions, and involve different forecasting methods. These differences are shown in Table 3-3.

Generally, the long-range planning process is a one-time, high-level, and highly judgmental process. It usually involves more external data inputs and a more dynamic and unpredictable environment. The plan is stated in general terms, such as total sales or the sales of aggregated groupings of products or services. Such planning efforts are used in long-range decisions, including facilities or capacity analysis, long-range projects, and the development of new products or new markets. Invariably, long-range decisions involve large capital commitments and difficult to recover (or sunk) investments.

The corresponding characteristics of the mid-range planning period are monthly quantitative and qualitative data, usually mixed from both internal and external sources and conducted for product groupings and families at the middle level of the product hierarchy. Decisions involve budgets, operations planning, the initial master schedule and operations plan, and mid-range purchasing commitments, such as blanket orders.

By contrast, short-range planning efforts are recurring (daily, weekly), highly detailed, and quantitative in nature. Short-range data usually comes from reliable internal sources and presumes stability of the external environment. Large numbers of individual

**TABLE 3-3 Long-, Mid-, and Short-Range Planning**

| LONG-RANGE | MID-RANGE | SHORT-RANGE |
|---|---|---|
| *CHARACTERISTICS* | | |
| One-time analysis | Periodic (monthly/quarterly) | Recurring |
| Mostly judgmental | Both quantitative and qualitative | Quantitative |
| External data | Some external data | Internal data |
| High level | Mid-level | Detail level |
| Dynamic environment | Varying environment | Stable environment |
| Few products/families | Product groupings/families | Many items or SKUs |
| Quarterly | Monthly | Weekly/daily |
| *DECISIONS* | | |
| Facilities analysis | Budgets | Inventory deployment |
| Long-range projects | Operations planning/master scheduling | Operations scheduling/final assembly scheduling |
| Capital investments | Blanket purchase orders | Material planning |

Adapted by permission, APICS, *Master Planning CPIM Review Course,* 1991, Transparencies 1-14, 1-15, and 1-16.

items are managed in the short range. Decisions often involve the scheduling and execution of the operations plan, and may integrate materials planning and purchasing decisions, scheduling, and inventory deployment through the distribution system.

## *Pyramids of Aggregation*

The importance of defining these three planning periods is overshadowed by the necessity of integrating them. This is often done through a process of aggregation and disaggregation. Three frameworks are customarily used for aggregation pyramids: time, product group, and geographic area. In the time aggregation, data is collected by day; then days are aggregated into weeks and months and quarters by using a variety of calendar-based algorithms, including the 4–4–5 rule (explained in the note to Figure 3-4). Similarly, geographic pyramids involve aggregations of store, district, regional, and global (or like designations), and product group pyramids involve aggregations of stock-keeping units (SKUs) or components, product items, and product families. Aggregation and disaggregation techniques may be used for one, two, or all three of the pyramids of aggregation. Figure 3-5 shows the commonly used increments of aggregation for time periods, geographic areas, and product groups.

A rather widely used application of aggregation–disaggregation is the pyramid forecasting technique. In that application, product forecasts are "rolled up" from the lower level to the higher level. Then, at the higher level, an adjusted or planning value is specified and "forced down" to the lower level. The adjustment may be determined by a variety of considerations, including the convenience of lot-sizing or bulk delivery volumes. A two-level example of the pyramid forecasting technique is shown in Decision Model Box 3-1. Note that products $X_1$ and $X_2$ are aggregated to the group level; then an

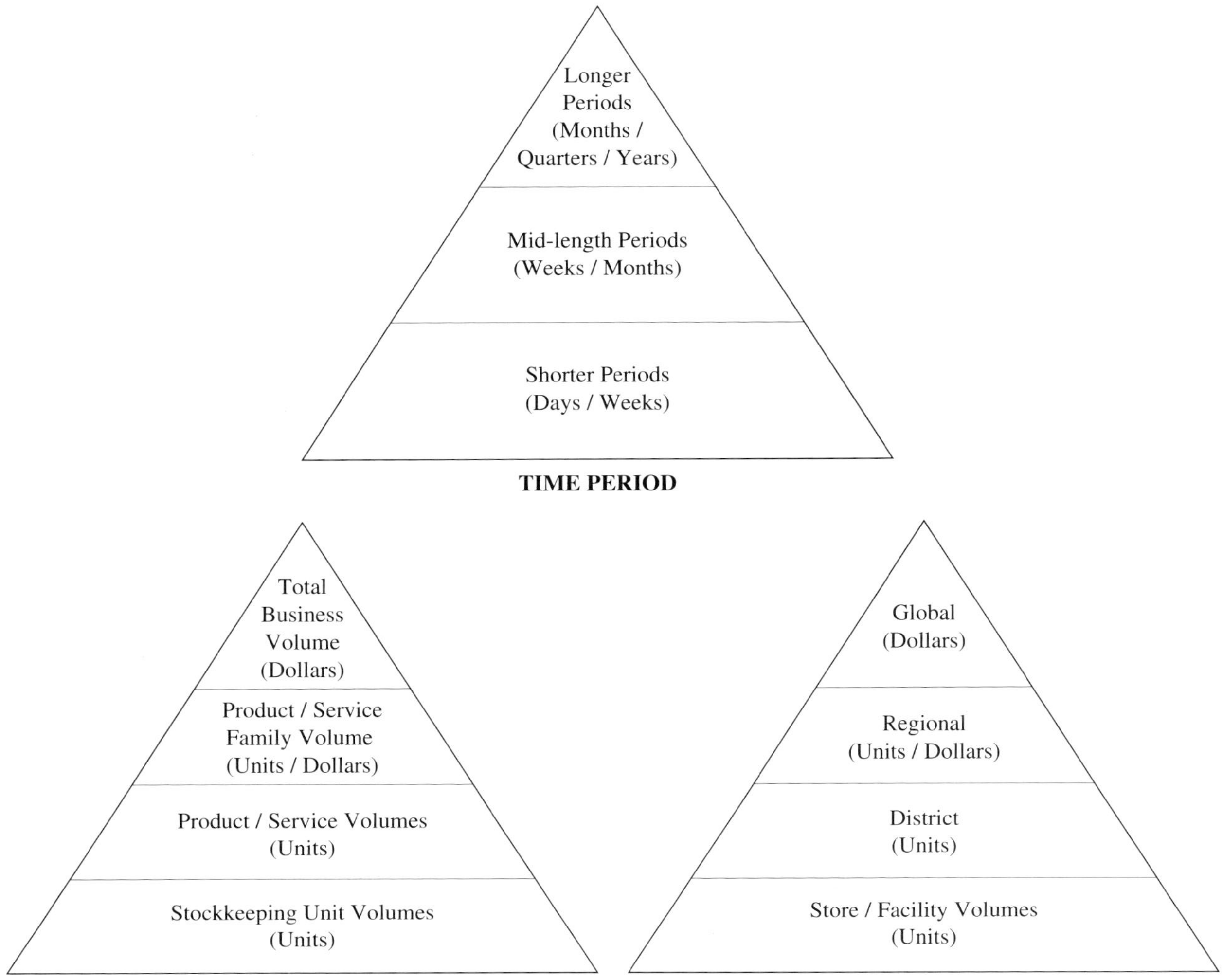


**FIGURE 3-5 The Pyramids of Aggregation**

Reprinted by permission, APICS, *Master Planning CPIM Review Course,* 1991, Transparency 1-12.

## DECISION MODEL BOX 3-1 Pyramid Forecasting at the Brand Central Retail Store

Brand Central, a national retail chain store, uses a pyramid forecasting process to integrate product item volumes for each product with the product family and total business volume forecasting process, and simultaneously to integrate geographic regions and time periods. The following data is a very small, but representative subset of Brand Central's forecasting process. Region forecasts of items $X_1$ and $X_2$ are given with the prices of those items. The number of units forecast is aggregated to a product family forecast, then adjusted, then forced back down in proportion to the original forecasts. The adjustment (in this case, to 15,000 units) may be purely judgmental, or based on some very mechanical consideration, such as efficient shipping lots, ranges of forecasting error, or seasonal demand. This example shows the integration of two levels of the product group pyramid, but it is common practice to simultaneously integrate several levels of two or three pyramids. Note that the slight difference between the adjusted dollar volume rolled up of $250,050.00 and the forced-down forecast of $250,041.69 results from a rounding variation.

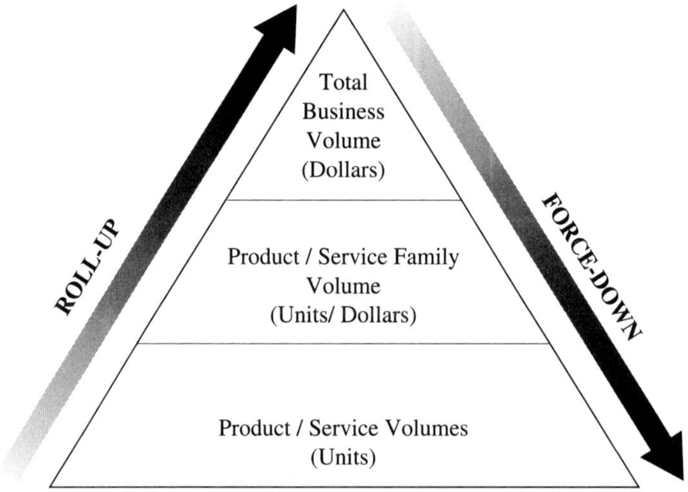


**Roll-Up**

| | Product | Units Forecast | | Price |
|---|---|---|---|---|
| Product level forecast for 1 month | | | | |
| | $X_1$ | 8,200 | | $20.61 |
| | $X_2$ | 4,845 | | 10.00 |
| Product family forecast for 1 month | $X_1 + X_2$ | 13,045 | Average | $16.67 |
| Adjusted forecast for product family for 1 month | | 15,000 | | $250,050.00 |

**Force Down**

| | | | | |
|---|---|---|---|---|
| Prorated forecasts from product family | $X_1$ | $\frac{15{,}000}{13{,}045}$ (8,200) = | 9,429 × $20.61 = | $194,331.69 |
| to product level for 1 month | $X_2$ | $\frac{15{,}000}{13{,}045}$ (4,845) = | 5,571 × $10.00 = | 55,710.00 |
| | | | | $250,041.69 |

adjustment is made at the group level (based, perhaps, on an intuitive evaluation) and the adjusted total volume is forced down to each of the two products, based on the prorated proportion of the initial forecasts.

## *Time Fence Management*

The concepts of impact evaluation and time dimensions are drawn together by time fence management. Time fences are critical junctures in future planning periods. They specify the times within which certain operations-related changes must be made. Three fences, the demand time fence, the planning time fence, and the capacity fence, are commonly defined (Greene, 1987). The *demand* fence is when physical or financial resources are committed to operations, and the *planning* fence is when planning effort is committed to operations. Inside the demand time fence (often the demand time fence corresponds with the short-range planning time frame), the schedule is "firm." No changes are permitted unless the cost of those changes is paid by the activity requiring the change. Between the demand fence and the planning fence, the schedule is somewhat fluid (or "slushy") and beyond the planning time fence it is "free," or easily changed. Capacity changes can be made beyond the capacity fence, which often corresponds to the long run. Forecasting is used to project future resource needs, but, as customer orders are received, they "consume" the forecast. These relationships are shown in Figure 3-6.

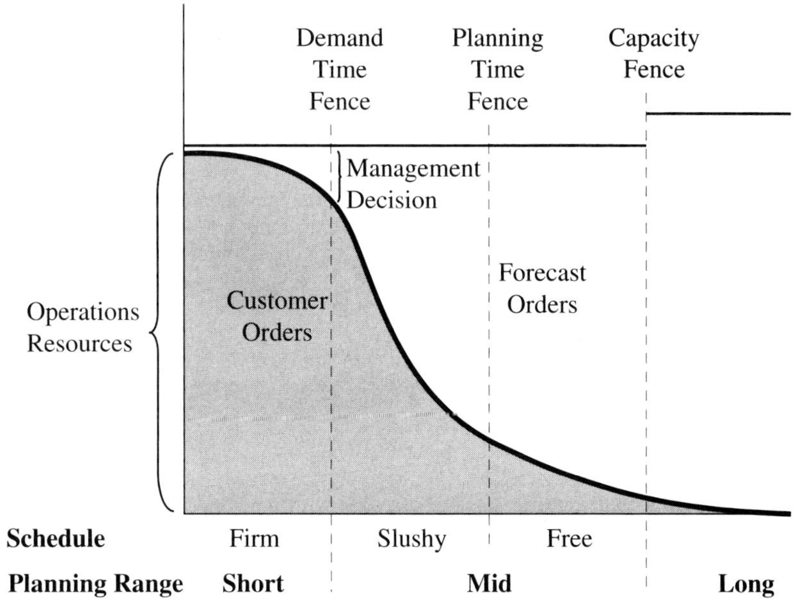


**FIGURE 3-6 The Use of Time Fences**

Reprinted by permission, APICS, *Master Planning CPIM Review Course,* 1991, Transparency 7-5.

Consider, for example, a make-to-order furniture factory that can final-assemble 1000 chairs per week. Because of variations in chair size, style, type of wood, finish, and covering, many components can be rough-cut and prepared for assembly, but not final-assembled. It takes eight weeks to dry the lumber and prepare the components, and an additional four weeks to assemble, finish, and cover a chair from components. Thus, inside the demand fence of four weeks, the schedule is firm; within the 12- (four plus eight) -week planning time fence, plans and materials are being prepared, but no resources (other than time) are *irrevocably* committed to final production. Beyond the 12-week planning fence, there is a period of visibility for planning purposes. The capacity fence, which might be defined at one year, is often defined between the mid-range and the long-range planning times.

In the mid- and long range, the firm uses forecasts to project the total number of chairs that will be demanded. A capacity increase is projected to 1200 units per week in the long range. In the mid-range, however, the forecast or current capacity of 1000 units per week is gradually absorbed, or "consumed," as customer orders are received. At the demand time fence, management must make the decision to produce at the level of existing customer orders or to produce to the forecast, hoping that subsequent orders will be forthcoming for the models that are produced.

Note that the demand time fence often coincides with a firm schedule and the short-range planning period, and that the long-range planning period defines the capacity fence and is driven almost entirely by the forecast. Capacity can be changed beyond the capacity fence, as shown in the diagram, for example, by adding more equipment or building an additional plant. Though time fences were initially designed as mechanisms to stabilize a production schedule, they are equally useful today as mechanisms to integrate and manage planning efforts.

## *Integrated Operations Decision Making*

The operations planning cycle uses the concepts of impact evaluation and time dimensions to integrate operations planning activities from the long-range business plan to the execution of the operations plan and evaluation of that process. It is divided into three time frames, corresponding to the long-, mid-, and short-range plans. In the long range, the business plan draws together plans for each of the major staffs and is specifically focused toward the accomplishment of corporate goals. Forecasting is a strategic activity, defining the management objectives of the business plan as a detailed statement of future requirements that are usable by all operating departments (Artes, 1992). Operations planning defines the operations contribution to the business plan and identifies, often by product family, the appropriate requirements by month or quarter. Resource planning assures that all key resources required by the operations plan are available. Thus, at the capacity fence, the general availability of resources is confirmed.

In the mid-range, the master production schedule and rough-cut capacity planning processes create an initial working schedule; then, as the planning fence is passed, the schedule becomes increasingly firm. Subsequently, material requirements planning and capacity requirements planning, respectively, identify all of the specific requirements for the operations schedule and evaluate available resources to assure feasibility. Within the planning time fence, planning assets are increasingly committed; for that reason, it is important to avoid spurious changes and adjustments. Thus, costs are often charged for changes in this range.

At the demand fence, the scheduled plan is affirmed, and planning is accomplished for short-range activities such as purchasing external components, shop floor planning (for example, input/output planning) of internal production, and performance measurement. Within the demand time frame, changes in the schedule can be made, but usually only if committed resources are paid for and if top management approves. The operations planning cycle is shown in Figure 3-7.

The individual plans and activities of the operations planning cycle will be described in detail in subsequent chapters. The introduction of the operations planning cycle here suggests the importance of the cycle as an integrative operations strategy tool. Concisely:

1. The activities of long-range, mid-range, and short-range planning are specifically differentiated but integrated by management-defined evaluative time fences.
2. The planning time fences contain several feedback and feed-forward loops that are based on key decision junctures.
3. The process demonstrates the use of an aggregate long-range planning perspective which leads to disaggregated mid- and short-range planning processes.
4. The planning cycle is focused toward the execution of an operation and the performance measurement of that operation, stated in terms of previously defined competitive priorities.
5. At each step of the cycle, conceptual perspectives and inherent risk management activities can be identified.

Though the representation of this integrative operations strategy framework varies (Leong et al., 1990) and the importance of various components may differ among industries and certainly among specific operations, it is absolutely important that the operations manager master and intuitively use this or some variation of the operations planning cycle. This cycle provides a planning framework based on high-level and long-term plans, iterated sequentially to mid- and short-range activities in a constantly reviewed process. This framework also provides the operations manager with a mechanism through which to evaluate and manage the focus of operations resources.

## *Focus of Operations*

The final element of operations strategy is a measure of implementation, defined as the focus of operations resources. Skinner may have been the first to coin the term *focus,* meaning a clear and sharply defined set of products, technologies, volumes, and markets (1974). The operations planning cycle, because it integrates impact evaluation and time dimensions, should focus the requirements of the production or service system. What

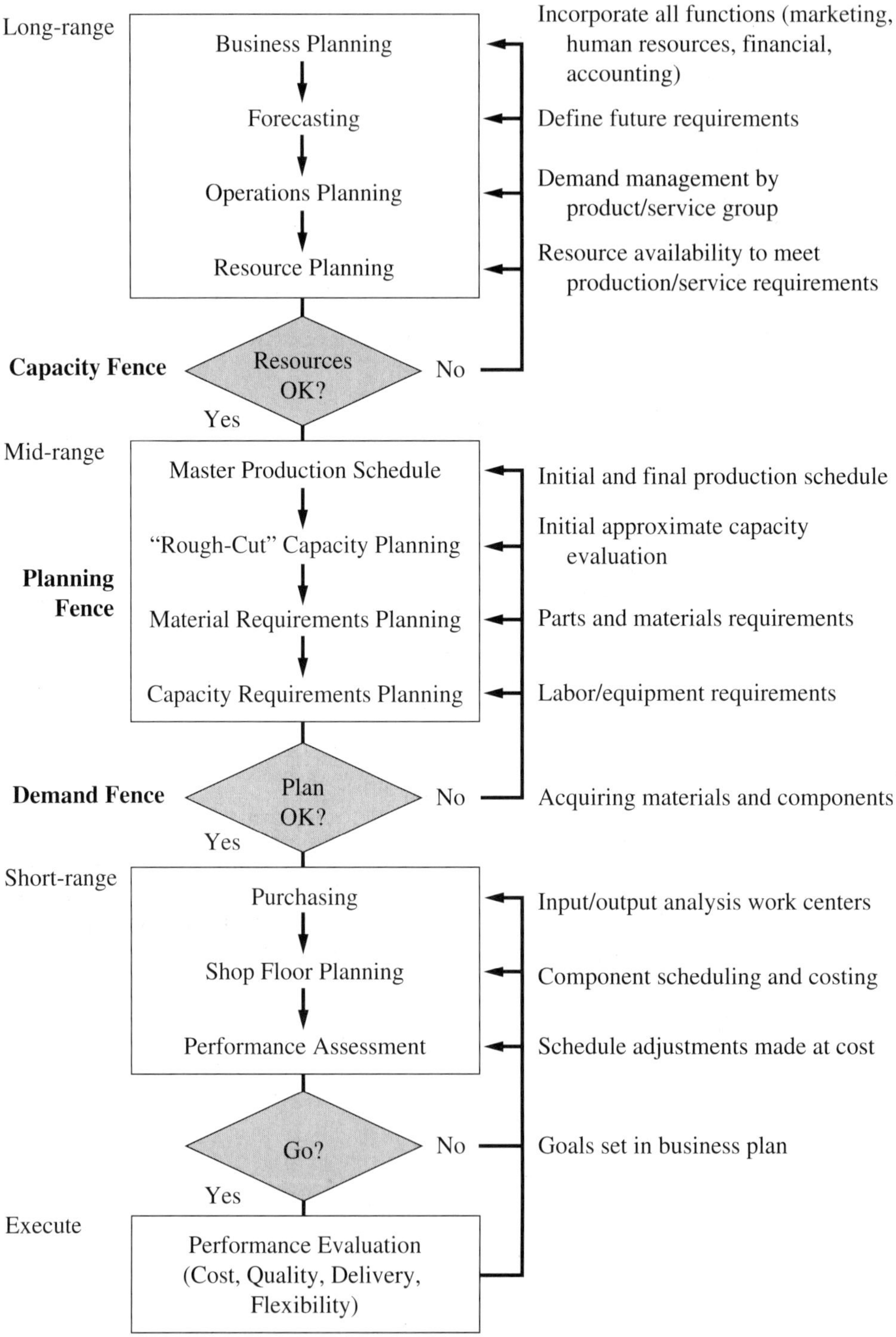


**FIGURE 3-7 The Operations Planning Cycle**

Reprinted by permission, APICS, *Master Planning CPIM Review Course,* 1991, Transparency 1-13.

remains is the important task of concentrating resources toward those requirements and establishing a critical mass or focus of resources sufficient to achieve an effective and efficient operation.

## *Focused Resources*

The three generic business strategies defined by Porter (1980) are cost leadership, product differentiation, and focus. Cost leadership is primarily based on process technology, process economies of scale, and linkages along the chain of transformations. Similarly, product differentiation relates to a unique aspect or characteristic of the product or service that is achieved in the value-adding process. Finally, focus is based on the selection of a narrower market segment or group of segments and tailoring the strategy "to serve that segment to the exclusion of others." Thus business cost strategies are primarily process technology-related, product differentiation strategies are primarily product- or service-related, and focus strategies are primarily market-related.

The operations manager must specify categories of those three dimensions. This is often achieved through project management techniques. For example, process technology groups may be classified as job shop through the discontinued line and fully automated line. Differentiated products may be defined as variations from the mechanical typewriter to the computer with word processing software. The customer or market for a product might be defined as "in house," local, regional, or international or by a range of segments or niches. Certainly more exact statements of these groups could be defined in specific businesses. This combination of product/service, process technology, and customer/market permits the company to define and focus one primary objective, with possibly a secondary objective for a particular facility—if not for the company. The selection of a specific product/service, process, and customer/market combination also suggests the competitive priority of cost, quality, delivery, or flexibility. For example, it would be difficult for most firms to have the same delivery capability for in-house and international markets. Cost, quality, and flexibility priorities would also likely differ between the in-house and international markets. The firm must concentrate its limited resources toward achieving competitive advantage in the market.

Within the specified distinctive competence, the operations manager should further classify the markets, processes, and products. For example, the models of an electronic typewriter might include those with a 24-character display, a 50-character display, a 3-line display, and a 10-line display. A regional market might be classified by major distribution zones, including states and cities, and the discontinuous-line process technology might involve several different production options, such as hot pressing, molding, and laser coring for the plastic liquid crystal display unit. These options, once selected, more specifically identify and constrain the cost, quality, flexibility, and delivery positions of the firm. A very fine discussion of this topic is offered by Sprague (1990). Figure 3-8 shows an application of the focus of operations resources.

When an operation is defined in these specific terms, it is much easier to understand the changes that would be associated with a proactive shift in strategy. For example, shifts in strategy such as the movement from the 24-character display model product market to a full 10-line screen display model, the opening of a new market region in Pennsylvania,

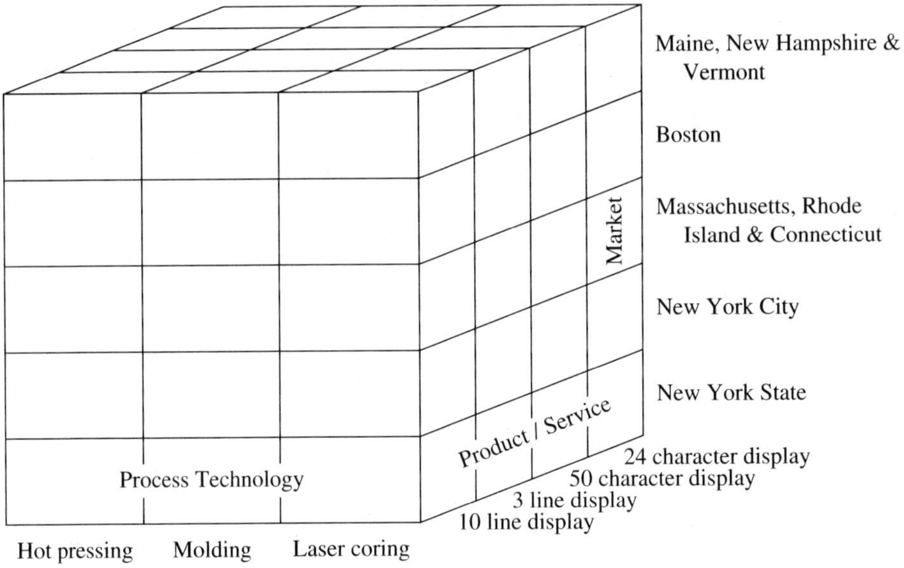


**FIGURE 3-8 The Focus of Resources**

or the implementation of a new process technology are all visualizable. Galbraith (1986) calls this the "population ecology" approach to strategic adaption and suggests a bio-ecological analog to the natural selection process. In operations strategy, such an approach would mean that the more costly, less efficient segments would be gradually replaced by better segments as market, process, and product conditions change.

## *Commitment Versus Risk*

Ultimately, the focus of committed operations resources and the risks associated with various strategic changes must be assessed. This process involves identifying and projecting the direction of the operation under the present conditions and with several given contingencies, based on plans, forecasts, or a combination of both. The current direction of the operation then is compared with several alternative possibilities and under various conditions of intervening events (recall Figure 3-2). This contingency analysis approach permits an examination of specific measures such as product quality or cost, market penetration, delivery rates, process flexibility, or others, and to assess the present direction of the firm against one or several alternative plans. The variation between the current projection and the specific plan (the gap) suggests an increased or decreased focus of resources with the associated risks. This contingency analysis is shown in Figure 3-9.

The current projection suggests a stable resource commitment to focus, say, a quality control program. Of course, this measure can be stated in very explicit terms, such as dollars for a new quality measurement system, or in less-defined terms, such as the use of a training program to develop personal commitment to identify all quality problems. Two

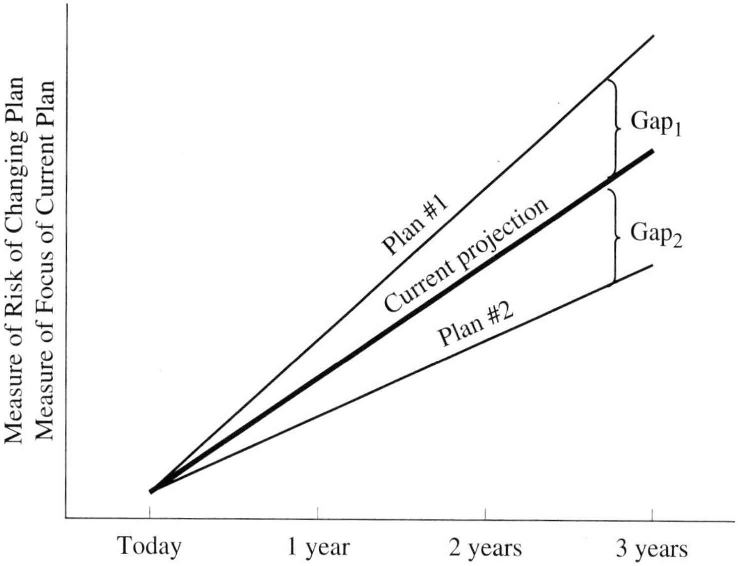


**FIGURE 3-9 Contingency Analysis**

alternative plans show different amounts of either per-period or cumulative resource commitment. But these plans are simultaneously associated with different risks. Though it would be easy to conclude that the less the commitment, the less the risk, that may not hold in all circumstances. A lesser commitment may be associated with a greater risk. For example, if a company makes a small commitment to the development of a new technology, a competitor may be encouraged to enter the market with a greater resource commitment and gain a competitive advantage. A more elaborate example of contingency analysis is given in Decision Model Box 3-2.

## *Flexibility as a Resource*

The Bredemeier Company application emphasizes the importance of the earlier description of the competitive priorities of cost, quality, delivery, and flexibility, and particularly the importance of flexibility. The ability to respond to changes in customer requirements is more than just technique-based. As Plossl (1992) notes, a sound strategy directed toward flexibility is also needed. Flexibility may be classified as product/service- or process technology-related, and further defined in six different ways, as shown in Table 3-4. This approach incorporates the concept of innovation, which has been separately identified by some researchers (Maidique and Hayes, 1984; Gerwin, 1987) as a fifth competitive priority.

Flexibility is either product/service- or process technology-related. Product/service-related flexibility, such as changes in the volumes, mixes, or product/service design, is very important in terms of responsiveness to customer delivery and quality requirements.

## DECISION MODEL BOX 3-2 Contingency Analysis—Bredemeier Samples

Bredemeier Samples is a small (100-employee) family-owned business that makes sample swatch books and cards. Swatch materials are used by many furniture, automobile, appliance, fabric, and rug retailers to show available color, covering, or wood grain alternatives. Manufacturing the sample books requires printing, cutting, pasting, and binding skills, and is generally labor intensive. Small volumes of 2,000 books per job are typical. Bredemeier currently plans to purchase a swatch cutter–paster machine that will automatically cut and mount up to 30 cloth or color paper swatches per page. This technology has been used successfully by an overseas competitor, but Bredemeier managers have identified as potential risks the sensitivity of the equipment to humidity and dust and the high labor training and skills required. Though the company has a policy to protect employees against layoffs, employee frustration with the high technology may be reflected in lower than expected efficiencies. One benefit of the new equipment is that the company could reduce delivery times and thus be more responsive to customer requirements.

The current plan calls for purchasing one new machine per year at a cost of $100,000 per machine, for each of the next five years. Bredemeier managers have estimated that the additional responsiveness provided by the first machine will increase the company profits by $40,000 per year. The second through fifth machines would increase company profits by $30,000, $20,000, $10,000, and $5,000, respectively. Additionally, managers have estimated that because of variations in receptiveness of current employees toward the equipment, the first machine would result in a 150% efficiency improvement over current methods, and that the additional machines would result in efficiency improvements of 120%, 90%, 60%, and 30%, respectively. The following table gives several decision options, stated in current dollars.

This very basic example only minimally introduces the issues of forecasting future sales and projecting future performance. The timing of the investment must be considered in terms of the

| Option | Description | Equipment Cost | Cost of Installation and Training | Benefit | | Benefit/Cost Ratio |
|---|---|---|---|---|---|---|
| 1 | 1 machine in first year | $100,000 | $150,000 | 5(40,000 × 1.5) | = $300,000 | $\frac{300,000}{250,000} = 1.2$ |
| 2 | 1 machine in each of first 2 yr | $100,000 × 2 = $200,000 | 160,000 | 5(40,000 × 1.5) + 4(30,000 × 1.2) | = $444,000 | $\frac{444,000}{360,000} = 1.23$ |
| 3 | 1 machine in each of first 3 yr | $100,000 × 3 = $300,000 | 170,000 | 5(40,000 × 1.5) + 4(30,000 × 1.2) + 3(20,000 × 0.9) | = $498,000 | $\frac{498,000}{470,000} = 1.06$ |
| 4 | 1 machine in each of first 4 yr | $100,000 × 4 = $400,000 | 180,000 | 5(40,000 × 1.5) + 4(30,000 × 1.2) + 3(20,000 × 0.9) + 2(10,000 × 0.6) | = $510,000 | $\frac{510,000}{580,000} = 0.88$ |
| 5 | 1 machine in each yr | $100,000 × 5 = $500,000 | 190,000 | 5(40,000 × 1.5) + 4(30,000 × 1.2) + 3(20,000 × 0.9) + 2(10,000 × 0.6) + 1(5,000 × 0.3) | = $511,500 | $\frac{511,500}{690,000} = 0.74$ |

**DECISION MODEL BOX 3-2** *Continued*

strength of the economy, the feelings of the employees about the equipment, and the possibility that if they do not offer more responsive delivery, a competitor will. Certainly the variables suggested by this situation can be extensively elaborated, as can the benefit/cost analysis. Of the five options, option 2 has the best benefit/cost ratio, yet many of the decision factors may change. Perhaps the least risky option is to purchase one machine in the first year, followed by a reevaluation of the plan.

**TABLE 3-4 Operations Flexibility**

| Product/Service/ Process Technology and Type | Definition and Examples |
|---|---|
| **Product/Service-related** | |
| Volume | The ability to respond quickly to changes in the amount of a particular product or service that is required. For example, a business card printer can easily respond to an order to print either 500 or 50,000 business cards, whereas the volume of an automobile assembly line is difficult to change rapidly. |
| Mix | The ability to react quickly to changes in mix or proportion of products of a product family that are produced. For example, a nut packaging operation can be changed to pack a different mix or product (100% peanuts to a cashew–peanut mix) more easily than a paint-can filling operation or a beer or soda bottling operation. |
| Modification | The ability to incorporate changes in product characteristics and to develop and produce newly designed products. For example, delivery of a redesigned automobile model would take a minimum of two years and as many as five years, whereas design and delivery of fashion clothing might take as little as several weeks. |
| **Process Technology-related** | |
| Changeover | The ability to respond rapidly to different production set-ups required for various products. For example, changeovers of heavy presses from one model of automobile fender or bumper to another may take 30 or more minutes, whereas changeover of a small drillpress can be done virtually without delay by computer-assisted-manufacturing systems. |
| Scheduling | The ability to vary the routing, sequence, or production lot-sizes to accommodate required production volumes. For example, a job shop typically has greater scheduling variability or flexibility than does an assembly line. |
| Innovation | The ability to define and implement new technologies in production processes with minimal disruption. For example, a firm with high employee skills would likely be able to implement a computer-assisted-manufacturing or material requirements planning system more rapidly than a firm with lower employee skills levels. |

Adapted from Gerwin (1987).

However, the related process technology flexibilities of changeover, scheduling, and process innovation are equally important because they ensure the process capability to produce the product or deliver the service flexibly at an acceptable cost, thus meeting delivery and quality requirements. A further description of different types of flexibility and a mathematical programming evaluation of the costs of trade-offs among those types of flexibility are provided by Ramasesh and Jayakumar (1991).

Because of the increasing dynamism of the global market, flexibility may emerge as the most important competitive priority of the 1990s and the first part of the twenty-first century. Over the past several decades, the key competitive priority in operations management has shifted. For example, in the decades of the 1950s and 1960s, many industries emphasized low cost with little flexibility of product or process, sometimes with a resulting subtle decline in quality. By the 1970s and 1980s, many American businesses were undercut by overseas producers who were able to produce higher-quality goods at low costs. Thus, quality became the critical production priority for many industries. However, as suggested by the Bredemeier application, high costs and the inherent risks of producing in increasingly dynamic international environments may increase the importance of flexibility as a competitive priority.

## *Summary*

Ultimately, the operations manager, as a management strategist, must be responsible for defining and implementing a strategy based on four elements: impact evaluation, time dimensions, integrating operations decisions, and focused operations. The technical expertise and eye for detail of the operations planner, who defines the measures and time dimensions, are necessary, but not sufficient preconditions for the success of the operations strategy process. The strategic management of an operation requires further integration and focus. At many points, the process involves the evaluation of incomplete and dynamic data and judgmental assessment and risks. The operations manager develops, with extensive experience, an intuitive appreciation for the subtleties of the environment, the product/service, and the process technology. Such an appreciation is clearly an art form.

Though the ability to structure a problem and use a variety of tools to establish a baseline is an important first step, the judgmental process of integrating information from a variety of measurable and unmeasurable sources is even more important. It is for this reason that Skinner and Sasser (1977), Drucker (1989), and Brightman and Noble (1979), among others, have identified the importance of the judgmental and subjective skills, including perspective, versatility, and communications as the key abilities of the strategic manager. As with forecasting, operations strategy involves a not clearly definable combination of science with art, of content with process, and of scientist with humanist.

The configurational approach to operations strategy, applied contingently, offers an important perspective of the operations strategy process. It focuses on key content structures, yet also on the internal dynamics of those activities. The operations management strategist may desire, in relatively stable environments, to emphasize the content aspects more heavily than process aspects. Alternatively, in dynamic situations, the operations management strategist may choose to use more process-oriented approaches. As noted in the quotations at the beginning of the chapter, operations strategy relies on both content and on process; however, it also requires behavioral flexibility and an overview perspective.

## Discussion Questions

1. Identify the characteristic differences between operations planning and operations strategy. Identify (by position) and describe a manager who represents each perspective.
2. From your personal experience or readings, identify several structural and infrastructural aspects of operations strategy.
3. List and define the four competitive priorities of the strategic analysis of the operation of a firm. Give an example of each.
4. What are the three competitive forces involved in the analysis of the strategy operations of a firm? Give an example of each.
5. As an organization projects its situation into the future, the effects of intervening variables or situations can take several general forms, as follows: random events; planned, yet difficult to predict events; and planned, patterned events. From your personal experience or readings, briefly describe an example of each category.
6. Identify several limitations inherent in all forecasting methods.
7. List several general characteristics of long-, mid-, and short-range planning activities; then note several examples of long-, mid-, and short-range planning activities.
8. Identify the three pyramids of aggregation and briefly describe each pyramid.
9. With regard to impact evaluation and time dimensions, define the three time fences and describe the production schedule within each time fence.
10. How is the operations planning cycle important as an integrative strategic management tool?
11. Describe a method that assesses the pervasiveness of commitment and the risks associated with various strategic changes. Briefly assess an organization decision in these terms.
12. List, define, and give an example of each of the six categories of operations flexibility.
13. Which type of flexibility is most important in terms of responsiveness to customer delivery and quality requirements? Give an example to support your position.
14. What do process flexibilities of changeover, scheduling, and process innovation provide and permit?

## Strategic Decision Situations

1. The Atlas Automobile Products Company distributes replacement automobile headlamps and taillight bulbs in a ten-state area in the mid-western United States. Dealerships and retailers are directly serviced on a weekly basis by several route trucks that carry an inventory of some sixty different regular and halogen headlamps and an assortment of some 100 taillight bulbs.

Due to the growth of the business and the increases in the numbers of different headlamps and bulbs, several of the routes are starting to require more product to ensure that the trucks do not run out of stock before the end of their route. The following table gives the demand data for the H0184 headlamp, a representative model.

Average Weekly Demands by Month

| | Jan | Feb | Mar | Apr | May | Jun | Jul | Aug | Sep | Oct | Nov | Dec |
|---|---|---|---|---|---|---|---|---|---|---|---|---|
| 1989 | 232 | 247 | 219 | 211 | 199 | 183 | 167 | 174 | 170 | 169 | 187 | 213 |
| 1990 | 239 | 256 | 237 | 221 | 199 | 182 | 185 | 174 | 172 | 177 | 198 | 228 |
| 1991 | 241 | 258 | 248 | 246 | 217 | 203 | 189 | 181 | 184 | 179 | 188 | 219 |
| 1992 | 249 | 261 | 257 | 257 | 235 | 222 | 231 | 215 | 202 | 188 | 217 | 227 |

**a.** Assist the operations manager to address this distribution situation. Note several operations concepts or theories that help explain how this situation relates to other operations variables. Consider the perspectives of the planner and the strategist. Which is more appropriate?

**b.** Plot the data and intuitively define the appropriate components of a forecasting system.

**c.** Using a computer program, establish a baseline forecast with a simple moving average and then define an appropriate measure of forecast error and evaluate several advanced forecasting methods to improve the accuracy of the forecast.

**2.** The Good Day Tire Company forecasts demand by company-owned and franchised retail outlets for approximately 90 different varieties and sizes of automobile tire. The tires are defined in three product lines which are stocked at seven local distribution centers throughout the state in standard tariffs (size mixes) based on the proportion of demand. Good Day wants to develop an effective, yet practical and easy way to understand and use a forecasting system for the distribution centers and keep inventory as low as possible. Since weekly demand for tires can vary positively or negatively by as much as 20% over the year (but generally is within ±10%), depending upon weather and other seasonal factors, it is difficult to forecast appropriate stockage for the distribution centers more than roughly two weeks ahead. The average number of units per week and price per tire are shown. Use the concepts of product mix and the pyramid forecasting method to develop an analytic approach with the following data and advise the director of inventory planning on the implementation and use of your recommendation.

| Product Line | Average Units/Week | Price/Tire |
|---|---|---|
| Ariba | 4950 | $40.00 |
| GLX | 2990 | 55.00 |
| Quantum | 1995 | 75.00 |
| | 9935 | |

**3.** The Watertown Toy Company builds plastic and composite rubber models and figurines for a variety of retailers, including Toys-R-You. They currently employ six people in their molding operation, and have six "flat pan" molding machines that they purchased in the 1970s. For efficiency, labor-machine cycles dictate that each machine be tended by an employee. The company wants to transition to an injection molding process because the new technology will eliminate the step of welding the two halves together and the unsightly seam in many, though not all, products. Each new machine costs $50,000 and installation and training is an additional $50,000 for any number of machines purchased. Management has estimated that the apparent higher quality of product produced by each new machine will increase company profits by $25,000, $20,000, $15,000, $10,000, and $5,000 per machine in each year of operation. The company expects to buy no more than one machine per year for five years.

**a.** Recommend how many units Watertown Toy should purchase.

**b.** Further situation: The vender has agreed to waive $30,000, which is the training portion of the installation and training fee if five units are purchased, one per year. Should the company take the offer? Consider the benefits of early payback and possible business condition changes.

## *References*


Adam, Everett E., Jr., and Paul M. Swamidass. "Assessing Operations Management from a Strategic Perspective," *Journal of Management.* Vol. 2, No. 15, 1989, pp. 181–203.

Artes, Richard. "Strategic Forecasting," *APICS: The Performance Advantage.* January 1992, pp. 33–38.

Brightman, Harvey, and C. Noble. "On the Ineffective Education of Decision Scientists," *Decision Sciences.* Vol. 10, No. 1, 1979, pp. 151–156.

Buffa, Elwood S. *Meeting the Competitive Challenge: Manufacturing Strategies for US Companies.* Homewood, Ill.: Dow, Jones and Irwin, 1984.

Collopy, Fred, and J. Scott Armstrong. "Rule-based Forecasting: Development and Validation of an Expert Systems Approach to Combining Time Series Extrapolations," *Management Science.* October 1992, pp. 1394–1414.

Drucker, Peter F. "The Coming of the New Organization," *Harvard Business Review.* January–February 1988, p. 45.

Drucker, Peter F. *The New Realities.* New York: Harper & Row, 1990.

Duncan, Robert M. "Quality Forecasting Drives Quality Inventory at GE Silicones," *Industrial Engineering.* January 1992, pp. 18–21.

Fahey, L., and H. K. Christensen. "Evaluating the Research of Strategy Content," *Journal of Management.* Vol. 12, 1986, pp. 167–183.

Fine, C. H., and A. C. Hax. "Manufacturing Strategy: A Methodology and an Illustration," *Interfaces.* Vol. 15, No. 6, 1985, pp. 28–46.

Fogarty, Donald W., John H. Blackstone, Jr., and Thomas R. Hoffmann. *Production & Inventory Management.* Cincinnati, Ohio: South-Western Publishing Co., 1991.

Fogarty, Donald W., Thomas R. Hoffmann, and Peter W. Stonebraker. *Production and Operations Management.* Cincinnati, Ohio: South-Western Publishing Co., 1989.

Galbraith, J. R., and R. K. Kazanjian. *Strategic Implementation: Structure, Systems, and Processes.* St. Paul, Minn.: West Publishing Co., 1986.

Gerwin, D. "An Agenda for Research on the Flexibility of Manufacturing Processes," *International Journal of Operations and Production Management.* Vol. 7, No. 1, 1987, pp. 38–49.

Greene, James H. *Production and Inventory Control Handbook.* New York: McGraw-Hill, 1987.

Hayes, Robert H., and Steven C. Wheelwright. "The Dynamics of Process-Product Life Cycles," *Harvard Business Review.* March–April 1979.

Hayes, Robert H., and Steven C. Wheelwright. *Restoring Our Competitive Edge.* New York: John Wiley and Sons, 1984.

Hayes, Robert H., Steven C. Wheelwright, and Kim B. Clark. *Dynamic Manufacturing.* New York: The Free Press, 1988.

Jenkins, Carolyn. "Accurate Forecasting Reduces Inventory," *APICS—The Performance Advantage.* September 1992, pp. 37–39.

Leong, G. K., D. L. Snyder, and P. T. Ward. "Research in the Process and Content of Manufacturing Strategy," *Omega: International Journal of Man-*

*agement Science.* Vol. 18, No. 2, 1990, pp. 109–122.

Leong, G. Keong, and Peter T. Ward. "Multifaceted View of Manufacturing Strategy." Columbus, Ohio: The Ohio State University: College of Business, Working Paper Series 90-50, June 1990.

Maidique, Modesto A., and Robert H. Hayes. "The Art of High Technology Management," *Sloan Management Review.* Vol. 25, No. 2, 1984, pp. 17–31.

Makridakis, Spyros, and Steven Wheelwright. *Forecasting Methods for Management.* New York: John Wiley and Sons, 1989.

Miller, D. "Configuration of Strategy and Structure: Toward a Synthesis," *Strategic Management Journal.* Vol. 7, No. 3, 1986, pp. 233–249.

Miller, D., and P. H. Friesen. *Organizations: A Quantum View.* Englewood Cliffs, N.J.: Prentice Hall, 1984.

Miller, J. G., and W. Hayslip. "Implementing Manufacturing Strategic Planning," *Planning Review.* July/August 1989, p. 22.

Paine, Frank T., and Carl R. Anderson. *Strategic Management.* Chicago, Ill.: The Dryden Press, 1983.

Plossl, George W. *Production and Inventory Control: Principles and Techniques.* Englewood Cliffs, N.J.: Prentice Hall, 1985.

Plossl, George W. *Managing in the New World of Manufacturing.* Englewood Cliffs, N.J.: Prentice Hall, 1991.

Plossl, George W. "Flexibility Is Now the Key to Survival for Manufacturing," *APICS—The Performance Advantage.* April 1992, pp. 37–42.

Porter, Michael E. *Competitive Strategy: Techniques for Analyzing Industries and Competitors.* New York: Free Press, 1980.

Ramasesh, R. V., and M. D. Jayakumar. "Measurement of Manufacturing Flexibility: A Value Based Approach," *Journal of Operations Management.* October 1991, pp. 446–468.

Skinner, Wickham. "Manufacturing—Missing Link in Corporate Strategy," *Harvard Business Review.* May–June 1969, pp. 136–145.

Skinner, Wickham. "The Focused Factory," *Harvard Business Review.* May–June 1974, p. 113.

Skinner, Wickham. *Manufacturing: The Formidable Competitive Weapon.* New York: John Wiley and Sons, 1985.

Skinner, Wickham. "The Productivity Paradox," *Management Review.* September 1986.

Skinner, Wickham, and W. Earl Sasser. "Managers with Impact: Versatile and Inconsistent," *Harvard Business Review.* November–December 1977, p. 140.

Sprague, Linda G. "Strategic Analysis for Global Manufacturing," in Patricia E. Moody, *Strategic Manufacturing.* Homewood, Ill.: Dow-Jones Irwin, 1990.

Stonebraker, Peter W. *Master Planning Certification Review Course.* Falls Church, Va.: American Production and Inventory Control Society, 1991.

Valentine, Lloyd M., and Dennis F. Ellis. *Business Cycles and Forecasting.* Cincinnati, Ohio: South-Western Publishing Co., 1991.

Venkataraman, N., and J. E. Prescott. "Environment–Strategy Coalignment: An Empirical Examination of Its Performance Implications," *Strategic Management Journal.* Vol. 11, No. 1, 1990, pp. 1–23.

Ward, Peter T., Deborah J. Bickford, and G. Keong Leong. "Configurations of Manufacturing Strategy, Business Strategy, Environment, and Structure." Columbus, Ohio: The Ohio State University: College of Business, Working Paper Series, 90-77. September 1990.

# Case 1

# Operations Strategy at Waste Management

## *Introduction*

Garbage handling is big business. More than 432,000 tons of trash, the equivalent of 200,000 automobiles, are discarded *each day* in the United States. Considering this large and growing market, Waste Management, Inc. (WMI),* the nation's largest garbage hauler, with 12% of the $25-billion U.S. disposal market, is positioning itself for the rapidly growing international recycling business and global competition. Incorporated in 1968, WMI has aggressively acquired many companies in the garbage hauling business; in 1987 alone WMI acquired 107 businesses. By the end of 1990, the disposal giant employed over 62,000 people.

Simultaneously, increasing public and governmental concern over the nation's colossal garbage pile has broadened the scope of the waste disposal industry. With tighter regulation, more costly litigation, and increased public responsibility and awareness, industries are terminating careless methods of waste riddance and implementing more responsible, but more costly techniques. Hazardous waste disposal is a prime example; companies in this area have grown at an annual rate of 25% to 30%, a rate that is not expected to vary significantly in the future. However, the available pool of trained employees in hazardous waste disposal has not kept up with the growth of demand. The hazardous waste industry created 267,000 jobs in 1990 and is expected to employ as many as three-quarters of a million persons by the year 2000.

Due to the growing shortage of landfill space, higher costs of solid waste disposal are inevitable. Along with shortages and higher costs, recycling and waste minimization programs are receiving increased public visibility and attention by government regulators. The industry must react to regulations, government policies, and judicial interpretations, each of which is constantly changing. For example, the federal Superfund act, which has

*This case is prepared as a basis for class discussion rather than to illustrate either effective or ineffective management of an operational situation.

authorized $15.2 billion to be appropriated from 1980 to 1994 for hazardous waste cleanup, contributes to increased growth of the industry but also imposes tight regulations and oversight of operations.

## *Waste Management, Inc.*

In 1971, when WMI went public, it had a market value of $20 million. Twenty years later, the company is worth $19 billion, an increase in value of 95,000%. By the end of 1988, the company employed 36,750 people in almost every state and in more than a dozen countries. In 1990, WMI's revenue was $6.03 billion, three times that of 1986; in the same period, earnings doubled to $684.8 million.

The organization is structured with an 11-member board of directors, a chairperson, a president, three senior vice presidents, and eight vice presidents. In addition, the corporate staff includes a general counsel, chief financial officer and treasurer, controller, and secretary. The board of directors is heavily involved in strategic planning to help anticipate markets and regulatory changes. Each year in September the top nine executives gather for one week to reevaluate the company's strategic direction.

Through its three principal subsidiaries, Waste Management of North America, Inc., Chemical Waste Management, Inc., and Waste Management International, Inc., WMI provides a mix of solid and chemical waste management services for commercial, industrial, and municipal customers. The services entail the collection, storage, transfer, interim processing, resource recovery, and disposal of waste. Moreover, WMI supplies street-sweeping services, portable lavatories and related services, and solid and chemical waste resource recovery operations. Through its Chem-Nuclear Systems, Inc. subsidiary, the company has provided low-level radioactive waste disposal since 1982.

WMI's closest competitor is Browning-Ferris Industries (BFI), which is approximately half WMI's size. BFI has been plagued by permit problems at several large garbage dumps and lack of dumps for its sanitation business, which have resulted in the shutting down and selling of some hazardous waste sites. In addition, Browning-Ferris's profits have slumped. In the quarter ending March 31, 1991, Browning-Ferris's revenue netted $57.3 million compared with the year-earlier period profits of $71.9 million. As of September 30, 1987, Browning-Ferris had an estimated 20,000 employees located at subsidiaries and affiliates in approximately 245 locations in the United States, Austria, Canada, Kuwait, Germany, Puerto Rico, Saudi Arabia, the United Kingdom, and Venezuela.

WMI, on the other hand, has been expanding almost continuously. In 1982, the company merged its hazardous waste recovery business with Chem-Nuclear Systems. Two agreements were signed in 1989 which significantly increased the company's international presence. In January, the company agreed to purchase PLM Sellbergs, which operated a leading solid waste management service in Sweden and Spain. One month later, WMI purchased 49.5% ownership in a major French industrial and chemical waste treatment and disposal company, PEC Engineering. In addition, WMI established a joint venture with Wheelabrator Technologies to form a waste-to-energy enterprise.

Wheelabrator is a developer of trash disposal facilities and had been in great need of WMI's disposal sites. The new enterprise will manage facilities that deal with air- and water-pollution control and the conversion of rubbish to energy sources.

In its bid to become "the premier pest-control company" in the nation, WMI has quietly purchased an estimated $12 million worth of pest-control firms in South Florida. Though initial efforts concentrated on three counties (Dade, Broward, and Palm Beach), WMI expects to spend between $25 million and $100 million to establish its presence in the lucrative extermination business. When WMI purchased the pest-control firms, it also purchased and retained the previous firm's name; thus, few people are aware of WMI's presence in the industry. WMI has also diversified into the lawn-care business, using the same methods.

In 1988, WMI was making pickups at seven million homes and 558,000 businesses in 800 communities in the United States. Approximately 350 of the nation's 500 largest trash markets are controlled by WMI. Although its reputation may not be the best with environmentalists and prosecutors, WMI is highly preferred among customers because of its professionalism and ability to work with various types of waste. The company's size is an essential requirement in many of the markets that it serves.

Though consumers are becoming more environmentally conscious and responsible, a "not in my backyard" (NIMBY) syndrome also is highly prevalent. With landfills reaching capacity and a shortage of new landfill sites, WMI is the only firm with the capital to invest in large rural plots and with the hauling equipment necessary to avoid the backyards of major urban areas. For example, in order to win a quarter-billion-dollar contract in the three-county Portland, Oregon, area, WMI purchased a rural landfill site 140 miles away and designed an intermodal truck and rail hauling operation. The rural residents agreed to the arrangement after being promised more than $2 million annually in payroll and fees.

It has been estimated that federal regulations promulgated during the 1990s will shut down approximately half of the United States' 6000 garbage dumps for noncompliance. However, WMI has already met the new regulatory guidelines, thereby increasing the property values of its landfills and enhancing the company's ability to expand its market share. This success is due in part to its staff of attorneys and lobbyists who have facilitated, if not defined, many of the federal and state regulations relating to disposal operations.

The company has also developed profitable and rapidly growing recycling programs under the advertising slogan, "Helping the world dispose of its problems." In 1990, WMI signed an agreement with American National Can Company to accept the metal and glass containers that WMI receives through its curbside recycling programs. Moreover, in a joint-venture with E. I. du Pont, a Plastics Recycling Alliance facility has been established in Chicago to develop the sorting technology and define new end-use markets for all grades of plastic. Currently the operation is sorting and processing high-density polyethylene (HDPE) and polyethylene teraphthalate (PET) plastics with plans to include polyvinyl chloride (PVC) and polypropylene. Most of the recovered material is PET plastic in the form of two-liter soda bottles. Recycling ventures such as these are a direct result of an Environmental Protection Agency requirement for a reduction in disposal volumes of solid waste in landfills. Furthermore, increasingly stringent state guidelines, which supersede and, in many cases, are tighter than federal requirements, have forced municipalities and industries to find new uses for solid waste.

WMI operates in a dozen foreign countries. In addition to operations in Europe, WMI has established a regional office in Hong Kong in an attempt to gain more Asian business. WMI wants to handle the chemical treatment business and also to build and operate a waste transfer station in Hong Kong with future expansion into China, Taiwan, and Japan. WMI believes that the Asian market will replace North American operations as its largest customer in the next two decades.

Immediately following the conclusion of the 1991 Persian Gulf War, WMI beat several international competitors to Kuwait and landed that country's disposal business. Not surprisingly, WMI won the contract by having 100 sanitation workers begin the clean-up process before an agreement was signed. When WMI presented the Kuwaitis with a $500,000 bill for one month's service, the country accepted and signed a $12-million annual contract for basic sanitation services for Kuwait City.

## High Technology Applied to an Earthly Problem

WMI has its own institution for higher learning, Landfill University. The landfill concept is becoming increasingly complex as dumps are reaching capacity and federal and state legislation is intensifying. WMI gathers its managers at Landfill University to inform them of changing regulatory and design issues. Moreover, managers are given extensive training in public relations and crisis management to blunt adverse effects of targeted publicity by environmental and citizen-action groups.

The range of WMI operations has necessitated a centralized information services staff of 400 and a decentralized regional information management organization of ten employees in each region. Starting with an IBM System/38, WMI expects to upgrade its system to a total of 500 Application System/400s. Computers are used to schedule 14,000 collection and transfer trucks, to maintain local customer lists, and to manage some of the 125-plus company-owned landfills. WMI's largest centralized data base, the customer information system, records and tracks approximately 3.5 million bills per month.

With increases in recycling, research in the area of plastics sorting is simultaneously being intensified. Sorting a diverse mix of materials quickly and accurately is essential to making the recycling of plastics practical. The mixing of plastic types results in recycled products that have less value; as a result, WMI views current plastic recycling methods as not "economically sustainable." Currently, plastics are analyzed as they move on a line at 150 to 200 feet per second by light sensors which monitor each container by chemical type and color. As each container approaches the appropriate bin, a blast of compressed air is released that blows the container off the line and into the bin. However, WMI is projecting a much larger second-generation sorting and recovery system that would initially analyze the plastic on a moving line, then, at the right moment, air-blast the item into the correct container.

In addition to recycling, WMI has actively encouraged waste minimization. A subsidiary, Chemical Waste Management, assists companies to manage hazardous waste rather than disposing of it. WMI is attempting to educate consumers of solid waste to be aware that if they do not precycle and recycle today, they will be paying higher disposal costs tomorrow.

In 1990, an agreement was signed with Cascade Engineering to mold 95-gallon high-density polyethylene (HDPE) solid-waste containers on Cascade's 9000-ton injection molding machine. WMI supplies virgin and recycled HDPE plastic from its plastic recycling joint venture with du Pont. One of the main reasons that Cascade landed the contract was because of its "totally integrated manufacturing and engineering" (TIME) program, which enables Cascade to assist customers in the design, as well as the manufacture, of products.

## *Compliance Versus Litigation*

Despite WMI's size and technologically advanced position, the company has not been exempt from prosecution and fines. To date, the company has paid in excess of \$50 million in fines with \$32 million being assessed from 1982–1987 for violations in environmental regulations. The company has also been notorious for leaking landfills and price-fixing convictions. Even though such a slap on the hand hardly makes a dent in WMI operations, the company has created a group of 80 attorneys to defend the company. That staff is so powerful that Citizen's Clearinghouse for Hazardous Wastes, Inc. allegedly tells those opposing WMI not to try to contest the company in court. Rather, grass-roots political tactics are recommended.

WMI maintains a Washington-based lobbying organization of 22 staffers. To gain goodwill, the company's political action committee contributed over \$1 million in the past four years to various political campaigns. In what may be an attempt at cooption, environmental and wildlife groups have received \$1.5 million of contributions from WMI during the same period.

WMI has attempted to polish its image with environmentalists by being the first company in the industry to appoint a vice president of environmental policy and ethical standards. This position is held by a former general counsel to the U.S. Environmental Protection Agency and the U.S. Department of Health and Human Services, Jodie Bernstein. With her on WMI's executive environmental committee are a former director of the Environmental Defense Fund and a former National Resource Defense Council attorney.

WMI seems to thrive on regulation. As the largest company in the waste disposal industry, the company possesses the capital to upgrade its sites to compliance level. Due to WMI's active lobbying effort, government regulations may favor WMI operations but make compliance more difficult for smaller companies. WMI is a state-of-the-art business organization and, because of its positioning, as more and more stringent regulations are promulgated, WMI is expected to be one of the few businesses with the prerequisites to compete in the ever-expanding international trash market.

## *Discussion Questions*

**1.** What is the nature of WMI's business?

**2.** In what ways is WMI a service operation? A manufacturing operation?

3. What operations transformations does WMI perform? What are the inputs? Outputs?
4. Which is the critical resource for WMI? Support your answer.
5. Considering Figure 2-1, what are WMI's technical core, external factors, and key resources?
6. What activities does (should) WMI plan at the middle management level? At the top management level?
7. In what areas does (should) WMI forecast?
8. Does it make sense to knowingly violate the law if the costs of doing so are low?
9. What specific directions is WMI strategically and proactively pursuing to ensure its growth and fit with the expected business environments of the twenty-first century?

## *Primary References*

Bailey, Jeff. "Tough Target; Waste Disposal Giant Often Under Attack, Seems to Gain from It," *Wall Street Journal.* May 1, 1991, p. A1.

Bremmer, Brian. "Recycling: The Newest Wrinkle in Waste Management's Bag," *Business Week.* March 5, 1990, pp. 48–50.

Kirkland, Carl. "Cascade Wants Designers to Think Big," *Plastics World.* June 1990, pp. 13–14.

Myers, Laura. "Waste Management Is Quietly Buying Up Pest Control Firms," *South Florida Business Journal.* August 15, 1988, pp. 1–2.

Weiner, Steve. "Garbage In, Profits Out," *Forbes.* December 12, 1988, pp. 47–48.

# Case 2

# *Business Planning at Elco Manufacturing*

## *Introduction*

Bob Anderson, vice president of operations of Elco Manufacturing,* looked around the table. "Well, frankly," he said, "our business forecasting system is a mess. We really don't have a good handle on demand patterns, we don't have a good measure of accuracy, and we don't have an effective method to monitor the forecasting process. If the truth must be known, operations responds to customer demands by keeping high inventories of raw materials, components, and end items. To say that we have a forecasting system that identifies and projects historical demand patterns is just not true. Because we don't have a good handle on demand, evaluation of the capacity options identified here would be pure speculation."

Bob paused, knowing that he had spoken heresy, yet feeling that it had to be said. Elco had been struggling for several years as a manufacturer and distributor of several high-quality lines of exercise and outdoor sports equipment. Though some components (for example, digital readouts and computers) were outsourced, most items were cut or formed in rather simple metal working or plastic molding operations. The final assembly for most products was done by manufacturing cells or on a small moving assembly line. The three major product lines, exercycles, bench apparatuses, and basketball backboards, varied significantly in demand pattern. Exercycles sold well in the fall and winter, bench apparatuses were stable throughout the year except for heavier demand during the holiday

*To protect proprietary information, the company described in this case (a major U.S. corporation) has requested that its name and other identifying information be changed. However, the basic relationships have been retained. This case has been prepared as a basis for class discussion rather than to illustrate either effective or ineffective management of an operational situation.

period, and basketball equipment was seasonally high in the spring and summer. Each product line had several models, however; some variations were achieved through modular upgrades or the addition of digital readouts and computers. Many basic sheet metal and plastic parts were common to most products within a line.

Bob had joined Elco two months ago with the charter to turn the operations function around. He was responsible for the purchasing, production and assembly, inventory management, and shipping operations through to regional warehouses. Because of their weight, most units were shipped by truck from the manufacturing facilities located in Columbus, Ohio (exercycles), Dallas, Texas (bench apparatus), and Sacramento, California (basketball backboards) to ten regional warehouses. From those warehouses Elco shipped directly to customers such as major department stores and sports specialty stores. Sales had been growing at a healthy rate, but profits had been squeezed due to price competition in the market and, Bob felt, manufacturing inefficiencies.

## The Initiative

"Well, what do you think we should do, Bob?" asked Roderick Elvington II, the CEO and scion of the founding family, after a short hush.

"Initially," responded Bob, "I need to work much more closely with the marketing people and probably establish a periodic, formal meeting with Susan Clarke and her staff." He paused and looked for an expression of support from the vice president of marketing. As they had agreed, Ms. Clarke was nodding in approval. "One problem is that manufacturing and marketing have each been using their own projection methods. Marketing forecasts may, for example, be based on optimistic sales expectations, and manufacturing forecasts may reflect the need to facilitate setups or the availability of materials or labor. Manufacturing and marketing must have one set of forecasting numbers."

"We also need to accurately capture the historical demand pattern for product lines and individual items, and then forecast those demands and identify the forecast error. Those numbers, along with the resources required to produce those volumes, should be focused. Then we can get a better handle on long-range business planning issues, such as purchasing new equipment or planning new facilities. Of course, this would involve inputs from the human resource and finance staffs. I have heard such a meeting called a 'business planning meeting.' Given that numerous strategy issues are involved, such a meeting should be chaired by the CEO."

"Yes," replied Roderick Elvington, hesitantly. "It would appear so. But I'm not sure that this business planning meeting, as you call it, would be worth the time. It seems to me that we have enough meetings around here as it is. Let me think about it; I'll get back to you."

Several other agenda items were discussed, including the planned advertising schedule for the next two quarters, the upcoming modifications to the health care plan, and the annual golf tournament. As the meeting broke up, Jim Piachowski, the executive officer and a close friend of the family, commented to Bob, "Thanks for speaking out. Junior really didn't want to hear what you said, but I think that we need that type of session. I'll talk with Rod Senior, and see what we can do."

Subsequently, Bob talked with Linda Chavez, the assistant operations manager, and with the help of the staff was able to develop monthly production data for all product lines and most products, though there were several periods with unavailable and likely inaccurate data. Bob passed this information as a tentative data base to Susan Clarke, suggesting that if nothing else was available, the production data could be used as a starting point. Several days later, Susan returned the three-year historical market demand data shown in Table C2-1.

As Bob had expected, his production data varied, in some cases significantly, from the actual marketing demand data. These differences were reflected in differences between customer desired delivery dates and actual shipping dates, between monthly sales in dollars and manufacturing volumes in units, and demand for stocked-out units, particularly when there were promotions. Also, units delivered to Canada were carried on the books of the Eastern Sales District, but were actually delivered to western Canada through the Northern California District. Bob did not see any indication that the numbers were understated so that sales people could look good by beating the forecasts. Bob made a note to discuss the source and the definition of the forecast data with Susan.

About a week later, it was announced at a staff meeting that the CEO would schedule a business planning meeting for Tuesday morning, two weeks hence. The flow of the meeting would start with a marketing/manufacturing demand forecast, followed by a discussion by manufacturing, human resources, and finance of the necessary resource management actions. The first meeting would be designed to identify what data were needed, what data were available, and to develop evaluation formats.

**TABLE C2-1 Elco Manufacturing—Business Planning**

| | Exercycles | | | Bench Apparatus | | | Basketball Backboard | | |
|---|---|---|---|---|---|---|---|---|---|
| | Year | | | Year | | | Year | | |
| Month | 1 | 2 | 3 | 1 | 2 | 3 | 1 | 2 | 3 |
| 1 | 1582 | 1702 | 1624 | 1902 | 2032 | 1893 | 464 | 253 | 432 |
| 2 | 1201 | 1496 | 1823 | 2145 | 2830 | 2034 | 678 | 379 | 546 |
| 3 | 1405 | 1602 | 2031 | 1803 | 1945 | 1773 | 923 | 845 | 956 |
| 4 | 602 | 746 | 1034 | 2342 | 2063 | 2168 | 1803 | 1978 | 2034 |
| 5 | 778 | 821 | 1203 | 1964 | 2159 | 2301 | 4582 | 4327 | 4512 |
| 6 | 1034 | 1148 | 1483 | 1845 | 1934 | 1824 | 6791 | 7284 | 8237 |
| 7 | 1293 | 1473 | 2304 | 1773 | 1831 | 1934 | 7205 | 8958 | 8403 |
| 8 | 1462 | 1983 | 2905 | 1948 | 1739 | 1845 | 3681 | 3012 | 3582 |
| 9 | 4972 | 3592 | 6245 | 2034 | 1862 | 1903 | 1406 | 1567 | 1745 |
| 10 | 6236 | 5025 | 8052 | 2183 | 2235 | 2374 | 1574 | 1923 | 2052 |
| 11 | 9021 | 8235 | 9743 | 2583 | 2304 | 2593 | 2890 | 2690 | 4167 |
| 12 | 7037 | 6294 | 8235 | 2420 | 2504 | 2464 | 3218 | 3500 | 2389 |

## *Forecasting Issues*

Bob realized that the forecasts were in error, but he was concerned primarily with the amount of the error and with the expected accuracy of several different forecasting methods. He began to review the data and the different forecasting methods and accuracy evaluation formats. He defined three criteria to evaluate the forecast methods:

1. The selected forecast method must fit the pattern of the data.
2. The selected forecast method must be easy to understand and to use.
3. The selected method must not take a great deal of time to evaluate for accuracy.

Bob recalled that averaging worked well with level data and was rather straightforward, but that the accuracy was not particularly good with trended or seasonal data. Differencing and regression worked well with trended data, but were more difficult to use, particularly regression. Finally, indexing was particularly good for a stable seasonal pattern, and was not particularly difficult to use. Ultimately, he would use a computer model to facilitate computations, but he would have to be absolutely sure that he could explain the method and logic to the CEO and others.

Bob also reviewed the definition and interpretation of several measures of forecast error, including:

*Bias:* The tendency to over- or underforecast. Overforecasting the actual demand assured stock availability in response to shop requirements or customer demands, but carrying costs were higher. Underforecasting reduced carrying costs, but increased stockouts.

*Mean Absolute Deviation:* Average historical error of a forecasting method. Both positive and negative errors are taken as an absolute value, then averaged, giving an expected range of the forecast error.

*Mean Square Error:* The average of the squared error. Generally, this method is not widely used, except to compare the error of several different forecasting methods with the same data series.

*Mean Absolute Percent Error:* The average percent error is useful to indicate the average proportion of the absolute error.

Bob was also concerned that a judgmental contribution be included in the process, because things like economic conditions, weather, and other subjective factors were important contributors to forecast accuracy. The product lines could be expected to be more stable than the disaggregated product items and, because customer relations policies encouraged discounting around unavailable units, a pyramid forecasting technique was suggested to integrate forecast system management. Bob initially looked at the exercycle data because, with only two primary models, the Deluxe and the Super, the process would likely be less complex. The initial data are presented in Table C2-2.

Bob was encouraged by the data in Table C2-2 because it suggested that there was some consistency of the product mix, or the proportion of model A to the total and the

**TABLE C2-2 Elco Manufacturing—Product Mix**

| Month | Deluxe | Super | Total | Month | Deluxe | Super | Total |
|---|---|---|---|---|---|---|---|
| 1/1 | 815 | 767 | 1582 | 2/7 | 1101 | 372 | 1473 |
| 1/2 | 656 | 545 | 1201 | 2/8 | 1405 | 578 | 1983 |
| 1/3 | 792 | 613 | 1405 | 2/9 | 2475 | 1117 | 3592 |
| 1/4 | 483 | 119 | 602 | 2/10 | 3790 | 1235 | 5025 |
| 1/5 | 398 | 380 | 778 | 2/11 | 6210 | 2025 | 8235 |
| 1/6 | 734 | 300 | 1034 | 2/12 | 4874 | 1420 | 6294 |
| 1/7 | 921 | 372 | 1293 | 3/1 | 1205 | 419 | 1624 |
| 1/8 | 1114 | 348 | 1462 | 3/2 | 1463 | 360 | 1823 |
| 1/9 | 2736 | 2236 | 4972 | 3/3 | 1703 | 328 | 2031 |
| 1/10 | 4753 | 1483 | 6236 | 3/4 | 903 | 131 | 1034 |
| 1/11 | 7134 | 1887 | 9021 | 3/5 | 845 | 358 | 1203 |
| 1/12 | 5034 | 2003 | 7037 | 3/6 | 905 | 578 | 1483 |
| 2/1 | 1203 | 499 | 1702 | 3/7 | 1784 | 520 | 2304 |
| 2/2 | 934 | 562 | 1496 | 3/8 | 2056 | 849 | 2905 |
| 2/3 | 1304 | 298 | 1602 | 3/9 | 4568 | 1677 | 6245 |
| 2/4 | 451 | 295 | 746 | 3/10 | 6373 | 1686 | 8059 |
| 2/5 | 500 | 321 | 821 | 3/11 | 7035 | 2708 | 9743 |
| 2/6 | 745 | 403 | 1148 | 3/12 | 6105 | 2130 | 8235 |

proportion of model B to the total. But he also noted some periodic variation in the product mix.

## *Capacity Issues*

The evaluation of capacity would prove more troublesome, Bob thought. The plants were generally machine constrained. That is, it was more costly and difficult to get a machine operational than to hire a new employee, or get more materials. Thus, planning for expansion and contraction of capacity would primarily involve numbers of units of equipment available rather than labor or materials. The situation was particularly acute at one plant in the stamping work center, generally regarded as the plant bottleneck. The analysis would have to show the incremental benefits of purchasing additional, more efficient equipment. A cost–benefit analysis would, however, demonstrate in simple terms the proportional payback of a new equipment purchase. Of course, increased demand would have to drive the change in capacity, and some additional cost information, such as interest rates on the borrowed money and labor costs, would have to supplement the analysis. The cost data that Bob developed are shown in Table C2-3.

Currently most of the metal stamping and cutting is done by medium presses, which were purchased some 20 to 30 years ago. Though the equipment performed well, it required an operator, and thus was more costly than automated equipment. The purchase of the next level of technology would permit interfacing the equipment with automated controls and subsequently with a computer-assisted manufacturing system, if desired.

**TABLE C2-3 Elco Manufacturing—Contingency Analysis**

| Cost of Unit $150,000 | | Efficiency and Increased Profits of Machines | |
|---|---|---|---|
| | | Efficiency | Profits |
| Purchase one unit per year until number of desired units has been purchased | First year | 1.5 | $40,000.00 |
| | Second year | 1.2 | $30,000.00 |
| | Third year | 0.9 | $20,000.00 |
| | Fourth year | 0.6 | $10,000.00 |
| | Fifth year | 0.3 | $5,000.00 |

| | Number of Units | Total Cost | Total Benefit | Benefit/Cost Ratio |
|---|---|---|---|---|
| Option 1 | 1 | $150,000.00 | ______ | ______ |
| Option 2 | 2 | $300,000.00 | ______ | ______ |
| Option 3 | 3 | $450,000.00 | ______ | ______ |
| Option 4 | 4 | $600,000.00 | ______ | ______ |
| Option 5 | 5 | $750,000.00 | ______ | ______ |

Planning for the business planning group meeting continued at a breakneck pace. Bob spoke daily with Susan Clarke to ensure accuracy of data and coordination of formats. Both tried to balance the amount of staff effort versus the potential savings in inventory and scheduling, as well as improved responsiveness to customer demands.

On Friday, a week before the first BPG meeting, Bob received the memorandum on page 103 from the CEO.

## *Discussion Questions*

1. Intuitively suggest several forecasting methods that would be most appropriate to project demand for exercycles, bench apparatuses, and basketball backboards. State the rationale for your decision.
2. Which error measurement method do you recommend for these data series? What considerations would you offer in support of your decision?
3. Under what circumstances is the pyramid forecasting technique useful? How would stability or periodicity of the product mix pattern be helpful in inventory management?
4. Consider the contingency analysis data. Determine the machine purchase option that you find most appropriate, and then support that decision. Recognize several strengths and several weaknesses of your analysis.
5. Give several reasons, from your own experience, or from your readings, why marketing and manufacturing may desire to have two or even several forecasts. What is the problem with this approach?
6. Identify several bases for forecast error that Bob and Susan should be vigilant to identify.

# ELCO MANUFACTURING

Office of the Chief Executive Officer

MEMORANDUM

Subject: Business Planning Group Meeting

From: Chair, Business Planning Group

To: Business Planning Group

Vice President, Finance

Vice President, Marketing

Vice President, Human Resources

Vice President, Manufacturing

Computer Information Manager

The business planning group (BPG) will meet in the Fogarty Conference Room at 1:30, Thursday, 25 April. Addressees should attend, and are requested to invite two or three key staff.

Since this is the first meeting of the BPG, attendees are encouraged to address process issues of the meeting and to ensure that the meeting defines appropriate and effective levels of staff interaction. Additionally, though it is recognized that our initial estimates may be tentative, attendees should attempt to develop the basics for an integrated staff planning process.

The agenda of the meeting will be

| | | |
|---|---|---|
| 1. | Introduction of the process and participants | CEO |
| 2. | Product line forecasts | VP, Mktg/VP, Mnfg |
| 3. | Product mix forecasting | VP, Mktg/VP, Mnfg |
| 4. | Production resources | VP, Mnfg |
| 5. | Resource availability and costing | VP, Fin/VP, HR |

This initial meeting will be particularly effective if participants review the meeting agenda and format, and submit suggestions for improvement in information-gathering processes, presentation of data, and integrated usage of data, as well as any other suggestions.

**7.** Note several areas of forecasting system definition where marketing and manufacturing are likely to disagree.

**8.** Why would the marketing demand data likely be a better input for the forecast than the manufacturing shipping data?

## *Computer Assignment*

**1.** Forecast exercycle demand. Define several techniques and select the best method based on a supported criteria of forecast error. Support your decision by an analysis of the error measures.

**2.** Forecast bench apparatus demand. Define several techniques and select the best method based on supported criteria of forecast error. Support your decision by an analysis of the error measures.

**3.** Forecast basketball backboard demand. Define several techniques and select the best method based on supported criteria of forecast error. Support your decision by an analysis of the error measures.

**4.** Present a discussion to identify the appropriate product mix of the Deluxe and Super models. Consider how you would define the judgments (*Hint:* Consider the prior forecasting methods and whether the product mix is stable or if it varies from month to month). Identify the pattern and how it can be used.

**5.** The operations manager must recommend a decision as to which of three different types of equipment must be purchased and how many units of each item. Present a discussion of the rationale and the decision as to how many new pieces of equipment should be budgeted for.

| | |
|---|---|
| Option 1 | |
| Cost of different equipment | $175,000 |
| Efficiencies | 1.8; 1.4; 1.0; 0.6; 0.2 |
| Profits | $50,000; $40,000; $30,000; $20,000; $10,000 |
| Option 2 | |
| Cost of different equipment | $150,000 |
| Efficiencies | 1.5; 1.2; 0.9; 0.6; 0.3 |
| Profits | $40,000; $30,000; $20,000; $10,000; $5,000 |
| Option 3 | |
| Cost of different equipment | $200,000 |
| Efficiencies | 1.6; 1.4; 1.2; 1.0; 0.8 |
| Profits | $50,000; $35,000; $20,000; $5,000; $5,000 |

What additional factors should be incorporated into this analysis?

# Chapter 4

# *Integration of Organization Design*

*It is our thesis that the selective advantage of one intra- or interorganizational configuration over another cannot be assessed apart from an understanding of the dynamics of the environment itself. It is the environment which exerts selective pressure. "Survival of the fittest" is a function of the fitness to the environment. The dinosaurs were impressive creatures, in their day.* —Shirley Terreberry (1968, p. 613)

## *Objectives*

After completing this chapter you should be able to:

- Define organization design and discuss the four dimensions of organization design.
- Name and describe five different organization design alternatives for operations.
- Show the relationship of the environment, size, and technology with organization design.
- Differentiate the use of focusing and fitting variables in the management of organization design.
- Apply proactively the concept of the chain of transformation and the concept of integrating operations management functions to design an organization.

## *Outline*

***Introductory Case: Sears, Roebuck—The Big Store***

***The Design Continuum***

*Interactivity of Design*

*Definition of Design*

*Dimensions of Design*

## *Introductory Case: Sears, Roebuck—The Big Store**

Sears, Roebuck is the epitome of an American business institution; it has defined and catered to the tastes of Americans for more than a century. Sears conceived and developed industry practices in merchandising, retailing, distribution system management, and customer service. In the 1970s, as the Sears Tower became the tallest building in the world, so did Sears, Roebuck, by every measure, dominate the manufacturing, distribution, and customer delivery aspects of operations management. Two of three Americans shopped Sears in any three months of 1972, more than half of American households had a Sears credit card, and one-third of American families owed an average $256 for past purchases at Sears. Thirty-five hundred major retail stores, smaller retail locations and catalog outlets, and over 100 warehouse locations distributed goods that, in many cases, Sears-owned companies manufactured to Sears' specifications.

Yet, by the early 1980s, it was apparent that Sears was in trouble. Profits had stagnated or declined, and growth in the emerging markets was nonexistent. The stock price had fallen to less than one-half of its prior value. Massive and slow-moving inventories were costing the firm 20% to 30% per year, and a top-heavy, yet diversified staff gave Sears the highest overhead costs in the retailing business and often resulted in internecine feuds. Simultaneously, Sears' position in the distribution and retail area slipped as more focused competitors with lower operating costs grew more rapidly than Sears. Sears' volumes were down and operating costs remained high.

*Materials drawn from Katz, *The Big Store,* 1987, and Strom, 1992.

In January 1986, Edward A. Brennan was promoted to chairman and chief executive officer of Sears, Roebuck, replacing the retiring Edward R. Telling. Brennan, the son of a Sears salesman, joined Sears in 1956, after working through college and for several additional years in a men's clothing shop. There, Brennan learned the retail business skills that he applied to sales management in the Sears "field" organization. Brennan's career ranged from store management, "parent" headquarters purchasing staff and staff section management, to district, region, and territory management. In all cases, Ed Brennan found ways to reduce costs and to return to profitability long-ignored areas, even territories, of the business. Simultaneously, he was exposed to the often byzantine politics of "The Big Store."

Though many of the current initiatives, designed to reposition Sears for the 1990s and the next century, were defined and initiated under Ed Telling, it is Ed Brennan's job to implement them. The once far-flung and highly independent territories have been brought under central control, without destroying the incentive to seek and exploit the local or regional markets. Dramatic downsizing and restructuring of the firm is ongoing, with the reorganization of the distribution network and the creation of "Brand Central" and numerous other product-focused groups. The merchandising activities have moved from Sears Tower to a new suburban headquarters. The structural and rejuvenating integration of this vast retailing network of durable goods, optical goods and services, automobile service, insurance, real estate, and investments is clearly necessary to avoid further decline of the firm to the position of a second-class merchandiser. Recent decisions to sell the financial services and real estate portions of its business and to close the catalog sales division herald a refocusing toward the core merchandising domain. Redesigned stores, low-cost copies of upscale fashions, and new marketing programs are part of the effort. The challenge today, to revitalize this leaner organization, is perhaps the greatest of any in the 100-year history of the organization that has survived on wits and flexibility.

## *The Design Continuum*

Terreberry's comment, quoted on the chapter title page, forcefully links the environment to the design of an organization. The restructuring experiences of Sears, Roebuck, noted in the introductory case, have been repeated at General Motors, International Business Machines, U.S. Steel (now USX) and the American Telephone and Telegraph Company, as well as many other of the flagships of American business. Each of these companies has downsized by 20% or more and has redesigned its organization in an effort to redirect its resources toward greater competitiveness in the global marketplace.

However, many other factors, in addition to the environment, should be considered in the design of an organization. Steiner (1977) presents strong arguments that size and organization goals drive organization design, whereas Galbraith and Kazanjian (1986) summarize research which concludes that environment, technology, market structure, size, and other variables are all importantly related to organization design. Though the terms "structure" and "design" are used somewhat interchangeably in the organization theory and general management literature, this text will use *organization design* to refer to the features and linkages of the organization and thus avoid confusion with the broader "structure considerations" of Part II. This chapter defines the organization design of a production/service operation as a variable that is controllable by management and, in fact, one of the more directly manageable variables in a dynamic operations environment.

## *Interactivity of Design*

Though organization design is not usually considered to be a topic within the purview of operations strategy (it is often left to organization theory), the extreme volatility of the business environment during the past decade requires that operations managers understand organization design. As a result of this environmental volatility, many changes in the design of operations organizations have occurred, including the general downsizing of American firms, the rapid growth of more specialized and entrepreneurial firms, the massive reduction of middle management, the emerging communications technologies, and the dramatic changes in process technologies, service delivery systems, and labor skills. Each of these changes has significantly affected the operations organization. Additionally, the organization design is among the more directly controllable of the management variables.

Peter Drucker (1989, p. 207) describes the "information-based organization," which reduces the number of levels of the organization by one-half and increases the specialized contribution of the knowledge-based individual. Drucker projects that these changes in organization design will continue and, more importantly, that the behavioral styles to manage such organizations must also shift. Because the operations manager will have less control over the dynamic effects that impact the organization, understanding the forms and processes of organization design is very useful. This chapter develops the definitional foundations and dimensions of organization design for the operations management function. Five design forms are identified and the situations are described in which these forms are appropriate. The subsequent section describes the major processes to manage various designs and notes the interrelationships of those processes. The final section addresses the integration of the operations function through the chain of transformations.

## *Definition of Design*

For clarity and to provide a common foundation, the term *organization design* is defined, following the approach of Hofer, Chandler, Lorange, and Galbraith and Kazanjian [a very fine elaboration of this approach appears in Galbraith and Kazanjian (1986)] as:

> *The mechanisms which define the features of the organization and which serve to link the different parts of the organization.*

Two aspects of this definition should be elaborated:

*Mechanisms which define the features.* Design mechanisms which define the functions of an organization include the definition of behaviors and roles of individuals or groups and the allocation of tasks and responsibilities to those individuals or groups, often on a functional or geographic basis. These aspects are generally considered to be the form of organization design.

*Mechanisms which link the parts.* The different features or entities of the organization must be drawn together through a variety of linking mechanisms, which establish both formal and informal reporting and communication relationships, and permit the flow of information in both directions.

The terms *differentiation* and *integration* are used to state this distinction. An early definition of differentiation is "the differences in cognitive and emotional orientations among managers in different functional departments and the difference in formal structures among these departments." Correspondingly, integration is defined as "the quality of collaboration between departments" (Lorsch, 1970, pp. 5, 7). These ideas are related to the definition of design because differentiation refers to "mechanisms which define features" and integration is the "mechanisms which link the parts." These activities are necessarily simultaneous. For example, the establishment of an engineering group to evaluate a product/service or technology would involve structural differentiation; however, the reports required or submitted by that group are integrative mechanisms.

In the traditional context, the notion of differentiation concerned horizontal differencing among sections, and integration concerned vertical relationships to pull together subordinate sections. However, both integration and differentiation can be applied either vertically or horizontally in defining the operations design. In the following sections, integration and differentiation are used as the basis to build a descriptive foundation of the nature of the design of an operation. Subsequently, these two aspects of design are interrelated and applied.

## *Dimensions of Design*

The organization design of an operation may be described in terms of centralization, formalization, complexity, and configuration (span of control and level). These dimensions are generally, though by no means universally, accepted as the key dimensions of design (Miles, 1980; Robbins, 1990; Daft, 1989). Centralization and formalization are the outcomes of linking processes, while complexity and configuration are related to the form or shape of the organization. As operations downsize, these dimensions provide operations managers with the key mechanisms of control. Figure 4-1 shows a representative organization design and labels these concepts.

Figure 4-1 shows an operation with three levels, level 1, level 2, and level 3. Departments are described according to their level as 2A, 2B, and so on, and each of the dimensions is exemplified. *Centralization* is defined as "the locus of decision-making authority along the vertical dimension" (Miles, 1980, p. 23). Centralization is a relative measure of the amount of concentration or dispersal of either formal authority or less formal power in the vertical hierarchy. In addition to the formalized decision-making prerogatives, centralization can refer to other activities, including participation or informal discretion. For example, formal expenditure authority may be delegated in different amounts to different levels of the organization, with the approval of large expenditures retained at higher levels. However, the degree of centralization may be informally defined, it may be visible or subtle, and it may be founded on substantive (knowledge-based) or inconsequential (purely titular) considerations. The measurement of centralization is often

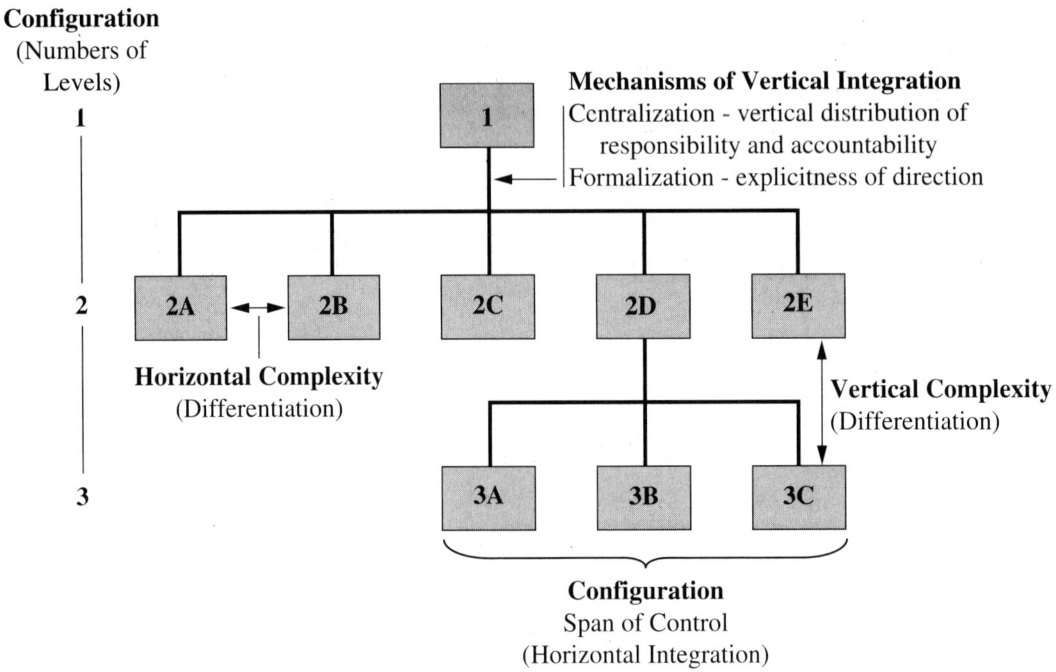


**FIGURE 4-1 The Dimensions of Organization Design**

difficult because many activities contribute to decision-making processes but are short of formally making the decision. Those less-direct aspects of the decision-making activity include information input, interpretation and advice, selection of alternatives, and implementation.

*Formalization* is defined as the "explicitness of expectations regarding work means and production." Formalization may involve work rules, policies, procedures, or oral instructions. The level of formalization is important because high formality is associated with a greater potential for punishment if the desired behavior is not met. Formalization reduces the amount of individual discretion, and thus, sometimes indirectly, increases task standardization. Additionally, excessive formalization may stifle initiative and limit the experiential value of the task or responsibility to the individual. However, too little formalization of design can give the appearance, if not the reality, of lack of design or disorganization. Thus, the amount and type of formalization is central to motivation and the perception of efficiency.

*Complexity* refers to the number of different components or subsystems in an organization and to the amount of functional differentiation between those components. Of course, uncomplex organizations are functionally simple and generally have fewer components. Complexity may be based on the amount of horizontal differentiation between units at the same level or on the amount of vertical differentiation from one level of the hierarchy to another. A complex operation might consist of many slightly different units or a few, highly varied units. Complexity results from the greater amount of interaction that is required with many or varied units and from fewer opportunities for standardization.

*Configuration* refers to the shape of the organization and includes the number of levels and the span of control (the number of subordinates reporting to one supervisor). Operations can be configured as "tall and thin" or "short and fat," depending upon the number of levels and the width of the span. Organizations change configuration as they grow, becoming taller or shorter, developing bulges or thin spots, and changing the process flows and relationships. Currently, many organizations are downsizing, particularly by reducing middle management and staff. Thus organization designs are getting flatter.

Numerous other dimensions could be suggested, but most would be somewhat redundant with centralization, complexity, formality, or configuration. A strong relationship has been found among these dimensions of design (Robbins, 1990). As might be expected, less centralization is associated with high complexity and greater centralization with less complex environments. The relationships of centralization and complexity with formality depend upon the skill level of the employees. Unskilled employees generally require greater formality, which is associated with less complexity and greater centralization. Skilled employees require less formality, which is associated with greater complexity and less centralization. High levels of complexity are also associated with less span of control and more levels, thus with generally taller designs.

The relationship, or congruence, among these variables is important because it reduces the friction and wasted motion of the organization, thereby improving efficiency. For example, the use of unskilled labor in an environment of low centralization, high complexity, low formality, high number of levels, and low spans of control would not be efficient. That would be the equivalent of an untrained apprentice doing a skilled, highly complex and technical job without guidance or supervision. The organization design process involves fitting the organization design variables within themselves and then adjusting the fit of these variables to the emerging needs of the organization in its environment.

## Forms of Design

The literature is somewhat consistent in the identification of five specific design forms. Those forms, named the simple, functional, divisional, conglomerate, and hybrid (or matrix) designs, are briefly defined here; subsequently the evolution of these forms is described. Depictions of the five forms of organization design are shown in Figure 4-2.

### Simple Designs

The simple design is characterized by one manager with two to eight or possibly more subordinates and generally not more than three or four levels. It is small in size and has little formalization, low complexity, and centralized authority. Simple designs almost

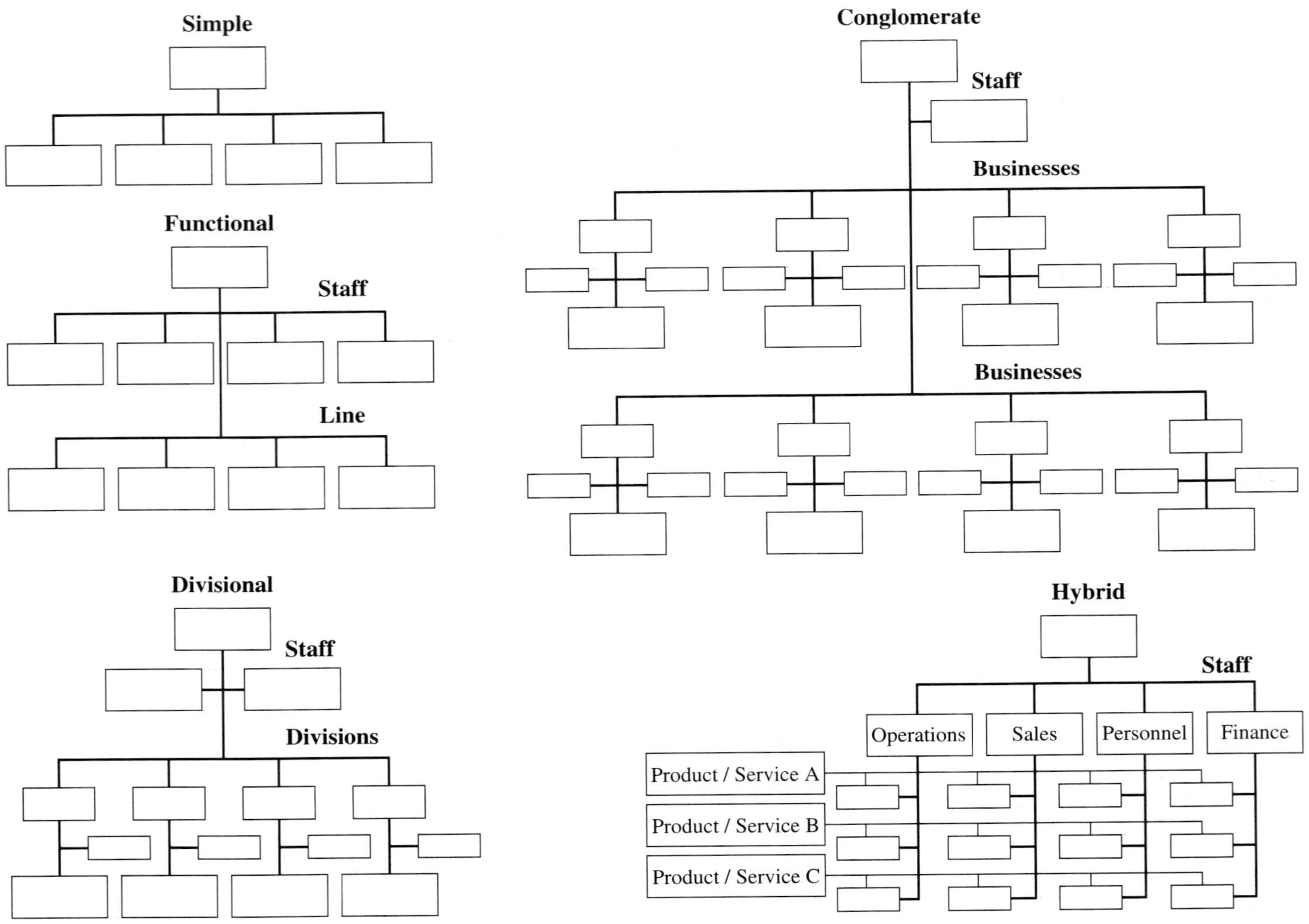


FIGURE 4-2 Alternative Organization Design Forms

always have fewer than 500 employees, and usually fewer than 100 employees. Simple designs respond rapidly to environmental changes, have clear, though often informal accountability, and are usually rather goal focused. As simple designs grow larger, they invariably develop staffs and become more like functional designs. Examples of simple organizations include most sole proprietorships, partnership organizations, and family-owned businesses. An example of a simple design is given in Application Box 4-1.

## *Functional Designs*

Functional designs are used in larger organizations; they are distinguished by several defined staff functions as well as a line organization. The simple design tends to break down with increasing size because there are limits of the span of control and the number of levels that one individual can manage. Additionally, as the firm gets larger, often operations management problems are more complex, thus requiring functional specialists. This division into specialized activities increases the complexity of the functional organization. Centralization is lower; however, the formality of a functional design normally is higher than that of the simple design. Functional organizations can be classified as either administrative or professional in nature.

In both administrative and professional functional organizations, processes are highly standardized, but administrative functional designs involve simple and stable tasks which, for reasons of efficiency or safety, are closely governed by rules, policies, or procedures. Thus, the administrative design is generally quite centralized. However, the professional functional design has little centralization, because decentralization is virtually required in environments of high and diversified knowledge content. One of the principal difficulties of functional designs is that they create differentiated groups which may be a source of organizational conflict. Examples of functional designs include most government agencies, libraries, hospitals, and schools and universities. A functional design is shown in Application Box 4-2.

## *Divisional Designs*

Divisional designs are created when the horizontal differentiation or complexity of an organization becomes so great that several separate functional groups must be defined. Unique support requirements necessitate that each of these groups have its own supervision and separate functional staff. These groups are often called "self-contained business units" because each has all of the functional staff necessary for its own operation. The groups of the divisional design may be distinguished by different products or services, by different levels of process technology, or by location. Each group represents a decentralized, though often rather formalized, authority. A weakness of the divisional design is that some of the technical and administrative functions within each group may be redundant or insufficiently employed. Examples of the divisional design are found in many large organizations whose focus is directed toward one area of business. For example, General Motors primarily builds automobiles, trucks, and locomotives. Though the products are somewhat different, they involve very similar production technologies. The key distinc-

## APPLICATION BOX 4-1 The Simple Design

Bredemeier Samples makes sample "swatch" books and cards. These sample books and cards contain small cuttings of fabric, materials, or paint chips of rugs, upholstered furnishings, and painted color samples for a variety of products. Depending on business conditions, the company employs as few as 80 persons or as many as 130 persons. This expansion and contraction of the work force is achieved through a network of employees' families, friends, and neighbors, and is possible because of the relatively unskilled nature of the cutting, gluing, and printing operations. Though some sales representatives are used, new sales in this highly specialized business often come through word of mouth. The employees are organized in two major sections, as shown by the following chart, though the organization is rather informal. Many functions, such as accounting and finance, are performed under contract, thus reducing the size of the staff.

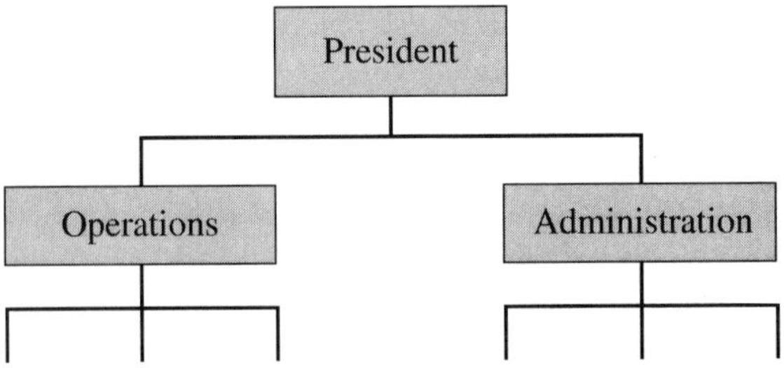


tive feature of the divisional design is that the groups are designed to provide similar products or services, to use similar or related process technologies, or to service different market regions. An example of a divisional design is shown in Application Box 4-3.

## *Conglomerate Designs*

The conglomerate design is like the divisional design, except that there is little task or output dependency among the groups of the conglomerate, as there is with the division. Each group of the conglomerate receives resources from the conglomerate and each returns revenues to the conglomerate, but in other regards, the groups function independently. For this reason, the conglomerate staff will often be limited to financial and administrative functions. In fact, the conglomerate may be a combination of several divisional organizations. The conglomerate design gives large firms the opportunity to distribute risk over several different business domains. Decentralization is almost complete and complexity is very high. Because each business retains much of its inherent identity and organizational culture, the conglomerate may acquire and sell businesses with relative ease. The organization chart of the conglomerate is like a combination of several divisional organizations, managed by a small corporate headquarters. The conglomerate design is shown in Application Box 4-4.

### APPLICATION BOX 4-2 The Functional Design

Southwestern University is located in Phoenix, Arizona and has approximately 20,000 students and 4000 employees, 1600 of whom are faculty. The university is organized, at the vice president level, into three functional groups: academics, students, and facilities, and has a number of special staff functions. Within each functional activity, there are numerous subfunctions. Note that, in addition to a more developed hierarchy, the functional organization typically has more extensive and more specialized staffs. The activities of the Vice President for Academic Affairs would likely be more representative of the professional functional design, while those of the student affairs and facilities areas would likely be a more administrative functional design. The university is organized as follows:

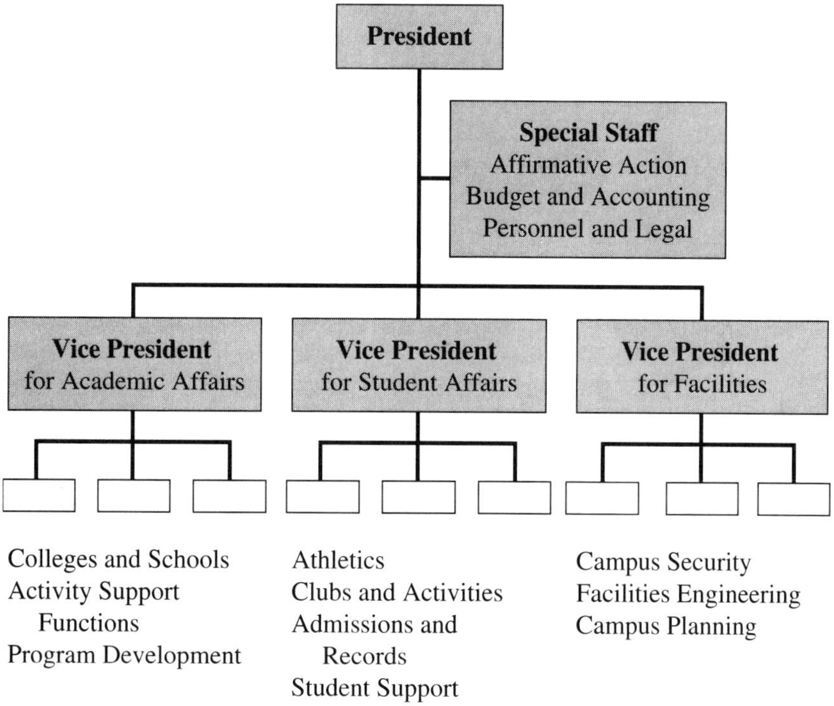


## *Hybrid Designs*

The hybrid design is also termed "simultaneous" by Miles (1980) and "matrix" by Robbins (1990). The hybrid design arises from the need to integrate several functional designs in a complex environment. The hybrid design defines a duality of responsibility; that is, each person or functional activity reports to two different proponents. As shown in Application Box 4-5, those different proponents are often defined from a functional and

## APPLICATION BOX 4-3 The Divisional Design

The 101st Airborne Division has approximately 15,000 soldiers. The organization consists of a general staff, a special staff, three very similar infantry brigades, and three support units. There are two assistant commanders, one for operations functions and one for support functions. The division general staff, called the G-(number) staff for personnel, intelligence, operations, and logistics, deals with the indicated general functional area; separate functional staff activities consider a variety of more specific areas. The three subordinate brigades (roughly 2000 soldiers each) have separate geographic or functional missions. The three division support organizations, Division Artillery, Division Support Command, and Division Aviation Group, have subunits with direct support missions to the infantry brigades as well as the general support of the division. A simplified representation of the division is shown in the following organization chart.

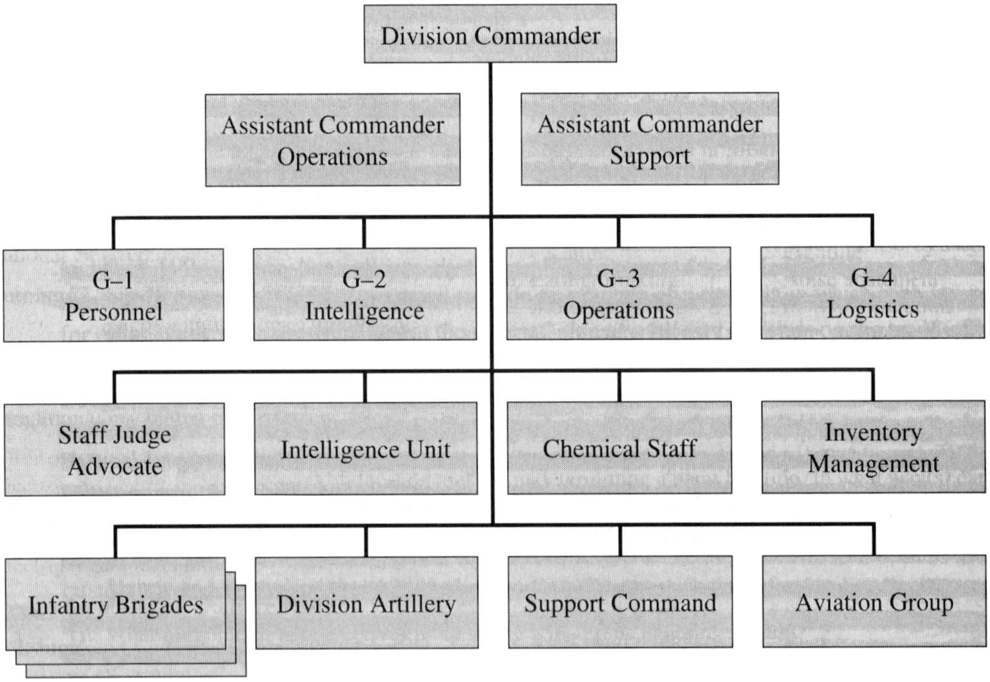


a divisional orientation. The hybrid is usually decentralized and has very low formality. However, because of the potentially conflicting objectives of the two proponents, complexity is often very high. The hybrid design was initially viewed as a transitional form, which might be used to develop a response to a short-term crisis or to make adjustments to an organization design.

For example, a task force might be created to address a business crisis. The members would temporarily have a dual responsibility to their functional section and to the task

## APPLICATION BOX 4-4 The Conglomerate Design

Sears, Roebuck has grown to be one of the largest conglomerates in the world. Through the 1980s, Sears was organized with a variety of businesses, including the Sears Merchandise Group, the Allstate Insurance Group, the Coldwell Banker Real Estate Group, and the Dean Witter Financial Services Group, as well as ownership in many smaller businesses. Typical of a conglomerate, the headquarters organization has only some 150 persons, consisting of the president and chief executive officer, support functions, and some limited legal, financial, and accounting functions. The separate businesses are almost entirely independent, each having a full line and staff organization. However, each separate business is responsible to the president for legal and accounting reporting and for the accomplishment of fiscal goals. Several recent Sears, Roebuck decisions suggest that the company which grew from a simple design to a conglomerate is reversing the process and proceeding to downsize. The recent divestiture of the financial services and real estate groups and the sale of up to 20% of the Allstate Insurance Group suggest that Sears is refocusing on its core merchandising operations.

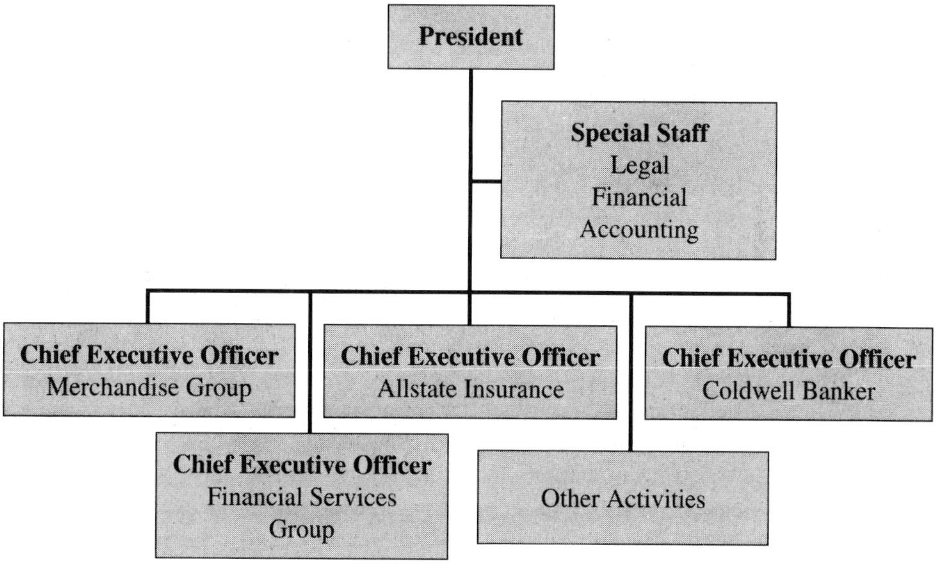


force. When the crisis was resolved, several members of the task force might be reassigned to a new section to implement the solution proposed by the task force. Recently, however, as operations have experienced increasingly complex and dynamic environments, the hybrid form has become more permanent and has sometimes taken the name of "technology platform" or "project implementation team" (see Chapter 13). Examples of "permanent" hybrid organizations are often found in high technology areas, such as aerospace and computers, but have also been used in retailing operations, such as in divisions of Sears, Roebuck. Though the hybrid design permits flexibility and interactivity

### APPLICATION BOX 4-5 The Hybrid Design

The Unisys Corporation was formed in 1986 when the Sperry and Burroughs Corporations merged. The integration of the two companies was difficult because each firm brought different technologies, different business approaches, and a different area of business to the combined organization. However, each organization also brought with it a great deal of redundancy, particularly in the more basic functions, such as human resources management, accounting, and sales. In many areas, the hybrid organization format was used to facilitate the integration of separate activities. The matrix of the combined cell shows the integration of several different projects with several functional areas. The integration of Sperry and Burroughs personnel was achieved by such a hybrid organization, in this case a transitional structure. For example, for a short time during the integration, a combined planning cell composed of both ex-Sperry and ex-Burroughs employees worked for a Sperry project chief and a Burroughs functional chief. Subsequently, a simple or functional design with simple processes and functions emerged.

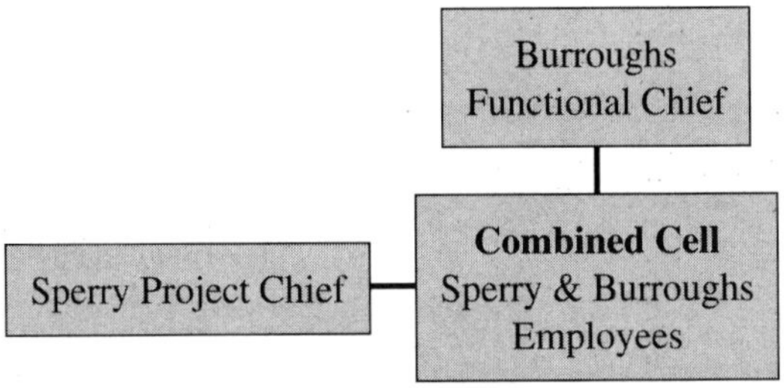


without bureaucratic impediments, its weakness is the duality of responsibilities and the potential for confusion and subtly divergent objectives of the two proponents.

Mintzberg (1983) has developed a very effective way to depict the forms of organization design using five basic components of an organization design: top management, middle management, the technical core, technical support staff, and administrative support staff.[1] These five components make varying contributions to the organization, depending upon the design. Thus, the size, positioning, and shape of the component may be represented by using the Mintzberg "graphics." In Figure 4-3, the generalized position and form of the five basic components are noted; then the five design types are shown, with adjustment of the components to describe the alternative design forms. Note, for example, that the simple design does not have any staff. The functional, divisional, conglomerate, and hybrid designs are also shown with the five basic organizational components represented.

[1]Mintzberg defines five slightly different organizational forms: the simple form, the machine bureaucracy, the professional bureaucracy, the divisionalized form, and the "adhocracy." As used here, the simple and divisional forms correspond to those of Mintzberg, and the hybrid corresponds to the Mintzberg's adhocracy. Mintzberg's bureaucracies are defined as the two types of functional organizations here (for example, the professional and administrative functional design) and Mintzberg describes, but does not separate, the conglomerate form.

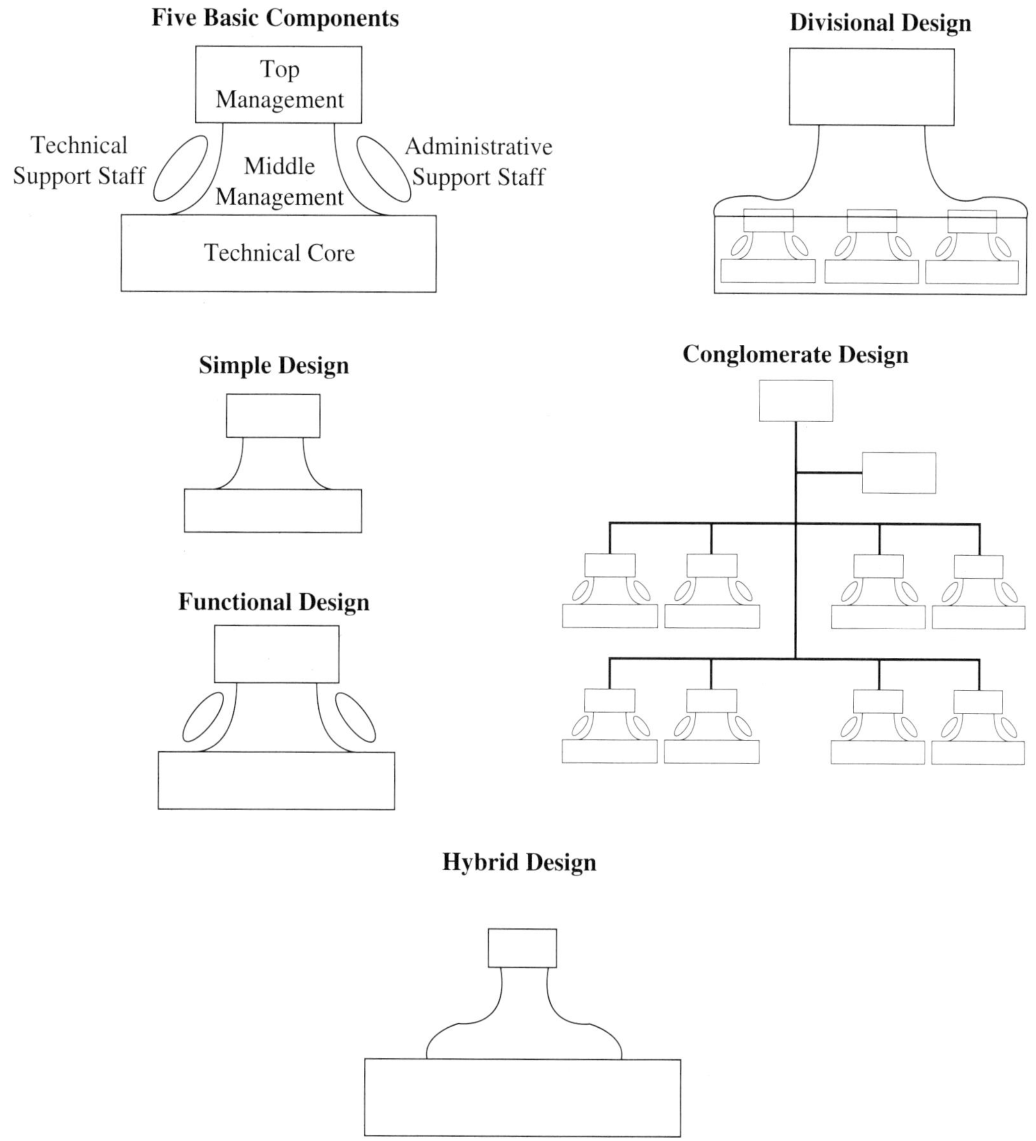


**FIGURE 4-3 Five Components of the Organization and Example Forms**

Adapted from Henry Mintzberg, *Structure in Fives: Designing Effective Organizations,* © 1983, pp. 11, 159, 170, 194, 225, 262. Reprinted by permission of Prentice Hall, Englewood Cliffs, New Jersey.

The graphic depiction of these structural forms emphasizes the general characteristics of the "pure" organization design. Certainly, variations would be found in each of these formats. Additionally, these structural forms may be used together. For example, an organization may be a conglomerate at the highest level, but each business might use a different organizational form, one that was selected because it best fit the situation. The sales organization of a firm might be divisional, based on marketing regions, while the manufacturing organization might be functional and the human resources staff might be a hybrid.

Each of the organizational forms has different strengths and weaknesses, and is appropriate for use in different circumstances. Additionally, each of the forms differs with regard to the dimensions of design and characteristics. These relationships are generalized in Table 4-1.

For example, a simple organization would likely be highly centralized and with low formalization and complexity. Additionally, most simple organizations are characterized by few levels and a generally wide span of control. They are usually small and with little specialization among the employees. There are few, if any, staff, and the organization environment is very dynamic. Bredemeyer Samples, in Application Box 4-1, exemplifies the characteristics of a simple design. Alternatively, the divisional and conglomerate design are less centralized with higher formalization and complexity. Most divisional and conglomerate organizations are characterized by many levels and varying spans of control. They are generally large and highly specialized. The staff varies from few to many and the organization environment tends to be stable. The 101st Airborne Division and Sears, Roebuck, in Application Boxes 4-3 and 4-4, exemplify the divisional and conglomerate organizations.

The historical growth of a firm can be approximated by using Table 4-1. Generally organizations start with simple designs that have the design dimensions and characteristics indicated (for example, high centralization, low formalization, and so on); as they grow

**TABLE 4-1 Dimensions and Characteristics of Various Design Forms**

| Dimension | Simple | Functional | Divisional | Conglomerate | Hybrid |
|---|---|---|---|---|---|
| Centralization | high | ←————— | ————— | —————→ | low |
| Formalization | low | ←—————→ | high | ←—————→ | low |
| Complexity | low | ←————— | ————— | —————→ | high |
| Configuration | | | | | |
| Number of levels | few | ←————— | —————→ | many | n/a* |
| Width of span | wide | ←—————→ | narrow | wide | n/a* |
| **Characteristics** | | | | | |
| Size | small | ←————— | —————→ | large | varies |
| Specialization | low | ←————— | —————→ | high | varies |
| Staff | none | ←—————→ | many | few | n/a* |
| Environment | dynamic | ←—————→ | stable | ←—————→ | dynamic |

*As indicated by the n/a, the hybrid design cannot be clearly defined on some dimensions or characteristics.

to functional and divisional designs, the dimensions and characteristics gradually shift. Often these patterns of design change are more apparent in younger, more rapidly growing organizations than in older, more stable organizations.

Though the emphasis of this section has suggested that organization design flows from simple to functional, to divisional, to conglomerate with hybrid designs used in special situations, the process can also be applied to contracting organizations. That is, an organization might downsize from a conglomerate to a divisional design by selling off unrelated businesses and focusing on a specific series of related vertically integrated businesses. Similarly, a divisional design might become more functional by increasing the prerogatives of the central organization. As the organization further downsized, elimination of areas of functional and specialist staffs would increasingly suggest a simple design. Thus, as demonstrated in Table 4-1, these pure organizational designs may be used to describe the evolution of the organization over time.

According to Weitzel and Jonsson (1989), declining organizations go through five identifiable stages, based on the organization's response to internal or external pressures. The first three stages of decline (blinded stage, inaction stage, and faulty action stage) involve internal and external scanning systems and corrective mechanisms to implement procedural changes. The fourth stage (crisis) involves a major reorganization of the firm. Finally, the dissolution stage requires decision makers to manage an orderly closing or liquidation of the business. At any of these stages, the firm can resolve key issues and recover. The Sears, Roebuck merchandising operation, a declining organization, has gone through several downsizings, but, because of its size, its diverse resource base, a strong home products market, and its significant efforts at renovation, it is expected to recover (Weitzel and Jonsson, 1991).

Organizations may also change their designs to compete in specified domains. The creation of a separate business by General Motors to manage the Saturn Project ("Why a . . . ," 1985) and the buy-back of Harley-Davidson from the American Machine and Foundry Corporation in 1983 (Reid, 1990) are both examples of the use of organization design processes as a mechanism to better fit the production organization to its environment. The following section considers the management of dynamically evolving organization designs.

## *Management of Design Through Process*

Since the late 1950s, the relationship of organization design to other organizational variables and with the environment has been studied intensely. From these studies, it appears that organization design is related to size, technology, and strategy. There is strongly supported evidence that congruence among these variables is important for organization efficiency and that organization goals (developed through the strategy formulation process) and designs are the two most easily controllable variables for management. Because of the increased availability of knowledge and increasingly dynamic and turbulent environments in many areas of business, operations managers are able to design their operations more proactively. That is, they define what the operation should be at some future period; then they redesign the organization structure of their operation toward that goal. The process of redesigning, by itself, enables the organization and facilitates movement toward the goal. The strongest relationships of design, not surprisingly, are found with size, technology, and the environment; these variables are particularly important to operations management, given organization downsizing and very dynamic process technologies. Additionally, vertical or horizontal integration requirements of the environment significantly constrain the design of the operation.

## *Size and Technology*

In the early 1960s, successful firms were found to be designed differently than unsuccessful firms, success being measured by various indices of profitability or return on investment. The landmark study by Woodward (1965) categorized firms by the type of technology used (unit production, mass production, and continuous process production). Chapter 7 gives a more detailed description of these process technologies. Woodward's findings are shown in Table 4-2.

The key finding of Woodward's research was that successful firms in each technology category were designed so that they approximated the characteristics for their group (Woodward, 1965). That is, successful firms using a unit production technology would closely approximate four management levels, while successful firms using the continuous process technology would closely approximate six levels. The other variables in Wood-

**TABLE 4-2 Structural Characteristics and Technology**

| Structural Characteristics | Technology | | |
|---|---|---|---|
| | Unit | Mass | Continuous |
| Number of management levels | 4 | 4 | 6 |
| Supervisory span of control | 23 | 48 | 15 |
| Worker skill | high | low | high |
| Formalized procedures | low | high | low |
| Centralization | low | high | low |
| Verbal communication | high | low | high |
| Written communication | low | high | low |
| Overall structure* | organic | mechanistic | organic |

*Burns and Stalker (1961) define mechanistic structures as highly centralized, formalized, and stable bureaucracies, and organic structures as decentralized, informal, and dynamic.

*Source:* Joan Woodward, *Management and Technology* (London: Her Majesty's Stationery Office, 1965); and *Industrial Organization: Theory and Practice* (London: Oxford University Press, 1980).

ward's study and the criteria for success are noted in Table 4-2. Subsequent research, reviewed in Fry (1982), suggested that the more important variable was size, and that process technology was only an indirect or moderating variable. However, as Galbraith and Kazanjian (1986) conclude, the rather obvious relationship of size with design should not detract from the importance of the technology and design relationship to the operations management functions. If a unit, batch, or continuous process is used, Woodward's findings suggest that the operation should be configured with the indicated design characteristics.

## *Environment*

Burns and Stalker (1961) found that successful organizations adopt design forms and processes that best fit the conditions of the environment, notably stability or dynamism. Burns and Stalker provided the initial definition of mechanistic and organic designs. Mechanistic designs were characterized by high centralization and formalization and a highly specialized, but stable, bureaucracy. Alternatively, the organic form was characterized by low centralization and formality, and high and dynamic interactivity.

Lawrence and Lorsch (1986) further defined the organization response to its environment. They evaluated 30 firms (10 firms each in three different industries) and identified the amounts of integrative and differentiative effort by each firm. Differentiating mechanisms were measured in terms of division of labor and technological specialization. Integrating mechanisms were measured in terms of the formality of the hierarchy, the volume of standardized policies, rules, and procedures, and the amount of time spent on liaison roles, committees, and like mechanisms.

The Lawrence and Lorsch study found that successful firms had different levels of differentiative and integrative effort than did less successful firms, depending upon the nature of the environment. In an uncertain environment, successful firms had greater differentiation and more integrative effort than low performers; however, in a more certain environment, successful firms had less differentiation and less integrative effort than other firms. Thus, the amounts of differentiation and integration, or relating to the definition of design, respectively, the *mechanisms which define features* and the *mechanisms which link the parts,* should be adjusted depending upon the complexity and dynamism of the environment. In complex and dynamic environments, it is necessary to expend greater differentiating *and* greater integrative effort.

Galbraith (1973) categorized the horizontal and vertical functioning of these integrating mechanisms. Vertical integrating mechanisms, such as hierarchical referral or reporting requirements, ensure the linkage of components and the communication between vertical levels. Similarly, rules, procedures, plans, schedules, and even the addition (or insertion) of levels also permit establishment of greater linkages among vertical components. Alternatively, horizontal linkages are encouraged by such mechanisms as liaison requirements, intergroup task forces, and various types of organization-to-organization coordinators. These design mechanisms are important tools of the operations manager to facilitate or enhance the effectiveness of either vertical or horizontal integration.

## *Strategy*

The idea that "structure (design) follows strategy" was identified by Chandler (1962), who specified four growth strategies as the basis for long-term survival of the organization. Chandler described these strategies in terms of growth; however, it is equally relevant to consider them in terms of contraction. These strategies, identified in Table 4-3, pose different administrative problems and thus tend to lead to adoption of a specific type of design.

The first strategy, expansion of volume, involves increasing sales within an existing market. Little change in the product or market is involved; however, the increase in volume may permit greater process efficiencies. A simple or functional design is likely to be sufficient for this growth objective.

The second growth strategy, geographic dispersion, involves entry into distinctly different markets with the same product or service. This strategy may also involve defining different marketing regions or, possibly, process technology enhancements for some regions. Alternatively, a second but parallel production/service facility may be built. The functional or divisional design is appropriate for this growth strategy.

The third strategy, vertical integration of linked businesses, means movement forward or backward along the transformation chain. If this movement involves the same process technologies and production volumes, the organization may be able to be restructured toward a divisional design. If notable changes in the process technology occur (either in Woodward's unit, batch, or continuous process terms, or in terms of the technology of the transformation), a conglomerate design would likely be more appropriate. This is because the differences in technology or volume required to move forward or backward on the chain of transformation call for different management skills and orientations.

The fourth growth strategy, product/service diversification, involves the development of new businesses or products that are less related to the core domain of the organization. Because there is less direct relationship or linkage between the businesses, such strategies encourage the use of the conglomerate design.

More recently, the concerns of firms have been directed toward downsizing, rather than growth, and, though there is little research on this topic, several tentative conclusions

**TABLE 4-3 Product/Service Strategies and Associated Designs**

| Strategy | Associated Design | Direction of Growth | |
|---|---|---|---|
| Expansion of volume | Simple or functional | | |
| Geographic dispersion | Functional or divisional | | |
| Vertical integration of linked businesses | Divisional or conglomerate | Growth ↓ | Decline ↑ |
| Product/service diversification in related or unrelated businesses | Conglomerate | | |

*Note:* The hybrid design, not shown here, could be used to temporarily change the organization from one design to another.

can be drawn. Initially, the downsizing process is much too complicated and subtle to be managed by reversing the processes that were used to facilitate the growth of the organization. Additionally, employee perceptions and motivation are quite different in a downsizing organization than in a growing firm. Cameron et al. (1991) characterize the alternative types of downsizing strategies as work force reduction, organization redesign, and systemic reevaluation. They suggest that the most successful downsizing efforts involve aspects of all three strategies.

The vertical integration of operations poses different problems, depending upon whether the integration is forward (downstream) toward the customer or backward (upstream) toward the raw material. These problems are related to the different attitudes and "mindsets" based on whether the integrative movement is upstream or downstream. These mindsets, shown in Table 4-4, are also appropriate for groups or activities of divisional organizations which integrate operations from upstream or downstream.

Typically, an upstream-integrated firm or activity will view its product as a standardized commodity. The market is sales-driven to maximize the number of end users. Financial controls are applied as per-unit costs and capital expenses, and the process is line-driven and encourages process innovation through technological know-how. Key skills include supply, trading, manufacturing, and engineering. Alternatively, the downstream integrated firm or activity is concerned with proprietary and customized products, targeted toward end users, and often developed in conjunction with those end users. High profit margins are sought to cover research and development and advertising activity. Product innovation is encouraged through employee participation in product development and marketing activities.

This difference of emphasis in the operations mindset of upstream- and downstream-directed activities, as well as different process volumes and scientific technologies, usually creates enough horizontal complexity as to require a divisional or conglomerate

**TABLE 4-4 Contrasting Emphases of Upstream and Downstream Integrated Companies**

| Attitude toward | Upstream | Downstream |
|---|---|---|
| Product/service | commodity<br>standardize | proprietary<br>customize |
| Market | maximize end users<br>sales push | target end users<br>marketing pull |
| Process | line-driven structure<br>process innovation<br>technological know-how<br>supply and inventory management; operations and engineering | line/staff structure<br>product/service innovation<br>marketing skills<br>product/service development/marketing |
| Financial | low-cost producers<br>capital budget | high margins<br>R&D/advertising budget |

*Source:* Adapted from Jay R. Galbraith and Robert K. Kazanjian, *Strategy Implementation, Structure, Systems and Process.* St. Paul, Minn.: West Publishing Co., 1986.

organization. Such highly differentiated and complex activities would likely be more successful as vertically integrated conglomerates, while less diversified or complex activities would more likely be managed by divisionalized designs.

This section emphasizes the contingencies imposed on the design of the operations function by technology, size, the environment, and by the strategy itself. Based on the discussion in Chapter 2 (Figure 2-7), the variables of task, technology, design, people, and the environment should be as congruent as possible. Once the domain is specified, the environment is given, as are most aspects of technology. Environment and technology impose significant constraints on organization design. However, operations managers do have some flexibility, within the constraints of those variables to contingently adjust the design, tasks, and processes of the operations function.

## *Designing the Operations Function*

Before selecting the appropriate design for an operation, the operations manager must define the primary task, or transformation process, of the plant or facility. From Chapter 1 (Figure 1-1) seven principal transformations were noted: extraction, physical transformation, location, storage, exchange, physiological transformation, and information. For durable goods and nondurable goods, and for most services, these transformations can be viewed as a sequential chain of transformations starting with creation, followed by the physical processing, manufacturing and assembly, distribution, and service/delivery.

### *Chain of Transformations*

Though the specific parts of each transformation activity vary, often the activities can be defined as: purchasing (for input resources); planning, scheduling, and process management (for the transformation); and distribution (for the output). Though other functions may be defined, including maintenance and quality control, the specific function names will certainly vary from business to business. Location, storage, and exchange transformations occur at various points along the chain, but extraction, physical transformation, location, physiological transformation, and information are the primary transformations at specific points on the chain. The chain of transformations with the primary transformations is shown in Figure 4-4.

In Figure 4-4, a durable or nondurable good or service moves along the supply chain from initial creation to manufacture, assembly, distribution, and finally delivery of a package of goods or services. The amount of value added at different stages of the chain varies. For example, much of the value of soft drinks or candies is added through distribution and service delivery, and relatively less value is added in other transformation processes. Alternatively, a greater proportion of the value of bulk steel is added through the extraction and manufacturing processes. Similarly, in services, the proportion of value added varies at different stages. The primary value added in video film making is in the production of the video, rather than in the distribution; however, the value added by the dentist's skills (delivery/service) is much greater than the value of the metals that are used to fill a cavity.

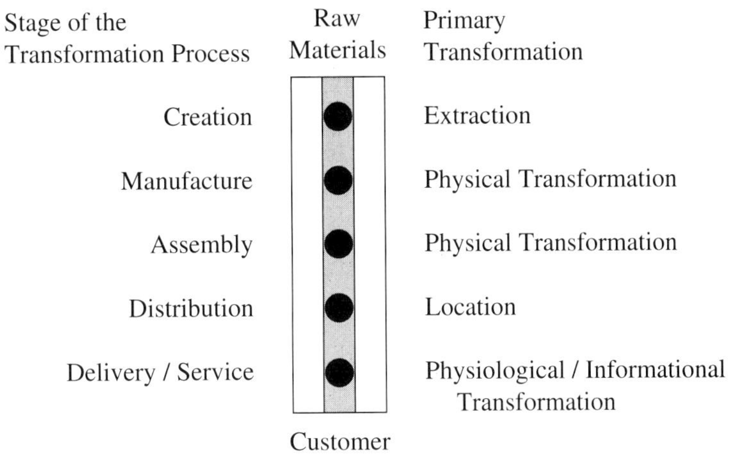


**FIGURE 4-4 The Chain of Transformations**

Reprinted by permission from page 51 of *Strategy Implementation,* 2e, by Jay R. Galbraith and Robert K. Kazanjian; Copyright © 1986 by West Publishing Company. All rights reserved.

Because of the volume or technology, some companies can manage one, or a few, products over the entire length of the chain of transformations, while other companies concentrate on only one stage of transformation. For example, several oil companies manage the entire transformation process from crude oil exploration and extraction to retail selling at service stations. In services, a restaurant chain may own a beef ranch or a potato farm and manage the entire chain of transformation for those goods, thereby ensuring a stable supply or a specified quality. However, the more common situation is that a firm will manage only one stage or several vertically linked stages. A clothing manufacturer might weave and dye input cotton thread and might manage a clothing distribution system or retail store network but would rarely own a cotton farm. An amusement park operator would not build or distribute the rides, and a steel mill operator would rarely produce stamped parts (at least not at the same facility), let alone distribute finished consumer goods made from rolled steel products.

A very complete study by Pandya (1992) differentiates three water irrigation systems in California, Maharashtra (India), and northern China by the design and methods of vertical integration. The California system integrates separate governing bodies through clearly enforceable contractual obligations, making the system hierarchically accountable, with resulting high performance. The northern China system, though organized with a centrally governing administrative mechanism, ensures performance through decentralized control and homogeneity among the users. However, the Maharashtra water system is governed by an administrative monopoly with control over water from production to consumption, and with limited accountability and poor system performance. Thus, vertical integration requires more than just design or administrative linkages for efficiency; hierarchical accountability and independence of producing and consuming organizations are necessary as well.

A transformation may be defined on the supply chain by length and breadth. For example, because an oil producer/distributor is principally concerned with the management of one product line through the entire length of the process, its chain of transformation is long and narrow. Alternatively, a retail products distributor would be primarily involved in the final production (assembly) and distribution of various food, drink, soap, and paper products. The focus of the retail products distributor should be a relatively short and wide presence on the transformation chain, primarily at the distribution and delivery/service point. These examples are depicted in the left and center parts of Figure 4-5.

On the right-hand side of Figure 4-5, the arrows show several acquisition and divestiture activities. Horizontal diversification results primarily from acquiring or developing new markets, process technologies, or products, though it can also result from developing additional extraction rights. Similarly, horizontal divestiture results from withdrawing from markets or the sale of facilities, process technologies or product lines and rights, as well as extraction properties. For example, a food conglomerate manages a product line from raw material to delivery/service and also owns a paper company and a distribution business that handles soaps, nonprescription drugs, and soft drinks. Figure 4-5 shows three transactions: the paper company builds a power generation business on its land, the food packager purchases a drug manufacturer to diversify into packaging nonprescription pharmaceuticals, and the paper packaging and distribution company sells a magazine printing business.

The term *center of gravity,* defined as "the driving force, such as market served, product offered, or process technology" (Galbraith and Kazanjian, 1986, p. 51), is used to

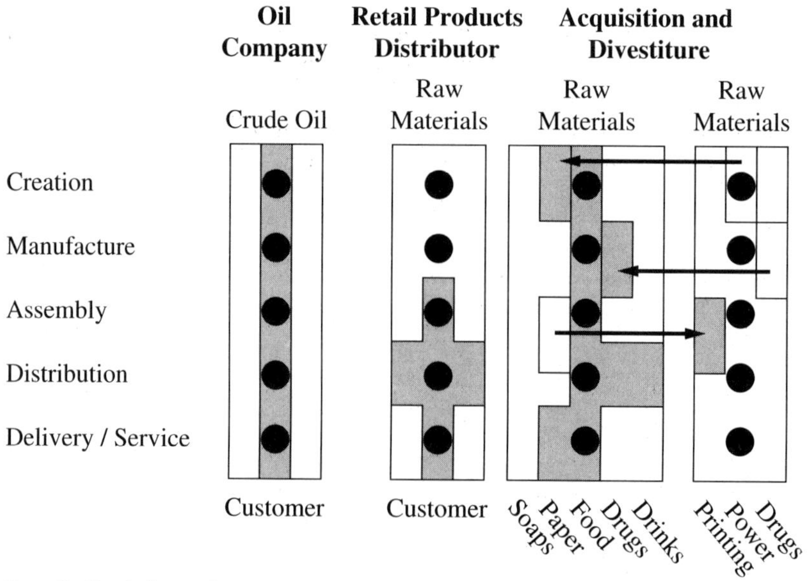


*Note:* Shading indicates the company domain.

**FIGURE 4-5 Chain of Transformations Applied to an Oil Company, a Retail Products Distributor, and Acquisition/Divestiture**

identify the primary focus of the firm's business. After the center of gravity is specified, acquisition and divestiture activities can be identified as "related," "intermediate," and "unrelated" to the primary focus of the business. Related businesses involve the same stage of the transformation chain. For example, Quaker Oats' Stokely Van Camp Inc. bought the food-related producer of Gatorade in 1984. ("How Swallowing . . . ," 1990, p. 56). Intermediate and unrelated diversifications respectively involve acquisitions or divestitures in different areas of the transformation chain, or where different industry practices exist. For example, the purchase by USX Corporation of Marathon Oil in the mid-1980s was an unrelated diversification because USX Corporation processes basic steel products, while Marathon is primarily in the refined petroleum products distribution business. Thus, the chain of transformations graphically depicts the extent of vertical and horizontal integration of a firm.

## *Trade-offs in Integrating Activities*

Given the nature of the transformation, the operations function should be designed to manage that transformation. The operation may be viewed as an input or purchasing activity, a transformation, an operations activity, and an output or distribution activity. For efficiency, materials and services should flow smoothly through the process with minimal scheduling, inventory, or quality disruptions. To ensure the smoothness of this flow, logic would suggest that these traditionally separate functions be fully integrated, yet that may depend upon the situation.

Miller and Gilmour (1979) report that successful operations management involves the correct organization of purchasing, planning and production inventory control, and distribution functions. In the traditional design, these three functions were separated; however, in contemporary operations, the operations manager must make decisions pertaining to the integration of functions. Design alternatives include:

***Partially Integrated***

1. Purchasing with operations planning and inventory control
2. Operations planning and inventory control with distribution
3. Purchasing and distribution

***Completely Integrated***

1. Purchasing, operations planning and inventory control, and distribution

Note that the purchasing and distribution functions, though normally not sequential, may be partially integrated in support of the operations function. The conditions in which these four partial or complete integrations are most effective depend upon the contingencies or trade-offs of each functional area. The incentive to integrate would be based on the amount of process disruption or cost associated with a particular trade-off decision. These trade-offs are noted in Figure 4-6.

The cells on the diagonal (cells 3, 5, and 6) represent the traditional trade-offs within each separate function. That is, the procurement cost versus the quality of the purchased

| | **Purchasing** | **Operations Planning & Inventory Control** | **Distribution** |
|---|---|---|---|
| **Distribution** | 1<br>Transportation Costs vs Procurement Costs | 2<br>Transportation Costs vs Inventory Costs | 3<br>Transportation Costs vs Customer Service |
| **Operations Planning & Inventory Control** | 4<br>Inventory Costs vs Procurement Costs | 5<br>Inventory Costs vs Production / Service Delivery Costs | |
| **Purchasing** | 6<br>Procurement Costs vs Quality | | |

**FIGURE 4-6 Trade-offs Among Operations Activities**

Adapted from Miller and Gilmore (1979).

good (cell 6) is the traditional trade-off managed by the purchasing function. The decision of inventory cost versus manufacturing cost (cell 5) is the traditional operations planning (level-chase) trade-off. The decision of transportation cost versus customer service, or customer service level (cell 3) is the traditional distribution center trade-off. If these three trade-offs, taken separately, are of equal importance, then the traditional organization, likely a functional or divisional design, with each function reporting to a separate staff director, is appropriate. There is no need to integrate the functions.

Cells 1, 2, and 4 represent trade-offs that cross traditional functional lines. If the inventory versus procurement (economic order quantity) trade-off (cell 4), for example, is critical to the competitive priority of the firm, then the operations planning and inventory control function should be integrated with purchasing. If the transportation cost versus procurement cost trade-off (cell 1) is critical, then the distribution and purchasing activities should be integrated. Finally, if the finished goods transportation and inventory cost trade-off (cell 2) is critical, then the operations planning and inventory control function should be integrated with distribution.

These partial integrations involve two activities. However, if one or more of the costs from each activity is involved in a more complex trade-off decision, then it makes sense to integrate all three functions under one manager. Alternatively, the long- and mid-range decisions might be periodically addressed by a combined planning team. As material flows from input, through transformation, to output are smoothed and speeded, integration of these three, directly related materials management functions makes sense. This is particularly true in complex, dynamic, and global environments and with higher-cost inventories. Thus, contemporary operations designs, which are moving toward just-in-time methods, would likely want to place all of the operations trade-offs under one function.

Miller and Gilmour address operations design of one corporation. However, this same rationale applies when a decision is made to forward- or backward-integrate or to divest. Generally, if the volumes and process technologies are roughly the same, the materials flow will be smooth and the integration will be manageable. However, if the quality specifications, volumes, or process technologies are very different, then the flow will likely be disturbed and less easy or more costly to manage. Vertical integration of a process is dependent upon efficiency of process flow; thus, with greater ranges of integration, there are more potential cost savings if those responsibilities are designed under one activity.

In summary, the decision of when to integrate different operations activities hinges on the trade-off costs involved. Within the firm, Figure 4-6 clearly expresses the trade-offs associated with integrating the purchasing, operations planning and inventory control, and distribution activities under one manager. This same rationale can be applied to evaluating the integration of external activities. If product or service volumes, quality, and process technologies are roughly the same, then the activities would likely be easily manageable by operations and understood by management. Alternatively, if the volumes, quality, and process technologies are different, then the activities would be less easily integrated. Normally, volume, quality, or process technology will differ if the integration involves a large jump either forward or backward on the transformation chain or because practices vary among different industries.

The efficiency of integration and flow of operations activities apply equally to service areas. For example, the product design function may be treated either as a manufacturing or a service activity. Apple Computer has traditionally done much of its product design work through consultants and outside designers. The results were either excellent or design "bombs," such as an 18-pound "portable" Macintosh computer. In 1989, Bob Brunner was appointed the manager of industrial design at Apple. He brought much of the design work in-house by tripling the design staff. This staff produced the very effective design of the Power Book. Additionally, the team is working on the Time Band, a wristwatch-sized computer with radio links to other computers. Similar considerations apply to maintenance or service teams, component assembly, and distribution system management. The operations strategy should thus weigh the advantages and disadvantages of integration or outsourcing of all parts of the manufacturing and service system (Hamilton, 1991).

## *Integration of Operations with the Environment*

Organization design provides the mechanisms to define structural features and also the mechanisms to link those features with themselves and with the environment. The operations function, as a key element of the organization, must be similarly integrated. Figure 4-7 summarizes the major relationships described in this chapter. The design of an organization is defined in terms of integration and differentiation. Successful firms should have roughly equivalent integration and differentiation efforts. Similarly, the environment and technology are defined by the level of complexity and dynamism, which can each be either low or high, though low complexity is most often associated with low dynamism and high complexity with high dynamism. Strategy, then, provides the critical intermediate link between the organization design of the operations function and the dimensions of the environment and technology.

The operations strategist would initially specify the quadrant of the environment and technology, if not a more accurately measured increment. The strategy may, in some cases, be used to change the environment; however, a more realistic option for most businesses is to accept the environment and technology as given and install the mechanisms that define features (differentiation) and those that link the parts (integration) of the organization design. This process is called fitting the organization design to the environment, including technology. The necessity for congruence of the organization design with the

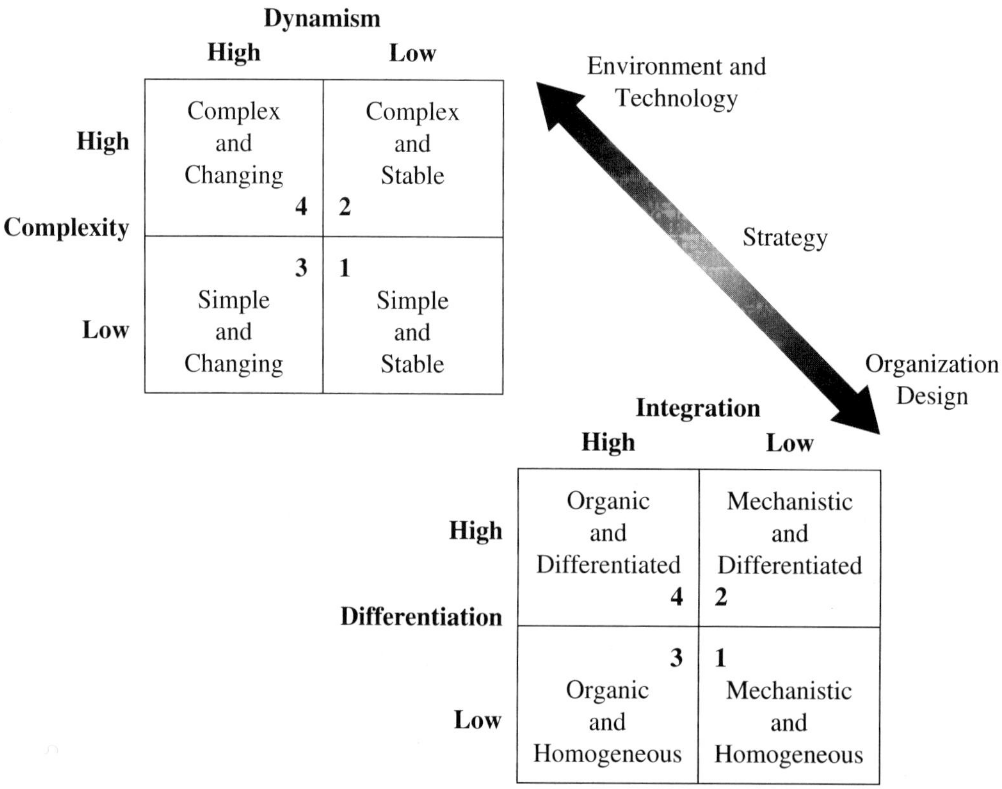


**FIGURE 4-7 Relationship of Environmental and Design Variables**

environment and technology leads to what Miles (1980, p. 273) calls the first and second general contingency principles of design:

1. Effective organizations match the complexity of their external environments with internal structural differentiation.
2. Effective organizations deal with environmental dynamism by creating flexible "organic" structures (or those with integrating mechanisms).

These two principles are key to the strategic design of production operations. In Quadrant 1 in Figure 4-7, the environment is simple and stable; thus the design of the organization should have low differentiation and little integrative effort. The organization design is mechanistic and homogeneous, for example, a cardboard box maker. Quadrant 2 has a complex, yet relatively stable environment, and the operation responds by structuring differentiated processes that are integrated by a relatively inflexible (mechanistic) bureaucracy. Examples are a bank, a mortgage operation, and an insurance company. In the simple, yet changing environment of Quadrant 3, the design of effective firms should be undifferentiated, but highly integrated and organic, as with fashion clothing producers or toy distributors. Finally, Quadrant 4 has a highly complex and changing environment, and thus is highly differentiated and simultaneously highly integrated and organic. Examples of Quadrant 4 are a computer manufacturer, an information processing firm, and an aerospace firm. Note that the extreme corner positions of Quadrants 2 and 3 may be difficult to successfully manage because high integration is generally best used with highly differentiated activities and vice versa. In this manner, the design of the operations function must be adjusted to strategically fit the environment, including technology, of the firm.

## *Summary*

This chapter develops an integrated approach to the management of the organization design of the operations function. Initially, design is defined and dimensionalized vertically and horizontally, then five structural forms are identified and four dimensions of design are clarified. These structural forms represent pure types on a continuum of design alternatives. Certainly, in application, variations and combinations will be found.

These alternative design forms are loosely associated with growth strategies of the organization and with the mindsets of forward (downstream) or backward (upstream) integrated operations or firms. Though there are limits to the amount of possible vertical or horizontal integration, the chain of transformations suggests the range of alternatives and a graphical way to depict those alternatives. The definition of cost trade-offs in a particular situation among materials management activities suggests the appropriateness of partial or complete internal integration of operations activities. The same rationale applies for external integration, which should generally consider activities that have the same product or service volumes, quality levels, and process technologies. Alternatively, as product/service volumes, quality, or process technologies differ, or as industry practices vary, the increasing complexity of the business would suggest the greater effectiveness of the conglomerate design, with independence of businesses or profit centers.

The environment and technology are presented as the two key and integrated external factors that contribute, with effectiveness of strategy as a moderating variable, to the design of the organization. The initial definitional and descriptive activities of organization design and structural alternatives are critical to the management of the operations function. Identifying the position of an operation on the chain of transformations and understanding its relationship with forward and backward integrated activities are the necessary foundations for subsequent efforts by the operations manager to design the operation to fit its environment and technology. Like AT&T, General Motors, IBM, and Sears, Roebuck, firms must use operations strategy to adjust the design to changes in the environment and technology.

## *Discussion Questions*

1. What does Terreberry state is an important consideration when one is evaluating organization designs? Give an example that supports Terreberry's conclusions.
2. There are four key dimensions to an organization design: centralization, formalization, complexity, and configuration. Describe the interrelationship of these dimensions.
3. Identify an organization that you are familiar with, and then show the key design dimensions of that organization. A rough sketch of that organization chart might be helpful.
4. Name and differentiate the five design forms.
5. Give an example of each of the five design forms. Briefly discuss the characteristics of the organization and why it fits that design.
6. Name and describe the five basic parts of the organization, according to Mintzberg.
7. Show how a chain of transformations may be used to describe a situation or business that you are familiar with.
8. Identify a typical customer product; then use the chain of transformations to trace the operations transformations that have occurred to the product from raw material to finished good.
9. Discuss the trade-offs in integrating the purchasing, operation planning and inventory control, and distribution activities. Identify the job of one operations manager and describe the degree to which that job is integrated.
10. Describe how the environment, size, and technology can affect how successful firms are designed.
11. Give three examples of firms that have changed their design because of environmental or technological influences.
12. Discuss the use of "focusing" and "fitting" variables in the design of an operations organization.

## *Strategic Decision Situations*

1. Verbally define the design of an operation that you are familiar with, and then depict the organization, using Mintzberg's five components. Describe and support the five basic components and configuration of your drawing.

2. Describe the operations activities of a large organization that you are familiar with; then use a drawing of the chain of transformations (like Figure 4-5) to depict those activities. Support your drawing.

3. From your readings and research, prepare a description of the design change of an organization (perhaps like Sears, Roebuck, General Motors, or Apple Computer) over time. Your discussion should include the interaction of technology and the environment as the organization grows and downsizes.

## *References*


Burns, Tom, and G. M. Stalker. *The Management of Innovation.* London: Tavistock Publications, 1961, Chapter 6, pp. 119–125.

Cameron, Kim S., Sara J. Freeman, and Aneil K. Mishra. "Best Practices in White Collar Downsizings: Managing Contractions," *The Academy of Management Executive.* Vol. 5, No. 3, 1991, pp. 57–73.

Carroll, Peter J. "The Link Between Performance and Strategy," *Journal of Business Strategy.* Spring 1982, pp. 3–20.

Chandler, A. D. *Strategy and Structure.* Cambridge, Mass.: MIT Press, 1962.

Daft, Richard L. *Organization Theory and Design.* St. Paul, Minn.: West Publishing Co., 1989.

Drucker, Peter F. *The New Realities: In Government and Politics/in Economics and Business/ in Society and World View.* New York: Harper and Row, 1989.

Fry, L. W. "Technology–Structure Research: Three Critical Issues," *Academy of Management Journal.* 1982, pp. 532–552.

Galbraith, Jay R. *Designing Complex Organizations.* Reading, Mass.: Addison-Wesley, 1973.

Galbraith, Jay R., and Robert K. Kazanjian. *Strategy Implementation, Structure, Systems and Process.* St. Paul, Minn.: West Publishing Co., 1986.

Hamilton, Joan O'C. "Design: Computers," *Business Week.* November 11, 1991, p. 142.

Hayes, Robert W., and Roger W. Schmenner. "How Should You Organize Manufacturing?" *Harvard Business Review.* January–February, 1978, pp. 105–118.

"How Swallowing Gatorade Gave Quaker Oats a Boost," *Business Week.* January 15, 1990, p. 56.

Katz, Donald R. *The Big Store.* New York: Viking Penguin, 1987.

Lawrence, Paul R., and Jay Lorsch. *Organization and Environment.* Boston, Mass.: Harvard Business School Press, 1986.

Lorsch, Jay W. "Introduction to the Structural Design of Organizations" in Gene W. Dalton, Paul R. Lawrence, and Jay W. Lorsch, eds. *Organization Structure and Design.* Homewood, Ill.: Irwin and Dorsey, 1970.

Miles, Robert H. *Macro Organizational Behavior.* Glenview, Ill.: Scott, Foresman and Co., 1980.

Miller, Jeffrey G., and Peter Gilmour. "Materials Managers: Who Needs Them?" *Harvard Business Review.* July–August 1979.

Mintzberg, Henry. *Structure in Fives: Designing Effective Organizations.* Englewood Cliffs, N.J.: Prentice Hall, 1983.

Pandya, Anil. "Vertical Marketing Systems: Non-Profit Marketing in the Public Sector," *Research in Marketing.* Vol. 11, 1992, pp. 147–194.

Reid, Peter C. *Well Made in America: Lessons From Harley-Davidson on Being the Best.* New York: McGraw-Hill, 1990.

Robbins, Stephen P. *Organization Theory: Structure, Design, and Applications.* Englewood Cliffs, N.J.: Prentice Hall, 1990.

Steiner, George A., and John B. Miner. *Management Policy and Strategy.* New York: Macmillan Publishing Co., Inc., 1977.

Strom, Stephanie. "Signs of Life at Sears, Roebuck," *The New York Times.* October 25, 1992, Section 3, p. 1.

Terreberry, Shirley. "The Evolution of Organizational Environments," *Administrative Science Quarterly.* Vol. 12, 1968, pp. 590–613.

Weitzel, William F., and Ellen Jonsson. "Decline in Organizations: A Literature Integration and Extension," *Administrative Science Quarterly.* March 1989, pp. 91–109.

Weitzel, William F., and Ellen Jonsson. "Reversing the Downward Spiral: Lessons from W. T. Grant and Sears, Roebuck," *Academy of Management Executive.* Vol. 5, No. 3, 1991, pp. 7–22.

"Why a Little Detroit Could Rise in Tennessee," *Business Week.* August 12, 1985, p. 21.

Woodward, Joan. *Management and Technology.* London: Her Majesty's Stationery Office, 1965.

Woodward, Joan. *Industrial Organization: Theory and Practice.* London: Oxford University Press, 1980.

# *Chapter 5*

# *Evaluation of Capacity Strategies*

> *We can break production . . . management down into two essential problems:* priorities *and* capacity. *Priorities in this context implies something more fundamental than determining which jobs are the "hottest." It means knowing* what *material is needed and* when, *and keeping this information up to date. This is what many people mean when they use the word "scheduling." Capacity means knowing how much man and/or machine time is needed to meet a schedule.*
>
> —Oliver W. Wight (1984, p. 5)

## *Objectives*

After completing this chapter you should be able to:

- State the importance of capacity decisions and identify three levels of capacity evaluation.
- Define capacity and show several applications of ways that capacity can be varied.
- Relate capacity costs to the best operating level curve.
- Differentiate required capacity and available capacity and show how the four-step process of resource evaluation resolves differences of required and available capacity.
- Identify and exemplify timing and size considerations of strategic capacity changes.

## *Outline*

***Introductory Case: Lordstown—A Historical Perspective***

***Capacity—A Costly Necessity***

***Theory of Capacity Strategy***

*Levels of Planning and Capacity Analysis*

## *Introductory Case: Lordstown—A Historical Perspective*

There is nothing more awesome than a smoothly tuned automobile assembly line—and nothing more obvious when things have gone awry. The Lordstown Vega assembly operation of the early 1970s is likely one of the best examples of industrial anarchy and the woes of modern technology. Simultaneously, the experience and knowledge gained at Lordstown have been widely applied to revitalize assembly methods. Envisioned at the time as a "factory of the future," the Vega assembly operation was designed by engineers for maximum production and efficiency, with an average production time of 36 seconds per car, or 100 cars per hour and 1600 cars per day from two shifts. There were 43% fewer parts to assemble due to careful product design, which was required by high-speed assembly methods.

Unfortunately, the zeal for efficiency and productivity felt by the engineers was not shared by the workers on the assembly line. The younger, better-educated work force had difficulty with the 36-second repetitive-cycle tasks and the very tightly specified assembly procedures. By late 1971 and early 1972, absenteeism, tardiness, turnover, and defective production of the sort that suggested industrial sabotage were at such levels that plant

Materials drawn from "Lordstown Plant of General Motors (A) and (B)" by Lee (1974) and "How GM's Saturn Could Run Rings Around Old Style Carmakers," 1985.

management was concerned. Labor grievances were at a record 15,000 per month. Something had gone wrong with this state-of-the-art high-capacity process.

By March of 1972, after a three-week strike, General Motors and the United Auto Workers agreed upon a multipart resolution of the problem. Recognizing the widespread distrust and insecurity of labor, coupled with boredom and lack of information about jobs and company objectives, GM instituted an extensive communication program, including daily plant radio announcements, information meetings, and supervisor training programs. These programs gradually reduced the levels of hostility and improved most measures of productivity, including absenteeism, production efficiency, and warranty cost ratings.

The program stopped short, however, of the revolutionary automobile assembly processes pioneered by Volvo at the Kalmar and Uddevalla (Sweden) plants. There, independent assembly teams of 15 to 25 workers set their own work schedules and used an innovative battery-powered dolly to move the automobile to various assembly sites. This reduced the pressures of the automated line and made the process rather like a job shop; however, as planned, the facility was projected to produce at a lower rate than a conventional assembly line but with higher quality. Improvements in job satisfaction were immediately apparent. Though fixed costs of the Kalmar facility were slightly higher than those of a conventional plant, variable costs were lower due to reduced scrap, higher quality, and greater worker productivity. It is notable that the Volvo production design worked well with a relatively low-volume production facility, but may not be competitive with a higher-volume facility. In fact, in the mid-1990s, the Kalmar and Uddevalla plants were closed due to high costs and low volumes.

Saturn, the strategic successor to Lordstown, suggests that GM considers effectively managed, highly automated facilities to be the best method to produce automobiles in a high-capacity environment. Though the ultimate production rates and labor productivity are expected to exceed both Lordstown and Kalmar, Saturn is starting up slowly and is ensuring that the automation is correctly managed. Voluntary recalls are initiated for seemingly trivial reasons and the inconvenience of the recall is minimized by available loan automobiles and hospitality suites. While Lordstown may have been close to industrial anarchy, the experience gave GM valuable insights into how to manage a highly automated, high-capacity facility. Recently announced plans to close 21 aging and less productive assembly plants suggest the continuing need to integrate capacity, facilities, and operations system design decisions in an environment of changing market demand.

## *Capacity—A Costly Necessity*

All manufacturing and service delivery organizations, regardless of the type of process, must consider available capacity and how they will use that capacity to produce the required goods or services. As the introductory quotation from Wight indicates, capacity and scheduling are closely interrelated and these, in turn, are driven by facilities and processes. This interrelationship is exemplified by the dilemma of General Motors noted in the Lordstown case. GM has excess capacity and expects to close 21 less productive automobile assembly plants over a five-year period; however, the high-tech Saturn plant does not presently have sufficient capacity to meet demand. Changes in capacity, either in volume or by product mix, are very costly because fixed assets must be reallocated, and, as shown by the Saturn example, quality, flexibility, and delivery are all affected. For this reason, operations capacity must be recognized as a strategic resource, and the effective management of capacity is a high priority for operations managers.

Capacity is a measure of the transformation process; it may be stated in volume (for example, units), time (hours or days), product range (number of products), process adaptability (rapidity of changeovers), or any combination of those measures. Though capacity is often thought of as a short-term or implementation variable, as in number of units per hour, it is even more important as a long-term planning variable. This is because today's capacity may require two or more years of planning lead time to ensure that all resources are available and efficiently integrated. Errors or failures of this process, if not quickly identified and corrected, can be extremely costly.

One of the most obvious distinctions between manufacturing and service businesses is the amount of flexibility in the use of capacity. As Bill Evans, general manager of the Bahia Resort Hotel in San Diego, states: "We have a commodity—a room—that's only got a one day shelf life, so we have to move it." This usually means that, as bookings drop, price breaks and promotions increase (Grover et al., 1992). Manufactured goods generally have a longer shelf life, which gives manufacturing greater flexibility in the timing of resource utilization.

This chapter introduces capacity as a necessary "cushion" to accommodate varying rates of the transformation process and of customer demands. The concern is not whether to have capacity, but rather how much capacity is necessary and at what cost. The importance of capacity decisions is noted and several levels of capacity decisions are described. Subsequently, cost analysis, economies of scale and scope, and the best operating level are related to strategic capacity analysis. These foundations are the basis for resource planning, which evaluates available capacity against required capacity. The final section applies these issues to the timing and extent of capacity changes. Capacity decisions are directly interrelated with facilities strategies, production system design, operations planning, materials management, just-in-time, and other subsequent topics of this book. Those relationships will be highlighted and pursued more specifically in subsequent chapters.

Capacity decisions may be considered to be more related to marketing or financial strategies; yet, as this chapter shows, the operations function makes a critically important, often overriding, contribution to capacity evaluation. The argument, simply stated, is that capacity decisions define the measure of the transformation process for which the operations manager is responsible and thus constrain the selection and pursuit of competitive priorities. Operations management must be directly involved in capacity decisions.

More specifically, capacity decisions involve fixed costs. The commitment to a particular level of technology requires a large and long-term investment, for example, in plant and equipment, which is not easily recoverable. Further, once such capacity commitments are made, they are difficult and costly to change. Consider, for example, the cost of reconfiguring a building to double loading-dock capacity. Thus, capacity decisions are costly because they cannot be easily recovered or changed. Further, from a practical perspective, once a particular capacity decision is made, managers usually do not want to readdress the issue for at least several years.

Additionally, capacity decisions set a limit on the ability to do a job by defining the primary costs of the operations process. The investment in a specific transformation process, such as capital equipment, commits the organization to a fixed cost and implicitly sets future per-unit costs, such as for labor or other variable-cost resources. For example, it is possible to build a road by using labor-intense methods and little equipment. The Romans built an extensive network of very fine roads, some of which are still used today. However, modern road-building operations use more capital-intense methods, involving expensive earth-moving and paving equipment, with a relatively lower contribution of labor to the production process. Once the specific technology is selected and the costs are committed, then the associated variable cost is also set. Additionally, numerous other capacity-related factors, such as the number of locations, the character of operations at each location, and the integration of facilities and processes, must be considered. Thus, the capacity decision involves a choice of technology, locations, process, and systems integration, all of which directly affect the fixed costs and the per-unit process time of the operation.

## *Theory of Capacity Strategy*

Traditionally, capacity is defined in terms of the rate of output of a facility or process. However, that very general definition must be amplified to consider the levels of capacity planning and capacity analysis in an integrated process, the capacity activities at each level, the measurement of capacity, and the types of operations capacity. These dimensions are generally discussed here and are amplified in the following sections.

### *Levels of Planning and Capacity Analysis*

Chapter 3 introduced the levels of the operations planning cycle from the long-range business plan, through the mid-range operations plan, to the short-range master production schedule and materials requirement planning activities (Figure 3-7). At each level, these planning activities should be evaluated by capacity activities to ensure that the plan is "doable." Additionally, capacity planning is directly related to the establishment and development of the distinctive competence of the firm. Generally, capacity strategy is defined as:

> *the process of identifying, measuring, and adjusting the limits of the transformation process to support competitive priorities such as cost, quality, delivery, and flexibility.*

Planning efforts should proceed from the long range, to the mid-range, and then to the short range. Once long-range plans are in place, mid-range and short-range plans can be prepared toward those defined goals and directions. As Plossl (1985) comments, capacity should first be managed in the largest possible aggregations. At each level of planning, then, an appropriate capacity process is used to evaluate the plan for feasibility, efficiency, and acceptability. The capacity strategy answers the basic questions:

1. Is the plan feasible, or "doable"?
2. Is the plan efficient, measured in terms of resource utilization, costs, or other stated competitive priorities?
3. Is the plan acceptable, in terms of meeting operating schedule, delivery, quality, and other customer-specified requirements?

Of course, if the answer to any of these questions is no, then the capacity process may be used to define the necessary actions to achieve the plan or to suggest alternatives or adjustments to the plan (Greene, 1987).

At each level, a dialogue occurs between the planning proposals and the capacity constraints. When the plan satisfies each of the capacity constraints and, as planning time fences are reached, the higher-level plan is approved and the process proceeds to a lower, more disaggregated capacity planning level, where the evaluation continues. This capacity evaluation process using "finite" resources smooths the production schedule and permits a more accurate link of the demand forecast with materials requirements, often yielding significant efficiencies (Casella and Barnes, 1992). However, as Levenbach and Thompson (1992) note, this process puts greater pressure on the accuracy of the forecast. Finally, after all capacity issues have been resolved, the plan is executed and managed through input/output control and sequencing. These techniques will be considered in more detail in subsequent chapters; this chapter focuses on the capacity strategy process. The levels of planning and capacity management are shown in Figure 5-1.

Note that Figure 5-1 shows the most common usage, though there is an increasing tendency, because of the availability of computers, to use each level of capacity to evaluate a higher level plan. For example, rough-cut capacity planning might be used to evaluate

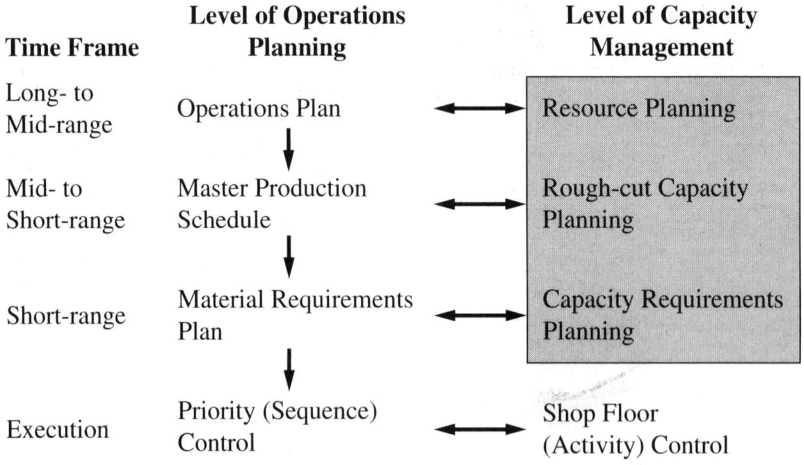


**FIGURE 5-1 Levels of Planning and Capacity Management**

Reprinted by permission, APICS, *Master Planning Certification Review Course,* 1991, Transparency 4-3.

an operations plan, particularly in situations with shorter time frames or more dynamism. Under all circumstances, however, capacity strategy must be driven from the top down; that is, long-range planning must precede mid-range efforts, and mid-range efforts must precede those in the short range (Correll, 1991).

The capacity evaluation process integrates operations and capacity plans from the long range to the short range and to execution. Resource planning has strategic implications because it defines the long-term capabilities of the firm. Rough-cut capacity planning (RCCP) and capacity requirements planning (CRP) delimit operations plans in the mid-run and short run. Finally, shop floor control (SFC) or activity control defines the limits of operations capabilities in the execution stage. This capacity strategy process both influences and is influenced by operations strategy (Melnyk and Narasimhan, 1991).

## *Capacity Activities*

At each level, the capacity activities are similar, but there are some distinctions in terms of time periods, inputs, and outputs, and in the detail of the resource management method. At the highest level, resource planning evaluates an operations plan, usually on a monthly or quarterly basis. Such evaluations deal in product families or groups and in monthly or quarterly time periods. Because of these long time periods, it is not necessary to offset the operations requirements for lead times. At this high level of aggregation, resource planning provides a general check of all resources and identifies those which may, when scheduled in greater disaggregation, cause problems of availability, either of quantity or timing.

In the mid-term, the RCCP is used to assess the viability of the master production schedule (MPS), which is defined in daily or weekly time periods and in product items. Lead-time effects are computed and a process load profile, if not a bill of materials, defines product structure information. The RCCP assesses capacity needs for all key resources, including components and raw materials, finance, labor, machine time, storage, and others. The rough-cut process is the highest level of planning at which management can affirm that the schedule is feasible.

CRP is used to evaluate the materials requirement plan (MRP) in the short term. MRP defines the orders, both internally to the shop and externally to suppliers, that are necessary to meet the MPS. CRP translates these orders into work center commitments (defined either as labor or machine hours) per time period (days or sometimes weeks). Other capacities are also checked, including available warehouse space, adjustments for scrap, and materials or components availability. Similarly, techniques such as priority and capacity control address the same requirements as operations systems are executed. The planning activities are summarized in Table 5-1.

At each level of capacity, management must answer four key questions. Those questions are considered by various types of planning activities and are:

*How much* volume is needed?
*Where* will the volume be needed?
*When* will the volume be needed?
*How* (or with what technology) will the product or service be produced?

**TABLE 5-1 Capacity Activities**

| | Resource Planning | Rough-cut Capacity Planning | Capacity Requirements Planning |
|---|---|---|---|
| Period | quarterly/ monthly | weekly/ daily | daily/ "bucketless" |
| Time Offset | no offset | lead-time offset | lead-time scheduled |
| Inputs | operations plan | master production schedule | materials requirement plan |
| Detail | family/group to items | items to components | components raw materials |
| Outputs | resource requirements | rough-cut capacity requirements | dispatch list purchase orders |
| Method | general resource profile | detailed process load profile | bill of materials |

These questions are considered by the appropriate long-range, mid-range, and short-range plans, each of which states the volume of production required per facility or work center per time period, and by process technology. Additionally, the planning process should identify communication channels, process flows, and other relationships to ensure that operations are fully integrated. This process of capacity design, scheduling, schedule adjustment, and continuous capacity improvement is called *total capacity management* (Wortman, 1992).

## *Measurement of Capacity*

Capacity strategy is generally defined as the process of identifying, adjusting, or measuring the limits of the transformation process toward competitive priorities. More specific statements of this definition, however, increase its usefulness to operations managers. Three different ways of defining capacity have emerged in the body of knowledge: design capacity, effective capacity, and actual capacity.

*Design capacity* is the output per time period under ideal or design conditions.

*Effective capacity* is the output per time period that can be realistically achieved, given various constraints, such as product/service mix, maintenance, quality, setups, and other known or anticipatable scheduling realities.

*Effective capacity* is less than design capacity due to known or anticipatable inefficiencies.

*Actual capacity* is the output of a process; it is usually less than effective capacity due to unanticipated processing inefficiencies.

These capacity distinctions permit the definition of the efficiency and utilization of a facility or a process, the key measures of capacity.

$$\text{Efficiency} = \frac{\text{actual capacity}}{\text{effective capacity}}$$

$$\text{Total utilization} = \frac{\text{actual capacity}}{\text{design capacity}}$$

Thus, efficiency is a measure of "how closely predetermined standards are achieved," while total utilization is a measure of "how intensely fixed resources are being used." These measures are exemplified by Decision Model Box 5-1.

Though the T&G example shows only one work center, these measures can also be applied to multiple processes or to facilities. In fact, a process usually involves a flow through several work centers, not just the load behind one machine or work center. Thus, the measurement of capacity and load must be considered in a system of several sequential or concurrent processes.

Capacity, the rate of flow, is also differentiated from load, which is the amount of planned, scheduled, and actual work in the system, measured either in total or at a particular point. The importance of the distinction between load and capacity is most apparent in just-in-time operations. Though other elements (such as human resource management and training) contribute to effective just-in-time operations, capacity considerations, including small loads or work-in-process, rapid setups and changeovers, low breakdown rates, ongoing preventive maintenance schedules, and high quality all are critical to the continuous improvement of just-in-time operations. Specifically, JIT reduces setups and changeovers and improves scrap rates and unexpected mechanical down time. JIT thus increases actual capacity and reduces the load behind each operation, thus decreasing inventory and storage requirements and lessening confusion. JIT operations often permit the processing of a greater variety of products/services through less costly setups (see Chapter 10).

The flow through the process is only as rapid as the flow through the slowest, or "bottleneck" work center. Process efficiency thus requires a reasonably smooth and continuous flow through required work centers or, in an integrated processing system, facilities or modules. A key consideration of the capacity of sequential activities is the fact that losses of efficiency in earlier processes in the sequence cannot be recovered in later sequences (Goldratt, 1986). Consider the effect of inefficiencies or lost utilization suggested by Decision Model Box 5-2.

## *Types of Operations Capacity*

Capacity can also be defined in more general product/service, market, and distribution system terms. A classic study by Hayes and Schmenner (1978) on the growth of capacity identifies four ways that management can strategically define and modify capacity to fit the goals of the organization.

1. Increase or decrease volume within a given market area.
2. Broaden or contract product/service lines.

## DECISION MODEL BOX 5-1 The Definition of Capacity at T&G Manufacturing Company

The T&G Manufacturing Company makes parts from raw titanium and other alloys for critical aircraft and airframe braces, such as wing and stabilizer supports. A milling machine in Work Center M is designed to produce three parts per hour during an eight-hour shift. With one shift per day, the machine has a design capacity of 24 units per day and 480 units in a 20-day month.[1]

However, the machine must be taken out of service for maintenance for one hour every 20 hours of operation. Thus, the maintenance schedule results in a loss of six units per week or 24 units per month. Similarly, the adjustment of the feeding unit and milling machine controls for different types of jobs requires an average of one-half-hour setup between jobs, resulting in a loss of ten units each week. Machine breakdown and quality defects, due to both defective materials and human error, result in a further loss of an average of five units per week or 20 units per month. The design capacity, effective capacity, and actual capacity, and the computations for efficiency and total utilization, are shown.

Design capacity: 24 units/day x 20 days/month = 480 units

Effective capacity: 480 units/month – 24 (maintenance downtime) – 40 (setup) = 416 units

Actual capacity: 416 units/month – 20 defects/month = 396 units

$$\text{Efficiency} = \frac{\text{actual capacity}}{\text{effective capacity}} = \frac{396}{416} = 95.2\%$$

$$\text{Total utilization} = \frac{\text{actual capacity}}{\text{design capacity}} = \frac{396}{480} = 82.5\%$$

[1]Note that, for purposes of defining capacity, T&G uses a simplified reporting month of 4 weeks × 5 days per month and 12 months per year. The remaining four weeks per year are lost time due to holidays and other uncontrollable reasons.

3. Increase or decrease span of process (vertical integration).
4. Expand or contract geographic market areas.

The traditional approach to capacity strategy suggests an hydraulic analogy, with product sequentially flowing from work center to work center as inputs, loads, and outputs, and with process capacity adjusted to provide for smoothing of the flow. These four components are shown in Figure 5-2. Note that the classic hydraulic analogy has been supplemented with a process variability "valve." Process variability exists, to some degree, in all processes. However, it only becomes visible when, as in the case of Work Center 3 and part YB 142 (Decision Model Box 5-2), it reduces system throughput. As variability of the process increases, either capacity or throughput, or both, are reduced. Similarly, as transfer batch or lot size increases, either capacity or throughput, or both, are lost. If, in the T&G example, part YB 142 was transferred from WC3 to WC4 in containers that required exactly 30 units, transfers would occur during periods 2–3, 4–5, and 6–7,

## DECISION MODEL BOX 5-2 The Capacity of Sequential Operations at T&G Manufacturing Company

The T&G Manufacturing Company processes parts YB 141 and YB 142 through two sequential work stations. The first work station of each process is human paced and the second is machine paced. The work stations have been extensively studied to determine the amount of time that each process takes. The following table shows the production of the two parts with a schedule based on those studies. Note that for simplicity, this example considers only daily production, with hourly transfers and no carry-overs. Production in work centers 1 and 3 is not considered for hour 7–8 because that production would not be finished during the particular day and production in work centers 2 and 4 is not considered in hour 0–1 because no work is available.

Parts YB 141 and 142–Capacity Planning

| Work Center | Human/ Machine Paced | Units/ Hour | 0–1 | 1–2 | 2–3 | 3–4 | 4–5 | 5–6 | 6–7 | 7–8 | Total Units |
|---|---|---|---|---|---|---|---|---|---|---|---|
| | | | Hour of the day | | | | | | | | |
| **Part YB 141—Planned Run** | | | | | | | | | | | |
| 1 | Human | 15 | 15 | 15 | 15 | 15 | 15 | 15 | 15 | | 105 |
| 2 | Machine | 15 | | 15 | 15 | 15 | 15 | 15 | 15 | 15 | 105 |
| **Part YB 142—Planned Run** | | | | | | | | | | | |
| 3 | Human | 15 | 15 | 15 | 15 | 15 | 15 | 15 | 15 | | 105 |
| 4 | Machine | 15 | | 15 | 15 | 15 | 15 | 15 | 15 | 15 | 105 |

According to the plan, T&G expects to be able to produce 105 units by the end of the day. However, T&G supervisors report that variances occur in both of the human-paced operations. They are concerned that, if the output of the human-paced operations varies, the lower volumes in one time period will not be absorbed by higher volumes in later time periods. They argue that, when lower capacities occur in a sequential operation, lower capacity continues throughout the process. These effects usually result from either worker slowness or poor-quality production. One supervisor provides the actual schedule from a similar job completed several weeks ago.

Parts YB 141 and 142–Actual Run—February 14

| Work Center | Human/ Machine Paced | Units/ Hour | 0–1 | 1–2 | 2–3 | 3–4 | 4–5 | 5–6 | 6–7 | 7–8 | Total Units |
|---|---|---|---|---|---|---|---|---|---|---|---|
| | | | Hour of the day | | | | | | | | |
| **Part YB 141–Actual Run** | | | | | | | | | | | |
| 1 | Human | 15 | 20 | 15 | 10 | 15 | 20 | 15 | 10 | | 105 |
| 2 | Machine | 15 | | 15 | 15 | 15 | 15 | 15 | 15 | 15 | 105 |
| **Part YB 142–Actual Run** | | | | | | | | | | | |
| 3 | Human | 15 | 10 | 10 | 15 | 20 | 15 | 15 | 20 | | 105 |
| 4 | Machine | 15 | | 10 | 10 | 15 | 15 | 15 | 15 | 15 | 95 |

*Continued*

**DECISION MODEL BOX 5-2** *Continued*

The initial run in work center 1 is over capacity; thus there is an excess during the entire day at work center 2. However, the initial runs by work center 3 are under capacity; thus work center 4 cannot make up the lost capacity during the day. This example shows the logic of the theory of constraints. The operations manager should define capacity in terms of the bottleneck work center and should fix the bottleneck to attempt to smooth production. In this case, the bottleneck at work center 3 should be addressed to ensure that its output is never so low that it affects work center 4.

resulting in an additional loss of 15 units (from 95 to 80 because the first transfer would occur at 2 hours and 40 minutes, leaving only 5 hours and 20 minutes for production in WC4. At 15 units per hour, 80 units would be produced). High process variability and large lot sizes both impede smooth production flows and reduce capacity (Williams, 1991).

A closely related concept is process flexibility, which permits the process to be rapidly changed so that different parts may be produced by the same work center. With process flexibility, both throughput and capacity are likely to be increased, because the flow of the processing system is smoothed. Flexible capacity permits the same facility to process a wide variety of products/services. Examples include automobile assembly lines that can produce a mix of products/services, including sedans, hatchbacks, convertibles, and station wagons, or a photo processing center that uses a specific mix to process one type of film, and sequentially adds several chemicals changing the concentration or mix for other types and speeds of film.

Vertical integration would be represented by increasing the number of sequential troughs (see Figure 5-2). An oil producer might have many sequential troughs, from exploration to retail, while a soap producer might only have one trough producing bulk soap powder from purchased ingredients that are packaged in bulk and sold to distributors. The fourth dimension of capacity, the development of several geographic markets, could be represented by the modification of the "buckets" to include additional output valves.

To summarize, capacity is measured as design, effective, and actual capacity. These measures are used for planning, whereas load is both planned and released work in the system. Capacity measures are used to calculate efficiency and utilization. In addition to those computational assessments of capacity, the dimensions of capacity change include volume, range of products/services, extent of vertical integration, and number of markets. The hydraulic analogy is useful to depict the capacity strategies of the organization.

## *Management of Capacity*

The preceding definitional and conceptual constructs are used by the operations manager to evaluate capacity. Operations management should regularly review key capacity concerns such as the cost of production, the related best operating level, economies of scale

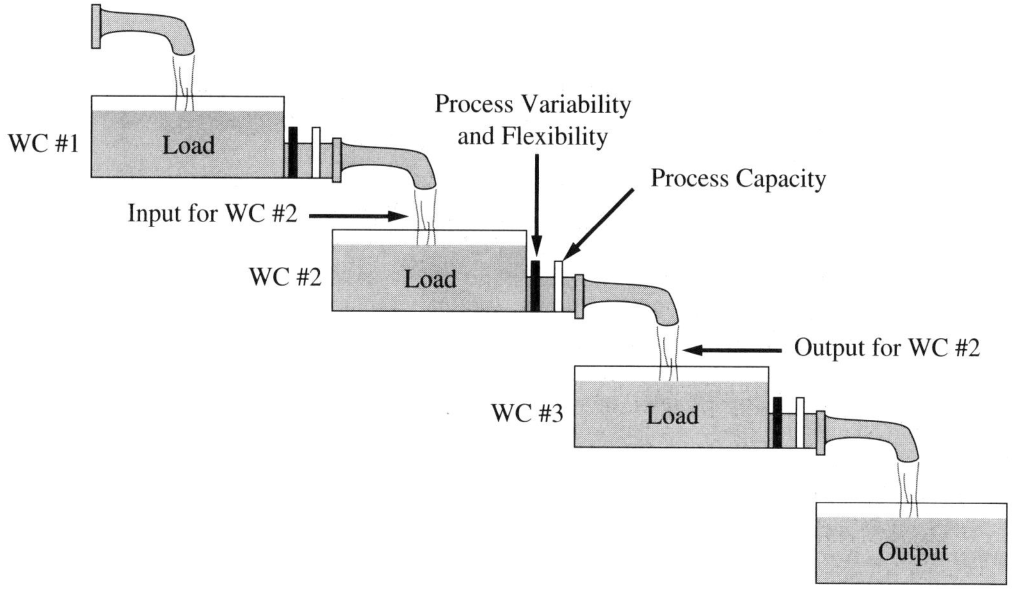


**FIGURE 5-2 The Hydraulic Analogy**

Adapted from Orlicky, 1975, p. 265, and Williams, 1991.

and scope, and the required versus the available capacity. These variables, taken together, form the foundation for periodic capacity decisions.

## *Cost Analysis*

The selection of process technology directly affects capacity. Because each process alternative requires a sunk or fixed cost investment in technology and constrains the further per-unit variable cost, the selection of the process technology significantly delimits the unit cost of the item. Consider, for example, the description in the introductory case of the Volvo Kalmar or Uddevalla facilities, compared with the General Motors Lordstown facility and its logical successor, the Saturn plant. Each facility uses a different proportion of fixed and variable cost contributions to production. The Kalmar facility, though viewed by some as a "step forward" at the time, was never able to demonstrate the competitiveness of a relatively labor-intense, job-shop-like process to build standardized automobiles (see Chapter 12 for a further discussion of Kalmar). Alternatively, General Motors' experience in building for a different segment of the market emphasizes the use of minimal labor (or variable cost) contributions and high fixed-cost contributions. Thus, both Lordstown and Saturn have relatively high fixed costs, and lower per-unit variable costs, compared to Kalmar or Uddevalla. Of course, the number of units of production is a key planning variable in determining the total cost. These different cost proportions are shown in Figure 5-3.

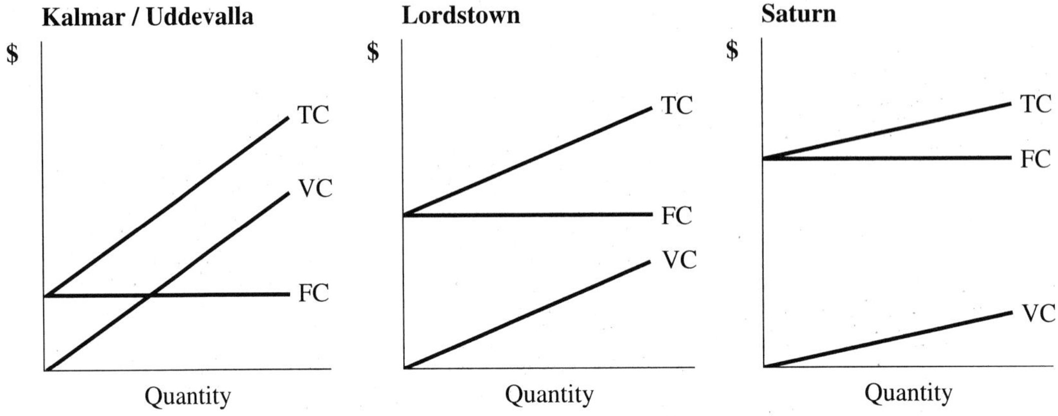


**FIGURE 5-3 Relative Fixed and Variable Costs of Automobile Facilities**

The break-even point (BEP) for any production process is defined by the volume, where total cost equals total revenue, or where fixed costs plus variable costs equal the price per unit times the number of units produced. These formulas are:

$$TC = TR$$

or

$$FC + VC \times U = P \times U$$

where

$TC$ = total costs of production of $U$ units
$TR$ = total revenues from the sale of $U$ units
$FC$ = fixed costs
$VC$ = variable costs per unit
$P$ = price per unit

A mathematical adjustment of the above formula gives the volume at the break-even point ($V_{BEP}$), which is more useful.

$$V_{\text{BEP}} = \frac{FC}{P - VC}$$

These relationships are shown graphically in Figure 5-4. Note that the variable cost has the same slope as the total cost.

Several different technology alternatives can be viewed together, as shown in Figure 5-5, suggesting a volume range over which a particular process technology should be selected. For example, for volumes in the range from the origin to $Q_1$, the lowest total cost alternative is technology 1. Technologies 2 and 3 are respectively best for the volume ranges $Q_1$ to $Q_2$ and above $Q_2$. These technology alternatives might roughly correspond

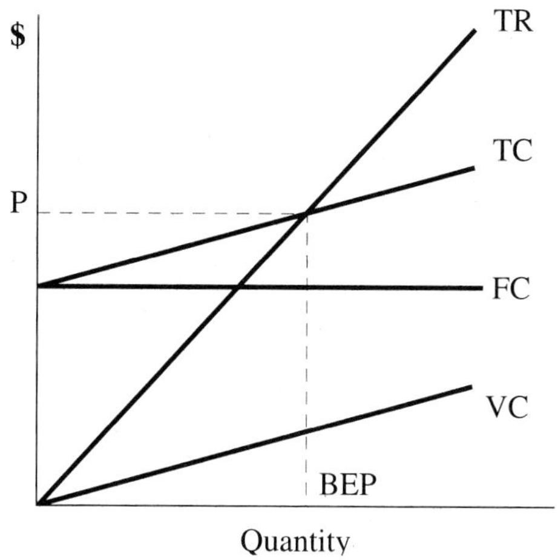


**FIGURE 5-4 Break-even Point**

to the Kalmar, Lordstown, and Saturn facilities. This lowest total cost at a particular volume is shown by the heavy solid line.

The point at which a decision maker is indifferent between process alternatives is identified by equating the total cost of one method to that of the second method, or

$$TC_1 = TC_2$$

or

$$FC_1 + VC_1 = FC_2 + VC_2$$

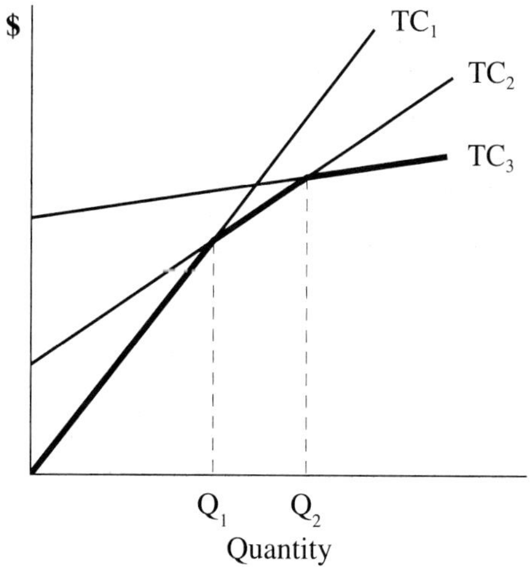


**FIGURE 5-5 Multiple Total Cost**

Though it is often assumed that questions of fixed facility costs and the corresponding variable labor costs are the realm of corporate financial analyses, the preceding discussion shows that these costs are directly related to capacity and to the performance of the operations function. Note that Figure 5-5 shows several total cost alternatives, which form a broken total cost line, not a continuous curve, which would be suggested if there were many technology alternatives. Schmenner (1976) uses the term "indivisibilities" to suggest that only a small number of technology and process alternatives are available. In most environments, it is not possible to add small increments of capacity. Of course, the break-even point can also be identified on the multiple technology line at the point where total revenue intersects the composite total cost line. Clearly, capacity decisions are a major contributor to the efficiency and effectiveness of the operation—the operations manager must be directly involved.

## *Best Operating Level*

After a volume decision has been made and the appropriate production method or process technology has been selected and installed, the operations manager must manage the facility at the volume of greatest efficiency for the given technology. This most efficient volume is called the best operating level (BOL). The BOL addresses the economies of the process and considers the cost per unit over a range of units produced. For example, if a particular process were selected with a \$1000 fixed cost, a \$10 per-unit variable cost, and a price of \$12, the break-even volume and total cost, calculated by the previously defined formulas, would be \$1000/(\$12 – \$10) or 500 units and \$1000 + 500(\$10), or \$6000 in total costs. This gives a cost per unit of \$6000/500 or \$12, which, as would be expected at the break-even point, equals the price. However, if the demand had not been forecast accurately, and only 250 units were required, the total cost would be \$1000 + 250(\$10) or \$3500 and the cost per unit would be \$3500/250 or \$14 per unit, a diseconomy of \$2 per unit. The diseconomy results because there was insufficient volume over which to efficiently prorate the fixed cost investment.

Similarly, if the number of units required increases notably above the projected 500 volume, for which the technology was chosen, diseconomies would also occur. Faster machine speeds may require greater maintenance and result in more breakdowns, and a second shift would likely cost more than the regular shift, both in pay and in greater confusion and training requirements. Due to these diseconomies associated with significant variance from the selected process volume, the cost per unit will rise, creating a U-shaped BOL curve, as shown in Figure 5-6.

Though the BOL curve is inelastic in the vicinity of the minimum point, the BOL point, there are clear cost penalties if a particular process deviates significantly from the BOL. If the volume is notably less than the BOL (insufficient units over which to prorate the fixed costs), or if the volume is notably above the BOL (the inability of the process to efficiently handle volumes for which it was not designed), diseconomies of scale occur. The diseconomies of scale were initially identified by C. Northcote Parkinson in what is called Parkinson's law (Parkinson, 1957).

More recently, these diseconomies of scale have been defined by Hayes and Wheelwright (1984) in four categories: distribution, bureaucracy, confusion, and vulnerability

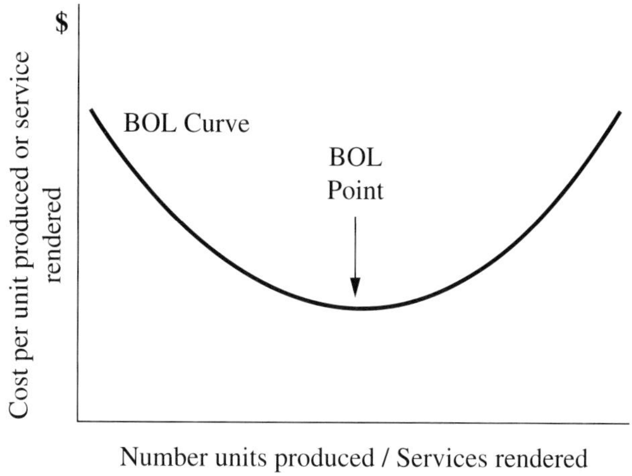


**FIGURE 5-6 The Best Operating Level Curve**

to risk. In each situation, an "overhead" increases disproportionately with greater unit volumes, resulting in a less cost-effective process. For example, in a distribution diseconomy of scale, a large factory must distribute higher volumes over a greater distance to a less densely populated area. Similarly, larger organizations often have greater bureaucracies and thus more confusing management processes. Additionally, a single facility is potentially more vulnerable to natural, as well as human, disasters such as earthquakes or strikes.

One BOL curve defines the cost of a specified technology. Movement along the BOL curve away from the BOL point, and the associated cost-per-unit and volume changes, results from inefficiencies or misutilization of the process. For example, all else being equal, if the number of employees in a one-shift, five-machine/five-employee work center were decreased, the number of units produced per period would decrease and the cost per unit would increase as the number of units produced moved left along the BOL curve. Similarly, if the number of employees increased above the required five persons, diseconomies of scale would gradually result as the greater number of employees got in each other's way. Thus, if the technology of the process is constant, a single BOL curve is defined and notable variation from the BOL volume will result in diseconomies of scale.

The BOL curve is derived from the total cost structure of a product or service. The BOL represents per-unit cost at various production volumes, whereas the total cost structure identifies the total fixed and variable costs for a specified volume of production. Thus, if there are multiple process technology alternatives, several total cost structures and the corresponding BOL curves would result, as shown in Figure 5-7. Note that each BOL curve is applicable to the range of production quantities from the associated total cost line. For each technology, as the production quantity increases, the cost per unit decreases to the BOL point. Then, as volume increases, diseconomies set in and the BOL curve increases.

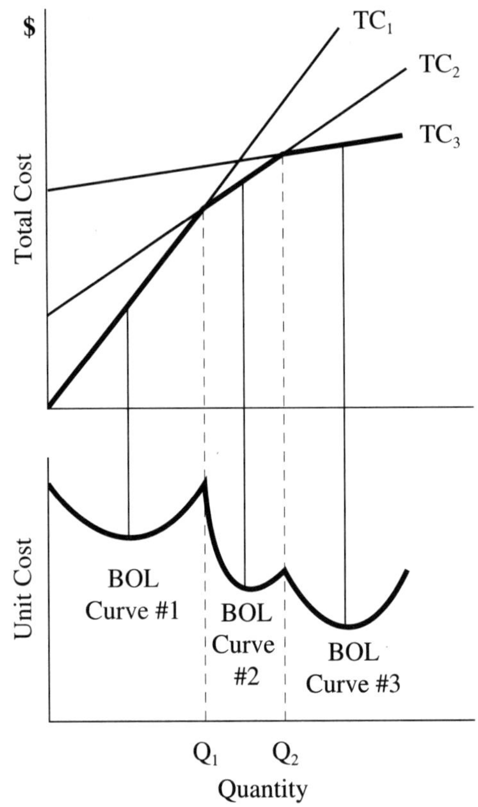


**FIGURE 5-7 The BOL and Multiple Process Technologies**

Based on the description of multiple process technologies in Figure 5-5, the change of technology from a low-volume process (low fixed costs, high variable costs) to a high-volume process (higher fixed costs, lower variable costs) will usually result in a downward and outward shift of the BOL curve. However, the exact shift of the curve depends upon the change in the fixed cost, the variable cost, and the diseconomies per unit associated with the specified technology. Figure 5-7 depicts the usual situation. When the process changes to a higher technology, greater unit volumes are produced, and thus the outward movement of the BOL curve. Additionally, because the incremental TC curve is increasing, but at a decreasing rate, the per-unit cost is decreasing at a decreasing rate and the BOL curve shifts in a downward as well as an outward direction. Note that the BOL, which is defined by the costs of the technology choice, does not necessarily correspond to the break-even point, which is defined by both costs and revenue.

## *Economies of Scale and Economies of Scope*

The economies and diseconomies of the BOL curve can result in either changes of scale or changes of scope. The traditional BOL rationale related to economies of scale, but recently developed operations practices have broadened the application to include economies of scope. These terms are defined as:

> *Economies of scale:* the efficiencies of prorating processing costs over greater volumes of a single product/service.
>
> *Economies of scope:* the efficiencies of prorating processing costs over a greater number of different products/services, which are processed in smaller item volumes but at greater total volumes.

Schmenner (1976) identifies three ways to achieve economies of scale, called *economies of volume, economies of capacity,* and *economies of process technology.* Economy of volume is the traditional approach of "spreading fixed costs" over a greater number of units. This corresponds to movement along the BOL curve from the upper left toward the BOL and the resulting lower per-unit costs. Economy of capacity, the second type of economy of scale, results because larger operations can function using proportionately fewer resources. Schmenner uses the example of inventory. Because the economic order quantities increase only as the square root of volume, not in direct proportion to volume, the per-unit costs of larger facilities, such as warehouses, are less. Similarly, the incremental cost of adding a second and a third shift is generally less than the costs of setting up a new first shift, because much of the overhead is already in place. Economies of process technology, the third type of economy of scale, result in a different contribution of fixed and variable costs and cause a shift of the BOL curve, as described in Figure 5-7.

In recent years, operations have increasingly used more flexible equipment to produce different, but functionally similar, products or services (for example, a product group or service line). Thus, though the volume of each product/service, considered separately, is lower, the volume of the group or line is the same or higher. This concept is the foundation for economies of scope, as exemplified by recent innovations of variable production lines, flexible manufacturing systems, and computer integrated manufacturing. If a single technology or a single process were redesigned to produce two items instead of one item, the resulting BOL situation would be as shown in Figure 5-8.

BOL curve 1 represents one inflexible process technology and various operating volumes with the corresponding cost per item. BOL curve 2 represents the use of that same equipment, but with a minor variation to produce two different products, represented by BOL curves A and B. Note that the BOL volumes of products A and B sum to the BOL of curve 2. BOL curve 2 is often located downward and to the right of BOL curve 1 because the potentially greater markets for differentiated products would permit greater production volumes and lower per-unit costs. However, lower volume and higher costs could result from poorly managed or marketed situations. The efficiencies of economies of scope are particularly important for applications like laser-cutting machines, which can be programmed to do multiple operations, such as cutting, etching, drilling, or finishing metal or other materials. An application of the BOL is described in Decision Model Box 5-3.

The discussion of the BOL has assumed, so far, a static decision environment. That is, one process technology alternative is selected; then the operations manager implements

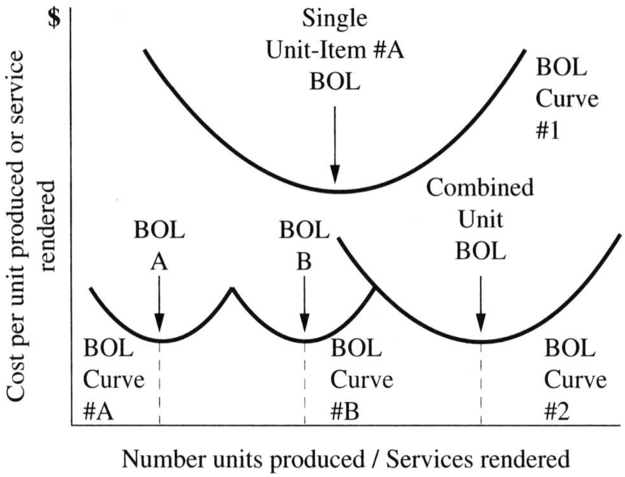


**FIGURE 5-8 The BOL with Economies of Scope**

the changeover to the selected process and operates the process at or near the BOL. However, there are a number of economies of either scale or scope that can result from unexpected or dynamic factors. For example, changes in the process to produce a second model may have varying effects on the demand for the first model. Product differentiation often results in greater total markets for both products; however, the second model may reduce the market for the first, resulting in only marginally greater total sales. Similarly, output productivity improvements would also likely occur due to learning curves, particularly in the long run. However, movement of the learning curve may be spiked due to numerous effects on the learning process (Hirschmann, 1964). Additionally, the integration of labor and equipment may result in some greater or lesser amount of synergy, or the enhanced productivity or effectiveness due to joint or combined effects. These dynamic effects would likely move the BOL curve downward and outward, adding to the effect of the static process economies described above.

## *Required Capacity versus Available Capacity*

Capacity strategy considers two distinct, yet closely related quantities: required capacity and available capacity (Blackstone, 1989). Required capacity identifies the amount of resource that will be required for each product, job, or family of products. This information is used to evaluate the plan (operations plan, master production schedule, or material requirements plan) and to determine the amount of capacity necessary to process the required number of products/services. Alternatively, the available capacity evaluation starts from the resources available, then adjusts the resources to reflect the realities of labor, materials, or machine unavailability. Capacity evaluation is the analytic process that identifies and measures processing production requirements and resource availability and then makes adjustments in one or both so that resources meet requirements.

## DECISION MODEL BOX 5-3 The Best Operating Level for The 'Copyrite' Print Shop

The 'Copyrite' Print Shop is a small job printer located in a university town. Their color printing equipment is five years old and, though dependable, is relatively labor intense. Management is considering purchasing new, less labor-intense equipment. Their initial step is to review only the fixed and variable costs of equipment options; subsequently, they expect to evaluate a range of financial, maintenance, and other support system costs as part of an overall decision. The current equipment is compared with two alternative upgrades. For each, the fixed cost, the variable cost, and a cost associated with incremental loss of efficiency is given in current dollars. Data are given in hundreds of dollars and for hundred-thousands of units of production (color copies).

| Current Equipment | Improvement Option 1 | Improvement Option 2 |
|---|---|---|
| Fixed cost (current $) = $100 | Fixed cost = $200 | Fixed cost = $200 |
| Variable cost = 10 | Variable cost = 5 | Variable cost = 2 |
| Diseconomy/unit = 5 | Diseconomy/unit = 2.5 | Diseconomy/unit = 1 |

Note that the loss of efficiency sets in after the second hundred-thousand units of production, and the diseconomy/unit occurs with every additional hundred-thousand units.

| Unit Cost | | | | Unit Cost | | | | Unit Cost | | | |
|---|---|---|---|---|---|---|---|---|---|---|---|
| Number of Units | Total Cost | Cost/ Unit | With Inefficiency | Number of Units | Total Cost | Cost/ Unit | With Inefficiency | Number of Units | Total Cost | Cost/ Unit | With Inefficiency |
| 1 | $110 | $110 | $110 | 1 | $205 | $205 | $205 | 1 | $202 | $202 | $202 |
| 2 | 120 | 60 | 60 | 2 | 210 | 105 | 105 | 2 | 204 | 102 | 102 |
| 3 | 130 | 43.3 | 48.3 | 3 | 215 | 71.7 | 74.2 | 3 | 206 | 68.7 | 69.7 |
| 4* | 140 | 35 | 45 | 4 | 220 | 55 | 60 | 4 | 208 | 52 | 54 |
| 5* | 150 | 30 | 45 | 5 | 225 | 45 | 52.5 | 5 | 210 | 42 | 45 |
| 6 | 160 | 26.7 | 46.7 | 6 | 230 | 38.3 | 48.3 | 6 | 212 | 35.3 | 39.3 |
| | | | | 7 | 235 | 33.6 | 46.1 | 7 | 214 | 30.6 | 35.6 |
| | | | | 8 | 240 | 30 | 45 | 8 | 216 | 27 | 33 |
| | | | | 9* | 245 | 27.2 | 44.7 | 9 | 218 | 24.2 | 31.2 |
| | | | | 10 | 250 | 25 | 45 | 10 | 220 | 22 | 30 |
| | | | | 11 | 255 | 23.2 | 45.7 | 11 | 222 | 20.2 | 29.2 |
| | | | | | | | | 12 | 224 | 18.7 | 28.7 |
| | | | | | | | | 13 | 226 | 17.4 | 28.4 |
| | | | | | | | | 14* | 228 | 16.3 | 28.3 |
| | | | | | | | | 15* | 230 | 15.3 | 28.3 |
| | | | | | | | | 16 | 232 | 14.5 | 28.5 |

*Asterisks show the best operating level.

The BOL for the current equipment is between four and five hundred-thousands of units and the unit cost, including inefficiencies, is just below 4.5¢. For option 1, the BOL is at 9 ten-thousands

*Continued*

**DECISION MODEL BOX 5-3** *Continued*

of units, and the unit cost including inefficiencies is 4.47¢; for option 2, the BOL is between 14 and 15 hundred-thousands of units and the unit cost, including inefficiencies, is just less than 2.83¢. In the above data sets, the cost per unit represents the economies of volume, and the unit costs with inefficiency represent the progressively increasing effects of inefficiency on the costs of volume. This is the diseconomy of volume. The fixed cost of option 1 is double that of the current equipment, while the variable cost is one-half that of the current equipment and the inefficiencies of option 1 are half those of the current equipment. These effects counteract each other, resulting in a best operating level which, though at a higher volume, is at the same cost/unit. The fixed cost of the second option is double that of the current equipment, but the variable costs and the inefficiencies are both one-fifth those of the current equipment. The lower variable costs and inefficiencies result in a lower unit cost and a higher volume of the BOL.

**Available Capacity.** The critical or constraining resource in a factory is often machine or materials availability and in a service business, it is often labor hours. This concept is generally introduced in Decision Model Box 5-1. If labor were required to feed, set up, or maintain the machine, and were not available for a second or third shift, the process would be called *labor constrained.* Alternatively, if the machine could be operated without significant human involvement, it could be used for a second and third shift (maintenance would be performed only during the day shift), and the process would be called *machine constrained.* In a three-shift environment, the available capacity in Decision Model Box 5-1 would be 396 units × 3 shifts, or roughly 1188 units per 20-day working month.

Labor-constrained capacity is computed by determining the total number of labor hours available, and then adjusting that value for various factors, including direct labor rates, efficiency, and absenteeism. Alternatively, materials/machine-constrained capacity is computed by identifying the total amount of machine time or materials possible and factoring the amount of actual availability. Resource availability factors for machines, materials, or labor are often stated in terms of resource efficiency and resource utilization rates. A commonly used formula for computing available capacity is

$$\begin{matrix}\text{Available} \\ \text{capacity}\end{matrix} = \begin{matrix}\text{time} \\ \text{available}\end{matrix} \times \begin{matrix}\text{resource} \\ \text{efficiency}\end{matrix} \times \begin{matrix}\text{resource} \\ \text{utilization}\end{matrix}$$

Decision Model Box 5-4 gives an example of the available capacity computation.

**Required Capacity.** Once the available capacity of the process is determined, the process is loaded with job requirements. Required capacity is computed for each job, or, in the long range, capacity evaluations are developed for expected product family volumes in each time period. Decision Model Box 5-5 shows a simple, though classic, representation of required capacity in a work center.

However, as shown in Decision Model Box 5-2, the flow of jobs through a process is not necessarily stable. Jobs moving through a process, particularly if the process involves

## DECISION MODEL BOX 5-4 Available Capacity at T&G Manufacturing

The T&G Manufacturing Company has organized a final assembly inspection operation in work center F. That operation employs five workers, including a group supervisor. Thus, work center F has a total of 5 workers × 8 hours per day × 20 days or 800 labor hours available in a 20-day month. However, the supervisor must spend two hours per day coordinating the work of the others. This 40 hours (2 hours × 20 days) of supervisory time is often expressed as a direct labor inefficiency. In this case, the available direct labor divided by total labor equals 760/800, or 95% labor utilization.

Efficiency is computed from resource availability. Records show that one-half hour per worker per day is wasted due to labor unavailability. This would be 4.75 workers × .5 hours × 20 days or 47.5 total hours lost per month. Note that four workers produce 20 days per month, but the supervisor produces product only 75% of the time, thus the 4.75 (rather than 5) workers. Machine/materials unavailability results in an additional 40 hours per month being lost. Thus, the efficiency would be reduced by 87.5 hours per month, which is 672.5/760 or 88.5%. The traditional computation of available capacity uses these efficiency and utilization calculations; the formula is

$$\begin{aligned}\text{Available capacity} &= \text{time available} \times \text{resource efficiency} \times \text{resource utilization}\\ &= 800 \times 0.885 \times 0.95 \approx 672.5 \text{ hr}\end{aligned}$$

These computations are detailed as follows.

Design capacity or time available = 8 hr/day × 5 workers × 20 days = 800 labor hr

Effective capacity = design capacity – supervisory time = 800 – (2 × 20)
= 760 hr

Actual capacity = effective capacity – labor unavailability – machine/materials unavailability

Labor unavailability = 4.75 × 0.5 hr × 20 = 47.5 hr lost

and

Machine/materials unavailability = 40 hr/month = 40 hr lost
87.5 hr lost

thus

Actual capacity = 760 – 87.5 = 672.5

$$\text{Resource efficiency} = \frac{672.5}{760} \approx 88.5\%$$

$$\text{Resource utilization} = \frac{760}{800} = 95\%$$

$$\text{Total utilization} = 800 \times 0.95 \times 0.885 \approx \frac{672.5}{800} = 0.841$$

## DECISION MODEL BOX 5-5 Required Capacity at T&G Manufacturing

The capacity requirements of six jobs at T&G are calculated based on the number of items required and the standard hours per item, and then adjusted for efficiency. These computations are shown. For example, the computation of job A, 200 units, is due in month 1 and would take 200 × 0.2 or 40 total standard hours. Dividing 40 by the efficiency of 0.95 gives a required capacity of 42.105 hours. The requirements are represented, often by a histogram, for each time period. With the present data, if a cap of 672.5 hours of available capacity per month were placed on the process (calculated in Decision Model Box 5-4), it would cause the process to be overloaded in month 2 and underloaded in months 1, 3, and 4. Though additional future requirements may be defined for months 3 and 4, this comparison of required and available capacity suggests that the plan currently should be adjusted by rescheduling or expediting roughly 200 hours of either job C or D to month 1.

This example shows the identification, measurement, and adjustment of a plan. Of course, more extensive capacity shortages would be resolved with overtime, additional shifts, machine speeds, outsourcing, or using flexible equipment, among other approaches. This application could be similarly, and in much more detail, applied to a plant or an industry.

| Job | Due Month | Number of Units | Std Hr/Unit* | Total Std Hr | Efficiency* | Capacity Required (hr) |
|---|---|---|---|---|---|---|
| A | 1 | 200 | 0.2 | 40 | 0.95 | 42.105 |
| B | 1 | 500 | 0.75 | 375 | 0.90 | 416.667 |
| C | 2 | 1000 | 0.4 | 400 | 0.85 | 470.588 |
| D | 2 | 600 | 0.6 | 360 | 0.90 | 400.000 |
| E | 3 | 2000 | 0.3 | 600 | 0.95 | 631.579 |
| F | 4 | 150 | 2.5 | 375 | 0.90 | 416.667 |

*Data based on historical records.

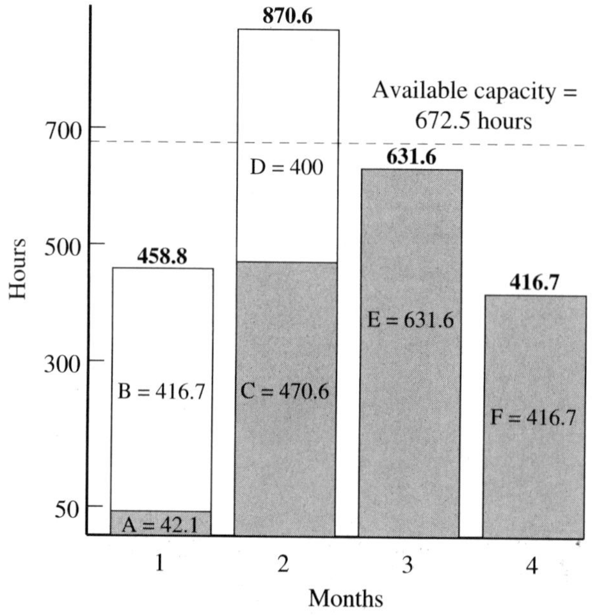

many steps, may be viewed as a series of random inputs and outputs, rather like the logic of queuing theory. The jobs may show extensive variance, or, in fact, randomness of arrival time due to the situation at upstream work centers. For this reason, Blackstone (1989) convincingly argues that the definition of available capacity should be restated to categorize utilization into factors of resource availability and facility activation, or:

$$\text{Available capacity} = \text{time available} \times \text{resource efficiency} \times \text{resource availability} \times \text{facility activation}$$

where resource efficiency = standard hours of output divided by hours worked (the classic efficiency computation)

resource availability = 1 – the fraction of time down due to machine breakdown or labor unavailability

facility activation = 1 – the fraction of time down due to lack of work

The use of a facility activation factor to adjust capacity, based on the availability of work, is the foundation of the theory of constraints. If capacity is not activated at a particular work center in a particular time period, that represents a constraint on the throughput or flow of the process. The term *bottleneck* is traditionally used to describe the buildup of load behind activated work centers; however, the term *constraint* more precisely describes the capacity evaluation of multiple system processes, because it includes the notion of both load and inactivity. When multiple products, multiple work centers, or multiple flows are involved, the resolution of constraints requires extensive interaction and evaluation of the process.

## Resource Planning

Resource planning is the process of establishing, measuring, and adjusting levels of mid- and long-range capacity, both required capacity and available capacity. It is often driven by the operations plan, but may be based on higher-level business plans. It is distinct from the rough-cut capacity plan, which operates in the mid- and short range, and from capacity requirements planning, which operates in the short range. The techniques of rough-cut capacity planning and capacity requirements planning correspond, albeit in much greater detail, to those of resource planning.

### Concepts of Resource Planning

Resource planning evaluates available and required capacity in the mid- and long run. Initially, the operations manager must identify the key resources. Though the evaluation will usually involve either machine or labor hours, or possibly both, it may also involve components or processes for which there is a long lead time, raw materials or components with uncertain availability, constrained warehouse or storage facilities, or financial assets.

## *Four-Step Resource Evaluation Process*

There are several different procedures that may be used in developing the capacity plan. These procedures are generally identified in Table 5-2 and further described in Orlicky (1975) and Fogarty et al. (1991). As shown in Table 5-2, the amount of information and complexity differ rather significantly among procedures. Using a simulation to evaluate different capacity planning approaches and considering the criteria of missed due dates, capacity deviations, and time fence requirements, Schmitt et al. (1984) conclude that the simple capacity planning method using overall factors (CPOF) worked as well as the capacity bill (CB) or resource profile (RP) methods. Capacity requirements planning (CRP) worked better than the other methods, but required a computer-based system. These findings are consistent with the intuitive conclusion that, for long-range resource planning efforts, the simpler CPOF method is sufficient, but for mid- and short-range capacity management, the more detailed, computer-based system is appropriate. It also suggests the benefits of using capacity planning methods to evaluate longer-range plans.

Regardless of the level at which it is conducted, the resource evaluation process involves four general steps. These steps are

1. Obtain the planned production for each product family or group by period (day, week, month, quarter).
2. Determine the product structure (resource profile or bill of materials) for each product family or group.
3. Determine the bill of resources (resources per unit) for each product, family, or group.
4. Calculate the total resource requirements.

The first step of resource planning involves obtaining the planned production for each product group or family by time period. This information comes from the operations plan, the master production schedule, or the material requirements plan. The second step is determining the product structure, defined as a listing of the amounts of key resources necessary to produce an item or family. The product structure describes a product group

**TABLE 5-2 Information Used by Capacity Planning Procedures**

| Capacity Planning Procedure | MPS | Accounting Direct Labor Summary | Routing & Time Standards | Bill of Materials | Manufacturing Lead Times | On-hand, In-Process Inventory, Lot Size, Safety Stock |
|---|---|---|---|---|---|---|
| CPOF | X | X | | | | |
| CB | X | | X | X | | |
| RP | X | | X | X | X | |
| CRP | X | | X | X | X | X |

*Note:* MPS—master production schedule; CPOF—capacity planning using overall factors; CB—capacity bill (which is the materials profile as used here); RP—resource profile, uses lead time associated with rough-cut planning; CRP—capacity requirements planning, which assesses all of the preceding and inventory status and is used with materials requirement planning.

in terms of the mix of specific product items, major work processes, and components of the product mix. More detailed capacity evaluation methods substitute the resources profile or the bill of materials (bill of labor) and approximate lead times for this purpose.

The third step, determining the bill of resources for each product family or group, identifies the per-unit time (machine or labor time, or lead time), cost (financial cost or planning time), or risk (uncertainty of success or probabilities of greater costs) of each key resource. For machine or labor times, the following formula is often used:

$$\begin{matrix}\text{Average} \\ \text{assembly time}\end{matrix} = \begin{matrix}\text{product mix} \\ \text{proportion}\end{matrix} \times \sum \begin{pmatrix}\text{standard assembly} \\ \text{hours/unit}\end{pmatrix}$$

The formulas for cost- or risk-measured resources would be similar, though the cost factor might be stated in dollars per unit.

The final step, calculating the resource requirements, multiplies the number of units required by the per-unit resource measure and determines the total resource requirement, broken down by work center or process. This total required capacity is compared to the measure of available capacity, however developed, and permits the computation of the capacity overage or shortage. An example of this process is shown in Decision Model Box 5-6.

In summary, capacity strategy involves two general computations, capacity requirements and resource availability. These decisions should be sequentially considered at the long-, mid-, and short-range time periods. To use rough-cut capacity planning, or capacity requirements planning, which are mid- and short-range techniques, to evaluate longer-range planning processes, such as operations planning, or long-range business planning is certainly possible, but may be overkill. Capacity processes are designed to provide the appropriate level of specificity for the operations planning method.

## *Implementation of Capacity Decisions*

Implementing capacity decisions involves three issues: the amount of the capacity cushion, the timing of the capacity change, and the size of the capacity increment. In most situations, such decisions are considered on a quarterly basis, and major decisions are rarely made at less than one-year intervals. Thus, the decisions, when made, are very important.

### *Capacity as a Cushion*

Initially, capacity must be considered to be a cushion, much as inventory safety stock is used. Capacity is particularly important as a cushion in make-to-order and assemble-to-order environments as well as in many services. Available capacity permits the operations manager to "gear up" for an unexpected short lead-time requirement. Depending upon the key resource, the operations manager may schedule at only 90% of actual capacity or may have several units of long lead-time components set aside against such an unexpected requirement.

## DECISION MODEL BOX 5-6 Resource Evaluation at T&G Manufacturing

The T&G Manufacturing Company uses a variety of titanium and alloy materials to build joints and other parts for airframe manufacture. Because of the cost of the metals involved, and the labor hours required to build them, these parts are considered to be key resources. Thus, T&G uses the four-step resource planning process to evaluate the milling operations of those resources. Given the following values:

| | |
|---|---|
| Product mix for product group A of products 1, 2, and 3: | 0.50, 0.30, 0.20 |
| Standard assembly hours of products 1, 2, and 3 of Product Groups A, B, and C: | 0.342, 0.294, 0.210 |
| Efficiencies for surface A, surface B, and final milling: | 0.95, 0.95, 0.95 |
| Available capacity for surface A, surface B, and final milling: | 320, 280, 300 |

### *Step 1. Obtain the planned production for each product family or group by period.*

The planned production for product group A in the specific month is 720, for product group B is 240, and for product group C is 160. This information would be obtained from the production plan.

### Step 2. Determine the product structure for each product family or group.

The product structure for a particular family of airframe parts would be given in process documents and is

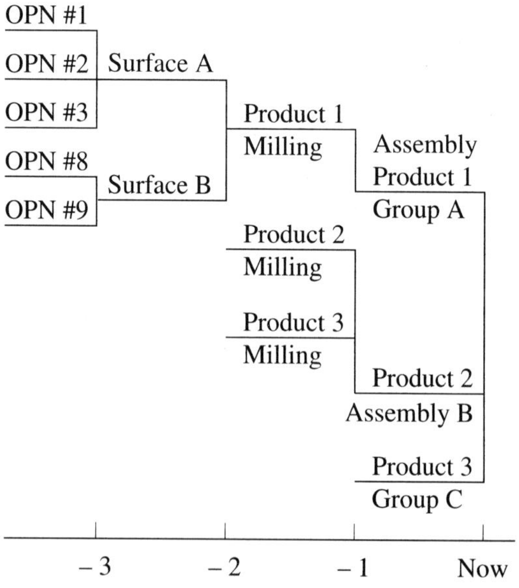


### Step 3. Determine the bill of resources for each product family or group.

The bill of resources is computed with the formula:

Product mix proportion × standard assembly hr/unit = average milling time

*Continued*

## DECISION MODEL BOX 5-6 *Continued*

| Product | Product Mix (given) | Standard Assembly Hr/Unit (given) | Average Assembly Time |
|---|---|---|---|
| 1 | 0.5 | 0.342 | 0.171 |
| 2 | 0.3 | 0.294 | 0.088 |
| 3 | 0.2 | 0.210 | 0.042 |
| | | | 0.301 |

Bill of Resources Analysis[1]

| | Surface A | Surface B | Final Milling |
|---|---|---|---|
| Product Group A | 0.274 | 0.250 | 0.301 ◄ |
| Product Group B | 0.222 | 0.185 | 0.285 |
| Product Group C | 0.241 | 0.241 | 0.256 |

### Step 4. Calculate the resource and materials requirements.

Thus, to build 720 of product group A in one month, the following capacity is required.

| | | | |
|---|---|---|---|
| Bill of resources analysis | 0.274 | 0.250 | 0.301 |
| Number of units | 720 | 720 | 720 |
| Total capacity required | 197.28 | 180.00 | 216.72 |

Similar computations would result in the data for each product group.

| | | | |
|---|---|---|---|
| Product group A | 197.28 | 180.00 | 216.72 ◄ |
| Product group B[2] | 53.28 | 44.40 | 68.40 |
| Product group C[2] | 38.56 | 38.56 | 40.96 |
| Total hours | 289.12 | 262.96 | 326.08 |
| Efficiency (given) | 0.95 | 0.95 | 0.95 |
| Plan[3] | 304.34 | 276.80 | 343.24 |
| Available capacity[4] | 320 | 280 | 300 |
| Shortfall | | | 43.24 |

Thus, there is a shortfall of capacity for final milling. The production plan must be adjusted, or supplemental resources planned for.



[1]The computations for product groups B and C correspond to those for product group A, though the necessary input data is not provided.

[2]Though not explicitly shown here, the total capacity required for product groups B and C would be found by multiplying the production plan requirement (step 1—240, 160) times the bill of resources (step 3) for surface A, surface B, and final milling.

[3]The resource requirements of the plan are calculated as total hours divided by efficiency.

[4]The available capacity would be calculated as in Decision Model Box 5-4; but for this problem, it is given.

## *Capacity Time Changes*

A capacity change decision can occur before the need for a changed capacity, can be concurrent with that need, or can be lagged behind the need. There are numerous ways to popularly describe these capacity timing strategies. For example, the lagging strategy is described as a "don't build it until you need it" approach, and the concurrent strategy might be called a "build for current demand" approach. The leading strategy might be labeled "build because it is the right thing to do" or "build because the market is going to turn." Figure 5-9 shows a stable increase in demand pattern over time, with the leading strategy creating capacity in anticipation of the increased demand, and the concurrent and lagging strategies respectively positioned with and behind the movement of demand. A more realistic representation of requirements would likely involve some amount of cyclical variation. If demand fluctuates extensively on an annual or other cycle, anticipating those swings to bring new capacity on line may be very difficult. For this reason, some companies may select to build capacity during the down-cycle, which is called a "contracyclical" capacity expansion.

The timing of capacity changes is related to the BOL because the leading, concurrent, and lagging strategies suggest that the firm will be operating at different positions on the BOL. Firms using a leading strategy will shift to a greater capacity approximately when they reach the BOL, and will generally operate on the left side of the BOL curve. Firms with concurrent strategies will operate at the center of the BOL curve, incrementing capacity at some point of increasing inefficiency. Finally, the lagging strategy changes its process technology and capacity by moving directly to the BOL of the lower curve and operating to overcome the inefficiencies of scale or scope. These strategies are depicted in Figure 5-10.

Of course, there are a variety of risks and advantages associated with each strategy. The leading capacity strategy is analogous to safety stock inventory in that it permits the manufacturing or service company to immediately or rapidly respond to changing market demands or to a growing market. These advantages, however, are counterbalanced by the associated risks that the up-front investment is higher and that a change may occur in the environment that reduces per-period revenues and slows the return on investment. Alternatively, a firm that decides on a lagging strategy reduces the risks of investment in potentially unused capacity or products that don't sell, but bears the risk of not being able

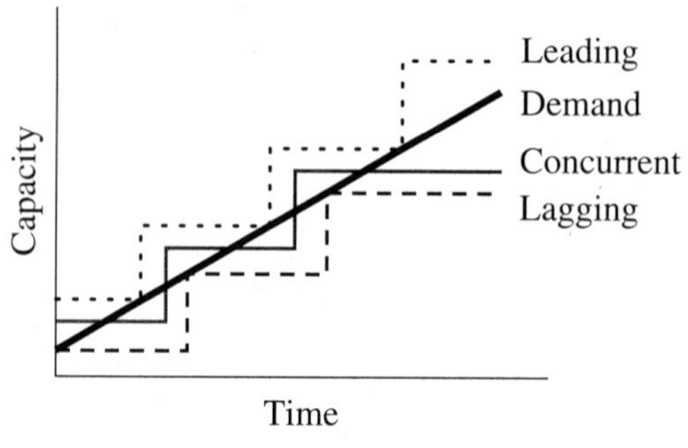


**FIGURE 5-9 Timing of Capacity Changes**

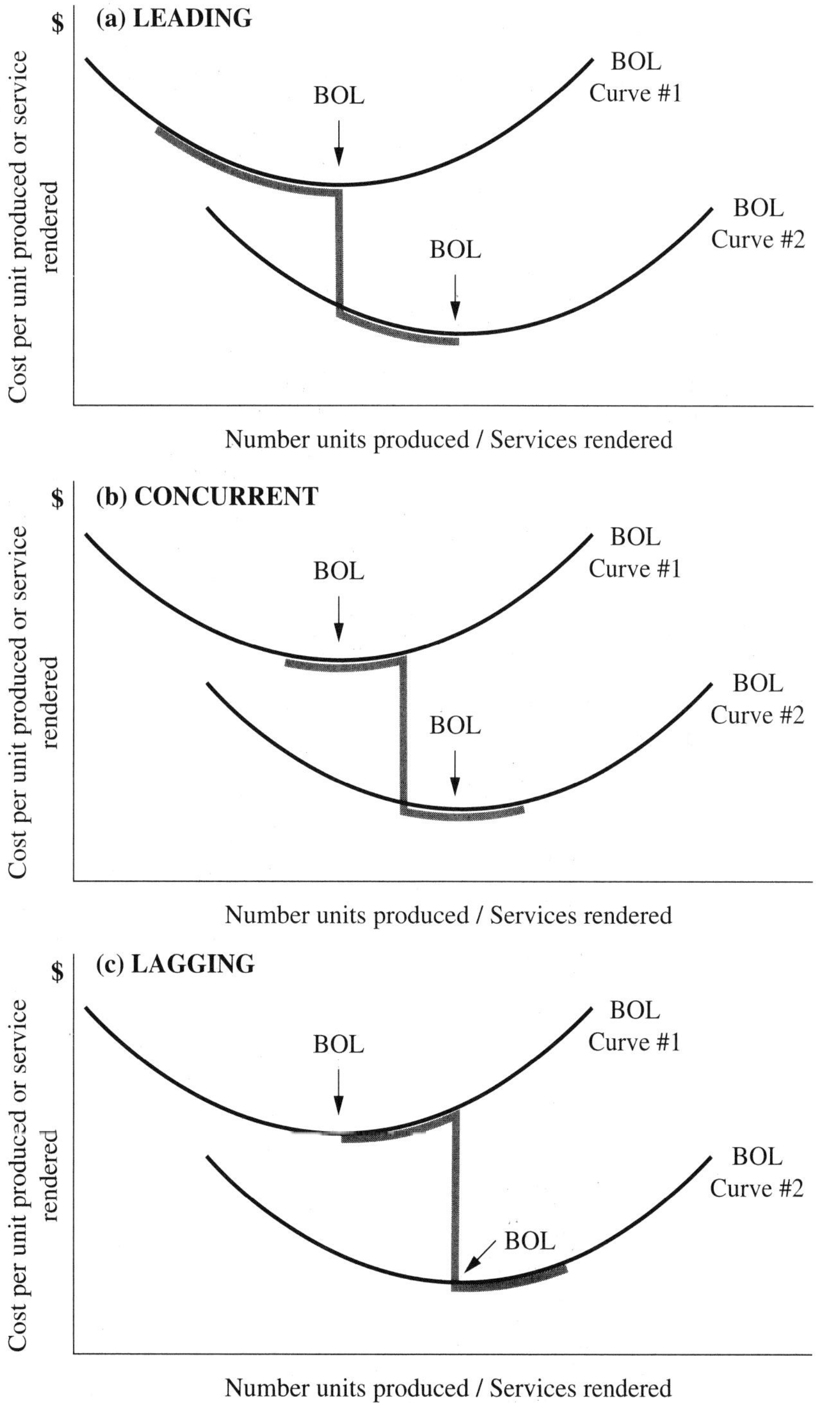


**FIGURE 5-10 Capacity Change Timing and the BOL**

to respond to customer demand—and the ensuing potential of back-order costs or lost sales (Leone and Meyer, 1980). The strategic capacity decisions of leading and lagging firms are shown in Table 5-3.

Leone and Meyer (1980) further suggest that, in addition to its representation of the economics of one or several processes, the BOL curve can be applied to the economic costs and risks in a multibusiness environment. During the 1950s and 1960s, productivity improvements associated with increasing volume, new technologies, learning curves, and general factors commonly outpaced inflation and other cost increases. Computers, communications, chemicals, and metals, among other industries, are examples of such "declining cost" industries. However, by the late 1960s and 1970s, the economic environment of many businesses began to change. Productivity improvements no longer could be counted on to offset cost increases due to inflation, capital costs, energy, or government regulation, and firms were not able to easily recover investments in capacity.

## *Size Increment of Capacity Changes*

Similarly, the size of the capacity increment also can be controlled by management, though within some limits. Capacity increments cannot be managed as a continuous function; they must be added in discrete chunks. The questions that arise are "how often?" and "what increments?" Figure 5-11 depicts that issue.

For various reasons, including organization structure, facilities availability, or process technology, it may not be possible to increment capacity in small amounts. However, the greater the capacity increment, the greater the risk of process or product obsolescence. Correspondingly, the longer the wait, the greater the risk that firm may not be able to get to the market first with a sufficient concentration of products and may have to overcome a competitor's advantage of an early-established and well-entrenched product. The costs of larger increments in longer time frames, and the associated risks (and costs) of catching up to and overcoming a competitor's strategic advantage are traded off against the costs

**TABLE 5-3 Capacity Decisions of Leading and Lagging Firms**

| Leading | Lagging |
|---|---|
| Build large-scale facilities | Build small-scale facilities |
| Build new facilities | Renovate or acquire existing facilities |
| Compete on basis of price | Compete on the basis of quality, delivery, or other criteria |
| Locate in developing areas | Locate in existing markets |
| Choose capital-intense technologies | Choose variable-cost or labor-intense technologies |
| Forecast demand using simple, less accurate methods | Forecast demand using sophisticated and likely more accurate methods |

Adapted from Leone and Meyer, 1980.

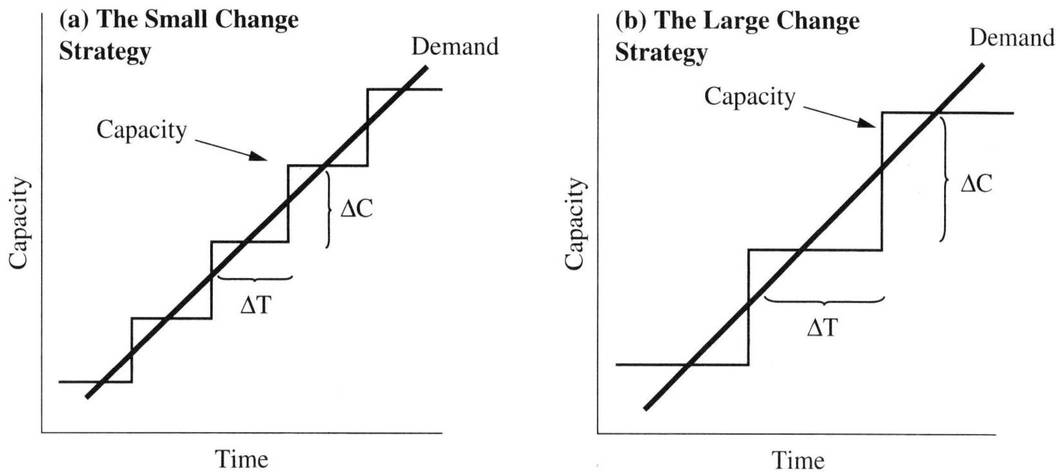


**FIGURE 5-11 The Increment and Periodicity of Capacity Change**

of continually directing assets to a capacity decision and the risks associated with building capacity too far ahead of demand.

## *Summary*

In summary, the capacity strategy must be evaluated for each business environment. It is clearly one of the most important decisions that a firm makes and must involve top management, because they involve the long-range direction and financial viability of the firm. Unfortunately, operations involvement in capacity decisions has traditionally been limited, even though the decision is central to the performance of the operations function. The selection of a capacity alternative is directly related to efficiency and facility utilization. It is founded in the analysis of fixed-cost and variable-cost process alternatives and the associated BOL curves of the selected process technology.

The capacity strategy must also address the advantages of static economies of scale and of scope and the potential dynamic economies of scale and scope that may ensue. Recent emphases on flexibility and innovation are explicitly based on the concept of economies of scope. Resource planning is one of the essential methods of capacity evaluation; it identifies and measures required and available capacity and adjusts either or both so that requirements can be met with available resources. This adjustment involves a four-step process that disaggregates production requirements into resource needs. At a minimum, the capacity evaluation process must assess the general question of leading, concurrent, and lagging demand requirements and the resulting capacity cushions that are created. Though risks of incorrectly diagnosing the environment are costly, the costs of not addressing capacity questions are greater. Few operations managers can successfully manage an operations process if they have not actively participated in the decisions that led to the selection of the process.

## Discussion Questions

1. Capacity has been called a costly necessity. Give several examples of capacity (both in services and in manufacturing operations) from your own experience and state the costs of that capacity and why they are necessary.
2. What basic questions do capacity strategies answer?
3. Identify several levels at which capacity activities occur and describe an example from your readings or experience which shows what these capacity activities do at each level.
4. Identify three specific definitions of capacity and show how they are helpful to the operations manager.
5. What are the four ways that operations capacity may be dimensionalized? Give an example from your experience of each of these dimensions.
6. Why are the fixed and variable costs of a particular operations process important to the operations manager?
7. Considering Figures 5-6, 5-7, and 5-8, define and give an example of economies of scale, multiple process technologies, and economies of scope.
8. Differentiate required capacity and available capacity. Give an example of each.
9. List the four steps of resource evaluation. From your experience, give an example of each step. (*Note:* Resource evaluation can be applied to as simple and widespread an example as preparing for a backyard barbecue, managing a charity carwash, or scheduling classes or social activities.)
10. Relate the best operating level to the timing of capacity change decisions. Describe operations that would tend to lead demand, those that would tend to be concurrent with demand, and those that might lag demand.
11. Using the concept of best operating level, graphically relate total costs to produce a quantity of units with per-unit costs to produce that number of units.
12. Discuss the circumstances under which a lower-level capacity evaluation process would be used to evaluate a longer-term (higher-level) operations planning process. Are there advantages of using rough-cut capacity planning to evaluate an operations plan and capacity requirements planning to evaluate a master production schedule? What are the disadvantages?

## Strategic Decision Situations

1. The North LaSalle Bank and Trust Company suggests guidance for its suburban branch banks on how many tellers should be scheduled for drive-through lane operations at different times of the day. The local suburban branch has four drive-through lanes; however, those lanes are

staffed at different levels during the day because, during low-volume periods, bank personnel can be better used at other duties. Typically, an open lane can service one customer every five minutes. The drive-through windows are open from seven o'clock in the morning until seven o'clock in the evening, Monday through Friday, and staff are scheduled for three-hour shifts in the drive-through. Bank policy permits employees to take one 20-minute break during the three-hour period, and, because employees bring their cash trays to the drive-through window area, shift changeover time is nominal. The bank has found that some customers bring multiple transactions or transactions that require greater processing times; these "high-density" transactions require an average of seven and one-half minutes each, and are estimated to occur at the indicated rate per line per hour. Evaluate the daily design capacity, effective capacity, actual capacity, efficiency, and utilization of the local suburban branch. Be prepared to advise management on their current use of resources.

| | Time | | | |
|---|---|---|---|---|
| | 7:00–10:00 | 10:00–1:00 | 1:00–4:00 | 4:00–7:00 |
| Number of employees | 2 | 3 | 2 | 4 |
| High density transactions per line per hour | 1 | 3 | 4 | 2 |

**2.** The downtown library is anticipating the installation of a new computerized book checkout system, which will replace their currently used manual system. The new system may be used to "wand" bar code identification panels on the inside covers of books. Given a normal manual operation with three librarians at three checkout counters, represent the following situations, using a BOL diagram.

**a.** The scheduling of five librarians to manually check out books at the checkout counter.

**b.** One of the three librarians calls in sick with the result that only two librarians are available to staff the three-position checkout operation.

**c.** The installation of the new computer system at the three stations and the gradual implementation of the system as the staff is trained to use it.

**d.** A power surge requires that manual operations procedures be used while the computer is reinitialized and the software is reloaded, a process that takes two to three hours.

**e.** The installation of software and bar code panels so that records, videos, and CDs can also be checked out with the computer system.

**3.** The Windy City Pump Company makes three sizes of valve in three different machine centers. With customizations, however, process standard hours and efficiency of specific jobs vary. The valve halves are initially cast and welded together, then machined in separate operations, each of which is done in a different machine center. The company operates one eight-hour shift per day on a 20-day monthly calendar, and has three employees in the casting area, four employees in the welding center, and five employees in the machine center. The senior employee in each area/center spends four hours per week on administration, and unplanned-for employee absenteeism results in one day per month lost per production center, while unavailable materials result in the loss of one labor day per month per employee in each center.

**a.** Find the available capacity of each center.

**b.** The following jobs are planned for the centers. Note that a job must be first cast, then welded, then machined. Determine the resource requirements and, considering available capacity (part 1), advise management. The current backlog in the welding center uses all available capacity in week 1, and the backlog in the machine center uses all available capacity in weeks 1 and 2. The jobs may be broken in any volume, but only at the end of the week, and they may be moved from work center to work center as "broken" jobs.

| | | | Cast | | Weld | | Machine | |
|---|---|---|---|---|---|---|---|---|
| Job | Due Week | Units | Std hr/unit | Efficiency | Std hr/unit | Efficiency | Std hr/unit | Efficiency |
| A | 3 | 200 | 0.3 | 0.95 | 0.15 | 0.85 | 0.30 | 0.95 |
| B | 3 | 400 | 0.2 | 0.90 | 0.50 | 0.80 | 0.70 | 0.90 |
| C | 4 | 100 | 0.4 | 0.85 | 0.30 | 0.90 | 0.80 | 0.90 |
| D | 5 | 300 | 0.3 | 0.90 | 0.25 | 0.80 | 0.60 | 0.85 |
| E | 6 | 250 | 0.5 | 0.90 | 0.55 | 0.85 | 0.50 | 0.90 |
| F | 7 | 330 | 0.3 | 0.95 | 0.30 | 0.90 | 0.30 | 0.95 |

4. The South Lake Steel Company manufactures three product groups of metal kitchen cabinets, which require rolled steel inputs and milling, mechanical assembly, and final assembly. The production plan data is provided below, as is a bill of resources. If the total capacity of the final assembly operation is 2.6 units/day, the mechanical assembly is 4.3 units/day, the milling operation is 2.5 units/day, and the steel is 4 tons/day, advise the South Lake management on the feasibility of the production plan.

**Production Plan of Family**

| Product Group | Jul. | Aug. | Sep. | Oct. | Nov. | Dec. |
|---|---|---|---|---|---|---|
| Number of days/mo | 17 | 23 | 19 | 22 | 20 | 16 |
| X | 85 | 115 | 95 | 110 | 100 | 80 |
| Y | 170 | 230 | 190 | 220 | 200 | 160 |
| Z | 85 | 115 | 95 | 110 | 100 | 80 |

**Bill of Resources**

| Product Group | Work Center | Description | Unit of Measure | Quantity/ Unit | Months Lead Time |
|---|---|---|---|---|---|
| X | 001 | final assembly | hours | 0.2 | 0 |
| | 002 | mechanical assembly | hours | 0.2 | 1 |
| | 003 | milling | hours | 0.1 | 1 |
| | 004 | steel | tons | 0.1 | 2 |
| Y | 001 | final assembly | hours | 0.1 | 0 |
| | 002 | mechanical assembly | hours | 0.2 | 1 |
| | 003 | milling | hours | 0.1 | 1 |
| | 004 | steel | tons | 0.2 | 2 |
| Z | 001 | final assembly | hours | 0.1 | 0 |
| | 002 | mechanical assembly | hours | 0.2 | 1 |
| | 003 | milling | hours | 0.1 | 1 |
| | 004 | steel | tons | 0.3 | 2 |

## *References*


Blackstone, John H., Jr. *Capacity Management.* Cincinnati, Ohio: South-Western Publishing Co., 1989.

Casella, Bill, and Todd Barnes. "Finite Capacity Scheduling Is also a Forecasting Tool for Beth Forge," *APICS, The Performance Advantage.* January 1992, pp. 20–23.

Correll, James G. "Capacity Management: The Answer to 'Do the Best You Can,' " *APICS, The Performance Advantage.* September 1991, p. 50–54.

Fogarty, Donald W., John H. Blackstone, and Thomas R. Hoffmann. *Production & Inventory Management.* Cincinnati, Ohio: South-Western Publishing Co., 1991.

Fogarty, Donald W., Thomas R. Hoffmann, and Peter W. Stonebraker. *Production and Operations Management,* Cincinnati, Ohio: South-Western Publishing Co., 1989.

Goldratt, Eliyahu M., and Jeff Cox. *The Goal.* Croton-on-Hudson, N.Y.: North River Press, 1986.

Greene, James H. *Production and Inventory Control Handbook.* New York: McGraw-Hill, 1987.

Grover, Ronald, Sandra D. Achison, and Gail DeGeorge. "Heartbreak Hotel for Tourism," *Business Week.* January 20, 1992, p. 36.

Hayes, Robert H., and Roger W. Schmenner. "How Should You Organize Manufacturing?" *Harvard Business Review.* January–February 1978.

Hayes, Robert H., and Steven C. Wheelwright. *Restoring Our Competitive Edge: Competing through Manufacturing.* New York: John Wiley and Sons, 1984.

Hirschmann, Winfred B. "Profit from the Learning Curve," *Harvard Business Review.* January–February 1964.

"How GM's Saturn Could Run Rings Around Old-Style Carmakers," *Business Week.* January 28, 1985.

Lee, Hak-Chong. "Lordstown Plant of General Motors (A) and (B)." State University of New York at Albany, 1974.

Leone, Robert A., and John R. Meyer. "Capacity Strategies for the 1980s," *Harvard Business Review.* November–December, 1980, pp. 133–140.

Levenbach, Hans, and James G. Thompson. "Tying the Forecasting Process into Finite Scheduling," *Production & Inventory Management.* January 1992, pp. 17–20.

Melnyk, Steven A., and Ram Narasimhan. "Uniting Capacity, Shop Floor Control and Strategy," *APICS: The Performance Advantage.* November 1991, pp. 33–45.

Orlicky, Joseph. *Materials Requirement Planning.* New York: McGraw-Hill, 1975.

Parkinson, C. Northcote. *Parkinson's Law.* Boston, Mass.: Houghton-Mifflin, 1957.

Plossl, George W. *Production and Inventory Control: Principles and Techniques.* Englewood Cliffs, N.J.: Prentice Hall, 1985.

Plossl, George W. *Managing in the New World of Manufacturing.* Englewood Cliffs, N.J.: Prentice Hall, 1991.

Schmenner, Roger W. "Before You Build a Big Factory," *Harvard Business Review.* July–August 1976.

Schmitt, Thomas G., William L. Berry, and Thomas E. Vollmann. "An Analysis of Capacity Planning Procedures for a Materials Requirement Planning System," *Decision Sciences.* Vol. 15, 1984, pp. 522–541.

Vollmann, Thomas E., William L. Berry, and D. Clay Whybark. *Manufacturing Planning and Control Systems.* Homewood, Ill.: Irwin, 1992.

Wight, Oliver W. *Production and Inventory Management in the Computer Age.* New York: Van Nostrand Reinhold Company, 1984.

Williams, Blaire R. "Understanding Available Resource Capacity in the Manufacturing Sector," *APICS: The Performance Advantage.* November 1991, pp. 39–41.

Wortman, David B. "Managing Capacity: Getting the Most from Your Company's Assets," *Industrial Engineering.* February 1992, pp. 47–49.

# Chapter 6

# Facilities Strategy

*Taking advantage of the speed and flexibility offered by modern air cargo carriers, manufacturers are no longer limited by distance. They can gather materials from all over the globe; . . . parts, components, subsystems, products, services, and information are continuously intermingled, . . . bypassing traditional warehousing facilities.*

—Fred Smith, President and CEO, Federal Express

*And Japanese multinationals . . . are pouring staggering amounts of money into manufacturing plants in developing countries. They are in Tijuana on the U.S.–Mexican border, throughout South America, in Southern Europe, and in Southeast Asia. The standard explanations for moving manufacturing out of Japan are "foreign protectionism" and "Japan's growing labor shortage." Both explanations are legitimate, but they are also smoke screens. The real reason is the growing conviction among Japan's business leaders and influential bureaucrats that manufacturing work does not belong in a developed country such as Japan.*

—Peter F. Drucker

## Objectives

After completing this chapter you should be able to:

- Explain the contribution of facilities strategy to operations strategy.
- List the four components of facilities strategy.
- Discuss the major factors that influence facilities location decisions.
- Link facilities layout with performance and analyze the different types of facilities layout.
- Describe the benefits of focused facilities.
- Describe the contribution of handling systems to improved productivity.

## Outline



## Introductory Case: The General Motors Saturn Plant*

When General Motors announced plans in January 1985 for its $5 billion Saturn small car project, Tennessee played it cool. GM was trying to pull together the most advanced technology possible in a bid to revolutionize automobile manufacturing, and gain a competitive advantage. Where the plant was to be located remained a question. Unlike other states, Tennessee officials did not dispatch caravans of politicians and state officials to Detroit to tantalize GM with concessions. Tennessee state officials coveted the Saturn plant, but they believed that temporary incentives would not change the decision. Rather, GM's location decisions would be based on more fundamental factors.

*Materials drawn from: David Whiteside, Richard Brandt, Zachary Schiller, and Andrea Gabor, "How GM's Saturn Could Run Rings Around Old-Style Carmakers," *Business Week,* January 28, 1985, pp. 27–28; Pete Engardio and Maralyn Edid, "Why a 'Little Detroit' Could Rise in Tennessee," *Business Week,* August 12, 1985, p. 21; Alex Taylor III, "Back to the Future at Saturn," *Fortune,* August 1, 1988, pp. 67–72; Majorie A. Sorge and Stephene E. Plumb, "Can Saturn Keep the Revival Meeting Going?" *Ward's Auto World,* Vol. 5, 1990, pp. 43–49.

As it turned out, Tennessee was correct. The lack of tax breaks or free giveaways had little to do with the location decision. GM never asked for any incentives. The decision to locate the Saturn facility and its 6000 workers on some 2400 acres of rolling countryside south of Nashville, near the one-stoplight town of Spring Hill, apparently had little to do with the state's promotion efforts and a lot to do with fundamentals.

Spring Hill, Tennessee, was selected by a process that evaluated various factors. GM and state officials said Spring Hill was chosen because of central Tennessee's strategic location, climate, ample supplies of water and electricity, and its eager work force. A University of Tennessee study showed that state manufacturers rated their employees as having "good worker attitude" and high productivity. The president of Nissan USA, Marvin T. Runyon, said, "The people here are just very good, loyal workers." Saturn president William E. Hoglund called Tennessee "absolutely perfect for the type of people we want to hire."

Low property taxes is another reason Tennessee was chosen. But the primary factor may have been simple geography. According to state figures, central Tennessee is close to GM's suppliers and within 500 miles of 76% of the U.S. population. Three interstate highways crisscross nearby Nashville, and there is a rail link to the 234-mile-long Tennessee–Tombigbee Waterway, a new $2 billion barge canal to the Gulf of Mexico. That means low freight costs, which Hoglund cited as the most important economic factor in the selection. Another factor was the infrastructure. Nissan USA makes light trucks and the Sentra car in nearby Smyrna, Tennessee. The proximity of Nissan, say state officials, also may have weighed heavily in the decision. Since the Japanese company's arrival, dozens of parts suppliers have sprung up, making everything from car seats to catalytic converters.

The Saturn plant represents the largest single construction project in GM history and covers an area of 4.4 million square feet, roughly the size of 100 football fields. The mile-long installation combines all essential operations on one site, similar to what the Japanese do in many facilities. The Spring Hill site houses sheet-metal stamping and body assembly, a foundry for casting engine blocks, a power-train assembly line, a plastics-molding unit, and an interior trim shop. Each operation is surrounded by dozens of loading docks so that material and parts can be delivered just in time close to the assembly lines. A unique feature of the plant is the ergonomically designed skillet conveyor, which moves the auto spaceframes along the assembly line. Employees work on the spaceframes while riding along with the moving line at speeds of 14–18 feet per minute. There are four skillet lines and 17 transfer points. Two of the lines use "scissor" skillets, which can be raised or lowered to the height that is best for the assembly team. The auto spaceframes are placed "door to door" instead of "bumper to bumper" to maximize use of space. Moving the partially assembled vehicles from one line to another involves lifting the skillets off the floor and moving them overhead to the next line to keep aisles clear for delivery of materials, for easy movement of plant personnel, and for safety reasons. Overall, 350 robots are used for welding, painting, and material-handling applications. Artificial vision is used in the paint shop and body-system areas, but there are no automated-guided vehicles.

Though the Saturn plant has had some quality problems, management has moved quickly to minimize the inconvenience of recalls. The Saturn project has shown that a quality car can be designed and built in America at a competitive cost.

## Facilities Strategy

Total business expenditures for new plant and equipment in the United States accounted for 11% of national output, compared with 14% in Germany and 21% in Japan. Investment by U.S. firms in new plant and equipment now trails Japan by $60 billion a year, and the U.S. advantage over Europe in new plant and equipment is decreasing steadily. This low investment in new plant and equipment is one of the primary reasons for the lack of competitiveness of U.S. manufacturers. Most experts attribute this low investment rate to a focus on short-term financial goals. Hugh L. McColl, Jr., National Bank Corporation chairman and CEO, says, "We need to find a way to make it more attractive for companies to get back in the business of doing the things they did historically to build their companies. If we want to be successful as a country, we need to be encouraging investment" (Mandel and Farell, 1992).

A facilities strategy will fall short if it fails to identify innovative opportunities for improving the operating efficiency of a new facility and also to consider that facility's potential effects on competitiveness. For example, it is estimated that between 20 and 50% of total operating expenses are attributed to materials handling. An effective facilities strategy can decrease these costs by 10 to 30% (Tompkins and White, 1984). A manufacturing facility often represents a company's largest and most expensive asset and, therefore, must be planned carefully. Firms often make facilities decisions in response to changing conditions, a reaction that could result in facilities decisions that are inconsistent with the manufacturing tasks and which could lead ultimately to the facilities' demise. Hayes and Wheelwright (1984, p. 109) suggest that "rather than waiting until the growth in one's own market makes it imperative to add additional capacity, or increasing unprofitability of an existing facility requires a major change in technology or organization, firms should think of their facilities decisions as some of their most powerful levers for achieving their long-term objectives." Facilities strategy must be regarded as a *proactive* component of the overall operations strategy. By any measure, facilities strategy has major cost, productivity, and competitive implications for an organization.

The term *facility* is often taken to mean "factory"; however, facilities equally apply to distribution warehouses and retail or service locations. Facilities strategy and decisions must include all real properties of the firm and must integrate operations, distribution, and service delivery activities.

### An Overview of Facilities Strategy

There are four components of facilities strategy: size and structural design, location, layout, and materials handling systems. These are the four primary topics of this chapter. Facilities strategy must be integrated with operations strategy as well as with other elements of the business strategy. Figure 6-1 shows the major inputs to the facilities strategy. For example, investment decisions regarding the facility are directly dependent on both the financial and marketing strategies. Product and packaging decisions have an impact on processing, material, and information needs, which in turn influence layout and material handling decisions. In service organizations the facility must be designed to facilitate customer interaction and to present a positive impression of service activities.

Vertical integration affects the make–buy decisions and thus the size and layout of the facility. Production scheduling and control decisions determine the lot sizing and timing of production, which affects the layout and handling system. We have seen in Chapter 5 how the capacity decision affects the size of a facility. The organization design determines overhead and support staff, and work force size, which impacts the structural design, size, number, and location of the facilities. A facilities strategy must support operations and purchasing in the way materials are received, stored, and moved through the production system, and in the way finished goods are shipped through the distribution systems. An information system is required to keep track of materials as they flow through the system and must be integrated with accounting and operations planning systems.

## Facilities Life Cycle

A facility, much like a product, goes through a life cycle. The facilities life cycle consists of four stages: design and start-up, progressive expansion, maturation and reinvestment, and renewal or shutdown (Hayes and Wheelwright, 1984). These stages roughly correspond to stages 4 through 7 of the product–process life cycle explained in Chapter 2. As Schmenner (1983, p. 129) states, the life cycle's "usefulness comes from recognizing that plants are subject to all kinds of changing forces, many of which are related to age but all

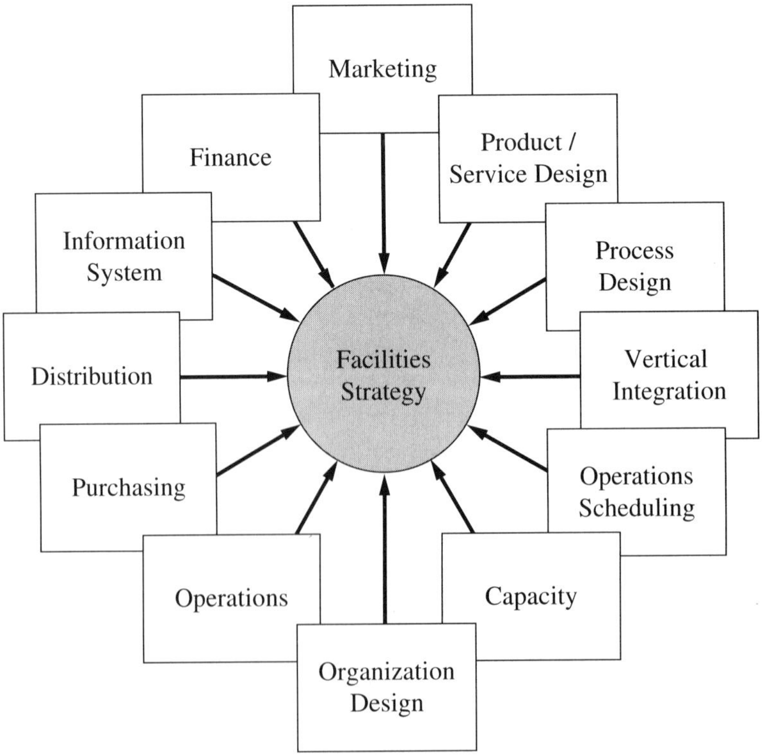


**FIGURE 6-1 Inputs to Facilities Strategy**

of which must be carefully considered and coped with. Anticipating a plant's needs in this way is sound preventive medicine."

Stage one involves planning and designing a new facility. There are several reasons why a new facility may be needed: competitive pressures, shifting markets, expected increase in demand, inability of the present facility to be cost competitive, obsolescence, steadily increasing transportation costs, and inability to service customers properly. We should note that the majority of these factors are related to changes in the market for products or services. This is an important stage since it affects future efforts to improve the facility and operations. Facilities typically represent the largest and most costly assets of a company, which once constructed represent a long-term commitment. Therefore, the facilities strategy must be integrated with operations, marketing, human resources, and financial strategies and must be consistent with the overall business strategy.

After the initial start-up, the utilization of a facility is expected to increase with an increase in market share of the product. This growth stage is the most profitable stage of a facility's life cycle and is marked by investment and incremental expansion of the facility to cope with increasing demand. There are three possible pitfalls at this stage. The first is that management may be too preoccupied with incremental expansion and fail to recognize the need for renewing the facility, improving worker skills, and upgrading operating systems. The second is that the addition of new products/services may be inconsistent with the long-run capabilities of the facility. This is the stage where a facility can become unfocused and lose its competitiveness. To cope with this type of situation, Skinner (1974) proposes the concept of "focused facilities," which will be discussed later in this chapter. The final pitfall is that the facility may be overexpanded to the point where it exceeds its optimal size.

Gradually, expansion of the facility slows down and the facility moves into the third stage, maturation and reinvestment. At this stage, not only is the facility maturing, but so are the work force and production/service delivery processes, especially if management has focused on incremental investment in new products/services and process technologies instead of maintaining existing products/services and processes. An important consideration at this stage is whether some of the products or services can be transferred to other facilities. Ultimately, the facility will be at the stage where management must decide whether to continue to renew, to overhaul, or to shut down the facility. The continued renewal of the facility is largely dependent on whether management has laid the groundwork for ongoing, incremental expansion. Failure to plan for this eventuality would mean that an overhaul is necessary, involving major changes in products/services and markets and investments in new process technologies at the facility. Such changes usually take several years to accomplish and are seldom successful. Schmenner (1983) reports that 46% of the respondents in his survey of plant closings cited inefficient or outdated process technology, layout, or materials handling as the primary reasons. Other reasons for plant closings are significant increases in labor cost, transportation cost, raw material cost, and union- or labor-related problems.

For example, Kmart realized that sales were stagnating in the 1980s and profits were down. Customers perceived the stores' appearance to be dull and antiquated. Kmart's stores were thought to be in the mature and declining stages of their life cycles. Competitors such as Wal-Mart and Sears were using larger spaces to display more merchandise. In response, Kmart formulated a facilities strategy that included modernizing its more than

2000 discount stores and experimenting with a new layout with better signs and lighting and bar-code scanning technology.

## *Facility Size and Structural Design*

As discussed in Chapter 5, the size of a facility is largely dependent on the capacity strategy because the size of capacity expansion, whether incrementally or in large chunks, impacts the facilities decision. Similarly, the decision on the number of locations is interrelated with the size of a facility. If multiple facilities are to be built, should each facility be identically sized? The solutions to these problems are industry and company specific. For example, Hewlett-Packard's strategy is to build identical facilities around the world such that "if you've seen one, you've seen them all." McDonald's, Hertz, and Marriott Hotels all have similar strategies.

A question that is often raised concerns the optimal size of a facility. Although the optimal size is difficult to identify exactly, an understanding of the factors that affect it is useful. External factors that have an impact on size include government regulations, market conditions, and the competitive environment, whereas internal factors include work-force size, process technology, and organization structure. The well-established trend is toward smaller and more focused facilities (Skinner, 1974; Schmenner, 1976). Lieberman (1989) finds that 96% of U.S. manufacturing plants are small in size, each with less than 500 workers, but collectively these plants account for 61% of total manufacturing employment.

Lieberman (1989) suggests that the optimal size of a facility depends on the trade-offs among the three dimensions of *volume:* (1) scope—the number of items, (2) scale—the total annual volume, and (3) vertical integration—the average number of processing steps that is carried out in the facility. Differences in facility size are motivated primarily by vertical integration economies rather than economies of scale or scope. Businesses with heavy or complex products or services typically pursue vertical integration economies and have the largest facilities, both in number and size. However, it is often necessary to subdivide a large facility into smaller focused units.

Hayes and Wheelwright (1984) observe that the optimal size of a facility lies somewhere between the *minimum* and *maximum* size of a facility. At the facility start-up stage, management is concerned with the *minimum* size that allows the facility to be operationally viable and competitive. As demand increases, the facility moves into the growth stage, characterized by incremental expansion to take advantage of economies of scale. Management must be careful not to expand beyond the threshold, or *maximum* size of a facility, where significant diseconomies of scale set in. Chapter 5 shows the best operating level approach to size.

## *Facility Location*

Facility location is the determination of the best possible placement of a facility relative to its customers, suppliers, and other related facilities. The decision to locate a facility should be consistent with the long-term strategic direction of the company and not focused strictly on operating cost and/or marketing issues. The objective is to provide a firm with a competitive advantage obtained by virtue of its location.

Location is strategically more important in industries such as retailing, lodging, and distribution than in others, such as the consulting industry. Ghosh and McLafferty (1984, p. 5) note that "a well-designed location strategy is an integral and important part of corporate strategy for retail firms. Whether selling goods or services, the choice of outlet location is perhaps the most important decision a retailer has to make. . . . Even slight differences in location can have a significant impact on market share and profitability." For example, Wal-Mart's strategy to locate in small communities and avoid direct competition with major discount stores in large metropolitan areas has been very successful. By providing better service and quality products at reasonable prices to its customers, Wal-Mart has a competitive advantage over the small independents and less efficient discounters found in small towns.

## *Levels of the Location Decision*

There are three levels of decisions to be addressed in the plant location problem: (1) selection of the global region or country, (2) selection of the subregion or state, and (3) selection of the community and site. This sequential process is intuitively clear. The "big picture" location factors at the country selection phase are examined first, followed by the more detailed aspects of state and community and site selection. Various location factors are associated with each level; these can be overlapping, with differences in the level of detail. A list of the location factors is provided in Table 6-1. Typically, a company will generate a list of factors that can be further subdivided into: (1) critical factors that must be present for a location even to be considered, and (2) desirable factors that are nice to have but not absolutely essential and can be traded off against one another. The list of factors that are considered critical is both industry and company specific.

### *Selection of Global Region or Country*

The first phase involves deciding whether to locate a facility in the home country or abroad. The global market can be broken up into three key geographic regions: North America, western Europe [European Community (EC) and European Free Trade Association (EFTA) countries], and Pacific Rim. The trend is toward greater global integration; U.S. firms are buying European companies, European companies are investing in the United States, and the Japanese are very active on both sides of the Atlantic. A *Wall Street Journal* survey on the appeal of globalization shows that 20% of CEOs from U.S. companies said they would open a new plant abroad compared to 42% of CEOs in Japan, 36% of CEOs in Europe, and 25% of CEOs in the Pacific Rim countries (Anders, 1989). This indicates that foreign firms appear to place a higher emphasis on a global facility strategy than U.S. companies.

In Harris Bank's series of *Conversations for the 90s: Simple Truths About International Competition,* several experts suggest that in going into a foreign market a corporation should not only look at return on capital but also look at the reasons for the investment—"What are the opportunities?" and "What are the threats if the company does

**TABLE 6-1 Location Factors and Importance at Different Levels of Decision Making**

| Location Factor | Global Region or Country Selection | Sub-Region or State Selection | Community and Site Selection |
|---|---|---|---|
| Stability of government | * | | |
| Political structure | * | | |
| Economic growth | * | | |
| Trade barriers—tariff protection, import duties | * | | |
| Federal government policies and regulations | * | | |
| Federal government incentives | * | | |
| Currency exchange rates | * | | |
| Cultural issues | * | | |
| Access to markets | * | * | * |
| Availability and cost of transportation system | * | * | * |
| Availability and cost of materials | * | * | * |
| Availability and cost of labor | * | * | * |
| Climatic influences | * | * | * |
| Availability and cost of utilities | * | * | * |
| Proximity to company's facilities | * | * | * |
| Environmental regulations | * | * | * |
| Construction cost | | * | * |
| Community attitude | | | * |
| Labor union setup | | | * |
| Labor productivity | | | * |
| Labor turnover | | | * |
| State/local government incentives | | | * |
| Availability and cost of land | | | * |
| Services—health, fire, and police | | | * |
| Educational, recreational, and civic facilities | | | * |
| Residential housing | | | * |
| Banking services | | | * |

not do it?" Companies are now finding it necessary to invest in offshore facilities to get better access to markets because of tariff restrictions and other trade barriers imposed by countries or regional blocs to protect their own industries. Some manufacturers have taken advantage of foreign tariffs that enable them to set up facilities while excluding competition from local foreign markets. Before making such a commitment, firms should consider the stability of the government and political system, general attitude, incentives, and policies of the host country toward foreign investors. Other factors to be considered are competitor strategies, major supplier locations, distribution costs, and major customer locations (see Table 6-1).

Many services, unless embodied in goods, are intangible and not storable. As a result, services require simultaneous processing and consumption at the same place and time.

Thus, foreign direct investment (FDI) is the predominant mode of delivery in foreign markets. Physical proximity to customers is essential. Thus, if McDonald's wants to sell hamburgers in a particular market, they must set up facilities at the places of demand for its service or engage in franchising. This explains why McDonald's restaurants are found around the world, in far-flung cities such as London, Hong Kong, Kuala Lumpur, Tokyo, and Moscow. Leasing, advertising, investment banking/brokerage, accounting, insurance, and retail trading are examples of services that predominantly use FDI. The information, communication, construction, consulting, software, and transportation industries use a combination of exports and FDI. Table 6-2 provides the competitive advantages of various service industries, important country advantages, and an explanation of the organization form used to penetrate foreign markets.

Setting up facilities in foreign countries requires that management be sensitive to local traditions and customs. For example, when Motorola was close to finishing its $400 million Silicon Harbor complex in Hong Kong, a soothsayer was summoned by the Chinese president of Motorola's Asia-Pacific semiconductor division to check the facility's *feng shui,* (Chinese for wind and water) for good luck. The prognosis was good—the facility was built on reclaimed land, so the project had water, which is a symbol for wealth. Another good omen was the mountains that surround the facility—a source of power to the Chinese. The soothsayer did find that the layout of the executive suite was inappropriate. This required a major renovation to give the president a direct view of the bay with the Horse Shadow Mountain in the background. By going to such lengths to honor local traditions, Motorola has shown its determination to succeed in Japan's backyard. The Hong Kong division is currently one of Motorola's most profitable and fastest-growing semiconductor units (Engardio et al., 1991).

**Foreign Investment in the United States.** The United States has been able to attract FDI because of the size of its market. Foreign investment in the United States has been increasing steadily and is predicted to exceed $400 billion per year for the remainder of the decade. The countries with the greatest amount of FDI are the United Kingdom with approximately 30% of the total, Japan with 16%, and the Netherlands with nearly 15%. Although Japan is not the largest foreign investor in the United States, it is worth noting that as much as 50% of corporate Japan's foreign investment ends up in this country. The manufacturing sector accounts for the largest share, with more than 35% of total FDI.

In the early 1980s, Japan was not a major investor in the United States. However, the investment scenario changed dramatically when the U.S. and Japanese governments set up a voluntary restraint agreement to limit the shipment of vehicles into the United States. Japanese firms realized that they have to locate manufacturing facilities in the United States if they wish to continue to increase their share of the U.S. auto market. Honda led the way by building an auto assembly plant in Marysville, Ohio, in 1982. Today, there are eight Japanese transplant facilities assembling automobiles in the United States. Each transplant has a long-term global strategy of locating manufacturing facilities in the markets they serve. For example, Subaru-Isuzu Automotive Inc., which is the smallest and least productive of the transplants, is willing to wait seven years to recover their investment of $550 million (Miller, 1990). According to the Japan External Trade Organization, Japanese corporations have a 10% ownership in more than 1500 U.S. factories. California

**TABLE 6-2 Competitive Advantages and Country Advantages in Selected Service Industries**

| Industry | Competitive Advantages | Country Advantages | Organizational Form |
|---|---|---|---|
| Accounting, auditing | • Access to transnational clients<br>• Experience of standards required<br>• Professional expertise<br>• Branded image of leading accounting firms | • On-the-spot contact with clients<br>• Accounting tends to be culture sensitive<br>• Adaptation to local reporting standards<br>• Oligopolistic interaction | • Mostly partnerships or individual proprietorships<br>• Overseas subsidiaries loosely organized, little centralized control |
| Hotels | • Experience in home countries of supplying up-market services<br>• Experience with training key personnel<br>• Quality control<br>• Referral systems<br>• Economies of geographical specialization, access to inputs | • Location bound when selling a "foreign" service | • Vary, but mainly through minority ventures or contractual relationships |
| Insurance | • Reputation of insurer, image (e.g., Lloyds of London)<br>• Economies of scale and scope; sometimes specialized expertise (e.g., marine insurance)<br>• Access to transnational clients | • Need to be in close touch with insured (e.g., life insurance, shipping, and finance)<br>• Oligopolistic strategies among large insurers<br>• Government prohibits direct imports; regulatory provisions<br>• Economies of concentration (in reinsurance) | • Mixture; strongly influenced by governments, types of insurance, and strategy of insurance companies |
| Investment banking | • Reputation of insurer; professional skills<br>• Substantial capital base<br>• Knowledge of and interaction with international capital markets<br>• Finance innovations | • Need to be close to clients<br>• Need to be close to international capital/finance markets, and also main competitors<br>• Availability of skilled labor | • Mainly via 100 percent subsidiaries |
| Restaurant | • Brand name, service image, quality control<br>• Reputation and experience<br>• Referral systems<br>• Economies of scale and scope<br>• Tie up deals with airlines and hotels | • Location bound | • As with hotels |

*Continued*

**TABLE 6-2** *Continued*

| Industry | Competitive Advantages | Country Advantages | Organizational Form |
|---|---|---|---|
| Software, data processing | • Linked to computer hardware<br>• Highly technology/ information intensive<br>• Economies of scope<br>• Government support | • Location of high skills agglomerative economies often favor home country<br>• Government incentives encourage offshore data entry | • Often part of computer companies |
| Transportation, shipping, airlines | • Highly capital intensive<br>• Government support measures, and/or control over routes of foreign carriers<br>• Economies of scope and coordination<br>• Linkages with producing goods firm (in shipping) | • Essentially location linking<br>• Need for local sales office, terminal maintenance, and support facilities (at airports and docks) | • Mostly 100 percent subsidiaries<br>• Some consortia of transnational corporations |

Adapted from *Foreign Direct Investment and Transnational Corporations in Services,* United Nations Center on Transnational Corporations, United Nations, New York, 1989.

has the most Japanese companies with 287, followed by Ohio with 121, and Illinois with 112 (Kinni, 1992).

**Western Europe.** The Single European Act, ratified July 1, 1987, has established the guidelines for creating a single market "without internal frontiers in which the free movement of goods, persons, services, and capital is ensured" in the 12-nation European Community (EC). In addition, an agreement has been reached between the EC and the European Free Trade Association (EFTA) to create a free trade zone of 19 nations. A unified Europe will have a population of over 355 million and a combined GNP of $5 trillion compared to the U.S. GNP of $4 trillion, potentially making it the world's largest market. A unified Europe presents new opportunities as well as challenges for both European and non-European companies. It has tremendous implications for a firm's location strategy. Increased protectionism is expected to result in more non-European companies setting up manufacturing facilities within the 19-nation customs area.

An established multinational corporation would now need to reconsider the opportunities for greater efficiencies of production and transportation, and more integrated marketing efforts in the EC. Specifically, firms would be encouraged to locate within the area to bring access to the market or to consolidate in one regional facility. In the past, the fragmented markets required local strategies, but a unified Europe calls for a European strategy. For example, Bayer, the German chemical company, is currently producing chemicals in several EC countries but intends to merge production for some of its product lines. Bayer plans to expand its production in Spain for export to other EC countries instead of making products solely for the Spanish market. There is a gradual shift of labor-intensive industries toward southern Europe to take advantage of lower labor costs, with services and high-value-added specialties concentrated in northern Europe. The trend is similar to the migration of industries to the Sunbelt in the United States in the 1950s to 1970s (Magee, 1989).

**Pacific Rim.** Whereas a unified Europe may emerge as the world's largest integrated market, the Pacific Rim is the world's fastest-growing economy. Japan is the largest market in the Pacific Rim region; however, its protective policies have limited the opportunity for U.S. firms to penetrate the Japanese market. Yet, companies such as IBM, Motorola, Schick, Coca-Cola, Toys-"Я"-Us, and Amway have shown that it is possible to succeed in Japan.

Many other Pacific Rim countries have probusiness policies, which include offering investors highly attractive incentives, grants, and loan programs to set up manufacturing facilities in the region. For example, Singapore offers investors tax holidays, investment credits, and reimbursement of a substantial portion of employee training costs. The newly industrialized countries of South Korea, Taiwan, Singapore, and Hong Kong, often referred to as the "four tigers," have been the focus of U.S. investments. However, as labor costs rise in the increasingly prosperous economies of the four tigers, manufacturers have in recent years opted for other Asian offshore manufacturing sites such as Malaysia, Thailand, and Indonesia, where wages are relatively lower.

It has been projected by trade experts that U.S. investment in east Asia will exceed $4.4 billion annually. According to Hubbard, Texas Instruments's (TI) president for Asia, "unless you invest in manufacturing capacity, you cannot gain market share" in this region (Kraar, 1991). TI's strategy is to locate design centers and factories close to prime customers in South Korea, Singapore, and Taiwan. Colgate-Palmolive's investments in manufacturing facilities in Thailand have enabled the company to garner 40% of the shampoo market, formerly dominated by the Japanese. Investments in service industries in this region have also taken off. Today, McDonald's sees sales growth coming from overseas markets, especially the Asia-Pacific region. The number of McDonald's restaurants in the region is impressive: 809 in Japan, 277 in Australia, 58 in Hong Kong, 49 in Taiwan, 37 in Singapore, 23 in Malaysia, 6 each in South Korea and Thailand, 1 each in China and Indonesia. Citibank has expanded banking facilities throughout the region, offering a variety of services such as automated teller machines, credit cards, and home equity loans.

**North America.** North America (United States, Canada, and Mexico) is one of the world's largest markets. To increase bilateral trade and economic activity, the United States and Canada signed a free trade agreement that took effect in 1989. Shortly thereafter, the United States, Canada, and Mexico began negotiations on the North American Free Trade Agreement (NAFTA) to eliminate a broad range of tariffs and trade barriers. This agreement has been approved by the United States Congress in November, 1993. North American unity has been pursued for more than a quarter century.

Mexico initiated the maquiladora industrial plan in 1965 to encourage foreign investments and to provide more jobs for its people. A maquiladora is a manufacturing facility in Mexico that produces goods from predominantly imported materials, which are then reexported. These manufacturing facilities can have 100% foreign ownership. As noted by Groff and McCray (1991), the major advantages of the maquiladora program are

- *Low labor cost.* A recent U.S. Labor Department study indicates that the hourly wage rate including benefits in Mexico is \$1.85 compared with \$14.77 in the United States, \$21.53 in Germany, \$12.64 in Japan, \$3.82 in South Korea, and \$2.64 in Brazil.
- *Preferential tariff treatment.* Raw materials imported into Mexico are not subject to tariff or duty; only the value added in Mexico is liable. Goods returned to the United States are entirely or partially exempt from tariff, provided that certain conditions are met.
- *Easy transportation and communications links.* Maquiladoras are located near the Mexican–U.S. border and are close to U.S. interstate highway systems. Communication with U.S. companies is generally by phone, although satellite links are becoming popular.

The United States owns nearly 70 percent of the maquiladoras, although European and Japanese firms have invested in similar operations. Ford, General Motors, Chrysler, IBM, Hewlett-Packard, Thomson, Nissan, Matsushita, Sony, Volkswagen, and Samsung are examples of companies that operate maquiladoras in Mexico. Growth in the number of maquiladoras has been phenomenal, with more than 1500 plants operating today. Recently, Zenith announced plans to shift its TV-assembly operations from Taiwan to Mexico, possibly marking the beginning of a trend for U.S. manufacturers with offshore plants in Asia to locate operations "closer" to home.

The North American Free Trade Agreement is expected to continue the growth of this regional market. However, there are concerns in the United States whether NAFTA will create more high-paying jobs to offset displaced workers. In addition, many Americans are concerned with the environmental impact of the agreement.

### *Selection of Subregion or State*

Once the global region or country has been determined, the facility location decision considers a subregion or state inside the country. Markets for most industries tend to be focused on a subregion or state rather than on specific localities. For example, the location of a major hub for an airline company determines how well it is able to serve the needs of customers in that region, increase its customer base, and improve profits. Factors in analyzing the attractiveness of a subregion or state are proximity to market, labor availability and cost, materials availability and cost, transportation system availability and cost, and so on (see Table 6-1).

Changing demographics have dramatically altered the market potential for most businesses. Over the last two decades, the United States has seen a net migration to the South which can be attributed to changes in the economy and life-style. Numerous industries have shifted from the "Rustbelt" to the "Sunbelt" to take advantage of tax incentives and cheaper, nonunionized labor. The South has also seen growth in the electronics industry, which does not rely heavily on rail transportation but rather on trucking and air freight. Other contributing factors are improved communications, climatic influences, widespread use of air conditioning, improved cultural amenities, increased educational opportunities, narrowing of regional differences in standards of living, and lower costs of living.

***Selection of Community and Site***

After the desired subregion or state has been determined, the community and site must be selected. The community and site selection are grouped in one level because the factors influencing these decisions interact to a large extent. Note that a bad subregion or state choice cannot be remedied by the site selection decisions since the *best* site will not be achieved; instead only the best site within the designated subregion or state is chosen. The objective of site selection is to determine the best possible site over the useful life of a facility. A number of tangible and nontangible factors shown in Table 6-1 must be evaluated before the final choice is made. The challenge is in merging tangible and intangible factors in the decision process.

The selection of a facility site has tremendous long-term social and economic consequences not only for the organization but for the community as well. For example, Kentucky gave Toyota incentives totaling $140 million for worker training, purchase of the 1600-acre plant site, and site improvements. Toyota's investment in the auto plant amounted to nearly $2 billion. Benefits to the community include payroll and other taxes of $1.5 million annually, and payment to the Scott County school system of $15 million over 20 years (O'Boyle, 1991).

Three significant site selection trends are described below:

- *Movement to the suburbs.* Traffic congestion, higher city taxes, and a rise in crime rates, especially in the inner city areas, combined with improved transportation and communication systems, have resulted in a migration of organizations to the suburbs. The advantages are a lower cost of living for employees, better quality of life, and easier plant expansion.
- *Industrial parks.* Industrial parks are large plots of land which are planned and maintained for use by several industries. These parks are usually located next to a major highway or close to a major airport, are industrially zoned with an established infrastructure and utilities, and provide the community with greater employment.
- *Movement to locate close to user.* The Just-in-Time (see Chapter 10) philosophy, which requires suppliers to make more frequent and reliable deliveries to the customers, has greatly influenced the facility location decision. For example, when Honda located its manufacturing plants in the midwestern United States, other Japanese suppliers quickly set up shop nearby.

## *Evaluation of Alternate Locations*

Solving the location problem is a complex process requiring good business judgment and experience, because it involves examining a large number of factors, evaluating data that are often contradictory and conflicting, and reconciling tangible and intangible factors. The tangible factors include those for which estimated costs can be made, such as labor, taxes, utilities, transportation, insurance, pollution control, and sewerage. Although it is important to assess the costs involved, that should not be the only criterion. A recent survey of 600 executives concerning America's best cities for business identified the following attributes as most demanded for a city: (1) a flexible, high-quality work force, (2) proximity to markets, (3) a strong local probusiness attitude, (4) a good public education system, (5) convenient air service to key cities, (6) low costs—housing, labor, facilities, and taxes, (7) an efficient highway system, and (8) "quality of life" (Huey, 1991). Thus, other noneconomic factors must be considered in the evaluation of location alternatives.

When United Parcel Service (UPS), which specializes in package delivery, wanted to move from its home in Connecticut, the final choices were Atlanta, Baltimore, and Dallas. One of the quantifiable factors that led to basing in Atlanta over Dallas/Fort Worth was the travel time and cost involved. The choice of Atlanta would save UPS over two person-years of travel time annually, based on 18,000 commercial air trips per year out of its headquarters. UPS's planned expansion into the European market would also make Atlanta, which is closer to Europe, a better choice than Dallas. Nelson, CEO for UPS, had this to say about the final selection of Atlanta, "I think it was the trees and the rolling hills. They reminded everybody of Connecticut" (Huey, 1991).

### *Single Facility Location*

This section involves the location of a single facility relative to a number of existing facilities. Examples are the location of: new equipment in a machine shop, a copying machine in an office building, a new storage area within an existing plant, a new warehouse to service production facilities and customers, a new plant relative to suppliers and customers, or a hospital, police station, library, or fire station in a city. The objective is to minimize the travel distance, time, or cost. In this case, travel distance is a surrogate for transportation or material handling costs.

Travel distances can be measured in two different ways: rectilinear and euclidean. Euclidean distance is the straight-line measure between two points. Air travel, pipeline design, and conveyor systems are examples of euclidean distances. Another measure is rectilinear distance, which is also referred to as rectangular, metropolitan, or Manhattan distance. It is applicable to machine location problems, where travel in a factory is limited to aisles arranged in rectangular patterns parallel to building walls. Downtown streets in most cities are orthogonally arranged. Hallways and aisles in most offices are arranged similarly.

Techniques abound for solving the single facilities location problem. A solution method using subjective judgment of the location factors is presented in Decision Model Box 6-1. The weighted factor technique permits the simultaneous evaluation of both qualitative (access to market and community attitude) and quantitative (taxes and land costs) factors in one integrated model. A quantitative solution technique, the center of gravity method, is given in Decision Model Box 6-2. The center of gravity method may be used to minimize transportation costs incurred between the proposed facility and the existing facilities. Although the least transportation cost approach ignores other nontangible factors, nonetheless it provides the basis for judgmental modifications when other considerations are included.

## DECISION MODEL BOX 6-1 Weighted Factor Technique

The Buckeye Supply Company has identified five cities within Franklin County as possible locations for its new facility. Four factors have been identified by management as important to the location decision. Weights are given to each location factor to reflect its relative importance. The weights that are solicited from management must sum to 100%. A score (1 = poor to 10 = best) is given to each location based on how well the site is rated on each factor. What is the best location?

Scores of the five locations are shown below.

| Location Factor | Weight | Columbus | Upper Arlington | Worthington | Bexley | Gahanna |
|---|---|---|---|---|---|---|
| Access to market | 40 | 9 | 10 | 8 | 7 | 6 |
| Community attitude | 30 | 5 | 7 | 10 | 8 | 9 |
| Taxes | 20 | 6 | 9 | 9 | 9 | 10 |
| Land | 10 | 10 | 6 | 8 | 5 | 7 |

The operations manager computed the following weighted score (weight × factor score) for each location.

| Location Factor | Weight | Columbus | Upper Arlington | Worthington | Bexley | Gahanna |
|---|---|---|---|---|---|---|
| Access to market | 40 | 360 | 400 | 320 | 280 | 240 |
| Community attitude | 30 | 150 | 210 | 300 | 240 | 270 |
| Taxes | 20 | 120 | 180 | 180 | 180 | 200 |
| Land | 10 | 100 | 60 | 80 | 50 | 70 |
| Total weighted score | 100 | 730 | 850 | 880 | 750 | 780 |

Worthington has the highest total weighted score and is therefore selected. If the two best sites have identical total weighted scores or the difference in scores is minimal, further investigation might be warranted. For example, additional location factors could be included for further evaluation of these two sites.

## DECISION MODEL BOX 6-2 Center of Gravity Method

The McCreery Company is investigating where to locate a new plant relative to two warehouses (A and B) and two suppliers (C and D). The following information has been obtained.

| Location | Coordinates in miles $(x_i, y_i)$ | Weight of Goods in tons $(W_i)$ |
|---|---|---|
| Warehouse A | (50, 120) | 1000 |
| Warehouse B | (80, 50) | 1500 |
| Supplier C | (110, 90) | 3000 |
| Supplier D | (120, 70) | 2500 |
| Total | | $\sum_i W_i = 8000$ |

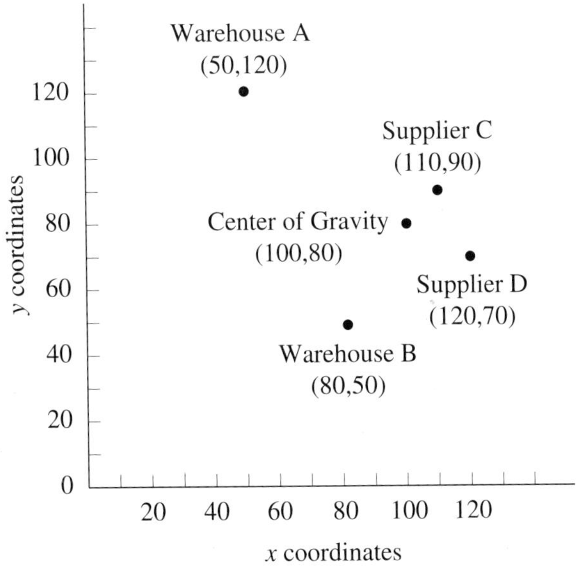


Management decided to use the center of gravity approach to locate the new facility. The center of gravity approach determines the location that minimizes the euclidean squared distance. The coordinates of the center of gravity are computed as:

*Continued*

**DECISION MODEL BOX 6-2** *Continued*

$$X^* = \frac{\sum_i W_i x_i}{\sum_i W_i} = \frac{50(1000) + 80(1500) + 110(3000) + 120(2500)}{(1000 + 1500 + 3000 + 2500)} = \frac{800{,}000}{8000} = \underline{\underline{100}}$$

$$Y^* = \frac{\sum_i W_i y_i}{\sum_i W_i} = \frac{120(1000) + 50(1500) + 90(3000) + 70(2500)}{(1000 + 1500 + 3000 + 2500)} = \frac{640{,}000}{8000} = \underline{\underline{80}}$$

where $X^*$ = $x$-coordinate of the center of gravity
$Y^*$ = $y$-coordinate of the center of gravity
$x_i$ = $x$-coordinate of the location $i$
$y_i$ = $y$-coordinate of the location $i$
$W_i$ = load (e.g., number of trips, volume of goods) traveling between the new facility and location $i$

The "best" location for the new facility is (100, 80). If, however, subjective factors required that the facility be located near a major population center, judgmental adjustment of the site by, possibly, five miles in any direction should be considered.

### *Multifacility Location*

When an organization has several facilities, management must decide on the effective allocation of particular products/services, processes, customers, and markets to specific facilities. Geographical network analysis can be used by firms in the basic materials or heavy commodity industries, where transportation costs dominate the total delivered cost of a product, or by companies customizing products or in service industries, where proximity to markets and customers is a prerequisite.

Schmenner (1982) suggests four types of multiplant manufacturing strategies: product plant, market area plant, process plant, and general purpose plant. In the product plant strategy, each plant focuses on manufacturing a distinct set of products or product lines to serve a well-defined market niche. This strategy allows process technology, equipment, and organization to be consistent with the appropriate competitive priorities, such as cost, quality, product flexibility, and delivery performance, that are associated with the plant's products. When a company has several product lines, each with high demand, it makes sense to use this strategy. By focusing on only a limited set of manufacturing tasks, the plant can benefit from economies of scale or scope. Typically, these plants are located in one or two regions around the country. Examples of companies using the product plant strategy are Colt Industries, Fairchild Industries, and Insilco.

A market area plant strategy calls for a plant to manufacture a majority or all of the company's products to serve a particular market. This strategy is applicable when transportation costs are high relative to the product's cost, demands are spread over a large geographic area, or customers require fast delivery. Companies that manufacture food, glass, can, and building products are likely to use the market area plant strategy. For example, Anheuser Busch has breweries located at several geographic locations to cater to regional market needs.

Process plants can be viewed as a series of feeder plants that manufacture the components to be sent to one or more final assembly plants. This approach allows a plant to take advantage of economies of scale by scheduling high-volume production of the products on specialized equipment. The strategy is applicable to the auto, computer, and machine tools industry, where the products are complex, and to industries such as shoes, apparel, and chemicals, where significant economies of scale can be realized. This strategy is also appropriate for vertically integrated industries such as aluminum and forest products which are linked closely to sources of energy or natural resources.

The general-purpose plant strategy involves responsibility for a variety of products, market areas, process segments, or some combination of these responsibilities. The concern here is with flexibility of the facility and the ability to adapt to frequently changing product needs. Government defense contractors in the aerospace and shipbuilding industries use this strategy.

***Network Approaches***

Trus Joist Corporation (Wheelwright, 1975), a manufacturer of customized roof and floor support systems, was under tremendous competitive pressures from two fronts—small as well as large firms in the construction industry. The smaller firms had numerous local sales and distribution outlets and thus were able to provide faster delivery service to customers. The larger firms took advantage of economies of scale and were very cost competitive. Trus Joist realized that to compete in this market against both the large and the smaller firms it would have to develop cost effective, low-volume production processes and then set up a network of small production facilities all over the United States to improve customer service delivery. The "spider web" facilities strategy permitted Trus Joist to improve its market position. Improved sales in a particular region enabled them to expand the facility to take advantage of economies of scale.

The "hub-and-spoke" network strategy has been particularly popular in the airline industry. Airlines identify major hubs to serve a region. Major airline hubs in New York and Washington serve the northeastern United States; Chicago and Detroit serve the midwestern United States; Atlanta, Miami, and Dallas serve the southern United States; and Seattle, Los Angeles, and San Francisco serve the western United States. Federal Express uses a similar approach in the package delivery industry. Packages are collected nightly by Federal Express offices all over the United States, transported to the hub at Memphis and then rerouted to their final destinations. Although the hub-and-spoke strategy was extremely successful in the United States, it did not work particularly well in Europe, because regulations imposed by different countries made it difficult to centralize operations. This difficulty might ease when EC integration is realized.

## *Facility Layout*

Facility layout involves the optimum arrangement of a facility to obtain a smooth flow of goods, services, people, and information. A well-planned layout can lead to an increase in product and process flexibility, improvements in product/service quality, reductions in manufacturing/service delivery cost, good housekeeping and maintenance, effective use of space, improved safety and employee morale, better communication between workers and supervisors, and a reduction in material handling costs. Thus, layout of a facility can directly impact the performance areas of cost, quality, flexibility, and customer delivery. In addition, facility layout has long-lasting effects because product/service, process technology, operations, marketing, distribution, and human resource plans will be impacted by and will have an impact on the layout.

Although often neglected, safety is a very important consideration in designing the layout of a facility. For example, Du Pont estimates it saves between $150 to $200 million annually as a result of its stringent safety program (Calise, 1991). Du Pont's policy statement, established in 1911, states: "No employee may enter a new or rebuilt mill until a member of top management has personally operated it." The design of a layout must be closely integrated with product or service, process technology, schedule, and handling systems design. It should be evaluated for its impact on personnel requirements in terms of space, separation of workers, and special facility features. For example, the paint shop or sand-blasting facility should be located away from other work areas for environmental and safety reasons.

### *Types of Layout*

There are three basic types of layout for a facility: fixed position, process, and product. Hybrid approaches such as the cellular and modular layouts are becoming increasingly popular and are also discussed. The three basic layouts and the cellular layout are shown in Figure 6-2. The selection of a particular layout is greatly influenced by the type of industry it supports. The physical organization of the layout of a facility is discussed next. The more conceptual process differences of these layout strategies will be discussed in Chapter 7.

#### ***Fixed Position Layout***

In this type of layout, the position of a product or customer is fixed and materials, equipment, workers, and the like are transported to and from the product or customer. Fixed position layouts favor industries where the products are very bulky, massive, or heavy, and movement of the product is problematic. Examples are shipbuilding, large aircraft assembly, oil drilling, and most construction projects. In construction projects, a portion of the fabrication work may be done in the factory before the fabricated pieces are transported to the customer's site for final assembly work.

In some service industries, it is often necessary to make repairs at the site of the problem. For example, stores offer in-house repair of large-screen TV sets, furnaces, or other large appliances. Convenience is another reason for using a fixed position layout.

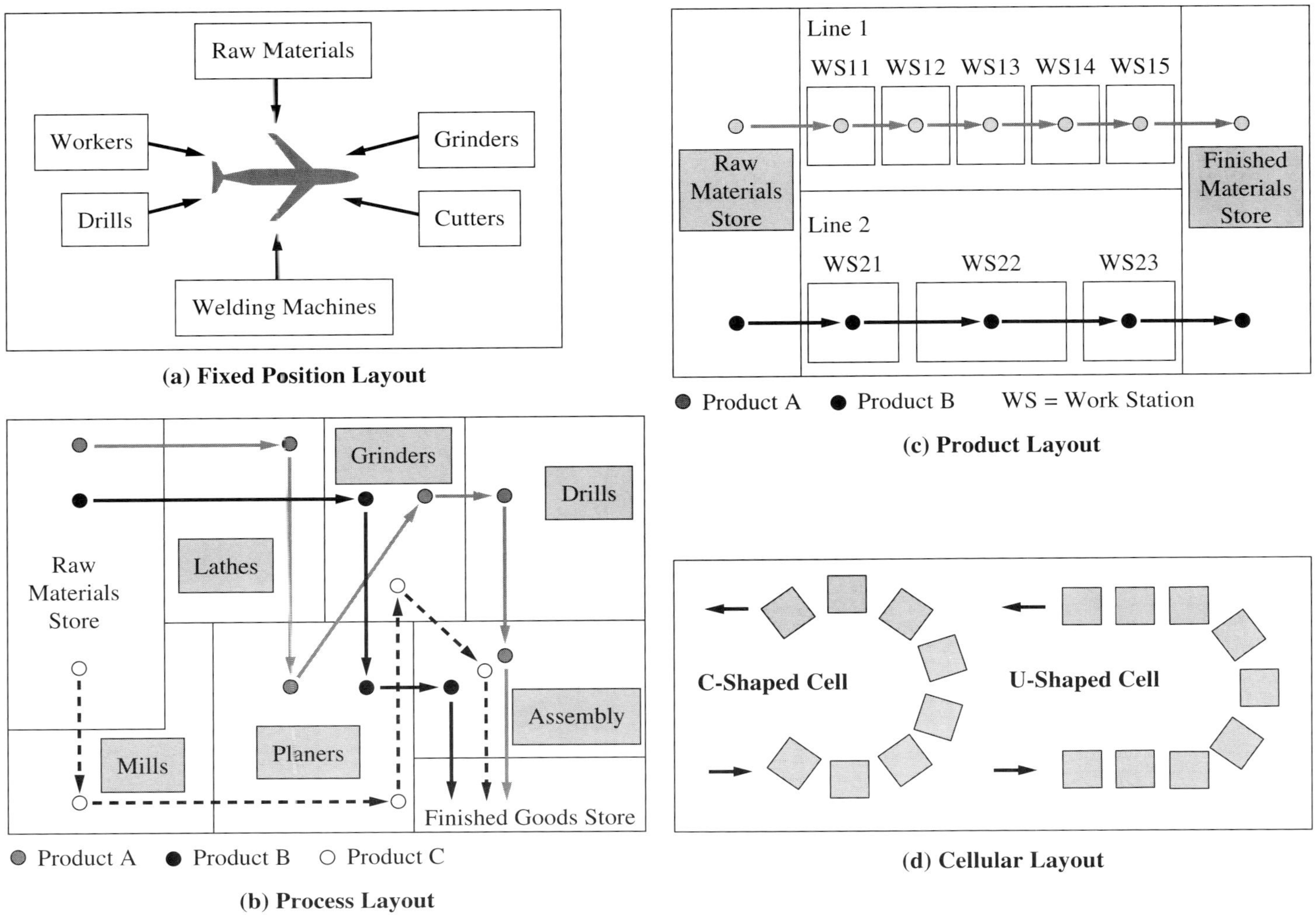


**FIGURE 6-2 Four Types of Layout**

Recently, several auto-lube companies have begun experimenting with customer site routine maintenance service. The service crew drives to the customer's location, provides the necessary service, and leaves for the next assignment. The customer pays a premium for the service of not having to turn in and collect the car at the service facility.

### *Process Layout*

In a process or functional layout, similar processes or functions are grouped together. This layout is often called a "job shop" layout. A process layout is used when the volume of parts to be produced does not warrant the use of a product or cellular layout. The flow of the products or customers through the departments does not follow any fixed pattern. Examples are machine shops, hospitals, universities, automobile repair shops, tailor shops, department stores, and supermarkets. In a machine shop, lathes, milling machines, drills, and so on are grouped together by function. The flow of jobs through the shop is best described as a jumbled flow. In a hospital, X-ray machines are located in one department, laboratories in another, and so on. Patients are moved from one area to another depending on the type of service required. A university is organized by colleges and departments. Students pursue different degrees and attend different classes, moving from one room or building to another. A process layout for Kmart's hypermarket is illustrated in Application Box 6-1.

The biggest advantage of a process layout is the flexibility that helps the facility to cater to the production of nonstandard items or provide customers with a variety of services in the same facility. The objective is to maximize the utilization of the equipment. The disadvantages are greater handling of material/customers, more complex scheduling and control activities, problems in one department not readily visible in another department, higher work-in-process or the build-up of customers in front of departments.

### *Product Layout*

The product layout arranges the processes or work stations in the sequence in which the product is manufactured or the service is rendered. This layout is also referred to as a production line or assembly line. Although a straight line appears to be the most logical for the shape of the layout, the Japanese have suggested using U- or C-shaped lines, which provide for closer communications. In a manufacturing environment, the raw materials enter at one end of the line and exit at the other end as finished products. In a service environment, customers are serviced in an orderly sequence as they move from one station to the next before exiting the facility. This type of layout is suitable for high-volume production with standardized products or services. Work-in-process and handling of materials/customers are minimized. The equipment is highly specialized and capital intensive. Manufacturing examples are automobile assembly and small appliances assembly. Service examples are: processing of mail by the U.S. Postal Service, check processing by a bank, and preparation of hamburgers in a fast-food restaurant.

The output of a production line is dependent on the slowest work station. To maximize the line output, the line must be balanced, that is, activities are assigned to each work

## APPLICATION BOX 6-1 Layout of Kmart's Hypermarket (American Fare)

In 1989, the first American Fare hypermarket was opened in Stone Mountain, outside Atlanta, Georgia. American Fare is a joint venture between Kmart and Bruno's, a leading food retailer in the Southeast. The hypermarket is simply a typical Kmart discount store integrated with a supermarket. American Fare operates in a trading area of over one million consumers living within a 30-minute drive of the store. According to Larry Parkin, Kmart's executive vice president of warehouse and grocery operations, "We will be known for food, children's clothing, toys, leisure adult apparel and footwear, home decorating, home improvement, horticulture, sporting goods, and health and beauty aids. Our perishables, apparel, horticulture, and toys will be particularly impressive and go beyond anything currently being offered in a super store format."

Customers can be assured of speed and accuracy because the store is equipped with 80 scanning checkouts. Reordering for inventory is done electronically through the point of sales system. The food section is organized to create a marketplace atmosphere as if people were shopping on a street in a little town. A large portion of the merchandise is featured on mobile modules, allowing changes to be made to the presentation quickly, and to replenish goods in the stockroom. The store is willing to invest extra money on lighting and fixtures but saves with concrete floors.

The store occupies 244,000 square feet and there is a parking lot that can hold 1800 vehicles. Spaces on the perimeter of American Fare are leased to companies such as: a Handleman operated

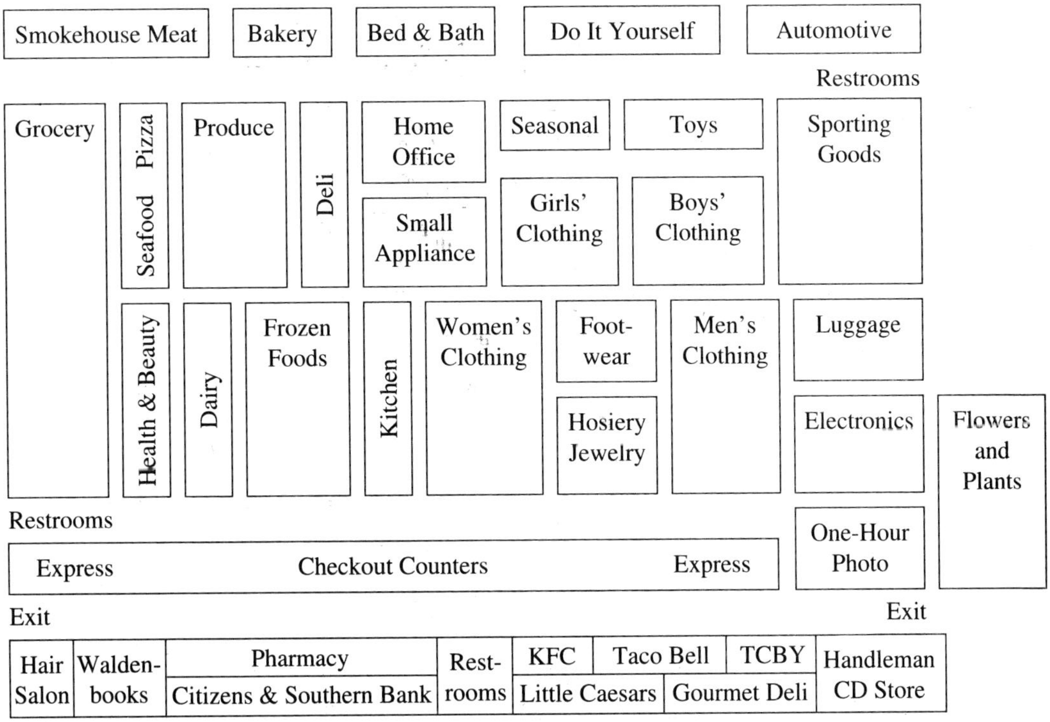


Continued

**APPLICATION BOX 6-1** *Continued*

store that carries CDs, movies, and tapes; a Waldenbooks bookstore; a Citizens and Southern Bank; a card and gift specialty shop; a pharmacy; and a hair salon. There is a food court that includes Taco Bell, TCBY, Kentucky Fried Chicken, and food stands run by Little Caesars, Gourmet Pizza, and Gourmet Deli.

Materials drawn from Jay L. Johnson, "American Fare Opens in Atlanta," *Discount Merchandiser,* February 1989, pp. 28–30, and from Jay L. Johnson, "Kmart's Hypermarket: American Fare," *Discount Merchandiser,* March 1989, pp. 32–40.

station to obtain similar work cycle times at all work stations. An unbalanced line means that there are resources that are not fully utilized, representing waste that should be eliminated. Because of the large number of ways that tasks and operations can be assigned to several work stations, line balancing is a challenging and complicated problem. Although numerous techniques such as linear programming and dynamic programming are available, less complicated heuristic and trial-and-error methods are commonly used. An example of a heuristic procedure for balancing an assembly line is presented in Decision Model Box 6-3.

### *Cellular Layout*

The cellular layout involves grouping a number of machines in a cell to produce a family of parts that require similar processing (see Figure 6-2). This layout is a hybrid layout representing a cross between the product and process layout. Cellular layout often uses group technology (GT), which groups parts according to similarities in processing requirements. Part grouping criteria include size, shape, and routing sequence. The machines are arranged for line flows in a U- or C-shaped layout to minimize the workers' walking distance and to improve communication flows for quicker identification of manufacturing inefficiencies. With this layout, one or more workers can operate several machines in a cell. A major advantage of the U-shaped layout is that it provides flexibility in moving workers within the cell to balance operations. Other advantages include reductions in space requirements, material handling, setups, lead time, and work-in-process inventories.

### *Modular Layout*

When a layout has to be reconfigured frequently to accommodate changes in requirements for space, equipment, and people arising from a redesign of existing products/services, elimination of existing products/services, or introduction of new products/services, it is advantageous to plan for change and develop a flexible layout. A flexible layout is one that can be changed, expanded, or reduced without much difficulty. The modular design concept is one approach to achieving layout flexibility. Modular designs are applicable to offices, industrial plants, and service facilities. Texas Instruments has designed several manufacturing facilities by applying the modular design concept to its production/service

## DECISION MODEL BOX 6-3 Assembly Line Balancing

The Lewis Company plans to produce whistling tea kettles on its assembly line at its Nittany Lion manufacturing facility. Management has identified the following operations required to produce the kettle.

| Operation | Description | Time (minutes) | Immediate Predecessor(s) |
|---|---|---|---|
| A | Fabricate body | 1.13 | — |
| B | Fabricate base | 0.51 | — |
| C | Weld body to base | 2.55 | A, B |
| D | Fabricate spout | 0.21 | — |
| E | Weld spout to body | 2.55 | C, D |
| F | Grind off excess weld | 1.75 | E |
| G | Buff | 2.45 | F |
| H | Construct handle | 4.58 | — |
| I | Construct lid lever | 2.96 | — |
| J | Construct lid | 3.65 | — |
| K | Assemble handle, lid, and lid lever | 1.25 | H, I, J |
| L | Screw handle to body | 1.52 | G, K |
| M | Inspection | 2.65 | L |
| | Total | 27.76 | |

The assembly line must be able to handle an output rate of 60 tea kettles per day. Although the factory works an eight-hour day, the actual productive time is only seven hours after deducting time for lunch and coffee breaks. Holly, a graduate operations management major, balanced the line using a six-step process with a primary rule of "largest number of following operations" and a secondary rule of "longest operating time." What is the performance of the line?

**Step 1.** Diagram the sequential relationships. Nodes represent operations and arcs denote the sequence.

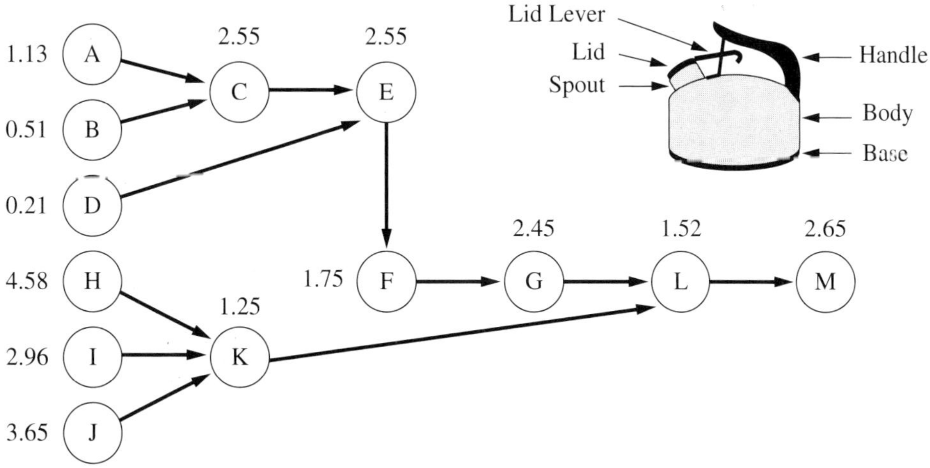


*Continued*

## DECISION MODEL BOX 6-3 *Continued*

**Step 2.** Calculate the cycle time ($C$) based on the desired output rate and the theoretical minimum number of work stations ($N^*$) (round fractional values up).

$$C = \frac{\text{total operation time per day}}{\text{units of output per day}} = \frac{7 \text{ hours (60 minutes per hour)}}{60 \text{ units}} = \underline{\underline{7.00 \text{ minutes/unit}}}$$

$$N^* = \frac{\text{sum of all operation times } (T)}{\text{cycle time } (C)} = \frac{27.76}{7} = 3.97 = \underline{\underline{4}}$$

**Step 3.** The primary decision rule to assign operations to a work station is the "largest number of following operations." Ties are broken with the secondary rule of "longest processing time."

| Ranking of Operation | Primary Rule Largest Number of Following Operations | Secondary Rule (Tie Breaker) Longest Processing Time |
|---|---|---|
| A | 6 | 1.13 |
| B | 6 | 0.51 |
| C | 5 | 2.55 |
| D | 5 | 0.21 |
| E | 4 | |
| H | 3 | 4.58 |
| J | 3 | 3.65 |
| I | 3 | 2.96 |
| F | 3 | 1.75 |
| G | 2 | 2.45 |
| K | 2 | 1.25 |
| L | 1 | |
| M | 0 | |

**Step 4**. Assign each operation to a work station, starting with the first station, based on the specified decision rules so that the sum of all operation times in the station does not exceed the cycle time and precedence relationships are satisfied. Proceed to the second station when no more operations can be added because of time or sequence requirements. Stop when all operations are accounted for.

*Continued*

**DECISION MODEL BOX 6-3** *Continued*

| Work Station | Time Remaining | Feasible Operations | Selection (Time) | Cumulative Time | Idle Time |
|---|---|---|---|---|---|
| 1 | 7.00 | A, B, D, H, J, I | A (1.13) | 1.13 | 5.87 |
| | 5.87 | B, D, H, J, I | B (0.51) | 1.64 | 5.36 |
| | 5.36 | C, D, H, J, I | C (2.55) | 4.19 | 2.81 |
| | 2.81 | D, H, J, I | D (0.21) | 4.40 | 2.60 |
| | 2.60 | E | E (2.55) | 6.95 | 0.05 |
| 2 | 7.00 | H, J, I, F | H (4.58) | 4.58 | 2.42 |
| | 2.42 | F | F (1.75) | 6.33 | 0.67 |
| 3 | 7.00 | J, I, G | J (3.65) | 3.65 | 3.35 |
| | 3.35 | I, G | I (2.96) | 6.61 | 0.39 |
| 4 | 7.00 | G, K | G (2.45) | 2.45 | 4.55 |
| | 4.55 | K | K (1.25) | 3.70 | 3.30 |
| | 3.30 | L | L (1.52) | 5.22 | 1.78 |
| 5 | 7.00 | M | M (2.65) | 2.65 | 4.35 |

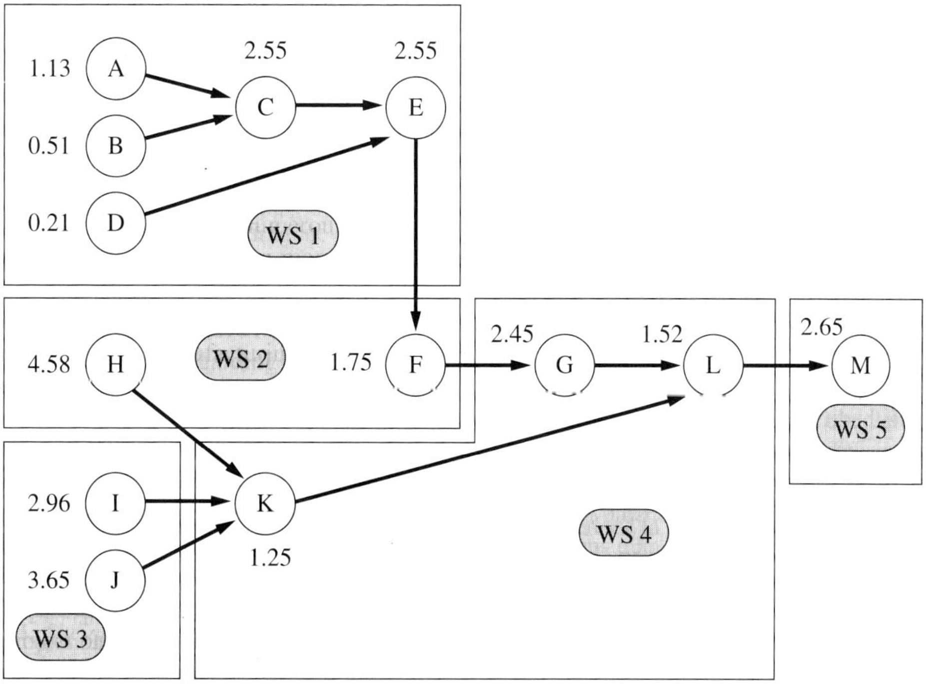


Continued

**DECISION MODEL BOX 6-3** *Continued*

**Step 5.** Compute the performance of the line as:

$$\text{Line efficiency } (E) = \frac{\text{sum of all operation times } (T)}{\text{number of work stations } (N) * \text{cycle time } (C)} = \frac{27.76}{5(7)} = \underline{\underline{0.793}}$$

$$\text{Line imbalance} = 1 - E = 1 - 0.793 = \underline{\underline{0.207}}$$

$$\text{Idle time} = N * C - T = 5(7) - 27.76 = \underline{\underline{7.24}}$$

**Step 6.** The line can be rebalanced by using some other rules, such as select operation with the shortest time first, and select operation with the highest positional weight first. The positional weight is the sum of the operation's time and all following operation times. General Electric's Assembly-Line Configuration (ASYBL$) program uses this decision rule. Determine if the line balancing result is sensitive to changes in operation times. Note that this solution used five stations, while the theoretical minimum number of stations is four. There is not always a solution that uses only the theoretical minimum. In this case $N^* = 3.97 = 4$. Since $N^*$ is so close to a whole number, it is unlikely that there is a solution that uses only four stations. However, if we can reduce the inspection time for operation $M$ to less than 1.78 minutes, the fifth station can be eliminated.

areas, offices, and warehouses. TI's objective is to "achieve a system effect—a facility in which all functions are served by a system of components using the fewest parts to satisfy the most demand. This modular system is composed of small elements that allow us [TI] to meet custom requirements with off-the-shelf components, rather than creating equipment dedicated to a single function" (Tompkins and White, 1984, p. 248).

## *Focused Facilities*

When a company is growing rapidly, a proliferation of products/services can occur over time. The facility could be saddled with an increasing number of products/services to meet diverse market needs. Firms try to expand on site to minimize capital investments and spread overhead over a wider range and volume of products/services. The objective is to take advantage of "economies of scale," a concept that is often poorly understood and misapplied by managers. Schmenner (1976, p. 77) notes that the phrase "economies of scale" is "so vague that it can be used to justify any number of decisions, which all too often turn out to be wrong." The increased product mix results in increasing complexity and conflicting manufacturing tasks within one facility. Skinner (1974, p. 114) notes that:

> *A factory that focuses on a narrow product mix for a particular market niche will outperform the conventional plant, which attempts a broader mission. Because its equipment, supporting systems, and procedures can concentrate on a limited task for one set of customers, its costs and especially its overhead are likely to be lower than those of the conventional plant. But more importantly, such a plant can become a competitive weapon because its entire apparatus is focused to*

*accomplish the particular manufacturing task demanded by the company's overall strategy and marketing objective.*

When a company is faced with multiple product/service lines, process technologies, markets, or volumes, Skinner (1974, p. 121) suggests using the plant-within-a-plant (PWP) concept to achieve focus: "Each PWP has its own facilities in which it can concentrate on its particular manufacturing task, using its own work-force management approaches, production control, organization structure, and so forth. Quality and volume levels are not mixed; worker training and incentives have a clear focus; and engineering of processes, equipment, and materials handling are specialized as needed." The PWP approach, or other techniques to focus a facility, allows management to easily realign operations and system elements as market needs change over time. Application Box 6-2 describes how Cummins Engine has refocused its factory.

## Systematic Layout Planning

Systematic layout planning (SLP) is a qualitative approach to layout planning developed by Muther (1973). An analysis is performed initially to determine the process flow. The analysis of material flows is especially important when large and bulky materials are handled, when handling costs are high compared with cost of operations, or when a large number of moves is required. Next the intensity of the flows between departments is established. The resulting flows are converted into traditional A-E-I-O-U-X closeness relationships and placed into an activity relationship chart. Basically, a relationship chart shows each of the activity's relationship with other activities, the importance of the closeness between these activities, and reasons for the proximity requirements. For example, in a manufacturing plant, the finished goods storage and shipping should be close together because of the flow of materials. The activity relationship chart is then converted into a space relationship diagram, which shows the size of the department and the magnitude of movement between departments. Based on practicality and feasibility considerations, several alternative layouts are developed using space templates representing each department. Often experience, judgment, and intuition are important elements in the generation of good layout alternatives. After careful evaluation, the preferred layout is then recommended. An example illustrating the SLP procedure is provided in Decision Model Box 6-4. For more complex layouts, computerized procedures, discussed in the next section, may be necessary to generate layouts based on the activity relationship chart.

## Computerized Layout Planning

Instead of using manual, analytical, or subjective procedures for solving the layout problem, computers can be used to generate a number of solutions quickly. In addition, a computer has the capability to solve much larger problems involving huge amounts of data. It should, however, be pointed out that the computer is an aid, not a substitute for human involvement in the decision process. In the final analysis, managers must make the

## APPLICATION BOX 6-2 Focusing of Factory at Cummins Engine

The Cummins Engine Company, a manufacturer of diesel engines, had tremendous success and held a 50% market share through the mid-1970s. Until that time, Cummins enjoyed a stable product line which enabled high-volume production on dedicated machining lines with high efficiencies. The environment changed quickly when federal regulations and intense competition from Komatsu and Caterpillar necessitated faster product introductions. This meant shorter product life cycles. The factory had to contend not only with producing replacement parts for existing models but also with manufacturing new engine families and options in the same facility. For example, for just one engine family there are 86 different flywheels, 49 flywheel housings, 17 starter motors, and 12 possible mounts, which explains why there are more than 100,000 parts in the sales catalogue. Compounding the problem of parts proliferation was the mandate from management to the factory to reduce lead time and cost. The conflicting demands placed on the factory by the variety of products required a reexamination of the factory organization. To accomplish the goals set by management, Cummins realized that it had to "focus the factory not only by product but also by volume." Cummins reorganized its facilities, using a four-step procedure (Venkatesan, 1990):

1. Lay out the factory into product-focused cells, routing families or similar products across tightly clustered groups of machines.
2. Once production is running smoothly, reorganize again, dividing the factory conceptually into different classes of production on the basis of volume, design stability, and predictability of demand.
3. Map each product, depending on its production requirements, onto the appropriate class of production machinery. Making parts on the wrong class of equipment—low-volume parts on transfer lines, for example—leads to a loss of flexibility, inefficiencies, and eventually, uncompetitiveness.
4. Continuously manage the transition of parts from one class of production to another as product life cycles evolve.

Benefits from the reorganization include: materials handling reduced by 95%; floor space reduced by 30%; work-in-process decreased by 50%; and lead time reduced by 50%.

Material drawn from Ravi Venkatesan, "Cummins Engine Flexes Its Factory," *Harvard Business Review*, March–April 1990, pp. 120–127.

critical decision on which layout best meets their objectives. The solutions from these computerized layout programs are only approximate, with the work centers or departments arranged in blocks. These outputs must be modified to guarantee a practical and useful design.

The solution procedures for the computerized layout planning use either construction or improvement methods. Construction techniques are normally used when a layout is being designed for the first time; they "construct" a feasible first layout. Improvement procedures require an initial design as input which they iteratively improved. The initial layout could be the existing layout or one generated by a construction procedure. However, none of these procedures can guarantee optimality of the solutions.

## DECISION MODEL BOX 6-4 Systematic Layout Planning

Berardi Custom Decor Corp. designs and manufactures a wide range of interior furnishings for many nationwide fast-food restaurants such as McDonald's and Hardees. Berardi used the systematic layout planning technique to develop the layout for its manufacturing facility, which has nine departments. Initially, a process flow analysis is used to define relationships among the activities. Then, an activity relationship chart for the nine departments is constructed. Next, a space relationship diagram is drawn. Based on this information, a layout is recommended.

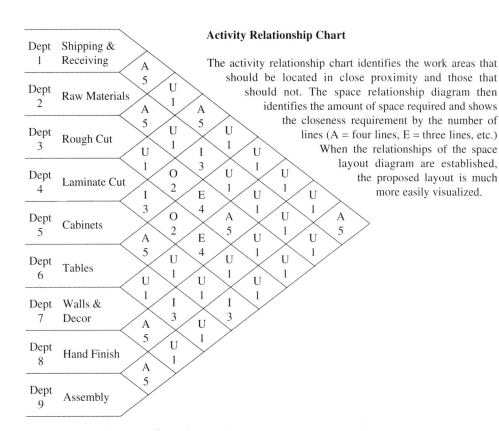

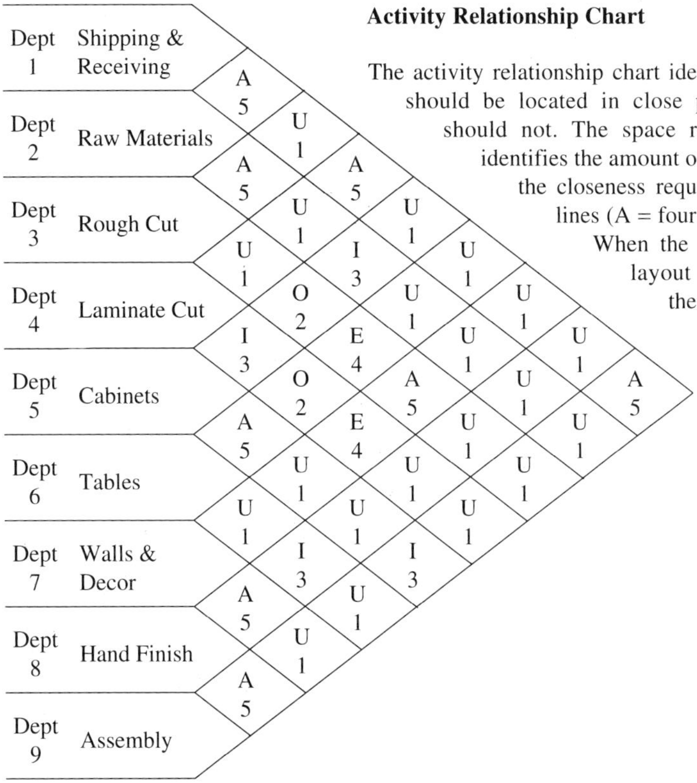


### Activity Relationship Chart

The activity relationship chart identifies the work areas that should be located in close proximity and those that should not. The space relationship diagram then identifies the amount of space required and shows the closeness requirement by the number of lines (A = four lines, E = three lines, etc.) When the relationships of the space layout diagram are established, the proposed layout is much more easily visualized.

| Code | Closeness Requirements | Symbol |
|---|---|---|
| A | Absolutely essential | ≣ |
| E | Extremely important | ≡ |
| I | Important | = |
| O | Ordinary importance | — |
| U | Unimportant | |
| X | Not desirable | ﹏ |

| Value | Reason |
|---|---|
| 5 | Highest flow |
| 4 | Extremely high flow |
| 3 | High flow |
| 2 | Ordinary flow |
| 1 | Low flow |

*Continued*

**DECISION MODEL BOX 6-4** *Continued*

**Space Relationship Diagram**

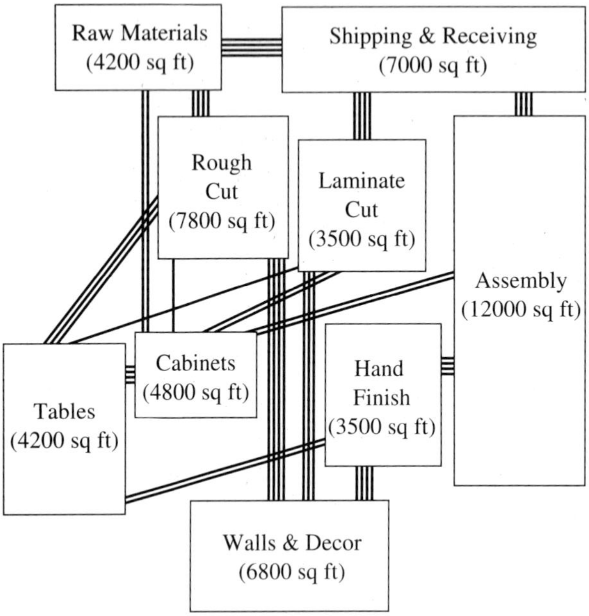


**Proposed Layout**

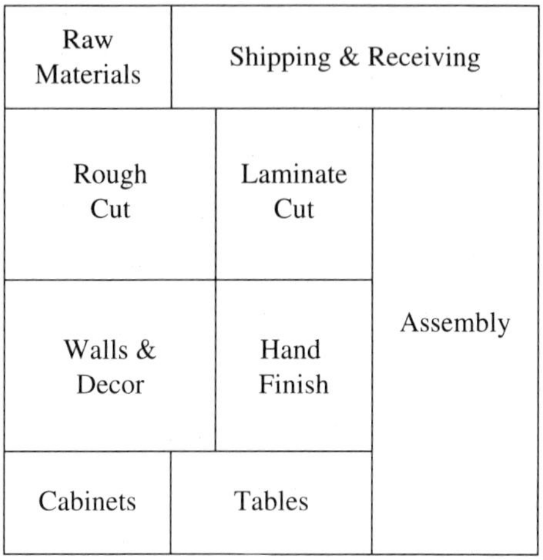


One of the earliest computerized layout planning programs is **CRAFT** (Computerized Relative Allocation of Facilities Technique), which is an improvement technique (Armor and Buffa, 1963). A pairwise interchange of departments is iteratively carried out until no further reduction in the total cost is possible. The cost is measured by the distance moved between departments. **COFAD** (Computerized Facilities Design) is an improvement procedure that jointly develops a layout and material handling system that tries to minimize both movement and handling costs (Tompkins and Reed, 1973). **SPACECRAFT,** which is an extension of **CRAFT,** allows large-scale layout planning problems in multistory buildings to be addressed (Johnson, 1982).

**ALDEP** (Automated Layout Design Program) is a construction program that seeks to maximize the closeness between departments (Seehof and Evans, 1967). The procedure uses a relationship chart to provide the subjective input to develop a layout plan. As shown in Decision Model Box 6-4, an activity relationship chart shows the interactions between departments and the reasons for the proximity of departments. **CORELAP** (Computerized Relationship Layout Planning) is another construction program that develops layouts based on subjective inputs provided by a relationship chart (Lee and Moore, 1967). The objective is to maximize the closeness between desired departments. **PLANET** (Plant Layout Analysis and Evaluation Technique) is a versatile construction program that allows three alternative methods of specifying material flow data and three algorithms for constructing layouts (see Deisenroth and Apple, 1972 for more details).

## Materials Handling Systems

Materials handling is an integral part of a facilities strategy. The term *material* is used broadly to refer to finished goods, work-in-process, raw materials, purchased parts, packaging materials, maintenance and repair supplies, scrap, and rework in a manufacturing plant; to products in a warehouse or distribution center; to checks, money, and customers in a service business; to mail in a post office; and to airline passengers in a transportation system. Tompkins and White (1984, p. 116) define materials handling as using "the right method to provide the right amount of the right material at the right place, at the right time, in the right sequence, in the right position, in the right condition, and at the right cost."

Materials handling involves more than just handling; it includes storage and control of materials. Therefore, materials handling must be integrated with facilities layout as well as with manufacturing/service, distribution, and information systems. For example, sufficient space must be provided for a conveyor system. Similarly, the structure and foundation of a facility must be strong enough to support an electric overhead crane running along gantry rails. Designing a facility without considering the storage and retrieval system seriously limits the amount of useful storage space. Fitting a materials handling system to a layout after construction is completed could present serious problems and involve considerable time and effort to remedy the situation.

It has often been stated that materials handling "adds cost but not value" to a product or service. The axiom is "Never move anything that does not need to be moved." With that in mind, there is a need to simplify handling by eliminating, reducing, or combining unnecessary movements. It is estimated that materials handling represents 10 to 80% of the product/service cost depending on the type of facility. Miller and Vollmann (1985) note that transaction costs represent 10 to 20% of total manufacturing overhead costs. Transaction costs include costs of ordering, execution, confirmation of materials movement from one area to another, costs of personnel in receiving, shipping, expediting, data entry, and processing, and so on. These costs are directly related to the materials handling system. Thus an improved handling system can have a major impact on the company's total operating system and presents significant potential for cost saving and improved productivity.

There are several objectives in choosing a materials handling system:

1. Increasing the speed and precision with which materials (customers) are moved through the facility, that is, removing any bottlenecks in the system.
2. Maximizing the use of space and equipment.
3. Increasing safety and working conditions to allow employees to work more efficiently.
4. Reducing damage.
5. Increasing the amount of control that managers have over the handling process by improving data gathering and processing.

The principles of materials handling are presented in Table 6-3.

**TABLE 6-3 Principles of Materials Handling**

1. Minimize the number of material moves.
2. Maximize the unit load handled, that is, move full as opposed to partial unit load.
3. Maximize safety of materials handling equipment.
4. Simplify the materials handling process.
5. Design materials handling equipment that will maximize space utilization.
6. Integrate storage and handling systems.
7. Integrate materials and information flows.
8. Minimize human effort in materials handling.
9. Design for improved operability, reliability, and maintainability.
10. Design materials handling equipment to be sufficiently flexible to operate under various conditions.

There are many reasons why an organization considers improvement of its present materials handling operations. Problems can arise that are not immediately perceived to be associated with materials handling. They often represent symptoms of inefficient materials handling such as excess idle time, crowded receiving areas, delays in shipping orders to customers, and high error rates. The more common materials handling devices are described in Table 6-4.

## *Financial Analysis of Facilities Investments*

Hayes and Wheelwright (1984) use a framework for evaluating the financial attractiveness of a proposed investment that comprises the following:

1. *Security—How quickly will the investment be recovered?*
   A common measure of security is payback, the number of years required to return the initial investment. For example, in the semiconductor industry it is common for companies to require paybacks on new investments to be less than two years. The volatile environment characterized by shorter product cycles, obsolescence of process technology, and shortage of capital due to rapid industry growth explains why a short payback is deemed necessary.
2. *Recompense—What is the return on investment?*
   After a company has decided that the payback period is acceptable, it is necessary to measure the expected earnings that will be generated from the project. Financial measures of recompense are return on investment (ROI), internal rate of return (IRR), net present value (NPV), and profitability index (PI).
3. *Predictability—What is the level of confidence regarding the anticipated returns from this investment?*
   Sensitivity analysis is carried out to deal with the impact of uncertainty on a proposed investment. For example, what is the impact on payback if the cash inflows are 10% lower than estimated, or what happens to the internal rate of return if the initial investment is 5% higher than predicted?

### TABLE 6-4 Materials Handling Equipment

1. **Automated Guided Vehicle (AGV)**
   Driverless vehicle that transports materials, guided by magnetic, chemical, or optical devices along defined routes on the floor. AGVs are used in assembly-line operations, flexible manufacturing systems, storage/distribution systems, etc.
2. **Automated Identification Systems**
   Automatic identification systems use various technologies to automatically collect product data for entry into a computer. The computer processes the data, which can be used to track, account for, and control movement of materials speedily and accurately. Examples are bar codes, machine vision, magnetic strips, optical character recognition, and radio frequency identification.
3. **Automated Storage/Retrieval System (AS/RS)**
   AS/RS is defined as "a combination of equipment and controls which handles, stores, and retrieves materials with precision, accuracy, and speed under a defined degree of automation" (The Material Handling Institute, 1977). The components of an AS/RS are the storage structure, the crane that stores and retrieves the materials, unit load containers such as pallets and bins, pickup and deposit stations, and computerized control system.
4. **Conveyors**
   Conveyors are best suited to move large volumes of material repetitively between fixed points in a facility and are used to transport bulk as well as discrete materials. Conveyors can be installed on the floor or overhead, depending on operating needs or space limitations. Typically, the flow of materials is in one direction only.
5. **Hoists and Cranes**
   Hoists are manually, electrically, or pneumatically driven devices that are used to lift and lower large and heavy materials. Cranes have hoists mounted on steel structures that run on rails installed on the floor or on gantries. Typically cranes are used to move and position materials in a limited area within the facility.
6. **Elevators**
   A cage or car attached to a hoist through cables to raise or lower people or materials in a building or mine. In high-rise buildings, hotels, and apartments, elevators are absolutely necessary to transport people between floors.
7. **Escalators**
   A moving stairway comprised of steps linked in a continuous belt used in buildings, department stores, subway stations, and the like to move people from one floor to another. Horizontal escalators are used in large airports to transport people quickly from one area to another on the same floor.
8. **Pipelines**
   Pipelines are used to transport fluids such as petroleum and natural gas over long distances using either electric pumps or gravity flows.
9. **Trucks**
   Trucks are termed *variable path equipment* and allow much greater flexibility in moving materials than conveyors in a facility. Trucks can be diesel, electric, gasoline, or manually powered.

An example of financial analysis of facilities investment is provided in Decision Model Box 6-5. It must be pointed out that financial analysis is not the only approach to support an investment. It is increasingly necessary to justify an investment based on strategic considerations where long-term market positioning is more important than short-term performance.

## DECISION MODEL BOX 6-5 Financial Analysis of Investment in a New Plant

The Minor Paper Company (MPC) is analyzing a proposal to build a pulp mill in Virginia. The initial cost of investment is incurred at the start of year 1. The plant is depreciated over an eight-year period using the straight line method. The plant is assumed to have no salvage value at the end of eight years. Estimated annual sales and variable operating costs are shown in the table below. Currently, the marginal income tax rate is 40%. MPC's cost of capital is 10%. Management would like to compute the following: payback period, ROI, NPV, PI, and IRR. There is some concern that the cost of capital could go as high as 12%.

### Proposal to Invest in a New Pulp Plant (in Thousands of Dollars)

| End of Year | Investment | Sales | Costs | Before-Tax Cash Flow[1] | Depreciation[2] | Profits[3] | Tax on Profits[4] | After-Tax Profits[5] | After-Tax Cash Flow[6] |
|---|---|---|---|---|---|---|---|---|---|
| 0 | $1600 | | | | | | | | |
| 1 | | $ 800 | $ 710 | $ 90 | $200 | $(110) | $(44) | $(66) | $134 |
| 2 | | 900 | 450 | 450 | 200 | 250 | 100 | 150 | 350 |
| 3 | | 950 | 500 | 450 | 200 | 250 | 100 | 150 | 350 |
| 4 | | 1000 | 500 | 500 | 200 | 300 | 120 | 180 | 380 |
| 5 | | 1100 | 500 | 600 | 200 | 400 | 160 | 240 | 440 |
| 6 | | 1100 | 500 | 600 | 200 | 400 | 160 | 240 | 440 |
| 7 | | 1100 | 600 | 500 | 200 | 300 | 120 | 180 | 380 |
| 8 | | 1200 | 800 | 400 | 200 | 200 | 80 | 120 | 320 |
| Total | $1600 | 8150 | 4560 | 3590 | 1600 | 1990 | 796 | 1194 | 2794 |

[1]Before-tax cash flow = sales − costs.
[2]Depreciation = (1600/8) = 200 per year.
[3]Profits = before-tax cash flow − depreciation.
[4]Taxes = (tax rate)(profits) = 0.40 (profits). A loss is indicated by a number in parentheses.
[5]After-tax profits = before-tax profits − taxes.
[6]After-tax cash flow = before-tax cash flow − taxes.

The operations officer assisted in calculating the following financial measures.

a. $\text{Payback} = \dfrac{\text{initial investment}}{\text{average after-tax cash flow}} = \dfrac{1600}{(2794/8)} = \underline{\underline{4.6 \text{ years}}}$

b. $\text{ROI} = \dfrac{\text{average annual after tax profits}}{\text{average beginning-of-year investment (book value)}} = \dfrac{(1{,}194/8)}{900} = 0.166 = \underline{\underline{16.6\ \%}}$

[*Note:* Average beginning-of-year investment
$= \dfrac{(1600 + 1400 + 1200 + 1000 + 800 + 600 + 400 + 200)}{8} = 900$]

*Continued*

**DECISION MODEL BOX 6-5** *Continued*

c. $$\text{NPV} = \left[\frac{\text{CF}_1}{(1+i)^1} + \frac{\text{CF}_2}{(1+i)^2} + \ldots + \frac{\text{CF}_n}{(1+i)^n}\right] - \text{initial investment}$$

$$= \left[\frac{134}{1.10^1} + \frac{350}{1.10^2} + \frac{350}{1.10^3} + \frac{380}{1.10^4} + \frac{440}{1.10^5} + \frac{440}{1.10^6} + \frac{380}{1.10^7} + \frac{320}{1.10^8}\right] - 1600$$

$$= 199.4 \Rightarrow \underline{\underline{\$199{,}400}}$$

where $\text{CF}_n$ = cash flow for year $n$
$i$ = cost of capital

d. $$\text{Profitability index (PI)} = \frac{\text{NPV}}{\text{initial investment}} = \frac{199.4}{1600} = \underline{\underline{0.125}}$$

e. IRR = discount rate for which NPV is equal to zero. For the new pulp mill, IRR = 13%.

f. If the cost of capital is 12%, the only changes are to NPV and PI. Payback, ROI, and IRR remain the same.

$$\text{NPV} = \left[\frac{134}{1.12^1} + \frac{350}{1.12^2} + \frac{350}{1.12^3} + \frac{380}{1.12^4} + \frac{440}{1.12^5} + \frac{440}{1.12^6} + \frac{380}{1.12^7} + \frac{320}{1.12^8}\right] - 1600$$

$$= 63.0 \Rightarrow \underline{\underline{\$63{,}000}}$$

$$\text{PI} = \underline{\underline{0.039}}$$

## *Summary*

This chapter has discussed the four components of facilities strategy: size and structural design, location, layout, and materials handling system. It has been emphasized that facilities strategy has major implications for the competitiveness of an operation, and thus for the firm. A facility typically represents a company's largest investment and therefore a company is committed to the facility for a long time once it is built. Facilities strategy must be integrated with operations strategy and other components of the business strategy. Inputs must be obtained from marketing, distribution, purchasing, product/service design, process design, production/staff scheduling and control, and so on. In addition, facilities strategy should be proactive instead of a piecemeal reaction to changing conditions.

In making location decisions, it is necessary to first identify the global region or country. The globalization of markets requires a rethinking of the way companies view their facilities strategies. Western Europe and the Pacific Rim represent tremendous growth markets for businesses, and failing to recognize these opportunities can be potentially disastrous. The formation of a free trade zone comprising Mexico, Canada, and the United States also has tremendous ramifications for a company's facilities strategy and profitability. In entering a foreign market a corporation should not only consider return on capital but also examine the consequences of not entering and the opportunities for entering the market. After a country has been selected a subregion or state is identified. This is followed by the selection of a suitable community and site.

Layout decisions are an important part of facilities strategy. This chapter has identified three basic layouts: fixed position, process, and product. The modular design concept (hybrid layout) provides for maximum flexibility to respond to change. The hybrid cellular layout has been shown to be efficient and to improve communications. Layout decisions must be integrated with materials handling decisions. Since materials handling adds cost but not value to a product or service, it is best not to move anything that does not need to be moved.

## *Discussion Questions*

1. What are the four components of facilities strategy?
2. What are the stages of a facilities life cycle?
3. Describe Kmart's approach to facilities strategy in its overhaul of more than 2000 discount stores. Is this strategy proactive or reactive?
4. What are the major advantages of building maquiladora plants in Mexico?
5. Discuss three trends that must be considered in determining community and site location.
6. What is the objective in single facility location? Also discuss the two types of measures used.
7. List five types of facility layout and provide an example of a situation in which each layout might be used.
8. How did Cummins Engine take advantage of the plant-within-a-plant (PWP) approach to develop a focused facility? Give the four steps that Cummins followed and the benefits realized.
9. Define the three phases of decision making in determining a plant location. In what way(s) can the list of location factors be subdivided into smaller groups?
10. Discuss some of the new opportunities and challenges offered by a unified European community.
11. What are some of the objectives in choosing a materials handling system?
12. Describe the factors that led General Motors to choose Spring Hill, Tennessee, as the location for its Saturn automobile plant.
13. What are the principles underlying the concept of the focused facility?

## *Strategic Decision Situations*

1. The Speedy Distribution Company is considering four midwestern cities as possible locations for its warehouse and distribution facility. Five factors have been identified by management as key variables in the location decision. Weights (which sum to 100) have been assigned by

management to each factor according to its relative importance. A score from 1 to 10 is given to each location based on its rating for each factor. A score of 1 signifies a poor rating, and a score of 10 is the best possible rating. Which location is most appealing to management?

| Location Factor | Weight | Chicago | Cincinnati | Detroit | Green Bay |
|---|---|---|---|---|---|
| Access to market | 30 | 6 | 5 | 4 | 3 |
| Access to suppliers | 30 | 7 | 5 | 6 | 3 |
| Community attitude | 10 | 3 | 7 | 4 | 9 |
| Taxes | 10 | 3 | 6 | 6 | 7 |
| Land | 20 | 2 | 3 | 2 | 8 |

**2.** The Hilo Company currently has four warehouses A, B, C, and D and is considering building a new plant to service these warehouses. The locations of the warehouses and the expected volume of goods transported between the new plant and the four warehouses are shown in the table below. Use the center of gravity approach to determine the location of the new plant.

| Location | Coordinates $(x_i, y_i)$ | Volume of Goods in Tons $(W_i)$ |
|---|---|---|
| Warehouse A | (6, 11) | 200 |
| Warehouse B | (11, 3) | 250 |
| Warehouse C | (12, 7) | 175 |
| Warehouse D | (10, 8) | 225 |

**3.** The SolarCalc Company is setting up an assembly line in its Indiana manufacturing facility for its solar calculators. Management has identified the following operations required to produce the calculators.

| Operation | Description | Time (seconds) | Immediate Predecessor(s) |
|---|---|---|---|
| A | Mount frame on jig | 10 | — |
| B | Insert solar-powered batteries | 15 | A |
| C | Insert power circuit | 20 | B |
| D | Insert chip into frame | 26 | A |
| E | Insert display into frame | 24 | A |
| F | Solder circuit connections | 45 | C, D, E |
| G | Insert keyboard | 20 | F |
| H | Install top body | 16 | G |
| I | Install bottom body | 16 | G |
| J | Test calculator | 30 | H, I |
| K | Packaging | 20 | J |
| | Total | 242 | |

The assembly line must be able to produce 1728 calculators per day. The factory runs on three shifts of 8 hours per day. Balance the line, using a primary decision rule of selecting the operation with the shortest processing time first and a secondary rule of selecting the operation with the largest number of following operations. What is the line efficiency? What steps can management take to try to improve the solution?

**4.** The ElbowGrease Company, makers of fine car wax, are considering investing in a new canning machine that would increase capacity. The following estimates have been made. The initial cost of the machine is $120,000; this investment is incurred at the beginning of year 1. Depreciation of the machine is over a 10-year period using straight line depreciation. It is assumed that the machine will have no salvage value at the end of 10 years. The increases in annual sales and operating costs are given in the table below.

| End of Year | Sales | Operating Costs | End of Year | Sales | Operating Costs |
|---|---|---|---|---|---|
| 1 | 60,000 | 36,000 | 6 | 80,000 | 48,000 |
| 2 | 70,000 | 42,000 | 7 | 80,000 | 48,000 |
| 3 | 80,000 | 48,000 | 8 | 80,000 | 48,000 |
| 4 | 80,000 | 48,000 | 9 | 80,000 | 48,000 |
| 5 | 80,000 | 48,000 | 10 | 60,000 | 36,000 |

The marginal income rate is 35%, and the cost of capital is estimated at 12%. ElbowGrease is looking for a payback period of 6 years. Should the project be authorized? What other financial measures should be computed? What would be the decision if the cost of capital is 15% instead of 12%?

## *References*


Anders, George. "Going Global: Vision vs. Reality," *Wall Street Journal.* September 22, 1989.

Armour, G. C., and Elwood S. Buffa. "A Heuristic Algorithm and Simulation Approach to Relative Location of Facilities," *Management Science.* Vol. 9, No. 2, 1963, pp. 294–309.

Calise, Angela K. "Du Pont Workers "Shocked" by Co.'s Tough Safety Plan," *National Underwriter.* August 12, 1991, pp. 8, 46.

Deisenroth, M. P., and J. M. Apple. "A Computerized Plant Layout Analysis and Evaluation Technique (PLANET)," *AIIE Technical Papers,* Twenty-Third Conference of the American Institute of Industrial Engineers, Anaheim, Calif., 1972.

Drucker, Peter F. "New Strategies for a New Reality," *Wall Street Journal.* October 2, 1991, p. A12.

Engardio, Pete, and Maralyn Edid. "Why a 'Little Detroit' Could Rise in Tennessee," *Business Week.* August 12, 1985, p. 21.

Engardio, Pete, Lois Therrien, Neil Gross, and Larry Armstrong. "How Motorola Took Asia by the Tail," *Business Week.* November 11, 1991, p. 68.

*Foreign Direct Investment and Transnational Corporations in Services.* United Nations Center on Transnational Corporations, United Nations, New York, 1989.

Ghosh, Avijit, and Sara L. McLafferty. *Location Strategies for Retail and Service Firms.* Lexington, Mass.: Lexington Books, 1987.

Groff, James E., and John P. McGray. "Maquiladoras: The Mexican Option Can Reduce Your Manufacturing Cost," *Management Accounting,* January 1991, pp. 43–46.

Hayes, Robert H., and Steven C. Wheelwright. *Restoring Our Competitive Edge.* New York: John Wiley & Sons, 1984.

Huey, John. "The Best Cities for Business," *Fortune.* November 4, 1991, pp. 52–70.

Johnson, Jay L. "American Fare Opens in Atlanta," *Discount Merchandiser.* February 1989, pp. 28–30.

Johnson, Jay L. "Kmart's Hypermarket: American Fare," *Discount Merchandiser.* March 1989, pp. 32–40.

Johnson, Roger V. "SPACECRAFT for Multi-Floor Layout Planning," *Management Science.* April 1982.

Kinni, Theodore B. "Keiretsu in America," *Quality Design.* December 1992, pp. 24–31.

Kraar, Louis. "How Americans Win in Asia," *Fortune.* October 7, 1991, pp. 133–140.

Lee, R. C., and J. M. Moore. "CORELAP—Computerized Relationship Layout Planning," *Journal of Industrial Engineering.* March 1967, pp. 194–200.

Lieberman, Marvin B. "Optimal Plant Size," Research Paper #1058, Graduate School of Business, Stanford University, August 1989.

Mandel, Michael J., and Christopher Farell. "How to Get America Growing Again," *Business Week.* 1992 special/bonus issue, pp. 22–44.

Miller, Edward K. "The Transplants: State of the Industry 1990," *Ward's Auto World.* January 1990, p. 23.

Miller, Jeffrey G., and Thomas E. Vollmann. "The Hidden Factory," *Harvard Business Review.* September–October 1985, pp. 141–150.

Muther, Richard. *Systematic Layout Planning* 2nd ed. Boston, Mass.: Cahner Books, 1973.

O'Boyle, Thomas F. "To Georgetown, Ky., Toyota Plant Seems a Blessing and a Curse," *Wall Street Journal.* November 26, 1991.

Schmenner, Roger W. "Before You Build a Big Factory," *Harvard Business Review.* July–August 1976, pp. 77–81.

Schmenner, Roger W. *Making Business Location Decisions.* Englewood Cliffs, N.J.: Prentice Hall, 1982.

Schmenner, Roger W. "Every Factory Has a Life Cycle," *Harvard Business Review.* March–April 1983, pp. 121–129.

Seehof, J. M., and W. O. Evans. "Automated Layout Design Program," *Journal of Industrial Engineering.* December 1967, pp. 690–695.

Skinner, W. "The Focused Factory," *Harvard Business Review.* May–June 1974, pp. 112–121.

Sorge, Majorie A., and Stephene E. Plumb. "Can Saturn Keep the Revival Meeting Going?" *Ward's Auto World.* Vol. 5, 1990, pp. 43–49.

Taylor III, Alex. "Back to the Future," *Fortune.* August 1, 1988, pp. 67–72.

Tompkins, James A., and John A. White. *Facilities Planning.* New York: John Wiley and Sons, 1984.

Tompkins, James A., and R. Reed, Jr. "Computerized Facilities Planning," *AIIE Technical Papers 1973,* Twenty-Fifth Conference of the American Institute of Industrial Engineers, Chicago, Ill., 1973.

Venkatesan, Ravi. "Cummins Engine Flexes Its Factory," *Harvard Business Review.* March–April 1990, pp. 120–127.

Wheelwright, Steven C. Trus Joist Corporation (Case 9-675-207), Boston: Harvard Business School, 1975.

Whiteside, David, Richard Brandt, Zachary Schiller, and Andrea Gabor. "How GM's Saturn Could Run Rings Around Old-Style Carmakers," *Business Week.* January 28, 1985, pp. 27–28.

# Chapter 7

# Operations System Design

*It is no trick to formulate strategy—the trick is to make it work.*

## Objectives

After completing this chapter you should be able to:

- Identify the stages of the operations system life cycle and show how those stages affect product/service, process technology, and facility decisions.
- List and describe the classical operations system alternatives.
- State the key variables of the product/service–process continuum and show the costs of operating "off the diagonal."
- Describe product/service and process focus and diffusion and note how emerging process technologies and business practices facilitate the diffusion of operations.
- Identify the levels of the operations system design hierarchy and how management decisions are integrated among the levels.

## Outline

## *Introductory Case: How Apple Grew*

In early 1976, two computer engineers pieced together parts of a television screen, a circuit board, a cassette tape recorder, and a typewriter keyboard to create a prototype personal computer. Steve Jobs and Steve Wozniak later presented the model at a computer hobbyist club. Jobs convinced this group of the value and potential market for his product. The first order was for 100 fully assembled and tested personal computers. Each circuit board was hand-assembled and then placed in a case. The first fifty machines were produced in Jobs' home, after which the work areas were moved to the garage. The product was simply named "Apple."

In the early years, Apple struggled to maintain its competitive edge in the new market. The primary focus was on the unique and innovative technology, evident in the second model, which offered an expandable memory from 4 thousand to 48 thousand bytes. As demand for the product increased, Apple and its approximately 25 employees moved to a nearby office building, where the small management team stringently curtailed operating costs and pursued their technological advantage. Apple's focus was on designing, educating, and marketing. Outside manufacturers were used to produce anything that Apple could not internally produce more cheaply. The business was growing rapidly, and neither

Materials drawn from Lee Butcher, *Accidental Millionaire,* 1988; and Regis McKenna, *Who's Afraid of Big Blue?* 1989; and John Markoff, *Beyond the PC: Apple's Promised Land,* 1992.

time nor expense could be spent to master the rudimentary skills necessary to produce reliable components. Large quantities of printed circuit boards were purchased externally and tested by outsiders in order to insure quality in the least costly and most time-efficient way.

In early 1979, operations were relocated to a new facility, 15 times the size of the prior space. The manufacturing department now consisted of one supervisor and 28 employees, who manually built approximately 30 computers per day at various work stations. Another group built and shipped 15 disk drives per week. New employees were being added each week to keep up with rapidly growing demand. However, flexibility of the production process decreased as management emphasized high volume at low cost and greater customer delivery responsiveness through efficient planning and scheduling.

By September 1980, 130,000 Apple IIs had been sold and the payroll topped 1000 employees. The company occupied 15 buildings in Silicon Valley, California; large-scale assembly-line manufacturing was accomplished in Texas. Warehouses existed throughout the United States and the Netherlands, and production plants had opened in Ireland and Singapore. Components were increasingly mass produced at company plants. In order to manage the business more effectively and pinpoint profit and loss areas, divisions were formed to produce disk drives, personal computer systems, and office systems.

Apple maintained its leading edge position through the 1980s with such innovations as the touch screen, laser disk storage, desk-top publishing, and graphics. What began as a project to build several prototypes has expanded through numerous stages of development, including job-shop and line assembly processes, to become a publicly held, divisionalized, multinational company—all in less than 10 years. Apple is expected to continue to grow through the 1990s with innovations in lap-top and miniature computers, including the powerbook portable computer and portable personal organizers like the Newton, and with programming and interface functions that make the products more friendly, versatile, and easy to use.

## *Design of an Operations System*

While capacity and location decisions involve the inputs and interactivity of most staff activities, as well as of top management, the design of the operations system, which includes manufacturing, distribution, and service delivery, more directly involves the operations function. In fact, the design of the operations system is likely the most important planning and control decision made primarily by the operations manager and operations staff. In addition, the system design is strategically important, because it is directly related to productivity and to the four competitive priorities, cost, quality, delivery, and flexibility. Typically, all director staffs will be involved in the higher levels of operations system design decisions, such as capacity and facilities location, but once those decisions are made, other decisions are usually made by the operations manager.

As the introductory quotation suggests, it is easy to formulate strategy for capacity and facilities strategy; the tough part is implementation of the operations system. The difficulty occurs because even the best capacity and location strategies provide only a rough framework; operations system design decisions establish the mechanisms of production or service delivery.

This chapter defines operations system design, describes the classic operations processes, and then introduces the product–process continuum, a matrix for strategic positioning of corporate resources. The conflicting requirements for flexibility and focus are discussed, and several emerging operations and system management methods and business practices are considered. Finally, the process technology selection hierarchy is introduced as a means of integrating long- and mid-range operations system decisions with short-range and scheduling procedures.

## *Operations System Life Cycle*

Like people and facilities (Chapter 6), operations systems, including products, services, and process technologies, have lives. Like the lives of people, these lives may be stable and successful, or turbulent and unsuccessful, depending upon how well they are managed. As Derks (1993) notes, the focus of the operations manager is to satisfy the customer and thereby the company stakeholders. The product/service–process technology life cycle, with seven identifiable stages, is the conceptual foundation for the classification and management of the operations system as it is conceived, grows, matures, then declines and is renewed. The seven stages of the life cycle, first introduced in Chapter 2, with their primary activities, are

| | |
|---|---|
| 1. Birth of the operations system | Identification of the need for the product or service, description of how the product or service works, and the conceptualization of process technology to produce or deliver it |
| 2. Product/service design and process technology selection | Definition of the form and appearance of the product or added value of the service and specification of the process technology |
| 3. Design of the operations system | Creation of the operations system and the system management facilities |
| 4. Start-up of the operations system | Building of the initial product on the production system or delivering the initial service |
| 5. Growth of volume | Modification of the product/service and expanding production and distribution systems to meet customer demand |
| 6. Stable state | Production in consistent volumes with carefully planned resources |
| 7. Decline and renewal of the system | Cessation of production or delivery, shut-down of the facility, and return of the resources to an acceptable state for subsequent reuse |

The classification of these seven stages is important because different decisions are made and different management capabilities are required at each stage. The first stage is a conceptualizing and planning stage, which involves extensive use of analytic and evaluative models to assess the feasibility of the product or service. In the second stage, prototype products, sample services, and scale models of the process technology are prepared to show product or service and process technology viability. Stage 3 involves a major funding commitment to build the facility. Chapter 2, Dimensions of Operations Strategy, describes the decisions of the first two stages and Chapter 6, Facilities Strategy, primarily describes the closely related third stage. This chapter makes some general comments about the third stage, and then concentrates on the final four stages of the life cycle.

Product/service and process technology each change in corresponding ways as the system grows through the last four stages of the life cycle. As the product or service evolves from initial production through growth and stable state to decline of the model and renewal by either redesign or a follow-on line, the process also may evolve from a fixed project to small batch mode, to a line flow, and then to continuous production. The correspondence of the final four stages of the product/service and the process technology life cycles and related industry characteristics is shown in Figure 7-1.

Note that, as the product/service and process technology are evolving, so too are the structure and competitive criteria of the industry. Initially, the industry consists of very small shops or offices that are competing on the basis of flexibility. As the market grows, demand tends to become more specific in product/service definition, and there is a consolidation as successful firms adopt standardized technologies and a fallout (or failure) of other firms. With mature markets, the competition among the few (not more than 10 or 15) major firms in the global marketplace is based on consistent delivery, as well as price (cost). In declining markets, price (cost) becomes the key competitive variable among the survivors. The management of the developing product/service and process technology interrelationship over the life cycle of the system is called *operations system design*—it is a very complex task, requiring both focus on system objectives and flexibility to adjust to changing environmental and technology conditions.

The introductory case describes the phenomenal growth of Apple Computers and the corresponding changes in production methods. Note that Apple Computers has sequentially gone through several life-cycle stages; however, if an organization has system design experience, it may move quite rapidly to the stable state. For example, despite the extensive product and process innovations, Saturn moved quickly through the start-up and growth stages. Yet examples of declining operations are also just as relevant. Though some firms are able to be successful by doing things in the traditional way, such tradition-oriented processes often become uncompetitive. For example, the Baxter Health Care Corporation Surgical Instrument manufacturing facility in Skokie, Illinois, was scheduled to close because the line manufacturing process was not cost competitive. At the last minute, a management team argued for a process redesign from the assembly line to a work cell. The change, initially implemented as a test on one line, resulted in labor reductions of roughly 50% and productivity improvement of about 400%. Though the final decisions have not been made, the redesign of other lines is proceeding and the reorganization will likely save the facility.

The facility life cycle (Chapter 6) corresponds very closely to the final four stages of the product/service and process technology life cycle, and facilities decisions are closely involved with stage 3, start-up of the operations system. Effective management of prod-

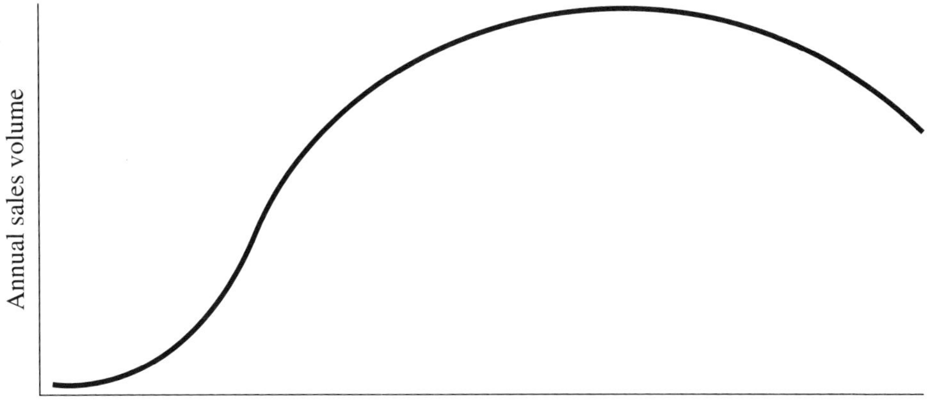


| | Start-up of the operations system | Growth of volume | Stable state | Decline and renewal of system |
|---|---|---|---|---|
| **Product Service** | | | | |
| **Volume** (chart above) | Low volume | Increasing volume | High volume | Declining volume |
| **Variety** | Unique products / services | Increasing standardization | Emergence of a dominant design | High standardization |
| **Process Technology** | | | | |
| **Organization** | Fixed project job shop | Small batch | Line flow assembly process | Line flow assembly process |
| **Innovation** | High | Medium | Medium | Low |
| **Integration** | Low | Medium | Medium | High |
| **Industry** | | | | |
| **Structure** | Small competitors | Consolidation and fallout | Few large companies | "Survivors" |
| **Competitive priority** | Flexibility | Quality and flexibility | Price (cost) and delivery | Price (cost) |

**FIGURE 7-1 Product/Service and Process Technology Life Cycles**

ucts/services and process technologies can prevent the early failure of a facility, enhance facility growth, and prolong the stable state stage, thus avoiding a gradual and insidious slide into mediocrity and decline. According to Schmenner (1983), the key symptoms of sliding into mediocrity are the proliferation of product variations, the ignoring of process technology advances, the repeated use of small expansions, and labor problems. One of the most important ways these difficulties can be controlled is by focusing the facility on one process technology. Thus, products/services and process technologies, and often the facility, are managed over several stages of the operations system life cycle with attention to the requirements of both focus and flexibility.

## *Definition of Operations System Design*

The design of an operations system involves products/services and process technologies, and often extends to entire facilities. Specifically, operations system design is defined as

> *the integration of products and service delivery with the facilities and process technologies over the life cycle of the operations system, which permits production of goods and services at desired quality, volumes, and costs.*

Operations system design is constrained by several considerations. Of course, there are the obvious issues of feasibility and acceptability. The availability of funding might preclude the acquisition of a new facility, and thus limit alternatives to modification of existing facilities. Alternatively, some process technologies might not be acceptable. The use of nuclear reactors for power generation, for example, has been unacceptable in some political jurisdictions. Within those limitations, however, there are further constraints on both the number and type of products or services that can be effectively produced by an operations system and the number and type of processes that can be effectively used by that system.

Though the operations system may not be limited to one technology, there is a constraint on the number or range of different process technologies that can be efficiently used in one facility. For example, Sasser et al. (1982) describe the experiences of the Time Products Division (TPD) of Texas Instruments Company. TPD separated the final assembly of watches and the assembly of the electronic components of those watches into two facilities because the technologies of those two processes were sufficiently different that they could not efficiently use one operations system or be managed by one management group. Additionally, as the TPD final assembly line was balanced, there were several "nonstandard operations" which, because of length or variability of task time, were done "off line." Further, the specifications of several parts could not be changed to facilitate assembly by TPD, even though those parts were produced by another division of Texas Instruments.

This example identifies the necessity to separate different process technologies, the importance of smooth and consistent production flows, and the requirement to integrate product/service design between two or more vertically integrated facilities. Operations system design thus involves the integration of product/service specification and process selection procedures over the life cycle of the operations system, though primarily starting with stage 3 and continuing to stage 7. The management of this process is constrained by the requirement to focus the facility, to control the production flow, and to be flexible in an often rapidly evolving environment.

## Classical Operations System Alternatives

Process technologies are classically defined as fixed position projects, process (or job shop) flows, and product (or line) flows. This distinction of classical process alternatives was described in Chapter 6 and is based on differences in equipment and materials movement, the nature and variety of labor skills required, and the information and process management characteristics. The typical physical layout pattern of these process technology alternatives is shown in Figure 6-2. The three classical process technology alternatives are supplemented by several more specific classifications, including small batch, large batch, continuous flow, intermittent lines, and repetitive flow. Though these elaborations add specificity and applicability, the three classical terms define the conceptual dimensions of process alternatives. The characteristics of classical process technology alternatives are listed in Table 7-1.

The project is exemplified by construction of a bridge, a highway, a large ship, an airplane or a building, a consulting project, property remodeling, an in-house maintenance program, custom-tailored clothing, or an entertainment production. The project is characterized by disposition of materials around a fixed production site and the flow of materials toward the site. High labor training and skill are required, and each hour of labor adds high value to the process. Projects usually have a large work in process and uncertain scheduling, which necessitate estimating, sequencing, and work-pacing evaluation methods.

The process, or job shop, flow is exemplified by printing or machine tools companies and some photographic processing. Service applications include most automobile maintenance and repair, fitting and tailoring of off-the-rack clothing, standardized consulting services, and restaurant food preparation and service. Job shops typically have numerous patterns of material flow, depending upon the requirements of the job, and require high skills and training with broad job content and high labor value added. Setups are frequent and the process is slow. Schedules are changed as jobs are expedited, delayed, or resequenced to make more efficient use of equipment or available materials or to respond to changing customer requirements. The challenge of the job shop operation is to minimize the effects of bottlenecks and to maximize the utilization of critical resources, often human skills, to deliver quality goods and services on schedule.

Finally, the line (product) flow is represented by a variety of different processes. Hydroelectric power generation or petroleum and sugar refinery operations represent a continuous flow of indistinguishable individual products. Alternatively, the assembly of most large durable goods uses a discrete line flow that may be broken at one or several points, like the Texas Instrument TPD line, to accommodate activities that are highly variable or take long periods of time. An intermittent line may be used when a flow is periodically broken, as with the printing of a newspaper. The line is set up for each edition by redefining the size of the paper and the content of the pages. Service examples of a line process include mail sorting operations and cafeteria-style meal selection. The classic product flow operation has a clear and rigid flow of materials with each product following in exactly the same sequence. The labor contribution is relatively low, particularly in highly automated operations, and material requirements and inventories vary predictably. Numerous tools are used to optimize resources in often inflexible and costly processes.

**TABLE 7-1 Classical Process Technology Alternatives**

| Characteristic | Project | Job Shop | Line Flow |
|---|---|---|---|
| *Equipment and Physical Layout Characteristics* | | | |
| Size of facility | varies | small | large |
| Process flow | from circumference | numerous patterns | rigid flow |
| Type of equipment | general purpose | general purpose | highly specialized |
| Capital intensity | varies | low | very high |
| Capacity addition | incremental | small changes | large chunks |
| Bottlenecks | constant shift | shifting | predictable, stationary |
| Speed of process | varies | slow | fast |
| Control of pace | worker | worker and supervisor | process design |
| Set-ups | each job | frequent, inexpensive | infrequent, expensive |
| Technology change rate | slow | average speed | fast |
| *Direct Labor and Work Force Characteristics* | | | |
| Labor value added | high | average | very low |
| Job content scope | large | average | small |
| Skill level | high | average | low |
| Wage rates | high | average | low |
| Worker training | very high | high | low |
| *Material and Information Control Characteristics* | | | |
| Material requirements | varies | unpredictable | very predictable |
| Vertical integration | none | limited | backward and forward |
| Inventories | | | |
| Raw materials | none | small | large |
| Work in process | large | large | very small |
| Finished goods | none | small | very high |
| QC responsibility | direct labor | direct labor | QC specialists |
| Product/service information | very high | high | low |
| Scheduling | uncertain | many changes | inflexible |
| *Process Management Characteristics* | | | |
| Challenges | estimating<br>sequencing<br>pacing | labor utilization<br>debottlenecking<br>learning curves | avoid downtime<br>time expansions<br>cost minimizing |
| Tools | PERT/CPM | load charts | line balancing<br>linear programming |

There are many different classifications of the operations processes, but all classifications assist in characterizing manufacturing, distribution, and service operations. With allowances for more specific process technology alternatives, the continuum from projects to process flow and to product/service flow operations is a useful way to structure process concepts. Thus, the potential flexibility of an operation is extremely important.

## Requirement for Process Flexibility

Chapter 3 introduced three ways in which a production process can be flexible: changeover flexibility, scheduling flexibility, and innovation flexibility (Table 3-4). These sources of flexibility were suggested as an increasingly important basis for the definition of competitive priorities, particularly as industry approaches the twenty-first century. Even today, in many industries, flexibility has become the key criterion, due to the costs and risks of the dynamic and global environment.

### Process Flexibility

Numerous definitions and categorizations of the term "flexibility" have been offered (Gerwin, 1982; Brown, 1984; and Leong et al., 1990). Simply stated, flexibility allows the operations manager to deploy or redeploy resources in response to variations in products/services, availability of resources, or process technology.

Each of the three types of process flexibility corresponds to a type of operation system variation. That is, changeover flexibility redeploys resources to different products or services, scheduling flexibility redeploys available resources in response to shortages or unavailability of other resources, and innovation flexibility redeploys resources to changed products/services or processes. These types of flexibility are further elaborated in Table 7-2.

Changeover flexibility allows greater response to product/service variations, either of product/service family volume, range, item mix, or product/service modification needs. Changeover flexibility can accommodate minor modifications of product specifications, but major modifications of product specifications would likely require resource (scheduling) and process (innovation) modifications as well. The different categories of process flexibility thus are highly interrelated. The requirement for changeover flexibility often occurs as a result of changes in the marketplace and thus is considered to be market driven. For example, manufacturers of durable goods, such as automobiles, diesel engines, appliances, and CRT tubes find that mixing different models of product in the production process sequence reduces inventory and improves productivity.

**TABLE 7-2 Categories of Process Flexibility**

| Type of Flexibility | Responds To | Subcategories of Flexibility |
|---|---|---|
| Changeover flexibility | product/service variations<br>(market driven) | product/service volume<br>product/service range<br>product/service mix<br>product/service modification |
| Scheduling flexibility | availability of resources<br>(resource driven) | materials<br>equipment<br>labor |
| Innovation flexibility | product/service, process technology, or information<br>(technology driven) | process technology<br>process control technology |

Scheduling flexibility is driven by the requirement to adjust for availability of resources, primarily materials, equipment, or labor skills. Examples of scheduling flexibility include the use of buffer stock, alternative routings, substitute components, labor cross-training, overtime, on-line equipment maintenance, and variable shift operations. The purpose of scheduling flexibility is to anticipate and minimize the effect of resource unavailability; thus it is resource driven.

Innovation flexibility is driven by changes in products/services, process technology, or the method of managing processes. For example, a laser may be used instead of cutting, drilling, and milling machines, in which case a programmable tool replaces three less automated machines. At the same time, a computer program may be used to control the laser, thus reducing the setup time and enhancing the flexibility of the equipment. Innovation flexibility is driven by process technology and the management information technology used to control the process. Technology innovation may be either within the firm or external to the firm; if it is external, it is less controllable. In general, each type of flexibility is sufficiently important that few firms can ignore for long their effects and stay in business. Changeover, scheduling, and innovation flexibility are each essential for operations in a dynamic and global environment.

## *Classical Product/Service–Process Technology Continuum*

The classic way to simultaneously represent flexibility of products/services and process technologies was proposed by Hayes and Wheelwright (1979). The stages of the product/service life cycle, as adapted from Hayes and Wheelwright, are linked to the corresponding process technology life cycle stages. The normal growth pattern was labeled as the diagonal. Thus, as a product or service evolved, a corresponding shift in process technology was expected. The product/service–process technology continuum is shown in Figure 7-2, which gives examples of different industry types along the diagonal.

For example, Apple Computers, noted in the introductory case, started in the upper left corner of the continuum with low volume fabrication of computers and with little process flow. As volume grew and as the product and process developed, Apple moved downward and to the right on the continuum. At some times, Apple moved very rapidly, while at other times the movement was not as dynamic. The key management tasks required by the project and batch environments are high flexibility and quality; those of continuous process industries are delivery and low cost. Similarly, the dominant competitive criteria of the industry differ among low-volume processes and high-volume processes. Though the Hayes and Wheelwright "dominant competitive criteria" are more elaborate than the business strategy distinctive competencies defined by Porter, the left side of the matrix generally is market focused, the center of the matrix is concerned with product/service differentiation, and the right side concentrates on cost-leadership-related factors. Because of differences in competitive priorities and management (and ultimately labor) tasks, it is difficult for an organization to rapidly change the product/service or the process technology. This is why the "focus" of an operation is important. Management and labor have difficulty adjusting from one environment to another. Similarly, it is

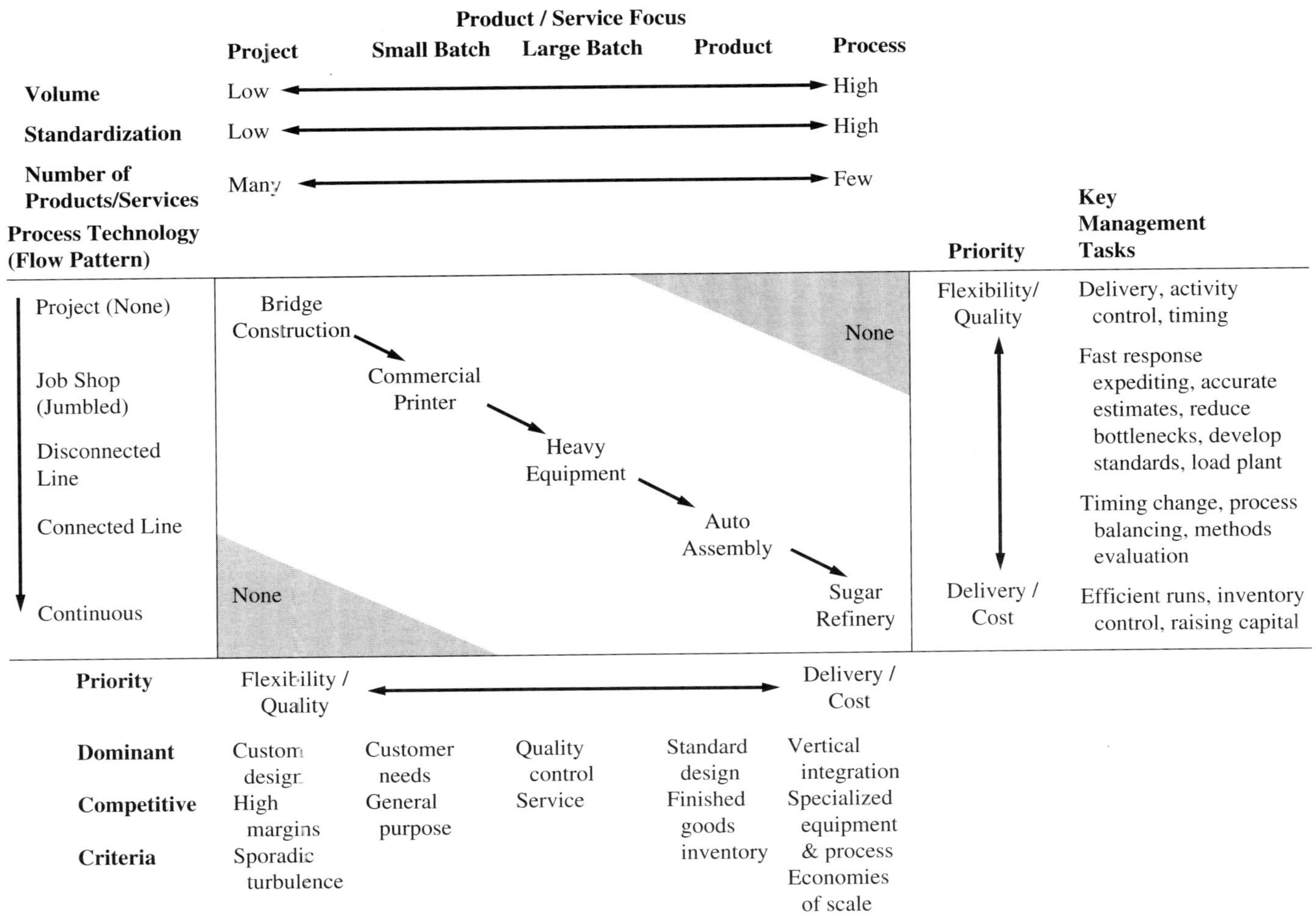


**FIGURE 7-2 The Product/Service–Process Technology Continuum**

Adapted from Hayes and Wheelwright, 1979.

difficult for most managers, particularly those at lower levels and in introductory positions, to move from one industry type to another.

The positioning of the firm on this matrix, and the corresponding fit of the management tasks and competitive criteria are an extremely important part of strategic assessment. Movement to the left and below the diagonal suggests greater product diversity and more standardized production methods, such as might be achieved through economies of scope (Noori and Radford, 1990). Alternatively, movement to the right and above the diagonal suggests greater product standardization, using a jumbled process. Once the current position of the firm or facility is defined, a further strategic step is to direct the firm or facility as it moves to dynamically reposition itself toward a better competitive niche.

### *Off-Diagonal Operations*

The product/service–process technology continuum emphasizes the difficulties of managing the repositioning of the operations system of a company or a facility. Despite management efforts to coordinate a change, it is not easy to change the position of a system on the product/service dimension and simultaneously on the process technology dimension. Movements tend to be linked to either the product/service dimension or the process technology dimension. An operation can rarely handle movement on both dimensions at the same time. Particularly with major projects, it may be easier to build an entirely new facility. General Motors made such a decision with the Saturn project (see Introductory Case, Chapter 6).

The classic product/service–process technology continuum suggests that there are cost penalties for moving an operation away from the diagonal. Below and to the left of the diagonal, there are the costs of unrecoverable investments in high-volume processes that produce products or services for which there is not sufficient total demand. A different interpretation of this situation is that the high-volume production process may be used for several different products, perhaps a product line, which would result in economies of scope. Alternatively, it is possible to use a fixed site or job shop to produce a highly standardized item, but because of the very flexible process, volumes would be lower and there is a cost of the volume lost, called the opportunity cost. These sunk and opportunity costs require, according to traditional operations management thought, that an operation to produce goods or services stay relatively close to the diagonal.

## *Requirement for Focus*

Realistically the repositioning of a firm may require the use of existing facilities. For example, the firm's financial situation may preclude construction of a new facility, yet the growth required by corporate goals may necessitate strategic repositioning despite the difficulties and risk exposure. The most obvious danger of repositioning is that the shift on one dimension will not be accompanied by a corresponding shift on the other dimension, resulting in a lack of focus. Often, through several successive shifts in one dimension, a company may be drawn significantly off the diagonal and incur substantial unforeseen costs. Typically, a company will automate a process in several increments, but retain the product or service variety that the previous nonautomated process permitted. Such piecemeal repositioning can have serious effects, though they may be insidious and difficult to identify.

The second danger of lack of focus is even more consequential. If a firm repositions itself on one dimension and simultaneously expands its range of activity on the other dimension, the result is an increased range over which the firm attempts to focus its operation. For example, the retail merchandise business has changed dramatically in the past 10 to 15 years with the advent of specialty stores and "factory warehouse" retail operations. Specialty stores are positioned in low-volume, customized, and high-cost situations within very narrowly defined areas of business. Examples would include specialty bicycle shops and jeans stores. However, simultaneously, the factory warehouse retail outlet has entered the high-volume, standardized, and low-cost range of operation. Examples include Office Max and Fedders or Silo appliance outlets. Several of the major retail distribution firms (including Sears, Roebuck, J. C. Penney, and Montgomery Ward) have tried to operate simultaneously with the product variety and image of the specialty stores, yet with the low costs of a warehouse operation. The resulting loss of focus has cost those major merchandisers. Such situations emphasize the need for both process and products/services focus.

## Process Focus

The necessity of focus was introduced by Wickham Skinner (1974), who stated that each facility should focus on a few tasks. The underlying concept is to identify a particular competitive priority (cost, quality, delivery, or flexibility) and a measure of that criterion (such as percent rejects or percent on-time delivery), and then to create an environment wherein simplicity and repetitive tasks are focused toward the criterion and those measures. Focus increases productivity and empowers the operation to be the best in its selected niche. Finally, to ensure focus, the characteristics of the products/services produced, in terms of quality and volumes, must be similar.

The rationale of process focus is that the diffusion of any resource beyond a narrow limit would require the facility to operate over an inefficient range of employee skills, equipment design, or even competitive priorities, resulting in loss of control. Another interpretation of focus is that the focused facility makes many different products/services through the use of a variety of process technologies. For example, the manufacture of a Rolls Royce automobile involves many different production processes to build a small number of highly customized products. Similarly, most job shops are process focused.

In practice, however, every facility faces some variability. However, there is a clear trade-off between high variability of the process and ease of control. Finch and Cox (1988) found that greater variability of process resulted in more frequently updated master production schedules, greater need for material requirements planning, greater need for a formal and detailed capacity planning function, and more frequent priority control reporting. More diffused processes are feasible, but require greater individual skill and effort to control. Simply, diffuse processes violate the rule of simplicity of operations; yet, with greater control efforts, they are possible, and in some situations, necessary.

## *Product/Service Focus*

The product/service, including product/service lines, can be focused in terms of the volumes, range, mix, and the rate of modifications. For example, a firm may choose to manufacture and market one type of automobile, a four-door sedan. Alternatively, the firm may select a product line of three or four different types of vehicles, including two-door models, hatchbacks, and station wagons, as well as the four-door sedan. The product mix of, for example, 30% four-door models, 20% hatchbacks, 10% station wagons, and 40% two-door models could be regularly adjusted, and the rate of product modification could also be varied. Some manufacturers modify the product/service line every several months, while others make changes every year or two. Of course, these ranges, volumes, mixes, and modifications affect the focus of the manufacturing or service delivery effort. Most line operations are product/service focused.

Just as diffusion of the process focus causes increased confusion and overload of people and equipment, so does product/service diffusion. Repeated but minor adjustments of product/service volumes or mix or excessive range can diffuse the product/service focus. Broad product/service range may be a matter of corporate pride or reputation, and likely will involve some strong stakeholder positions. However, excessive product/service range results in diffusion and higher operations and support costs. A criterion such as contribution to profit of each product may be an appropriate basis to evaluate product ranges and thereby assess product/service focus.

The rationale of greater product/service range is that, like economies of scope, it permits the spreading of fixed costs across a larger number and thus greater total volume of products or services. Though it may be difficult to measure exactly the proportion of overhead that should be costed against particular models, this sort of analysis may have a further shortfall because it fails to consider the marginal contribution to profit and the different transaction costs of each item within a product line. Considering the marginal contribution to profit, those products or services that provide the highest total revenue are generally high-volume items. Though some high-volume items may be temporarily sold as loss leaders, over time most make a relatively high marginal contribution to profits and require less overhead per unit. Thus, the contribution to profit of the product/service with the highest total revenue is likely larger than for products or services with lower total revenues.

Alternatively, low-volume products, unless sold with a hefty price mark-up, generally contribute only marginally to total revenue because per unit overhead costs are higher. Such products may be a drain on profits. This analysis suggests that there is a range beyond which the loss of focus results in decreasing marginal contribution to total revenue and increasing support costs. Though diffusion of product/service range may be undertaken for marketing or line image reasons, the costs of such diffusion should be recognized. Figure 7-3 presents a Pareto (sequenced by item from largest to smallest total

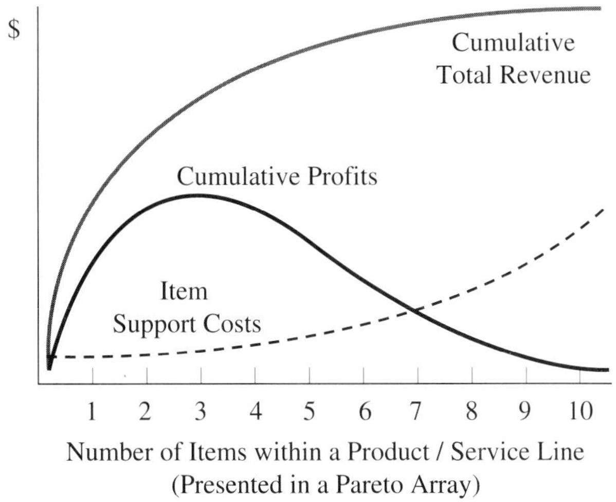


**FIGURE 7-3 Item Contribution to Product/Service Line Profitability**

revenue) analysis of this situation and shows the cumulative total revenue, the unit support costs, and the cumulative profits.

This type of analysis suggests that, as a product or service line grows, despite the continued increase of cumulative total revenue and because of increasing item support costs, cumulative profits may peak and decrease. Of course, this analysis is highly dependent upon an accurate statement of per unit overhead, yet it does suggest that there are limits of product/service diffusion.

## *Product/Service Versus Process Focus*

Over the life cycle of a production/service system, the emphasis toward a product/service or process focus will likely shift. As an operation starts up and moves toward the growth of volume stage, the emphasis is on the process. Modifications and volume, range, or mix changes are likely. However, as the product or service enters the stable state stage, increasing concern is directed toward efficient process technology or product focus. The sales volumes are higher and the process becomes more stable, both in volume and product mix and in quality and dependability. But, as the product further continues in the stable state and starts toward decline and renewal, a renewed emphasis on process becomes apparent. Schmenner's (1983) description of the "failing" stage of a facility life cycle has already been noted (Chapter 6). Often, however, it is easier to stop production abruptly than to try to reverse the movement on the product/service–process technology continuum and adjust the product/service and process technology back toward lower-volume positions.

In the case of several automobile manufacturers, the decision was made to close the facility, rather than to try to redirect the production system. The turnaround of a "declining system" requires the reintroduction of job-shop-like processes, with the labor skill, methods, equipment, and management style changes. Some companies are able, in special circumstances, to make the transition back up the product/service–process technology continuum. Studebaker, for example, closed its South Bend, Indiana, assembly line in the 1960s, but continues to build automobiles in small volumes using a job shop in Canada. And the Baxter Health Care Skokie (Illinois) plant reorganized from a line flow to work cells, adjusting back up the product/service–process technology continuum. This relationship of the process technology and product/service volume and mix over the life cycle is shown in Figure 7-1.

One important aspect of Figure 7-1 is that it identifies the focus of an operations system for a particular stage of its life cycle. That is, at the start-up and early growth stages, and in the decline and renewal stage, the system should focus on the product or service and then fit the necessary process technology. Alternatively, in the stable state stage, the system should focus on the process technology and fit the appropriate product or service characteristics. The exact mix of product/service and process technology focus will vary by industry, by stage of the operations system life cycle, and by the commitment of management. The product/service–process technology continuum dimensionalizes the options and alternatives for management to use in planning the development of the operations system life cycle.

## *Movement off the Diagonal*

The focused facility concept suggests that the specific product/service or process technology focus must be defined for each facility; then, using the product/service–process technology continuum, the corresponding point on, or off, the diagonal must be identified. Repositioning the operations system should be carefully planned, according to conventional operations management thought, to avoid movement off the diagonal or too much diffusion. However, the realities of operating in a dynamic environment may not permit the luxuries of this approach. Particularly where competition is intense and global, a firm may be required to position itself off the diagonal or to accept a certain amount of diffusion, particularly in the short run. In fact, off-diagonal and diffuse operations systems may be the basis for competitive advantage.

Movement downward along the diagonal of the product/service–process technology continuum enhances the economies of scale; however, positioning to the left and below the diagonal enhances economies of scope. This is one example of how operations managers may define an operations system off the diagonal as a way of seeking competitive advantage. Several techniques to position an operations system off the diagonal are described in the following paragraphs.

**Modular Structures and Variable Production Lines.** Both modular product or service structures and variable production lines will permit increased variation and customization of products or services from a continuous or connected line process. Modular structures use a few high-volume component modules produced with line processes. Final assembly, packaging, or customer selection integrates different groupings of those modules, giving the appearance of a small-batch, or even customized, product. Various electronic products, from radios to sound systems to televisions and computers, have used product modules for years. Additionally, modular production is used for many furniture items, including bookshelves, chairs, suite units, and modular office furniture. In services, modular options are commonly offered with credit cards, life and health insurance policies, and consulting packages. Modular components permit the appearance of a greater product range; however, the components are produced with standardized high-volume production processes.

Variable production lines use a single line, with minor process variations, to build different products. For example, Toyota uses the same "mixed model" assembly line to sequentially build a sedan, then a hardtop, then a sedan, then a station wagon (Wantuch, 1983). However, Ford's Wixom plant is a true mixed model plant, assembling Lincolns, Continentals, Town Cars, and Mark VIII automobiles on the same assembly line. Additionally, newspaper presses are used to publish many different editions and sizes of newspaper. Most major publications now print many highly customized products, defined by geographic area (often local government or zip code) and by the timing of the publication, on the same continuous production line. Some publications change and update headlines and articles over the three- or four-hour life of an edition. Other publications, including *The New York Times* and *USA Today,* disseminate copy electronically for local printing and distribution. Newspaper inserts, printed and assembled on a variable production line, may be defined for specific subscriber groups. Thus, they resemble product modules, their counterparts in manufacturing.

One of the more elaborate applications of variable production lines is the Allen-Bradley computer integrated contactor (industrial switches) facility in Milwaukee, Wisconsin. Though each job follows the same production line flow, different machine settings, controlled by a computer, are used at each step of the process to build different models. The same production line may be used for lot sizes as small as one and for a wide variety of products (see Chapter 13 for more details). Flexibility of the production facility and modular structure design directly contribute to economies of scope and are called *left lateral movement.* These methods are shown in Figure 7-4.

**Flexible Processes.** Numerous companies have found that they are able to improve productivity by designing more variation in the process technology. This may appear to be a "deautomation" of the system, in the sense that the process is being redesigned from a continuous process or line flow to a batch or even a project method. However, in converting to manufacturing cells or service teams, companies often include more extensive computer or human control systems and a higher level of process automation. An example is the Baxter Health Care Skokie Surgical Instruments plant, described previously. There an assembly line has been replaced with a manufacturing cell. The automation of the production controls, as well as of the production process, permits what would normally be a line process to function more like a batch or project operation. This is called *upward movement.*

**Enhanced Process Flows.** The third type of movement off the diagonal enables a project or job shop flow to acquire equipment or services and operate more like a line or continuous flow, but without the heavy front-end investment in facilities or equipment. For example, many agribusinesses find it less expensive to subcontract the services of

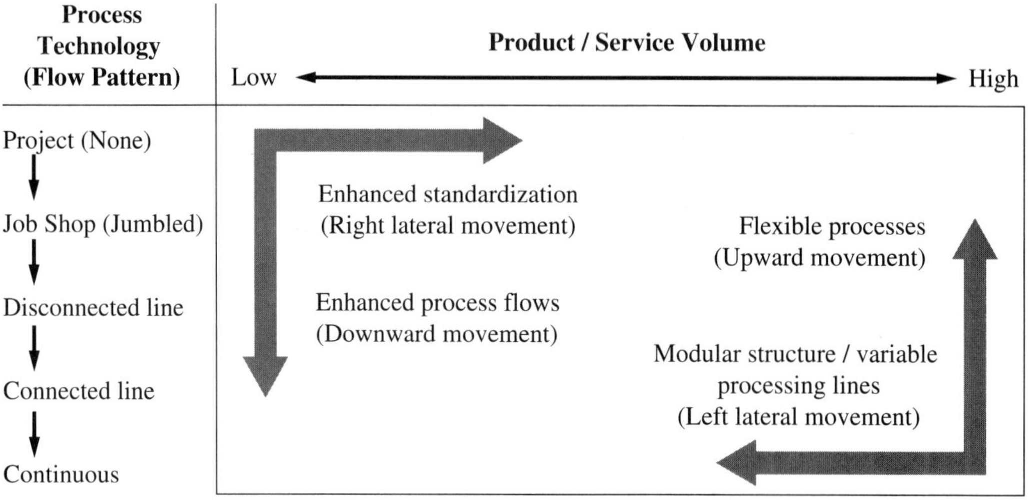


**FIGURE 7-4 Product/Service and Process Technology Diffusion**

harvesting companies than to own and maintain their own equipment. These subcontractors provide state-of-the-art equipment and trained operators to enable the farmer to rapidly harvest at the best possible moment, considering weather, market, price, and the state of the crop. Without such harvesting teams, farmers would have to use their own equipment, which likely would be older and less efficient. More importantly, however, the harvesting subcontractor, moving from farm to farm, uses a more continuous type of process than a single farmer could.

Similarly, many small businesses purchase telephone services (such as call waiting and call forwarding) and lease computers or information processing services, such as inventory management, payroll, or tax preparation. These methods permit a small proprietor to use expensive capital equipment and costly or diverse labor skills without the risk of capital commitment. For example, a university printer, anticipating higher demand for multi-color individualized instructor and student course packets, might contract to lease a high-speed four-color copy machine for a trial period of one year. The purchase of such equipment would be both costly and risky; however, leasing the equipment would permit a small entrepreneur to test the market for the product without extensive risk. This *downward movement* off the diagonal permits acquiring equipment or services to facilitate a smoother, faster flow of single and low-volume jobs, but with less risk.

**Enhanced Product Standardization.** The corresponding right lateral movement permits fixed or jumbled job shops to competitively offer a few high-volume, highly standardized products or services. Group technologies, such as the use of common parts, mounting bosses, or handling lugs, permit a firm to produce higher volumes at competitive costs in a manufacturing cell. In service operations, these facilitators of standardization are exemplified by a variety of franchise or cooperative agreements, such as motels, fast-food restaurants, chain stores, and real estate agencies. All are essentially fixed-site businesses; however, the franchise defines standardized products, permits bulk purchasing, centralizes many services, and establishes customer expectancies. This encourages, at a cost, a wider population of customers.

Similarly, various techniques permit entrepreneurs or job shop operators to provide a standardized product or service in direct competition with larger, more product-focused operations (Noori and Radford, 1990). For example, spreadsheet or data base management software programs, such as accounting packages, have enabled many individual tax preparers and consultants to provide quite standardized and higher-volume services. Desk-top publishing software, for example, permits an individual entrepreneur with a laser printer to compete in a higher-volume production market that previously was restricted to larger job shops. These *right lateral movements* permit a fixed-site small business to increase its volume.

In each case, these technologies and methods permit the operations manager to move the production system away from the traditional diagonal with less cost or risk. Thus, opportunities for a specified market niche or focus (either in cost, based on above-the-diagonal higher volumes, or in product differentiation, based on below-the-diagonal lower volumes) are increasingly available. Additionally, a wide range of emerging process technologies are facilitated.

## *Emerging Process Technologies*

Recent advances in information processing, and materials and data handling technologies permit redefinition, and allow greater diffusion, of traditional production systems. Four generalized manufacturing approaches have emerged, which deserve further emphasis. They are called *variable production lines, manufacturing cells, flexible manufacturing systems,* and *computer integrated manufacturing.* These process technologies are generally sequential and apply primarily to manufacturing operations, though service applications are rapidly developing. For example, the operations of consulting teams correspond to manufacturing cells or flexible manufacturing systems.

### *Variable Production Lines*

Variable production lines are dedicated high-volume lines that are reconfigured to permit some process variation and thus several different products or services. They usually incorporate a simple information system that gives the necessary process variability information to employees in sufficient time for them to make appropriate adjustments. For example, the Cummins diesel engine plant custom builds several different types of diesel engine, ranging from small automobile and light truck engines to large emergency power generators, on one assembly line. The line uses a product carrier frame and an information panel that is visible to downstream assembly employees. The panel, with color blocks at particular positions, indicates which components should be prepared for assembly to the particular unit. This information system, combined with accurate component usage factors, permits product variability on a continuous production line.

## *Manufacturing Cells*

Manufacturing cells are dedicated subsets of the manufacturing system designed to process part families or product groups. For this reason, they are sometimes called a plant-within-a-plant. Cells usually involve the designation of a small group of workers and machines to be responsible for one subset of the business and may be based on several high-volume and standard products or on one or several high-priority customers. Typically, a cell is responsible for all aspects of the particular category of business from order taking to scheduling, production, and shipping. Cells have a limited product flow and are often U- or C- (or horseshoe- ) -shaped, to permit better employee communication and movement in the cell area. (See Chapter 6.)

Cells are able to achieve economies of setup, employee learning, reduced work in process, shorter throughput times, and notably improved responsiveness to customers. They are particularly useful to reduce inventory costs or where short delivery times or high quality standards are required by customers. Manufacturing cells were initially designed to reduce manufacturing throughput time (New, 1977) and to minimize inventory. The John Deere Waterloo, Iowa, diesel engine plant (Spencer, 1980) is an often noted example. More recent examples have been designed to provide flexibility of response to customer needs and to reduce operating costs.

## *Flexible Manufacturing Systems*

A flexible manufacturing system (FMS) integrates and enhances the flexibility of manufacturing cells through the use of centralized control systems. Often a standard mounting boss or lug is used to simplify materials handling and permit computer-controlled machines to rapidly change setups for the specific job. Seventy-five percent of machine parts produced in the United States are produced in lot sizes of 50 or less (Jaikumar, 1986; Buffa, 1985). For cost efficiency, these jobs must be produced by using line flow techniques; however, each job requires a different setup. FMS is ideal for such situations. FMS is often called an "island of automation" because it involves activities that are fed by and feed to nonautomated systems. The premise of FMS is to provide flexibility approaching that of a job shop, but with the materials handling capabilities of a line flow (Jaikumar, 1986). A computer manages variable setups as well as the routing of those parts through the process.

The Quill Corporation, applying a similar concept to distribution systems, packages customer orders for national distribution from its warehouse in Lincolnshire, Illinois. A two-mile-long conveyor system moves presized boxes to some 30 stations, where items are either automatically or manually picked, based on a bar-coded order number. Orders are shipped within 36 hours of receipt, and the accuracy of the semiautomated pick system is almost 100%. In fact, most returns result because of customer error.

## *Computer Integrated Manufacturing*

Computer integrated manufacturing (CIM) is the application of a computer system to link several separate information systems and technologies at different functional levels. Though the technology is very complex, the purpose of CIM is to simplify, automate, and integrate. The CIM system connects several components of a production system into an integrated whole, as shown in Figure 7-5.

Computer integrated manufacturing draws information from several levels of the business and from various functional areas. Figure 7-5 describes the more common types

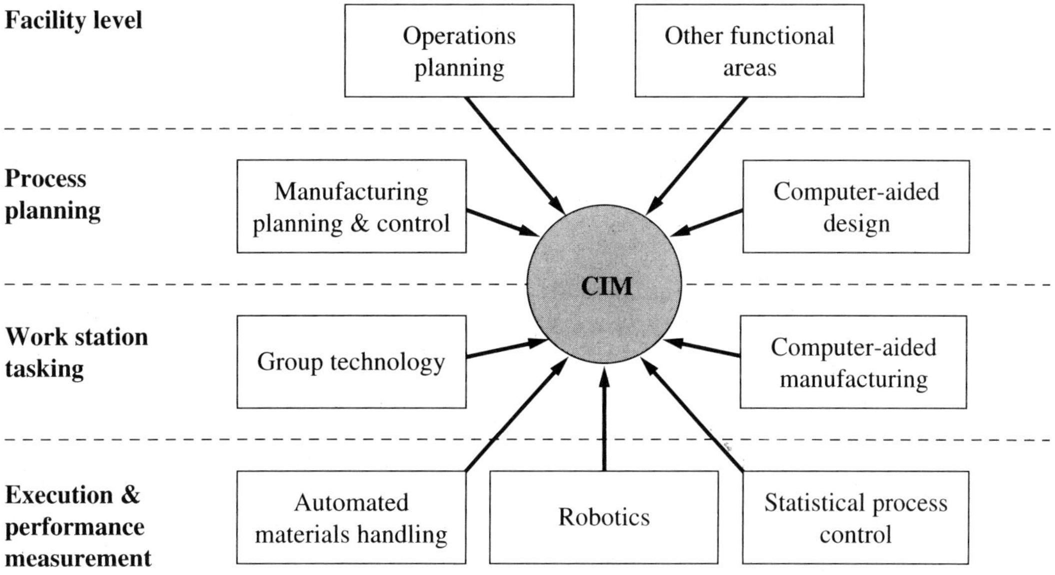


**Computer-aided Design:** the use of computers to draw and store engineering designs.

**Computer-aided Manufacturing:** the use of computers to program and control production equipment, often based on computer-aided designs.

**Statistical Process Control:** a system to monitor numerous process technology performance indicators and identify potential out-of-tolerance conditions.

**Robotics:** the use of programmable machines to handle materials or tools in the performance of manufacturing tasks.

**Automated Materials Handling:** equipment which permits the storage, retrieval, and movement of materials and parts.

**Group Technology:** an engineering method which identifies sameness of parts, equipment, or processes and uses that sameness in subsequent design of parts, equipment, or processes.

**Manufacturing Planning & Control:** the interface of the master production schedule with the production system to execute the production plan.

**Operations Planning:** evaluation of long- and mid-range information in terms of capacity and requirements.

**Other Functional Areas:** integration of various human resource, marketing, and cost measures with the operations function.

**FIGURE 7-5 Computer Integrated Manufacturing Systems**

of information that are used by a CIM system; however, other types of information may be useful in various specific applications. Few organizations could claim to have a fully integrated CIM system, because moving toward CIM involves simultaneous automation of process technologies (work station tasking and execution and performance measurement) and process control systems (facility level and process planning). This requires simultaneous growth of the process technology and the process control system, as shown in Figure 7-6.

As suggested by Figure 7-6, the growth from traditional manufacturing toward CIM is usually achieved in several stages, each of which permits the traditional line flow manufacturer to enhance the production variety. The information system gives greater process flexibility and greater control. In fact, a well-developed CIM system permits an operation to function efficiently at almost any position on the product/service–process technology continuum. Firms usually start movement toward a CIM system by increasing the variability of the traditional production process, then sequentially developing manufacturing cells, linking those cells with a flexible manufacturing system, and finally automating all parts of the system with a CIM system.

The use of CIM logic is becoming increasingly widespread in distribution and service systems. The automated storage and retrieval systems (AS/RS) which are used by major distributors, such as W. W. Grainger and Sears, Roebuck, are examples. Additionally, the use of bar codes for product identification, combined with automated credit validation, is a way that CIM concepts significantly speed customer order processing in most retail environments.

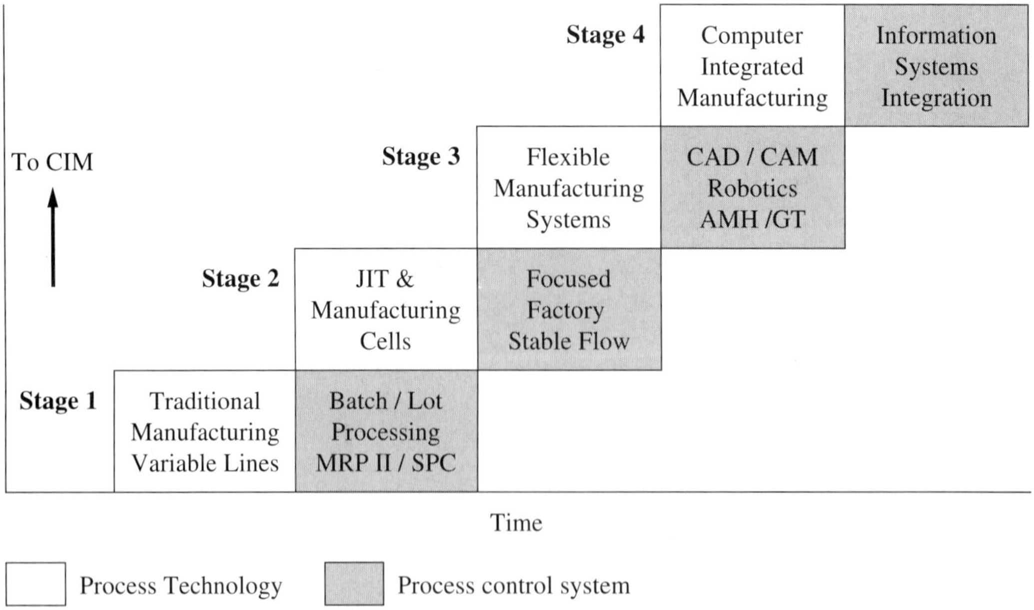


**FIGURE 7-6 Toward a CIM System**

The type of information and control system will depend upon whether the objective is materials planning or process control and upon the amount of lead-time variability or the flexibility required of the production system. Manufacturing cells and just-in-time systems work well in stable, continuous-flow, pull materials planning situations. Alternatively, if the system is push-oriented, or involves custom product design, then lead-time variability is likely to be higher and material requirements planning is more appropriate. At the shop-floor level, continuous and stable flow situations are best managed by Kanban or other visible mechanisms to pull materials, but if flexibility is high, then the shop floor should be managed by traditional operations scheduling. These dimensions of information system flexibility, adopted from Karmarkar (1989), are shown in Table 7-3.

## *Emerging Business Practices*

Though many large firms in traditional business environments require the efficiencies of purchasing and owning their own facilities and equipment, there is increasing support, even among large firms, for the use of leased or contracted facilities, equipment, and services. The advantages of leasing are most apparent in new and untested market areas or technologies, or with items that experience rapid technological changes or require frequent servicing. Of course, leasing is a common practice in situations where there is only a short-term need for the equipment or service, such as in the construction industry. In the 1960s and 1970s, computers were often leased because the costs were quite high, the technology changed rapidly, and the first applications were risky. More recently, as costs have decreased and applications have become accepted and proven, a greater proportion of computers is being purchased.

Of course, there are costs associated with leasing, yet surprisingly, the total cost of leasing may be well below the cost of purchasing a piece of equipment. A notable portion of the cost advantage of leasing is explained by the tax advantages of not owning the equipment and depreciation losses of ownership. Decision Model Box 7-1 shows the costs of leasing compared with the costs of purchasing computer equipment.

**TABLE 7-3 Process Information Systems**

| | Materials Planning | Process Control |
|---|---|---|
| Inventory pull systems<br>Continuous flow<br>Low lead-time variability | Just-in-time | Kanban |
| ↕ | | |
| Inventory push systems<br>Custom engineering<br>High lead-time variability | Material requirements planning | Traditional scheduling |

## DECISION MODEL BOX 7-1 The Lease–Purchase Decision at True Value Retail

The management of the True Value Retail Store wants to acquire a small computer system to manage sales and inventory records, with future applications in tax accounting and purchasing. The store expects to use the computer system for five years. Application Table 7-1-1 shows the computation of total costs to lease the computer, which is compared with the data in Application Table 7-1-2, the cost of owning the system. The lease cost, including maintenance, is $1200 per year, and the purchase price of the equipment is $10,000 with a salvage value of $6250 in five years. The maintenance contract is $300 per year. The value of tax write-offs is 40%, and the annuity factor is 20% (which may be somewhat higher than bank interest rates, but represents the opportunity costs—or rate of return of money invested in other ways—of the store). A fixed depreciation scale of 25%, 20%, 15%, 10%, and 5% is used; all costs incurred at end of year.

### APPLICATION TABLE 7-1-1 Cost of Leasing

| (1) Year | (2) Lease Cost | (3) Tax Advantage (40%) [0.4 × (2)] | (4) Lease Cost after Taxes [(2) – (3)] | (5) Net Present Value Factor* (20%) | (6) Adjusted Lease Cost [(4) × (5)] |
|---|---|---|---|---|---|
| 0 | $1200 | $480 | $720 | 1.0 | $720 |
| 1 | 1200 | 480 | 720 | 0.83 | 598 |
| 2 | 1200 | 480 | 720 | 0.69 | 497 |
| 3 | 1200 | 480 | 720 | 0.58 | 418 |
| 4 | 1200 | 480 | 720 | 0.48 | 346 |
| | | | | Total cost of leasing | $2579 |

*Calculated as $1/(1 + i)^t$.

### APPLICATION TABLE 7-1-2 Cost of Owning

| (1) Year | (2) Maintenance Cost | (3) Depreciation | (4) Business Cost [(2) + (3)] | (5) Tax Advantage [0.4 × (4)] | (6) Net Cost After Taxes [(2) – (5)] | (7) Net Present Value Factor (20%) | (8) Present Value of Money After Taxes [(6) × (7)] |
|---|---|---|---|---|---|---|---|
| 1 | $300 | $2500 | $2800 | $1120 | –$820 | 0.83 | –$681 |
| 2 | 300 | 2000 | 2300 | 920 | –620 | 0.69 | –428 |
| 3 | 300 | 1500 | 1800 | 720 | –420 | 0.58 | –244 |
| 4 | 300 | 1000 | 1300 | 520 | –220 | 0.48 | –106 |
| 5 | 300 | 500 | 800 | 320 | –20 | 0.40 | –8 |
| | | | | | Net cost of owning computer | | –$1467 |

Summarization

| | |
|---|---|
| Purchase price | $10,000 |
| Cost of owning computer | –1467 |
| Subtotal | 8533 |
| Salvage recovery ($6250 × 0.40) | 2500 |
| Total cost of ownership | $ 6033 |

*Continued*

**DECISION MODEL BOX 7-1** *Continued*

Note that the cost of leasing in Application Table 7-1-1 is adjusted for the tax advantage and for the net present value of money. Alternatively, the cost of ownership in Application Table 7-1-2 is based on the annual maintenance and depreciation costs, which sum to the business costs, and are the basis for the 40% tax advantage. The present value factor is applied to the maintenance cost minus the tax write-off, or net cost after taxes. The present value of these costs is summed over the five-year period and deducted from the purchase price, as is the salvage value of the equipment.

Very obviously, the cost of the computer equipment for five years is more than two times the cost to lease the equipment. The majority of the difference occurs because the value of the computer depreciates, and the owner bears that depreciation. However, these computations are dependent upon the cost of the item, the lease cost, maintenance and depreciation costs, the net present value factor, and other values of the store.

---

Firms may also lease services, such as payroll, security, and janitorial services. Information and education services are also widely demanded, as the plethora of consultants in almost every field and academic discipline attests. Firms find that, because of specialization, they can obtain such services at lower costs and greater quality with less risk and commitment than if they hire their own staff.

Each of these methods increases the process flexibility of the facility and decreases the potential risks of long-term resource commitments. These, combined with increased product/service flexibility, suggest that it is possible to operate on a greater range of the product/service–process technology continuum than in immediate proximity to the diagonal. Additionally, though there are still costs of operating off the diagonal, the costs and risks are both different and much reduced from the classical model. The key requirements for a firm to operate away from the diagonal are a highly educated and trained work force and a responsive information system. Though there are limits of movement off the diagonal, there are also opportunities and conditions that facilitate effective off-diagonal operations for those who have the work force and information systems. Figure 7-7 reflects the positioning of various example situations used in this chapter on the product/service–process technology continuum.

Though these technologies permit the operations function to operate away from the traditional diagonal, there may be some hidden costs. Such costs are often rather insidious in that they may be difficult to measure and aggregate. For example, software automation costs, such as training and implementation time, are usually not considered to be sunk capital investments and thus might not be measured or monitored as closely by management. For example, see the discussion of the Volvo Kalmar and Uddevalla plants in Chapter 12.

Ultimately, the greater flexibility of the system must be costed against the sometimes very high total system (including system development) costs. Additionally, the likelihood and costs of failure to implement a system (an MRP system, for example) can be rather high. An early study by Anderson et al. (1982) found that 60% of firms that implemented MRP systems classified themselves as class C or class D users (suggesting limited functioning of the system and numerous data errors) with average costs of more than

| Process Technology (Flow Pattern) | Product / Service Volume: Low | ← | → | → | High |
|---|---|---|---|---|---|
| Project (None) ↓ | | University Printers | Franchises & Cooperatives | Software Company | |
| Job Shop (Jumbled) ↓ | Avanti | | Desktop Publishing | Volvo Kalmar | |
| Disconnected line ↓ | | Modular Office Furniture | | | Baxter Health Care |
| Connected line ↓ | Allen-Bradley | Quill Distribution System | Cummins Diesel | | |
| Continuous | | | News Publishing | | |

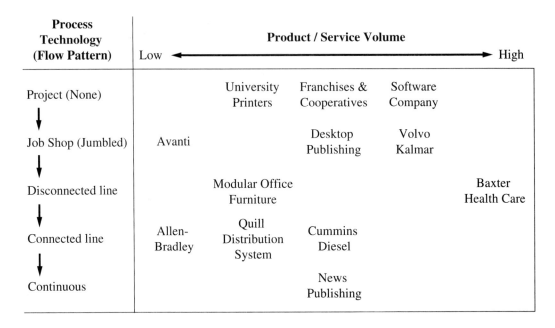

**FIGURE 7-7 The Product/Service–Process Technology Continuum with Diffusion**

one-half million dollars. However, if the effort is not made, there are long-range risks that a competitor may successfully implement a system and experience significant cost, flexibility, delivery, or quality improvements.

These emerging process technologies, information control systems, and business practices permit increased flexibility of process technology. The traditionally defined risks of lost opportunity costs or unrecoverable sunk investments are dramatically reduced; yet other risks appear to be taking their place, including the difficulty of cost measurement, the risk of information system failure, and the risk that a business will be strategically and competitively outflanked.

## *Operations System Decision-Making Hierarchy*

After the position or range on the product/service–process technology continuum and the direction and momentum of movement on the continuum have been identified, the operations manager must make some more specific decisions, among them, the major technological choice, the equipment and layout selection, and activity scheduling. These specific decisions, though time consuming, involve extensive computational algorithms and more direct management control. Thus, starting with the positioning of the operations system, these decisions are best accomplished sequentially as a hierarchy of operations system decision-making, as shown in Table 7-4.

**TABLE 7-4 Operations System Decision-Making Hierarchy**

| | |
|---|---|
| Position<br>↓ | Competitive positioning on the product/service–process technology continuum, definition of the position on the continuum, and identification of the direction and momentum of movement which are projected |
| Major technology choice<br>↓ | Selecting the process technology of the manufacturing or service operation and the supporting information system |
| Equipment selection and layout specification<br>↓ | Selecting either general-purpose or varying degrees of specialized equipment and allocating available facilities, using qualitative or quantitative methods |
| Operations planning | Creating a schedule, such as an operations plan or a master production schedule, and assessing that schedule through the appropriate capacity evaluation method |

## *Major Technology Choice*

As might be expected, long-range and strategic perspectives drive the operations system design effort. Once the focus or diffusion of the operations system is defined, then the process technology is selected. Table 7-5 classifies various alternative manufacturing and service processes. The manufacturing processes change the physical properties, shapes, dimensions, and surfaces of materials or join parts. The corresponding classification of service operations involves location, storage, exchange and physical, physiological, or information transformations. This list is not inclusive; it is offered only to suggest the range of different manufacturing and service processes.

## *Equipment Selection and Layout Specification*

The equipment selection and facility layout specification is an important, though particularly detailed and mechanical type of evaluation. As one operations manager stated, "Equipment selection is like buying the right tire, and facility layout is where the rubber meets the road." For example, a general service garage might use general-purpose equipment to change a car's oil, whereas a company which did only oil changes would use more specialized equipment.

The nature of the equipment selected can have a significant effect on the capacity, efficiency, and utilization of the operation (see Chapter 5). Similarly, the location of that equipment can have significant effects on organization productivity (see Chapter 6). In this regard, the topics of Chapters 5 through 7 are very closely related. From the process perspective, the alternatives apply to both manufacturing and service environments and span a range from general-purpose to specialized machines. Table 7-6 gives the general characteristics of those two "pure" alternatives. It is no surprise that Table 7-6 corresponds

**TABLE 7-5 Classification of Manufacturing and Service Processes**

## Manufacturing

**1.** Processes for changing physical properties

a. Chemical reactions
b. Refining/extraction
c. Heat treatment
d. Hot working
e. Cold working
f. Shot peening

**2.** Processes for changing the shape of materials

a. Casting
b. Forging
c. Extruding
d. Rolling
e. Drawing
f. Squeezing
g. Crushing
h. Piercing
i. Swaging
j. Bending
k. Shearing
l. Spinning
m. Stretch forming
n. Roll forming
o. Torch cutting
p. Explosive forming
q. Electrohydraulic forming
r. Magnetic forming
s. Electroforming
t. Powder metal forming
u. Plastics molding

**3.** Processes for machining parts to a fixed dimension

Traditional chip removal processes

a. Turning
b. Planing
c. Shaping
d. Drilling
e. Boring
f. Reaming
g. Sawing
h. Broaching
i. Milling
j. Grinding
k. Hobbing
l. Routing

Nontraditional machining processes

a. Ultrasonic
b. Electro-arc
c. Electrochemical
d. Optical lasers
e. Electron beam machining
f. Chem-milling
g. Abrasive jet cutting
h. Electrical discharge
i. Plasma-arc machining

**4.** Processes for obtaining a surface finish

a. Polishing
b. Abrasive belt grinding
c. Barrel tumbling
d. Electroplating
e. Honing
f. Lapping
g. Superfinishing
h. Metal spraying
i. Inorganic coatings
j. Parkerizing
k. Anodizing
l. Sheradizing

**5.** Processes for joining parts or materials

a. Welding
b. Soldering
c. Brazing
d. Sintering
e. Plugging
f. Pressing
g. Riveting
h. Screw fastening
i. Adhesive joining

## Service

**1.** Processes for relocating goods

a. Messenger
b. Airline
c. Auto or taxi
d. Bus or subway
e. Truck
f. Delivery service
g. Ship or boat
h. Railroad
i. Mail
j. Canal/river barge

**2.** Processes for storing goods

a. Bank account/vault
b. Storage rental unit
c. Freezer
d. Public lockers
e. Warehouse
f. Pipeline
g. Padlock
h. Data storage

**3.** Processes for exchanging items

a. Retail sales units
b. Banks
c. Credit card sales
d. Catalog sales
e. Barter/swapping
f. Retail/leasing
g. Contracts
h. Informal sales

**4.** Processes for physical transformation

a. Cleaning
b. Eating/drinking
c. Motel and hotel
d. Heating/cooling
e. Lighting
f. Noise abatement
g. Item modification
h. Item maintenance or repair

**5.** Processes for physiological transformation

a. Entertainment
b. Exercise
c. Medical
d. Dental
e. Appreciation (art)
f. Religious
g. Personal and vanity
h. Other clinical

**6.** Processes for information transformation

a. Telephone
b. Mail
c. Radio and television
d. Newspapers
e. Magazines/journals
f. Data links
g. Conferences
h. Face-to-face
i. Beeper
j. Education/training
k. Consulting
l. Fax

Note: Manufacturing classifications are adapted from Amstead et al., 1977.

rather closely to parts of Table 7-1. General-purpose equipment is often used in a job shop, while more specialized equipment is commonly associated with a continuous process. Thus, general-purpose equipment would be preferred in the start-up and growth stages, and more specialized equipment would be selected during the stable state stage.

The second equipment and layout selection decision is the method of deciding upon the location of the equipment. This two-step procedure involves identifying the amount of space or capacity of each center and, second, the configuration of the centers. None of the numerous methods is inherently optimizing, and the methods are measurement bound, particularly if the facility is large, or with multiple floors, and with many separate activities. Additionally, there are questions of variable routings, one-way and return trips, and multidestination trips. For these reasons, layout algorithms are appropriate as mechanical tools, but they must be supplemented by human evaluation.

## Operations Planning

Table 7-1 noted several of the process management characteristics and challenges for each of the classic process alternatives. A fixed process might use the program evaluation review technique/critical path method (PERT/CPM) to manage the flow of materials, while a job shop might use a variety of debottlenecking and scheduling algorithms, and line flow operations would use line balancing or linear programming (see Chapters 6, 8, 10, and 13). Though some of these decision methods are "optimal," they are dependent upon uncertain or variable input information. However, these approaches are very useful as estimation and evaluative tools. They offer an initial mechanical assessment that can be subsequently adjusted through judgmental processes or by trial and error.

The topics of layout specification and activity scheduling are dependent upon the higher decisions of the operations system planning hierarchy. Additionally, they are computationally bound. Dependence upon higher-level decisions is exemplified by the scheduling changes that would be required by a decision to replace assembly line processes with manufacturing cells or just-in-time systems. These topics will be discussed in Chapter 10.

**TABLE 7-6 Equipment Selection Alternatives**

| Cost | General Purpose<br>Low | Specialized<br>High |
|---|---|---|
| Operator skill and control | high skill, more control | low skill, less control |
| Output rate | low—human paced | high—system or machine paced |
| Setup time | lower—problems predictable and controllable | high—problems random and highly technical |
| Maintenance cost | low—lower skill required/ greater parts availability | high |
| Product/service quality | based on human control | high—based on machine accuracy |
| In-process inventory | high | low—fewer "run-ins" |
| Obsolescence | slower—easier updating/modification | high |

## Summary

This chapter has addressed the need for focus and simultaneously the positioning of product/service and process capabilities. The hierarchy of operations system design provides a long-range to short-range integrating framework of manufacturing and service operations systems. This chapter has emphasized the positioning and focus of the operations system with brief discussions of the other three levels of the operations system design hierarchy. The technological choice is not further discussed here because it is highly industry specific. The strategic considerations of equipment selection are very closely related, as noted, to process selection. Layout specification was discussed in Chapter 6; operations planning will be further discussed in Chapter 8, and operations control will be discussed in Chapter 10.

The product/service–process technology system life cycle provides a central starting point for product/service, process technology, and often facility analysis. The operations manager must define the position of a particular situation on the product/service–process technology continuum, then consider the amount of focus or diffusion and the direction and momentum of movement desired for the operations system. The risks and opportunities associated with each situation must then be gauged. The classical approach is that the facility or process must be focused for productivity and efficiency; yet emerging process technologies and practices may permit more diffused positioning. These emerging positioning approaches involve greater complexity and information flows, but possibly less cost and risk. Certainly, the costs and risks are of a different nature. There are very clear reasons for some diffusion, but the exact definition of focus or diffusion for a situation is a difficult and continual process, particularly in dynamic environments. Reassessment and repositioning must be considered regularly.

Once the position of the firm is determined, the remaining decisions are much more highly constrained and mechanical. The hierarchy of operations system planning identifies the three additional stages of that process. Clearly, any changes at the position/focus level will have major impacts at the lower levels of the hierarchy; yet simultaneously, lower levels of the hierarchy represent measures of efficiency and effectiveness by which the effectiveness of the operations system is evaluated.

## Discussion Questions

1. Identify the final four stages of the product/service–process technology life cycle. Give an example of a company that has dynamically adjusted the position of its operations system on the life cycle.
2. From your personal experience or readings, identify and briefly describe one company in each of the last four stages of the product/service–process technology life cycle.
3. Describe the corresponding changes that occur in the product/service and process technology life cycles along with the related industry characteristics. Give an example of a company that has experienced these changes.
4. Briefly note some possible constraints on operations system design.

5. What does an operations system design involve?
6. Name and describe the characteristics of the three classical process alternatives.
7. From your personal experience or readings, identify and briefly describe several products and several services that are built or delivered by using the classical processes.
8. List the three types of process flexibility and the driving factors associated with each. Give an example of each type.
9. Identify and support the key variables of the product/service–process technology continuum.
10. Describe briefly the cost penalties of operating off the diagonal.
11. Identify and describe from your experience or readings, a cost penalty that resulted from operating off the diagonal.
12. Briefly describe product/service and process focus.
13. Identify the relationship of product/service versus process emphasis with that of the product/service and process technology life cycle. Give an example of a company and explain how the company has positioned itself.
14. Why is a manufacturing cell sometimes called a "plant within a plant"?
15. Two advantages of leasing are the increases in process flexibility of a facility and the decreases in potential risks. These advantages, combined with the product/service flexibilities, suggest the possibility of operating on a greater range of the product/service–process technology continuum (that is, off the diagonal). What are the key requirements for a firm to operate away from the diagonal? Give an example of a successful application and an unsuccessful application.
16. Identify the levels of the process planning hierarchy and briefly describe the management decisions required at each level. Give an application of how a decision was made through the four levels. (*Note:* The primary discussion of the final two levels is in other chapters.)

## *Strategic Decision Situations*

1. The president of Xenon Industries is concerned about the focus of the company and has asked for a three-to-five-page summarization considering three topics: the focus, the major technology, and the type of equipment used by the company. Select a specific company that you are familiar with, or research a company in business publications and, using those details, respond to the president's concerns. Your comments should be directed toward the current situation of the company, and where you think the company should be in three to five years.
   a. Identify the product line of the company; then specify the position of the product/service line on the product/service–process technology continuum and state the degree of focusing or diffusion and the direction of movement on the continuum.
   b. Identify the major technology of the manufacturing or service process and the information system which supports that process.
   c. Identify the general-purpose or specialized equipment that is appropriate for the process and identify the allocation of facilities to be used.

*Note:* Appropriate appendices may be included to support your report with substantive capacity evaluation and layout information (see Chapters 5 and 6).

2. The Speedy Delivery Pizza Company plans to acquire company vehicles, which will replace personal vehicles that are used for home delivery of their products. The lease cost is $1000 per year and the purchase price per vehicle is $7000 with a salvage value of $2000 in five years. A maintenance contract for leasing is required, costing $300 per year, and insurance costs are considered to be equal under either option. The tax advantage is 30% and the annuity factor is 15%. A fixed depreciation scale of 25%, 20%, 15%, 10%, and 5% is used. Advise the company on the best option.

3. The West Side Publishing Company wants to upgrade its printing equipment with an integrated high speed printing unit that costs $60,000. The unit could be purchased and then sold to and leased back from an equipment holding company, which would cost $8000 per year for a five-year contract or $6000 per year for a ten-year term, with a required maintenance cost of $500 per year. For a five-year fixed contract, the company could get 10% on its money, while for a ten-year fixed contract, 12.5% would be the annuity factor. Using a tax advantage of 30%, a fixed depreciation rate of 14%, 13%, 12%, 11%, 10%, 9%, 8%, 7%, 6%, and 5%, which contract would be preferred? After five years, the unit is expected to have a value of $48,000 and after 10 years, the unit will have a value of $35,000.

## *References*


Amstead, B. J., P. F. Ostwald, and M. L. Begeman. *Manufacturing Processes.* New York: John Wiley and Sons, 1979.

Anderson, John C., Roger G. Schroeder, Sharon E. Tupy, and Edna M. White. "Material Requirements Planning Systems: The State of the Art," *Production and Inventory Management.* October–December 1982.

Brown, J. "Classification of Flexible Manufacturing Systems," *The FMS Magazine.* April 1984, pp. 114–117.

Buffa, Elwood S. "Meeting the Competitive Challenge with Manufacturing Strategy," *National Productivity Review.* Spring 1985, pp. 155–169.

Butcher, Lee. *Accidental Millionaire.* New York: Paragon House Publishers, 1988.

Dean, James W., Jr., and Gerald I. Susman. "Organizing for Manufacturable Design," *Harvard Business Review.* January–February 1989, pp. 28–37.

Derks, Richard P. "Purpose-Driven Product and Process Design," *Industrial Engineering.* January 1993, Vol. 25, No. 1, pp. 38–42.

Finch, Byron J., and James F. Cox. "Process-Oriented Production Planning and Control: Factors That Influence System Design," *Academy of Management Journal.* Vol. 31, No. 1, 1988, pp. 123–153.

Gerwin, Donald. "The Do's and Don'ts of Computerized Manufacturing," *Harvard Business Review.* March–April 1982, pp. 107–116.

Gerwin, Donald. "Manufacturing Flexibility in the CAM Era," *Business Horizons.* January–February 1989, pp. 78–84.

Goldhar, Joel D., and Mariann Jelinek. "Computer Integrated Flexible Manufacturing: Organizational, Economic, and Strategic Implications," *Interfaces.* May–June 1985, pp. 94–105.

Greene, James H. *Production and Inventory Control Handbook.* New York: McGraw-Hill, 1987.

Hayes, Robert H., and Steven C. Wheelwright. "Link Manufacturing Process and Product Life Cycles," *Harvard Business Review.* January–February 1979.

Hayes, Robert H., and Steven C. Wheelwright. "The Dynamics of Process–Product Life Cycles," *Harvard Business Review.* March–April 1979.

Hayes, Robert H., and Steven C. Wheelwright. *Restoring Our Competitive Edge: Competing through Manufacturing.* New York: John Wiley and Sons, 1984.

Hill, Terrence J., and R. M. G. Duke-Woolley. "Progression or Regression in Facilities Focus," *Strategic Management Journal.* Vol. 4, 1983, pp. 109–121.

Jackson, Richard H. F., and Albert W. T. Jones. "An Architecture for Decision Making in the Factory of the Future," *Interfaces.* November–December 1987, pp. 15–28.

Jaikumar, Ramchandran. "Postindustrial Manufacturing," *Harvard Business Review.* November–December 1986, pp. 69–76.

Karmarkar, Uday. "Getting Control of Just-in-Time," *Harvard Business Review.* September–October 1989, pp. 122–131.

Kotha, Suresh, and Daniel Orne. "Generic Manufacturing Strategies: A Conceptual Synthesis," *Strategic Management Journal.* Vol. 10, 1989, pp. 211–231.

Leong, G. Keong, and Peter T. Ward. "Multifaceted View of Manufacturing Strategy." Working Paper Series, WPS 90–50, Ohio State University, June 1990.

Leong, G. K., D. L. Snyder, and P. T. Ward. "Research in the Process and Content of Manufacturing Strategy," *Omega International Journal of Management Science.* Vol. 18, No. 2, 1990, pp. 109–122.

Markoff, John. "Beyond the PC: Apple's Promised Land," *New York Times.* November 15, 1992, Section 3, p. 1.

McKenna, Regis. *Who's Afraid of Big Blue?* Reading, Mass.: Addison-Wesley Publishing Co., 1989.

Moody, Patricia E. *Strategic Manufacturing: Dynamic New Directions for the 1990s.* Homewood, Ill.: Dow Jones Irwin, 1990.

New, C. Colin. "MRP and GT: A New Strategy for Component Production," *Production and Inventory Management.* Vol. 18, No. 3, 1977, pp. 50–62.

Noori, Hamid, and Russell W. Radford. *Readings and Cases in the Management of New Technology: An Operations Perspective.* Englewood Cliffs, N.J.: Prentice Hall, 1990.

Sasser, W. Earl, Kim B. Clark, David A. Garvin, Margaret B. W. Graham, Ramchandran Jaikumar, and David H. Maister. *Cases in Operations Management: Analysis and Action.* Homewood, Ill.: Irwin, 1982.

Schmenner, Roger W. "Every Factory Has a Cycle," *Harvard Business Review.* March–April 1983, pp. 121–129.

Skinner, Wickham. "The Focused Factory," *Harvard Business Review.* May–June 1974.

Spencer, Michael S. "Scheduling Components for Group Technology Lines," *Production and Inventory Management.* October–December 1980, pp. 43–49.

Wantuck, Kenneth A. "The Japanese Approach to Productivity," *Proceedings of the American Production and Inventory Control Society Annual Conference,* 1983.

Whitney, Daniel E. "Manufacturing by Design," *Harvard Business Review.* July–August 1988, pp. 83–91.

# Case 3

# Facilities Strategy at Courtyard by Marriott

## Introduction

The hotel business is worth around $40 billion a year in the United States, but the business is a mature one with limited growth potential. During the 1980s, there was a 40% increase in hotel rooms, that contributed to a growing gap between room availability and occupancy rates. This overexpansion was in part caused by tax-shelter incentives that encouraged developers to build hotels in excess of demand. These incentives were removed in 1986, and the market is expected to balance out by the mid-1990s.

The overbuilding of hotels has resulted in a surplus of available rooms and a decline in occupancy rates. In 1990, industry occupancy rates averaged 64%, about four percentage points below the break-even rate. One company that continues to exhibit strong growth despite industry difficulties is the Marriott Corporation.* Marriott had a fivefold increase in sales from 1977 to 1988. Much of this sales growth was based on the Courtyard by Marriott chain, which was created to target the midprice ($45–70 a night) segment of the lodging market. Over 190 Courtyard hotels have been opened by Marriott since 1983, which have helped it obtain a large percentage of the midprice market from competitors such as Holiday, Ramada, and Quality Inns.

## Marriott Corporation

Marriott was founded in 1927, on the same day that Charles Lindbergh made his historic transatlantic flight, by J. Willard Marriott Sr. as a franchise stand for A&W root beer. It

*This case is prepared as a basis for class discussion, rather than to illustrate either effective or ineffective management of an operational situation.

remained basically a fast-food and contract catering business for 30 years, until the first hotel was acquired in 1957. The company went public in 1953 and was listed on the New York Stock Exchange in 1968 with sales of approximately $100 million a year. Much of Marriott's success has been due to the strong management of Bill Marriott Jr., who took over as company president from his father in 1964 and became chief executive officer (CEO) in 1972. Between Bill Jr.'s appointment as CEO and the founder's death in 1985, sales rose from $84 million to $4 billion. Over the last 20 years, sales growth has been around 20% per year for the majority of this period.

In the early 1980s, Marriott was concerned that it was running out of good sites at which to locate traditional Marriott hotels at a frequent enough rate to assure a continued rate of high growth. A preliminary decision was made to develop a new hotel chain designed to appeal to customers who were not satisfied with current hotel offerings. Two target market segments were identified: business travelers (who travel at least six times a year and stay in mid-level hotels or motels) and pleasure travelers (who travel at least twice a year and stay in hotels or motels). In designing a new hotel chain, it was critical to determine the type of hotel facilities and services that Marriott should offer to attract these customers away from the competition. To develop an "optimal" hotel design, Marriott hired outside consultants to conduct a large-scale consumer study to determine the features that customers valued most in a hotel.

## *Developing a Design for Courtyard*

The study was designed to determine the features that customers most desired for each of seven sets (or facets) of hotel attributes: external factors, rooms, food-related services, lounge facilities, services, leisure facilities, and security factors. Overall, the study considered 50 attributes with each attribute being evaluated on the basis of from two to eight alternatives. Table C3-1 lists the seven sets of attributes, where each set consists of several different attributes. The alternative choices for each attribute are indented with the option chosen by the survey respondents underlined. The study was designed to provide answers to numerous questions, including:

- Of the hotel features and services listed in Table C3-1, which combination should be offered?
- What should be the location strategy for the new hotels?

To determine the features and services desired, customer preferences needed to be ascertained. This was accomplished by using a two-pronged approach. First, the respondents were asked to evaluate each of the seven sets of attributes one at a time. Included for each choice were the associated additional costs. For example, the entertainment attribute had two choices: a color TV would add no cost, or a color TV with HBO, movies, and so on would add 40 cents a night to the base price of a hotel room. The respondents were required to choose (1) the option for each attribute that best described their current hotel, (2) the option they wanted and were willing to pay for, and (3) the options that were completely unacceptable. In addition, each attribute level within the facet was to be ranked

**TABLE C3-1 Hotel Features and Services**

EXTERNAL FACTORS

Building Shape
- L-shaped w/landscape
- Outdoor courtyard

Landscaping
- Minimal
- Moderate
- Elaborate

Pool Type
- No pool
- Rectangular
- Free form shape
- Indoor/outdoor

Pool Location
- In courtyard
- Not in courtyard

Corridor/View
- Outside access/restricted view
- Enclose access/unrestricted view/balcony or window

Hotel Size
- Small (125 rooms—2 stories)

Large (600 rooms—12 stories)

ROOMS

Entertainment
- Color TV
- Color TV w/movies at $5
- Color TV w/30 channel cable
- Color TV w/HBO, movies, etc.
- Color TV w/free movies

Entertainment/Rental
- None
- Rental cassettes/in-room Atari
- Rental cassettes/stereo cassette playing in room
- Rental movies in-room BetaMax

Size
- Small (standard)
- Slightly larger (1 foot)
- Much larger (2.5 feet)
- Small suite (2 rooms)
- Large suite (2 rooms)

Quality of Decor (in standard room)
- Budget motel decor
- Old Holiday Inn decor
- New Holiday Inn decor
- New Hilton decor
- New Hyatt decor

Heating and Cooling
- Wall unit/full control
- Wall unit/soundproof/full control
- Central H or C (seasonal)
- Central H or C/full control

Size of Bath
- Standard bath
- Slightly larger/sink separate
- Much larger bath w/larger tub
- Very large/tub for 2

Sink Location
- In bath only
- In separate area
- In bath and separate

Bathroom Features
- None
- Shower massage
- Whirlpool (Jacuzzi)
- Steam bath

Amenities
- Small bar soap
- Large soap/shampoo/shoeshine
- Large soap/bath gel/shower cap/sewing kit
- Above items + toothpaste, deodorant, mouthwash

FOOD

Restaurant in Hotel
- None (coffee shop next door)
- Restaurant/lounge combo, limited menu
- Coffee shop, full menu
- Full-service restaurant, full menu
- Coffee shop/full menu and good restaurant

Restaurant Nearby
- None
- Coffee shop
- Fast food
- Fast food or coffee shop and moderate restaurant
- Fast food or coffee shop and good restaurant

Free Continental
- None
- Continental included in room rate

Room Service
- None
- Phone-in order/guest to pick up
- Room service, limited menu
- Room service, full menu

Store
- No food in store
- Snack items
- Snacks, refrigerated items, wine, beer, liquor
- Above items and gourmet food items

Vending Service
- None
- Soft drink machine only
- Soft drink and snack machines
- Soft drink, snack, and sandwich machines
- Above and microwave available

In-room Kitchen Facilities
- None
- Coffee maker only
- Coffee maker and refrigerator
- Cooking facilities in room

LOUNGE

Atmosphere
- Quiet bar/lounge
- Lively, popular bar/lounge
- Type of people
- Hotel guests and friends only
- Open to public—general appeal
- Open to public—many singles

Lounge Nearby
- None
- Lounge/bar nearby
- Lounge/bar w/entertainment nearby

*Continued*

**TABLE C3-1** *Continued*

SERVICES

Reservations
- Call hotel directly
- 800 reservation number

Check-in
- Standard
- Pre-credit clearance
- Machine in lobby

Check-out
- At front desk
- Bill under door/leave key
- Key to front desk/bill by mail
- Machine in lobby

Limo to Airport
- None
- Yes

Message Service
- Note at front desk
- Light on phone
- Light on phone and message under door
- Recorded message

Cleanliness/Upkeep/Management Skill
- Budget motel level
- Holiday Inn level
- Nonconvention Hyatt level
- Convention Hyatt level
- Fine hotel level

Laundry/Valet
- None
- Client drop off and pick up
- Self-service
- Valet pick up and drop off

Special Services (concierge)
- None
- Information on restaurants, theaters, etc.
- Arrangements and reservations
- Travel problem resolution

Secretarial Services
- None
- Xerox machine
- Xerox machine and typist

Car Maintenance
- None
- Take car to service
- Gas on premises/bill to room

Car Rental/Airline Reservations
- None
- Car rental facility
- Airline reservations
- Car rental and airline reservations

LEISURE

Sauna
- None
- Yes

Whirlpool/Jacuzzi
- None
- Outdoor
- Indoor

Exercise Room
- None
- Basic facility w/weights
- Facility w/Nautilus equipment

Racquet Ball Courts
- None
- Yes

Tennis Courts
- None
- Yes

Game Room/Entertainment
- None
- Electric games/pinball
- Electric games/pinball/ping pong
- Above + movie theater, bowling

Children's Playroom/Playground
- None
- Playground only
- Playroom only
- Playground and playroom

Pool Extras
- None
- Pool w/slides
- Pool w/slides and equipment
- Pool w/slides, waterfall, equipment

SECURITY

Security Guard
- None
- 11 a.m. to 7 p.m.
- 7 p.m. to 7 a.m.
- 24 hours

Smoke Detector
- None
- Lobby and hallways only
- Lobby/hallways/rooms

24-hour Video Camera
- None
- Parking/hallway/public areas

Alarm Button
- None
- Button in room, rings desk



according to its relative importance. After all seven facets were evaluated, the incremental costs were totaled. If the charges plus base room price were higher than what the customer was willing to pay, they were asked to go back and select the enhancements they were willing to forego in order to arrive at an acceptable total room price.

In the second phase, respondents were asked to evaluate "complete" hotel offerings consisting of various combinations of the seven facets. The combinations shown to each respondent were chosen to be balanced, providing unbiased, statistically significant information. The respondents were required to rate each combination depending upon the likelihood of their staying there. The choices ranged from "Would stay there almost all the time" to "Would not stay there." The information gathered from this portion of the study provided the basis for determining the features and services Marriott would offer (Table C3-1, underlined). The respondents even chose the name of the new hotel: "Courtyard by Marriott."

Another primary concern for Marriott was the location strategy for the new hotels. Respondents were asked for demographic information and for information on the hotel accommodations they currently used for business and pleasure stays. They were also asked to allocate 100 points among a set of locations based on their importance in selecting a hotel. The locations were defined in terms of proximity to business, shopping, sightseeing, nightlife, theaters, airports, major highways, and so forth. Marriott management used this information when deciding upon locations.

A key to the effectiveness of the study lies in the fact that it focused on not only what travelers wanted, but also on what they did not want to pay for. This focus on customer needs allowed funds to be spent on hotel features that customers actually wanted, rather than on features that management assumed the customers wanted. The best validation of the effectiveness of this approach is the success of Courtyard by Marriott. Competitors have opened numerous clone chains in this lucrative market segment as they scramble to catch up with Courtyard.

## *Capacity and Facilities Strategy for Courtyard*

Firms in service industries, such as Marriott, must define and assess the "service bundle," which is comprised of four components: (1) facilitating goods, (2) explicit services, (3) implicit services, and (4) supporting facilities. For a hotel, facilitating goods include tangible items such as beds, televisions, rooms, and general hotel facilities that are available for customer use. Explicit services are less tangible, including characteristics such as speed and quality of service. Implicit services are more difficult to define because they depend on customer preferences. Implicit services include the customer's perceptions of status or comfort. The supporting facility is the building.

The objective of Marriott's consumer study was essentially to define the service bundle that would be offered by the Courtyard chain. The goal was to appeal to customers in the mid-priced segment of the lodging market who tended to stay at hotels owned by the competition, such as Holiday, Quality, and Ramada Inns, without attracting customers from Marriott's namesake hotels, which focused on the high end of the market. As such, the consumer survey was used to develop a service bundle that would appeal to this market segment. Thus, the service bundle for Courtyard was designed to offer high-quality rooms at moderate prices without frills such as bellmen, room service, or extensive meeting facilities. For instance, guests at Courtyard hotels pick up their own room service trays. This helps keep expenses down and provides better food value. In this case, room service was an explicit service customers were willing to sacrifice, and were willing to go to the extra effort of picking up their own trays in order to save money.

## *Location*

Location proved to be a major factor in the success of the Courtyard chain. On the basis of consumer survey, important location factors were found to be proximity to restaurants, interstate exits, airports, other suburban growth corridors, and office parks. Locating near interstate exits, airports, and office parks allows Courtyard to provide easy access to the travel networks and business facilities that businesspeople are interested in. Marriott estimates that two-thirds of Courtyard's business comes from the business travel segment of the market. In addition, locating in suburban areas rather than in expensive downtown business districts helps to cut down on the costs of acquiring land. This is important, because the average Courtyard hotel occupies approximately four acres of land and urban district land can cost two to ten times the amount required for more suburban areas. Suburban locations also help prevent direct competition between Courtyard and the more upscale Marriott hotels, which tend to be located in downtown areas.

## *Facilities Layout and Room Capacity*

The consumer survey played a major role in determining the facilities layout and room capacity for Courtyard hotels. The study provided detailed guidelines for designing a facilities layout. For instance, the survey indicated that customers preferred a small (125 rooms), two-story hotel over a large high-rise hotel (12 stories, 600 rooms) with a large lobby and extensive meeting rooms. Other results of the survey showed that customers wanted enclosed central corridors and stairs, a rectangular pool in the courtyard of the building, and moderate landscaping. The resulting design for Courtyard hotels incorporated these preferences in a low-rise building with two or three floors, enclosed central corridors and stairs, with a courtyard in the middle containing a rectangular pool. The final design for Courtyard hotels is relatively standard, resulting in a cookie cutter model that can be constructed relatively inexpensively and is immediately recognizable to travelers who have previously stayed at another Courtyard.

Recently, Courtyard has begun modifying its standard format in order to tap the mid-priced market in urban areas. The revised format consists of a taller mid-rise building designed to use less land. The new urban mid-rise Courtyards use an average of one-third of an acre of land, which is one-twelfth the usual size. This approach was first introduced in an eight-story, 168-room hotel in midtown Atlanta, which opened in August 1991. Marriott hopes that the mid-rise hotel design for Courtyard will allow it to offer high-quality, moderately priced rooms in urban areas as well as suburban areas. But one thing will remain constant: the new mid-rise buildings will all have courtyards, although they will be significantly smaller and will require a good deal of imagination. In a Courtyard hotel under construction in Chicago the courtyard space will be on the roof of a parking deck.

## *Technology Issues and Cooperative Arrangements*

One of the important technological trends in the hotel industry is the increasing importance of information systems. During the 1990s it is predicted that the lodging industry will make more aggressive use of information systems to strike a balance between cost efficiency and customer service. Marriott's corporate plan calls for making use of automation techniques such as a worldwide data network, a relational data base of frequent Marriott guests, and a new property management system that will encompass check-in and check-out, food and beverage sales, catering, and accounting. A recently implemented guest recognition system provides information that can be used to improve customer service. Using this system, front desk or reservation personnel can call up information about guests who have stayed at a Marriott before, allowing special rates to be automatically offered to qualifying customers such as senior citizens, and individual customer preferences to be satisfied, such as a desire for a corner or nonsmoking room.

Information technology can be combined with a form of cooperative arrangement to improve sales. Marriott, in partnership with American Airlines' AMR travel services, Hilton Hotels Corp., and Budget Rent-A-Car, developed the Confirm Central Reservation System. The object is to link services together, allowing customers to make flight, rental car, and lodging reservations with a single phone call. This helps Marriott get customers, since a customer may reserve a room with Marriott when making a reservation with American Airlines or Budget. Another form of joint venture is a hotel such as Marriott cooperating with an airline in awarding "frequent stayer" points to customers who stay at that hotel after taking a flight on the cooperating airline. The customer is thus encouraged to stay at Marriott, rather than at a competing hotel, in order to earn more points, and is likely to return in the future to earn additional points.

Marriott is investigating potential uses of new technologies for providing better customer service. In the future, customers may encounter robots being used for hotel cleaning, especially vacuuming. Computer screens are being developed that will provide information in several languages. A voice mail system is currently being tested in a Marriott in Des Moines. If voice mail is successful, it will be installed systemwide. It is important to note that Marriott tries to take advantage of existing equipment wherever possible, such as the telephone or television, in order to decrease the amount of new equipment with which the guest needs to become familiar. Another use of technology to provide better service is a check-in program being utilized at the O'Hare International Airport hotel outside of Chicago. A terminal in the courtesy van communicates via cellular phone with the information systems at the hotel. Customers can use the terminal in the courtesy van to check in and receive their room keys on the ride from the airport to the hotel. Despite the introduction of such new technologies, Marriott is relatively cautious in implementing new technologies due to the potentially confusing impact on the customer.

According to Charles L'Esperance, Marriott's senior VP of hotel systems, this is probably because "we have an extra sensitivity to its [technology's] impact on guest services."

## *Marriott's Strategic Plans*

The Courtyard by Marriott chain has been a tremendous success, with over 190 hotels in operation and over 3000 new jobs created. Predictions are for the chain to grow to 300 hotels by the mid-1990s, with sales exceeding $1 billion. Courtyard hotels have caused a major restructuring of competition in the mid-price level of the lodging industry, with the following effects: (1) older hotels in Courtyard's price range found themselves losing market share; (2) relatively new and upscale hotels located near Courtyard hotels also experienced a loss of market share and were forced to refurbish or reduce rates; and (3) at least five new clone chains have been initiated by competing hotel chains to imitate and attempt to match the success of Courtyard by Marriott. An important question is "Where does Marriott go from here?"

The answer to the question concerning Marriott's future plans has several parts. First, as discussed earlier, Marriott is expanding the Courtyard concept by developing mid-rise hotels to tap the mid-priced, urban market. Second, in 1987 Marriott bought Residence Inns to complement the Courtyard chain in the mid-priced segment of the market. Residence Inns offer customers the extra privacy and space of suites for $60 to $90 a night. Finally, in an effort to cover all the bases, Marriott has developed Marriott Suites to cater to the high end of the market, and Fairfield Inns for the low end (under $40 a night) of the market. By using its proactive strategy, Marriott continues to increase sales in a competitive industry that is overbuilt and experiencing low occupancy rates.

## *Discussion Questions*

1. Why did Marriott want to develop a chain of hotels for the mid-price market of the lodging industry?
2. What are the major factors that are considered in determining a location for a Courtyard hotel?
3. Describe Marriott's plan for "covering all the bases," or tapping different market niches or segments.
4. Briefly describe the consumer survey that was used to determine the features that would be offered in Courtyard hotels.
5. What are some of the hotel features that have been incorporated into the Courtyard by Marriott chain as a result of the consumer survey?
6. Discuss Courtyard by Marriott's "service bundle."
7. Discuss how technology can be used to improve customer service.

## *References*

Chakravarty, Subrata. "Sails Reefed," *Forbes*. November 30, 1987, pp. 110–113.

Kennedy, Carol. "How Marriott Corporation Grew Five-fold in Ten Years," *Long Range Planning*. Vol. 21, No. 2, 1988, pp. 10–14.

Lewis, Robert C., and Michael Nightingale. "Targeting Service to Your Customer," *The Cornell Hotel and Restaurant Administration Quarterly*. August 1991, pp. 18–27.

Pike, Helen. "Restoring the Personal Touch," *Computerworld*. July 30, 1990, pp. 51, 54.

Shaw, Russell. "Marriott Moves Courtyard into Franchise Mode," *Hotel and Motel Management*. January 14, 1991, pp. 1, 60.

Shaw, Russell. "Marriott Moves Courtyard into Midrise Format," *Hotel and Motel Management*. September 9, 1991, pp. 1, 77.

Taylor, John. "Don't Stop Now," *Forbes*. July 9, 1990, pp. 36–37.

Wind, Jerry, Paul E. Green, Douglas Shifflet, and Marsha Scarbrough. "Courtyard by Marriott: Designing a Hotel Facility with Consumer-Based Marketing Models," *Interfaces*. January–February 1989, pp. 25-47.

Wolf, Carlo. "Talking Tech with Marriott," *Lodging Hospitality*. June 1991, pp. 38–39.

Case 4

# Capacity Evaluation, Facilities Strategy, and Operations System Design at Elco Manufacturing

## Introduction

Bob Anderson, vice president of manufacturing at Elco Manufacturing,* could not believe his ears. This was supposed to be an informal session of the Business Planning Group (BPG), followed by a company holiday and new year social. Susan Clarke, the vice president of marketing, had just suggested the possibility of a 50% increase in exercycle demand during the second, third, and fourth quarters of next year, and a 25% increase in demand for the bench apparatus starting with the fourth quarter. All eyes shifted to Bob as the CEO, Roderick Elvington, II, said, "Well, Bob, it looks like an unparalleled opportunity. What will it take to do the job?"

"A lot of luck," Bob answered spontaneously, but, he thought, too glibly. His initial reaction to Susan Clarke's estimates was to directly challenge them. Bob felt that he had developed a rather good working relationship over the past several months with the vice president of marketing. On the basis of an improved forecasting process, he had been able to more tightly schedule his production operation and reduce inventory. Susan was aware of these cuts and had started to pass the cost savings on to major customers in the form of discounts. Why would she throw out such a surprise announcement now, and, what was worse, in front of the CEO? On second thought, Bob reasoned, Susan Clarke did not control the market forces that were deriving demand, and, if these estimates were good—and Bob had gained a great deal of respect for Susan's judgment on such matters—the

*To protect proprietary information, the company described in this case (a major industrial corporation) has requested that its name and other identifying information be changed; however, the basic relationships have been retained. This case has been prepared as a basis for class discussion rather than to illustrate either effective or ineffective management of an operational situation.

opportunities for growth were there. The questions were, simply stated, could he deliver? And at what cost?

## *Capacity Evaluation and Resource Planning*

"I guess the question revolves around capacity evaluation and resource planning. We have been operating very close to capacity on an annual basis. I expect that overtime will get us through in the short run; however, overtime is costly. That will cut into margins. I believe that for long-run operations efficiency, we will have to consider additional capacity." Bob looked around the table and saw that all eyes were looking at him with concern. He felt it would not be appropriate to go into more detail on the facilities planning alternatives at this time. That would really ruin the company holiday social.

"We will have to review various options and evaluate the costs," Bob continued. "We currently have a design capacity at the Columbus Exercycle Plant of about 3500 units per month, but, for various reasons, that drops to about 2500 units per month of actual output. With overtime, we can get about 2950 units per month. I will have to take a look at the planning alternatives in more detail and assess the effect on resource utilization and costs. Once I have some solid numbers and have had a chance to talk individually with members of the staff, I will get back to this group. Additionally, I would like to provide some initial data on facilities options. Is next week all right?"

"Fine," Roderick Elvington beamed. He appeared increasingly comfortable in his new role as the chairman of the BPG. "We will hold an ad hoc session of the BPG two weeks from this coming Thursday. That should give you all an opportunity to consider the impacts of our capacity requirements. As general guidance, the board of directors is aware of the capacity tightness, and I believe that they would be disposed to consider facility alternatives in the range of $20 million total investment. We can look at some preliminary data then. Meeting adjourned."

"Hey, that was a bolt from the blue," Bob commented to Susan Clarke as they chatted during the holiday social.

"I'm sorry, Bob," Susan said sincerely. "We got a revised market evaluation this morning, which suggests that the current downturn may be over. I did put in a call to Chavez, but apparently she didn't catch you. Also, we have discussed the sales force indications that demand appears to be increasing as a result of the discounts. However, I forgot about the costs of the second shift."

The next morning, Bob sat at his desk and considered the options. Linda Chavez, the assistant operations manager, noted the unacceptably high cost of stockouts and backorder alternatives in the very tightly integrated retail networks that they sold to. "Most of our products are labor intense," she continued. "But there are limits to the amount that we can increase the labor force through overtime or additional shifts. The second and third shifts, respectively, factor 1.15 and 1.3 of first-shift costs, based on labor cost and productivity measures. We do build ahead and hold inventory, but the warehouse gets pretty full around September. Possibly we could rent some additional storage on a short-term basis."

"You've covered most of the alternatives, but nothing seems particularly good. I think we ought to work on our capacity. We need to show that we have done everything that we can in efficiency and utilization. I'm almost positive, however, that we will need to consider a new facility. Because Elco hasn't done this before, it may take a bit of educating to convince the staff, but this would seem to be a good time to do some facilities planning. We may want to show them the data from the CNC center to emphasize just how tight the load is. But the resource plan is what we have to use to show the need for a new facility."

"Let's see what falls out of the numbers," Bob continued. "We have a design capacity for one shift of 3496 units per month, based on 2.7 labor hours per unit, one 8-hour shift, 59 workers, and 20 days per month. We lose a total of 1660 hours of production time per month through controllables such as preventive maintenance (10 hours/day), setups (8 hours/day), employee rest (30 hours/day), materials in transit (15 hours/day), and other reasons (20 hours/day). Additionally, we lose roughly 1000 production hours per month through uncontrollable reasons such as defective material (20 hours/day), machine breakdown (10 hours/day), inventory shortage (15 hours/day), and other reasons (5 hours/day). These inefficiencies reduce actual units to about 2500 per month. We'll need to significantly tighten this up by looking at the two or three most important inefficiencies."

Bob paused, noting Linda's concern. "Oh, don't worry, this one is a piece of cake. Joe will go over capacity evaluation methods with you, and he has some software that might be helpful."

## *Facilities Strategy*

Early the following week, Bob and Linda met to look at the required capacity for the milling center and the resource requirements for the final assembly operation. Bob gave Linda the results of a quick site evaluation survey that they had conducted among top management of the five possible plant sites and some center of gravity data that related the sites to district warehouse and supplier information (Table C4-1).

**TABLE C4-1**

*Site Evaluation*
*Total Weighted Factor Method*

| | | Site | | | | |
|---|---|---|---|---|---|---|
| Location Factor | Weight | Durham (14, 5) | Boston (15, 9) | Denver (6, 7) | Tampa (12, 1) | Phoenix (3, 3) |
| Road access | 0.15 | 5 | 3 | 8 | 6 | 7 |
| Community | 0.05 | 6 | 7 | 6 | 8 | 8 |
| Taxes | 0.15 | 5 | 6 | 7 | 2 | 5 |
| Labor relations | 0.30 | 4 | 7 | 5 | 5 | 5 |
| Climate | 0.05 | 7 | 3 | 5 | 8 | 9 |
| Raw materials | 0.25 | 6 | 5 | 8 | 5 | 4 |
| Recreation | 0.05 | 7 | 2 | 4 | 9 | 8 |

*Continued*

**TABLE C4-1** *Continued*

*Site Evaluation*
*Center of Gravity Method*

| | Coordinates | | |
|---|---|---|---|
| Location | X | Y | Volume |
| Warehouse A | 5 | 12 | 100 |
| Warehouse B | 8 | 5 | 150 |
| Warehouse C | 11 | 9 | 300 |
| Warehouse D | 12 | 7 | 250 |
| Supplier 1 | 2 | 5 | 400 |
| Supplier 2 | 13 | 6 | 200 |
| Supplier 3 | 8 | 1 | 50 |
| Supplier 4 | 14 | 14 | 500 |

Linda was starting to get used to the rather entrepreneurial style of her boss. She realized that in the current very tight economic environment, there were opportunities for growth and profitability, but that those opportunities would result only from productive and effective operations management.

## Production System Design

"The milling center is a good example of a facility that is fully loaded," Bob continued. "We can't just rent some more equipment and it is costly to hire skilled machinists. Outsourcing is expensive, and we are dependent upon the quality of that part for smooth operation of the gears. For those reasons, we just have to do this one in house. The use of additional shifts in the milling center, with additional labor, is probably the only alternative, at least in the short run."

"Let's see what the milling center looks like." Bob referred to the milling center load report (Table C4-2). "OK, we're final scheduled through March, though we may have to pull in a few jobs to smooth production over the late spring. A load profile report would be helpful to evaluate capacity, but at this point, I'm not sure what the impact of the 50% and 25% increases would be and when they will come. I'm also not sure that I buy Susan Clarke's 50%—let's go with 40% until we can confirm the numbers. I'll give her a call on this. Until we get better numbers, let's assume that all jobs in the second through fourth quarters are increased by 40%."

**TABLE C4-2 Load Report—CNC Milling Center**

| Job | Due Month | Number of Units | Standard | Efficiency |
|---|---|---|---|---|
| A | 2 | 3500—F* | 0.015 | 0.95 |
| B | 2 | 4000—F | 0.011 | 0.80 |
| C | 3 | 3000—F | 0.013 | 0.90 |
| D | 3 | 3500—F | 0.026 | 1.10 |
| E | 3 | 1500—F | 0.046 | 0.90 |
| F | 4 | 5200 | 0.011 | 0.95 |
| G | 4 | 8500 | 0.004 | 0.85 |
| H | 5 | 1800 | 0.024 | 0.90 |
| I | 5 | 500 | 0.052 | 0.80 |
| J | 5 | 3000 | 0.035 | 1.00 |
| K | 6 | 4000 | 0.025 | 0.90 |
| L | 7 | 1500 | 0.026 | 0.80 |
| M | 7 | 2000 | 0.091 | 1.15 |

*F = final scheduled

Available capacity: 160 hrs

"The final assembly operation is a bit different. While the milling center is machine constrained, final assembly is relatively labor intense. We might use resource evaluation techniques to look at broader and higher-level applications, such as product mix and shifting resources among operations—it is product driven, not operation driven. We have to look at the desired monthly production plan for the four models of exercycle and see what that does to the labor requirement." The information is shown in Table C4-3.

**TABLE C4-3 Resource Evaluation—Final Assembly Operations**

| Planned Production Month | 01–04 | 05–08 | 09–12 |
|---|---|---|---|
| PG A (Exercycle) | 2000 | 4300 | 6600 |
| PG B (Bench apparatus) | 1500 | 2000 | 2500 |

| Resource Requirements | Subassembly 1 | Subassembly 2 | Final Assembly |
|---|---|---|---|
| Product group A | | | |
| Month 1 demand | 2000 | 2000 | 2000 |
| Average assembly time | 0.628 | 0.362 | 0.307 |
| Required capacity | | | |
| Product group B | | | |
| Month 1 demand | 1500 | 1500 | 1500 |
| Average assembly time | 0.552 | 0.384 | 0.296 |
| Required capacity | | | |
| Total capacity required | | | |
| Efficiency | 0.950 | 0.900 | 1.050 |
| Production plan | | | |
| Number of units of labor | 10 | 8 | 5 |
| Available capacity | | | |
| Short (+ = short) | | | |

After Linda had reviewed the data, Bob continued. "Susan Clarke also stated that, with the upturn in the economy, the demand for higher-cost units would increase; thus, we may want to change our product mix for exercycle products 1 (high end) through 4 from 0.20, 0.40, 0.30, and 0.10 to 0.25, 0.45, 0.20, and 0.10. The standard assembly times for final assembly are respectively 0.274, 0.357, 0.298, and 0.321. We need to show current projected requirements, and then see what that 40% increase in demand that is projected by marketing does to us."

"Well, do you think that you can carry the briefing from here?" Bob asked.

"All right, I'll try," Linda responded. "But I expect you to back me up on any surprises. After what Susan Clarke did to you, I am not sure that I trust any of those people."

"I agree, that forecast may have been out of left field," Bob acknowledged. "But, given that Susan may not yet have a clear sense of how we operate and, taken from a marketing perspective, it was perfectly reasonable for her to want to mention new demand and to relay a success story toward the end of the year. Remember, when a marketing person says 'indication' they may be quite confident, but we in manufacturing like to confirm such market swings. Unfortunately, people tend to stay in the confines of their discipline or job. Successful operations management involves integrating several functional areas into a solid team."

The next day, Bob and Linda met to discuss the financial data. "We need to show that the expansion is a secure investment and that it gives a reasonable rate of return. I expect that Junior's estimate of what the board will accept is rather close to the mark. You can use the corporate assumptions of 10% net present value rate and 40% tax rate, though Virginia Thompson in Finance may have some new tables. Another thing: It just may be worth our trouble to consider leasing some equipment, rather than buying it. You may want to develop some numbers like these for the roughly six million dollars' worth of equipment that we will need" (Table C4-4).

**TABLE C4-4 Elco Industries—Equipment Evaluation: Financial Analysis of Alternatives ($000)**

| | Cost of Leasing | | Cost of Ownership | | |
|---|---|---|---|---|---|
| Year | Lease Cost | Tax Advantage | Maintenance Cost | Depreciation | |
| 0 | 600 | 240 | | | Purchase |
| 1 | 600 | 240 | 150 | 1500 | price: |
| 2 | 600 | 240 | 150 | 1200 | 6000 |
| 3 | 600 | 240 | 150 | 900 | Salvage |
| 4 | 600 | 240 | 150 | 600 | value: |
| 5 | | | 150 | 300 | 1500 |

| Year | Sales | Costs |
|---|---|---|
| 1 | 4,000 | 5500 |
| 2 | 6,000 | 5500 |
| 3 | 8,500 | 5000 |
| 4 | 10,000 | 4500 |
| 5 | 12,000 | 4000 |
| 6 | 13,000 | 5000 |
| 7 | 13,000 | 6000 |
| 8 | 14,000 | 6000 |

## *Discussion Questions*

1. Why should the operations manager be somewhat skeptical of a surge in demand projected by marketing? What actions should the operations manager take to minimize the impact of such surprises?

2. If a surge in demand projected by the marketing department were to occur, what would be the potential effects on manufacturing? How should manufacturing respond?

3. To what degree should the manufacturing manager contribute to top-level management discussions on capacity and resource planning, facilities strategy, and operations system design? What contributions to these discussions would you expect from other functional staff members? What contributions to these discussions would you expect from the operations management staff?

4. How does the work station load report help the operations manager identify problems and resolve those problems before they occur?

5. Given the current load report and that jobs scheduled for delivery through month 3 are final-scheduled, what techniques would you use to adjust production schedules to smooth capacity?

6. Evaluate the effect of the product mix change on the required resource in subassembly 1, subassembly 2, and final assembly operations.

7. Describe how resource evaluation is a more inclusive evaluation process than is capacity management.

8. The CEO, Roderick Elvington II, called and indicated that he placed a high premium on the factors of climate and community. For that reason, he suggested that the weight structure noted in Table C4-1 be revised to road access, 0.05; community, 0.20; taxes, 0.10; labor relations, 0.15; climate, 0.25; raw materials, 0.15; and recreation, 0:10. What reaction do you have to the CEO's weighting structure?

9. What are the advantages and limitations of the site analysis and financial analysis suggested by Tables C4-1 and C4-4?

## *Computer Assignment*

1. *Capacity evaluation.* What are the present and projected required and available capacity, considering the design, effective and actual capacity, efficiency, and utilization? In order of priority, identify three actions that the operations manager should take to improve efficiency and utilization.

2. *Resource evaluation.* What is the effect of the 40% increase in volume, both of the milling center and the final assembly operation? How should the operations manager consider handling these situations?

3. *Site alternatives.* Which sites would appear to be better? What weight structure should be suggested, given the nature of the product?

4. *Site financing.* How should the new facility, if needed, be financed? What are the considerations under which the firm would be neutral between the leasing and owning of equipment?

# Part III

# Infrastructure Considerations of Operations Strategy

**Chapter 8**
*Operations Planning*

**Chapter 9**
*Improving Materials Management*

**Chapter 10**
*Just-in-Time*

**Chapter 11**
*Quality and Customer Service Management*

**Chapter 12**
*Productivity and Work Force Management*

**Case 5**
*Motorola—In Pursuit of Six Sigma Quality*

**Case 6**
*Operations, Inventory, and Quality Planning at Elco Manufacturing*

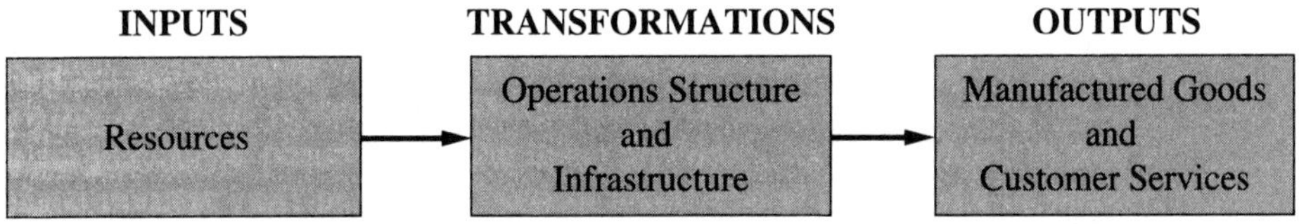
INPUTS
Resources
TRANSFORMATIONS
Operations Structure
and
Infrastructure
OUTPUTS
Manufactured Goods
and
Customer Services

# Chapter 8

# Operations Planning

*Decisions exist only in the present. The question that faces the long-range planner is not what we should do tomorrow. It is what we have to do today to be ready for an uncertain tomorrow. The question is not what will happen in the future. It is: what futurity do we have to factor into our present thinking and doing, what time span do we have to consider, and how do we converge them to a simultaneous decision in the present?*
—Peter Drucker

*The production plan is the "regulator." It regulates the amount of inventory or backlog that will exist by controlling the production rate. It regulates the amount of material that will be made and purchased because the master schedules, the material requirements plans, and the capacity plans are all derived from it. It regulates the level of work-in-process because it drives the master schedules and material requirements plans that release work into the factory. Because it is the regulator for all these activities, it regulates cash flow and is the foundation for the business plan.* —Oliver Wight

## Objectives

After completing this chapter you should be able to:

- Understand the importance of effective operations planning.
- Describe the interactions of operations planning with other plans.
- Identify the inputs to operations planning.
- List the options available to manage supply and demand.
- Discuss various operations planning strategies.
- Explain the concept of hierarchical planning systems.

## Outline



## Introductory Case: Operations Planning at Owens-Corning Fiberglas

Owens-Corning Fiberglas (OCF) is the world's leading producer of glass fiber products. The Anderson plant in South Carolina, one of OCF's largest manufacturing facilities, produces a large number of fiberglass mat products. The mat product line consists of over 200 distinct items sold in a variety of widths, weights, binder treatments, and edge trimmings. Mat products are used primarily in the construction of boat hulls, as a reinforcement in pipeline construction, and in bathroom fixtures such as bathtubs and showers.

In 1982, OCF implemented a computer-based model to address production planning and scheduling decisions at its Anderson plant. Since the initial development of this model, major advances in manufacturing and information systems and a drastic corporate reorganization have occurred. In 1986, OCF reorganized management and decentralized both customer service and information management functions. These forces have individually contributed to a dramatic change in production planning within OCF.

Owens-Corning Fiberglas uses the production switching rule (PSR), a heuristic procedure to develop production plans, because mathematical models tend to be too complex. The PSR has five shift settings from which production for a planning period can be selected. Management's preference to reduce the effects of work-force changes explains why the number of shift settings allowed over the entire planning horizon is limited to five. The fiberglass mat is manufactured on two production lines, each with different capacities and capabilities. Each line can be scheduled to run on four shifts. Three normal shifts are provided by working three eight-hour periods from Monday to Friday. A "fourth" shift represents the weekend shift, and 0 represents shutdown.

The fiberglass mat products can be aggregated easily into pounds. The time period is one month and the planning horizon is twelve months. Forecasted demand is provided by the marketing department. A production plan is generated every month when new information becomes available. In developing production plans, the PSR attempts to minimize the total of payroll costs, overtime costs, hiring and firing costs, and inventory costs in satisfying forecasted demand. An example of OCF's production plan showing the shift settings for the two production lines, the projected monthly aggregate ending inventories, and various cost elements is provided in the table.

**Production Plan at OCF**

| Period | Demand (lb)[1] | Production (lb)[1] | Inventory (lb)[1] | Shift Setting[2] | Regular Wages ($) | Hiring Cost ($) | Layoff Cost ($) | Inventory Cost ($) | Total Cost ($) |
|---|---|---|---|---|---|---|---|---|---|
| Jan. | 132 | 100 | 152 | (3, 0) | 90,000 | 0 | 0 | 20,400 | 110,400 |
| Feb. | 124 | 140 | 168 | (4, 0) | 120,000 | 12,000 | 0 | 23,600 | 155,600 |
| Mar. | 155 | 140 | 153 | (4, 0) | 120,000 | 0 | 0 | 20,600 | 140,600 |
| Apr. | 187 | 155 | 121 | (4, 1) | 130,000 | 7,000 | 0 | 14,200 | 151,200 |
| May | 174 | 170 | 117 | (4, 2) | 140,000 | 7,000 | 0 | 13,400 | 160,400 |
| Jun. | 194 | 170 | 93 | (4, 2) | 140,000 | 0 | 0 | 9,300 | 149,300 |
| Jul. | 169 | 170 | 94 | (4, 2) | 140,000 | 0 | 0 | 9,400 | 149,400 |
| Aug. | 132 | 155 | 117 | (4, 1) | 130,000 | 0 | 3,000 | 13,400 | 146,400 |
| Sep. | 151 | 155 | 121 | (4, 1) | 130,000 | 0 | 0 | 14,200 | 144,200 |
| Oct. | 167 | 155 | 109 | (4, 1) | 130,000 | 0 | 0 | 11,800 | 141,800 |
| Nov. | 97 | 140 | 152 | (4, 0) | 120,000 | 0 | 3,000 | 20,400 | 143,400 |
| Dec. | 140 | 140 | 152 | (4, 0) | 120,000 | 0 | 0 | 20,400 | 140,400 |
| Total | | | | | 1,510,000 | 26,000 | 6,000 | 191,000 | 1,733,100 |

Materials drawn from: Oliff and Burch (1985); Oliff and Leong (1987); and Leong, Oliff, and Markland (1989).

[1]Beginning inventory in January = 184. Beginning shift setting = (3, 0).

[2]$(i, j) = i$ is the number of shifts on line 1, and $j$ is the number of shifts on line 2.

Values for inventory, production, and demand are in 10,000 pounds.

A minimum aggregate inventory level of 900,000 pounds must be held in stock.

## Operations Planning

Operations planning links top management's strategic plans with manufacturing or service operations. We use operations planning to refer generically to production planning in manufacturing firms and staff planning in service organizations. A production plan attempts to set production, work-force, and inventory levels to meet sales objectives while minimizing manufacturing costs and effectively utilizing limited organizational resources over a specified planning horizon. A staff plan determines the work-force level and labor-related capacities that can satisfy customer demand by utilizing limited organizational resources over a specified planning horizon. Effective operations planning allows an organization to balance the sometimes conflicting objectives of maximizing customer service, maintaining a stable production or work-force level, minimizing inventory investment, and maximizing profits.

In today's highly competitive environment, delivering the right goods or services at the right time and in the right quantities to the customer at minimum cost requires a smooth flow of operations and information. The development of an effective operations planning and control system to support this flow can enhance customer service and provide a firm with a competitive advantage. An operations planning framework is presented in Figure 8-1. The objectives of operations planning are derived from the operations strategy interacting with the key functional areas of marketing, finance, and human resources. The overall objective for the company is to combine the inputs from all functional areas in order to maximize profits. Plant and equipment are considered fixed in the time period for operations planning. In the long run, operations planning provides the input for resource planning, involving the acquisition of new equipment, expansion of the existing facility, or construction of a new facility (see Chapter 6). Therefore, operations planning has strategic implications for allocating corporate resources such as materials, equipment, facilities, personnel, and money. The operations plan presents a broad framework for performing specific activities. For manufacturing, a master production schedule is developed which is consistent with the operations plan. In the case of service organizations, the operations plan is disaggregated into a master schedule or work-force schedule. Exact specification of time and work activity in which the operation is to be performed are not the concern of the operations plan. Such details are left to operations sequencing and dispatching, which are performed when more accurate and reliable data are available.

Drucker (1959, p. 239) explains that planning allows us to do things today "to be ready for an uncertain tomorrow." The operations plan helps management to focus attention on potential problems in advance. Discovering a problem after it has occurred is too late and is worrisome to management. Many manufacturing problems can be traced to operating in a "reactionary" or "fire-fighting" mode. For example, in response to delays in delivery, many companies hire expeditors to draw up shortage lists and focus on "hot jobs." Expediting seldom works because by pulling these "hot jobs" through the plant, other jobs are neglected. Additional setups are incurred, which compound the capacity and scheduling problem in the shop. Soon more jobs are added to the shortage list and more expeditors are needed to handle the increased number of "hot jobs." Work-in-process inventories are piled up all over the floor waiting for processing, and customer service suffers. By focusing only on expeditors to get jobs out through the door, companies can

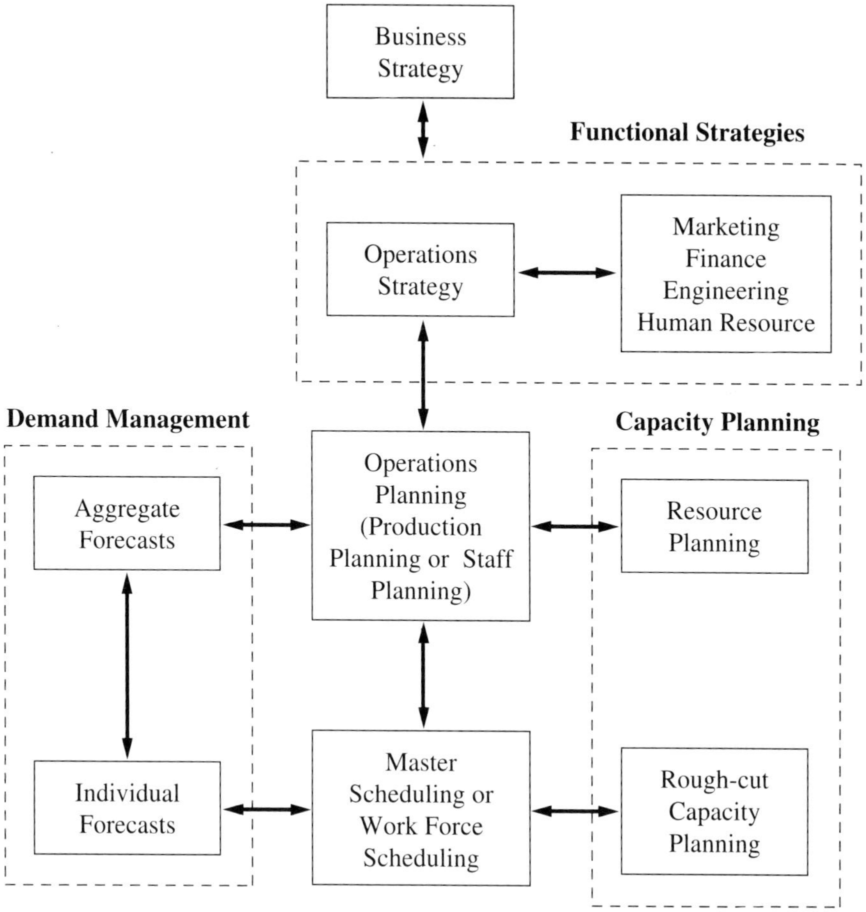


**FIGURE 8-1 Operations Planning Framework**

get trapped in a vicious cycle. An effective operations plan that attempts to match supply with demand will help management avoid these pitfalls.

Although operations planning is used in a majority of businesses, it is often an informal and incomplete process. As Oliver Wight (1974) notes, "Whether they explicitly recognize it or not, most companies establish some kind of production plan." While this is commendable, it is not enough in today's competitive environment. Without a formal system in place, an informal system will evolve to overcome inconsistencies and eventually get the job done. However, the operations plan is achieved at a price: increased organizational slack. Organizational slack is defined as anything that is in excess of what is effectively needed to get the job completed. Symptoms of organizational slack are excess inventories, excess workers, excess overtime costs, excess capacity, long lead times, and long new-product-introduction cycles. Examples of early warning signs of poor operations planning include:

- Marketing is complaining that the right quantities of the right products are not being produced at the right time, and wants an increase in inventories to prevent lost sales.
- Finance is unhappy about the high inventory levels and wants them reduced because of the high cost incurred.
- Purchasing is frustrated that numerous production schedule changes require frequent rescheduling of vendor shipments.
- Marketing cannot comprehend why manufacturing is not producing items in closer alignment with the sales forecast.
- Manufacturing is unhappy with the short, inefficient production runs necessitated by the product mix and quantities specified in the production schedule. Numerous additional machine setups are made, which are time consuming and costly.
- Manufacturing is asking for more expeditors to go after the "hot jobs," which are fast becoming "superhot jobs."
- Quality is being sacrificed to get jobs out to meet delivery dates.
- Evidence of a highly charged emotional environment includes severe tension and pressure in the last week of the month and numerous incidences of finger-pointing.
- Unplanned overtime costs are high.

Operations planning, if implemented successfully, can lead to numerous benefits, such as improved productivity and customer service levels, decreased expediting, and reduced setup and inventory costs. For example, in the early 1980s, Bendix Corporation implemented operations planning at all its manufacturing facilities. Benefits reported were the following: productivity at a European subsidiary improved by 9% and inventory turnover increased by 30% in three years; favorable investment ratios were maintained at a domestic subsidiary, even though customer orders decreased by 30%; customer service was improved at a Canadian subsidiary with a reduction of inventories of $4 million within the first year of implementation (Wantuck, 1989).

## *Functional Interface*

The operations plan provides a direct channel for consistent discussion and communication between manufacturing and top management as well as with other functions. An integrated approach to operations planning is the only way to ensure that all parties agree to one plan and that the operations manager can be held responsible for meeting the plan. A well-documented operations plan can help alleviate fear of the future and resistance to change. Using a comprehensive approach to operations planning can lead to the discovery of previously unknown inefficiencies. In the quest to achieve overall strategic goals, the collaborative approach with its "no stones left unturned" philosophy can spawn new ideas that could be used to improve the system's operations. In addition, a realistic and achievable operations plan discourages informal systems and suboptimal minimeetings from developing, and consequently, less time is spent in hand-wringing and second-guessing the plan. While it is desirable to have stability so that operations can justly be held responsible for meeting plans, there should be sufficient flexibility for the company to respond to actual customer requirements. What is needed is an overall, dynamic plan for the company which changes according to market conditions and at the same time allows each function to adapt accordingly.

An integrated approach is needed because functional conflicts often arise in meeting overall business strategic goals. The operations plan must be supportive of the operations and business strategies as well as the bottom line. For example, a company's objective is to produce "high-quality, customized products, with dependable delivery performance." Customization requires producing goods or services to customers' specifications, which in turn necessitates that operating processes be sufficiently flexible to accommodate the diversity of these requirements. The operations plan must be designed to consider all these factors to enable deliveries to be met and permit the company to be profitable. Several important areas of potential disagreements among different functions within an organization and their impact on the operations plan are discussed below. Shapiro (1977) provides a good discussion on potential conflicts between marketing and manufacturing.

### *Capacity*

Capacity is at the heart of the operations plan (see also Chapter 5). The classic trade-off is between having too much capacity and too little capacity. Either way, management is not going to be happy, and for different reasons. Insufficient capacity can lead to lost sales, and excess capacity can be costly. The issue of capacity is very important to operations planning. Given a choice, operations would prefer to work with excess capacity, since it is easier to schedule jobs and meet promised deliveries. Making significant changes to a plant's capacity is a long-term proposition involving capital investments. Therefore, marketing must provide accurate demand forecasts to ensure that capacity and facilities plans can be made effectively.

### *On-time Delivery*

On-time delivery is a major bone of contention between marketing and operations. The operations plan provides the basis for trade-offs and dialogue between marketing and operations. For example, if marketing requests to have some products or services delivered earlier than planned, operations would in turn require marketing to take delivery of some other products or services at a later time. This is the only possible outcome if capacity is constrained and cannot be increased easily. Without a new, revised operations plan, marketing and operations must work closely together to maximize the utilization of scarce resources to meet competing needs. Some companies resort to expediting to resolve delivery problems. Expediting basically implies that one customer is more important than another. Such a near-sighted policy seldom works in the long run. When sales are booming, the loss of sales from small customers is not considered critical by management. However, in periods of economic downturn, every customer, small or big, becomes extremely important as the company tries to maintain sales. The industry is marked by excess capacity as demand falls. Customers previously "spurned" in terms of delivery may be lost forever because they can shop elsewhere for better service. On-time delivery requires objectives regarding lead times to be defined clearly and understood by all parties involved. Reductions in setup time allow more productive utilization of equipment and can help simplify operations scheduling and reduce lead times. Setup reduction is an important element of just-in-time systems, which will be discussed in Chapter 10.

### *Inventory Levels*

Marketing may want to hold inventories at various distribution centers to provide fast delivery time, especially for make-to-stock products. Customers expect a high probability that their orders will be filled immediately from inventory for make-to-stock products. Management must decide the level of inventory needed and the financial budget that can support this investment. The operations plan is designed to reflect these objectives. Several operations plans with varying levels of inventory can be generated so that management can examine the cost trade-offs among the alternatives before deciding on the appropriate plan to achieve the strategic goals.

### *Breadth of Product/Service Line*

Marketing strategies regarding the breadth of a product/service line, the number of product or service variations, and the product or service mix have major implications for operations planning. A change in product or service mix could result in different processing requirements and cause capacity and scheduling problems, even though the total number of units produced or customers served could be the same. Purchasing would have to adjust orders for raw materials and parts. Trying to produce too many products or services in one facility could lead to a loss of focus. (A detailed discussion of "focused facilities" is provided in Chapter 6.) Operations planning allows problems associated with these strategies to be openly discussed so that attention can be focused on what needs to be done. For example, in 1986 Cummins Engine's sales catalog offered more than 100,000 parts (Venkatesan, 1990). In addition, in one engine family, there were 86 different flywheels, 49 flywheel options, and 17 types of starter motors with 12 possible mountings. Based on these options, there were approximately 1200 assembly combinations. Federal emissions regulations and intense competition from companies such as Komatsu and Caterpillar forced Cummins to introduce new products and be more responsive to the customers' needs. At the same time Cummins had to manufacture parts for discontinued products for existing customers. The result is a proliferation of parts and products. Cummins had to cut prices 20–40% in order to retain its market share. Senior management asked the factory to reduce costs and lead time, which meant that work in process had to be reduced at the time the factory was trying to cope with an increase in the number of parts produced.

### *New Product/Service Introductions*

New product/service introductions have major implications for operations and purchasing and should be included in the operations plan. While demand for new products/services should be a part of the marketing forecast, there may be marketing objectives regarding design changes on existing products/services. There is also the timing of new product/service introduction and the impact on existing capacity. Problems inherently present in new product/service introductions take more time to iron out, which can have an impact on process utilization. Engineering should interact with operations regarding processing requirements, time standards, quality levels, and the like. Purchasing input is required as to the availability of materials. An important question is whether the production of low-volume new products should be mixed in with the production of mature products that require high-volume production runs.

The interface with other plans allows potential problem areas to be identified and discussed so that operations can play a more *proactive* role instead of reacting to problems as they occur. Inputs from various functional areas to the operations planning process are summarized in Figure 8-2.

## *Influencing Supply and Demand*

If demand is constant, solving the operations planning problem is an easy task. However, companies are often faced with turbulent and seasonal demand. To deal with seasonal demand, companies may initially attempt to stabilize aggregate demand. After all efforts to stabilize demand have been made, various techniques to affect the supply through short-term adjustments to capacity can be used to meet demand.

**FIGURE 8-2 Operations Planning Inputs**

## Controlling Demand

There are several ways to control or influence demand, such as the use of complementary products/services, flexible pricing, promotions and advertising, reservations, and flexible delivery dates. Although managing demand is important to manufacturing, it is even more critical in service organizations, especially those offering a service bundle with a low percentage of facilitating goods.* The reason is that the build up of inventory in slack periods may not be a viable option.

### Complementary Products and Services

By providing complementary products or services, companies can even out the seasonal impact on existing capacities. Usually, manufacturers consider adding products that require similar processes. A manufacturer of snow blowers may want to build lawn mowers to balance aggregate demand. Manufacturers of air conditioners have developed heat pumps, which function as heaters in winter and provide air conditioning in summer. Demand for heat pumps should be less cyclical than demand for air conditioners only. However, companies must be cautious as they expand their market activities lest their facilities become unfocused, an issue discussed in Chapter 6.

Many busy restaurants now provide lounges with television sets where customers can sit and have a drink while waiting their turns at the dining tables. In addition to fewer complaints from customers about waiting in line, restaurants derive additional profits from the lounge. Fast-food restaurants are offering breakfast to complement lunch and dinner, and to increase the use of cooking facilities. After McDonald's introduced its breakfast services, Burger King was slow to respond, because the broilers used for meat patties were not suitable for preparing eggs. Burger King eventually overcame this problem and expanded into the breakfast market.

### Flexible Pricing

The objective of flexible pricing is to even out demand by reducing peak demand or to increase demand during "down" periods. Prices are raised during peak periods to discourage heavy demand and lowered to increase sales during off-peak periods. Examples include higher rates charged by electrical power utilities in summer to lower the use of air conditioning; heavily discounted tickets requiring a Saturday night stayover offered by airlines to attract nonbusiness travelers; discount prices for matinee shows; "happy hours" at bars; and differential rates offered by telephone companies which favor calling during evenings, weekends, and holidays. Golf courses often charge lower "winter" greens fees to prolong the golf season. Manufacturers facing seasonal demand generally give discounts for early season delivery of goods.

### Promotions and Advertising

The use of flexible pricing is closely coordinated with promotions and advertising. Advertising can be used to stimulate sales by offering discounted prices during nonpeak

*The service bundle consists of supporting facility, facilitating goods, explicit services, and implicit services. Facilitating goods are defined as "material purchased or consumed by the buyer" (Fitzsimmons and Sullivan, 1982, p. 17). The term "facilitating goods" was suggested by John Rathmell in *Marketing in the Service Sector* (Cambridge, Mass.: Winthrop Publishers, 1974).

or low-demand periods. Airlines heavily advertise their cheap winter fares to encourage nonbusiness travelers to fly instead of driving to their final destinations or to make additional trips because of affordable ticket prices. Sales promotions are advertised so that customers are made aware of the upcoming event. Ski resorts publicize the availability of snow machines to generate artificial snow on the ski slopes. This lets customers know in advance that their ski vacation is less dependent on nature to provide the snow needed for skiing. Thus snow machines allow demand to be spread over a longer season instead of concentrating demand on heavy snowfall days.

### *Reservations and Flexible Delivery Dates*

Customers are often asked to make appointments in advance to reserve capacity. This option allows the organization to match supply and demand as closely as possible. Appointments are common in service organizations such as medical practitioners, auto repair shops, law firms, airlines, and hotels. Although the reservation system has its merits, "no-shows" by customers not financially responsible for such actions have resulted in inefficient use of capacity and lost profits. Airlines have been known to overbook their capacities to compensate for no-shows and run the risk of alienating their customers. A customer who is "bumped" from a reserved seat is typically compensated by the airline with a free ticket to any destination in the continental United States. Airlines have also introduced nonrefundable, advanced purchase supersaver tickets targeted at nonbusiness travelers with inflexible departure and return flight dates and times. Customers are penalized for any changes made to confirmed flight schedules. Most hotels now require a one-night prepaid room charge for reservations made by the customers, but the down payment is refundable if cancellation is made at least one day in advance.

Sometimes customers are asked to wait for products that are not immediately available, which results in a back-order situation. When back orders occur, two things can happen. One scenario is the customer is mildly annoyed at the poor service but is willing to wait and there is an additional cost involved for the company to keep track of the order. This scenario, although costing the company a little, is much better than the second scenario in which the customer is lost. The cost of lost sales is much harder to assess but generally involves loss of goodwill and future sales and, therefore, future profits. Back orders allow production to be postponed to a period where slack capacity is available.

## *Controlling Supply*

In addition to the previous short-term techniques to affect demand, there are several short-term alternatives for affecting supply. These are hiring and layoffs, undertime and overtime, temporary and part-time workers, inventory, subcontracting, cooperative arrangements, and consumer participation.

### *Hiring and Layoffs*

When operations are labor intensive, changes in the work-force level can have an impact on the capacity. The ability to hire more workers is sometimes limited by other resources such as the availability of equipment that supports the workers. Also, some equipment requires a minimum number of workers to operate, thus placing a lower limit on the work-force level needed to maintain operations. Sometimes a second shift can be added. The disadvantages of a second shift are the difficulties associated with finding workers willing to work shifts and the generally lower productivity during the second or third shifts. In addition, union agreements may have an impact on hiring and layoff policies. Workers with more years of service may not be laid off ahead of newer employees; that is, layoffs follow the "last in first out" policy.

There are costs associated with hiring and layoff of workers. The costs of hiring new employees are costs of advertising, screening, interviewing, medical examinations, employment agency fees, company visitations, and training. Some localities have a severe shortage of skilled workers. This situation requires newly hired workers to go through an expensive training program. Newly trained workers may take several months to get up to speed and be fully productive. Frequent turnover of personnel can have a negative influence on the work force in terms of morale and negative feelings, which could result in a loss of productivity. Workers who are laid off are compensated on the basis of seniority and years of service with the company. Intangible effects such as poor public relations and image of the company in the community are more difficult to estimate. Instead of using layoffs, some companies offer attractive early retirement packages to trim the work-force size. In the auto industry, job security is now becoming an important issue because of the high level of layoffs arising from excess auto plant capacities. In 1990, the UAW negotiated an agreement that pays hefty compensations for workers laid off as a result of plants that are permanently closed.

Companies must be careful not to have highly erratic employment levels. In general, employees are more willing and feel more secure working for companies that maintain stable employment levels. The benefits of a stable work force include higher employee morale and increased company loyalty, both of which can have a significant impact on productivity and quality levels. The Japanese believe in a system of lifetime employment, where employees are retrained for new jobs if no longer needed in their current jobs. This system encourages worker loyalty; it is discussed in greater depth in Chapter 10.

### *Undertime and Overtime*

This alternative is one of the most common approaches to altering capacity. This approach can be easily and quickly implemented when compared to the hiring/layoff decision. Workers find overtime especially attractive, since they have an opportunity to earn more money. Manufacturers frequently use overtime to make up shortfalls in capacity. The company can maintain a stable work force and develop long-term relationships with its employees, which can lead to a loyal and productive work force.

On the down side, excessive overtime can cause worker fatigue, which can lead to poor performance, poor quality, and increased accidents. In addition, higher payroll costs are incurred, since a premium (50% to 100% of regular wages) is paid for overtime work. Union rules may permit workers to reject overtime work, making it difficult for a company to pull together a crew to work a production line after regular hours.

Undertime means that workers and equipment are not fully utilized; this situation is expensive to maintain for long periods of time. During periods of slow demand, workers may be asked to do housekeeping around their work area and routine maintenance.

Workers can also be provided with additional training to acquire new skills or improve current ones. The assumption is that workers are being paid their regular wages during undertime. Increasingly, we are seeing companies temporarily idling facilities in periods of low demand. Workers get little or no compensation during the time off but retain benefits such as health insurance, a situation that is better than being laid off permanently. This happens more frequently in industries where there is excess capacity and production is carried out in shifts. Chrysler, Ford, and General Motors have temporarily closed plants in an effort to match supply with demand. Government and state employees have been forced to stay home without pay for short periods of time, lasting from several days to a couple of weeks, to balance the budget.

### *Temporary and Part-Time Workers*

Depending on the level of training and skill needed, the use of temporary or part-time workers is an attractive and practical option. Temporary workers are often paid less and receive few or no benefits. The use of temporary workers is applicable to industries with highly seasonal demand and especially to service-related industries, such as department stores, fast-food restaurants, supermarkets, farms, recreational parks, and hotels. Post offices rely heavily on temporary workers during the Christmas season. Most worker unions are opposed to the hiring of temporary workers and typically build this provision into the collective agreements with their companies. The reason is that temporary workers do not pay any union dues and may actually diminish the influence of the union. The success of this option is dependent on the availability of a steady pool of temporary workers from which a company can hire at short notice. Students looking for part-time or summer work are a primary source of temporary workers.

There are several trends regarding the use of temporary and part-time workers worth noting here (Pollock and Bernstein, 1986):

1. The percentage of part-time workers in the airline industry has more than doubled since 1983, to 12% of employees.
2. "Contingent" workers account for 25% of the total work force.
3. Over 40% of jobs in the retail industry are filled by part-time workers.
4. The number of "telecommuters" who use technologies such as telephones, fax machines, and computers to stay in touch with the office while working at home has increased 400% since 1980.
5. A 10% to 15% annual growth in the number of temporary workers is anticipated to continue through the mid-1990s.

In addition to the above observations, the federal government has been allowed to hire temporary workers since 1989.

An example of a company that relies heavily on part-time workers is Tuesday Morning Inc., a retailing chain that specializes in upscale, limited quantity, closeout merchandise such as gifts and household items. The stores are open only four times a year for several months, yet the business is profitable. In 1990, annual sales totaled $107 million with net income of $4.7 million. Currently, there are 150 stores located in 22 states (mostly in the South), but plans are underway to expand throughout the United States to reach a target of 250 stores by 1995. Because the stores are open less than half a year, Tuesday Morning hires entirely part-time workers to staff the stores, except for store managers (Helliker, 1991).

The use of part-time workers is not without its drawbacks. Sears, in an effort to keep labor costs as low as possible, shifted its sales-force composition from 70% full-time employees to 70% part-timers. In the short term, this strategy led to aggregate wages and benefits being reduced significantly. The long-term effects are an increasing rate of employee turnover and a drastic drop in customer satisfaction (Schlesinger and Heskett, 1991).

#### *Inventory*

A company can use inventories to buffer production from seasonal demand. Inventories include raw materials, work in process, finished parts, assemblies, and finished goods. Because demand in peak periods exceeds the available capacity of a plant, inventories are built up in earlier periods when capacity exceeds demand to enable high demands in later periods to be met. Reasons for not holding excess inventories are discussed in more detail in Chapter 9. Obviously, the use of inventories is more applicable to manufacturing organizations, where goods can be stored, than to service organizations, where services (excluding facilitating goods) are not storable.

#### *Subcontracting*

Subcontracting is an effective method for a company to acquire temporary capacity. Problems associated with subcontracting are higher costs and less control over delivery and quality. The expertise of the subcontractor is an important consideration. If the facility's capacity cannot be increased without substantial investment and demand is not stable, subcontracting may be a viable approach. In manufacturing, a gear box producer may subcontract gears during peak demand periods. Many small and mid-size companies find it cost effective to subcontract janitorial services. The health-care industry makes extensive use of outside contract services such as food catering, laundry, and housekeeping. The contract management business in hospitals is expected to double to more than $8 billion a year by the mid-1990s. Hospitals are even subcontracting specialized services. For example, Psicor contracts with hospitals to provide equipment and supplies for open-heart surgery.

#### *Cooperative Arrangements*

This option is similar to subcontracting except that business could go either way. Hotels have been known to make arrangements where "overbooked" customers during peak holiday seasons are transferred to another hotel in the cooperating group. Power utility companies "buy" electricity from each other, depending on their ability to meet demand fluctuations. Aluminum manufacturers commonly "swap" customer contracts with each other to balance supply and demand. Customers receive their orders directly from the company to which their contracts have been swapped and not from the company where the original order was placed. This arrangement saves double handling and transportation costs, which could be passed on to the customers. Cooperative arrangements are more likely in industries where capacities have to be added in big chunks and which involve high capital investments.

***Consumer Participation***

This option is particularly applicable to the service industries. By transferring a portion of the service to the customer, the labor requirements for the delivery of services are reduced. Examples include self-service salad bars, self-service gas pumps, and self-bagging of groceries. Manufacturers are also taking advantage of increased customer participation by transferring parts of the assembly process to the customers. For example, bicycles, knock-down furniture, and gas grills are sold unassembled in cartons. By requiring customers to assemble the product, manufacturers can use their existing labor for other critical activities. Companies also benefit from lower packaging and transportation costs, because the unassembled products are less bulky. The use of this approach assumes that the assembly required is not complicated and customers can put the pieces together correctly by following the enclosed instructions. The downside risk is that customers are not adept at handling the assembly tasks and could be sufficiently frustrated to return the product for a full refund or exchange the product for another because they damaged the product during assembly.

## *Operations Planning Strategies*

The two basic strategies are level strategy and chase strategy. A comparison of these two strategies in terms of various characteristics is summarized in Table 8-1. In addition, an infinite range of compromise strategies may be selected from different combinations of the pure chase and level alternatives.

### *Level Strategy*

A level strategy involves setting a constant output rate or maintaining a stable work force. In manufacturing companies, a constant output is achieved by using a steady work force and by allowing inventories to absorb fluctuations in demand. An example of a level strategy for a manufacturing firm is presented in Decision Model Box 8-1. Because

**TABLE 8-1 Comparison of Chase and Level Strategies**

| | Chase Strategy | Level Strategy |
|---|---|---|
| Inventory costs | negligible (safety stock only) | high |
| Labor skill level | low | high |
| Job discretion | low | high |
| Quality of life | low | high |
| Worker compensation | low | high |
| Training per worker | low | high |
| Labor turnover rate | high | low |
| Hiring/layoff costs | high | negligible (attrition only) |
| Quality costs and problems | high | low |
| Supervision required | high | low |
| Capacity change costs | high | none |
| Forecasting requirements | short run | long run |

## DECISION MODEL BOX 8-1 Operations Planning at Lin Steel Company

The Lin Steel Company, a manufacturer of steel wires, is faced with cyclic demand for its products. The table below shows a monthly aggregate demand forecast for the next year. The following data have been collected. The production rate is 100 tons per worker per month. The average salary for a production worker is $2000 per month. Overtime is reimbursed at 150% of regular salary. Workers are limited to 25% overtime per month. The cost of hiring an additional worker is $800. Laying off a worker costs $1200. There is presently no inventory in stock. Inventory holding cost is $2 per ton per month. The inventory at the end of each month is calculated as: Ending inventory = beginning inventory + production – demand. All forecasted demand must be met; that is, no backorders are allowed.

Lin Steel wants to generate a production plan for the next 12 months to utilize its resources more effectively and to provide better customer service. Michelle, the materials manager, has been asked to prepare three alternatives for evaluation in an upcoming production planning meeting involving representatives from marketing, manufacturing, and finance. The production plans are generated by using: (a) a level strategy—maintain the current work-force level of 50 workers, using inventories to buffer demand, (b) a chase strategy—adjust the work force to meet demand exactly, (c) a mixed strategy—trim the work force to 48 workers, maintain this work-force level, and use overtime and inventory to buffer demand. Management would like the three plans to be presented in three formats: tabular, graphic, and cumulative. The costs of the three operations planning strategies should also be computed. If holding cost is 40% higher than estimated, what is the impact of this on the three plans?

| Month | Forecasted Demand (Tons) | Month | Forecasted Demand (Tons) |
|---|---|---|---|
| Jan. | 3000 | July | 6000 |
| Feb. | 4000 | August | 4000 |
| Mar. | 4000 | September | 4000 |
| Apr. | 4000 | October | 6000 |
| May | 7000 | November | 6000 |
| Jun. | 6000 | December | 6000 |

The materials manager computed the following plans.

(a) Level Strategy—Tabular Representation

| Period | Demand Forecast (tons) | Production (tons) | Inventory (tons) | Work-force Level | Regular Wages ($) | Overtime Cost ($) | Hiring Cost ($) | Layoff Cost ($) | Inventory Holding Cost ($) | Total Cost ($) |
|---|---|---|---|---|---|---|---|---|---|---|
| Jan. | 3,000 | 5,000 | 2,000 | 50 | 100,000 | 0 | 0 | 0 | 4,000 | 104,000 |
| Feb. | 4,000 | 5,000 | 3,000 | 50 | 100,000 | 0 | 0 | 0 | 6,000 | 106,000 |
| Mar. | 4,000 | 5,000 | 4,000 | 50 | 100,000 | 0 | 0 | 0 | 8,000 | 108,000 |
| Apr. | 4,000 | 5,000 | 5,000 | 50 | 100,000 | 0 | 0 | 0 | 10,000 | 110,000 |
| May | 7,000 | 5,000 | 3,000 | 50 | 100,000 | 0 | 0 | 0 | 6,000 | 106,000 |
| Jun. | 6,000 | 5,000 | 2,000 | 50 | 100,000 | 0 | 0 | 0 | 4,000 | 104,000 |
| Jul. | 6,000 | 5,000 | 1,000 | 50 | 100,000 | 0 | 0 | 0 | 2,000 | 102,000 |
| Aug. | 4,000 | 5,000 | 2,000 | 50 | 100,000 | 0 | 0 | 0 | 4,000 | 104,000 |
| Sep. | 4,000 | 5,000 | 3,000 | 50 | 100,000 | 0 | 0 | 0 | 6,000 | 106,000 |
| Oct. | 6,000 | 5,000 | 2,000 | 50 | 100,000 | 0 | 0 | 0 | 4,000 | 104,000 |
| Nov. | 6,000 | 5,000 | 1,000 | 50 | 100,000 | 0 | 0 | 0 | 2,000 | 102,000 |
| Dec. | 6,000 | 5,000 | 0 | 50 | 100,000 | 0 | 0 | 0 | 0 | 100,000 |
| Total | 60,000 | 60,000 | | | 1,200,000 | 0 | 0 | 0 | 56,000 | 1,256,000 |

*Continued*

**DECISION MODEL BOX 8-1** *Continued*

(b) Chase Strategy—
Tabular Representation

| Period | Demand Forecast (tons) | Production (tons) | Inventory (tons) | Work-force Level | Regular Wages ($) | Overtime Cost ($) | Hiring Cost ($) | Layoff Cost ($) | Inventory Holding Cost ($) | Total Cost ($) |
|---|---|---|---|---|---|---|---|---|---|---|
| Jan. | 3,000 | 3,000 | 0 | 30 | 60,000 | 0 | 0 | 24,000 | 0 | 84,000 |
| Feb. | 4,000 | 4,000 | 0 | 40 | 80,000 | 0 | 8,000 | 0 | 0 | 88,000 |
| Mar. | 4,000 | 4,000 | 0 | 40 | 80,000 | 0 | 0 | 0 | 0 | 80,000 |
| Apr. | 4,000 | 4,000 | 0 | 40 | 80,000 | 0 | 0 | 0 | 0 | 80,000 |
| May | 7,000 | 7,000 | 0 | 70 | 140,000 | 0 | 24,000 | 0 | 0 | 164,000 |
| Jun. | 6,000 | 6,000 | 0 | 60 | 120,000 | 0 | 0 | 12,000 | 0 | 132,000 |
| Jul. | 6,000 | 6,000 | 0 | 60 | 120,000 | 0 | 0 | 0 | 0 | 120,000 |
| Aug. | 4,000 | 4,000 | 0 | 40 | 80,000 | 0 | 0 | 24,000 | 0 | 104,000 |
| Sep. | 4,000 | 4,000 | 0 | 40 | 80,000 | 0 | 0 | 0 | 0 | 80,000 |
| Oct. | 6,000 | 6,000 | 0 | 60 | 120,000 | 0 | 16,000 | 0 | 0 | 136,000 |
| Nov. | 6,000 | 6,000 | 0 | 60 | 120,000 | 0 | 0 | 0 | 0 | 120,000 |
| Dec. | 6,000 | 6,000 | 0 | 60 | 120,000 | 0 | 0 | 0 | 0 | 120,000 |
| Total | 60,000 | 60,000 | | | 1,200,000 | 0 | 48,000 | 60,000 | 0 | 1,308,000 |

(c) Mixed Strategy (Trial-and-Error Approach)—
Tabular Representation

| Period | Demand Forecast (tons) | Production (tons) | Inventory (tons) | Work-force Level | Regular Wages ($) | Overtime Cost ($) | Hiring Cost ($) | Layoff Cost ($) | Inventory Holding Cost ($) | Total Cost ($) |
|---|---|---|---|---|---|---|---|---|---|---|
| Jan. | 3,000 | 4,800 | 1,800 | 48 | 96,000 | 0 | 0 | 2,400 | 3,600 | 102,000 |
| Feb. | 4,000 | 4,800 | 2,600 | 48 | 96,000 | 0 | 0 | 0 | 5,200 | 101,200 |
| Mar. | 4,000 | 4,800 | 3,400 | 48 | 96,000 | 0 | 0 | 0 | 6,800 | 102,800 |
| Apr. | 4,000 | 4,800 | 4,200 | 48 | 96,000 | 0 | 0 | 0 | 8,400 | 104,400 |
| May | 7,000 | 4,800 | 2,000 | 48 | 96,000 | 0 | 0 | 0 | 4,000 | 100,000 |
| Jun. | 6,000 | 4,800 | 800 | 48 | 96,000 | 0 | 0 | 0 | 1,600 | 97,600 |
| Jul. | 6,000 | 5,200 | 0 | 48 | 96,000 | 12,000 | 0 | 0 | 0 | 108,000 |
| Aug. | 4,000 | 4,800 | 800 | 48 | 96,000 | 0 | 0 | 0 | 1,600 | 97,600 |
| Sep. | 4,000 | 4,800 | 1,600 | 48 | 96,000 | 0 | 0 | 0 | 3,200 | 99,200 |
| Oct. | 6,000 | 4,800 | 400 | 48 | 96,000 | 0 | 0 | 0 | 800 | 96,800 |
| Nov. | 6,000 | 5,600 | 0 | 48 | 96,000 | 24,000 | 0 | 0 | 0 | 120,000 |
| Dec. | 6,000 | 6,000 | 0 | 48 | 96,000 | 36,000 | 0 | 0 | 0 | 132,000 |
| Total | 60,000 | 60,000 | | | 1,152,000 | 72,000 | 0 | 2,400 | 35,200 | 1,261,600 |

*Continued*

**DECISION MODEL BOX 8-1** *Continued*

**Graphic Representation of Operations Planning Strategies**

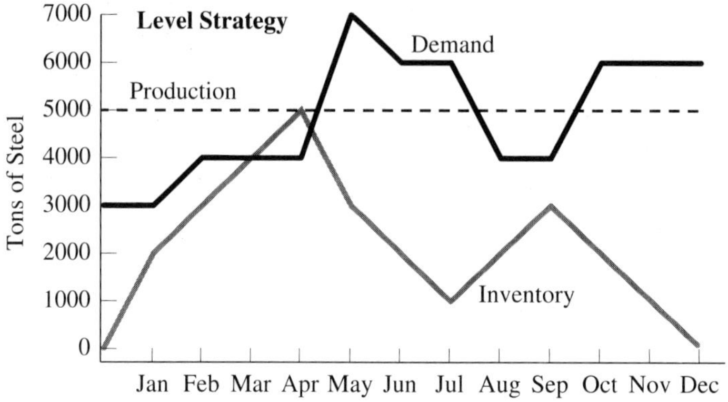


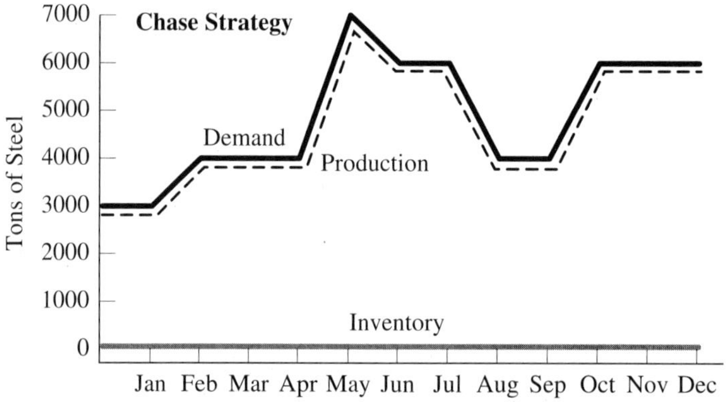


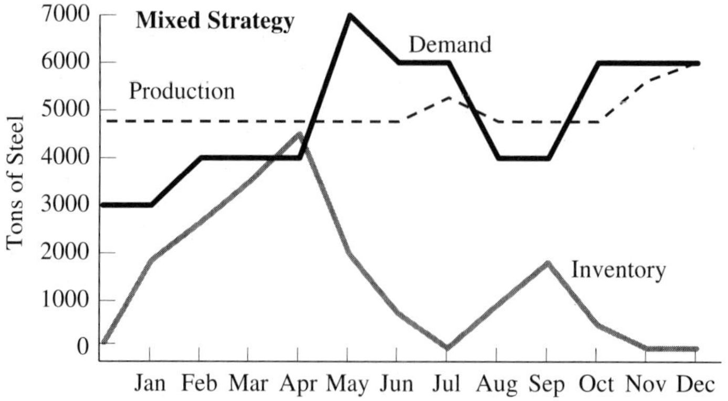


*Continued*

**DECISION MODEL BOX 8-1** *Continued*

**Cumulative Production–Demand–Inventory Chart**

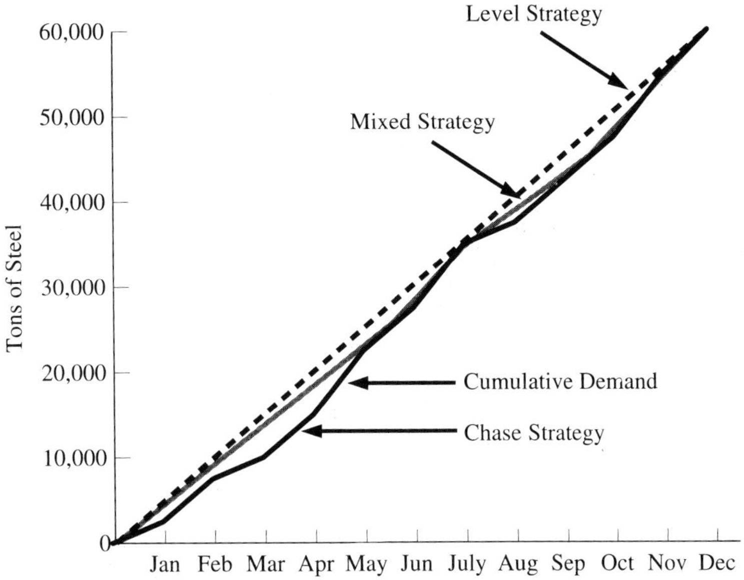


(d) Cost Comparison of the Three Operations Planning Strategies for Lin Steel

| Strategy | Regular Wages ($) | Overtime Cost ($) | Hiring Cost ($) | Layoff Cost ($) | Inventory Holding Cost ($) | Total Cost ($) |
|---|---|---|---|---|---|---|
| Level strategy | 1,200,000 | 0 | 0 | 0 | 56,000 | 1,256,000 |
| Chase strategy | 1,200,000 | 0 | 48,000 | 60,000 | 0 | 1,308,000 |
| Mixed strategy | 1,152,000 | 72,000 | 0 | 2,400 | 35,200 | 1,261,600 |

The least total cost incurred in this example is the level strategy. The reason is the high cost of hiring and laying off workers compared to the cost of holding inventory. Depending on the cost parameters such as holding cost, hiring/layoff cost, and the like, the outcome of the cost comparisons can vary widely. It should be pointed out that quantifiable costs are only one input used by management to decide on an acceptable production plan. The plan should be evaluated on how well it is able to meet the company's strategic goals.

*Continued*

**DECISION MODEL BOX 8-1** *Continued*

(e) Costs of the Three Plans When
Unit Inventory Holding Cost Is $2.80 per Month

| | Inventory Holding Cost ($2 per month) | | | Inventory Holding Cost ($2.80 per month) | | |
|---|---|---|---|---|---|---|
| Strategy | Level | Chase | Mixed | Level | Chase | Mixed |
| Regular wages | 1,200,000 | 1,200,000 | 1,152,000 | 1,200,000 | 1,200,000 | 1,152,000 |
| Overtime cost | 0 | 0 | 72,000 | 0 | 0 | 72,000 |
| Hiring cost | 0 | 48,000 | 0 | 0 | 48,000 | 0 |
| Layoff cost | 0 | 60,000 | 2,400 | 0 | 60,000 | 2,400 |
| Inventory holding cost | 56,000 | 0 | 35,200 | 78,400 | 0 | 49,280 |
| Total cost | 1,256,000 | 1,308,000 | 1,261,600 | 1,278,400 | 1,308,000 | 1,275,680 |

Note that the least cost plan is provided by the mixed strategy when the unit inventory cost is increased by 40%.

services cannot be inventoried, a level strategy in a service organization involves keeping a steady work force and using overtime and undertime to buffer fluctuations in demand. An example of a level strategy for a service firm is provided in Decision Model Box 8-2.

The level strategy is appealing for several reasons. The costs associated with hiring and laying off workers are eliminated. The level strategy avoids ups and downs associated with frequent hiring and layoffs and low morale as a result of high worker turnover. With a steady work force, workers are better utilized if they are cross-trained in a variety of skills.

## *Chase Strategy*

A chase strategy attempts to match supply with demand by varying the work-force size. Examples of a chase strategy in manufacturing and services are presented in Decision Model Boxes 8-1 and 8-2. In a manufacturing environment the use of this strategy avoids any inventory buildup and, therefore, saves on carrying cost. In a service environment the objective is not to have any undertime. A chase strategy is more applicable in an operating environment in which low-wage unskilled workers perform jobs with limited discretion. Training costs are much higher than for the level strategy because of the frequent turnover of employees. More supervision may be needed to ensure that the workers are carrying out their duties according to specifications, and chances for errors are usually much higher.

When the costs of hiring, layoff, overtime, and subcontracting are high relative to the costs of carrying inventory, the chase strategy becomes less attractive than the level strategy. The chase strategy is more prone to stockouts compared to the level strategy,

## DECISION MODEL BOX 8-2 Operations Planning at Boyer Construction Company

The Boyer Construction Company, which specializes in residential and commercial remodeling work, is facing seasonal demand for its services. The forecasted aggregate demand in labor hours for the next year are as follows: winter = 19,200, spring = 28,800, summer = 36,000, and fall = 24,000. Each employee works 480 hours per season. The average employee salary for a season is \$5760. Overtime is reimbursed at \$18 per labor hour. Workers are limited to 120 overtime hours per season. The cost of hiring an additional worker is \$3000. Laying off a worker costs \$2000. The company prides itself on completing all work within the season the service orders are due; that is, no back orders are allowed. The company currently has 50 workers. Boyer Construction wants to generate a staffing plan with a planning horizon of one year to utilize their resources more effectively and to provide better customer service. The staffing plans are generated using: (a) a level strategy—maintaining a stable work-force level and using overtime to buffer demand, (b) a chase strategy—adjusting the work force to meet demand exactly, (c) a mixed strategy—combination of hiring and laying off employees and using overtime. Which strategy would be the least expensive? If the costs of hiring and laying off a worker are \$1500 and \$1000, respectively, what are the effects on the three plans?

The following operations plans were computed.

(a) Level Strategy

| Season | Demand Forecast (hours) | Work-force Level | Available Regular Hours | Overtime Hours | Regular Wages (\$) | Overtime Cost (\$) | Hiring Cost (\$) | Layoff Cost (\$) | Total Cost (\$) |
|---|---|---|---|---|---|---|---|---|---|
| Winter | 19,200 | 60 | 28,800 | 0 | 345,600 | 0 | 30,000 | 0 | 375,600 |
| Spring | 28,800 | 60 | 28,800 | 0 | 345,600 | 0 | 0 | 0 | 345,600 |
| Summer | 36,000 | 60 | 28,800 | 7,200 | 345,600 | 129,600 | 0 | 0 | 475,200 |
| Fall | 24,000 | 60 | 28,800 | 0 | 345,600 | 0 | 0 | 0 | 345,600 |
| Total | 108,000 | | 115,200 | 7,200 | 1,382,400 | 129,600 | 30,000 | 0 | 1,542,000 |

To maintain a stable work force over the planning horizon, the focus is on the season with the peak demand. In this case, the summer season has maximum labor requirements of 36,000 hours. Each worker can work a total of 600 hours per season, made up of 480 regular hours and 120 overtime hours. Therefore, the total number of workers required is (36,000/600) = 60 workers. With this strategy there is undertime in the winter and fall seasons totaling 14,400 regular hours. This undertime is absorbed under regular wages.

(b) Chase Strategy

| Season | Demand Forecast (hours) | Work-force Level | Available Regular Hours | Overtime Hours | Regular Wages (\$) | Overtime Cost (\$) | Hiring Cost (\$) | Layoff Cost (\$) | Total Cost (\$) |
|---|---|---|---|---|---|---|---|---|---|
| Winter | 19,200 | 40 | 19,200 | 0 | 230,400 | 0 | 0 | 20,000 | 250,400 |
| Spring | 28,800 | 60 | 28,800 | 0 | 345,600 | 0 | 60,000 | 0 | 405,600 |
| Summer | 36,000 | 75 | 36,000 | 0 | 432,000 | 0 | 45,000 | 0 | 477,000 |
| Fall | 24,000 | 50 | 24,000 | 0 | 288,000 | 0 | 0 | 50,000 | 338,000 |
| Total | 108,000 | | 108,000 | | 1,296,000 | 0 | 105,000 | 70,000 | 1,471,000 |

*Continued*

**DECISION MODEL BOX 8-2** *Continued*

(c) Mixed Strategy (Trial-and-Error Approach)

| Season | Demand Forecast (hours) | Work-force Level | Available Regular Hours | Overtime Hours | Regular Wages ($) | Overtime Cost ($) | Hiring Cost ($) | Layoff Cost ($) | Total Cost ($) |
|---|---|---|---|---|---|---|---|---|---|
| Winter | 19,200 | 40 | 19,200 | 0 | 230,400 | 0 | 0 | 20,000 | 250,400 |
| Spring | 28,800 | 60 | 28,800 | 0 | 345,600 | 129,600 | 60,000 | 0 | 405,600 |
| Summer | 36,000 | 60 | 28,800 | 7,200 | 345,600 | 0 | 0 | 0 | 475,200 |
| Fall | 24,000 | 50 | 24,000 | 0 | 288,000 | 0 | 0 | 20,000 | 308,000 |
| Total | 108,000 | | 108,000 | 7,200 | 1,209,600 | 129,600 | 60,000 | 40,000 | 1,439,200 |

(d) Cost Comparison of the Three Operations Planning Strategies for Boyer Construction

| Strategy | Regular Wages | Overtime Cost | Hiring Cost | Layoff Cost | Total Cost |
|---|---|---|---|---|---|
| Level strategy | 1,382,400 | 129,600 | 30,000 | 0 | 1,542,000 |
| Chase strategy | 1,296,000 | 0 | 105,000 | 70,000 | 1,471,000 |
| Mixed strategy | 1,209,600 | 129,600 | 60,000 | 40,000 | 1,439,200 |

The total cost incurred in this example is the mixed strategy. The reason is the high cost of undertime incurred with the level strategy in response to highly seasonal demands. The chase strategy incurred a high cost associated with hiring and laying off workers. A different least-cost strategy will likely emerge with different costs associated with hiring, layoff, and overtime.

(e) Costs of the Three Plans When Hiring Cost Is $1500 and Layoff Cost Is $1000 Per Worker

| | Hiring/Layoff Cost ($3,000/2,000) | | | Hiring/Layoff Cost ($1,500/$1,000) | | |
|---|---|---|---|---|---|---|
| Strategy | Level | Chase | Mixed | Level | Chase | Mixed |
| Regular wages | 1,382,400 | 1,296,000 | 1,209,600 | 1,382,400 | 1,296,000 | 1,209,600 |
| Overtime cost | 129,600 | 0 | 129,600 | 129,600 | 0 | 129,600 |
| Hiring cost | 30,000 | 105,000 | 60,000 | 15,000 | 52,500 | 30,000 |
| Layoff cost | 0 | 70,000 | 40,000 | 0 | 35,000 | 20,000 |
| Total cost | 1,542,000 | 1,471,000 | 1,439,200 | 1,527,000 | 1,383,500 | 1,389,200 |

Note that the least-cost plan is provided by the chase strategy because of the lower hiring and layoff costs.

because companies often experience difficulty in adjusting capacity fast enough to match sales exactly. Union agreements that heavily penalize employee layoffs also discourage companies from adopting a chase strategy.

Although there are obvious disadvantages associated with the chase strategy, several service industries such as fast-food industries, amusement parks, and resort hotels rely heavily on this strategy for their survival. An example is the Disney World theme park in Orlando, which has been particularly successful in using a large pool of temporary workers during the peak tourist season and yet maintains a high level of customer service. By utilizing students in the summer months, the company is able to tap into a huge and ready reserve of temporary workers, pay relatively low wages, and get a good-quality work force. Students are looking for part-time jobs in the summer, and this temporary arrangement works well for both employers and students.

## *Mixed Strategies*

The basic level and chase strategies represent the two diametrical extremes of operations planning. Companies typically employ some combination of these two pure strategies. The level strategy with a steady work force in manufacturing can be modified to allow adjustments to the production rate, using overtime and undertime to respond to demand variations so that little or no inventory is maintained. Subcontracting can be used if overtime cannot solve the capacity problem. Another example of a mixed strategy is one that attempts to maintain a stable work force as long as possible, using overtime and undertime to meet demand, but recognizes that it is more realistic to keep some inventory and have some hiring and laying off of employees.

Whatever operations planning strategy is selected, it must be consistent with the operations and business strategies, and provide a firm with a competitive advantage. Japanese manufacturers are the biggest proponents of using smooth production techniques to apply the just-in-time (JIT) management philosophy to great competitive advantage. Many Japanese companies such as Toyota, Honda, and Sony have "lifetime employment" and no-layoff personnel policies. IBM is an example of a U.S. corporation which had a no-layoff policy for many years, though the recent downsizing has included layoffs. Japanese manufacturers prefer a level operations planning strategy that allows overtime and undertime to buffer against fluctuations in demand. Temporary workers are also used extensively. With smooth production and the kanban system, inventories are kept to a minimum. United States companies are now beginning to implement JIT (see Chapter 10), which favors leveling production as an operations planning approach. A discussion of operations planning in a JIT environment is provided in Application Box 8-1.

## *Operations Planning Decision Costs*

There are three broad categories of quantifiable costs relevant to operations planning: regular production costs, inventory costs, and production rate change costs.

**Regular Production Costs.** These costs apply to the production of one output unit during regular time. The applicable costs are the fixed and variable costs of production,

## APPLICATION BOX 8-1 Operations Planning at Toyota

Toyota's production system calls for smoothing of production to minimize disruptions and inventory. A production plan showing the number of cars to be produced in the current year is prepared by Toyota. The yearly production plan is translated into the monthly and daily plans. For example, if the annual production plan calls for 168,000 units, then the production each month is 14,000 units. The monthly plans are then translated into daily requirements. For a 20-day month, the number of cars produced per day is 700. At the daily level, the different mix of the 700 autos must be considered: 400 sedans, 200 coupes, and 100 wagons. A daily schedule is then developed that shows the sequence of assembling the various types of cars: for example, sedan–coupe–sedan–coupe–sedan–wagon–sedan, and so on (see also Chapter 10, Table 10-1).

To adapt to changes in demand occurring within a year, temporary workers can be hired or laid off. Ordinarily, machines are loaded at only 50% of their full capacities. Toyota has multifunctional workers who can typically handle several machines, sometimes as many as a dozen machines. In periods of increasing demand, temporary workers can be hired so that each worker now works on half the number of machines he or she was responsible for previously. Toyota can double the machine capacity utilization with this approach. It is important to have equipment that newly hired, unskilled temporary workers can become fully competent on within a short period of time. An interesting policy is that although Toyota believes in minimizing the number of workers used, it is not deemed necessary to have a minimum number of machines to meet demand. It is not unusual to have excess machine capacity so that only temporary workers are needed to effectively expand production capacity in response to increases in demand. On assembly lines, temporary workers can be added to reduce the cycle time and increase the production rate.

Toyota uses a two-shift daily schedule with the first shift between 8 a.m.–5 p.m. and the second shift from 9 p.m.–6 a.m. Short-term increases in production output can be achieved by having employees work overtime to fill the time slots between shifts. During periods of weak demand, temporary workers will be laid off. Toyota's policy is to let redundant workers take a rest rather than to allow production of unnecessary inventory just to keep workers busy and utilization high. In slack periods, workers can work on process improvements that will become useful when demand increases. Other activities that can be organized during slow periods are quality control circle meetings, practicing and improving setups, and routine machine maintenance. Another option is to use excess workers and equipment to manufacture parts that have previously been purchased from suppliers.

Materials drawn from Y. Monden, "Smoothed Production Lets Toyota Adapt to Demand Changes and Reduce Inventory," *Industrial Engineering,* August 1981, pp. 42–51.

direct and indirect material costs, and regular payroll costs. If all production is carried out during regular time, regular payroll cost is not a relevant cost and can be ignored in comparing various alternative strategies.

**Inventory Costs.** Inventory costs include the cost of carrying inventory, back-order and stockout costs, and cost of adding storage facilities beyond those required for level production. The inventory carrying cost includes costs related to storage, opportunity cost, insurance, taxes, obsolescence, breakage, pilferage, and deterioration (see also Chapter 9). Back-order and stockout costs are harder to estimate and include expediting costs, loss of goodwill, and loss of sales income.

**Production Rate Change Costs.** When production rates are changed there are costs involved in reorganizing and replanning for the new production level. For example, when a second shift is added, we may see an initial decline in labor productivity. A one-time cost of start-up and shutdown of a production facility may be incurred. Other items included in this category are costs associated with hiring and laying off of regular employees, overtime and undertime, temporary and part-time workers, subcontracting and outsourcing, cooperative arrangements, and customer participation.

Although we have looked at tangible costs, other intangible factors may need to be considered. An optimal solution that requires frequent hiring and firing of employees may not be acceptable to management either from a public image standpoint or because of restrictions imposed by the existing union agreement. The operations plan developed must be consistent with a firm's overall strategic goals.

## Methods of Solving the Operations Planning Problem

Many techniques are available for solving the operations planning problem. These methods can be broadly categorized as either optimal or nonoptimal techniques.

### Optimal Techniques

These techniques typically use mathematical programming to obtain optimal solutions to the operations planning problem. One of the earliest mathematical approaches is the linear decision rule (Holt, Modigliani, and Simon, 1955). The linear decision rule (LDR) assumes quadratic cost functions associated with hiring/layoff cost, inventory cost, and undertime/overtime cost and a linear regular payroll cost function. The optimum work force and production levels are obtained by differentiating the total cost function. Although the LDR was implemented at a paint factory, an evaluation of its performance several years later indicated that users overrode a large percentage of the plans generated because the logic of the LDR was not readily transparent. Linear programming, the transportation method, and goal programming are other optimal mathematical approaches that have seen limited applications. The limitations of these methods are the following: costs are not always linear, changes in the worker's productivity with time are not reflected in the formulation, and continuously changing the production rate may not always be possible.

### Nonoptimal Techniques

Included in this category are the trial-and-error approaches, heuristics, and simulation. Most organizations develop an operations plan by using a trial-and-error approach. Experience plays an important part in the solution process. A trial-and-error method typically includes the following steps.

1. Develop an initial plan based on demand forecasts and agreed guidelines.
2. Check if the plan can be satisfied using available capacity. Otherwise, revise the plan accordingly.
3. Compute the cost of the plan.
4. Modify the plan to obtain a lower-cost solution.
5. Perform sensitivity analysis to determine the cost implications of parameter changes such as inventory holding cost rate, and hiring and firing costs.

This approach is simple to implement, but it depends greatly on the skill and experience of the planner. It can also be time consuming. Although a feasible and satisfactory solution is obtained, there is no guarantee that it is an optimum one. Decision Model Boxes 8-1 and 8-2 provide examples of using a trial-and-error approach to solve the operations planning problem in a manufacturing and service environment, respectively.

Heuristics are similar to trial-and-error methods, with the exception that a more formalized reasoning is adopted. Heuristics attempt to simplify the solution process but cannot guarantee optimal solutions. An example is the production switching rule used to develop production plans at Owens-Corning Fiberglas described in the Introductory Case. Heuristics are often more acceptable to management due to their simplicity, transparency, and efficiency.

Simulation approaches overcome the unrealistic assumptions of mathematical programming techniques. Although simulation does not guarantee an optimal solution, it allows the planner to formulate a model with nonlinear cost relationships, time-varying cost parameters, or costs that change with production quantities. Thus simulation provides a more realistic approximation of the operations planning problem than is possible with mathematical programming. The availability of commercial spreadsheets such as Lotus 123©, VisiCalc, and Multiplan has simplified the model-building process and allows many alternative plans to be evaluated easily.

### *Sensitivity Analysis*

The operations plan is derived from demand forecasts and cost parameters, which are assumed to be deterministic. This situation is rarely true. Management's concerns are related to questions such as: If actual sales are higher or lower than forecasted demand, what is the cost impact of each on the operations plan? If costs associated with inventory or production rate changes differ from estimates used, will the operations plan be substantially different? The first question is related to the sensitivity of the operations plan to errors in demand forecasts; the second question addresses the robustness of the operations planning technique used. Management can use sensitivity analysis to focus attention on areas where forecast errors can be particularly problematic and to get a better handle on the operations planning problem. Examples of sensitivity analysis carried out in a manufacturing and service environment are provided in Decision Model Boxes 8-1 and 8-2.

## *Essentials of Effective Operations Planning*

Effective operations planning requires the integration of the operations plan with the business plan and other functional plans as well as good communications among all functions. For the operations plan to be widely accepted, it must be realistic, consistent, and feasible. In addition, there are several critical issues that must be addressed to ensure the effective planning of operations:

1. Accurate demand forecasts
2. Aggregation
3. Time period and planning horizon
4. Frequency of replanning
5. Formalizing and controlling the operations planning process

## *Accurate Demand Forecasts*

Demand forecasts are an important input to the operations planning process and are typically supplied by marketing. Without forecasts there can be no planning. The forecasting of aggregate demand is usually more accurate than forecasting for individual products or services. The further into the future forecasts are needed, the less they are likely to be accurate and reliable. The proportional decline in accuracy and reliability of individual forecasts is greater than for aggregate forecasts. It is precisely for these reasons that the use of aggregate forecasts is recommended for long-range planning.

Forecasts are expected to differ from actual demand. Minor variations from actual sales can often be absorbed by using overtime, inventory, or rescheduling orders. However, large mismatches can have a devastating effect on operations. If demand is overforecasted, the firm may be left with a high level of inventory or forced to lay off employees to bring output in line with actual sales. Equally undesirable is demand forecasts that are consistently low. The likely outcomes are the following: the facility's capacity is severely strained; orders are lost as a result of stockouts; deliveries are delayed, which lead to a loss of goodwill; quality is sacrificed to get orders out quickly. Thus accurate demand forecasts are critical to the overall performance of the operations plan.

When actual sales have exceeded forecasts for the previous periods, management must decide if customers were making purchases early or if the increased demand will continue. If the increased demand is attributed to early purchases, then no drastic action is needed, since demand is expected to be less than planned in the immediate future. On the other hand, if the increased demand is due to a sudden upturn in the economy or a strike at a competitor, the forecasts should be revised accordingly and the operations plan should be adjusted. Few forecasting techniques are available that can effectively track turning points that represent periods of extraordinary opportunity or caution. Managers should "incorporate subjective judgments in dynamic situations when the quantitative forecasting models do not reflect internal or external changes" (Georgoff and Murdick, 1986).

## *Aggregation*

In order to generate an operations plan, an aggregate unit of the various products or services must be developed. This can be a challenging problem, depending on the particular industry involved. The objective is to come up with a commonly understood aggregate unit that lies somewhere between the total dollars in the business plan and the individual products found in the master production schedule. Occasionally, dollars are used as an aggregating unit due to the type of products or services. The measure should be sufficiently broad that management does not get bogged down with too many details at this planning level. The units vary from company to company. Physical measures are appropriate when products are relatively homogenous. Examples are gallons of paint, tons of steel, cases of beer, square feet of tiles, and cubic feet of concrete mix.

The aggregation of products becomes more challenging when there are multiple products involved. A thorough understanding of the products and their associated processing requirements is necessary to generate meaningful groups. A good approach is to develop product families based on commonality of processing requirements. Products using like quantities of similar resources should be grouped in the same family. Typically, five to 15 product families are considered manageable. Another approach is to use the input side of production, such as equivalent labor hours or machine hours. In service organizations, the different services offered are aggregated into equivalent labor hours. An important requirement of any aggregation process is the ability to translate the units in the operations plan to dollars in the business and marketing plans to ensure that these plans are consistent with each other. In addition, the aggregate units in the operations plan must be disaggregated to individual products in the master production schedule or to individual workers in a work-force schedule.

## *Time Period and Planning Horizon*

A suitable time period is one month, although quarters have been used when longer planning horizons are desired. In some situations, such as the end of a peak sales season, companies may wish to use more precise time intervals, such as weeks, to enable inventories to be kept close to target. The planning horizon typically covers six to 18 months and is influenced by the time span of the business strategy. The availability and accuracy of demand forecasts is another factor impacting the planning horizon.

## *Frequency of Replanning*

In executing the operations plan, there are several key issues that must be considered: when to change the plan, frequency of replanning, and what portion of the plan to stabilize. Obviously, we would like the plan to be sufficiently flexible to respond to market conditions. However, frequent changes to the operations plan are highly disruptive in managing operations. Without stable plans, workers and machine capacities cannot be effectively utilized, and customer service and profits may suffer as a result. Frequent changes can also lead to more execution problems. An adequate review period is one month, although the review could be carried out more frequently if sales are not up to the operations plan. Once the commitment to production is made, any drastic change will be very costly. There is a fine balance between trying to maintain stability in the operations system and the ability to respond to market conditions. Time fences are established to serve as guidelines in revising the operations plan and represent points in the production process where changes become expensive. The setting of time fences is dependent on capacity and lead times. The longer into the future the change is required, the easier it is to make adjustments to the plan. When changes to the operations plan become costly, they must be approved by top management.

The just-in-time (JIT) inventory management philosophy, increasingly popular in the United States, requires a smooth operations plan for the pull inventory management system (see Chapter 9) to work. The objective is to maintain a steady flow of production each day for long periods of time. Changes to the plan are made after careful analysis has been carried out. JIT manufacturers have greatly benefited from the smooth operations plans, as evidenced by the reduced inventory levels. Smoothed production will be discussed in more detail in Chapter 10.

## *Formalizing and Controlling the Operations Plan*

For operations planning to work effectively, top management must play an active role in formalizing the planning process. The formal process enables top management decisions to be implemented on a focused, rigorous, and timely basis. Monthly operations planning meetings are held to discuss and review the operations plan, with the chief operating officer or general manager chairing these meetings. At these meetings, top and middle managers, including vice presidents from marketing, operations, finance, engineering, and other related areas, openly discuss problems, suggest alternative solutions, and make tough decisions. Inputs are sought from:

1. Marketing, regarding customer demands, significant changes in demand trends, upcoming promotions, new product or service introductions, competitors' activities, and market conditions.
2. Finance, regarding investment policy relating to inventory levels, new equipment, and facilities.
3. Operations, regarding actual production of goods or services, existing capacity, backlog of orders, frequency of equipment breakdowns, lead times, quality of manufactured items or services, work-force level, and inventory level.
4. Engineering, regarding new product/service introductions, engineering change orders, changes in process technology, routing changes, and new design changes.
5. Human resources, regarding labor problems and availability of a pool of skilled or temporary workers in the area.
6. Purchasing, regarding availability and delivery of materials, and the status of qualified subcontractors.

At the monthly operations planning meeting, several alternative plans are presented for discussion. The objective of this meeting is to resolve conflicts and build consensus in reaching an acceptable operations plan. When there is overall agreement, the chief operating officer or general manager signs off on the operations plan, indicating management's commitment. Copies of the signed operations plan are given to managers in charge of implementing the plan.

At the meeting, the past performance of the operations plan is evaluated, and the tentative operations plan, master schedule, resource plan, marketing, financial, and other associated plans are reviewed together. Monitoring the performance of the operations plan is vital to its acceptance and success. When a plan is frequently questioned with respect to its validity, managers lose faith in the formal process and resort to an informal system to overcome the deficiencies. Timely and accurate feedback of information regarding changes in demand, production rates, labor and material availability, and the like is necessary for monitoring the validity of the plan. Large variations in production rates, worker performance, frequency of equipment breakdowns, vendor lead times, and so on should be avoided, since they contribute to poor performance of an operations plan. To evaluate the performance of an operations plan, actual occurrences should be compared with planned outcomes.

Examples of performance categories are the following: forecasted sales against actual sales, planned production against actual production, planned work-force level against actual work-force level (or labor hours), and planned inventory against actual inventory, or planned backlogs against actual backlogs. Deviations from the plan should be analyzed and reasons provided to explain the source of the deviation to enable corrective actions to be taken. The results should be widely communicated to all relevant parties in the organization. The Tennant Company uses the following reports to control its operations plan: the conformity of the master production schedule to the operations plan (weekly), capacity utilization (weekly), delivery performance (daily), actual production to master production schedule performance (weekly), and inventory/backlog performance (weekly). Over the past few years, Tennant has met monthly operations plans in ten out of 12 months for each of these years and had not missed a quarterly operations plan (Vollmann, Berry, and Whybark, 1992).

## *Disaggregating the Operations Plan*

The operations plan uses aggregate units to examine general levels of work force, production, and inventory. Aggregate units are useful only at the higher planning level. The plan needs to be disaggregated to make it useful and meaningful for implementation by operations personnel. Disaggregation involves breaking down the aggregate units into individual items to be produced or services offered so that specific requirements for labor, materials, equipment, and inventory can be determined. To ensure feasibility, the total units in the disaggregated plan must sum to the total in the same time period in the operations plan. The outcome of disaggregating the operations plan is a master production schedule (in manufacturing), master schedule (in services), or a work-force schedule (in services).

A master production schedule (MPS) is a detailed plan of production that states the quantity and timing of individual end items over some specified time frame. The planning horizon for an MPS can vary from three months to one year, but normally covers a time frame much less than that for operations planning. The time periods are typically in weeks, although days, hours, or months can be used. As in operations planning, time fences play an important role in the master production scheduling process. Time fencing is often used to avoid inefficiencies and unnecessary disruptions on the shop floor. Many firms use three time fences: frozen, slushy, and free zones. The first few weeks of an MPS is typically frozen, meaning that no changes are allowed in this portion of the master production schedule except under exceptional circumstances. Any changes in the frozen period must be authorized by management because of the impact on other customer-order commitments, purchasing requirements, equipment utilization, open shop orders, and profitability. Schedule stability in the short run is important. Beyond the frozen period is the "slushy" zone, where changes to the MPS are allowed provided that one order is traded with another equivalent order, and required materials and components are available. The "free" portion of the MPS allows more drastic changes as long as the operations plan is not violated. A description of how Texas Instruments improved customer service by reducing the frozen interval of the MPS is provided in Application Box 8-2.

Service organizations typically use work-force schedules, although some service organizations use master schedules. For example, universities and colleges publish and circulate a master schedule of course offerings two to three terms in advance. The schedule is used to arrange for classroom capacity requirements and faculty to teach these courses, as well as to allow students to make long-term plans for completing their degrees. These schedules are quite rigid, and only minor changes such as classroom reassignments are made. An exception is the cancellation of a course in which the specified minimum enrollment has not been met. A family doctor or a beautician uses a master schedule that includes customer appointments and time set aside for walk-in customers. Airlines, railways, and tour companies also generate a master schedule of services for the next six to 12 months. Work-force schedules are prepared to meet these schedules of services. Accounting, engineering, and management consulting firms translate contracts that show completion times of services to work-force schedules.

## *Hierarchical Planning Systems*

Hierarchical planning systems adopt an integrated approach to address the operations planning and scheduling problem. The operations planning and scheduling problem is partitioned into a series of subproblems that are solved sequentially, often iteratively, with constraints established by higher-level decisions imposed on lower-level subproblems. Meal (1984, p. 106) notes that hierarchical planning systems "fit the organizational structure and provide for ease of review at each managerial level. Higher-level decisions have longer lead times, longer planning horizons, and are concerned with aggregates such as total manpower requirements and total product-line demand. The lowest-level decisions have shorter lead times, shorter planning horizons, and are concerned with individual items, machines, and workers." The hierarchical planning structure allows a clear delegation of the detailed decision making to subordinates at lower levels of the organization and yet enables top management to retain overall control of the entire planning process. Senior managers contend with aggregate data in allocating valuable resources to achieve corporate objectives. The detailed responsibility of job and task assignments are successively delegated to superintendents, supervisors, production control assistants, and shop floor workers. A description of the hierarchical planning system employed at American Olean Tile Company is provided in Application Box 8-3.

## APPLICATION BOX 8-2 Operations Planning at Texas Instruments

The Industrial Automation Division of Texas Instruments (TI) located in Johnson City, Tennessee, manufactures programmable logic controllers. In 1985, TI realized that a lack of functional linkage was preventing products and information from flowing smoothly through the system. To improve customer service, TI examined areas such as vendor deliveries, lead-time reduction, and the production planning process. An evaluation of TI's master production schedules (MPS) prior to 1985 showed a frozen interval of 16 weeks, which meant that changes could only be made beyond the 16-week window. The planning horizon of TI's MPS is six months. The frozen interval was needed to ensure that materials ordered could be delivered in time, labor could be made available, and machine schedules could be developed during that time. Supplier lead times were from 12–18 weeks, and manufacturing lead times ranged from four to eight weeks. TI realized that the long frozen interval was limiting the flexibility of the factory to respond to customer requirements. Combined with the volatile demand forecast and cyclical demand patterns, the problems that were created included expediting, high overtime costs in manufacturing, and poor customer service.

Over a five-year-period, TI improved the demand forecasting process, reduced the frozen interval, used a pull production system, and made more frequent adjustments to the plan. The frozen interval has been reduced to eight weeks for increases in demand and to three weeks for demand decreases. The disparity in the frozen intervals is because it is easier to decrease production than it is to increase capacity. The ability to reduce the frozen interval stems from a reduction in the vendor and manufacturing lead times. Long-term purchase orders were made with suppliers to provide better and more flexible deliveries. Manufacturing lead times were decreased by eliminating nonvalue-added processes, reducing lot sizes, using kanban, and so on. The benefits were the following: total inventory reduced by 45%; the number of orders completed within the standard lead time improved 26%; customer on-time deliveries improved 77%; past-due units decreased from an average of 2000 to 400; orders completed on time improved 50%.

Materials drawn from Mark Rose, "Production Planning at Texas Instruments Improves Service and Reduces Costs," *Industrial Engineering,* January 1991, pp. 33–34, 36.

# *Summary*

Ineffective or inadequate operations planning can lead to a "fire-fighting" mode of operating a business. The outcome is organizational slack, which translates to excess inventories, excess workers, excess overtime costs, excess capacity, long lead times, and long new-product-introduction cycles. For an operations plan to be effective it must be integrated with other plans and endorsed by top management. The operations planning process must be formalized to prevent suboptimal informal systems from evolving. An effective operations plan allows a company to better utilize its scarce resources to satisfy customer requirements. Operations planning, if implemented successfully, can lead to numerous benefits, such as improved productivity and customer-service levels, decreased expediting, reduced setup costs, and decreased inventory costs.

## APPLICATION BOX 8-3 Hierarchical Planning System at American Olean Tile Company

The American Olean Tile Company (AOTC) manufactures a wide array of ceramic tile products. Their products include tile for floors and walls, indoor and outdoor use, residential and commercial customers, and elaborate mural designs. They are grouped into three basic product lines: quarry tiles, glazed tiles, and ceramic mosaics. The company operates eight factories in the United States, which supply approximately 120 sales distribution points (SDPs). The factories utilize many different production processes, but all begin with a crushing and milling procedure, and ultimately lead to the kiln firing of the tiles. AOTC's distribution network has expanded quite rapidly in recent years, prompting management to begin using a modeling program to supplement manual planning of production and distribution. To improve the integration of the annual plan, short-term scheduling, and inventory control the company developed a hierarchical production planning (HPP) system shown in the figure below.

**Hierarchical Planning System at American Olean Quarry Tile Division**

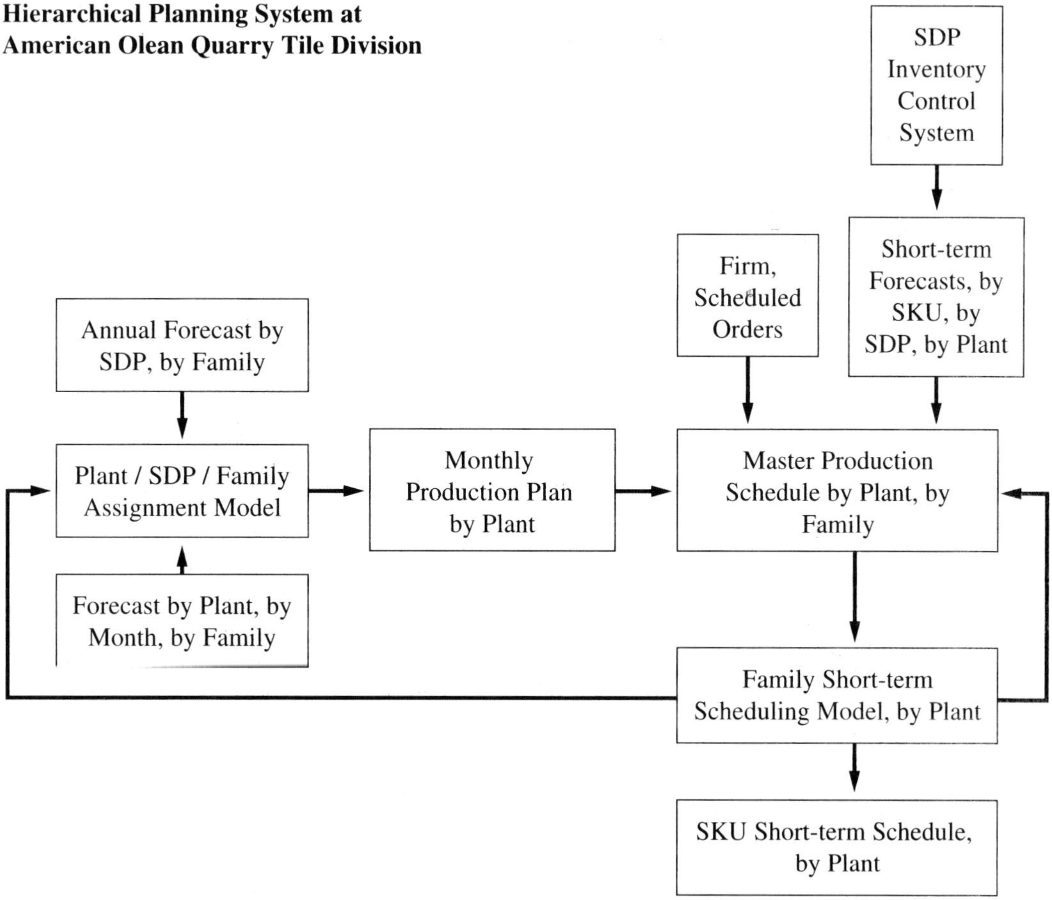




*Continued*

**APPLICATION BOX 8-3** *Continued*

AOTC's HPP system uses a simple aggregation–disaggregation scheme and a mixed-integer-programming model for short-term scheduling. The company first concentrated on the quarry tile division. Products that have similar seasonality patterns are grouped into a family. This aggregation procedure is appropriate for AOTC due to the nature of their products and its manufacturing process. The quarry tile line is grouped into ten product families, each consisting of several hundred stock-keeping units (SKUs), which accounted for over 98% of total quarry sales.

An annual subjective sales forecast for total quarry division sales in square feet of tiles provides the input necessary for production planning. The forecast is generated by the director of market planning and other top management on the basis of numerous inputs, including economic trends and market developments. The forecast is then applied to each of the ten product families on the basis of their percentage of total sales histories. From these forecasts, plus seasonal inventory targets and demand patterns, a monthly production plan is developed by the plant production personnel.

The monthly production plan, combined with large customer orders and short-range forecasts from the sales distribution points, form the master production schedule (MPS). The individual plant production assignments are then made to meet the MPS while minimizing the total of variable manufacturing, setup, and inventory costs. Using this hierarchical planning and scheduling system has improved coordination and communication between the marketing and manufacturing departments, enabled more consistent production planning and scheduling decisions to be made, reduced production and distribution costs, and saved the company between $400,000 and $750,000 annually. In addition, management can use the model to gauge the financial impact of various strategies such as capital investments in additional plant capacity and stopping the manufacturing of a specific product at a plant because the major raw material cost has become too high. Most importantly, the development of an integrated HPP system allows AOTC to significantly improve its capability to be more competitive in the market.

Material drawn from Matthew J. Liberatore and Tan Miller, "A Hierarchical Production Planning System," *Interfaces,* July–August 1985, pp. 1–11.

## *Discussion Questions*

1. What are some of the methods that are used to influence or control demand?
2. List some of the short-term alternatives for affecting supply.
3. Provide a short definition for the following strategies: level, chase, and mixed.
4. Why is product demand aggregated for determining the operations plan?
5. Define the terms time period and planning horizon.
6. Discuss the method of evaluating the performance of the production plan in terms of comparing actual occurrences with planned outcomes.
7. What inputs into the production plan are provided by managers of the following functional areas: marketing, finance, operations, engineering, human resources, and purchasing?
8. Discuss the interface between the production plan and the master production schedule (MPS).

9. What are some of the early warning signals of poor operations planning?
10. List some of the operations planning inputs.
11. State the individual objectives of manufacturing, marketing, and finance, as well as the overall company objective.
12. Discuss operations planning in a just-in-time (JIT) environment such as at Toyota.
13. Discuss some of the operations planning differences between a large manufacturer of ballpoint pens and a small neighborhood ice cream shop.
14. Compare a custom tailoring shop with a large chain of stores that offer mens' apparel in terms of aggregating product demand.
15. Explain why hospitals could be called the model of a chase strategy in action.

## *Strategic Decision Situations*

1. Lawncare Inc. is a manufacturer of electric-powered lawn mowers. Demand for lawn mowers is very seasonal, with the highest demand occurring in the spring and summer quarters. The table below shows aggregate demand forecasts for the next four quarters.

| Quarter | Forecasted Demand (Units) |
|---|---|
| Fall | 3000 |
| Winter | 2000 |
| Spring | 6000 |
| Summer | 5000 |

The following information has been collected. The production rate is 40 units per worker per quarter. The average salary for a production worker is $2200 per quarter. The overtime rate is 150% of the regular time rate, and workers are limited to a maximum of 25% overtime per quarter. The cost of hiring an additional worker is $1500, and the cost of laying a worker off is $1000. Currently there is no inventory in stock. Inventory is calculated at the end of the quarter as: Ending inventory = beginning inventory + production – demand. The holding cost is $20 per unit per quarter. All forecasted demand must be met and no back-orders are allowed.

The management of Lawncare wants to generate an effective production plan for the next fiscal year, which starts in the fall quarter. Abe Favre, the materials manager, has been asked to prepare three alternative plans to be evaluated by managers from finance, marketing, and manufacturing in the next production planning meeting. The production plans to be generated are (a) a level strategy—maintain the current work-force level of 100 workers, using inventories to buffer demand, (b) a chase strategy—adjust the work-force level to meet demand exactly, and (c) a mixed strategy—trim the work force to 90 workers, maintain this work-force level, and use overtime and inventory to buffer demand. The cost of each strategy should also be computed. There is some concern that the cost of capital may increase in the near future, which will increase the original inventory carrying cost by 20%. What is the impact of this on the three plans?

2. The Funtime Amusement Park provides a range of rides, games, and shows throughout the year, but experiences highly seasonal demand, with peaks occurring in May–September and December. The forecasted aggregate demand in labor hours for the next year is provided in the table below. Funtime wants to develop a staffing plan with a one-year planning horizon in order to most efficiently meet customer needs. Each employee works 160 hours per month at an average rate of $8 per hour. Overtime pay is $12 per hour. The maximum amount of overtime per month per employee is 30 hours. The cost to hire an additional worker is $700, and it costs $400 to lay a worker off. All forecasted demand must be met, or revenues will fall. The company currently has 250 workers.

Three alternative staffing plans are being considered: (a) a level strategy—using overtime to buffer demand and maintain a stable work-force level, (b) a chase strategy—adjusting the work force to meet demand exactly, and (c) a mixed strategy—a combination of hiring/laying off employees and overtime. These strategies are to be compared on the basis of cost, with the least expensive being chosen. In addition, if the cost to hire a worker is $1400, what is the impact on the three plans?

**Forecasted Demand**

| Month | Labor Hours | Month | Labor Hours |
|---|---|---|---|
| January | 21,600 | July | 54,000 |
| February | 21,600 | August | 54,000 |
| March | 27,000 | September | 43,200 |
| April | 32,400 | October | 27,000 |
| May | 43,200 | November | 20,000 |
| June | 54,000 | December | 37,800 |

## *References*


Buffa, Elwood S. "Aggregate Planning for Production," *Business Horizons*. Fall 1967, pp. 87–97.

Buffa, Elwood S., and Jeffrey Miller. *Production-Inventory Systems: Planning and Control*. Homewood, Ill.: Irwin, 1979.

Drucker, Peter F. "Long-Range Planning," *Management Science*. Vol. 5, No. 3, 1959, pp. 238–249.

Everdell, Romeyn, and Judith A. Ryde. "The Production Plan—The Top Management Interface," *APICS Twenty-Fifth Annual Conference Proceedings*, 1982, pp. 231–238.

Georgoff, David M., and Robert G. Murdick. "Manager's Guide to Forecasting," *Harvard Business Review*. January–February 1986, pp. 110–186.

Helliker, Kevin. "If There's Hardly Anything Left to Buy, It's Tuesday Morning on Christmas Eve," *Wall Street Journal*. December 23, 1991.

Holt, Charles C., Franco Modigliani, and Herbert Simon. "A Linear Decision Rule for Production and Employment Scheduling," *Management Science*. October 1955, pp. 1–30.

Leong, G. Keong, Michael D. Oliff, and Robert E. Markland. "Improved Hierarchical Production Planning," *Journal of Operations Management*. Vol. 8, No. 3, 1989, pp. 90–114.

Liberatore, Matthew J., and Tan Miller. "A Hierarchical Production Planning System," *Interfaces*. July–August 1985, pp. 1–11.

Meal, Harlan C. "Putting Production Decisions Where They Belong," *Harvard Business Review*. March–April 1984, pp. 102–111.

Monden, Y. "Smoothed Production Lets Toyota Adapt to Demand Changes and Reduce Inventory," *Industrial Engineering*. August 1981, pp. 42–51.

Northcraft, Gregory B., and Richard B. Chase. "Managing Service Demand at the Point of Delivery," *Academy of Management Review.* January 1985, pp. 66–75.

Oliff, Michael D., and Earl Burch. "Multiproduct Production Scheduling at Owens-Corning Fiberglas," *Interfaces.* September–October 1985, pp. 25–34.

Oliff, Michael D., and G. Keong Leong. "A Discrete Production Switching Rule for Aggregate Planning," *Decision Sciences.* Fall 1987, pp. 582–597.

Pollock, Michael A., and Aaron Bernstein. "The Disposable Employee Is Becoming a Fact of Corporate Life," *Business Week.* December 15, 1986, pp. 52–53, 56.

Root, Cary M. "Production Planning: Past, Present and Potential," *Inventories and Production.* May–June 1983, pp. 6–10.

Rose, Mark. "Production Planning at Texas Instruments Improves Service and Reduces Costs," *Industrial Engineering.* January 1991, pp. 33–34, 36.

Sasser, W. Earl. "Match Supply and Demand in Services," *Harvard Business Review.* November–December 1976, pp. 133–140.

Schlesinger, Leonard A., and James L. Heskett. "The Service-Driven Service Company," *Harvard Business Review.* September–October 1991, pp. 71–81.

Shapiro, Benson. "Can Marketing and Manufacturing Coexist?" *Harvard Business Review.* September–October 1977, pp. 104–114.

Venkatesan, Ravi. "Cummins Engine Flexes Its Factory," *Harvard Business Review.* March–April 1990, pp. 120–127.

Vollmann, Thomas E., William L. Berry, and D. Clay Whybark. *Manufacturing Planning and Control Systems.* 3rd ed. Homewood, Ill.: Irwin, 1992.

Wantuck, Kenneth. *Just-In-Time for America.* Southfield, Minn: KWA Media, 1989.

Wight, Oliver W. *Production and Inventory Management in the Computer Age.* Boston, Mass.: Cahners Publishing Company, Inc., 1974.

# *Chapter 9*

# *Improving Materials Management*

*The logic of MRP is universally applicable; the way it is applied depends upon the environment.* —George W. Plossl, 1985

*Parts is parts . . . is parts.* —A Shop Floor Colloquialism

## *Objectives*

After completing this chapter you should be able to

- Define materials management and describe four dimensions of materials management practices.
- Identify the four foundations of inventory decisions.
- Describe traditional inventory management methods and their shortfalls.
- Describe material requirements planning and difficulties in implementing material requirements planning systems.
- Describe ways to continuously improve materials management practices.

## *Outline*

## *Introductory Case: MRP Implementation at Helene Curtis*

Mike Garsombke looked around as he entered Room 2042C. He knew this would be a long meeting, yet there was no other way to ensure that every aspect of the program was coordinated. His implementation team, Don in scheduling, Laura in inventory, Roger in purchasing, Edna in automation, and Wayne on the shop floor, watched Mike enter. They also knew this would be a long meeting.

Helene Curtis*, a leading manufacturer and distributor of professional hair care products and beauty shop aids, had made the decision more than a decade ago to automate the punch card inventory control system. The first effort was a disaster. It seemed that the weekly printout was always late and inaccurate and never contained the needed information. Despite the difficulties of the first attempt, the nature of the product line almost required the use of an automated materials management system. Though its product would appear rather simple in structure (with components of base, soap, fragrance, colorizers, diffusers, softeners, and packaging), in fact, the company carries over 20,000 stock-keeping units.

Mike had joined Helene Curtis a bit more than seven years ago and since then, had spent what seemed to be more than one career in MRP. His first priority, as the assistant implementation team chief, had been to get the files in shape. Much of the early difficulties had been caused by inaccurate inventories of raw materials and schedule changes requiring supplier deliveries to be expedited. Mike remembered those early days. "Everyone had a small 'stash' of inventory; it was part of the company culture. The stash of inventory was like a bank account, you could draw on it to help a friend—or to get

*Materials drawn from conversations with "Mike."

yourself through a squeeze. It was almost like job security. . . . And that system worked well when inventories didn't cost much and were less complex."

"We also had to replace the primary consultant and set up a schedule of training small groups for ten to 15 hours per week. And that was after you did your normal job. We didn't even touch a computer until the files were good and the people knew their jobs, and how the human system interfaced with the computer system. Then they understood how MRP could help them. It took about 18 months to get the first phase (bill of materials, schedule, and inventory) on line. Despite the training and care in systems implementation, we had some glitches. We spent several months upgrading from a class C system to a class B; now we are close to an A system. It just has to be right, or it isn't worth doing." After his boss retired, Mike was promoted to the implementation team chief position and had directed the continuous improvement of the upgraded system.

Mike took a chair at the head of the table and leaned back. He looked thoughtfully at the flow charts on the wall and chuckled. They had come a long way. Inventory turns had tripled, costs had decreased, and stockouts, which used to constantly disrupt the manufacturing process, had been virtually eliminated. Reaching into his pocket, he pulled out a game spinner, the kind with a big arrow, and set it in the center of the table. "OK," he said. "Scheduling, who's up?" Don hit the spinner, and to the group's approval, it stopped at Laura. "You know," Mike said, as he nodded at Laura, "you just can't take this stuff too seriously."

## *Materials Management Systems*

The cost of materials has been estimated (Gunn, 1987) at roughly 50% of the total production cost with some variance depending upon the industry. The corresponding contribution of direct labor and overhead was estimated at 15% and 35%, respectively. However, by the year 2000, Gunn estimates that the cost of materials will increase to 75%, with labor and overhead shrinking to roughly 3% and 22%, respectively. Thus, the intensity with which materials resources are managed by operations managers can be expected to increase correspondingly.

Note that materials management is considered by some to be primarily a manufacturing concern; correspondingly, services are considered by those persons to be more concerned with the delivery of intangibles. This inaccurate stereotype seriously misrepresents the chain of transformations and the functions of an operations manager. Though service deliverables usually involve high proportions of intangibles, most services require some amount of inventory. For example, retail activities are at the end of a very long inventory distribution pipeline. A dentist cannot fill cavities without inventories of silver, replacement tools, and various drugs and liquids. Even telephone, electricity, gas, and other utility services require extensive inventories of spare parts and tools. The rapidly growing area of product distribution and service delivery involves extensive and often costly holdings of inventory.

Materials management systems are projected to become a more important and more visible operations resource in this decade because of increasing materials costs and the growing service economy. Materials management activities involve the flow of materials, including the volume and timing of materials transactions. As such, materials management incorporates purchasing, inventory control, and distribution systems. More formally, materials management is defined as:

> *Coordinated activities to* plan for and control *the* volume and timing *of materials flow through acquisition, transformation and movement (the* phases of materials management*) of raw materials, work-in-process, and finished goods (the* states of materials*).*

This definition emphasizes four dimensions of materials management. These are the primary topics of this chapter; other aspects of these topics are developed in the following chapter. Ed Heard (in Moody, 1990) describes the distinction between the materials and scheduling aspects of production as "visible" inventory (for example, units that are stored or awaiting use—or in inventory) and "invisible" inventory (for example, units that are currently being transformed—or scheduled for work). The significance of this distinction is that management usually counts only visible inventory. In fact, both visible and invisible inventory should be counted because visible inventory indicates the effectiveness of the forecasting–scheduling–distribution system, while invisible inventory is a measure of the effectiveness of the production process. The four dimensions of materials management are further defined as:

1. *Planning and Control.* Typically materials management planning activities extend a minimum of three months and often as much as two to three years into the future. Planning periods define the control mechanisms that are used in the execution of the plan.
2. *Volume and Timing.* Materials decisions involve both volume and timing, which, taken together, define the rate of flow. For example, if annual usage of a particular item is 500,000 units, then the movement of that item may be accomplished once yearly at volumes of 500,000, at quarterly volumes of 125,000, monthly volumes of 41,667, weekly volumes of 9615, or daily volumes, for 360 working days per year, of 1389.
3. *Phases of Materials Management.* The activities of materials management occur in various phases, which are functionally described as acquisition, transformation, and movement. These phases may also be categorized as purchasing, inventory management (storage, moving, queuing, setup, and transformation), and distribution.
4. *States of the Materials.* The states of the materials may be defined as raw materials, work-in-process, and finished goods.

Because of the differences in materials management situations and variations in the contribution of materials to the total production costs, numerous materials management techniques have emerged. This chapter initially describes materials management systems, and then notes the classic reasons for inventory and the categories of inventory management systems. Subsequently, various inventory management methods are discussed, including the traditional order quantity methods, automated materials planning techniques, and continuous improvement approaches. The central premise of the chapter, noted in the quotes on the chapter title page, is that the logic of materials management is universal, though applications vary extensively.

## *A Cushion against Uncertainty*

As defined, the materials management system is one of three components that are central to the execution of operations strategy.

1. *Materials Decisions*—use prepositioned, internal and external (to the firm) inventories, defined as items and volumes, to reduce costs, processing, or delivery times.
2. *Scheduling Decisions*—use available capacity and, through flexibility and delivery, respond to customer orders.
3. *Customer Service Decisions*—design, create, and deliver the product/service as specified by the customer.

These components are traditionally regarded as often conflicting in terms of their cost. For example, a low-cost schedule traditionally involves longer production runs (with fewer change-overs or setups), but longer production runs often result in higher inventory costs and, in some environments, may cause poorer responsiveness to customer requirements or service. Alternatively, more varied, higher-cost scheduling results in lower material costs and better service performance. Similarly, high levels of customer service can be achieved through either large inventories or very flexible scheduling, or a compromise position. Conventional operations theory suggests that a strategy must be selected from these alternatives.

No one strategy is appropriate for all situations. For example, a stationery store would likely periodically order larger inventories of the ubiquitous throw-away pen, but more frequently order smaller quantities of a costly designer pen. Figure 9-1 shows the three "pure strategies" and suggests an area of compromise alternatives or niches.

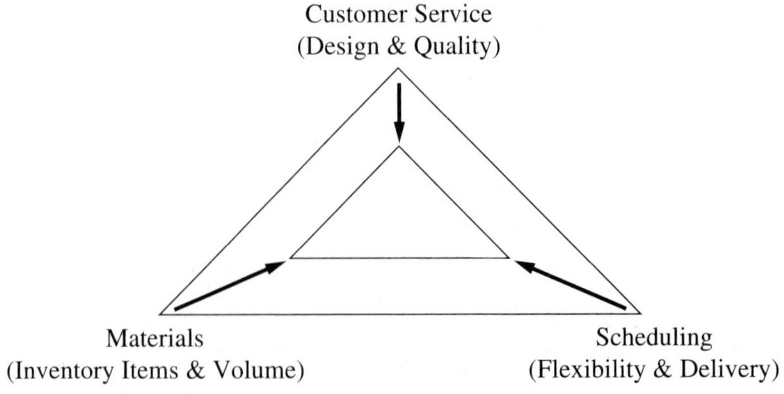


**FIGURE 9-1 The Components in the Execution of Operations Strategy**

Current operations strategy suggests that the operations manager competitively position the operations system in a strategically defined niche, considering materials, scheduling, and customer service requirements and costs. These three controllable components (materials management, operations scheduling, and customer service) must be mixed to achieve the best interests of the customer. Where the customer is involved, there can be no conflicts (Schaeffer, 1993). The materials management questions are closely related to the three components, as follows:

| | |
|---|---|
| What product is needed? | Customer service—design and quality issues |
| How much is needed? | Materials management—inventory and volume issues |
| When is it needed? | Operations scheduling—flexibility and delivery issues |

Many of the recent developments in materials management have emphasized continuous improvement of production systems to simultaneously reduce inventories, permit more flexible scheduling, and provide more responsive service to customer needs. Actions by a firm toward these goals can be shown as the smaller triangle in the center of Figure 9-1, which represents a smaller, yet more flexible and faster-moving pipeline.

The selected position of operations in Figure 9-1 also represents the type of cushion that will be used against the uncertainty of customer demand. Safety stock inventory and safety capacity are widely used by manufacturing managers; however, distribution managers regularly use no-cost trade-ups in the event of item stockouts. The ability of a firm to respond to customer demand uncertainty thus depends upon an aggregate of inventory, scheduling, and customer service decisions.

## *Inventory—Asset or Liability*

Inventory, or items that are stocked against future expected use, represents both a potential asset and a potential liability to an operations manager. On the one hand, inventory represents stored production (capacity) or value added that, when the product is sold, will produce a profit for the firm. If the demand or the price for the product or service is expected to increase, a firm would be encouraged to stock additional inventories. Conversely, inventories usually involve a heavy capital investment in materials, labor, and overhead, which incur financial or opportunity costs. Additionally, building a larger inventory than is immediately necessary may be risky, particularly if the potential for shrinkage, including obsolescence, deterioration, or pilferage of the item is high.

More specifically, reasons to carry inventory or to increase inventory holdings are the need for improved customer service, efficiencies of transportation, reduced per-unit ordering or setup costs, and smoothed resource utilization. Alternatively, the reasons to reduce inventories are high interest rates or opportunity costs, unavailability of storage or excessive handling costs, undesirable insurance and tax costs, and shrinkage costs. Thus, to determine the "best" level of inventory for an item, the costs of carrying inventory must be compared with the corresponding costs of not carrying inventory. A number of methods are available to evaluate this decision, from the traditional order quantity methods, to more recent materials planning methods, and the now widely practiced continuous improvement approaches. Today, most materials managers agree with Beddingfield (1992) that reducing inventory increases cash flow and reduces carrying costs, thereby enhancing competitiveness.

## *Foundations of Inventory Decisions*

Inventory is a fact of life. It is required for running water and is the reason for the use of refrigerators (to store food) and bank accounts (to store money). There are many situations that cause and require inventory, and thus there are many ways to classify inventory. Inventory results because of a need to smooth the flow of goods through the chain of transformations. Note that services are generally not storable and thus are usually not considered as an inventory item. Inventory can be classified as either dependent on or independent of other actions or decisions and may be categorized for varying amounts of management attention. This section describes the functions of inventory, differentiates dependent and independent demands, and evaluates inventory categories using ABC analysis.

### *Functions of Inventory*

Inventory, whether considered as goods on hand or managed as a back-order or backlog capability, is required for four reasons: to *anticipate expected variances* in requirements, to *provide safety against unexpected variance* in requirements, to *permit efficient use of lot-sizing,* and to *smooth inventory flow in transportation.* There are two general cases for each of these functions, as shown in Table 9-1.

**TABLE 9-1 Functions of Inventory or Backlogs**

Anticipation Inventory

- Respond to expected cyclic demand for goods or materials
- Accommodate expected cyclic supply of goods or materials

Safety Stock

- Cover unexpected supplier shortfalls
- Absorb unexpected demand variation

Efficiencies of Lot-Sizing

- Prorate order costs of external purchases
- Prorate internal setup costs and permit partial deliveries

Transportation Inventory

- Allow for pipeline inventories
- Account for work-in-process

Anticipation inventory accounts for *expected* variations in the flow of inventory usage. For example, in most parts of the northern hemisphere, few snowblowers are sold in the months of June or July, and few lawn mowers are sold in the months of December or January. However, manufacturers of snowblowers and lawn mowers (this combination of products might be expected because of the common production technologies and processes), with a one-month delivery lead time, might build lawn mowers from February to June. After a one-month line changeover in July, they would build snowblowers in August through December, with a changeover back to lawn mowers in January. The lawn mowers would be built and transported to retail outlets by March, in anticipation of the spring and summer sales period, and the snowblowers would be built starting in August in anticipation of sales in the fall and winter. Thus, an inventory buildup of lawn mowers would occur from February through April or May, when sales would increase; similarly, an inventory buildup of snowblowers would occur from August through October or November. This is anticipation inventory due to cyclical demand for the product. Similarly, because the supply of some goods, agricultural produce, for example, is cyclical, inventories are held until the item is demanded. In products that experience seasonal demand, anticipation inventories are established to smooth expected variations of demand or supply.

Safety stocks accommodate *unexpected* variations in supply or demand. Raw material safety stocks permit an operations manager to cover unexpected supplier shortfalls, for example, if a delivery truck is delayed by an accident or a supplier's equipment fails. Safety stock may also be used to protect against a stock-out due to an unexpected surge in demand, for example, after a major storm. Safety stock smooths inventory flow over random or uncontrolled events; it is a buffer which permits continued operation of a process.

Efficiencies of lot-sizing permit *prorating* of external purchase orders or internal machine setups over several or many units in an order or production lot. The more units that these one-time costs of purchasing or machine setup can be prorated over, the more efficient the processing, yielding economies of scale. However, with long runs and few setups, inventories increase. For example, it does not make sense for most businesses to order one box of business stationery. Given the costs of communicating the order, setting up a printing press, delivering the product, and setting up the payment, it is more efficient to purchase several boxes of stationery at one time. This example applies both to setting up an order for external purchase and to setting up a machine for internal production of a component.

Fourth, some transportation inventory will inevitably be required in the pipeline to *smooth* the materials flow. Perhaps the most apparent examples of pipeline inventory are the oil and gas stored in "pipelines," including rail and truck tankers and storage facilities. However, other less apparent pipeline inventories would include forestry and agricultural goods, foods such as milk or cheese, irrigation and commercial water supply systems, and many bulk raw materials. These materials may be held in external transportation or distribution systems or as internal work in process. Because of the bulk, weight, or perishability of an item, or to ensure a convenient flow of the product, the most efficient method of delivery or movement is by "pipeline."

## *Categories of Demand for Inventory*

Demand for inventory or services can be categorized as either dependent or independent. Dependent demand is driven by a manufacturing schedule, by a required service, or by retail demand for a related product. Directly scheduled demands generally involve manufactured end items, such as furniture, automobiles, appliances, and the like. For example, most chairs require four legs, most automobiles require four tires (excluding the spare tire), and most stoves have four burners. Thus, once an end item is scheduled, the parts required to build that item are dependent on the schedule. Similarly, some styles of chair are sold with the corresponding foot rest, and stereo speakers are built and priced individually, but often sold in pairs. In services, examples of dependent demand include medical and dental facilities and inventories that are committed based on appointments or scheduled procedures.

Alternatively, demand for many services and end items is independent of a schedule or of demand for a related product. Demands for medical care, telephone service, repair parts for automobiles and after-market accessories, or entertainment services are not directly dependent upon a schedule or tie-in sale. Demand for these items must be forecast.

The importance of the distinction between dependent and independent demand is that each approach uses different inventory management methods. If demands are treated as independent, then those demands are forecast over time and the inventory decision is based on an inexact estimate of the period demand. Assumptions must be made about the regularity of the flow of demand and replenishment times. Thus, independent demand management methods are imprecise about how much is needed and when it is needed. However, if demands for inventory are dependent, say, on a production schedule, then inventory management decisions can be more exact—unless the schedule changes.

The preceding description emphasizes the dichotomy of dependent and independent demand management environments. In practice, the demand for most products and services is both dependent and independent. For example, demand for automobile tires by an automobile manufacturer is dependent upon the manufacturing schedule, but demand for replacement of those same tires is independent. Similarly, the use of communication lines by private individuals is likely to be independent, but usage of these same lines for transmission of business or financial data is dependent upon the updating process, which is planned.

Because of the increased exactness of dependent inventory management systems, businesses have been motivated to capture information about their demand and thus treat those demands as dependent or schedulable. For example, in many areas, requirements for gas and electric power are both commercial and residential. Those requirements are carefully planned in close coordination with major commercial users, and the remaining (often as little as 20%) demand is forecast for residential areas. By segregating dependent and independent demands, utility operations are able to manage capacity-bound resources more efficiently. The demands for natural gas and heating oil can be similarly managed. As demand dependencies for inventory are established, requirements planning and scheduling methods are increasingly feasible.

## *ABCs of Inventory Management*

A nineteenth-century Italian economist, Wilfredo Pareto, found, in a study of the wealth distribution, that 20% of the population had 80% of the total wealth. The next 30% of the population had 15% of the wealth, and the final 50% of the population had 5% of the total wealth. Applied to inventory management, Pareto's "principle" suggests that there are the critical few high-cost items of inventory that should be carefully managed and the trivial many items, which are of less concern. So-called A items are the most costly, and should be carefully managed, while B and C items are less costly categories and receive less management attention. Note that in application, there may be more than three categories of items and that the proportion of items is set according to each situation.

Pareto analysis computes the total inventory value of the item, either in total dollars (the number of units times the item cost) or in item criticality (often measured by perishability, stockout penalty, the cost of closing a work center or facility, or the result of a quality defect) among several items; then the items are resequenced according to total cost. Applications of the Pareto principle include inventory management, quality control, forecasting accuracy, and other operations decisions. Simply stated, the operations manager should most carefully manage the categories that have the greatest cost or potential impact on the operation.

The highest-total-cost item would be given the most attention. The proportion of items defined in categories A, B, and C, and the proportional costs of those items, taken cumulatively, will vary among environments. For example, the inventory of a luxury jewelry store would likely be almost entirely A items, while most items of a feed and grain store would be managed as C items. Other operations might handle a wider range of items which, when categorized by cost, permit a more clear distinction of A, B, and C items. Decision Model Box 9-1 shows the computation and use of ABC analysis.

ABC analysis is widely used in support of cycle counting programs that are used in service distribution systems. The traditional physical inventory counting process is rarely used today because it requires the shutdown of major parts of an operation and because it may result in a greater number of counting errors.

Alternatively, cycle counting may be used to count some proportion of the inventory items each day on a cyclic schedule. Typically, a cycle-counting team is required to verify the inventory items (including part numbers, number of items, and storage location) of a fixed number of records each day. Of course, the inventory status of A items would be more regularly checked than those for B or C items. However, as Greene (1987) notes, there are a number of other circumstances when a count may be warranted. "Opportunity" counts are scheduled when inventory quantities are low because, with low inventories, the counting effort and potential confusion are reduced. "Low-cost" counts are generated if a stock person is working with the item at the storage site. For example, in the process of picking an item for an order, a stock person could count the remaining items at the storage site with little extra effort. "Special" counts may be required by an unexpected outage or a major discrepancy—either of which indicates a system error or other significant problem (possibly pilferage or faulty stocking action).

## DECISION MODEL BOX 9-1 The ABCs of Inventory at Compuserve Distributors

Compuserve Distributors stocks ten models of printer. Given the following data, determine which printers should be more intensely managed, using two ABC analysis approaches: one based on total inventory cost and the second based on the criticality of stocking out.

| Stock Number | Volume/ Year | Cost/ Unit | Stockout Penalty/Unit | Stock Number | Volume/ Year | Cost/ Unit | Stockout Penalty/Unit |
|---|---|---|---|---|---|---|---|
| 21 | 135 | 100 | 150 | 61 | 75 | 350 | 10 |
| 31 | 75 | 200 | 50 | 62 | 45 | 500 | 50 |
| 41 | 200 | 250 | 650 | 71 | 125 | 700 | 200 |
| 42 | 150 | 400 | 50 | 72 | 75 | 850 | 100 |
| 51 | 90 | 300 | 250 | 73 | 30 | 950 | 150 |

Total volume = 1000 Total cost: (volume × cost) = $394,000
Total cost: (volume × stockout penalty/unit) = $224,000

Generalized, the ABC procedure has three steps: (1) determine the input data values (annual volume, cost/unit, and, if needed, the stock-out penalty per unit) of each item. (2) Sum these values; then divide the unit cost or the unit penalty by the total value to find the percentage. (3) Resequence the values based on the percentages and categorize as A, B, or C.

ABC according to the percentage of total cost of inventory:

| Stock Number | Volume/ Year | Cost/ Unit | Total Cost | Percent Total Cost | Stock Number | Volume/ Year | Cost/ Unit | Total Cost | Percent Total Cost |
|---|---|---|---|---|---|---|---|---|---|
| 71 | 125 | 700 | $87,500 | 22.21—A | 51 | 90 | 300 | $27,000 | 6.85—C |
| 72 | 75 | 850 | 63,750 | 16.18—B | 61 | 75 | 350 | 26,250 | 6.66—C |
| 42 | 150 | 400 | 60,000 | 15.23—B | 62 | 45 | 500 | 22,500 | 5.71—C |
| 41 | 200 | 250 | 50,000 | 12.69—B | 31 | 75 | 200 | 15,000 | 3.81—C |
| 73 | 30 | 950 | 28,500 | 7.23—C | 21 | 135 | 100 | 13,500 | 3.43—C |

ABC according to the percentage of total cost of the stockout penalty:

| Stock Number | Volume/ Year | Penalty/ Unit | Total Penalty | Percent Total Cost | Stock Number | Volume/ Year | Penalty/ Unit | Total Penalty | Percent Total Cost |
|---|---|---|---|---|---|---|---|---|---|
| 41 | 200 | 650 | $130,000 | 58.04—A | 42 | 150 | 50 | 7,500 | 3.35—C |
| 71 | 125 | 200 | 25,000 | 11.16—B | 73 | 30 | 150 | 4,500 | 2.01—C |
| 51 | 90 | 250 | 22,500 | 10.04—B | 31 | 75 | 50 | 3,750 | 1.67—C |
| 21 | 135 | 150 | 20,250 | 9.04—B | 62 | 45 | 50 | 2,250 | 1.00—C |
| 72 | 75 | 100 | 7,500 | 3.35—C | 61 | 75 | 10 | 750 | 0.33—C |

*Continued*

**DECISION MODEL BOX 9-1** *Continued*

The ABC chart shows the *cumulative* percent of inventory items on the horizontal axis and the selected management criteria on the vertical axis. The left chart shows cumulative percent inventory cost, while the right chart shows cumulative percent stockout penalty. The determination of the number or percent of A, B, and C items is judgmental, but often approximates the 20%, 30%, 50% ratio found by Pareto. In this situation, ABC analysis would be particularly helpful in managing high-penalty items.

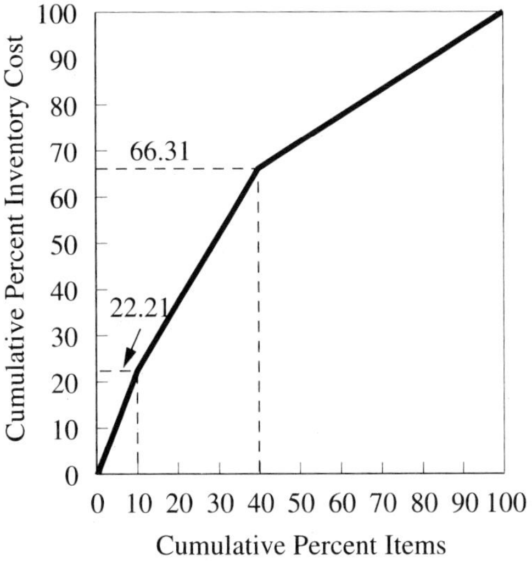


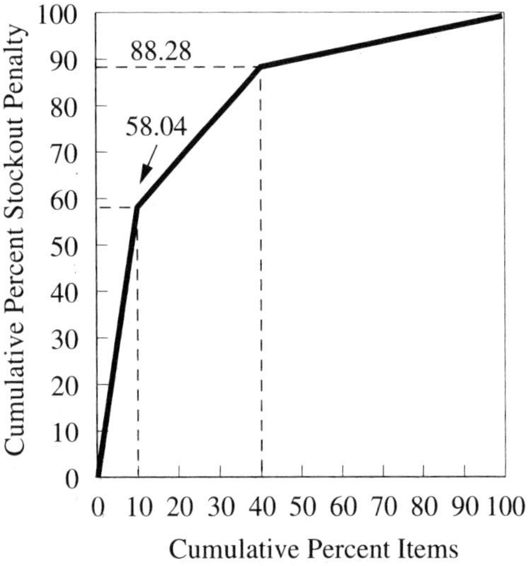


## *Traditional Inventory Management*

Traditional methods of inventory management involve inventory decisions directed toward reducing either the cost or the risk of holding inventory. Most traditional methods identify periodic demands (often annual) and calculate the minimum cost per unit based on the cost of ordering and a fixed per-unit carrying cost. Typically, such computations involve a trade-off between the cost of ordering (purchasing, delivery, inspection, and budget transactions) and the cost of carrying (interest, warehousing and security, and stock shrinkage, including pilferage, deterioration, and obsolescence). The traditional methods of inventory management classify inventory decisions in each of the three materials management questions (what product is needed, how much is needed, and when is it needed?). Unfortunately, traditional methods do not provide a complete analysis of these three questions.

### *Economic Order Quantity*

The economic order quantity is commonly represented in two ways: (1) as the inventory level over time, and (2) as the total cost of inventory management (including item cost,

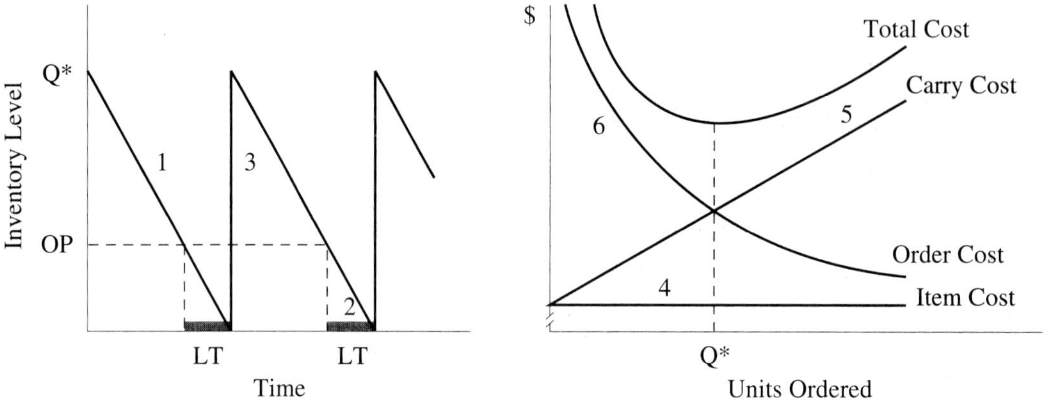


Note:
Q* = Economic order quantity
LT = Lead time
OP = Order point

**FIGURE 9-2 The Economic Order Quantity**

setup cost, and carrying cost) for different amounts of products ordered. These relationships are shown in Figure 9-2. The $Q^*$, the economic order quantity, is the order amount at which total inventory costs are minimized. The basic EOQ model requires seven assumptions, which are (1) constant demand for inventory, (2) constant order lead times, (3) one-time receipt of the entire order, (4) constant item cost per unit—no quantity discounts, (5) constant per-unit carrying costs, (6) a one-time fixed order/setup cost that units are prorated over, and (7) single (not multiple) transactions (Fogarty et al., 1991). These assumptions are represented in Figure 9-2.

These assumptions may appear to be rather constraining; however, the consequence of loosening some of these assumptions may not be severe. If the $Q^*$ varies by, say 10%, there is very little change in the total cost of inventory. This is because the total cost curve is "inelastic" in the vicinity of the EOQ.

Additionally, a variety of models have been developed which permit the convenience of discrete period (for example, a week, a month, and so on) ordering. The more commonly used of these models include the lot-for-lot ordering (order the number of units required for each period), the period order quantity (order for the discrete period volume that is closest to the EOQ), the least unit cost, the least total cost, and the part period balancing. Most introductory operations management or management science texts review several of these models. Decision Model Box 9-2 shows the EOQ calculation.

## *Limitations of EOQ*

Unfortunately, despite the extensive variations of the EOQ, this approach has several limitations. Even with the inelasticity of the total cost curve in the vicinity of the EOQ,

## DECISION MODEL BOX 9-2 Lot-sizing at the Mid-West Distributor

The Mid-West Distributor stocks and delivers Golden Eagle Beer in a three-state area. Demand is 200 cases/day, or, with 300 business days per year, 60,000 cases/year. The lead time for resupply from the brewery is one day, and the standard deviation of daily demand is 50 cases. If the annual interest rate is 15% and shrinkage is 5%, the cost is \$10.00 per case, and the order cost is \$20, calculate the economic order quantity, the interval between orders, the number of orders, and the safety stock (95% service level).

The formulas for the economic order quantity ($Q^*$) and reorder point with safety stock ($r$) are

$$Q^* = \sqrt{\frac{2DC_o}{C_h}}$$

$$r = \mu + z\sigma$$

where: $Q^*$ = economic order quantity
$D$ = demand rate in units *per period*
$C_o$ = cost of ordering in dollars
$C_h$ = period holding cost per unit [(interest rate ($i$) + shrinkage ($s$)] × item cost)
$r$ = reorder point
$\mu$ = demand over lead time
$z$ = number of standard deviations for a specified service level
$\sigma$ = standard deviation of lead time demand

*Note:* An annual period, as shown in this example, is commonly, though not mandatorily, used.

Solution, $Q$ system:

$$Q = \sqrt{\frac{2\ (C_o = 20)\ (\text{days/yr} = 300)\ (\text{daily demand} = 200)}{(\text{Cost} = \$10)(i = 0.15 + s = 0.05)}} = 1095.445 \approx 1100 \text{ cases}$$

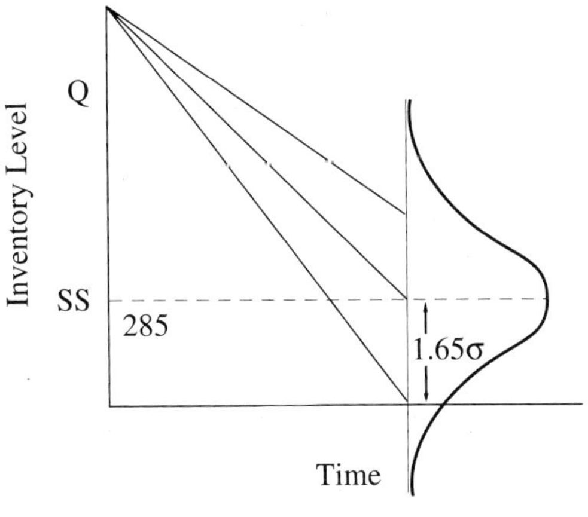


*Continued*

**DECISION MODEL BOX 9-2** *Continued*

With a 95% service level, the $z$ value is 1.65 (from a $z$ table). Because the lead time is 1 day, demand during the lead time is 60,000/300, or 200 cases. The reorder point, with safety, is $r = \mu + z\sigma$, or $200 + 1.65(50) = 282.5$, or 285 cases. The number of orders is 60,000/1100, or 54.5, roughly one order every 5.5 days. The $Q$ system places an order of 1100 cases when stock drops to 285 cases.

The period order quantity method adjusts the EOQ to a convenient discrete period. For example, if the order period were once per week (six-day business week), the POQ would be 1200 cases per order.

The relevant cost of inventory for one year would be the cost of holding plus the cost of ordering. Sometimes the annual item purchase cost is included in the formula. Including the annual item purchase cost, the total cost is:

Total cost = cost of holding + cost of ordering + annual item purchase cost

or

$$TC = QC_h/2 + DC_o/Q + DC$$

or

$$TC = 1095 + 1095 + 600{,}000 = \$602{,}190$$

the EOQ and the reorder point methods may be high-cost strategies. This is because they require the definition of a fixed annual demand (which would likely vary), they do not consider exactly when the demand occurs, and they overemphasize the minimum total inventory costs, rather than considering holding and order setup cost contributions to the total.

The total cost of inventory, given varying order sizes and different order quantity models, does not vary greatly because of the inelasticity of the total cost curve in the vicinity of the EOQ. This can be shown by calculating the total cost of an order policy of 10% or 25% greater or less than the EOQ, using the total cost formula in Decision Model Box 9-2, shown as follows:

| **Variance** | $Q$ | **Total Cost** |
|---|---|---|
| –25% | ≈820 | 820 + 1463.41 + 600,000 = \$602,283.41 |
| –10% | ≈985 | 985 + 1218.27 + 600,000 = \$602,203.27 |
| EOQ | 1095 | 1095 + 1095 + 600,000 = \$602,190.00 |
| +10% | ≈1205 | 1205 + 995.85 + 600,000 = \$602,200.85 |
| +25% | ≈1370 | 1370 + 875.91 + 600,000 = \$602,245.91 |

Note that a 10% variance in the EOQ amounts to a roughly \$12.00 variance in total inventory cost, which is about one-half of one percent of the inventory cost (\$12/2190 = 0.00548). For a 25% variance of the EOQ, the cost increment is about 4%. When the annual unit purchase cost of \$600,000 is included in the computation, the cost variance is trivial. Thus, it really does not make too much difference which order quantity or which models are used, particularly if the values used in the computation, such as the annual demand, the interest rate, or the cost (or procedures) for ordering, are subject to change.

The EOQ computation is dependent on stated values for annual demand, interest rates, costs of ordering, and of the item. Annual national economic projections, as aggregate forecasts, are often quite accurate; however, few operations managers would claim to forecast, with less than 25% error, disaggregate demand to item level or even regional sales level. Additionally, demand for most items is seasonal, which would require the computation of an EOQ for the higher season and another for the low season. The use of a quarterly or even a monthly period for EOQ computations is possible, but even this does not consider forecast errors.

Other areas of data inaccuracies are that the cost of the item may be stated as a standard cost, not the production cost, and shrinkage may be overstated or understated by the widely used 5% assumption. Further, several contributors to order setup costs, including ordering technologies, counting procedures, shipping methods, and internal machine setup technologies, have changed dramatically in the past few years, but may not be reflected in revised EOQ computations. In fact, it is very difficult to state several of the values used in the EOQ computation with accuracy (Rhodes, 1981). Thus, the EOQ is computed primarily from forecasts and estimates, which may be quite inaccurate. However, the inelasticity of the total cost curve in the vicinity of the EOQ makes it rather robust to changes or inaccuracies in the data. The square root radicai in the formula gives a stabilizing effect. For example, a quadrupling or reduction of demand by three-fourths would respectively double or halve the EOQ. Similarly, reducing the holding costs or item costs by three-fourths or quadrupling the holding costs or item costs would only double or halve the EOQ.

Unfortunately, this stabilizing effect may tend to discourage efforts to operate on the contributing factors to inventory costs. By focusing management attention on the algebraic minimization of the total cost curve, the EOQ directs attention away from the contributors to total cost, the various carrying and ordering costs. Though the unit carrying cost may be given (at least it is not directly controlled by the operations manager), efficiencies of ordering or internal setups are directly realizable by operations managers. Examples include the reduced costs and increased accuracy of cycle counting, long-term supplier contracts (for example, blanket contracts), telephone or fax ordering, computer-managed setups, external setups (for example, outside of the equipment, which can be prepared before the equipment is shut down), and shared deliveries. As order costs or setup costs are reduced, the total cost of inventory is reduced and the quantity of the $Q^*$ decreases, as shown in Figure 9-3.

Probably the most significant deficiency of the EOQ is that it disregards the exact timing of the annual requirements. It defines an annual time period, which, as an aggregate, is likely quite accurate, but assumes constant demand for the items. It does not specify exactly when the units are needed. This is particularly important for high-valued items with bills of materials that have many levels. In such cases, the lead times may be constant, but of long duration, permitting efficiencies of timing (dependent demand). For example, if 100 units of an item are needed once per week on Friday, an EOQ model would likely hold some stock of the item all of the time. But, a timed lot-for-lot method would hold zero units from Monday through Thursday and schedule deliveries of 100 units on Friday morning, reducing the average annual holding time of the inventory. Thus, the EOQ is the method of choice when demands are independent. Alternatively, if the bill of materials structure and item lead times can be used to accurately schedule when the part is needed (dependent demand), then material requirements planning is the method of

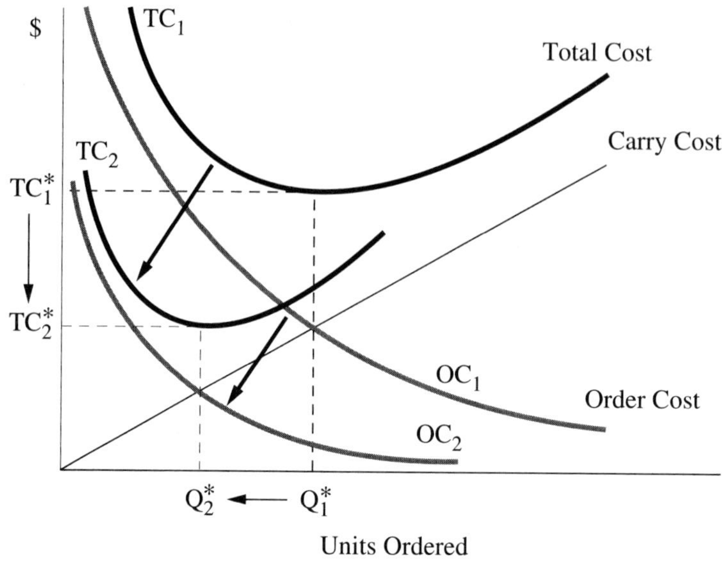


**FIGURE 9-3 Total Inventory Costs as Setup Costs Decrease**

choice. Material requirements planning resolves the deficiencies of EOQ models, but requires that accurate demand information, product structures, and inventory status be available.

## *Material Requirements Planning*

Basic material requirements planning (MRP) systems use the bill of materials, the master production schedule, and inventory data to calculate time period requirements for materials. Though MRP was originally developed as a method of ordering inventory, it has been extended to accomplish scheduling and management control functions as well. There is a wide range of applications for MRP, including service and small business operations (Davis, 1983). For example, today some hospitals are using MRP, based on activity schedules, to manage inventories of irregularly used or expensive items, with a small amount of safety stock for emergencies. Additionally, many small retailers are realizing inventory reductions, and the associated savings, because they order additional units using distribution requirements planning (DRP) as those items are sold.

Though a few MRP systems cost more than $5 million installed, some systems are available for $100.00 (Grey, 1986, and Melnyk, 1992). Several small business systems are available for $3500, and some very complete academic and training systems (which limit the number of parts that can be managed or the capabilities) may be purchased for less than $1000. The key, however, to MRP is recognizing that, as a computer-driven automated system, it will reduce the visibility, tangibility, and understandability of materials decisions on the shop floor and require different skills to effectively manage inventories. These difficulties are highlighted by the introductory case.

## *Historical Development of MRP*

The historical development of MRP has been associated with alternating periods of optimism and disillusionment, both among MRP consultants and technicians, and in the perception of the general public. These cycles of optimism and disillusionment are likely mirrored by companies as they go through an implementation process. Figure 9-4 represents the sequential developments of MRP and MRP II (manufacturing resource planning). Fully developed MRP II systems are a part of computer integrated manufacturing (CIM).

Though there were numerous early starts, according to Wight (1984) a key event in the development of MRP occurred in 1965, when IBM defined the production and inventory control system (PICS) approach, built around the bill of materials processor. Inventory and production schedule information were joined with the bill of materials and exploded. Those three key components, shown at the top of Figure 9-4, are driven by various manual or automated systems.

The basic parts explosion of MRP integrates the three key files in several logical processing steps. In a very simplified sense, those are

1. Identify the end item requirement in terms of units and due dates from the master production schedule.
2. Identify current and projected available inventory of the end item to meet that requirement.
3. If there is insufficient inventory of the end item:
   a. Use the bill of materials file to identify the availability of subcomponents of the end item (number required, lead time offset, safety stock and lot-sizing method).
   b. Use the inventory records to identify the current and projected available inventory of subcomponents of the item.
4. If there is insufficient inventory (excluding safety stock) of any subcomponent:
   a. Schedule the necessary production of that item, with appropriate lead-time offset and lot size.
   b. Identify the scheduled production (or parts of that job) with the job number of the higher-level component or end item so that the production can be "pegged" to the deliverable end item.
5. Repeat steps 3 and 4 for each lower level of the bill of materials and continue in this manner until sufficient units are available to produce (with lead time offsets) the requirements at all levels.

MRP II supplements the basic parts explosion by recommending purchasing and shop floor dispatch actions and by monitoring supplier deliveries and production management

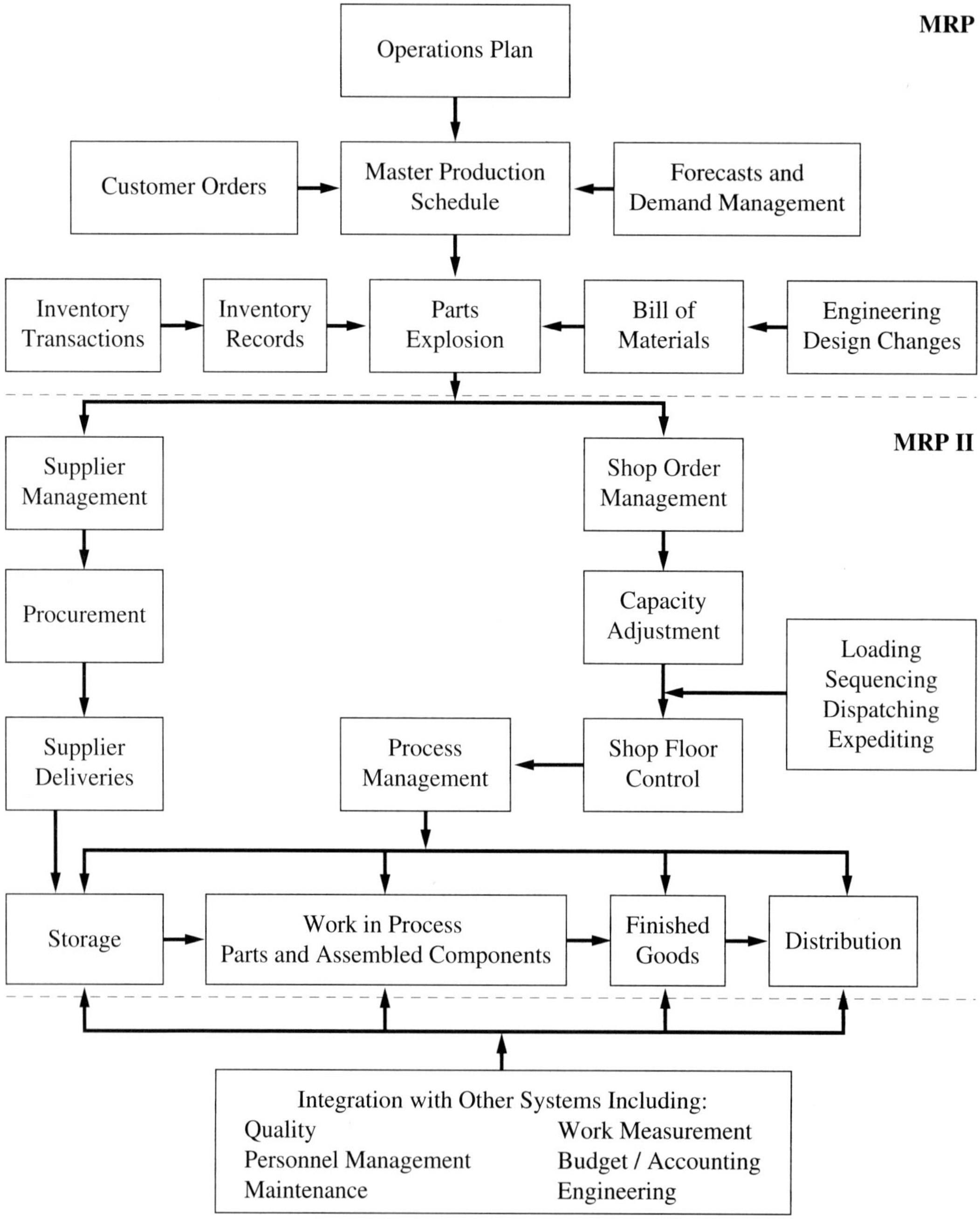


**FIGURE 9-4 The Components and Relationships of MRP Systems**

actions as the job moves from raw materials to finished goods and through the distribution network. Supplier management would include monitoring of procurement activities and supplier deliveries. Shop floor order management includes capacity adjustment and shop floor control, and then management of the production process. If exceptions or variations occur, the MRP system identifies those exceptions, and depending upon the software, recommends a "fix." The master scheduler manages this process.

More specifically, the parts explosion involves gross-to-net and projected-available-balance computations. These computations are shown in detail in Decision Model Box 9-3.

The lot-sizing rules of MRP can include various order quantity methods and safety stocks. Thus, if the cost advantages of prorating setups are used and, if demand variances require safety stocks, then, as Sauers (1990) comments, the improvement of MRP over the EOQ is that it uses the actual schedule and the timed actions of a fully exploded bill of materials. This results because MRP uses dependent demands. In many businesses, however, this is an important improvement and can result in significant inventory cost reductions.

Early MRP systems were based on weekly time "buckets"; that is, the MRP schedule was exploded and published once per week. Information processing capabilities are now sufficiently fast to permit "bucketless" (based on transactions, not on time periods) MRP systems. With bucketless systems, MRP is updated with each transaction, and every schedule change is immediately calculated and evaluated. However, once the schedule is computed and dispatched and purchase orders are released, the schedule must be executed as planned—changes are very disruptive. Bucketless systems permit on-line assessment of changes and execution adjustments as desired, but discipline is required to minimize the number of changes.

## *Future Directions of MRP*

Though the basic MRP processes are well established, much improvement can be achieved in implementation. The initial implementations of MRP systems were sometimes disappointing. An early study (Anderson et al., 1982) found that only 9.5% of respondents claimed to have Class A systems, a measure of system development and accuracy. Twenty-nine percent stated that they were Class B users, and fully 60% were Class C or D users. The Class A system, for example, is defined as "a closed loop system used by top management to participate in production planning, with deliveries on time, little or no expediting, and inventory under control" (Wight, 1981). The 9.5% of respondents who report Class A systems may be inflated because it does not include nonrespondents in a survey drawn from inventory managers and consultants.

A more recent and more optimistic report ("Computers . . . ," 1984) finds that in a survey of 3600 manufacturing and nonmanufacturing companies, 27% reported decreased materials costs and increased labor productivity, inventory turns, and customer service resulting from an MRP implementation. An even more recent study by Turnipseed et al.

## DECISION MODEL BOX 9-3 MRP at the Schmidt Shovel Company

Over the next ten weeks, the Schmidt Shovel Company is scheduled to deliver 150 common shovels. The product structure and indented bill of materials are given:

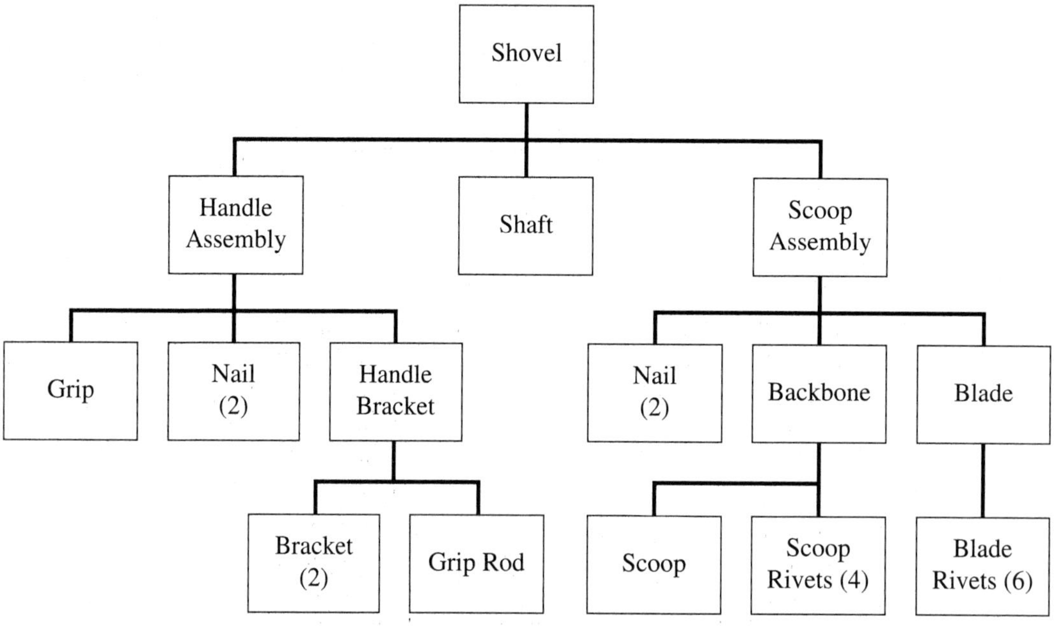


**The Common Shovel**

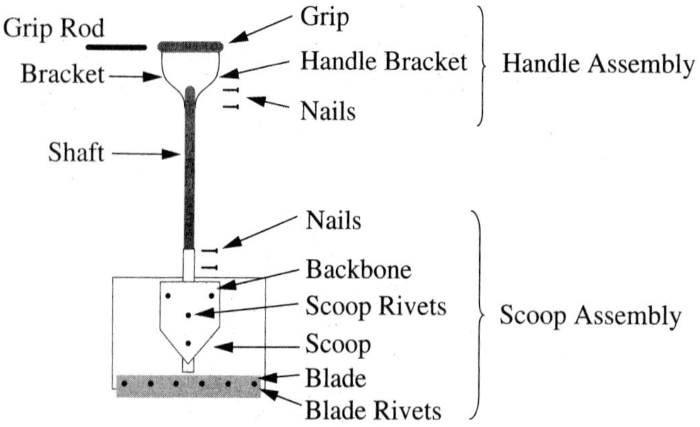


*Continued*

## DECISION MODEL BOX 9-3 *Continued*

**Indented Bill of Materials for a Common Shovel**

| Level | Nomenclature | Number Required |
|---|---|---|
| 0 | Shovel | |
| 1 | Handle assembly | 1 |
| 2 | Grip | 1 |
| 2 | Nail | 2 |
| 2 | Handle bracket | 1 |
| 3 | Bracket | 2 |
| 3 | Grip rod | 1 |
| 1 | Shaft | 1 |
| 1 | Scoop assembly | 1 |
| 2 | Nail | 2 |
| 2 | Backbone | 1 |
| 3 | Scoop | 1 |
| 3 | Scoop rivet | 4 |
| 2 | Blade | 1 |
| 3 | Blade rivet | 6 |

*Gross-to-Net Computations.* Gross-to-net computations permit component parts in inventory or scheduled receipts to be included in the available inventory computation. The computation starts with the 0 (highest) level of the bill of materials and progresses to the bottom of the bill of materials. The gross requirement is computed for each part at each level, then current and projected inventory (on-hand inventory and scheduled receipts) are subtracted to get the net requirement of that part. The following table shows the gross-to-net computation for the handle assembly that would support an order for 150 shovels. The net requirement is the aggregate number of each part that will be required to build the 150 shovels during the ten-week period. For example, 150 shovels require a net of 110 handles, after subtracting the 40 units in inventory. This information is helpful for planning, but it does not indicate when the demands will occur.

| Part Description | Number of Each | On-hand Inventory | Scheduled Receipts | Requirements Gross | Requirements Net |
|---|---|---|---|---|---|
| Handle assembly | 1 | 40 | — | 150 | 110 |
| Grip | 1 | 32 | 35 | 110 | 43 |
| Nail | 2 | 70 | 50 | 220 | 100 |
| Handle bracket | 1 | 47 | — | 110 | 63 |
| Bracket | 2 | 15 | 40 | 126 | 71 |
| Grip rod | 1 | 39 | 30 | 63 | — |

*Continued*

## DECISION MODEL BOX 9-3 *Continued*

*Lead Time Offset Using Projected Available Balance.* MRP records for the shovel show the exact timing of the demands. Gross requirements from the master production schedule and scheduled receipts are used to compute the projected available balance (PAB) and planned order release. The PAB is computed from period to period using the following formula and the handle assembly is calculated as an example for the second and fourth periods.

$$PAB_n = PAB_{n-1} - \text{gross requirements} + \text{scheduled receipts}$$

Handle assembly

$$PAB_2 = 40 - 35 + 0 = 5$$

$$PAB_4 = 5 - 35 + 30^{*} = 0$$

The use of varying lead times, different lot sizing and safety stock conventions, and a different number of components all cause variations in this basic calculation. The parts explosion uses the gross-to-net and lead-time-offset adjusted planned order releases of items at higher levels to compute the gross requirements for lower-level items.

Level 1

| | | | Week 1 | 2 | 3 | 4 | 5 | 6 | 7 | 8 | 9 | 10 |
|---|---|---|---|---|---|---|---|---|---|---|---|---|
| Handle assembly | Gross requirements (given) | | | 35 | | 35 | | 30 | 5 | | 35 | 10 |
| | Scheduled receipts | | | | | | | | | | | |
| Lead time = 2 | Projected available balance | 40 | 40 | 5 | 5 | 0 | 0 | 0 | 0 | 0 | 0 | 0 |
| Lot for lot | Planned order release | | | 30 | | 30 | 5 | | 35 | 10 | | |

Level 2

| | | | Week 1 | 2 | 3 | 4 | 5 | 6 | 7 | 8 | 9 | 10 |
|---|---|---|---|---|---|---|---|---|---|---|---|---|
| Grip | Gross requirements | | | 30 | | 30 | 5 | | 35 | 10 | | |
| | Scheduled receipts | | | 35 | | | | | | | | |
| Lead time = 2 | Projected available balance | 32 | 32 | 37 | 37 | 7 | 2 | 2 | 0 | 0 | 0 | 0 |
| Lot for lot | Planned order release | | | | | | 33 | 10 | | | | |

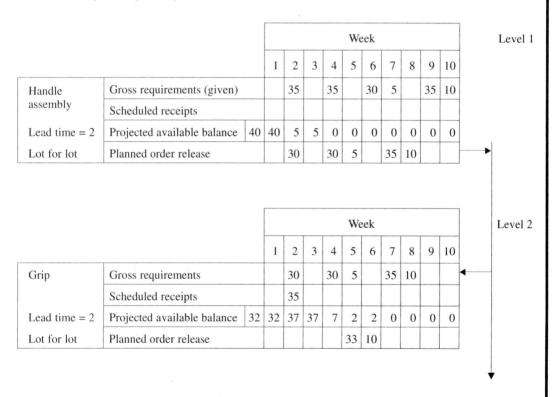

*Note that the scheduled receipt of 30 in week 4 is carried as a planned order release until week 2, when it is ordered and becomes a scheduled receipt.

*Continued*

**DECISION MODEL BOX 9-3** *Continued*

Level 2 × 2

| | | | Week 1 | 2 | 3 | 4 | 5 | 6 | 7 | 8 | 9 | 10 |
|---|---|---|---|---|---|---|---|---|---|---|---|---|
| Nail – 2 req | Gross requirements | | | 60 | | 60 | 10 | | 70 | 20 | | |
| | Scheduled receipts | | 50 | | | | | | | | | |
| Lead time = 1 | Projected available balance | 70 | 120 | 60 | 60 | 0 | 40 | 40 | 20 | 0 | 0 | 0 |
| Lot size = 50 | Planned order release | | | | | 50 | | 50 | | | | |

Level 2

| | | | Week 1 | 2 | 3 | 4 | 5 | 6 | 7 | 8 | 9 | 10 |
|---|---|---|---|---|---|---|---|---|---|---|---|---|
| Handle bracket | Gross requirements | | | 30 | | 30 | 5 | | 35 | 10 | | |
| | Scheduled receipts | | | | | | | | | | | |
| Lead time = 2 | Projected available balance | 47 | 47 | 17 | 17 | 0 | 0 | 0 | 0 | 0 | 0 | 0 |
| Lot for lot | Planned order release | | | 13 | 5 | | 35 | 10 | | | | |

Level 3 × 2

| | | | Week 1 | 2 | 3 | 4 | 5 | 6 | 7 | 8 | 9 | 10 |
|---|---|---|---|---|---|---|---|---|---|---|---|---|
| Bracket – 2 req | Forecast | | | 26 | 10 | | 70 | 20 | | | | |
| | Scheduled receipts | | 40 | | | | | | | | | |
| Lead time = 1 | Projected available balance | 15 | 55 | 29 | 19 | 19 | 0 | 0 | 0 | 0 | 0 | 0 |
| Lot for lot | Planned order release | | | | | 51 | 20 | | | | | |

Level 3

| | | | Week 1 | 2 | 3 | 4 | 5 | 6 | 7 | 8 | 9 | 10 |
|---|---|---|---|---|---|---|---|---|---|---|---|---|
| Grip rod | Forecast | | | 13 | 5 | | 35 | 10 | | | | |
| Lead time = 3 | Scheduled receipts | | | 30 | | | | | | | | |
| *SS = 20 Lot for lot | Projected available balance | 39 | 39 | 56 | 51 | 51 | 20 | 20 | 20 | 20 | 20 | 20 |
| | Planned order release | | | 4 | 10 | | | | | | | |

*SS = safety stock

(1992) found significant relationships between worker involvement and control of the implementation, particularly during the early stages of implementation, and the outcome of the implementation. Participant involvement was shown as a determinant of satisfaction and of the quality of the implementation. Because more is known about MRP implementation, success rates are high, particularly where there is a strong commitment by top management.

The use of MRP systems is expected to grow dramatically for the foreseeable future (Baer, 1989). The greater cross-functional emphasis of MRP II is consistent with integrated operations management because it facilitates interaction with human resources, financial, and accounting planning and administration, as well as quality control and work measurement. Well-developed MRP systems can integrate ten to fifteen major information systems, as well as numerous subsystems, typically upwards of 150 to 200 different program files.

Where interactive files are used, however, there is little tolerance of data error, and several errors can be multiplicative in effect. For example, 90% accuracy in each of production schedule, inventory records, and bill of materials files would result in 73% ($0.9 \times 0.9 \times 0.9$) overall system accuracy. This assessment prompted Grey (1986) to recommend that prospective adopters consider the ease of implementation of a particular software as a primary decision factor. Cingari (1992) suggests that a continuous improvement program be applied to the MRP data and that communication is one of the habitual weak links that management should address. Success of MRP implementation requires extensive employee training, the time and cost of which should not be underestimated.

One method of reducing errors in inventory counting is to relieve (or backflush) inventory records, which means to subtract out the parts and component inventories for each unit produced only after the unit has been shipped or placed in finished goods inventory. This technique reduces the errors in inventory, because it eliminates mistakes due to changed orders or volumes. However, with backflushing, inventories must be separately adjusted for scrap (Kutos, 1992). Additionally, Young and Nie (1992) identify an EOQ-like model that balances the costs incurred from cycle counting of inventory and those of stockout. They suggest that their model performs better than models that use traditional ABC logic. Under all circumstances both backflushing and effective cycle counting practices can reduce inventory counting errors significantly.

The complexity of MRP often takes inventory management functions away from the shop floor and places them in the purview of computer information systems. The understanding of the MRP system and the visibility of problems and solutions have been removed from the area where the solution must be implemented and from the people who must implement the solution. Typically, few people on the shop floor understand data processing, though most are very familiar with MRP. Increased use of PCs and local area networks, as well as employee training, resolves this question.

MRP system "nervousness" or instability results when seemingly minor changes of the master production schedule cause significant changes when they are exploded down through the bill of materials structure, sometimes affecting jobs or orders that have already been released and started. Bucketless systems are particularly prone to nervousness, because each transaction is considered as a time period, and subject to change. Schedule "freezing" and time fence management are used by the master scheduler to limit such adjustments. That is, within a designated time fence, say, one month, the production schedule is "frozen" and no further changes can be made, except within strict cost or approval constraints. "Necessary" changes often require approval by higher management.

Each of these directions relates to the quality of implementation. Poorly implemented systems with high levels of errors and limited capabilities (as defined in Figure 9-4) result in a variety of informal methods to bypass the system. The complexity and potential for problems with such methods are costly and just add to the errors of the formal system. Alternatively, well-implemented systems can result in tremendous cost reductions because of the ability to plan exact requirements (in terms of what product is needed, how much is needed, and when it is needed). Specifically, MRP corrects a key weakness in dependent demand methods by defining exactly when a requirement for specific volume occurs. For this reason, successful MRP implementation is a powerful source of strategic advantage for a firm. It is also a step in the direction of continuous improvement.

## *Continuous Improvement of Materials Management*

The materials management system can be improved by reducing the amount of inventory held, by stabilizing and smoothing the flow of inventory, and by reducing the loss of inventory (or value added) due to all causes (quality control, obsolescence, pilferage, and so on). Efforts toward these objectives generally have taken three forms—materials system integration, bill of materials restructuring, and just-in-time production.

### *Materials System Integration*

Ideally, to ensure smoothness of materials flow, the materials management system should be integrated from the creation of raw materials to the delivery and servicing of the end item. One of the most effective techniques to increase the efficiency and reduce the cost of a logistics flow path is to synchronize lot size, load sizes, package sizes, and item quantities along the steps of the flow path (Nicholl, 1992). Though one corporation may not necessarily manage all of these activities (see Chapter 4), the materials information system should vertically integrate suppliers, manufacturers, and distributors. That is, the system should be viewed as links in a chain, each of which adds value through transformation, and each of which is both forward and backward linked. Suppliers should be given production scheduling information, and distribution centers should be linked to the production system through distribution requirements planning (DRP). The organization structure aspects of linking the purchasing activities with manufacturing and distribution are discussed in Chapter 4. This integration of supplier and distribution systems is shown in Figure 9-5.

**Supplier Integration.** Supplier integration can smooth and reduce the complexity of the purchasing function. To emphasize the importance of the purchasing function, consider

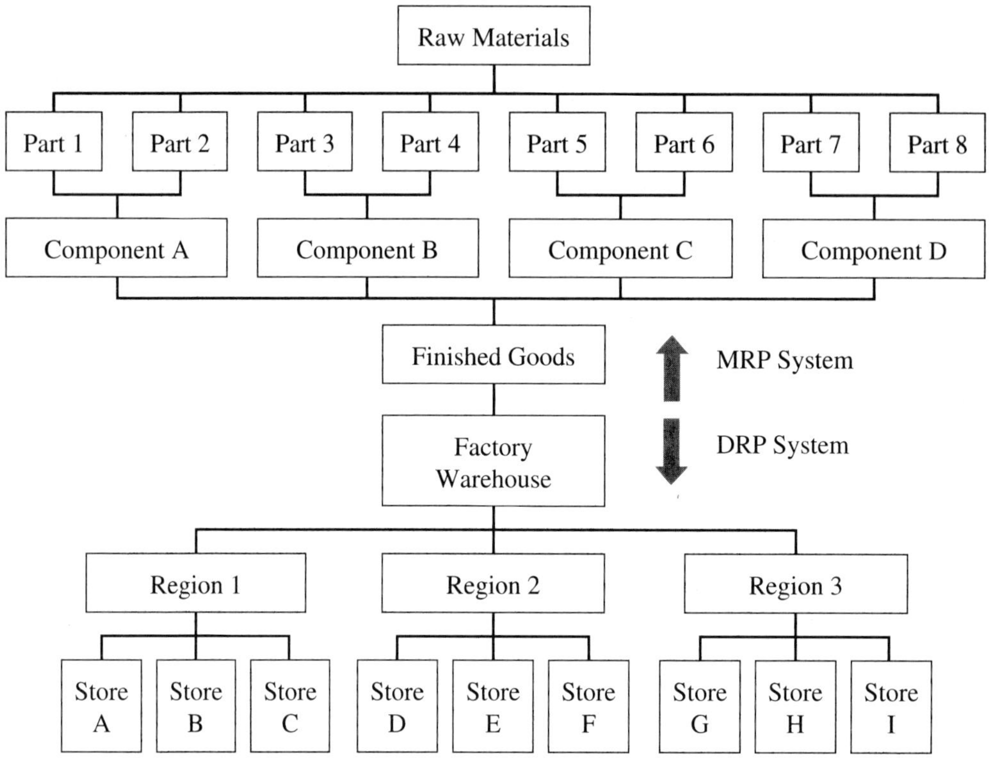


**FIGURE 9-5 Supplier and Distribution System Integration**

the potential for savings. Purchased parts and materials constitute between 30% and 60% of the cost of goods sold in the United States, depending upon the industry. Thus, a small percentage decrease in the cost of purchased items can result in a much larger percentage increase in profits. For example, consider a purchasing operation where the cost of purchased materials is 40% of the total sales, and profit is 10% of the total sales. If purchasing costs were reduced by 10% to 36% of total sales and other costs were constant, then profits would increase from 10% to 14%, or a 40% increase in profits. The significance of purchasing system savings is that such savings may be directly captured as profits.

Though the effects of improved product and process design, quality control, and inventory management process efficiencies would also be directly reflected in reduced costs and improved profits, the improvement of the purchasing function may be easier to achieve. Such cost savings in purchased materials are possible through a number of purchasing techniques. A starting point for purchasing system evaluation is to use ABC analysis to identify those purchased items that contribute the most to costs. The intense management of A items through such techniques as long-term contracts, integration of purchasing with design engineering to standardize and reduce the number of parts, improvement of purchasing lead times, and use of supplier evaluation methods (such as supplier certification) to reduce and manage the number of suppliers can yield notable cost reductions. Continuing reduction of purchasing costs is possible as analysis is applied to B and C items.

The purchasing process must be linked with the external environment, as well as with the operations system. Marketing likely will identify customer requirements and make the initial quality and quantity projection. If the product or process is complex, engineering will be required to write product specifications, including product configuration and quality requirements. Purchasing releases the contract, based on approval of the source's quality program, and delivery timing. Subsequently, based on production schedules, materials control releases specific orders, receives the order acknowledgment, receives and inspects the shipment, and places the item in stock or releases it for use. As the product is delivered, the distribution system will be involved with issues of product availability and quality. These linkages are shown in Figure 9-6.

Purchasing initiates order contracts through one of three types of systems: the cyclic order system, the fixed order quantity, and MRP. Cyclic orders are time-based, like the period order quantity; fixed order quantities are unit-size-based, using convenient lot sizes for transportation, or the EOQ, and MRP is requirements-based. Often purchasing contracts can be managed for longer periods (six months or a year) based on projected volumes. Subsequently, specific delivery schedules are defined on the basis of the requirement. There are four general types of purchasing contract arrangements.

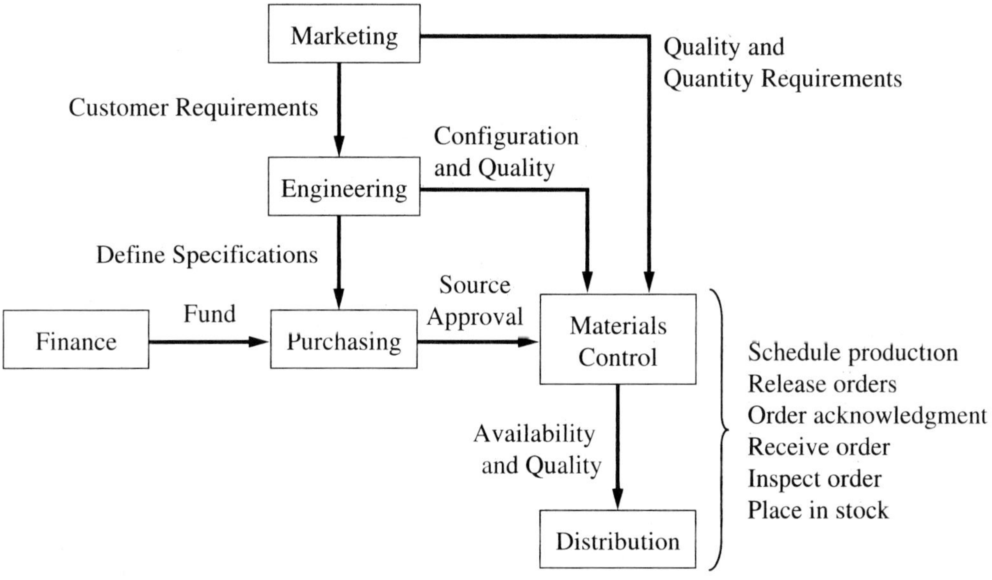


**FIGURE 9-6 Purchasing Integration**

1. *Blanket Order.* Minimum and sometimes maximum quantities are specified over a defined period (normally one year). Production then sends the requisitions directly to the supplier within the specified volumes and lead times. The blanket order reduces the administration required for separate orders.
2. *Standing Order.* The standing order is like a blanket order, except that it is defined for an indefinite period. Requisitions must be placed within specified lead times and volumes.
3. *Systems Contracts.* Suppliers maintain at buyer's facilities specified amounts of inventory and periodically refresh specified amounts of inventory. Contracts to stock vending machines are a simplified example of systems contracts. Often such approaches are used for consumables such as chemicals, glues, and small bulk parts such as nuts, bolts, expendable tools and instruments, and the like.
4. *Distribution Contracts.* Suppliers maintain specified amounts of inventory at their facilities, dedicated for your use. Delivery to buyer's facility is based on requisitions and must be within specified volumes and lead times. Distribution contracts define inventories off-site, but in sufficient volumes to ensure against stockout.

These different types of contract are particularly important as companies reduce inventory and smooth materials flow. They permit reduction of purchasing costs, more flexible response to changing demands, and reduced risk of stockout. However, care should be taken to avoid merely transferring the responsibilities and costs of inventories to "JIT warehouses," off-site, but closely located, storage operations whose only function is to hide large inventories of safety stock.

Supplier integration is achieved by extending the MRP schedule visibility to suppliers of components, parts, or raw materials. Similarly, distribution requirements planning extends the MRP logic through the distribution system, potentially to the retail level. This integration provides formal planning visibility throughout purchasing, operations, and distribution systems, with the associated benefits of inventory reduction, enhanced productivity, and improved customer service. The operations system becomes a fully integrated input-transformation-output structure throughout the length of the chain of transformations.

**Distribution System Integration.** According to industry estimates, distribution costs amount to more than 20% of the U.S. gross national product. The breakdown of the more than $400 billion per year of distribution costs is categorized as 47% in transportation costs, 21% in warehousing costs, and 21% in inventory carrying costs. An example of a DRP system is shown in Decision Model Box 9-4.

The significance of multilevel planning visibility is apparent as the "lumpy" demand from the warehouses is converted into reasonably stable and accurate planned requirements. Though the forecast for any aggregation of four weeks is rather accurate, the planned requirements project exactly when the demand will occur. Smaller lot sizes might reduce the lumpiness, but transportation costs would likely increase. The significance of DRP visibility is that it permits the distribution planner to look ahead at the regional demands and smooth them. Forward visibility permits the distribution manager to manage

## DECISION MODEL BOX 9-4 Distribution Requirements Planning at National Distribution

The National Distribution Company manages the distribution of durable appliances for a major retailer. National uses a central warehouse collocated with the factory and three regional warehouses. Demands are forecast at the regional level and are aggregated for long-range planning purposes at the central warehouse. However, a distribution requirements planning system is used to compute requirements for short-range demand at the central warehouse. Region safety stock, shipment size, and lead times are given. The central warehouse directly feeds the factory master production schedule.

| | | | Week | | | | | | | | | |
|---|---|---|---|---|---|---|---|---|---|---|---|---|
| | | | 1 | 2 | 3 | 4 | 5 | 6 | 7 | 8 | 9 | 10 |
| Region 1 | Forecast | | 15 | 15 | 15 | 15 | 15 | 15 | 15 | 15 | 15 | 15 |
| Safety stock = 10 | Planned receipts | | | | 25 | | | | | | | |
| Lead time = 3 | Inventory | 40 | 25 | 10 | 20 | 30 | 15 | 25 | 10 | 20 | 30 | 15 |
| Order size = 25 | Planned order release | | 25 | | 25 | | 25 | 25 | | | | |

| | | | Week | | | | | | | | | |
|---|---|---|---|---|---|---|---|---|---|---|---|---|
| | | | 1 | 2 | 3 | 4 | 5 | 6 | 7 | 8 | 9 | 10 |
| Region 2 | Forecast | | 50 | 50 | 50 | 50 | 30 | 30 | 30 | 30 | 60 | 60 |
| | Planned receipts | | 75 | | | | | | | | | |
| Lead time = 1 | Inventory | 25 | 50 | 0 | 25 | 50 | 20 | 65 | 35 | 5 | 20 | 35 |
| Order size = 75 | Planned order release | | | 75 | 75 | | 75 | | | 75 | 75 | |

| | | | Week | | | | | | | | | |
|---|---|---|---|---|---|---|---|---|---|---|---|---|
| | | | 1 | 2 | 3 | 4 | 5 | 6 | 7 | 8 | 9 | 10 |
| Region 3 | Forecast | | 35 | 35 | 35 | 35 | 35 | 35 | 35 | 35 | 35 | 35 |
| | Planned receipts | | | 50 | | | | | | | | |
| Lead time = 2 | Inventory | 40 | 5 | 20 | 35 | 0 | 15 | 30 | 45 | 10 | 25 | 40 |
| Order size = 50 | Planned order release | | 50 | | 50 | 50 | 50 | | 50 | 50 | | |

*Continued*

**DECISION MODEL BOX 9-4** *Continued*

| | | Week 1 | 2 | 3 | 4 | 5 | 6 | 7 | 8 | 9 | 10 |
|---|---|---|---|---|---|---|---|---|---|---|---|
| Total region requirements | Region 1 | 25 | | 25 | | 25 | 25 | | | | |
| | Region 2 | | 75 | 75 | | 75 | | | 75 | 75 | |
| | Region 3 | 50 | | 50 | 50 | 50 | | 50 | 50 | | |
| | Total of region requirements | 75 | 75 | 150 | 50 | 150 | 25 | 50 | 125 | 75 | |

| | | | Week 1 | 2 | 3 | 4 | 5 | 6 | 7 | 8 | 9 | 10 |
|---|---|---|---|---|---|---|---|---|---|---|---|---|
| Central warehouse<br>Safety stock = 100<br>Batch size = 200<br>Lead time = 2 | Forecast needs | | 100 | 100 | 100 | 100 | 80 | 80 | 80 | 80 | 110 | 110 |
| | Planned requirements | | 75 | 75 | 150 | 50 | 150 | 25 | 50 | 125 | 75 | |
| | Planned receipts | | | 200 | | | | | | | | |
| | Projected available inventory | 180 | 105 | 230 | 280 | 230 | 280 | 255 | 205 | 280 | 205 | 205 |
| | Master production schedule order | | 200 | | 200 | | | 200 | | | | |

Note that the use of planned requirements improves at the central warehouse based on the use of region planned orders, which give a more accurate projection than the aggregated region forecasted needs. Additionally, lot-sizing (lot for lot) methods at the central warehouse and reduced safety stock would improve this system even further, though possibly at greater risk of stockout.

demand turbulence. Further, visibility in the distribution system, when linked to the master production schedule, gives manufacturing those same capabilities (Martin, 1990).

Additionally, the DRP system permits the operations manager to consider seasonality of demand, pipeline buildup and depletion, restructuring the distribution network to more accurately reflect demand flow, product phase-outs, and back-ordering requirements. Of course, the effectiveness of a DRP system depends upon information accuracy, education of users, management support, and communications among the participants.

## *Bill of Material Restructuring*

The second dimension of continuous improvement is the restructuring of a product bill of material to permit increased plannability. The traditional bill of material is structured in the way that the product is manufactured. It includes a "list of all subassemblies, subordinates, parts, and raw materials that go into a parent assembly, showing the quantity of each required to make an assembly" (Cox et al., 1992). Traditional structuring activities involve product, parts and services definition, production instructions, engineering changes, service parts support, procurement planning, operations scheduling, and materials control.

However, recently developed methods of product structuring permit increased plannability. These methods, often involving modularization of the bill, permit optimal level scheduling, encourage more accurate product option forecasting, expedite order entry, allow more reliable product costing, and facilitate efficient data storage and system maintenance (Mather, 1989).

Simply, the traditional bill of material schedules at the highest, or end item, level of the product structure. Alternatively, modular bills schedule below that level, often at level 1 or 2, but potentially at the bottom level of the product structure. Product modules are defined for commonly purchased groupings of product options or alternatives. For example, an automobile air conditioning option module would include the compressor unit, tinted glass, dashboard switch options, different engine belts, and a supplement to the owner's manual. Other examples of modularly structured products are home entertainment and stereo racks and personal computers, which are sold with several sets of alternative component modules. These modules have standardized and pluggable interfaces with all other components. The definition of product modules permits item management at the module or component level and assembly of those modules with a much simpler final assembly schedule (FAS), or at the customer's site as part of the customer delivery process.

The value of modules is that they permit apparent product diversity based on the lower-level scheduling of a reduced number of items. Consider a grandfather clock. The traditional grandfather clock might have twelve different face plates, eight different pendulum and weight casing styles, four different cabinet styles or finishes, among other variations. Building and holding end item inventory of all possible product variations, or even a reasonably diversified product range, would be very costly. However, if these products were built and stored as modules, and then assembled or packed to customer specified options, the reduction of inventory and increased responsiveness to customer specifications would be tremendous. With traditional management techniques, each design variation requires a separate bill of material, and the total number of different bills and clocks is a *multiplicative* function of the number of component alternatives. But, if the product is managed at the module level, then the number of modules is *additive.* In the clock example, modularization reduces the number of bills and separate end items from as many as 7680 to 37. This reduction of bills and end items significantly reduces the time spent in inventory management—and cost of inventory. This comparison is shown in Figure 9-7.

Initial research (Stonebraker, 1991) tentatively suggests that modular bills can assist in improving inventory turns by a factor of five with a corresponding reduction of inventory costs. Additionally, modularized products show a twenty-fold reduction in product family size (and thus reduced product complexity). However, the complexity of the modular bill may result in a reduction of quality and delivery performance. Further research is necessary in this area.

An extension of the modular bill of material is the configurator. Instead of predefined modules (stated as part numbers, bills, and routings), as used by modular bills, the configurator bill uses algorithms, rule-based techniques, and conditional logic to define

**Traditional BOM**

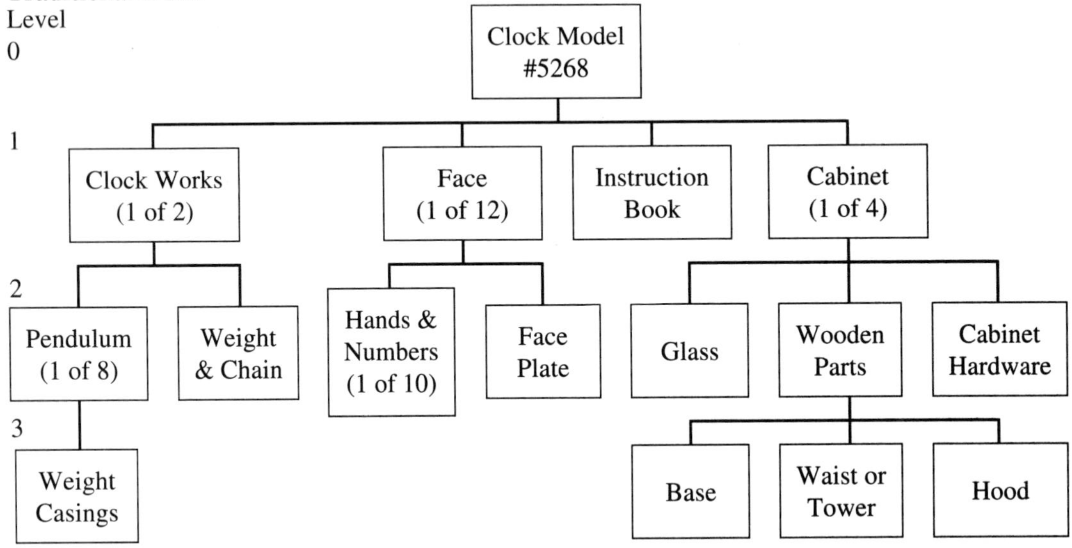


Note: Total number of products using traditional bills of material is potentially $1 \times 2 \times 12 \times 4 \times 8 \times 10 = 7680$. This is because products are managed at the end-item level of the bill of material.

**Modular BOM**

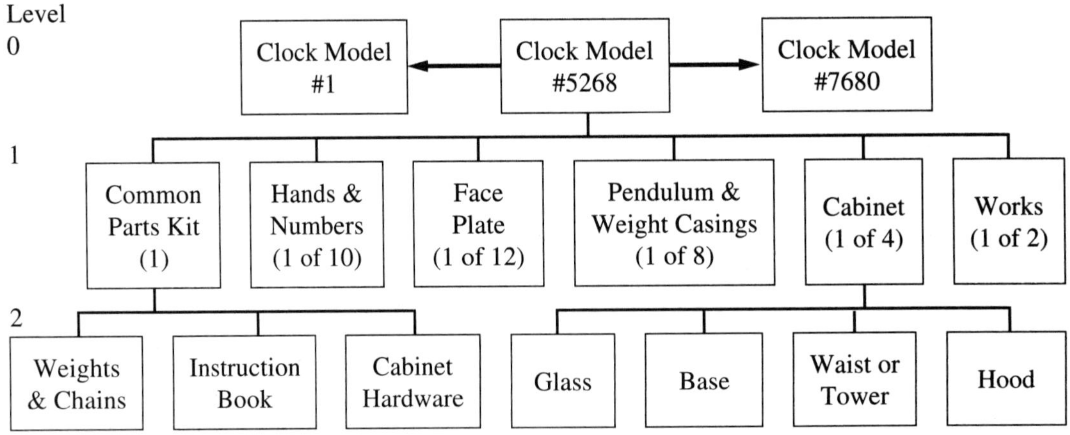


Note: At the end-item level of the bill of material there may potentially be 7680 different models; however, the total number of product modules managed using modular bills of material is equal to $1 + 10 + 12 + 8 + 4 + 2 = 37$. Products are managed at an intermediate level of the bill of material.

**FIGURE 9-7 Traditional and Modular Bills of Material**

the product and manufacturing requirements. For example, a round table might be defined only as glass-topped or plastic, and, if plastic, then by color. The diameter of the table, along with these characteristics, would be used to specify all components. Iron legs, instead of wooden legs, would be required if the table were greater than three feet in diameter. The molding for the edge of the plastic table would be determined by $\pi d$, the formula for the circumference. If the top of the plastic table were white, the molding would be black; otherwise the molding would be white. The configurator bill logic replaces the modular bill with variable- or algorithm-based relationships (Lieberman, 1992). Configurator bills also have been shown to give a special advantage in make-to-order and assemble-to-order operations (Burke, 1991; Burke, 1992).

## *Just-In-Time Operations*

Just-in-time (JIT) may be one of the most used—and misused—buzzwords of the 1980s and early 1990s. One somewhat ludicrous application has extended JIT to the scheduling of learning activities just-in-time for an examination, otherwise called *cramming*. Other "fables" and misunderstandings about JIT include that it is entirely a Japanese idea, that it involves production only, and that it necessitates geographic collocation (nearness) of suppliers and users. As Ackerman (1988) clarifies, JIT was widely practiced in the United States well before World War II. JIT is a philosophy of management extending from suppliers through production to distribution systems. A carefully managed transportation system can reduce the need for proximity of supplier and user. This section will briefly introduce JIT as it relates to materials management; Chapter 10, Just-in-Time, will elaborate the JIT management philosophy.

As an inventory management technique (distinct from the broader definition of JIT as a philosophy of management), JIT reduces inventories by creating an unbuffered pull inventory management system. The pull system defines a linkage from retail distribution back to the raw material, or on a less global scale, among related production activities. As such, because it backward-links the production process, the pull system serves the function of a bill of materials. That is, as an end item is scheduled for assembly, production of components is required, which, in turn, drives demand for the subcomponents, and so on. For this reason, Goddard (1982) initially suggested that JIT would be applicable primarily in a repetitive environment. Zangwill (1992) found that the use of JIT in a highly dynamic environment may, in fact, result in an increase of inventory. JIT inventory management systems have been very effective in a variety of operations and distribution environments, though care must be taken with dynamic or nonrepetitive environments. These differences between traditional and JIT systems are shown in Table 9-2.

Though JIT production systems espouse a goal of zero inventories, most inventory management situations require some safety or buffer stocks at selected locations (Hall, 1983). The theory of constraints (Goldratt and Cox, 1986; Fogarty et al., 1991) evaluates use of buffer inventories to smooth or protect constrained processes, shipping requirements, and assembly operations. Thus, though reducing inventories to zero may not be possible, JIT does increase the visibility of inventory decisions, particularly for shop floor

**TABLE 9-2 Comparison of Traditional and JIT Methods**

| Factor | Traditional Methods | JIT |
|---|---|---|
| Shop Floor | | |
| Inventories | Large, asset, safety stock | Small, liability |
| Setups | Slow | Fast |
| Lot size | Balance setup vs. hold costs | Small, immediate needs |
| Queues | Preclude feeding problems | If problems, stop line |
| Quality | Statistics identify the problem for rework | Producing quality products the first time |
| Human Resources | | |
| Management process | Management by edict | Management by consensus |
| Worker skill | Single function, routine | Multifunction |
| Communications | Complex, computer managed | Simple, visible |
| External | | |
| Vendors | Adversaries (many sources) | Partners (few sources) |
| Deliveries | Few | Many |
| Distribution decisions | Push | Pull |

Adapted from Goddard, 1982.

personnel. In a repetitive and reasonably stable environment, the increased system visibility and simplicity permit control through problem identification and correction at a lower level of management.

As firms look to improvements in materials management processes, the efficiencies of demand chain integration, modular product structuring, and JIT production can potentially result in cost and flexibility improvements, but quality and delivery performance must be carefully monitored. With reference to Figure 9-1, improvements of the materials management system are likely to be accompanied by corresponding improvements of scheduling and customer service. In effect, the smoothed flow of inventory is moving more rapidly in a smaller pipeline, represented by the inner triangle of Figure 9-1. Continuous improvement methods reduce the costs associated with the traditional inventory questions: What product is needed, how much is needed, and when?

## *Summary*

Materials management practices affect both manufacturing costs and service delivery performance of a company; effective materials management directly contributes to a competitive edge. This chapter has initially defined several fundamental issues of materials management, including push and pull systems, dependent and independent demand, and evaluation of product lines for high-value items (ABC analysis). The historical development of materials management systems was traced by successively evaluating traditional lot-sizing methods, the development of automated material requirements planning models, and various continuous improvement approaches, including JIT. Each method was evaluated by the measure of how well it considers the key materials management questions: What is needed, how much is needed, and when is it needed? Each succeeding approach improves upon previous methods in some ways, but also has limitations, in terms of cost, appropriateness, accuracy, and employee skills and management effort. The decision of which system to implement is dependent upon the costs of implementation and the productivity criteria that the materials management system must meet.

Traditional lot-sizing methods are likely appropriate with product structures that have high volumes and stable requirements for a few low-cost end items. A plastic parts molder or a print shop might use traditional lot-sizing methods to order raw materials. Alternatively, if inventory costs are high and the production process is high volume and repetitive, then JIT would seem more appropriate. The manufacture of most durable goods, particularly high-cost durables, such as automobiles, has significantly profited from JIT. If the range of products and product options is wide and the market dynamic, as is the case with electronics and computer items, MRP may be the best method. The increasing complexity and dynamism of most production environments encourage materials managers to move toward inventory planning methods such as MRP and JIT and reduce the applicability of traditional methods, particularly if used alone. This variety of different methods to manage materials is supported in practice; Newman and Sridharan (1992) found that a wide range of materials management methods were used with varying performance, as evaluated by inventory turns, lead times, and other measures. To paraphrase the opening quotation from Plossl, though the logic of materials management is universal, the way that logic is applied varies depending upon the environment, or "parts is parts . . . is parts."

## *Discussion Questions*

1. Define four dimensions of materials management practices.
2. From your personal experience or readings, identify and give several examples of pressures to increase and decrease inventory holdings and the rationale for that action.
3. What is the difference between a push system and a pull system? Give an example of each.
4. List and describe four general reasons that require the maintenance of inventories or the maintenance of backlogs. Give an application of each.
5. From your personal experience or readings, list several examples of dependent and independent demands for inventory or services.
6. Why is the distinction between dependent and independent demand important?

7. Describe how ABC analysis focuses the inventory manager's attention to those items that are most costly, or most critical to the operation.

8. What is the most significant deficiency of the EOQ method of inventory management?

9. List the three essential components utilized to calculate requirements for materials in basic material requirements planning systems. Briefly describe the interaction of these components.

10. What do "bucketless" systems permit? How is MRP managed with such systems?

11. How can the typical material requirements planning system be improved? Select an example system from your experience or readings; describe the system and suggest improvements.

12. Distribution requirements planning (DRP) links the distribution center to the production system, thereby extending the MRP logic through the distribution system. What advantages are provided from such integration?

13. Briefly describe JIT's contribution to the continuous improvement of materials management.

14. Explain, using as an example a product with which you are familiar, how a reduction in inventory is accomplished through the implementation of product modules.

## *Strategic Decision Situations*

1. Comdisc, Inc. has organized its CD players into ten product lines. The following table shows the stock number, the annual volumes in units, the unit cost/item, the stockout costs, based on executive judgment, and order costs. The company is concerned about the dynamic market and that they are not managing the inventory effectively.

   a. Using inventory cost and stock-out penalty ABC methods, identify the product lines that should be the most carefully evaluated. Which technique would you recommend? Why?
   b. If the current interest rate is estimated at 20%, compute the economic order quantity for each product line.
   c. Make a recommendation to management of the best inventory management practices.

| Line | Annual Volume (units) | Unit Cost | Stockout Cost | Order Cost |
|---|---|---|---|---|
| 14 | 15,000 | $39.00 | $ 50.00 | $679.00 |
| 21 | 800 | 52.00 | 75.00 | 462.00 |
| 35 | 5,500 | 132.00 | 300.00 | 396.00 |
| 42 | 12,000 | 145.00 | 300.00 | 428.00 |
| 56 | 2,100 | 160.00 | 75.00 | 285.00 |
| 69 | 650 | 240.00 | 250.00 | 484.00 |
| 73 | 8,000 | 280.00 | 500.00 | 524.00 |
| 87 | 250 | 420.00 | 600.00 | 124.00 |
| 90 | 1,200 | 670.00 | 1200.00 | 243.00 |
| 108 | 400 | 935.00 | 3000.00 | 324.00 |

**2.** The Round Lake Grocery Store stocks six-packs of canned beer from five distributors. Local ordinances permit the sale of alcohol on Sunday, and because tourism is a major industry in the three summer months, sales are relatively constant during the seven weekly sales days. The management uses a 10% quarterly cost of money and desires to maximize the use of its limited storage space and delivery capabilities through the use of economic lots. Given the data in the table,

**a.** Calculate the economic order quantity.
**b.** Calculate the safety order point (weekly orders, lead time = 2 days, the standard deviation of daily demand = 15 units, safety level = 95%).
**c.** Calculate the total quarterly cost of inventory, including the cost of the item.
**d.** Advise management on an ordering policy.

| Beer | Quarterly Demand | Cost/Unit | Cost/Order |
|---|---|---|---|
| International Imports | 1500 | 20 | 40 |
| Golden Eagle | 550 | 5 | 10 |
| Western Water | 950 | 12.5 | 20 |
| Milwaukee's Finest | 1300 | 7.5 | 5 |
| Bush's Best | 1200 | 9 | 6 |

**3.** The National Chain Distribution Company manufactures and markets a line of bench saw. The company has three sales regions and the saw consists of two primary parts, a saw and a bench. Given the following region forecasts, plan demand for the product and make a recommendation.

| | | | Week | | | | | | | | | |
|---|---|---|---|---|---|---|---|---|---|---|---|---|
| | | | 1 | 2 | 3 | 4 | 5 | 6 | 7 | 8 | 9 | 10 |
| Region 1 | Forecast | | 30 | 30 | 30 | 30 | 30 | 30 | 30 | 30 | 30 | 30 |
| Safety stock = 10 | Planned receipts | | 50 | | 50 | | | | | | | |
| Lead time = 3 | Inventory | 40 | | | | | | | | | | |
| Order size = 50 | Planned order release | | | | | | | | | | | |

| | | | Week | | | | | | | | | |
|---|---|---|---|---|---|---|---|---|---|---|---|---|
| | | | 1 | 2 | 3 | 4 | 5 | 6 | 7 | 8 | 9 | 10 |
| Region 2 | Forecast | | 25 | 25 | 50 | 50 | 30 | 30 | 45 | 45 | 60 | 60 |
| Safety stock = 20 | Planned receipts | | 75 | | | | | | | | | |
| Lead time = 1 | Inventory | 25 | | | | | | | | | | |
| Order size = 75 | Planned order release | | | | | | | | | | | |

| | | | Week 1 | 2 | 3 | 4 | 5 | 6 | 7 | 8 | 9 | 10 |
|---|---|---|---|---|---|---|---|---|---|---|---|---|
| Region 3 | Forecast | | 35 | 35 | 55 | 55 | 35 | 35 | 25 | 25 | 45 | 45 |
| Safety stock = 15 | Planned receipts | | 70 | | | | | | | | | |
| Lead time = 2 | Inventory | 40 | | | | | | | | | | |
| Order size = 70 | Planned order release | | | | | | | | | | | |

| | | Week 1 | 2 | 3 | 4 | 5 | 6 | 7 | 8 | 9 | 10 |
|---|---|---|---|---|---|---|---|---|---|---|---|
| Total region requirements | Region 1 | | | | | | | | | | |
| | Region 2 | | | | | | | | | | |
| | Region 3 | | | | | | | | | | |
| | Total of region requirements | | | | | | | | | | |

| | | | Week 1 | 2 | 3 | 4 | 5 | 6 | 7 | 8 | 9 | 10 |
|---|---|---|---|---|---|---|---|---|---|---|---|---|
| Central warehouse | Forecast needs | | | | | | | | | | | |
| Safety stock = 100 | Planned requirements | | 200 | 200 | | | | | | | | |
| Batch size = 200 | Planned receipts | | | | | | | | | | | |
| Lead time = 2 | Projected available inventory | 150 | | | | | | | | | | |
| | Master production schedule order | | | | | | | | | | | |

| | | | Week 1 | 2 | 3 | 4 | 5 | 6 | 7 | 8 | 9 | 10 |
|---|---|---|---|---|---|---|---|---|---|---|---|---|
| Saw assembly | Gross requirements | | | | | | | | | | | |
| Lead time = 2 | Scheduled receipts | | | | | | | | | | | |
| Lot for lot | Projected available balance | 250 | | | | | | | | | | |
| Safety stock = 50 | Planned order release | | | | | | | | | | | |

| | | | Week | | | | | | | | | |
|---|---|---|---|---|---|---|---|---|---|---|---|---|
| | | | 1 | 2 | 3 | 4 | 5 | 6 | 7 | 8 | 9 | 10 |
| Bench assembly | Gross requirements | | | | | | | | | | | |
| Lead time = 2 | Scheduled receipts | | | | | | | | | | | |
| EOQ = 300 | Projected available balance | 32 | | | | | | | | | | |
| Safety stock = 32 | Planned order release | | | | | | | | | | | |

## *References*


Ackerman, Ken. "Just-in-Time's American Practitioners," *Management Review.* June 1988, pp. 55–57.

Anderson, John C., Roger G. Schroeder, Sharon E. Tupy, and Edna M. White. "Materials Requirement Planning Systems: The State of the Art," *Production & Inventory Management.* October–December 1982.

Baer, Tony. "Closing the Loop: MRP II Takes the Next Step," *Managing Automation.* January 1989, pp. 60–62.

Beddingfield, Thomas W. "Reducing Inventory Enhances Competitiveness," *APICS—The Performance Advantage.* September 1992, pp. 28–31.

Black, J. T. *The Design of the Factory with a Future.* New York: McGraw-Hill, Inc., 1991.

Bourke, Richard W. "Configurators: Rule-based Product Definition," *APICS—The Performance Advantage.* December 1991, pp. 51–54.

Bourke, Richard W. "Configurators: An Update," *APICS—The Performance Advantage.* August 1992, pp. 38–39.

Cingari, John. "What Is the Role of MRP II in Quality?" *APICS: The Performance Advantage.* February 1992, pp. 24–26.

"Computers Take Control in Manufacturing and Warehousing," *Modern Materials Handling.* November 19, 1984, pp. 46–54.

Cox, James F., John H. Blackstone, and Michael S. Spencer. *APICS Dictionary.* Falls Church, Va.: American Production and Inventory Control Society, 1992.

Davis, Charles H. "Production and Inventory Processing: Material Requirements Planning," *Journal of Small Business Management.* July 1983, p. 25.

Fogarty, Donald W., Thomas R. Hoffmann, and Peter W. Stonebraker. *Production and Operations Management.* Cincinnati, Ohio: South-Western Publishing Co., 1989.

Fogarty, Donald W., John H. Blackstone, Jr., and Thomas R. Hoffmann. *Production & Inventory Management.* Cincinnati, Ohio: South-Western Publishing Co., 1991.

Goddard, Walter E. "Kanban vs. MRP II: Which is Best for You?" *Modern Materials Handling.* November 5, 1982.

Goldratt, Eliyahu, and Jeff Cox. *The Goal: A Process of On-going Improvement.* Croton-on-Hudson, N.Y.: North River Press, 1986.

Greene, James H. *Production and Inventory Control Handbook.* New York: McGraw-Hill, 1987.

Grey, Chris. "MRP II Software: Blueprint for Optimizing Manufacturing," *Computer World.* January 27, 1986.

Gunn, Thomas. *Manufacturing for Competitive Advantage: Becoming a World Class Manufacturer.* Cambridge, Mass.: Ballinger Publishing Company, 1987.

Hall, Robert. *Zero Inventories.* Homewood, Ill.: Dow Jones-Irwin, 1983.

Heard, Ed. "Competing in Good Times and Bad" in Patricia Moody, *Strategic Manufacturing.* Homewood, Ill.: Dow Jones-Irwin, 1990.

Hill, Terry. *Manufacturing Strategy, Text and Cases.* Homewood, Ill.: Irwin, 1989.

Karmarkar, Uday. "Getting Control of Just-in-Time," *Harvard Business Review.* September–October 1989, pp. 122–131.

Kutos, Scott. "Inventory Control in the 1990s," *Production & Inventory Management.* January 1992, pp. 23–26.

Lieberman, Mark. "Configuration Control: A New Way to Look at MRP II Manufacturing," *APICS: The Performance Advantage.* March 1992, pp. 35–38.

Martin, André. *DRP: Distribution Resource Planning: Distribution Management's Most Powerful Tool.* Essex Junction, Vt.: O. Wight Ltd. Publications, 1990.

Mather, Hal. *Bills of Materials.* Homewood, Ill.: Dow Jones-Irwin, 1987.

Melnyk, Steven A. "The State of MRP II Software," *APICS: The Performance Advantage.* February 1992, p. 33.

Moody, Patricia E. *Strategic Manufacturing: Dynamic New Directions for the 1990s.* Homewood, Ill.: Dow Jones-Irwin, 1990.

Newman, William, and V. Sridharan. "Manufacturing Planning and Control: Is There One Definitive Answer?" *Production and Inventory Management Journal.* Vol. 33, No. 1, 1992, pp. 50–54.

Nicholl, Andrew D. "Determining Optimum Logistics Costs," *APICS—The Performance Advantage.* February 1992, pp. 50–54.

Orlicky, Joseph. *Material Requirements Planning.* New York: McGraw-Hill, 1975.

Plossl, George W. *Production and Inventory Control: Principles and Techniques.* Englewood Cliffs, N.J.: Prentice Hall, 1985.

Rhodes, Philip. "Inventory Carrying Cost May Be Less Than You've Been Told," *Inventory Management Review.* October 1981.

Sauers, Dale. "Analyzing Inventory Systems" in Ahmad Ahmadian, Rasoul Afifi, and William D. Chandler, *Readings in Production and Operations Management.* Boston: Allyn and Bacon, 1990.

Schaeffer, Randall. "A New View of Inventory Management," *APICS—The Performance Advantage.*

Stonebraker, Peter W. "Configuring the Bill of Materials for Productivity," unpublished research papers, 1991.

Turnipseed, David L., O. Maxie Burns, and Walter E. Riggs. "An Implementation Analysis of MRP Systems: A Focus on the Human Variable," *Production and Inventory Management Journal.* January–March 1992, pp. 1–5.

Vollmann, Thomas E., William L. Berry, and D. Clay Whybark. *Manufacturing Planning and Control Systems.* Homewood, Ill.: Irwin, 1992.

Wight, Oliver W. *MRP II: Unlocking America's Productivity Potential.* Boston, Mass.: CBI Publishing Co., Inc., 1981.

Wight, Oliver W. *Production and Inventory Management in the Computer Age.* New York: Van Nostrand Reinhold Company, 1984.

Young, Scott T., and Winter D. Nie. "A Cycle Count Model Considering Inventory Policy and Record Variance," *Production and Inventory Management Journal.* Vol. 33, No. 1, 1992, pp. 11–16.

# Chapter 10

# Just-in-Time

*I have a friend who is responsible for two factories, one in Japan and one in the United States. He explained why the factory in Japan always outperforms the one in the United States: "They both set the same target, and they both may hit it. But when the Japanese hit it, they keep going, whereas the Americans tend to stop and rest on their laurels before pursuing the next goal. So in the end, the Japanese achieve more." They continuously strive for perfection with the goal of achieving excellence.* —John E. Rehfeld,
President and Chief Operating Officer, Seiko Instruments USA, Inc.

*Total Quality Control (TQC) is not a miracle drug; its properties are more like those of Chinese herb medicine.*
—Kaoru Ishikawa

## *Objectives*

After completing this chapter you should be able to:

- Discuss the JIT philosophy.
- Explain why JIT firms have a competitive advantage.
- Identify seven types of waste in an organization.
- List key JIT practices.
- Discuss the importance of continuous improvement.
- Describe the implementation process.
- Explain how JIT is applicable to services.

## *Outline*

## *Introductory Case: Toyota Drills Illinois Firm to Build Bumpers Faster and Cheaper**

Besides investing heavily in manufacturing and research and development facilities, Toyota also invests heavily in supplier firms to build a world-class network of quality suppliers. Toyota has a supplier development outreach program (SDOP) in the United States, which includes training on Just-in-Time (JIT), workshops, and seminars on total quality management. One U.S. company that has benefited from Toyota's SDOP is

*Materials drawn from Joseph B. White, "Japanese Auto Makers Help U.S. Suppliers Become More Efficient," *Wall Street Journal,* September 9, 1991; and Francis J. Gawronski, "Toyota Suppliers a Key Component of Long-Term Strategy," *Automotive News,* April 1, 1991, p. 16.

Bumper Works (BW), a small factory in Danville, Illinois, which employs about 100 workers producing lightweight pickup-truck bumpers. It took Shahid Khan, founder and owner of BW, five years of sales calls to Toyota before landing his first contract in 1985. Then, in 1987, Toyota informed Shahid and two other bumper makers to design new bumpers with specifications considerably more durable than those required by General Motors, Ford, or Chrysler. Such demands from Japanese companies are not uncommon. "We were the only ones who could demonstrate we could do that," Shahid says. In 1988, BW became the sole supplier of bumpers to Toyota's U.S. auto manufacturing facilities.

Bumper Works' relationship with Toyota seemed secure, but Toyota wanted more: annual price reductions despite rising costs for materials and labor, better bumpers, and more punctual deliveries. "We [had] benchmarked ourselves against the American industry," Shahid says. "I don't think we knew how bad we were." Toyota agreed to help BW and in September 1989, Shahid flew to Japan to get a first-hand look at the Toyota production system in operation. He discussed with Toyota management improvements that could be made at BW. "Their question," Shahid recalls, "was, 'Is there something inherently Japanese about the system? Or is it possible to export it?' "

In March 1990, Hiroshi Ginya, a manufacturing expert from Toyota headquarters, made the trip to Danville. Ginya pointed out that there was little Toyota could do for BW until it reduced the setup time for dies in the metal stamping presses to less than 22 minutes from 90 minutes or more. The reduced setup time would allow BW to be sufficiently flexible to make 20 different bumper models each day. BW could not afford new presses with quick-change features. However, with Toyota's help, the workers improvised by welding homemade metal tabs to their nine-ton dies. This made the job of aligning the dies on pins attached to the presses easier. Workers videotaped the die-change procedures and prepared an instruction manual so that other workers could learn from it. "We had no organization," recalls die coordinator David Harmon. "There were a lot of simple things we didn't think about until the Toyota team came in."

After BW achieved the die-change objective in July 1990, Toyota sent two more consultants from Japan to lead what Shahid calls a "boot camp." Shahid and his staff worked for about two weeks putting in 16-hour days to reconfigure the layout of the BW plant. This involved moving nearly every piece of equipment in the plant except the gigantic metal presses. The objective was to improve the process flow, with raw materials coming in at one end and leaving the other side of the plant as a finished bumper the same day. With the old layout, the bumpers were stamped, moved by forklifts to a holding area at the far end of the plant, and returned several days later for welding. With the new layout, bumpers go from presses to welding with only a brief stop in between. When a batch of bumpers is shipped, a card (kanban) is returned to the press operators to authorize more production. The operators now schedule their own work instead of waiting for instructions from a supervisor.

The next improvement program at BW involved operating with less inventory. BW encountered difficulties in implementing the program, and Toyota had to send another team to help iron out some of the problems. BW consults with Toyota whenever problems occur. "They call it open kimono discussions," Shahid says. The JIT system is paying off for BW with improved bumper quality and costs. For example, wasted material cost per bumper has been reduced from $1.28 to 73 cents, productivity has increased 60%, and the number of defects has gone down by 80%. These cost savings benefit both BW and

Toyota. BW is able to keep Toyota's business and Toyota has a dependable, low-cost supplier and can pass the cost savings through to their customers.

## Just-in-Time—Path to World-Class Operations

Just-in-Time (JIT) was developed in the early 1960s as the Toyota production system by Taiichi Ohno and his colleagues at Toyota, though it can be traced to American manufacturing practices in the 1930s. In Japan, it resulted from a need to improve quality and productivity after World War II and to catch up with more established automobile manufacturers in America and Europe. Japan is a land of limited natural resources and space. Constrained by this environment, the Japanese realized that there is no place for waste and inefficiency in their society. This philosophy has been extended to the workplace. Although the Toyota production system has been around for a long time, it was not until after the 1973 oil crisis that the system, now known as JIT, was adopted by other companies in Japan. JIT became more prominent after the second oil shock in 1978. Japan came out of that economic crisis in better shape than most other developed countries, and the world began to take notice of JIT.

In the face of increasing global competition, American firms have recently realized that traditional manufacturing philosophies are no longer meeting the needs of the marketplace. It is imperative that firms make dramatic changes in manufacturing philosophies and techniques. Companies must strive to be world-class manufacturers to gain a competitive edge. The path to world-class manufacturing requires firms to make fundamental changes in how they view elements of operations such as management–labor relations, job classification, training, quality, inventory management, maintenance, scheduling, automation, and supplier/customer relations. In addition, manufacturing must be sufficiently flexible to respond to changing customer needs. To achieve the status of world-class manufacturer requires "continual and rapid improvement" in quality, cost, lead time, and customer service (Schonberger, 1986). JIT is one way for firms to achieve excellence in manufacturing and to become world-class manufacturers by satisfying their customers.

Schonberger (1982) reported that JIT was reintroduced in the United States in the early 1980s. Today, JIT is used in various forms by both manufacturing and service companies. The success of Apple Computers, Black & Decker, Deere and Company, FMC Corporation, General Electric, Harley-Davidson, Hewlett-Packard, 3M, Omark Industries, and Xerox (Hall, 1983, 1987; Sepheri, 1986; Schonberger, 1983, 1986; Wantuck, 1989) has proved that the strategies of JIT are not culturally dependent, that in fact they work right here in America. Further, JIT is applicable to all parts of the chain of transformations from resource creation to service delivery. The following four specific examples show the benefits to manufacturing facilities that have implemented JIT (Sheridan, 1990).

1. Corning Inc., Corning, New York
   - Reduced defect rates from 1800 to 9 parts per million.
   - Reduced customer lead times from 5 weeks to several days.
   - Achieved customer delivery dates 98.5% of the time.
   - Reduced process losses 50%.

2. Dana's Valve Plant, Minneapolis, Minnesota
   - Reduced manufacturing throughput time 92%.
   - Increased productivity 32%.
   - Trimmed customer lead times from 6 months to 6 weeks.
   - Consolidated two plants into one, producing comparable output in half the manufacturing space.
   - Pared quality costs 47%.
   - Trimmed total inventory 50%; slashed inventory of subassemblies 94%.
   - Improved return on investment 470% and return on sales 320%.
3. Motorola, Boynton Beach, Florida
   - Reduced manufacturing cycle time 85%.
   - Improved "out-of-box" quality 250% and field reliability 350%.
   - Reduced 300 candidates to just 22 "best-in-class" sole-source suppliers, chosen for their willingness to commit to extremely high quality levels.
   - Achieved five sigma quality level (fewer than 200 defects per million).
4. Toledo Scale, Worthington, Ohio
   - Reduced manufacturing cycle time in its focused factory printed circuit board (PCB) area from 2 weeks to 3 days; reduced cycle time for the weight-indicator devices from 2 days to 30 minutes.
   - Reduced work-in-process inventory 67%.
   - Reduced defect rates in the PCB line 85%.
   - Achieved customer delivery dates 99% of the time.
   - Increased productivity 24% over a 2-year period, based on value of shipments per employee.

## Elements of JIT

As shown by the above examples, the essence of JIT is to improve productivity and quality, cut costs, and make money for a company. These ultimate objectives can only be achieved by focusing on four key and closely intertwined elements of JIT: elimination of waste, respect for people, continuous improvement, and focus on customer.

### Elimination of Waste

Waste is defined by Fujio Cho of Toyota as "anything other than the minimum amount of equipment, materials, parts, space, and worker's time, which are absolutely essential to add value to the product" (Suzaki, 1987, p. 8). This definition implies that waste can be viewed as any "nonvalue-added activity." One reason why companies have difficulty making money is the failure to recognize wastes that are present in the work environment and the associated opportunities for improvement. In order to eliminate waste, a company should first establish what does and does not add value from the customer's perspective. Then it should eliminate activities that add cost but not value to the product and focus on activities that are directly related to things the customer sees and cares about. Toyota identified seven types of waste.

***Waste from Overproduction***

Overproduction is the biggest culprit in terms of waste in the factory. The reason is that overproduction hides other basic problems in the system. Overproduction is the result of producing goods before they are required or producing just to keep machine utilization high. Traditionally, American manufacturers have been guilty of allowing output to increase in order to create an illusion of improved efficiency, although production may be quite inefficient in reality. Toyota called this "an efficiency improvement for the sake of appearance." Resources are consumed that could be used more effectively elsewhere. Unnecessary inventories are created, which require additional paperwork, storage space, holding costs, and so on. Overproduction could lead to a situation where we have too much of something that is not needed, and not enough of something that is needed.

***Waste from Waiting***

Waiting is a common occurrence found in many workplaces. Numerous examples include: a worker waits at a work station when the preceding process is unable to deliver required parts to the present process; a part waits for machine availability to be processed; a machine operator waits for maintenance personnel to repair broken equipment. Wastes arising from waiting are clearly visible, and are therefore easy to identify and eliminate.

***Waste from Transportation***

Transportation wastes are caused by an item's having to be moved unnecessarily, stored temporarily, or rearranged. These wastes result mostly from poor layout design that requires goods to be transported over long distances. Often we are surprised to learn how far a product must travel through a facility before it is completed. It is not uncommon for incoming shipments from the suppliers to be delivered to a warehouse and then transported to the work station where the parts are finally processed. This involves multiple handling and loading/unloading activities before the goods arrive at their final destination. Improvement in layout, transportation methods, workplace organization, coordination of activities, and the like can help eliminate this form of waste. For example, incoming parts could be transported several times a day directly to the line for processing.

***Waste from Processing***

Another source of waste may be the method of processing the product. Often the manufacturability of a product is not considered during the product design stage. Additional workers could be required to correct problems in the process itself. For example, plastic containers produced by an injection molding machine may require additional grinding to remove excessive flash. If the mold is of a better design and quality, the additional labor required for finishing could be minimized or eliminated. Tools, fixtures, or dies not properly installed could contribute to the expenditure of considerable time and energy in processing the materials. Certain defects in the product may arise from improper processing procedures.

***Waste from Inventory***

Carrying excessive inventory has tremendous impacts on cost and profitability, as discussed in Chapter 9. Figure 10-1 illustrates the "water and rocks" analogy; rocks represent

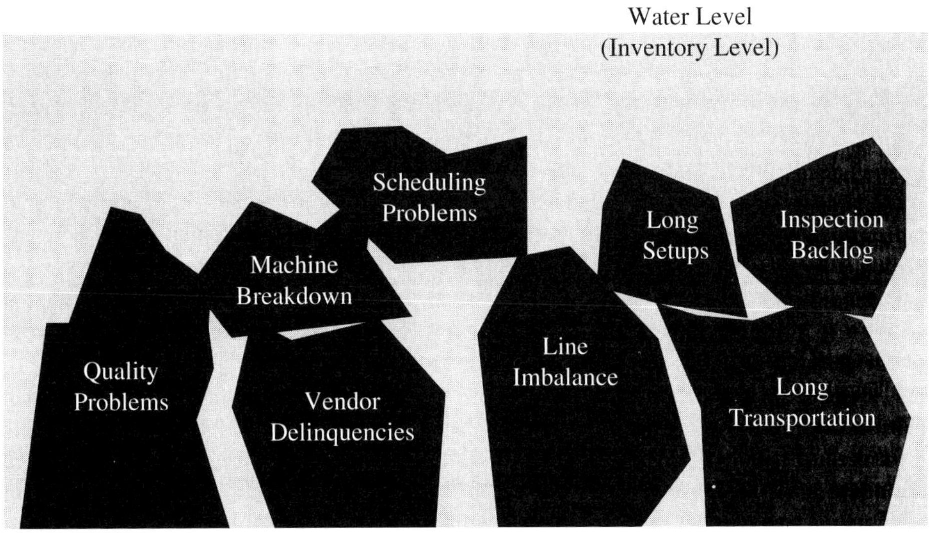


**FIGURE 10-1 Excess Inventories Hide Problems**

problems and water represents inventories that have been traditionally used to protect and buffer these problems. Excess inventories hide problems such as poor quality, poor scheduling, line imbalances, vendor delinquencies, long setups, long transportation, and the like. Thus, excess inventory can be said to be the "root of all evil." Lowering the inventory level exposes problems in the shop. These problems need to be solved before further reductions in inventory can be made. The objective is to lower the inventory gradually so that problems can be uncovered, brought to the attention of the whole organization, and finally corrected.

The impact of inventories extends far beyond the walls of a manufacturing facility. In fact, most economists view excessive inventories as a major cause of the U.S. recession in the early 1980s. American firms have since learned from the inventory debacle of that recession and have improved their inventory turns. The objective for firms is to provide better service with less inventory.

***Waste from Motion***

Unnecessary motion is time spent on movements that do not add value to the product/service. All work involves some motion. However, at Toyota, there is a clear distinction between "to work" and "to move." Ohno puts it this way: "Moving about quite a bit does not mean working. To work means to let the process move forward and to complete a job. In work there is little waste and only high efficiency" (Lu, 1986, p. 10). Therefore, in work there are two types of movement: one is necessary for making the product and the other is *wasted motion,* which does not move the manufacturing process forward or add any value to the product. For example, an operator can look busy searching for misplaced tools, dies, or fixtures without adding any value to the product. This wasted activity can lead to an increase in production cost and lead time.

***Waste from Defective Parts***

Failure to produce the product right the first time has serious consequences for the manufacturer. If the defects are discovered in the factory, then corrective action can be taken, but at a cost. Defective products found by the customer after delivery present the most serious problems. These include the possibility of lawsuits, warranty costs, and loss of future sales. A complete discussion of costs associated with poor quality is found in Chapter 11. The Japanese believe in "quality at the source." Any defective part should never be passed to the next process. The underlying philosophy is "The next process is your customer," a phrase first used by Ishikawa while attempting to solve quality problems at a steel mill in 1950. By treating the next process as your customer, all employees work with the same customer-driven quality goal. There is no ambiguity regarding how quality is viewed within an organization.

## *Respect for People*

In addition to eliminating waste in the workplace, JIT is based on respect for people. Productivity improvements cannot be achieved without employee support (see Chapter 12). It is people who make things happen, people who are responsible for the success of an organization, and people who have ideas for quality improvements and waste elimination. Vern Pearson, Omark's production manager, says, "If we're talking about priorities in terms of Just-in-Time, I guess people would be number one. I'm only as good as the people in my organization. If we don't have people involvement we don't have anything. The people out in the plant make it happen" (Goddard, 1986, p. 15).

The question is "How do we get people to work to their fullest potential?" An important element is good people management, which starts with respect for the individual. Respect for the individual is demonstrated by eliminating wasteful operations, creating a safe and equitable work environment, and encouraging people to show their talents by giving them greater responsibility and authority. At Toyota, respect for people extends beyond the more tangible signs: all employees are referred to as associates; all associates wear the same uniform; there are no reserved parking spaces; all associates eat in the same cafeteria; there are no private offices; and desks are in one large room with no walls. In order for employees to be the best they can be, the fear of making and reporting mistakes must be eliminated. When things go wrong, the tendency is to find a scapegoat. This is a negative approach that should be avoided. Instead, management should focus on solving the problem instead of resorting to finger-pointing. This creates an atmosphere of respect for the individual's achievement, intelligence, hard work, and commitment.

## *Continuous Improvement (Kaizen)*

The driving force behind continuous improvement or *kaizen* is that we should not rest on our laurels. No matter how good we think we are, there is always room to be better. If we stand still, the competition will pass us by. The goal is to set a benchmark and keep raising it. JIT is not a project with an end. Rather, it is an ongoing process, much like a lifelong journey. The Japanese strongly believe that little things add up to big things, while Americans have a tendency to go for the home run. As Shoichiro Irimajiri, president of Honda of America Manufacturing, said in his speech at Stanford University on April 7, 1987:

> *Mr. Honda used to say, "In a race competing for a split second, one tire length on the finish line will decide whether you are a winner or a loser. If you understand that, you cannot disregard even the smallest improvement." The same thing is true in the products we design and build for our customers. So many times the highest efficiency is achieved in design, in manufacturing, in service, by a series of improvements, each one of which seems small. We are now making major improvements in the efficiency of our automobile plant in Marysville, not from any single big change, but rather from thousands of improvements made by our associates. When added together, they will significantly increase our production efficiency and our competitiveness.*

Although continuous improvement involves making incremental changes that may not be highly visible in the short run, they can lead to significant contributions over the long run.

The achievement of continuous improvement requires a long-term outlook and the support of top management. It also requires the involvement of all employees in the organization. Firms adopting this approach must have the necessary support structures of training, management, resource allocation, measurement, and reward and incentive systems (Dingus and Golomski, 1988; Hayes and Wheelwright, 1984; Melcher et al., 1990). Employees must be motivated to accept continuous improvement as a means for the organization to achieve a competitive advantage in the marketplace. To increase performance, firms must "continuously push at the margins of their expertise, trying on every front to be better than before. Standards to them are ephemeral milestones on the road to perfection. They strive to be dynamic, learning companies" (Hayes, Wheelwright, and Clark, 1988, p. 25).

Motorola believes that the "company that is satisfied with its progress will soon find its customers are not." It is this belief that has resulted in a hundred-fold improvement in quality at Motorola since 1981. Motorola's formula consists of three steps: (1) banish complacency; (2) set heroic goals that compel new thinking; and (3) raise the bar as you near each goal, setting it out of reach all over again. The pursuit is total customer satisfaction.

## *Focus on Customer*

Focus on the customer is the driving force behind quality, productivity improvements, and the success of the organization. Meeting the customer's need means delivering a high-quality product that will minimize the customer's overall cost of purchasing and using the product. The focus on the customer goes beyond just taking orders and being a good listener. Organizations must strive to be responsive to customer needs, which requires an understanding of the customer's internal operations and future requirements.

Many organizations see a need to be closer to their customers as a way of keeping customers happy. In traditional manufacturing organizations, employees are often not in touch with the customers and have little opportunity of seeing how the quality or a lack of quality of their work impacts the customer. Since employees work exclusively for specific departments such as fabrication, shipping, quality control, and the like, their main concern is to meet immediate goals of their department. By allowing factory workers the opportunity to have direct and continuous contact with the customers, employees can find out first-hand from them what their requirements and expectations are so that improvements can be made to address the customers' concerns. This employee–customer connection conveys the message that the company sincerely cares about their customers.

The "service factory" concept proposed by Chase and Garvin (1989) is one approach of offering better customer service and improving competitiveness. The factory personnel can work closely with the customer in areas such as manufacturability, troubleshooting quality problems, and solving production problems. For example, Tecktronix, an electronic equipment manufacturer, has a toll-free telephone number so that customers can call the factory and talk directly to shop floor personnel to get answers regarding quality problems, use of their oscilloscopes, and other Tecktronix products. Customers are invited to the factory to witness first-hand the superiority and quality of its manufacturing processes. Using the factory as a showroom serves to reinforce the customer's perception of product quality.

## *Key JIT Practices*

The four elements of JIT, elimination of waste, respect for people, continuous improvement, and focus on customer, are supported by 12 JIT practices. Understanding how waste occurs in the factory and the impact it has on operations is basic to the process of elimination of waste through "management by sight" or "visual control." Waste must be made visible so that everyone in the organization is aware of the problem, and new and creative ideas to solve these problems can be found. Key elements and practices of the JIT philosophy are illustrated in Figure 10-2.

### *JIT Production*

Just-in-Time means producing exactly what the customer demands and delivering the good exactly when and where the customer wants. The objective of JIT is to "produce the right products, at the right quantity, at the right place, and at the right time" with the goal of achieving zero deviation from the assigned schedule. JIT production is a pull system, which refers to the "production of items only as demanded for use, or to replace those taken for use" (Cox et al., 1992). In a pull system, you produce exactly what you need, nothing more, nothing less. Simply stated, "If you don't need it, don't build it." The pull system works well for firms such as Toyota with high-volume repetitive production processes and well-defined material flows. With the pull philosophy, overproduction is essentially eliminated, and unnecessary inventories in the factory are minimized. Consequently, inventory turns will increase and holding costs will be reduced.

Toyota uses the *kanban* (Japanese for card or visual record) as a tool to implement JIT. Kanban is an information system used to control the production quantities in each process. The system is very simple, yet highly visible, and most importantly it is cost effective. Generally, there are two types of kanban used: withdrawal and production. A withdrawal kanban authorizes a container of parts to be withdrawn from the preceding process. A production kanban authorizes the processing of a container of parts. Figure 10-3 shows the use of these two kanbans to control the production flow.

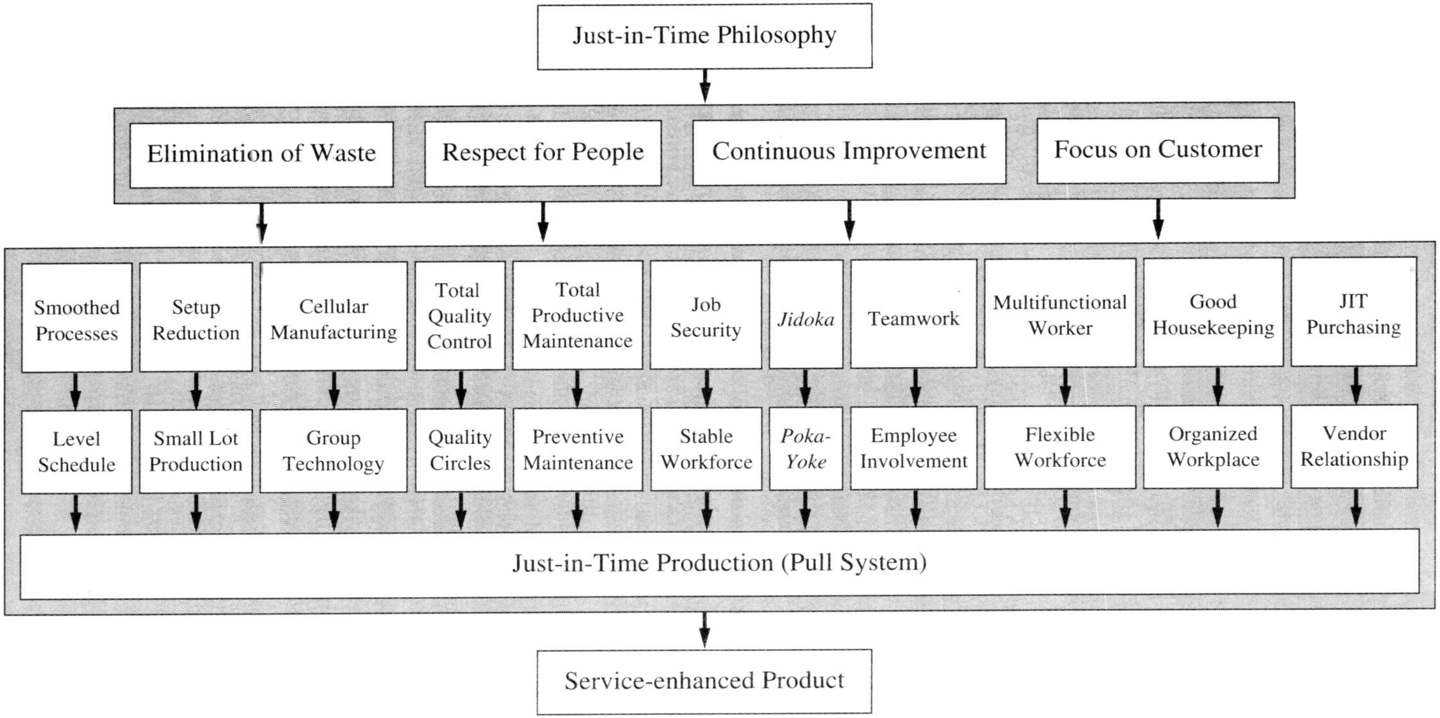


**FIGURE 10-2 JIT Elements and Practices**

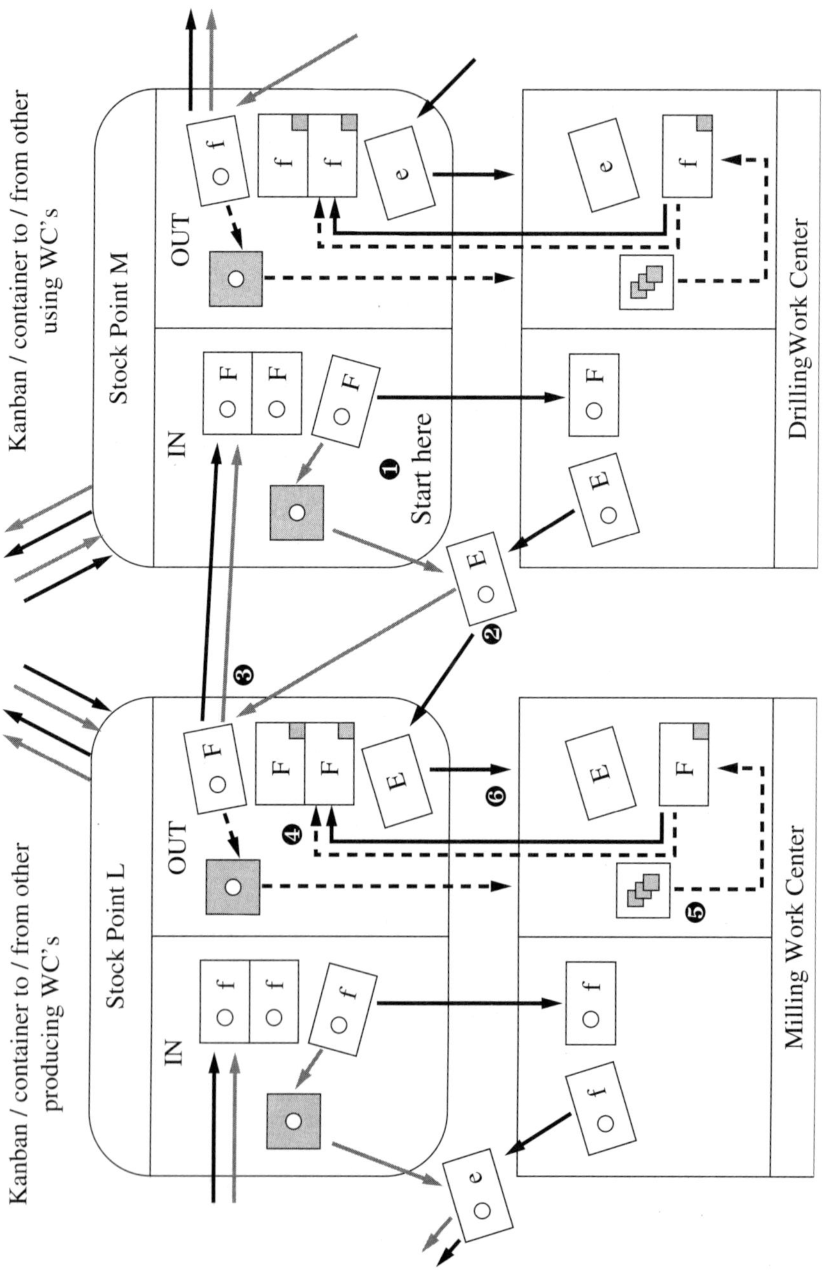
Kanban / container to / from other using WC's
Stock Point M
IN
OUT
Start here
Drilling Work Center
Kanban / container to / from other producing WC's
Stock Point L
IN
OUT
Milling Work Center

**Key**

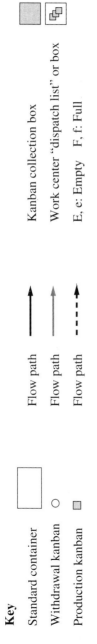

| | | |
|---|---|---|
| Standard container | Flow path | Kanban collection box |
| Withdrawal kanban ○ | Flow path | Work center "dispatch list" or box |
| Production kanban | Flow path | E, e: Empty F, f: Full |

This example shows a milling work center supplying milled heads to a drilling center that drills bolt holes in them. Stock point L serves milling (and other nearby work centers); stock point M serves drilling (and other nearby work centers). The flows of parts containers and kanban between milling and drilling are labeled in upper case; other movements are labeled in lower case.

Parts for drilling are obtained as follows:

❶ A full parts container is about to be moved into drilling. Detach withdrawal kanban and place it in a collection box for stock point M.

❷ Attach withdrawal kanban from stock point M to container most recently emptied in drilling.

❸ Take empty container with withdrawal kanban to stock point L. Transfer kanban to a full container and take container back to stock point M.

This last act also triggers production activities as follows:

❹ The full container just taken had a production kanban attached to it. Before leaving stock point L, detach and place production kanban in a collection box.

❺ Take production kanbans (that apply to milling) to milling and place them in the dispatch box. The production kanbans are worked on in the order of receipt from stock point L.

❻ Place parts for each completed job into an empty container taken from stock point L. Attach the production kanban to the full container and move container to stock point L.

**FIGURE 10-3 The Dual-Card Kanban and Container Flow Pattern**

Reprinted by permission of Richard J. Schonberger, "Applications of Single-Card and Dual-Card Kanban," *Interfaces,* Vol. 13, No. 4, August 1983. Copyright 1983 the Operations Research Society of America and The Institute of Management Sciences, 290 Westminster Street, Providence, Rhode Island 02903.

To manage the workplace effectively by using the kanban system requires several operating conditions to be followed. These operating rules are

1. No defective items may be sent to the subsequent process. If a problem is identified, it should be solved to prevent its recurrence.
2. The subsequent process is allowed to withdraw only the exact quantity as required by the kanban from the preceding process, nothing more or less. No withdrawal can take place without a kanban, and a kanban must always accompany each container of parts withdrawn.
3. The preceding work station should produce only what has been withdrawn by the subsequent process. Production occurs in the sequence in which the cards are received.
4. The number of kanbans used should be a minimum. The maximum level of inventory is determined by the number of kanbans. Consequently, all attempts should be made to keep the number of kanbans as small as possible.

The formula for calculating the number of kanbans ($K$) required to support production of each part at a work center is provided in Decision Model Box 10-1. In general, the value of $K$ seldom comes out as an integer and should be rounded up to the next whole number, which creates a small amount of safety stock. Therefore, it is good practice to start off the computation by assigning a zero value to $V$ (policy variable) in the formula.

For JIT production to work effectively, it must be supported by the key practices described in the remainder of this section.

## *Smoothed Processes*

Smoothed processes are the cornerstone for JIT production. The objective of smoothed processes is to eliminate the peaks and valleys in the work load. If we maintain capacity to meet peak rather than average demand, there is waste inherently embedded in the system. Such waste is in the form of slack associated with the work force, equipment, and work-in-process. The final assembly process is the most important starting point for production smoothing as it provides the signal for subsequent production at all preceding processes. By leveling production at final assembly, the variation in the quantity of each part withdrawn at each subassembly station is minimized. This then allows the subassembly stations to produce each part at a level rate in smaller daily lots.

At Toyota, the process for production smoothing involves first taking the total number of vehicles in the monthly production schedule and dividing it by the number of working days to determine the average daily production rate. Then, for each day, the goal is to produce in the same sequence the same mix of vehicles. Table 10-1 shows an example of a smoothed production schedule. Toyota also takes advantage of flexible machinery and reductions in production lead times to further smooth production. Reductions in lead time can be achieved with quicker setup times, improved layout, production in small lots, and so on.

**DECISION MODEL BOX 10-1 Calculating the Number of Kanbans at Butler Bumper Co.**

The Butler Bumper Company is using a kanban production system. The demand is 500 bumpers per day. Each container holds 25 bumpers. Typically, a container of bumpers requires 0.4 day for processing, and 0.1 day for wait time, which includes materials handling time. Compute the number of kanban sets to be authorized if the system is operating in an ideal environment free of external interference. If the operating system is exposed to external interference corresponding to 10% of daily demand, what is the number of kanban sets required and the level of inventory?

The formula for the number of kanban sets is

$$K = \frac{D(T_p + T_w)(1 + V)}{C}$$

where $K$ = number of kanban sets
$D$ = average daily demand for the part as determined by a uniform schedule
$T_p$ = processing time including setup (decimal fractions of a day) for one container of parts
$T_w$ = waiting time (decimal fractions of a day) in process and between process per container
$C$ = container capacity (typically not to exceed 10% of daily demand)
$V$ = policy variable set by management to reflect possible external interference (should be no more than 10%). This variable impacts the level of safety stock in the system.

Given $D = 500$, $T_p = 0.4$ day, $T_w = 0.1$ day, $C = 25$, and $V = 0$, then

$$K = \frac{500(0.4 + 0.1)(1 + 0)}{25} = \frac{500(0.5)(1)}{25} = \frac{250}{25} = \underline{\underline{10 \text{ kanban sets}}}$$

$$\text{Amount of inventory in the system} = KC = 10(25) = \underline{\underline{250 \text{ units}}}$$

If there is external interference, $V = 0.10$, and

$$K = \frac{500(0.4 + 0.1)(1 + 0.1)}{25} = \frac{500(0.5)(1.1)}{25} = \frac{275}{25} = \underline{\underline{11 \text{ kanban sets}}}$$

$$\text{Amount of inventory in the system} = KC = 11(25) = \underline{\underline{275 \text{ units}}}$$

Note that the system now has 25 additional units (safety stock) to cover contingencies.

## *Setup Reduction*

High setup time promotes overproduction, since it necessitates production in large lots, which result in higher levels of inventory. Reducing the setup time would effectively increase machine capacity, eliminate overproduction, and reduce both finished goods as well as work-in-process inventories. In addition, setup reduction is a major requirement

**TABLE 10-1 Example of an Ideal Smoothed Production Cycle for Toyota Camry**

To smooth the production cycle for Toyota Camrys, production engineers calculate the monthly volume of each model and then define that volume in daily quantity and units per minute. These calculations are shown as follows:

| Model | Monthly Quantity | Daily Quantity | Units per 9.6 Minutes |
|---|---|---|---|
| Sedan | 8,000 | 400 | 4 |
| Coupe | 4,000 | 200 | 2 |
| Wagon | 2,000 | 100 | 1 |
| | 14,000 | 700 | 7 |

There are 20 working days per month and two 8-hour shifts per day.

$$\text{Cycle time} = \frac{(480 \text{ minutes})(2 \text{ shifts})}{700 \text{ units}} = 1.37 \text{ minutes per unit}$$

The cycle repeats itself after 9.6 minutes (= 7 units × 1.37 minutes per unit).
Sequence per 9.6-minute cycle: sedan–coupe–sedan–coupe–sedan–wagon–sedan

in promoting smooth production. Shorter setup times allow for small lot production, which reduces the production lead time and enables factory operations to become more flexible.

Suzaki (1987) suggests a three-pronged approach to improvements: simplify, combine, and eliminate. Thus, in any setup reduction program the goals are to: (1) simplify the process as much as possible; (2) combine several operations to reduce the number of steps; and (3) determine if any unnecessary steps can be removed. For example, Bumper Works achieved significant reductions in the setup time for dies on the stamping presses, not with new equipment but by making the alignment of the dies simpler and easier to carry out. The Japanese, with the assistance of Shigeo Shingo, developed SMED (Single Minute Exchange of Die), which means that all setups should be less than ten minutes. Similar terms that are often used are "single setup" or "one-touch setup." Examples are the following: Toyota reduced the setup time for a 1000-ton press from 4 hours in 1941 to 3 minutes in 1971; Hitachi's setup time for a die-casting machine decreased from 1.25 hours in 1976 to 3 minutes in 1983; Yanmar Diesel machining line's setup time was decreased from 9.3 hours in 1975 to 9 minutes in 1980 (Suzaki, 1987).

## *Cellular Manufacturing*

In a JIT system, the layout of the plant is organized to minimize materials handling, transportation, work-in-process inventory, cycle time, and most importantly, to improve feedback of information. For these reasons, the Japanese prefer a product layout instead of a functional (process) layout (see Chapter 6). The problem with the process layout is that similar machines are grouped together in such a manner that the material flow is not immediately visible. With this type of arrangement, consecutive processes could be some distance apart. Thus, the layout inhibits effective communication between workers at these processes, which makes it harder to ensure that the "next process is your customer." With a product layout, the processes are arranged in the sequence of production so that there is no confusion in terms of where the material is going next. Since the processes are placed close together, total travel distance for production is minimized, and communication between processes is significantly improved. Wastes and problems inherent in the process layout are eliminated and the result is a substantial improvement in the shop's performance.

In developing a product layout, the Japanese organize the production of parts or families of parts in a number of cells with U-shaped lines. This is called *cellular manufacturing,* where one or more workers are assigned to work on several machines in each cell dedicated to the production of a family of parts. Although cellular manufacturing has been equated with group technology, Goddard (1986, p. 20) says, "Technically, cellular manufacturing is the linking of machines and operations to produce a part, whereas group technology is primarily concerned with the production of like parts, grouped by design." The benefits of cellular layouts are discussed in Chapter 6. It is not uncommon to have a cell with several machines dedicated to the production of one part by a single worker. The worker starts processing on one part and, when it is completed, moves the part to the next machine for processing. Each worker has a route that is determined by the machines worked on. The worker is always handling and processing one part at a time. This is called *one-piece production.* Suzaki (1987) explained how a sporting goods factory on the West Coast reorganized its machines into U-shaped layouts to improve process flow. The benefits were a reduction of work-in-process inventories from 30 units to one unit, space savings of 50%, a big reduction in lead time, an improvement in labor productivity of 30%, and significant improvements in quality.

## *Total Quality Control and Quality Circles*

Since JIT requires delivery of the right part at the right time, quality is extremely important. Bad parts mean that good parts are not available when needed. With pull production, small lot sizes, and small inventories, there is a strong possibility that the production line will be shut down if poor-quality parts are accepted for production. For JIT to work it must not only be "doing things right the first time" but "doing things right the first time and all the time."

The concept of total quality control (TQC) or total quality management (TQM) was originated by Armand Fiegenbaum, who defined it as "an effective system for integrating the quality development, quality maintenance, and quality improvement efforts of the various groups in an organization so as to enable production and service at the most economical levels which allow for full customer satisfaction." Fiegenbaum envisioned that TQC would be under the auspices of a management function devoted solely to product quality. The Japanese approach differed from Fiegenbaum's in that TQC activities are not the sole domain of QC specialists; all employees and divisions are deeply involved with studying and promoting QC. The goals of TQC are

1. Improving the corporate health and character of the company. Top management defines the goals, pointing out which part of the company's character requires modification, or which aspect must be improved.
2. Combining the efforts of all employees to establish a cooperative system.
3. Establishing a quality assurance system and obtaining the confidence of customers and consumers. Its primary goal is "quality first."
4. Aspiring to achieve the highest quality in the world; developing new products/services for that purpose.
5. Establishing a management system that can secure profit in times of slow growth and can meet related challenges.
6. Showing respect for humanity, nurturing human resources, considering employee happiness, and providing a cheerful workplace.
7. Utilizing statistical methods for QC (for example, statistical process control).*

Motorola believes that "to get people to care about quality, you have to care about them." Motorola invests heavily in employee training programs that respond to changing work environments. Employees are taught new creative skills, which enhance their sense of individual worth and well-being. The training programs show that Motorola is well aware of their employees' concern for personal development and advancement. Consequently, Motorola's employees can now reach a potential that was not thought possible before. In 1988, Motorola received the Malcolm Baldrige National Quality Award in recognition of its commitment to quality.

The *quality circle,* a concept which originated in Japan in the early 1960s, is the cornerstone for implementing TQC. The Japanese Union of Scientists and Engineers (JUSE) (1987) reported that quality circle activities have spread to more than 50 countries worldwide. A quality circle is a small group of employees who voluntarily work together on areas of common concern such as quality, safety, communications, work environment, efficiency, and the like. The group meets on a regular basis, identifies problems, discusses potential solutions, and then forwards its proposals to management. The group is led by a facilitator rather than the traditional authoritarian decision maker. The facilitator's responsibilities include getting everyone involved, preventing domination by any one individual, dealing with negative comments, maintaining focus, keeping enthusiasm high, and managing conflict. At Toyota, the ultimate purpose of quality circles is to "promote a worker's sense of responsibility, provide a vehicle to achieve working goals, enable each worker to be accepted and recognized, and allow improvement and growth in a worker's technical abilities" (Monden, 1983, p. 132). The principles that justify the existence of quality circles are provided in Table 10-2.

One of the earliest reported attempts to introduce quality circles in the United States was made by Lockheed Missiles and Space Company in 1973 (Rieker, 1975). However, it was not until the late 1970s that quality circles became popular in the United States. Although quality circles are found in the United States and in Japan, there are some differences worth highlighting. In the United States, a quality circle is often initiated by

*These seven goals are adapted from Ishikawa, *Total Quality Control: The Japanese Way* (translation by Lu), 1985, pp. 95–96.

**TABLE 10-2 Principles of Quality Circle Activities**

1. Quality circles should be initiated in the workplace on a voluntary basis. It is a group activity that accommodates everyone, not just the most capable, outgoing, or prominent workers. Sharing problems should be encouraged with participation according to individual capability.
2. Quality circle activities should occur during working hours—not before or after.
3. Quality circles should not be monopolized by either supervisors or management. Discussions should be entered into freely and frankly and seen as an opportunity for all members to listen with open minds. The goal is to bring harmony to the workplace.
4. Specific—not abstract—problems should be studied, beginning with immediate yet small, concrete issues. Solving problems should give members a feeling of confidence and accomplishment.
5. A stable, controlled operating environment should be established. Steps should be taken to stop recurring problems and to anticipate new ones. Problem-solving techniques require the application of quality control and industrial engineering methods, among others.
6. A work area is not simply a place for physical labor, but a place where the worker's creativity can be utilized. Workers are encouraged to think and generate new ideas.
7. Management should provide training to improve workers' skills.
8. Management should provide an environment where workers can find pleasure and meaning in life in their work.
9. Managers should be committed to giving guidance, training, and support, and to showing respect for people. Managers must reject their traditional distrust of shop workers.
10. Management should emphasize the spirit of give and take. Quality circles can help transcend corporate boundaries while still developing friendly rivalry.

Adapted from Akira Ishikawa, "Principles of QC Circle Activities and Their Effects on Productivity in Japan: A Corporate Analysis," *Management International Review,* Vol. 25, No. 3, 1985, pp. 33–40.

management as a *formal* organization, while in Japan, it is an *informal* group among workers. There is full participation by Japanese workers due to group pressure, even though it is voluntary. Managers in the United States have to be more persuasive in convincing workers to join in quality circle activities. The frequency of turnover and layoffs in the United States makes it difficult for members to belong to the same circle for a long period of time, thus limiting the opportunity for consistent education on a long-term basis (Ishikawa, 1985).

## *Total Productive Maintenance*

Just-in-time systems have very little work-in-process inventory, and any equipment breakdown is very disruptive to production. The old adage of "don't fix it if it ain't broke," or breakdown maintenance, must be changed, since this approach promotes waste. The use of breakdown maintenance stems in part from the near-sighted focus of managers intent on putting off maintenance to improve short-term capacity utilization and profits.

Preventive maintenance is a proactive approach to making adjustments and repairs to equipment before problems occur, in order to eliminate unexpected downtime, eliminate processing variation, increase the life of equipment, avoid major equipment repairs, and ensure a smooth flow of products. The objective of preventive maintenance is to enable processes to be operable at the time they are needed. *Total productive maintenance* or *total preventive maintenance* (TPM) stresses achieving overall productive system effectiveness through preventive maintenance and total involvement of all employees in an organization. TPM is similar to TQC from the perspective of total employee commitment with the goals of improving quality and productivity. These ultimately lead to increased profitability of a plant. At the Mikuni plant, Washing Machine Division of Matshushita Electric Company in Japan there is a slogan associated with the TPM program that reads: "Maintenance for Profit" (Takatsuki, 1986).

Manufacturing personnel must be involved in the careful planning and scheduling of preventive maintenance to ensure that it happens regularly without disrupting production. There must be a spirit of cooperation between machine operators and the maintenance department. The machine operators should be trained to do routine maintenance such as machine cleaning, adding lubricant, bolt tightening, and the like to avoid premature deterioration of the machine. In addition, operators should be aware of early warning signs of machine degeneration by checking for excessive wear, oil leaks, listening for telltale sounds, and so on that suggest the onset of some serious problems. The job of maintenance personnel is to assist the operators with self-maintenance activities, repair broken equipment, specify machine operating procedures, determine machine design weaknesses, and take corrective actions.

## *Job Security and Stable Work Force*

In Japan, employment is viewed as a "social commitment," while in the United States, employment is treated as a "contract." The lifetime employment system used by Japanese companies ensures that the company will have a reliable and stable pool of loyal, knowledgeable, and motivated workers. Workers benefit from the job security that the system guarantees. With lifetime employment, the company can invest in the long-term development of the individual without fear of the individual's being hired away by a competing firm. A comprehensive training program can be provided to mold the employee to best suit the needs of the company. Over time, the employee develops more and more capabilities. The premise is that an employee who has been with the company for ten years would have ten years of experience, and not ten times one year of experience. Although the ultimate objective is to provide lifetime employment for all employees in the company, a more realistic goal is to provide the highest level of job security that is possible for a core group of employees. In Japan, lifetime employment applies only to permanent workers, who represent only a portion of the Japanese work force.

In the "contract" system, a company hires when there is a position vacant. The applicant's qualifications must closely match the job's requirements. Basically, the individual is "selling" his/her skill, knowledge, and experience to the company. The employee does not feel obligated to the company and will switch jobs when he or she gets a better offer from another company. Turnover of employees in the workplace is higher with the contract system. According to Boyett and Conn (1991), an average American beginning a career in the 1990s will probably work for five or more employers and in ten or more jobs over the course of a lifetime.

During the economic recession that started in 1991, U.S. corporations were forced to cut costs and downsize the work force. Announcements of layoffs have raised the anxiety level among U.S. workers about their job security. With downsizing, the danger is that employees feel demoralized and tend to work for themselves rather than providing the collaborative effort needed to meet corporate goals. This situation is bad for long-term competitiveness. For example, the announcement in December 1991 by General Motors that it plans to close 21 plants and lay off more than 74,000 employees over the next few years has sent shock waves through its rank and file. Although layoffs of such magnitude are rare in Japan, the deepening global recession has caused several Japanese companies to force managers into early retirement or to be transferred to lower-status jobs at subsidiary companies (Neff et al., 1993).

The fear of layoffs resulting from employee suggestions for improving the product or process should be allayed by management. Otherwise, it is unlikely that employees will make further suggestions for productivity improvement. Employees whose positions are made redundant should be moved to other areas that best suit their skills or should be retrained to develop new skills. Layoffs should be considered as the absolute last resort. Omark and Hewlett-Packard are U.S. companies that have a policy of no layoffs of their work force resulting from productivity improvements. At NUMMI, employees assisted the plant's assembly-maintenance crew in building a robot that eventually worked alongside humans doing the same work. The workers feel confident that no jobs will be lost even with the addition of more robots. The reason is a provision in NUMMI's agreement with the United Auto Workers union that states: "The company agrees that it will not lay off employees unless compelled to do so by severe economic conditions that threaten the long-term financial viability of the company." In addition, counter measures such as reducing the salaries of its officers and management will be taken before any layoffs can occur (Sheridan, 1990).

## *Jidoka*

Toyota likes to refer to *jidoka* as "automation with a human touch," or *autonomation.* Most automated machines require operators to watch the machines run, and thus do not add value. In jidoka the machines are upgraded so that when an abnormal condition such as defects, tool breakage, or a shortage of parts occurs, the machine stops and gives a warning signal informing the operator to take the necessary action. The Japanese believe in "visual control" where abnormal conditions are made visible so that they can be eliminated. The jidoka concept can be extended to the production line. When an abnormality is found, both workers and machines must stop immediately. The andon light is a "visual control" used to signal problems on the line. When a problem occurs or the work cannot be completed in time, the operator pushes a button, which causes a yellow light to flash, signaling for help from the supervisor. If the supervisor cannot solve the problem after some time, the line is stopped and a red light comes on automatically. All efforts will be made to correct the problem and to prevent a similar recurrence.

*Poka-yoke* is Japanese for a "foolproof mechanism" that is incorporated into a machine to carry out 100% inspection and to provide immediate feedback when something abnormal occurs. Thus, poka-yoke is an example of a "visual control" tool which prevents defective parts from passing on to the next process and thus supports the goal of quality at the source. A warning signal is turned on when abnormalities occur, and the machine stops automatically. When this happens, the root cause of the problem is identified and solved to prevent it from recurring. Shingo (1986) describes numerous examples of actual poka-yoke devices installed in Japanese companies.

### Teamwork

People learn best when they are given the opportunity to participate actively in decision making and problem solving. It is through active participation and involvement that people develop a sense of achievement and ownership through successfully solving a problem. This in turn creates the motivation and commitment necessary to attack and eliminate wastes at all levels in an organization. The idea behind the team approach is that synergy is created such that the "whole is greater than the sum of the parts."

The required traits of group consciousness and a sense of equality explain why the team approach to solving problems is extremely successful in Japan. Teamwork implies that all functions must work together for the common good of the company. Without people working together on the same team, the communications required to integrate the various elements of JIT will not be there. A team effort provides an environment conducive to generating more and better ideas for improvements than a group of individuals working independently. At Toyota, employees generate millions of suggestions annually, with over 90% of them adopted (Suzaki, 1987).

The teamwork approach is gaining increasing popularity in the United States. In 1985, NUMMI, the joint venture between GM and Toyota in Fremont, California, was formed to experiment with the JIT system, using unionized American workers and suppliers. According to Osamu Kimura, NUMMI president, the key to cultivating a team spirit is "to involve all team members in everything—that means quality, cost, safety, . . . everything. It is important to ask them to think and to make a plan by themselves. Nobody knows the situation—the problems—better than the team members. Management's role is to help and support them" (Sheridan, 1990). At GM's Saturn plant, teams are responsible for "hiring" workers, approving parts from suppliers, and handling administrative matters such as the team's budget, in addition to their regular assembly work (Woodruff et al., 1992).

Frank Ostroff and Douglas Smith of McKinsey & Company, envision a *horizontal organization,* where virtually everyone would "work together in multidisciplinary teams that perform core processes" to be more responsive to customers (Byrne, 1993). In moving toward this innovative form of "boundaryless" organization, companies such as Eastman Chemical, Lexmark International, Motorola, and Xerox are using cross-functional, self-directed teams to manage their operations horizontally. This concept fits nicely with the JIT philosophy.

### Multifunctional Worker

The changing demands of the marketplace with shorter product life cycles bring about a need for manufacturing systems and workers that are sufficiently flexible to respond to the wide-ranging needs of the customers. Changing demands can cause the loads at work centers in the plant to change over time. To respond to these changes and use only the minimum number of workers may require workers to be transferred from one assembly area to another. Workers need to be cross-trained to be competent at a variety of processes in their work area. The objective is to develop a flexible work force with multiple skills.

The importance of a flexible and cross-trained work force becomes more apparent when companies use cellular manufacturing. Each worker basically operates several machines in the manufacturing cell and is responsible for setting up the machines, doing routine maintenance, and checking the quality of the parts. When a worker falls behind schedule, a fellow worker may be moved over to assist in restoring equilibrium. This requires workers to develop a variety of skills. To encourage employees to cross train, Toledo Scale instituted a "pay-for-skills" program. When a worker completes training and certification in a new skill, the worker's pay is increased by 18 to 22 cents per hour (Barnet, 1992).

## *Good Housekeeping and Organized Workplace*

Housekeeping is more than just keeping shop floors clean and racks well organized. Housekeeping should not be considered as an expense item or an activity that could be avoided because "we cannot afford it." The benefits derived from good housekeeping far exceed the cost incurred. Clean floors and machines not only create an impression of good appearance but can expose problems such as oil leaks and surface cracks. These early warning signs lead to the detection of problems that can be corrected before major breakdowns can occur.

A clean and organized work environment improves workers' morale and instills in the employees a sense of pride in the workplace. An organized workplace also improves management–labor relations. The effort put into housekeeping is closely linked to the quantity of defective parts produced, the frequency of machine breakdowns, inventory level, number of employee suggestions for improvement, absenteeism level, number of accidents, and so forth. Thus we see how housekeeping can help reduce the cost of making a product. Housekeeping should be everybody's job because of its wide-ranging impact.

The Japanese place a high value on cleanliness and orderliness, and it is no coincidence that we find Japanese factories to be well organized, clean, and quiet. This philosophy extends even to Japanese factories in America. Any visitor to Honda's manufacturing facilities at Marysville, Ohio, will find a relatively quiet shop floor, employees dressed in clean overalls, aisles that are clearly marked and laid out, clean machines, floors, and rest rooms, and so on. As Hayes and Wheelwright (1984, p. 356) note: ". . . the personal attitudes of the Japanese worker, as impressive as they are, are not the major reason behind the almost total sense of order that is observed. Instead, it is more a reflection of the attitudes, practices, and systems that the managers of those plants have carefully put into place over a long period of time. The evidence of management ingenuity and hard work is everywhere."

## *JIT Purchasing*

For JIT to work there must be a close working relationship with the suppliers. Buyers and sellers should develop long-term partnerships that are mutually beneficial. Instead of the traditional arms-length, adversarial relationship with suppliers, manufacturers should consider their suppliers as an extension of the factory. It has often been said that you are only as good as your suppliers. Companies should take advantage of supplier expertise to help with specifications, manufacturability, selection of materials, and the like. For example, Xerox now encourages their engineers to communicate with suppliers, where previously they had a policy of prohibiting this interaction. In addition, Xerox has a program that provides assistance to suppliers to improve their capabilities. There must be free flow of information between buyers and sellers. The benefit for Xerox is better quality and lower purchase prices. In the introductory case at the beginning of this chapter, Toyota provided assistance to one of its suppliers, Bumper Works, to implement JIT. During the implementation phase, things that went wrong were resolved by *open kimono* discussions between Bumper Works and Toyota. *Open kimono* implies that "there are no secrets" between the buyer and seller. The end result of this cooperative effort is that quality has improved and costs are coming down. Table 10-3 provides a comparison of conventional and JIT purchasing practices.

Companies are recognizing the need to have fewer but better suppliers. With fewer suppliers, companies are resorting to supplier certification to maintain high quality and to eliminate incoming inspections. For example, Ford Motor Company not only has a vendor certification program but gives a *Total Quality Excellence* award to the top echelon among Ford's suppliers in recognition of their "excellence and continuous improvement in quality, engineering expertise, delivery performance, and customer relations." Such recognition provides encouragement for the suppliers to continue their excellent work.

In a survey of JIT purchasing practices in the United States, Freeland (1991) identifies six dominant roadblocks to implementing JIT purchasing. The percentages shown for each of the factors represent the proportion of respondents who felt that the factor has impaired the company's ability to implement JIT purchasing. It should be noted that a respondent may select more than one factor as contributing to the problem.

1. Erratic end-user demand (70%)
2. Substantial distances between the company's facilities and available suppliers (43%)
3. Supplier quality (35%)
4. High frequency of product changes and updates (30%)
5. Wide variety of customer production options (30%)
6. Product that must be made to order (22%)

In Japan, major corporations have expanded the basic long-term supplier–vendor relationship and created a distinctive business practice known as *keiretsu.* Briefly, keiretsu is a long-term business alliance by which members are linked together through ownership of each other's stock and members enjoy preferential treatment in business transactions. Keiretsu can have either a horizontal or vertical orientation. *Horizontal keiretsu* is often referred to as *financial keiretsu,* where a bank, other financial institutions, and a giant trading company could link together with some unrelated companies, such as a consumer electronics manufacturer or brewery. Although keiretsu companies comprise less than 0.1% of all companies in Japan, they account for 78% of the value of all shares on the Tokyo Stock Exchange. The six major financial keiretsu of Mitsubishi, Mitsui, Sumitomo, Fuyo, DKB, and Sanwa have been responsible for nearly one-quarter of Japan's GNP (Rapoport, 1991). For example, the DKB group is comprised of major companies such as

**TABLE 10-3 Conventional and JIT Purchasing**

| Conventional Purchasing | Just-in-Time Purchasing |
|---|---|
| 1. Large delivery lot sizes typically covering several weeks of requirements. Deliveries are infrequent. | 1. Small delivery lot sizes based on the immediate needs for production usage. Deliveries are very frequent, e.g., several times a day. |
| 2. Deliveries are timed according to the buyer's request date. | 2. Deliveries are synchronized with the buyer's production schedule. |
| 3. There are several suppliers for each part. Multiple sourcing is used to maintain adequate quality and competitive pricing. | 3. Few suppliers are used for each part. Often, parts are single-sourced. |
| 4. Typically, inventories are maintained for parts. | 4. Little inventory is required, because deliveries are expected to be made frequently, on time, and with high-quality parts. |
| 5. Purchasing agreements are short-term. Pressure suppliers by threat of withdrawing business. | 5. Purchasing agreements are long-term. Pressure suppliers through obligation to perform. |
| 6. Products are designed with few constraints on the number of different purchased components used. | 6. Products are designed with great effort to use only currently purchased parts. Objective is to maximize the commonality of parts. |
| 7. Minimal exchange of information between supplier and buyer. | 7. Extensive exchange of information with regard to production schedules, production processes, etc. |
| 8. Purchasing agent is the primary focus of communication with supplier. | 8. Purchasing agent is the facilitator of many points of communication between design engineers, production engineers, etc. |
| 9. Prices are established by suppliers. | 9. Buyer works with supplier to reduce supplier's costs and thereby reduce prices. |
| 10. Geographic proximity of supplier is not important for the supplier selection decision. | 10. Geographic proximity is considered very important. |

Reprinted with the permission of APICS, Inc., "A Survey of Just-in-Time Purchasing Practices in the United States," *Production and Inventory Management,* James R. Freeland, April–June 1991, p. 45.

Dai-Ichi Kangyo (the world's largest bank), Asahi Chemical (the world's largest textile company), Fujitsu (the world's second largest computer company), Kawasaki Steel, Isuzu Motors, and cosmetics maker Shiseido.

*Supply keiretsus* are vertical alliances involving an interlocking network of suppliers dominated by a major manufacturer and are well entrenched in the auto, electronics, and machinery industries. The amount of intragroup trade in a supply keiretsu is strong; industry experts estimate that at least 30% of the business of member companies is carried out within the group. For example, Matshushita accounts for more than 20% of the Japanese VCR market, with its strongest domestic competitor, JVC, having just under 20% of the market. What is intriguing is that Matshusita owns 51% of JVC, which also designs many of Matshusita's products (Ferguson, 1990).

Keiretsu-like ties are emerging in the United States. When the Japanese automakers decided to set up manufacturing facilities in the United States, numerous Japanese parts suppliers were quick to emulate them. Since 1982, the Japanese have built eight auto assembly plants in the United States, mostly in the midwest. Following closely on their heels were more than 250 Japanese suppliers (Rapoport, 1990). These suppliers are careful to locate close to the vendors' facilities so that delivery can be on a JIT basis. Environmentalists are concerned that the increased number of trips made to deliver purchased parts contribute to increased pollution and global warming. This concern must be balanced with improved efficiencies on the shop floor. Tougher standards set by the Environmental Protection Agency for auto manufacturers on fuel economy and emission control should help alleviate this problem.

## *Functional Interactions*

Just-in-time necessitates that operations interact with other functions or departments such as marketing, design engineering, and accounting to support the concept of continuous improvement. Traditionally, each function operates within its narrowly defined territorial boundaries established by the organization. By focusing narrowly on functional or departmental efficiency without considering total organizational goals, local optimization results as opposed to the global optimization possible when all functional areas work together for the well-being of the organization.

### *Marketing Interface*

The marketing function involves such activities as product management, sales, customer service, and marketing research. The marketing contribution to a successful JIT implementation is to obtain feedback from the customers in terms of their expectations and requirements in order to supply the information necessary to optimize the design engineering and production processes. Reduction of order processing time is another important area of support. A quick response with order-promise information can translate into a marketing competitive advantage. The process of order entry, credit checking, and other paperwork associated with the order must be streamlined and made error-free. Marketing must understand that customer orders provide the starting point for any operations activity. Customer orders are the vehicles that trigger the "pull" of the product through the factory.

Just-in-time is an excellent marketing tool, providing a company with a competitive edge over non-JIT competitors. A JIT manufacturer delivers products directly to the customer's assembly line, or on a more timely basis to the stocking point, without receiving inspection, which effectively reduces the customer's internal production costs. The sales department must seek out customers who want JIT goods or services and are willing to make long-term commitments with a reasonable amount of stability in delivery quantities and delivery dates. The sales policy should support JIT production, that is, the top priority for sales personnel is to secure firm contracts, since schedules are difficult to alter without major consequences and disruption to the production system. Marketing's support of the operations function in a JIT environment is summarized in Table 10-4.

## *Design Engineering Interface*

The objective for design engineering is to design a product that not only meets customer requirements and needs but is also easy and cost effective to manufacture. The ability to meet customer requirements requires a close link to the customer. Marketing plays a critical role in providing inputs from the market in terms of customer requirements. Manufacturability of a product is important, because it determines the ease of fabrication

**TABLE 10-4 Marketing's Support of Operations**

| Marketing Activity | Marketing's Support of Operations |
|---|---|
| Sales | Helps smooth production/service delivery schedules. Avoids end-of-period "hockey sticks" in orders. Develops a base of customers who want JIT goods or services and are willing to commit to long-term contracts with reasonably stable delivery quantities and dates. |
| Order entry and customer service | Reduces lead time in order processing. |
| Product/service management | Coordinates product/service strategy with operations in order to emphasize quality and on-time delivery. |
| Marketing research | Provides feedback to operations on quality variables relating to product/service quality. |
| Physical distribution* | Adheres to shipping schedules. Evaluates alternatives of warehouse location, fleet expansion and management, and third-party carriers. Increases visibility of customers' operations. Balance shipping loads with production batches for frequent deliveries. Coordinates customer carrier pickups. Implements pull system from warehouse. |
| Advertising and promotion | Coordinates promotions with operations to stabilize shop schedules. |

*The distribution function is part of materials management in some organizations.

Adapted from R. Natarajan and J. Donald Weinrauch, "JIT and the Marketing Interface," *Production and Inventory Management,* July–September 1990, p. 43.

or assembly of the product, the amount of scrap and defects generated, the type of inspection required, the level of production yields, and the production cost. Thus design engineering has a significant impact on the long-term cost, quality, and profitability of the product. At Hewlett-Packard's plant in Roseville, California, a "cost-of-complexity" analysis found that the selection of components for a printed-circuit assembly can impact the cost of production. One alternative, which involves inserting a part by using an automatic insertion machine, costs 15 cents. Another alternative, which adds the part after the wave-soldering operation (that is, backloading a part), costs $1.50. Chris Barmeir, the controller at HP, says, "If you can change a design to make a part auto-insertable and avoid the backload process, the process becomes less costly" (Sheridan, 1990). To design the 1990 Lincoln Town Car, Ford built more than 110 prototypes on the assembly line in the auto plant at Wixom, Michigan. Ford's workers helped to fine-tune the design to improve quality and ease of assembly. More than 2600 employee suggestions were incorporated into the final design (Sheridan, 1990).

An objective of product design is to reduce the number of parts used, because it has a major impact on cost and quality. With fewer parts, the benefits for the organization are wide-ranging: purchasing of parts is simplified; workload is reduced; finished goods and work-in-process are reduced; plant and warehouse storage space is decreased; fewer quality details have to be contended with; scheduling is simplified; and communication is simplified. For example, Texas Instruments's TI-25 calculators have been designed for ease of assembly with only seven components, the fewest number of parts in any scientific calculator in the world. The TI-25 calculators have five models, which are priced from $5 to $10. Production of these calculators at the Lubbock plant in Texas is approximately 2 million units per year (Sheridan, 1990).

Simultaneous or concurrent engineering has been suggested as a means of shortening the design-to-manufacture cycle time through the involvement of all functional areas in the design process. For example, Lee Iacocca announced in a recent TV commercial that it took Chrysler only two years to move from design to production of its sleek Viper sports car, using the teamwork approach involving personnel from engineering, marketing, and production.

## *Accounting Interface*

Recently attention has focused on the appropriateness of traditional accounting practices in a JIT environment. Accounting plays an important role in providing valuable performance information. Japanese companies, like their American counterparts, must value inventory for tax and financial purposes. The difference is that the Japanese do not allow these accounting procedures to affect their measurement and control of organizational activities. Japanese companies do a better job of using their management control systems to augment and enhance their manufacturing strategies. In essence, there is a more direct link between management accounting practices and corporate goals.

Hiromoto (1988) notes that Japanese companies appear to utilize accounting systems as a means to motivate employees to perform in support of long-term manufacturing strategies rather than to provide senior management with precise data on costs, variances, and profits. Thus, accounting plays the role of an "influencer" rather than that of an "informer." For example, senior Japanese managers are less concerned about whether an overhead allocation system depicts the exact demands each product places on corporate resources than about how the system impacts the cost-reduction efforts of middle managers and workers on the shop floor.

Accounting in Japan has also exhibited an overwhelming commitment to "market-driven management." Japanese firms have long recognized that the design stage represents the most promising area for realizing low-cost production. The emphasis is on designing and building products that will satisfy the price predicted for market success. Many Japanese companies estimate costs of new products by making it a point not to rely solely on current engineering standards. Instead, they determine target costs based on competitive market price estimates. As a result, these target costs are normally much below prevailing costs, which are computed based on standard technologies and processes. Benchmarks are then set by managers to gauge incremental progress toward achieving the target cost objectives. Hiromoto (1988) observes, "How efficiently a company *should* be able to build a product is less important to the Japanese than how efficiently it *must* be able to build it for maximum marketplace success." The lesson here is that accounting policies should be supportive of corporate strategy, not independent of it.

## *Implementation Issues*

There is no ideal approach to implement JIT, since it depends to a large extent on the business environment and manufacturing processes involved. However, trying to implement all key JIT practices simultaneously would not be a wise decision. Management should be cautious not to bite off more than they can chew in the early process of JIT implementation. Wantuck (1989) suggests following the *ten-step game plan for change* to ensure success in designing a JIT implementation program.

1. *Top management leadership.* Management must not only provide leadership but also show visible commitment and involvement in the whole implementation process.
2. *Steering committee.* The steering committee is formed to formulate policy, select the pilot area, provide resources, and guide the project.
3. *Education program.* Widespread education is necessary, since JIT affects the entire organization. The objective is to get people to buy into the project.
4. *Pilot project planning.* The project team recommends the key JIT practices such as setup reduction, group technology, and smoothed production that are to be included in the pilot.
5. *Steering committee approval.* The project team makes a formal presentation to sell top management on the project with the goal of securing formal approval.
6. *Employee training.* After project approval, employees in the pilot area must be properly trained to enable them to understand the project. Employee participation and suggestions are extremely critical to the success of the project.

7. *Pilot implementation.* During implementation, progress should be monitored and recorded. Feedbacks should be used to revise the plan.
8. *Pilot post mortem.* A post mortem provides for an evaluation of the causes and effects of the project. An official report documents the major problems encountered and how they were solved.
9. *Feedback to steering committee.* Lessons learned from the post mortem are communicated to management. The presentation meeting marks the formal closeout of the project.
10. *Expansion to next project.* This step signals the beginning of the next project cycle. The process is ready to start over by building on knowledge gained so far.

Scott et al.'s (1992) empirical study at the Wilson Sporting Goods plant shows that levels of satisfaction tend to increase for production workers as their involvement with JIT practices increases. Inman and Brandon (1992) note that an undesirable effect of JIT is stress brought about by rapid changes in the workplace. Klein (1989) also argues that line operators experienced a higher level of stress under JIT. Unnecessary stress can be reduced by practicing better time management and having a good support system to attend to worker concerns. Ultimately, "Attitudes must change first. You have to accept the need for JIT, want it, believe you can do it, and commit that you will do it before it can happen" (Wantuck, 1989, p. 364).

## *JIT and MRP*

Just-in-time and material requirements planning (MRP) related systems are not incompatible with each other. The kanban pull system is relatively simple and cheap to operate, since it does not need a computer. MRP II (manufacturing resource planning) systems do an excellent job of planning and coordinating materials flow at higher levels and providing a common basis for communication among the various functional areas. Additionally, MRP systems can help managers better understand the impact of changes in the master production schedule and lot-sizing decisions on capacity and inventory. In a repetitive production environment with fairly steady schedules, effective production control can be achieved with a hybrid approach of MRP and JIT (Karmarker, 1989). In this environment, MRP works well, because frequent materials planning is not necessary. At the same time, the pull system performs well on the shop floor, keeping inventory to a minimum. Examples of hybrid systems are "synchro-MRP," "rate-based MRP II," and "JIT-MRP."

The Manufacturing Quality Assurance Organization (MQAO) at Kodak Park in Rochester, N.Y., provides services, such as product-quality information and test-development expertise, to Eastman Kodak's photographic supply chain. MQAO operates in an environment faced with increasing demand, costs of material, space, equipment, and labor. At the same time, MQAO's customers are demanding improved service quality, cost, delivery, and customer satisfaction. MQAO turned to JIT and MRP II to improve their operations. Reported benefits include reduced lead times, service costs, and space requirements (Wasco et al., 1991). MQAO's success shows that combining MRP II with JIT is doable and can lead to improved productivity and customer service.

## JIT in Services

Just-in-time is applicable to services as well, because it emphasizes elimination of all types of waste. The seven types of waste identified earlier in the chapter can be found in service organizations as well. The second element of JIT, respect for people, is most obvious in a service environment, where contact between employees of an organization and customers is high. How well a firm manages its work force determines to a large extent the quality of service delivered. In essence, service quality is hard to "standardize," since it depends to a large extent on the provider of the service. Continuous improvement is another JIT philosophy that works in a service setting. There is always room for improvement in anything we do, be it manufacturing or services. The final element of JIT is the focus on customer, a concept that is widely practiced in the service industry. A point worth noting is that service sector productivity has been lagging behind that of the manufacturing sector. This indicates that there is plenty of room for improvement to be made in the service sector in terms of continuously eliminating wastes, by focusing on getting the maximum potential out of employees, and emphasizing meeting the needs of the customers.

Benson (1986) notes that service organizations such as banks and hospitals are applying the JIT philosophy. Application Box 10-1 shows how JIT is being used in hospitals. With health care costs soaring and insurance companies getting tougher on reimbursement of claims by hospitals, there is a need to control costs. Controlling spiraling costs through inventory reduction in the health care industry is where the JIT philosophy has its biggest potential. Inman and Mehra (1991) present three cases of JIT application for service environments: a telecommunication services corporation, a government contractor to the Department of Energy, and an overnight package delivery service company. Another example is the use of several key JIT practices by fast-food chains such as McDonald's, Wendy's, and Burger King to prepare and deliver "quality" burgers at an affordable price to customers on a timely basis. The banking industry with its repetitive, high-volume check processing operations and its electronic processes used to debit credit card purchases is another likely JIT candidate. Benefits resulting from JIT implementation for these service companies include improved quality, improved service, improved communication, lower costs, reduction in storage space resulting in the elimination of warehouse space, quicker resolution of problems, and decreased carrying costs. As Chase and Aquilano (1992, p. 298) state, "Once we start thinking of services as an organized system of production processes, we can consider the use of JIT-type concepts to re-engineer service delivery operations. The result will be consistent services of high quality and excellent value, produced with high productivity."

## Summary

Although many of the JIT concepts have been developed after World War II in Japan, many of the principles and practices work just as well in the United States. JIT requires people to challenge the way things have been traditionally done. JIT requires a new way of thinking, a new corporate culture, and a new philosophy. Continuous improvement is

## APPLICATION BOX 10-1 JIT at St. Luke's Episcopal Hospital

In 1990, the nation's 6700 hospitals spent $15 billion on supplies such as disposable gloves and gowns, sutures, and therapeutic solutions. The major players in the lucrative hospital supplies market are Baxter International, Johnson & Johnson, and Abbott Laboratories. Baxter is the largest manufacturer of hospital supplies, with 29% of the market. J&J's share is 11% and Abbott Laboratories has about 10%. Baxter is also the leading distributor with 28% of the market.

Hospital supply expenditures only begin with the cost of the purchases. "For every dollar spent to buy a product, hospitals spend another dollar moving that product through the system," said David Cassak, hospitals editor for *In Vivo Business and Medicine Report,* a trade magazine. Hospitals are resorting to just-in-time (JIT) deliveries to cut down on the amount of inventories held at the stockroom. Expected savings accrue from reduced holding and handling costs as well as improved space utilization.

St. Luke's Episcopal Hospital, a 950-bed facility in Houston, has historically kept a high level of inventory of expensive medical supplies in its 20,000-sq-ft warehouse. Like all hospitals, St. Luke's cannot afford to run short of vital items, least of all in the operating rooms. Doctors at St. Luke's perform open-heart surgery on 3000 patients each year, using enormous quantities of supplies. However, the recent nationwide squeeze on health-care costs has put tremendous pressures on St. Luke's to control costs. As a result, St. Luke's shut its warehouse and sold the inventory to Baxter International.

Baxter runs a service called Valuelink at St. Luke's, which involves managing, ordering, and delivering products from Baxter as well as from 400 other suppliers. Initially, Baxter provided daily JIT deliveries to the hospital loading dock. The JIT supply method provided more frequent deliveries from the supplier and reduced inventory levels in the hospital's storeroom. Ultimately, the objective is to move towards a stockless supply system, where all inventory responsibilities are shifted from the hospital to the distributor, and deliveries are made daily. Baxter fills orders in exact quantities and delivers directly to the departments, including operating rooms and nursing floors, inside St. Luke's.

"We think we have saved $1.5 million a year since 1988 from just-in-time deliveries alone," said Randy Jackson, a St. Luke's vice president, "with another $500,000 likely once the stockless system is fully implemented. Annual savings of $350,000 are achieved with a reduction in staff and $162,500 from eliminating inventory. In addition, the hospital has converted storerooms to patient care and other income-generating use."

Materials drawn from Milt Freudenheim, "Removing the Warehouse from Cost-Conscious Hospitals," *New York Times,* March 3, 1991.

the cornerstone of JIT and world-class operations. Firms are continually looking for ways to eliminate waste. With continuous improvement comes continual change, which can be painful, but is absolutely necessary for the survival and growth of the business. This mindset must be conveyed to all employees and nourished through continual education, communication, feedback, and support. Continuous improvement requires the involvement of all employees in an organization. Respect for people is the key ingredient that enables a firm to extract the maximum potential from its employees. Ultimately, it is satisfying the customers' needs and requirements that provides the driving force behind the JIT philosophy.

## Discussion Questions

1. What key elements of JIT are demonstrated in the introductory case describing Bumper Works' relationship with Toyota? How are key JIT practices used to support these key elements?
2. What are the key elements of JIT, and how does each contribute to improving productivity and quality?
3. Why is reducing setup times a key JIT practice, and what is the three-pronged approach to improvements suggested by Suzaki?
4. Define the term *poka-yoke.*
5. List some of the benefits of good housekeeping and an organized workplace.
6. Discuss the use of JIT in services in general and hospitals in particular.
7. What are the operating rules necessary to effectively use a kanban system?
8. What are the seven goals of total quality control (TQC)?
9. Define the concept of jidoka, or autonomation, and provide some examples of actual applications of the concept.
10. Discuss how a fast-food restaurant such as McDonald's, Wendy's, or Pizza Hut can make use of the principles of JIT to improve service.
11. Why is excess inventory "the root of all evil"?
12. Discuss the use of JIT in a continuous process environment, such as the beer and steel industries. Give some reasons for success or failure in such an environment.
13. Compare the differing attitudes toward employment in Japan and the United States.
14. There are two types of kanban. What are they and what is the purpose of each?
15. Define the term *open kimono* and describe how it relates to JIT purchasing.
16. JIT necessitates that manufacturing interact with other functions or departments within the company. Give three examples of interaction and explain the importance of developing cooperation among functions.
17. Discuss the human element of JIT and the resulting attitude toward mistakes.
18. Give another term for kaizen and discuss the basic philosophy underlying this concept.
19. Smooth production is a cornerstone for JIT production using kanban. What are the objectives and benefits of smooth production?

## Strategic Decision Situations

1. The BiPed Bicycle Company is using a kanban production system. One part of the plant is dedicated to the production of bicycle seats. The demand is 100 bicycle seats per day. Each container holds four bicycle seats. Typically, a container of bicycle seats requires 0.03 day for

processing, and 0.10 day for wait time, which includes materials handling time. Jay, the line supervisor at BiPed, has been assigned the task of computing the number of kanban sets to be authorized, assuming ideal conditions. What is the level of inventory in the system? Jay feels strongly that the materials handling system can be improved so that the wait time can be reduced to 0.05 day. Assuming this improvement can be carried out, describe the effects on the number of kanban sets required and the level of inventory in the system.

**2.** The Yopet Company manufactures three types of recreational vehicles: Yopet Gold, Yopet Silver, and Yopet Platinum. Yopet has determined the monthly demand as: Yopet Gold = 9000 units, Yopet Silver = 6000 units, and Yopet Platinum = 3000 units. The plant is working 20 days per month and three 8-hour shifts. Yopet is currently using the JIT method of production. Management would like to develop a smoothed daily production schedule for the recreational vehicles. What are the cycle time and an acceptable daily schedule?

## *References*


Barnet, D. Wolf. "Flexible Work Environment Improves Productivity," *Columbus Dispatch.* January 26, 1992.

Benson, Randall J. "JIT: Not Just for the Factory," *APICS 29th Annual International Conference Proceedings.* 1986, pp. 370–374.

Boyett, Joseph H., and Henry P. Conn. *Workplace 2000: The Revolution Reshaping American Business.* New York: Dutton, 1991.

Byrne, John A. "The Horizontal Corporation," *Business Week.* December 20, 1993, pp. 76–81.

Chase, Richard B., and Nicholas J. Aquilano. *Production and Operations Management: A Life Cycle Approach,* 6th ed. Homewood, Ill.: Irwin, 1992.

Chase, Richard B., and David A. Garvin. "The Service Factory," *Harvard Business Review.* July–August 1989, pp. 61–69.

Cox, James F., John Blackstone, Jr., and Michael Spencer, eds. *APICS Dictionary,* 7th ed. Falls Church, Va.: American Production and Inventory Control Society, 1992.

Dingus, V. R., and W. A. Golomski. *A Quality Revolution in Manufacturing.* Norcross, Ga.: Industrial Engineering and Management Press, 1988.

Ferguson, Charles H. "Computers and the Coming of the U.S. Keiretsu," *Harvard Business Review.* July–August 1990, pp. 55–70.

Freeland, James R. "A Survey of Just-in-Time Purchasing Practices in the United States," *Production and Inventory Management.* April–June 1991, pp. 43–49.

Freudenheim, Milt. "Removing the Warehouse from Cost-Conscious Hospitals," *New York Times.* March 3, 1991.

Gawronski, Francis J. "Toyota Suppliers a Key Component of Long-Term Strategy," *Automotive News.* April 1, 1991, p. 16.

Goddard, Walter E. *Just-in-Time: Surviving by Breaking Tradition.* Essex Junction, Vt.: Oliver Wight Limited Publications, 1986.

Hall, Robert W. *Zero Inventories.* Homewood, Ill.: Dow Jones-Irwin, 1983.

Hall, Robert W. *Attaining Manufacturing Excellence.* Homewood, Ill.: Dow Jones-Irwin, 1987.

Hayes, Robert H., and Steven C. Wheelwright. *Restoring Our Competitive Edge: Competing Through Manufacturing.* New York: John Wiley and Sons, 1984.

Hayes, Robert H., Steven C. Wheelwright, and Kim B. Clark. *Dynamic Manufacturing.* New York: Free Press, 1988.

Hiromoto, Toshiro. "Another Hidden Edge—Japanese Management Accounting," *Harvard Business Review.* July–August 1988, pp. 22–26.

Inman, R. Anthony, and Larry Brandon. "An Undesirable Effect of JIT," *Production and Inventory Management.* January–March 1992, pp. 55–58.

Inman, R. Anthony, and Satish Mehra. "JIT Applications for Service Environments," *Production and Inventory Management.* July–September 1991, pp. 16–20.

Ishikawa, Akira. "Principles of QC Circle Activities and Their Effects on Productivity in Japan: A Corporate Analysis," *Management International Review,* Vol. 25, No. 3, 1985, pp. 33–40.

Ishikawa, Kaoru. *What Is Total Quality Control?: The Japanese Way,* translated by David J. Lu. Englewood Cliffs, N.J.: Prentice Hall, 1985.

Karmarkar, Uday. "Getting Control of Just-in-Time," *Harvard Business Review.* September–October 1989, pp. 122–131.

Klein, Janice A. "The Human Cost of Manufacturing Reform," *Harvard Business Review.* March–April 1989, pp. 60–66.

Lu, David J. *Kanban: Just-in-Time at Toyota.* Stamford, Conn.: Productivity Press, 1985.

Melcher, Arlyn, William Acar, Paul DuMont, and Moutaz Khouja. "Standard-Maintaining and Continuous Systems: Experiences and Comparisons," *Interfaces.* May–June 1990, pp. 24–40.

Monden, Yasuhiro. *Toyota Production System: Practical Approach to Production Management.* Atlanta, Ga.: Industrial Engineering and Management Press, Institute of Industrial Engineers, 1983.

Natarajan, R., and J. Donald Weinrauch. "JIT and the Marketing Interface," *Production and Inventory Management.* July–September 1990, p. 42–46.

Neff, Robert, Neil Gross, and Larry Holyoke. "Japan: How Bad?" *Business Week.* December 13, 1993, pp. 56–59.

Rapoport, Carla. "Why Japan Keeps on Winning," *Fortune.* July 15, 1991, pp. 76–85.

Rieker, Wayne. "Trip Report for Study of Quality Control Circles in Japan," *JUSE Reports of Statistical Application Research.* Vol. 22, No. 2, 1975, pp. 33–48.

Schonberger, Richard J. *Japanese Manufacturing Techniques: Nine Hidden Lessons in Simplicity.* New York: Free Press, 1982.

Schonberger, Richard J. *World Class Manufacturing: The Lessons of Simplicity Applied.* New York: Free Press, 1986.

Schonberger, Richard J. "Applications of Single-Card and Dual-Card Kanban," *Interfaces.* August 1983, pp. 56–67.

Scott, Allan F., James H. Macomber, and Lawrence P. Ettkin. "JIT and Job Satisfaction: Some Empirical Results," *Production and Inventory Management.* January–March 1992, pp. 36–41.

Sepheri, Mehran. *Just-in-Time, Not Just in Japan: Case Studies of American Pioneers in JIT Implementation.* Falls Church, Va.: American Production and Inventory Control Society, 1986.

Sheridan, John H. "America's Best Plants," *Industry Week.* October 15, 1990, pp. 27–64.

Shingo, Shigeo. *Zero Quality Control: Source Inspection and the Poka-Yoke System,* translated by Andrew P. Dillon. Cambridge, Mass.: Productivity Press, 1986.

Suzaki, Kiyoshi. *The New Manufacturing Challenge: Techniques for Continuous Improvement.* New York: Free Press, 1987.

Takatsuki, Ryoichi. "Productivity and Quality Innovation with TPM (Total Productive Maintenance), in *Applying Just in Time: The American/Japanese Experience,* Yasuhiro Monden (ed.). Norcross, Ga.: Industrial Engineering and Management Press, 1986.

Wantuck, Kenneth. *Just-In-Time for America.* Southfield, Mich.: KWA Media, 1989.

Wasco, W. Calvin, Robert Stonehocker, and Larry Feldman. "Success with JIT and MRP II in a Service Organization," *Production and Inventory Management Journal.* October–December 1991, pp. 15–21.

White, Joseph B. "Japanese Auto Makers Help U.S. Suppliers Become More Efficient," *Wall Street Journal.* September 9, 1991.

Woodruff, David, James Treece, Sunita Wadekar Bhargava, and Karen Lowry Miller. "Saturn: GM Finally Has a Real Winner, But Success Is Bringing a Fresh Batch of Problems," *Business Week.* August 17, 1992, pp. 87–91.

# Chapter 11

# Quality and Customer Service Management

*Get a customer through price and promises; keep the customer through quality and delivery.*
—An Instructor at a Sales Conference

*All quality control does is catch our mistakes. I want to avoid them!* —Hewlett-Packard Training Materials

## Objectives

After completing this chapter you should be able to:

- Define the components of quality and customer service management.
- Identify several ways to segment the market and note the corresponding manufacturing focus to support those segments.
- Describe three different quality control methods and suggest the conditions under which they should be used.
- Differentiate customer service operations in make-to-stock and make-to-order environments.

## Outline

## *Introductory Case: What Price Quality?**

Two companies have been visible in their concerns with quality and customer service management in the past several years. On the surface, the companies have much in common; both are large, nationally known, and well established in consumer-sensitive markets such as personal care items and food products. There, however, the similarity ends. Senior executives of one company were convicted of fraud and felony charges and jailed. In the second company, the creation of a position of vice president of product integrity may have prevented minor problems from becoming major ones and involving the company in such a scandal.

### *The Beech-Nut Nutrition Corporation*

In 1981, Beech-Nut incurred an annual loss of $2.5 million; its number two position in the baby food market (behind the industry giant, Gerber Products) was sliding. Beech-Nut's best-selling apple juice line accounted for 30% of company sales. To reduce costs, Beech-Nut signed a "too good to be true" contract for apple concentrate at a price that was 20% below the market. Later that year, Beech-Nut's director of research and development reported conclusive evidence that the apple concentrate was a blend of synthetic ingredients. The CEO, Neils Hoyvald, and vice president of manufacturing, John Lavery, received the report but took no action.

*Materials drawn from Richard Martin, "The Watchdog. Gillette's Giovacchini Rules on the Quality, Safety of 850 Products," *The Wall Street Journal,* Eastern Edition, December 12, 1975, p. 1, and Chris Welles, "What Led Beech-Nut Down the Road to Disgrace," *Business Week,* February 22, 1988, pp. 124–128.

The truth later surfaced, however, and in 1988 the two executives were convicted of selling phony apple juice. Though labeled as "100% pure," the product consisted of beet sugar, apple flavor, caramel coloring, and corn syrup—no apple juice at all. In addition to the individual convictions and fines, Beech-Nut paid more than $10 million in fines and damages, and company sales plummeted from the negative publicity.

### *Gillette Corporation*

Millions of Gillette products are sold each year from a product line of more than 850 different items, mostly personal care products. More than 20 years ago, however, Gillette recognized its vulnerability to product liability. Robert Giovacchini was appointed as the first vice president of product integrity. Mr. Giovacchini was empowered to: pull any product off the market whenever standards were not met, halt the introduction of new products, challenge advertising claims, change product packaging, and veto proposed corporate acquisitions. On matters of product integrity, he could overrule any research scientist, quality-control expert, plant manager, or marketing executive. He reports to the president.

On one occasion, Mr. Giovacchini, who believes his job "fulfills a real social need," halted the introduction of a new shaving cream when he found that the aerosol pump would deliver only three ounces of the can's four-ounce contents. Though the product was correctly labeled, "Net Weight 4 oz," only three ounces could be used by the customer. The likelihood that customers would realize the difference was small, but the product was not given the go-ahead until the propellant pumps were corrected. Mr. Giovacchini's reasoning was "The fact that customers don't know the difference doesn't make it right."

## *Product and Service Delivery*

Robert Giovacchini was the first quality-control manager of a major corporation to be promoted to vice president of product integrity. This personnel action by Gillette recognized the strategic importance of total quality management and positioned the firm to emphasize concern for customers. Following Gillette, many American companies have changed their perspective of quality from an inspection-based, manufacturing-focused, blue-collar responsibility to a defect-prevention, company-focused, top management concern (Leonard and Sasser, 1982). According to Reddy (1980), this transformation has occurred over several stages. Prior to World War II, quality was based on craft skills; products were made to provide satisfaction. Between the 1940s and 1960s, however, quality management increasingly involved inspection and reliability management. The 1970s and 1980s emphasized customer assurance, international competition, and legal liabilities. Today, quality incorporates understanding and defining customer requirements of all operations outcomes.

This evolution may be more apparent in the marketplace. Conspicuous consumption, spontaneous purchasing, and promotional hype were the marketing watchwords through the 1980s. However, quality, service, and value are likely to be the keys to selling in the 1990s. The product must sell itself by its apparent value, defined as performance, guarantees, and reasonable prices, supported by long-term customer loyalty and factual advertising. Wal-Mart stores built such customer loyalty on the motto of "The low price on the brands you trust." Wal-Mart is now the world's largest retailer (Power et al., 1991).

For almost half a century, W. Edwards Deming and J. M. Juran have been the preeminent gurus of quality. While Deming has championed statistical quality control, Juran is more closely associated with the broader notions of total quality management. Both men have been extensively recognized, though for different reasons. While Deming's 14 points (see Table 11-1) may have won more notice, there is a heavily subscribed point of view that the "higher-level" perspective of total quality management, espoused by Juran, may have more influence over the years. Certainly, each of those pioneers, in very different ways, has had a profound influence on the quality revolution.

In 1987, the Baldrige National Quality Award was established by Congress to recognize outstanding quality achievements by U.S. companies in manufacturing, service, and small business categories. The award is based on seven criteria: leadership, information and analysis, strategic quality planning, human resource utilization, quality assurance, quality results, and customer satisfaction. These criteria are evaluated by independent teams of experts from industrial, professional, and trade organizations, and universities. Between two and four companies have won the award each year since 1988. The nature of the award and its positive effects on a company are noted in greater detail in Case 5, which discusses Motorola, one of the winners. However, not all award-winning compa-

**TABLE 11-1 Deming's Fourteen Points**

**1.** Create consistency of purpose within the company.
**2.** Learn the new philosophy.
**3.** Require statistical evidence of process control along with incoming critical parts.
**4.** The requirement of statistical evidence of process control in the purchase of critical parts will mean in most companies drastic reduction in the number of vendors that they deal with.
**5.** Use statistical methods to find out, in any trouble spot, what are the sources of trouble.
**6.** Institute modern aids to training on the job.
**7.** Improve supervision.
**8.** Drive out fear.
**9.** Break down barriers between departments.
**10.** Eliminate numerical goals, slogans, pictures, posters urging people to increase productivity or sign their work as an autograph, so often plastered everywhere in the plant. ZERO DEFECTS is an example.
**11.*** Look carefully at work standards.
**12.** Institute a massive training program for employees in simple, but powerful statistical methods.
**13.** Institute a vigorous program for retraining people in new skills.
**14.** Create a situation in top management that will push every day on the above thirteen points.

*There are several different statements of the fourteen points. Possibly the most controversial point is point 11, which is stated in *Out of the Crisis* (1986) as: "Eliminate work standards (quotas) on the factory floor. Substitute leadership." This has been interpreted by Mundel (1992) as "Throw out work standards." Work standards, if interpreted as quotas, may be challenged as counterproductive. However, if work standards are used as benchmarks, they can be very helpful, both to employees and to management.

nies are successful. The Wallace Company, a distributor of fittings for the oil and chemical industries, may have incurred serious financial difficulties resulting from its effort to win the Baldrige award. Though the effort toward the Baldrige award significantly contributed to quality improvement, that effort may have distracted attention from the serious financial problems of the company, which filed for bankruptcy shortly after winning the award (Hill and Freedman, 1992).

## *Quality and Customer Service*

The concepts of quality and customer service are inseparable, because quality is defined by the customer, often through subjective and preconceived values. Though a durable good may have some inherent quality or value, it is usually sold with a bundle of supplemental services, such as options, installation, and service support, all of which contribute to the perceived quality of the product. For this reason, the traditional manufacturing notions of quality must be considered in the context of the customer service environment in which the product is delivered.

### *Quality*

In its simplest form, quality is defined as "fitness for use" (Crosby, 1988), though even that definition ignores what is meant by fit and for whose use. A more precise definition is

> *Product or service quality requires a* total system *which* identifies customer requirements, *which* designs the product/service to those requirements, *and which* establishes a production or service delivery system to produce in conformance *with the specifications.*

This definition emphasizes the systemic approach to quality, which is called total quality assurance (TQA) or total quality management (TQM). These names are given to the aggregate system or perspective of all quality and customer service activities. The TQM system integrates customer-defined requirements with the technical activities of product or service design and the conformance to those specifications. TQM must be linked to strategic planning through specific defined goals received at periodic meetings and by focusing on results which are carefully documented and measured (Sharman, 1992). Quality must always be customer driven; it is defined by the customer and varies from use to use. Quality incorporates some amount of subjective and intangible evaluation, which is often based on perceived reputation or loyalty to the good and associated service. In all cases, the development and implementation of a TQM program requires a total cultural change within the company, starting with top management. Continuous improvement approaches and employee involvement programs must be implemented and regularly measured for effectiveness (Frank and Halle, 1992).

Juran (1980) categorizes product or service quality as structural, sensory, time-oriented, commercial, and ethical. Garvin (1987) defines the eight dimensions of quality as performance, features, conformance, reliability, durability, serviceability, aesthetics, and perceived quality. An even more elaborate categorization of some 25 service quality variables is found in Zeithaml et al. (1988). Other product or service characteristics include safety, service personnel behaviors and appearance, apparent knowledge and personal skills, ease of use, efficiency, and environmental and ecosystem impact. Though these groupings of quality characteristics are widely applicable and generally helpful, the definition of quality must be separately specified for each product/service and each customer situation.

The second aspect of the definition of quality is design. The design of major products may take five years and cost as much as 70% to 80% of the final production costs (Corbett, 1986). However, more recent approaches to quality design have emphasized reduced design times by careful control of the design process. Traditionally, design has been a function of product engineering alone; however, most products today require that the design activity integrate other functional areas. The product must work (engineering), must be sellable (marketing), must be profitable (finance), and must be buildable (manufacturing). These requirements suggest the integration of product design activities.

The integration effort may involve one individual, a cross-functional team, or a product/process design department (Dean and Susman, 1989). The choice among these methods often depends upon the organization size, but may involve other factors. Individuals (sometimes called product managers) are usually preferred by smaller firms. This method focuses responsibility, but, depending on the individual background, may encourage a more manufacturing, engineering, or marketing-oriented perspective. Cross-functional teams are preferred by mid-sized and larger organizations, particularly if the team reports to top management. Each member represents a proponent area (marketing, finance, purchasing, engineering, operations, quality, and others). To avoid conflicts, such teams may be required to define specific goals. The use of a product design department means greater overhead, but it places the responsibility and resources with one manager. Departmental structures for the design function are often found in larger organizations. Sometimes, the type of organization structure selected will be driven by the importance of the design function and fit with organization requirements.

The third aspect of quality is conformance to specification or design. After a product or service is specified and designed and the process is developed, it must be produced in conformance with the specification. The term *quality control* is often used to describe the measurement of product or service conformance to the design characteristics. Different phases of the product/service-process technology life cycle necessitate various different qualitative and statistical approaches. The total quality system and the three components of quality described here (customer, design, and conformance) correspond to the transcendent, user-based, product-based, and manufacturing- and value-based categories of quality as defined in Garvin (1984).

### *Customer Service*

Customer service includes the value-adding transformations of location, exchange, physiological change, storage, or information that often accompany and facilitate the sale of durable goods. Services may be categorized by tangibility and customer involvement. Generally, the more tangible the service, the less involved the customer. For example, vending machines, self-service sales, garbage pickup, and retail or fast-food delivery generally relocate a tangible good and little else. Alternatively, health services and entertainment are generally not tangible and require immediate customer participation. Services may also be categorized as equipment- or labor-intense, depending upon the contribution of each. A health or recreation club is primarily equipment- or facility-based, though the presence of an equipment supervisor may be necessary. Alternatively, a psychiatrist offers a unique personal service, though specialized diagnostic equipment may also be used.

## *Manufacturing versus Service Environments*

Although service operations have much in common with manufacturing based on the chain of transformations, some differences exist. Most services are created at the customer interface portion of the chain of transformations, and, for that reason, services differ from resource creation, manufacturing, and assembly operations. The traditional distinctions between manufacturing and service environment are shown by Table 11-2.

Generally, the manufactured good is produced at few locations near key resources by technically oriented employees, with little customer contact or participation. The deliverable is generally tangible and not perishable; it requires high fixed-cost and lower variable-cost facilities. Alternatively, service environments often involve many locations near the customer, with more extensive customer participation. The service is often perishable and intangible, with lower fixed costs and higher variable costs. Other possible

**TABLE 11-2 The Traditional Characteristics of Manufacturing and Service Environments**

| Characteristic | Manufacturing | Service |
|---|---|---|
| Nature of location | | |
| Number of locations | few | many |
| Placement of locations | near key resources | near customer |
| Nature of employee | | |
| Skill type | technical | behavioral |
| Nature of customer involvement | | |
| Physical contact | little | great |
| Customer participation | low | high |
| Nature of deliverable | | |
| Perishable | no | likely |
| Tangible | yes | mostly intangible |
| Constraining resource | equipment, materials | labor |
| Nature of capital structure | | |
| Fixed costs | high | low |
| Variable costs | low | high |

differences between manufacturing and service operations include the amount of standardization, the method of costing added value, and the measures of effectiveness (Murdick et al., 1990). Perhaps the critical strategic difference between manufacturing and service organizations is that few services have the ability to use capital as a barrier to competition. Manufacturers, through capital investments, costly product and process design, and other such activities, are able to limit the ability of other manufacturers to develop competitive products. However, service organizations must rely on proprietary technologies, licenses, service differentiation (often through reputation), or cutting costs by automation or substitution of cheap labor for expensive labor (Thomas, 1978).

Another important difference between manufacturing and service environments is the measure used to evaluate quality. As defined, quality is measured by three components (definition of customer requirements, design toward those requirements, and establishment of a system to ensure conformance with the design). Table 11-3 differentiates quality measures in manufacturing and services.

The measures of quality in service organizations are generally more subjective, intangible, and human-based; while the factors in manufacturing tend to be more objective, tangible, and machine-based. For example, customer requirements for a product might involve reliability, maintainability, or durability; however, in a service environment, those requirements are more likely to consider the apparent behaviors, reputation, or knowledgeability of service personnel. In both cases, a product/service must ultimately be designed toward the customer-specified requirements.

**TABLE 11-3 Examples of Quality Measures***

| Manufacturing | Service |
|---|---|
| *Definition of Customer Requirements* | |
| Reliability | Behavior |
| Maintainability | Reputation |
| Durability | Knowledgeability |
| Delivery | Ease of use |
| Functions and features | Access/availability |
| Safety and performance | |
| *Design the Product/Service toward Those Requirements* | |
| Physical dimensions | Customer features |
| Material properties | Smoothness of operation |
| Electrical/mechanical | Component capability |
| Efficiency of design | Pleasantness and acceptability |
| *Establishment of a System to Ensure Conformance with the Design* | |
| Inspection | Organization |
| Measurement | Dependability |
| Variables | System visibility |
| Attributes | Training of personnel |

*These are specific examples of quality measures in manufacturing and service situations; however, in application, a mix is often needed.

In reality, however, these differences between manufacturing and service measures of quality may not be as apparent, particularly if the chain of transformations is considered. For example, Sears, Roebuck's "wearout warranty" offers free replacement of more than 70 brand-name children's clothing items if the item wears out while the child is still in the same size. This concept of quality extends from manufacturing quality through to customer specification. The program was initiated as a result of focus groups that Sears formed to define customer requirements. As such, it combines the durability of manufactured quality with the quality reputation of the service business (Power, 1991).

## *Manufacturing and Service System Design*

Manufacturing system design emphasizes both product and process efficiency; these are directly related to the cost and quality of the good and the corresponding delivery and process flexibility, which define the service system. For example, production of high-volume standardized products would involve a high-efficiency production process. Alternatively, service system design emphasizes responsiveness to customer requirements, including price and service variability, perceived quality, and availability. Thus, there are important, though subtle differences in the criteria of evaluation of manufacturing and service organizations. Price is differentiated from manufacturing cost through two mechanisms, market-based profit markups and value-added service. Additionally, manufacturing quality is differentiated from service-related notions of *perceived* quality. Effective organizations will define both manufacturing and service systems in such a way as to emphasize either and integrate customer responsiveness or process efficiency (Kuhn, 1990). These variables are shown in Figure 11-1.

Figure 11-1 is useful as a mechanism to classify a firm's strategy as service- or manufacturing-oriented. Additionally, it helps to focus any mismatch of the components of the strategy, to define strategy shifts over time, to identify product/market niches, and to compare two businesses. The vertical dimension identifies the variables of service system design, while the horizontal axis defines the variables of manufacturing design.

Consider, for example, the strategies of Ethan Allen furniture and Rolls Royce automobiles. Those products are demonstrated in showrooms and must be custom-ordered. Availability is low, and price and product variability are high. Extensive product variation is possible because the products are custom-built. The low-volume manufacturing process of each does not involve process efficiencies. Costs are high, and so is the apparent quality of craft-based production methods. This strategy is described at position 1 in Figure 11-1.

A very different strategy has been developed by O'Sullivan (a manufacturer of partially assembled furniture) and Chevrolet. O'Sullivan furniture is available through mail-order companies and warehouse furniture outlets; though some Chevrolets are special ordered, most are purchased from available stock. Both products have a broad product line, but with limited variability and rapid delivery. They are relatively low-priced and of basic perceived quality. Considering the manufacturing system design, each firm uses highly efficient, machine-based production methods in a make-to-stock environment, with

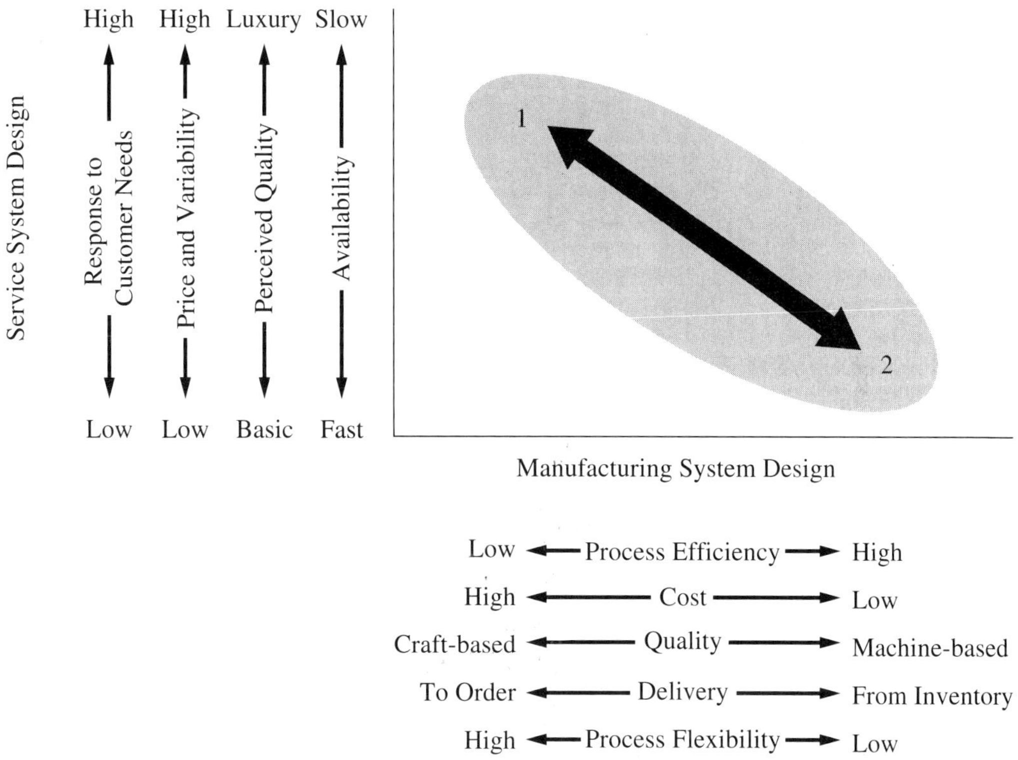


**FIGURE 11-1 Manufacturing and Service System Design**

low process flexibility and low per-unit costs. These strategies are defined at position 2 in Figure 11-1.

Figure 11-1 corresponds in some ways to the product/service–process technology continuum (Figure 7-2). The most notable difference, however, is that here the vertical axis is defined as service system design and in the product/service–process technology continuum, that axis is the process. Additionally, the manufacturing system is more generally defined. However, the figure does correspond in orientation and can be used to supplement the continuum. The arrow between positions 1 and 2 suggests a continuum between the two strategies. Most firms will attempt to find a competitive niche in this area along or adjacent to the diagonal, represented by the shaded oval, though recently developed technologies, described in Chapter 7, allow companies to operate away from the diagonal. Figure 11-1 provides a mechanism to label the corporate-level strategic positioning and competitive niche with regard to operations strategies.

The relationship of cost and quality must be further clarified. The previous discussion considers only the manufacturing basis for quality, not the issue of "high" or "low" quality performance and its association with cost and price. The traditional expectation is that low cost would be associated with low quality and high cost with high quality. That is an oversimplification. In an engineering context (conformance to specification) the traditional approach is easily refuted. Consider an operation that produces 100 parts per day at a cost of \$10 each and for which the rework of rejects costs \$5 each. If there are 20% first-run rejects, one-half of which can be reworked, the cost of a good part is

$$\text{Cost/good part} = \frac{10(100) + 5(10)}{90} = \$11.67$$

However, if first-run rejects are reduced to 10%, one-half of which are reworkable, then the cost of a good part is decreased as follows:

$$\text{Cost/good part} = \frac{10(100) + 5(5)}{95} = \$10.79$$

In this sense, higher quality is associated with lower costs. Reddy (1980) provides several applications in which improved quality was achieved simply and with dramatically reduced product costs. Similarly, and in a more intuitive vein, process variance on a high-volume, low-cost-per-unit operation would likely be much tighter (for example, higher quality) than that for a low-volume, higher-cost-per-unit operation. Further, if all costs of faulty quality are considered (lost sales, returns, litigation, scrap, and rework), high conformance quality makes sense as a low-cost strategy.

However, with regard to "perceived quality" in a customer purchasing situation, Hagerty (1978) found that the likelihood of purchasing an item increases as perceived quality increases and decreases as price increases. Little interaction of quality and price were found. Another study (Levin and Johnson, 1984) found that among 47 subjects who were given either quality or price information in meat selection situations, increases in perceived quality were associated with increases in price estimates. These market situation findings pertaining to price and quality contradict the cost–quality relationship found in manufacturing. Low cost corresponds to high quality in a manufacturing environment, but low price corresponds with perceived low quality in simple marketing situations.

The strategic positions of high quality and cost leadership may, in fact, be independent. In a study of more than 600 companies in the PIMS (profit impact of marketing strategy) data base, Phillips et al. (1983) found little relationship between product quality and either direct costs or relative marketing expenditures. The independence of cost and quality permits firms to identify separate marketing strategies, one directed toward an image of low cost, the other directed toward an image of high quality. Porter (1980) and Kotha and Orne (1989) provide strong theoretical arguments to differentiate the low-cost and high-quality market segments as separate strategies. Porter categorizes market segments as low cost and a chosen form of product differentiation (such as quality or style). Kotha and Orne amplify Porter's categorization with the finding that cost-driven firms have simple product lines and highly integrated processes whereas differentiation-driven firms have discontinuities in the process and complex product lines.

## *Costs of Customer Satisfaction*

The quality strategy must focus on each of the three dimensions of quality—customer requirements, product/service research and design, and production in conformance to design specifications. Responsiveness to customer requirements can be achieved by such strategies as broader product/service lines, superior performance, flexible production systems, higher inventories, and more elaborate high-speed distribution systems. The costs of design include product research and development, and process design and innovation. Finally, the costs of producing in conformance to requirements include expenses of process control, maintenance, laboratories, inspection, and equipment. A firm can choose to invest heavily in these areas and expect to have low rates of customer service failure.

Alternatively, the costs of failure of the quality system are product/service lines that do not satisfy customer needs, inflexible and unresponsive manufacturing systems, low product availability, and a limited distribution service system, all of which result in lost volume. The costs of design failure include customer defection, ill will, returns, field repair and replacement of poorly performing items, warranty claims, and litigation. Finally, the costs of internal defects are scrap and rework. A firm might feel obliged to choose between the costs of emphasis on quality and the failure of the quality system. These decisions are, in fact, highly interrelated. A firm must either invest in quality emphasis (for example, product availability, performance, design, and conformance) or bear the potential costs of failed quality (product shortfall, product failure, and internal defects). Table 11-4 shows this relationship and emphasizes the total cost of customer satisfaction. Gillette and Beech-Nut (in the introductory case) exemplify these two strategies.

Several important conclusions are apparent from Table 11-4. Initially, there might be an intuitive reaction to define a strategy of customer satisfaction that minimizes total costs of emphasizing quality and failure of quality. However, these variables are very difficult to measure, particularly the costs of quality failure. Additionally, in today's increasingly customer- and demand-driven markets, the minimum cost method of defining quality level is unacceptable. Increasingly, firms are recognizing that both marketing and manufacturing must work together toward zero defects and high responsiveness to customer requirements.

**TABLE 11-4 Costs of Customer Satisfaction**

| Cost Category | |
|---|---|
| *Costs of Responsiveness to Customer Requirements* | |
| Flexible production systems | Purchasing systems |
| Inventory level | Maintenance systems |
| Elaborateness of distribution systems | |
| *Costs of Product/Service Research and Design* | |
| *(Cost of Prevention)* | *(Cost of external failure)* |
| Research and development | Customer ill will, returns |
| Process design and innovation | Field repair, replacement |
| Employee training | Warranties, litigation |
| *Costs to Ensure Conformance to Design Specifications* | |
| *(Cost of Appraisal)* | *(Cost of internal failure)* |
| Inspection, process control | Scrap |
| Laboratories and equipment | Sorting, downgrading, and rework |

## *Linking Marketing and Operations*

Market focus, or segmentation, is the strategic decision to divide customers into smaller categories to better customize the delivered product/service bundle. It permits more direct response to customer requirements, thereby assuring greater satisfaction. However, taken to an extreme, it suggests a different product/service for each customer. Though customer satisfaction and perceived quality likely would be improved by extensive market focus, the effects on operations might be disastrous. Similarly, limited market segmentation might ease operations' job, but make marketing the product/service increasingly difficult. Segmentation concentrates operations and marketing assets toward a competitive niche, selected on the basis of competitive strengths and weaknesses through TOWS analysis (see Chapter 2).

Unfortunately, firms do not place enough emphasis on the linking or coordination of marketing and operations strategies (Berry et al., 1991). Clearly, marketing is a critical first step to the formulation of both a marketing and an operations strategy. However, the research in this area is primarily directed toward descriptive and conceptual efforts and model building, characteristic of the early stages of this research.

The total market may be divided into several segments, each of which is defined in several ways. Two key strategies for selecting a market segment are the size and the growth rate (Paine and Anderson, 1983). For example, a firm can go after:

1. Large size—the largest segment of the market. Of course, the largest segment may be where the competition is most intense.
2. Small size—a small, but easily defended segment of the market. The firm thus may be able to avoid competitive pressures.
3. High growth rate—finding a currently small, but rapidly growing segment of the market.
4. Increasing number of segments—developing a position in an increasing number of segments based on one or several product/service variations. Typically, such firms try to increase small and relatively stable market segments.

Market segmentation may be based on product/service lines, geographic areas, order volume and price, and customer types. For example, main frame and personal computers are treated as separate market segments by most computer manufacturers. Similarly, geographic regions are commonly used to segment markets, and high-volume customers are often separated from low-volume customers. In some businesses, the individual customer or customer type (for example, government versus private, level of school system) is used to define market segments. For example, textbook publishers often structure their organization and product lines by grammar school, high school, and university markets.

Most writers agree with Schnaars (1991) that there is "no one best way to segment a market." In fact, the basis for market segmentation should consider what the firm desires to accomplish in terms of corporate positioning or competitive agenda. Moran (1974) notes that the definition of market segments must be driven by corporate strategy. Each segment of the market, shown in the top part of Figure 11-2, must be focused toward a defined competitive niche.

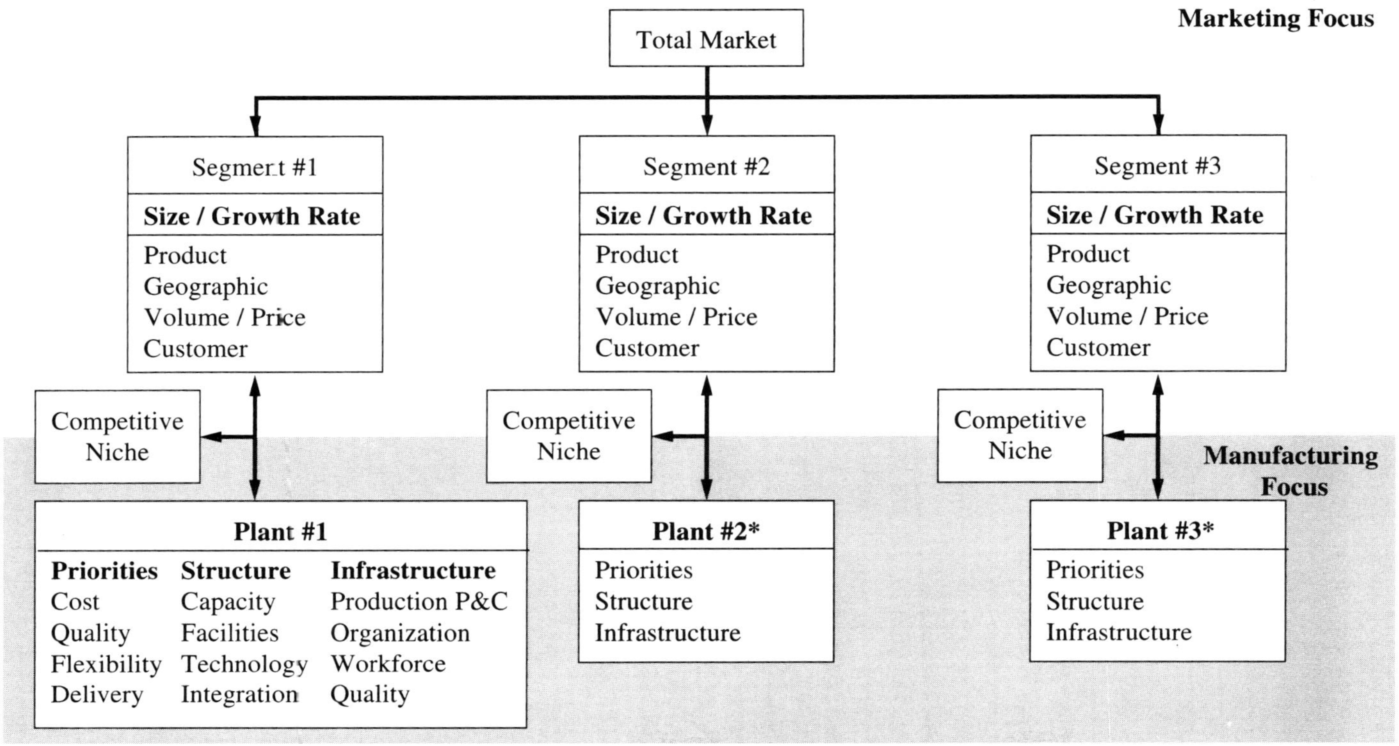


* Plant 2, which supports the hardwood market, has relatively less structure and greater infrastructure than plant 3, which supports the softwood lines. Similarly, the competitive priorities differ. Because the focus of each market segment differs, the supporting plant must have an appropriate manufacturing focus, defined in terms of competitive priority, structure, and infrastructure variables.

**FIGURE 11-2 Marketing Focus and Manufacturing Focus**

But market segmentation is only part of the process. The manufacturing focus, shown in the bottom half of Figure 11-2, is defined to support a specific market segment. Market segment 1 and the supporting manufacturing focus of plant 1 are fully elaborated in Figure 11-2, whereas market segments 2 and 3 are only roughly suggested. The emphasis of manufacturing on structural and infrastructural activities also varies, as do the competitive priority and criteria.

Manufacturing focus is based on the competitive priorities of cost, quality, flexibility, and delivery and further decisions about structure and infrastructure. As shown in Figure 11-2, the specific structural and infrastructural combinations that are necessary to support a particular market niche will differ, just as market segments differ. For example, a national furniture maker has several lines of furniture designed around different types of wood. Hardwood furniture (oak, maple, and cherry) items are sold through name brand distributors, many of which use sales galleries. Another line, composed primarily of pine and other softwood items, is sold through catalogs and retail chains. These two product lines are sold with different price structures and are focused toward different segments of the furniture market.

The manufacturing focus, defined in terms of the competitive priority and structure and infrastructure, required to support these market segments also differs. Because greater labor skills, better equipment, and more time are required to work hardwoods, the hardwood furniture manufacturing facility has higher levels of work force skills, a less formal organization, more operations planning and control, less automation and technology, and smaller facilities and annual capacity than does the softwood plant. These different focuses are best achieved through separate plants. In Figure 11-2, plant 2, which supports the hardwood market, has relatively less structure and greater infrastructure than plant 3, a larger-volume plant that supports segment 3, the softwood segment. If, in addition to the hardwood and softwood lines, the company also developed a line of customer-assembled metal furniture, such as shelving or office furniture, this line would likely be managed as a different market segment and would be supported by a plant with a different competitive priorities structure and infrastructure.

The market focus cannot change more rapidly than the supporting manufacturing organization. Market focus is driven by strategies of price or product differentiation and must be integrated with the manufacturing focus. These segments may be relatively stable over time, as in the furniture and automobile businesses, or they may be more dynamic, as in the electronics and computer businesses.

Ultimately, the firm must define whether it is manufacturing- (including engineering) or market-driven. That is, does the company sell what it builds, or does it build what it sells? Figure 11-2 shows the integration of marketing and manufacturing forces toward a specific competitive niche. Whether the niche is marketing- or manufacturing-driven, the strategic issue is that the marketing focus and the corresponding manufacturing focus must fit each other. For example, a high-capacity facility should not be used to support a small and declining market segment.

The marketing-driven company differs from the manufacturing-driven company in several key ways. Marketing-oriented companies focus on important customers, and buying influences permeate every corporate function. Alternatively, in manufacturing-focused companies, production capability and product design information tend to be more visible. In all cases, however, strategic and locational decisions should be made interfunctionally and interdivisionally and executed in an integrated manner. A manufacturing-driven company is exemplified by Lincoln Electric, described in Application Box 11-1.

## *Quality of Design*

The second component of quality and customer service management is the quality of the product/service design and manufacturing process or service delivery system. To revitalize its sluggish sales in the late 1980s, the German automobile manufacturer Bavarian Motor Works (BMW) thoroughly overhauled product design activities to emphasize the craft skills and technical specifications of their manufacturing process. The design of cars with "soul" has permitted BMW to compete head-to-head with Japanese manufacturers and to overtake Mercedes Benz in European markets (Templeman, 1991). Quality of design is important in different ways during each of the seven steps of the product/service–process technology life cycle.

In the birth stage, the general product or service capabilities and functioning are defined. In addition to the necessary engineering and research and development activities, numerous business decisions must be made, including market studies, economic and safety evaluations, materials and methods evaluations, environmental impact studies, and others. The birth process identifies the product/service, the general process technology, and market concerns and opportunities.

The second stage is product/service design and process technology selection. The product or service is first designed and built as a prototype, then redesigned and rebuilt—often ten or more times. In each iteration, three concerns are addressed: functioning, technology, and manufacturing/delivery methods. Product/service functioning includes such items as size, weight, appearance, maintainability, ease of use, and employee training. Technology includes the type of materials and methods of production—different materials require different production methods. Finally, the product or service must be designed so that it can be manufactured or delivered reliably and economically. This stage should involve some initial conclusions about the production process; for example, estimates of volume, materials, and methods might suggest appropriate process alternatives.

The production/service delivery system also is designed and evolves through numerous modifications. Stage 3, the production/service delivery system design, involves layout and line balancing considerations, work design and measurement, learning curves, technology, and equipment (general or specialized) selection. Once these decisions have been made, equipment is purchased and installed; then pilot runs and testing are conducted with the likely result that the process will be modified several times before it is released for production. For example, as noted in Chapter 10, more than 110 prototype models of the 1990 Lincoln Town Car were built, resulting in more than 2600 employee-suggested design changes before the final design was released (Sheridan, 1990).

Depending upon the product, start-up may be very complex or very simple. Start-ups of a nuclear power generator or an automobile assembly line involve a very careful

### APPLICATION BOX 11-1 Definition of Competitive Niche at Lincoln Electric

Lincoln Electric Company has become the largest manufacturer of arc-welding equipment in the world as a result of its deeply established philosophy to produce and sell high-quality products at competitive prices. "We want to be number 1 in any business we're in," states the company president; this has been accomplished by installing state-of-the-art automation technology and running the system with motivated, highly trained, and loyal employees.

Quality runs rampant at Lincoln; it has long been committed to hiring "the best" employees, designing and manufacturing with "the best" technology, using "the best" raw materials and components, and producing "the best" welding machines and motors. To ensure continued improvement, Lincoln offers its employees "the best" profit-sharing incentive system, which has contributed to achieving "the best" productivity record in its industry.

Lincoln Electric constantly focuses on manufacturing costs as well. Parsimony and efficiency are built into the Lincoln organization at all levels. Automation is designed around workers, thereby decreasing the number of employees required to assemble each motor. (Lincoln employees do not have to worry about losing their jobs to greater technological efficiency; Lincoln has a long-standing policy of no layoffs.) Scrap from metal-working operations is recycled, thus eliminating waste. Because each operation of each motor is done by a single identifiable person, defects are traceable to the responsible operator. With regard to employee benefits, there are no dental coverages, no paid holidays, and no sick days. Executives are "perkless" too, with no company cars, no club memberships, and limited expense accounts. Such frugality reduces Lincoln's costs, which are passed on to the customer. As a result, Lincoln has long been the industry price leader.

Lincoln's products are sold by an engineering-oriented sales force, because its customer base is highly technical. Regardless of their academic or professional background, all new sales, executive, and staff employees begin on the assembly line. This introduction provides them with the hands-on experience to better serve Lincoln customers. Due to their expertise in technology and productivity, in 1989, Lincoln signed a potential $6 million plus per year contract with General Motors to facilitate productivity improvement in other companies using GM's robots.

The 96-year-old company has been run on an elementary and unyielding strategy to produce "the best" products in its market at the most competitive price, and to reward its employees for their contribution to the company's reputation and success. As one senior executive commented, "Our distinctive competence is manufacturing. We are not a marketing company or a service company. We concentrate on manufacturing and try to be 'the best' manufacturing company in the world."

Materials were drawn from Stanley J. Modic, "Fine-tuning a Classic; Don Hastings Helps Lincoln Electric Shed Its Shroud of Conservatism," *Industry Week,* March 6, 1989, pp. 15–18, and David Prizinsky, "Lincoln Hitches Star to GM in Bid to Sell Robots," *Crain's Cleveland Business,* August 7, 1989, p. 1.

"hand-off" of the operation from the technical people to line operators and extensive training activities. This process takes several months, if not more, and often requires continued involvement of technicians even after the line is running. Start-up of a service operation is likely to take less time and require a less complex hand-off, though training of service operators is equally important.

Products and services are then sequentially moved through growth of volume, stable state, and decline and renewal phases. Firms would want to have several products/services at different stages of development, because that strategy distributes both the work and the risk. For example, a firm might have a growth product or service, one or two items in stable state, and several moving toward decline and renewal. Additionally, a firm might have ten or more products/services moving through the first four stages. Often the growth and termination market segments will have similar characteristics, such as low and unstable volumes, product variation, dynamic changes in customer types and geographic requirements, and so forth. For this reason, it is common to have one plant, focused on process, to support these two segments and one or several other product-focused plants to support the more stable steady-state products and market segments. The product and production process must be designed to support the market segment.

## *Control for Conformance*

Once customer requirements are expressed and defined in technical specifications, operations must build the product/deliver the service in conformance with those requirements. Conformance activities involve product/service and process technology evaluation, defect measurement, and quality control. This evaluation considers cause and effect relationships of various production methods and the costs of various contributors to the overall level of quality. Defects in product characteristics are then measured. Finally, quality control methods measure deviation and adjust the process so that product/service quality is in conformance with the required design.

### *Product/Service and Process Evaluation*

The two specific concerns of product/service and process evaluation are (1) what is the cause and effect relationship among quality variables? and (2) which, if any, "defects" should be considered first as part of the continuing improvement effort? The "fishbone" analysis (also called Ishikawa analysis) and Pareto evaluation of the cost of defects address these concerns. Fishbone analysis interrelates the functional activities of an operations process and assists in defect identification through cause and effect evaluations. The primary line (backbone) of the fishbone diagram is the principal quality characteristic of concern. Major and minor fishbone lines represent various categories and subcategories of functionally related defects. Fishbone diagrams may be used to effectively focus a group discussion from the outcome (poor quality) back to the causes of defects. Application Box 11-2 shows the use of a fishbone diagram to evaluate an adhesive stickiness problem.

Pareto analysis focuses the manager's attention on the cost of errors and categorizes defects by proportion of total quality costs. Pareto analysis can be applied in other areas, including inventory management and forecast errors. (Decision Model Box 9-1 describes an inventory situation.) In the quality management application, the Pareto concept of the critical few and the trivial many is used to identify the areas where effort could be most effectively committed toward quality improvement. Though zero defects is the goal, Pareto analysis may be used to suggest how to proceed toward that goal. An example of Pareto evaluation is shown in Decision Model Box 11-1.

## APPLICATION BOX 11-2 Fishbone Analysis at Mead Quick Release

Lynne McKiernan, quality manager of Mead Quick Release, adjusted the projector and turned to the screen. "As you can see," she began, "defective release values of our labels can result from four possible causes, strength of the label paper, strength of the release adhesive, coating of the carrier paper, and surface of the recipient object." The market for release products had grown rapidly in the past 5 years. Sometimes called "gumless labels," release technologies have been adopted for use in many preprinted price, brand name, and disposable labels, such as those used with computer, medical and fruit products. The release adhesion value is important because it must be high (sticky) enough to adhere to the designated surface, but low enough so that it will not destroy the surface when removed. Unfortunately, the company had experienced stickiness quality problems in recent shipments to United Banana. Lynne's chart, shown below, identified four contributors to the release value.

"Clearly," Don Jacobs, the customer service manager, interrupted, "one primary factor is missing. You have to consider the number of times that a label is moved. Each time the label is moved, the adhesive picks up wax, dust, and chemicals from the recipient object."

"But," countered Susan Gordon, the research chemist, "the lack of surface water/wax is shown as a secondary bone on the diagram. A separate primary bone may not be necessary."

Lynne nodded appreciatively at Susan and acknowledged the question of how the 'Lack of Surface Water/Wax' bone was placed and defined. The fishbone chart was designed to show variable interrelationships, and the positioning of the 'Lack of Surface Water/Wax' bone might help in showing the reason for defective release values of the United Banana contract.

After a short pause, Walt Carlson, the production manager, commented, "You know, it might be helpful if we had some numbers to describe the surface of the banana. Like Don and Susan, I think that the surface is our problem, but it would be helpful to have some measure of the porousness of banana skins, the flatness of the surface, the regularity of the surface, and the amounts

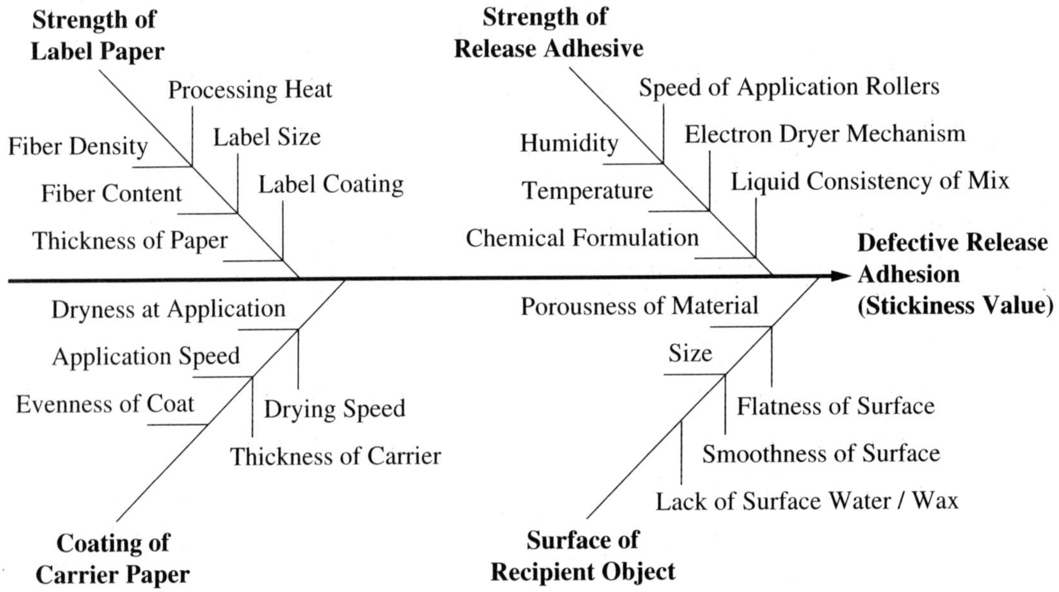


*Continued*

**APPLICATION BOX 11-2** *Continued*

of moisture or wax on the surface. We may find extensive variance in the surface, which might result in the quality variance that we have experienced."

As the discussion proceeded, Lynne became increasingly convinced that she would have to work with the United Banana people to get some additional product data. She expected that the banana skins varied widely in porousness, flatness, regularity, and amount of surface wax and liquid and wax. She wondered to herself if they would have to formulate an adhesive with variable stickiness to fit the characteristics of each shipment or type of banana.

## *Defect Measurement*

Process controls measure key product characteristics—attributes or variables—and, if product/service defects are found, the production processes are adjusted to improve quality. Attributes are binary characteristics; that is, they can be categorized with a simple yes/no (good/bad, present/not present). Variables are measured as a central (or design) value and an acceptable range around that value. For example, "Does the light bulb work?" (attribute—yes, no) versus "What is the average life or intensity of the light bulb?" (variable—central value ± range).

Variation from the standard is measured in two ways, both of which define a central characteristic and a lower and upper control limit. Control limits are distanced from the central value by statistical deviations or a range. The traditional approach assumes that there is no loss of quality within the limits; however, beyond the limits, a defect exists. For example, if a specification is 3.5 mils thickness, with a limit of ± 0.05 mils, then the product is accepted within the range of 3.45 to 3.55 mils and rejected outside that range. This approach may encourage operators to rework rejects only to minimally acceptable limits.

Taguchi stated that any deviation from the standard must be costed in terms of customer satisfaction, ease of assembly, and operational and functional variances. Thus, Taguchi's credo is to make products so "robust" that they avoid random variation during manufacturing activities. The emphasis of Taguchi methods is to "look upstream" to the materials and product design. Variations eliminated there will reduce defects in the final product. This cost is called the "Taguchi loss function." Taguchi suggests that by identifying the costs of even the slightest deviation, the resulting distribution of the quality standard is much closer to the target value than if the traditional "no cost" method were used (Kachar, 1985). The costs of defects for each method and the associated expected distributions of these defects are shown in Figure 11-3.

The Taguchi approach increases the robustness of quality systems by encouraging manufacture to the central value rather than to the limits. However, either technique may be used to encourage continuous improvement because the control limits can be tightened. For example, an initial definition of 3 standard deviations = ± 0.25 could be tightened to 3 standard deviations = ± 0.15. Motorola has improved its quality conformance program to the point that it manufactures many items to six sigma (six standard deviations), which is equivalent to only three errors per billion parts (see Case 5).

## DECISION MODEL BOX 11-1 Pareto Evaluation of Quality Control at Hercules Tool & Die

The Hercules Tool & Die Company manufactures a wide range of metal stamped parts and plates to customer specification. In addition, they do some grinding and finishing work on plates, though that may also be done by the customer. Monthly scrap involves some $3400 (measured as an aggregate of material costs, wasted time, and prorated overhead) and is a major contributor to productivity loss and to foregone profit opportunities. Hercules has determined that defects are due to six causes (shown in the table and the associated Pareto diagram).

Jim Henkle, the director of quality control, advised that scrap reduction efforts should be directed toward the bad materials and poor machining, because they are the most costly basis for rejects. His rationale was that effort in those areas would result in greater scrap reduction. The company committed to a review of supplier quality procedures and to an intensive training session for the machinists. The resulting effort reduced the total scrap cost by $1530 from $3400 to $1870, a 45% overall improvement. Materials scrap was reduced to $612 and poor machining scrap was reduced to $408, a 60% improvement in each. The revised Pareto evaluation shows the updated contributions to scrap. One focus of the quality control effort should be toward defining the potential opportunities for improvement. The first efforts should be to solve the most consequential problems. Though subsequent areas get increasingly tougher to address, as indicated by the revised Pareto percentages, continuous improvement is a very important part of a quality control program. Note that the A, B, and C categories are arbitrarily selected.

| | Original Data | | Revised Data | |
|---|---|---|---|---|
| Reason for Reject | Cost of Scrap | Percent of Total | Cost of Scrap | Percent of Total |
| Bad materials | $1530 | 45 | $ 612 | 32.7 |
| Poor machining | 1020 | 30 | 408 | 21.8 |
| Improper cutting | 340 | 10 | 340 | 18.2 |
| Poor finishing | 272 | 8 | 272 | 14.6 |
| Flaw along edge | 170 | 5 | 170 | 9.1 |
| Faulty deburring | 68 | 2 | 68 | 3.6 |
| | $3400 | 100.0 | $1870 | 100.0 |

*Continued*

**DECISION MODEL BOX 11-1** *Continued*

Initial
Pareto
Evaluation

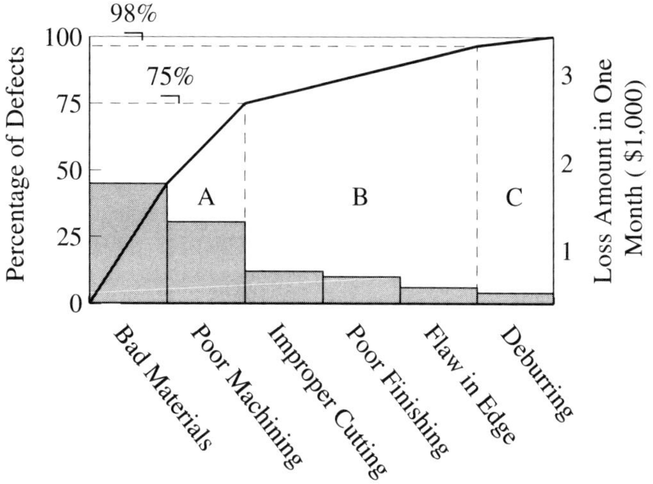


Revised
Pareto
Evaluation

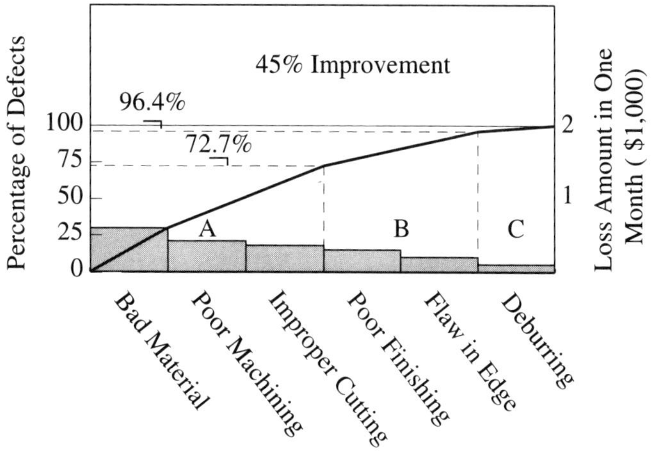


## *Quality Control*

Quality control involves either a process constraint or source inspection. In process constraint, the process is designed in such a way as to prevent or preclude quality defects. *Poka-yoke* is the Japanese term that means defect prevention. An English definition is "mistake-proofing techniques such as a manufacturing or setup activity that is designed to prevent an error from resulting in a product defect" (Cox et al., 1992). *Poka-yoke* often involves product attributes; for example, a sensing mechanism or template may be used

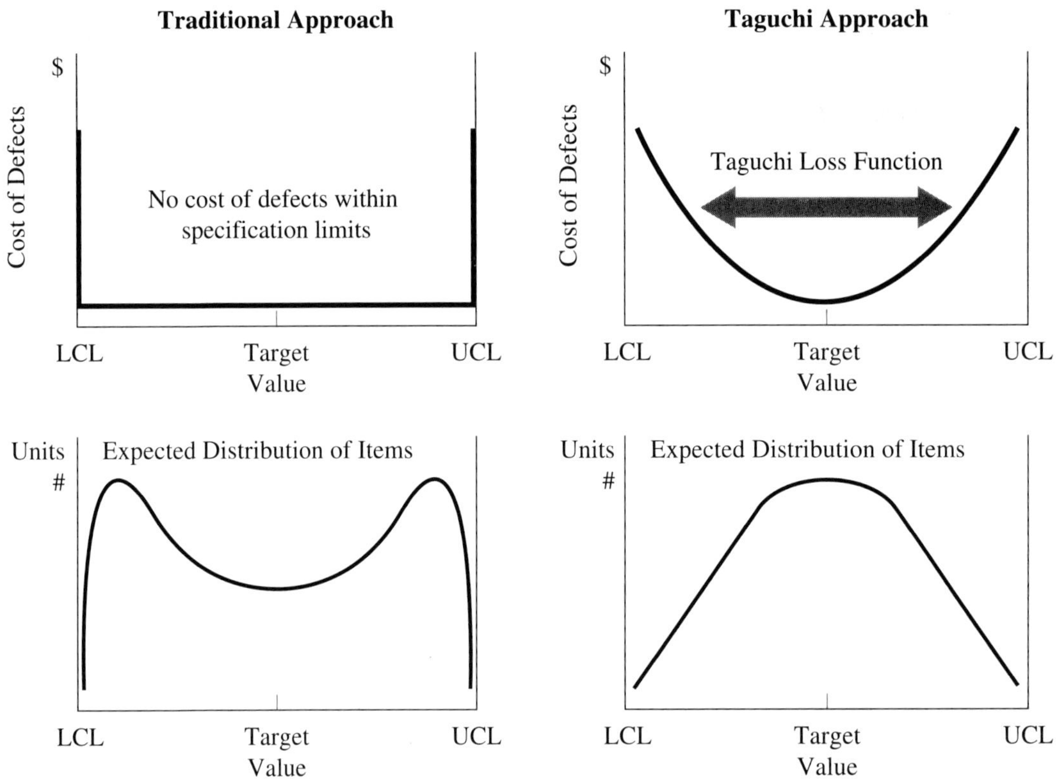


**FIGURE 11-3 Measurement of the Cost of Quality Variation**

to prevent the assembly of a wrong part to a component. However, *poka-yoke* may also involve product variables, such as a jig to prevent overdrilling. Source inspection methods evaluate process deviations and may self-correct or shut the process down before the defect becomes significant. Such an adaptive control process is called "precontrol." Thus, *poka-yoke* is a restraint on the process, while source inspection measures process variance and adjusts or precontrols the operation.

The method of source inspection is based on the stage of the life cycle. During life cycle stages 2–5 (product/service design and process technology selection, production/service delivery system design, start-up, and growth of volume), little is known about the nature of the process, and the product/service quality definition may be changing based upon marketplace requirements. Thus, design of experiments (DOE) is used to identify the appropriate quality variables. However, as the product/service and process technology become more stable, the product/service attributes and variables, and the process setups and methods become increasingly well defined. During the stable state stage, statistical process control (SPC) is more likely to be used to evaluate quality control. Finally, the product and process may become so stable and well understood that the full sampling of the lot may not be necessary. Lot acceptance sampling (LAS) techniques are widely used with such stable processes and with distribution activities of all types. Figure 11-4 shows the evolution of quality control methods over the product life cycle.

### *Design of Experiments*

Design of experiments involves complex statistical methods, such as multiple regression, factorial analysis, or orthogonality to identify key process variables and their relationship to product variance. DOE evaluations often start with a variables research and definition stage. Up to 100 or more variables are evaluated by using paired comparison or similar techniques (Montgomery, 1985). The resulting assessment isolates key variables, ideally to between five and twenty. That limited set of variables then is evaluated by using multivariable analysis techniques to find the strongest relationships. Factor analysis may also be used to gradually focus the process and product/service variables to four or fewer key measures. These variables are then validated, often by sample splitting or other such techniques. The variables that most reliably define the quality characteristic are retained and used to develop control charts or scatter plots.

Design of experiments is as much associated with defining the quality of a product/service as it is with compliance. DOE should be started during the product design/process selection stage, and then developed during the operations system design stage, the startup stage, and possibly the growth stage. As reliable quality variables or attributes are defined, the emphasis of DOE shifts from identifying all variables to defining and validating a few key variables, which is a compliance activity. The use of factor analysis in process evaluation is described in Decision Model Box 11-2.

### *Statistical Process Control*

Statistical process control is an on-line sampling (sometimes a 100% sample, which is a complete census) to monitor and adjust a stable production process. Three types of charts, the percent chart (*p*-chart), count chart (*c*-chart), and units chart (*u*-chart) evaluate differ-

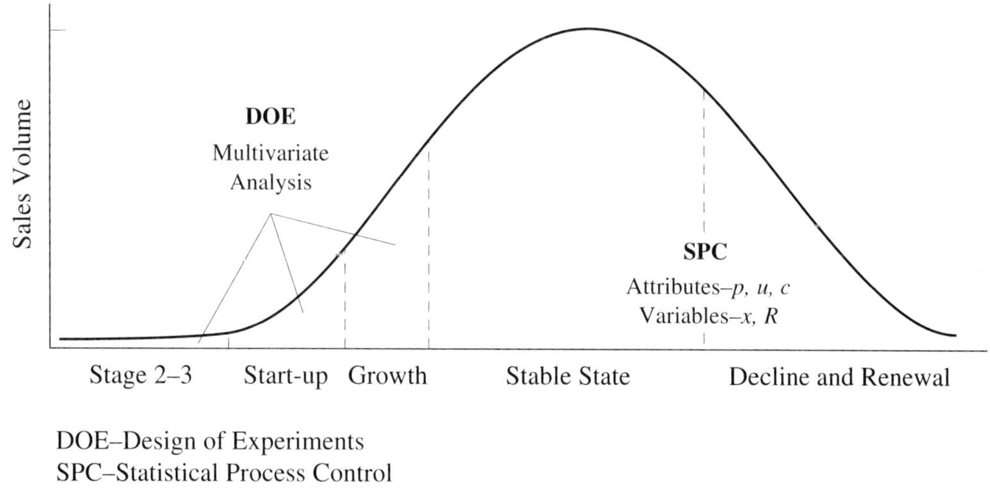


**FIGURE 11-4 Statistical Quality Control and Product Life Cycle**

## DECISION MODEL BOX 11-2 Factor Analysis at GERCO

The GERCO Manufacturing Company contracts molded plastic and veneer installations for a major conversion van outfitter. GERCO's counter and closet assemblies are constructed of various composite materials with a fashion veneer. For durability, most corners and joints are fastened with screws or staples, but where possible, glue is used because of its light weight. One particular unit, a molded shelf glued to the corner of a veneer cabinet, has had an unacceptably high failure rate. Bob Gershon, vice president of operations, reviewed the defect data for 22 days of work, consisting of approximately 100 units per day, with daily temperature and humidity data.

| Day | % Defects | Temperature | Humidity | Day | % Defects | Temperature | Humidity |
|---|---|---|---|---|---|---|---|
| 1 | 6 | 78 | 46 | 12 | 4 | 83 | 72 |
| 2 | 12 | 87 | 51 | 13 | 10 | 93 | 66 |
| 3 | 9 | 76 | 51 | 14 | 5 | 81 | 68 |
| 4 | 15 | 96 | 45 | 15 | 11 | 94 | 62 |
| 5 | 11 | 84 | 38 | 16 | 14 | 86 | 51 |
| 6 | 4 | 81 | 62 | 17 | 5 | 76 | 56 |
| 7 | 8 | 88 | 71 | 18 | 8 | 79 | 73 |
| 8 | 16 | 91 | 38 | 19 | 7 | 94 | 76 |
| 9 | 10 | 83 | 42 | 20 | 8 | 82 | 46 |
| 10 | 10 | 87 | 54 | 21 | 6 | 77 | 54 |
| 11 | 9 | 89 | 65 | 22 | 8 | 96 | 74 |

Though Bob had taken a number of statistics courses and was familiar with multiple regression and analysis of variance, he needed a simple, quick, and—most importantly—easily understood solution. Jane Simmons, the quality control inspector, suggested that the temperature and the humidity data each be split into two groups, low and high, creating four test groups and permitting direct evaluation of the relationship of heat and humidity to defects. That information is shown below.

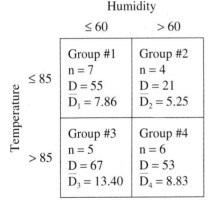

| Temperature | Humidity ≤ 60 | Humidity > 60 |
|---|---|---|
| ≤ 85 | Group #1<br>n = 7<br>D = 55<br>$\bar{D}_1 = 7.86$ | Group #2<br>n = 4<br>D = 21<br>$\bar{D}_2 = 5.25$ |
| > 85 | Group #3<br>n = 5<br>D = 67<br>$\bar{D}_3 = 13.40$ | Group #4<br>n = 6<br>D = 53<br>$\bar{D}_4 = 8.83$ |

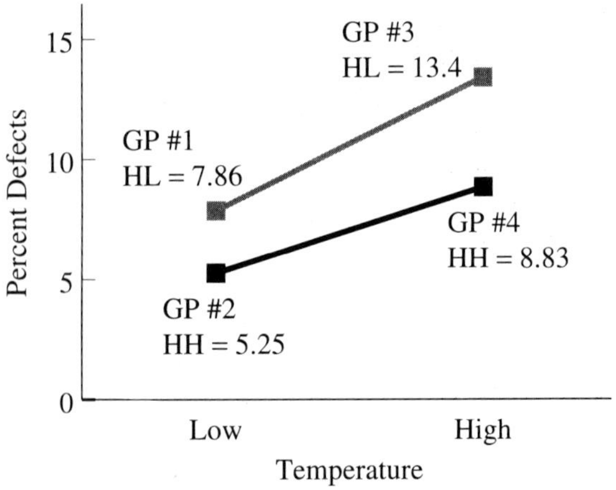


*Continued*

**DECISION MODEL BOX 11-2** *Continued*

For the four groups, the sample size, *n*, the total percent defects, *D*, and the average defects, $\bar{D}_i$, are given in the box. The graph shows the average defects for the low and high temperature ranges and the low (HL) and high (HH) humidity ranges. On the basis of this analysis, Jane concluded that both temperature and humidity affect defects. As temperature increases so do defects, and as humidity decreases, defects increase. But Jane was particularly interested in the interaction of variables, apparent because the plotted lines are not parallel. As temperature increases and humidity decreases, defects increase most dramatically. Bob beamed at his QC inspector and interjected: "Of course, it's summer, and in the heat, the glue is drying too fast."

With a further review of the data and a small mechanical humidifier, they were able to identify the best humidity range for the particular glue compound in use. Humidity control in gluing operations reduced the defects to less than one-quarter of one percent. Jane was encouraged by this method and looked for further ways to continue improvement of quality.

ently defined product attributes. Two additional charts, the $\bar{x}$- and *R*-charts, are used to evaluate product variables. These charts all define a central value and upper and lower process specification limits. An example of a generic process control chart is shown in Figure 11-5.

Typically, control charts measure a central value ($\bar{p}$, $\bar{u}$, or $\bar{c}$ for attributes and $\bar{\bar{x}}$ and $\bar{R}$ for variables) and define the process limits (upper and lower control limits), which are often two or three standard deviations from the central value. The chart defines each dot as the central value of one of several sequential product groupings, often stated in units of time, lots, or items. Because the definition of the population differs, distribution assumptions of the model differ, as do the computational formulas, though they are quite similar in concept. The process control chart identifies observations that are outside the specified limits, which may be analyzed for cause.

**Control Charts for Attributes.** The *p*-chart is used to measure the percent of nonconforming items in the population and to define the upper and lower control limits of the process. The *p*-chart assumes the properties of a binomial distribution. That is, the

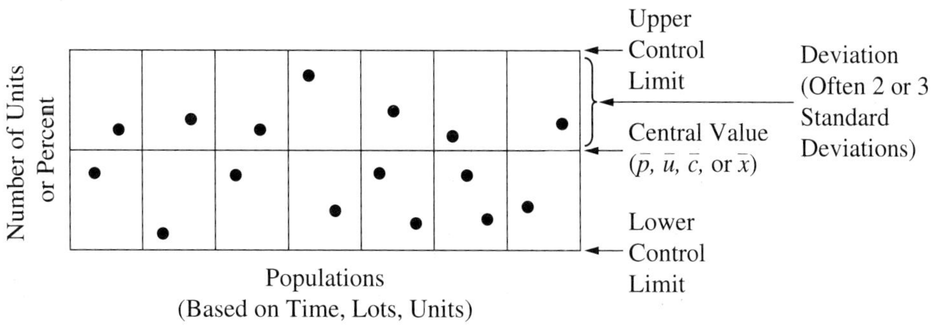


**FIGURE 11-5 An Example Process Control Chart**

evaluation consists of a small number of samples from sequentially evaluated very large populations. The successive samples are independent, and each evaluation may have two outcomes: acceptable or defective.

The *c*- and *u*-charts assume the properties of the poisson distribution and are based on an inspection of several independent samples, each of which has the same small and constant probability that a defect exists. The *c*-chart defines the sample as the count of defects drawn from one unit, such as a production lot, a box of apples, or a case of eggs. The *c*-chart would also be used for defective elements of a computer hard drive or the energizing sources of a video screen. Alternatively, the *u*-chart defines the average of several different samples drawn from one group, for example, several $6 \times 6$ in. samplings of a carpet for pattern defects or several $3 \times 3$ in. samplings of a plate glass window for burrs. Decision Model Box 11-3 gives examples of control charts for attributes.

**Control Charts for Variables.** If the source inspection involves variables, rather than attributes, then the data are evaluated by using the $\bar{x}$ and $R$ charts. This process assumes that the data are normally distributed and that a small number of samples (usually between three and eight) are randomly drawn from ten or more sequential lots. The sequential lots are also assumed to be created by an unvarying process. The data are first evaluated for range or process variability, because, if the range is not in control, then the computation of the central value may be inaccurate. Decision Model Box 11-4 gives an example of the control chart for variables.

***Lot Acceptance Sampling***

Lot acceptance sampling involves identifying a sufficiently large sample size so that the risk that the sample inaccurately represents the state of the population is low enough as to be acceptable. There are two possible types of sampling error: that a good lot will be rejected (the producer's risk) and that a bad lot will be accepted (the consumer's risk). The operating characteristic curve assumes a binomial distribution and that a sample is drawn from an infinitely large population. The greater the effort to appraise and prevent (for example, the larger the sample), the greater the control and the reduced probability of product or service failure. Application Box 11-3 gives a description of the use of the operating characteristic curve.

Precontrol may be used with process control techniques to verify the process and ensure operator training. The movement of sequential observations within specification limits is evaluated to determine if the pattern indicates, for example by a sequence of increasing or decreasing values, that the process is getting out of control. Precontrol is further described in Application Box 11-4.

Because current emphases such as JIT encourage smaller lot sizes and zero defects, a line-stop quality control strategy has been increasingly used in manufacturing and services. That is, each product/service is produced/delivered in a lot size of one. If an item is defective, the process is stopped and the cause is investigated. Shin and Min (1993) identify productivity and cost reduction as a benefit of stop-line quality systems. Though a stop-line system may incur greater costs, for example, greater process disruption, in the short term, long-term benefits are significant.

## DECISION MODEL BOX 11-3 Statistical Process Control at the Mid-West Steel Company—Attributes

**1.** The $p$-chart. The Mid-West Steel Company builds steel office furniture items. In one work center, a metal bracket used to mount desk drawers is cut and rolled. Sample sizes of 50 are selected from each sequential lot of one thousand units with the following results. The number and percent of defective units are shown in the table.

| Sample | Number of Defects | % Defects ($p$) | Sample | Number of Defects | % Defects ($p$) |
|---|---|---|---|---|---|
| 1 | 3 | 6 | 6 | 7 | 14 |
| 2 | 4 | 8 | 7 | 3 | 6 |
| 3 | 6 | 12 | 8 | 4 | 8 |
| 4 | 9 | 18 | 9 | 5 | 10 |
| 5 | 5 | 10 | 10 | 3 | 6 |

The sample average percent defects ($\bar{p}$) and the upper and lower control limits (UCL and LCL) for $\bar{p}$ are calculated as follows:

$$\bar{p} = \Sigma p/n = 98\%/10 = 0.098$$

$$s_{\bar{p}} = \sqrt{[p(1-p)]/m} = \sqrt{[(0.098)(0.902)]/50} = 0.042$$

$$\text{UCL} = \bar{p} + 3s_{\bar{p}} = 0.098 + 3(0.042) = 0.098 + 0.126 = 0.224$$

$$\text{LCL} = \bar{p} - 3s_{\bar{p}} = 0.098 - 3(0.042) = 0.098 - 0.126 = 0.000$$

where $s_{\bar{p}}$ = the standard deviation of $\bar{p}$
$m$ = the sample size
$n$ = the number of lots

Analysis (3 standard deviations) shows that the average number of surface defects per lot is 0.098, the standard deviation is 0.042, and the control limits are 0.000 and 0.224. Because all samples are within that range, the variation is considered random and the process is in control. This analysis could be done for other ranges.

**2.** The $c$-chart. In a second work center, surface defects are sampled on 24 lots of rectangular (24 in. × 36 in.) steel plates. A lot consists of 10 plates. The total number of surface defects in each lot is shown in the table.

| Lot Number | Surface Defects ($c$) | Lot Number | Surface Defects ($c$) | Lot Number | Surface Defects ($c$) | Lot Number | Surface Defects ($c$) |
|---|---|---|---|---|---|---|---|
| 1 | 1 | 7 | 5 | 13 | 8 | 19 | 4 |
| 2 | 0 | 8 | 0 | 14 | 0 | 20 | 7 |
| 3 | 4 | 9 | 2 | 15 | 2 | 21 | 3 |
| 4 | 2 | 10 | 1 | 16 | 1 | 22 | 1 |
| 5 | 1 | 11 | 1 | 17 | 3 | 23 | 0 |
| 6 | 2 | 12 | 0 | 18 | 5 | 24 | 2 |

Continued

**DECISION MODEL BOX 11-3** *Continued*

$$\bar{c} = \Sigma c/n = 55/24 = 2.29$$
$$s_{\bar{c}} = \sqrt{\bar{c}} = 1.51$$
$$\text{UCL} = \bar{c} + 3s_{\bar{c}} = 2.29 + 3(1.51) = 2.29 + 4.53 = 6.82$$
$$\text{LCL} = \bar{c} - 3s_{\bar{c}} = 2.29 - 3(1.51) = 2.29 - 4.53 = 0.00$$

where $c$ = the count of surface defects
$n$ = the number of lots

Analysis shows that the average number of defects per lot was 2.29, the standard deviation was 1.51, and the control limits (3 standard deviations) were 0.00 and 6.82. Because lots 13 and 20 had more defects than the upper control limit, this process is out of control and should be reviewed for cause.

**3.** The *u*-chart. The *u*-chart would be used for a sample average defect. For example, if four 3 in. × 3 in. samples were drawn from one plate of each lot in section 2, and the total number of defects found were the same data as in situation 2, the computations for the u chart estimators are:

$$u = c/n = 55/24 = 2.29$$
$$\bar{u} = (c/n)/m = 2.29/4 = 0.57$$
$$s_{\bar{u}} = \sqrt{\bar{u}/m} = \sqrt{2.29/4} = 0.757$$
$$\text{UCL} = \bar{u} + 3s_{\bar{u}} = 0.57 + 3(.757) = 0.57 + 2.271 = 2.84$$
$$\text{LCL} = \bar{u} - 3s_{\bar{u}} = 0.57 - 3(.757) = 0.57 - 2.271 = 0.00$$

where $c$ = total count of defects per unit (plate number 1 = 1, etc.)
$n$ = number of lots
$m$ = number of samples per lot

Analysis shows that the average number of defects per sample on one plate was 0.57, the standard deviation was 0.757, and the control limits were 0.00 and 2.84. Given this definition of the sampling process, eight lots (numbers 3, 7, 13, 17, 18, 19, 20, and 21) are out of control for three standard deviations.

## *New Developments in Quality and Customer Service Management*

The increasingly customer-driven or demand-constrained markets have required goods and services that meet the highest of quality standards, produced and distributed at reasonable costs. Thus, all components of the operations system are striving for market, product/services, and process advantages in an environment that is less and less tolerant of quality defects in goods or failures of customer service. These concerns have led to greater interest in ISO 9000, the global standard of quality certification, quality function deployment, and customer service management.

## DECISION MODEL BOX 11-4 Statistical Process Control at the Mid-West Steel Company—Variables

Another work center at the Mid-West Steel Company involves a part for which the quality standard is a mean length of 564 mm and a mean range of 7 mm. Five observations are taken from ten sequential lots.

| Lot Number | Observation Number 1 | 2 | 3 | 4 | 5 | Lot Number | Observation Number 1 | 2 | 3 | 4 | 5 |
|---|---|---|---|---|---|---|---|---|---|---|---|
| 1 | 570 | 572 | 569 | 571 | 568 | 6 | 561 | 566 | 568 | 559 | 652 |
| 2 | 562 | 564 | 562 | 565 | 561 | 7 | 571 | 559 | 563 | 561 | 564 |
| 3 | 570 | 571 | 572 | 570 | 565 | 8 | 558 | 562 | 563 | 567 | 557 |
| 4 | 568 | 564 | 563 | 564 | 567 | 9 | 560 | 561 | 563 | 559 | 558 |
| 5 | 554 | 558 | 553 | 558 | 559 | 10 | 559 | 569 | 567 | 563 | 561 |

The computations of the upper and lower control limits for the range ($R$) and the mean ($\bar{x}$) are based on sample size. The formulas, which use several parameters based on sample size, are

$R_{UCL} = D_4\bar{R}$ where $D_4$ is a parameter based on sample size for three standard deviations
$R_{LCL} = D_3\bar{R}$ where $D_3$ is a parameter based on sample size for three standard deviations

$\bar{x}_{UCL} = \bar{\bar{x}} + A_2\bar{R}$ where $A_2$ is a parameter based on sample size for three standard deviations
$\bar{x}_{LCL} = \bar{\bar{x}} - A_2\bar{R}$ where $A_2$ is a parameter based on sample size for three standard deviations

Given the sample size of five observations from each of ten lots, the values for $D_3$ and $D_4$, respectively, are 0 and 2.114, and the value for $A_2$ is 0.577. These table values are found in many quality control textbooks. Five observations is a commonly used sample size because it provides relatively high confidence without excessive sampling effort. The computations for the samples and the control limits are

| Lot Number | $R$ | $\bar{x}$ | | |
|---|---|---|---|---|
| | | | $\bar{R}$ | = 15.6 |
| 1 | 4 | 570 | | |
| 2 | 4 | 562.8 | $\bar{\bar{x}}$ | = 565.42 |
| 3 | 7 | 569.6 | | |
| 4 | 5 | 565.2 | $R_{UCL}$ | = 32.9784 |
| 5 | 6 | 556.4 | | |
| 6 | 93 | 581.2 | $R_{LCL}$ | = 0 |
| 7 | 12 | 563.6 | | |
| 8 | 10 | 561.4 | $\bar{x}_{UCL}$ | = 574.4212 |
| 9 | 5 | 560.2 | | |
| 10 | 10 | 563.8 | $\bar{x}_{LCL}$ | = 556.4188 |

Because the range for lot 6 is out of control, the subsequent computation of $\bar{\bar{x}}$ is likely inaccurate. The fifth observation of lot 6 may have two inverted digits (that is, data entry). As an exercise, recompute the problem with a value of 562 and check for control.

Your results should give a revised $\bar{R}$ of 7.2 and $\bar{\bar{x}}$ of 563.62. The $R_{UCL\ \&\ LCL}$ = 0 and 15.22, which is in control; however, the recomputed $\bar{x}_{UCL\ \&\ LCL}$ equals 559.4656 to 567.7744, suggesting that lots 1, 3, and 5 are out of control. A further evaluation of the process is necessary.

## APPLICATION BOX 11-3 Operating Characteristics Curves

Unless the sample is 100% of the lot, it will, with some probability, misrepresent the actual state of the lot, as shown by the following table:

| | Conclusion Based on the Sample | |
|---|---|---|
| Actual State of the Lot | Accept | Reject |
| Good | $X_1$ | Producer's risk<br>Type 1, alpha error |
| Bad | Consumer's risk<br>Type II, beta error | $X_2$ |

The sample accurately represents the state of the lot in situations $X_1$ and $X_2$. The producer's risk (type I, alpha error) is if the sample rejects good lots; the consumer's risk (type II, beta error) is if bad lots are accepted. The operating characteristic (OC) curve is used to evaluate a lot for a particular attribute. The manager must give some initial risk assessment information, as follows:

| | |
|---|---|
| Acceptance quality level (AQL) | Seller's maximum percent defects in an acceptable lot |
| Lot tolerance percent defect (LTPD) | Buyer's maximum percent defects in an acceptable lot |
| Alpha risk ($\alpha$) | Risk that a sampling error causes a good lot to be rejected |
| Beta risk ($\beta$) | Risk that a sampling error causes a bad lot to be accepted |

After these values are specified, a sampling plan table is used to find a sample size ($n$) and an acceptance count ($c$), which is the maximum number of defects for the lot to be accepted. Twelve common plans are as follows:

| Plan | $\alpha$ | AQL | $\beta$ | LTPD | $n$ | $c$ | Plan | $\alpha$ | AQL | $\beta$ | LTPD | $n$ | $c$ |
|---|---|---|---|---|---|---|---|---|---|---|---|---|---|
| 1 | 0.1 | 0.01 | 0.2 | 0.1 | 18 | 1 | 7 | 0.05 | 0.01 | 0.1 | 0.08 | 80 | 2 |
| 2 | 0.1 | 0.03 | 0.2 | 0.1 | 45 | 3 | 8 | 0.05 | 0.02 | 0.1 | 0.08 | 96 | 4 |
| 3 | 0.05 | 0.01 | 0.2 | 0.1 | 25 | 1 | 9 | 0.05 | 0.01 | 0.1 | 0.05 | 120 | 3 |
| 4 | 0.05 | 0.01 | 0.1 | 0.1 | 40 | 1 | 10 | 0.01 | 0.01 | 0.1 | 0.05 | 200 | 6 |
| 5 | 0.05 | 0.01 | 0.1 | 0.08 | 55 | 2 | 11 | 0.05 | 0.02 | 0.1 | 0.05 | 250 | 9 |
| 6 | 0.05 | 0.02 | 0.1 | 0.1 | 60 | 3 | 12 | 0.01 | 0.01 | 0.05 | 0.03 | 700 | 14 |

The OC curve is used to relate risk and defect data to the sample size and acceptance count values. It is defined by four variables, $\alpha$, $\beta$, AQL, and LTPD. Each OC curve represents a different sample size ($n$) and acceptance count ($c$). As the AQL and LTPD move closer together (or as $\alpha$ and $\beta$ get smaller), the OC curve becomes more vertical. The more vertical curve gives a more accurate sampling plan but requires a larger sample size. The following steps are used to develop a sampling plan:

*Continued*

**APPLICATION BOX 11-3** *Continued*

1. Define acceptable risks ($\alpha$, $\beta$) AQL, and LTPD.
2. Find the appropriate $n$ and $c$ (either table values or through a computer program).
3. Observe n samples from a lot. If $c$ or less defects are found accept the lot; otherwise reject.

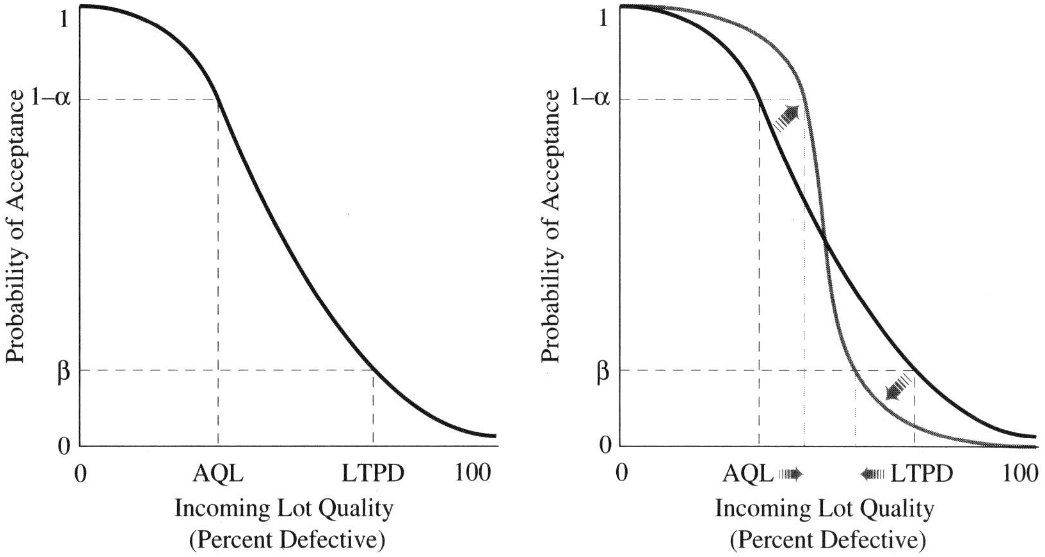


## *ISO 9000*

Many quality management systems have been developed over the years. The first widespread use of acceptance sampling dates to World War II, when Bell Laboratories technicians worked with the Army Corps of Engineers to define the Army Ordnance Tables (which were used to prevent ammunition failure). Subsequently those tables were modified to apply to a broad range of military equipment and were adopted as standard by an American–British–Canadian group as the ABC Military Standard. Later, the standard was accepted by the American National Standards Institute and the International Standards Organization (ISO). ISO is a worldwide agency, now representing 91 countries through their national standards bodies and consisting of 180 technical committees. Certification by ISO 9000, the current standard, is an almost mandatory step for companies entering international business.

There are, in total, five standards defined by ISO 9000 series, the most recent series of specifications, which fall into three groups. The first group (ISO 9000) is a general description of the approach and organization of the standards. The second group (ISO 90001–9003) defines the obligations between suppliers and buyers in terms of manufac-

## APPLICATION BOX 11-4 Precontrol

One approach to precontrol establishes a warning at 1.5 standard deviations from the mean on a normal distribution. Within this precontrol line is the green area, which represents about 86% of the observations. Between 1.5 and 3 standard deviations on either side of the mean is the yellow area, which includes a total of 14% (7% on each side) of the normal distribution. Outside 3 standard deviations from the mean are the red areas. Approximately twelve of 14 random observations will statistically occur within the green range, two of 14 observations will occur in the yellow range, and less than one in 100 observations will occur in the red range. Establishing precontrol of a process can be explained in four simple steps.

### *Precontrol Steps*

1. Define the process mean and actual or desired standard deviation. Draw 2 precontrol lines at ± 1.5 standard deviations.
2. Determine process capability by taking five sequential samplings to validate the precontrol lines. These samplings must all be within the green zone; if not, use diagnostic tools to reduce the process variation.

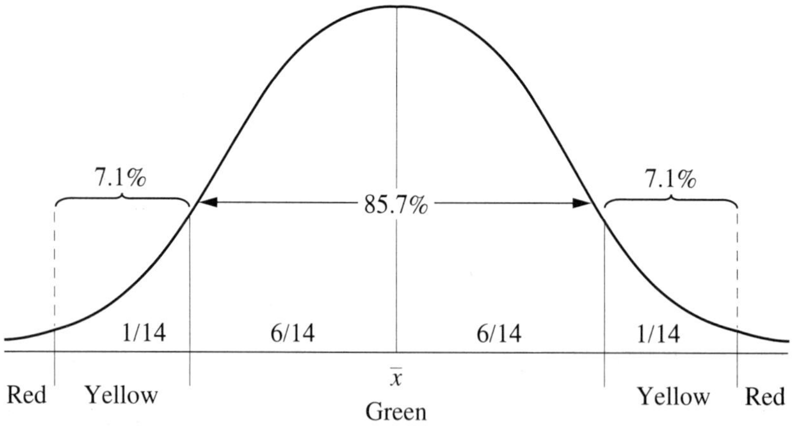


3. After the process is validated, sample two units consecutively. The frequency of sampling is determined by dividing the time interval between two stoppages by 6. Use the following table to determine appropriate actions.

| Condition | Action |
|---|---|
| 2 green | Continue |
| 1 green; 1 yellow | Continue |
| 2 units in yellow | Stop |
| 1 unit in red | Stop |

4. If required to stop, to resume, redefine process capability by returning to step 2.

turing design, production and installation processes, and final product testing or inspection. The third group (ISO 9004) identifies internal quality program development and management systems. These standards define 20 elements that must be met and a process of initial registration and periodic assessment (Greene, 1991). An audit by a qualified independent registration organization confirms compliance with ISO 9000 standards, whereupon a supplier receives a registration certificate, and is published in a directory of registered suppliers. ISO 9000 thus provides an assurance that suppliers have complied with internationally accepted standards of process quality. This distinction is a key competitive edge in the global marketplace (Kuhn, 1991).

The significance of ISO 9000 is that it provides the mechanism for a global standard to register suppliers. This mechanism has, to a large extent, been accepted by national quality governing bodies. One further effect of the widespread standardization, however, has been to encourage movement toward the metric dimensions. Future global marketplaces will rely more heavily upon registration and standardization, and globally competitive firms must meet these measurement standards. This is particularly important for firms doing business in Europe. Specifically, Du Pont, Union Carbide, General Electric, and 3M have developed exemplary programs (*ISO 9000,* 1992). Through ISO 9000, quality is becoming an increasingly visible input to the firm's global strategy.

## *Quality Function Deployment*

The concept of quality function deployment (QFD) was developed at Mitsubishi's Kobe (Japan) shipyards in the 1960s. QFD permits an organization to focus the competitive priorities of quality and flexibility toward customer requirements, and thus to improve productivity at a faster rate. QFD emphasizes a process of evaluating and responding to customer requirements. However, the initial steps of the QFD process are often more time-consuming than conventional approaches because QFD requires more extensive evaluation of customer requirements prior to the start of product design (Stocker, 1991). The QFD effort has four phases, each of which may have up to 14 steps. The four phases sequentially define customer requirements, product specification, parts characteristics, and process characteristics. Each phase of the process operates to translate a requirement (what is required) into an acceptable outcome (how the requirement will be satisfied).

This very systematic approach focuses all functional areas to the common goal of satisfying customer requirements. The benefits, both tangible and intangible, include reduced manufacturing and defect costs, less waste in development and process time, and increased customer satisfaction. An application of QFD is shown in Application Box 11-5.

Quality function deployment can also be used as a strategic planning tool. The Application Box shows a manufacturing example of QFD; however, QFD may be more broadly defined as a "system for designing a product or service which focuses customer requirements and integrates appropriate members of the producing or supplier organization" (Maddux et al., 1991). Taken as a system, QFD may be used to design an intangible service, such as a program or an activity. At the highest level, it is an integrative and sequential analytic and evaluative process.

## APPLICATION BOX 11-5 Quality Function Deployment at the Bar Soap Company

The Bar Soap Company has manufactured and distributed fewer bars of soap in the past several quarters as a result of new product introductions by several competitors. Bar Soap must redefine its image and position in the market, or lose significant market share points. The president assigned a multifunctional task force to evaluate Bar Soap quality.

Based on written and telephonic customer surveys and several in-house sensory evaluations, the QFD team defined the customer requirements. These general requirements were further categorized and specified, and then prioritized. At the same time another part of the team used "reverse engineering" and "benchmarking" to evaluate the functional characteristics of Bar Soap and competitor products. The customer demand information, benchmarks, functional characteristics, and current customer satisfaction data, as integrated by the team, are shown on the QFD matrix.

| | | Functional Characteristic | | | | Importance index | Customer Satisfaction | | | | |
|---|---|---|---|---|---|---|---|---|---|---|---|
| | | Slippery % incline | % Lye | Texture (index) | Shape (fit index) | | Bar soap (now) | Competitor A | Competitor B | Bar soap (+6 months) | |
| Customer Demands | Easy to hold | ❑ | | ❑ | ☆ | 4 | 3 | 4 | 5 | 5 | |
| | Long lasting | ❍ | ☆ | | ❍ | 5 | 2 | 5 | 5 | 5 | |
| | Lathers well | ❍ | ☆ | ❑ | | 3 | 4 | 3 | 4 | 3 | |
| | Feels good | | | ☆ | ❑ | 2 | 5 | 3 | 2 | 4 | |
| Benchmarks | Bar soap (now) | 3 | 4 | 5 | 2 | | Market Information | | | | |
| | Competitor A | 2 | 6 | 2 | 4 | | 60 | 65 | 55 | 55 | Price (¢) |
| | Competitor B | 1 | 7 | 3 | 4 | | 26 | 28 | 41 | 32 | Share (%) |
| | Bar soap (+6 months) | 1 | 8 | 4 | 5 | | 5 | 8 | 9 | 9 | Profits (¢) |

☆ Strong Relation
❑ Some Relation
❍ No Relation

Indexes 1–5, 5 = high

*Continued*

**APPLICATION BOX 11-5** *Continued*

The matrix shows that, according to the customer satisfaction data, the most important evaluative criterion, long lasting, places Bar Soap clearly behind the competition. Additionally, the long-lasting characteristic is closely correlated with the percent of lye. Bar Soap can then use the diagram to identify where they want to be in six months and what they will have to do to get there. Of course, many more specific plans and analyses will be developed as supplemental and elaborative of this diagram, including product characteristics definition, process characteristics definition, and process control definition. However, the process of redefining quality at Bar Soap has started.

## *Customer Service Management*

Ultimately, the three components of quality and customer service management (identify customer requirements, define quality of design, and establish manufacturing conformance) must be integrated in a customer service delivery system, the exact nature of which depends on whether the environment is make-to-stock or make-to-order. With make-to-stock methods, a product is manufactured or prepared prior to the customer order and is held in stock (inventory). With make-to-order methods, the final product is not prepared until the customer order is received. A special case of the make-to-order method is the assemble-to-order method, which prebuilds some components, but, like the make-to-order method, does not finally build the product or deliver the service until the customer order is received.

For example, McDonald's restaurants prepare many food items in advance, particularly during periods of heavy business. The food is held for a short period of time in warming equipment, just as finished goods inventory would be held by a manufacturer. This permits McDonald's to respond rapidly to customer orders with a standardized make-to-stock product line. Additionally, with some meals, McDonald's offers a pre-boxed option to which some items are assembled-to-order. Burger King offers a more customized line, but generally takes longer to serve a customer. Wendy's strategy is full customization based on customer orders, but with the corresponding greater preparation times. Many service businesses have adapted the make-to-order, make-to-stock, and assemble-to-order methods to their particular environments.

In all cases, production must be directed toward defined customer requirements. This truth prompted Chase and Garvin (1989) to suggest that production and service delivery systems must compete by bundling services with products in such a way as to anticipate and respond to a comprehensive range of customer needs. Computer information systems and manufacturing processes are easily transferred or imitated, and thus cannot be for long the basis of competitive distinctiveness. For this reason, the uniqueness of the manufactured good itself is a necessary but not sufficient basis for the long-term competitiveness. Companies must find a competitive edge in service-enhanced products. Thus, a customer-driven operations strategy, which integrates the manufacturing, marketing, and service delivery efforts, is the key to competitive success. The major concepts of this integration are summarized in Table 11-5.

## *Summary*

The concepts of quality and customer service management are inseparable, because quality cannot be defined until it is stated in terms of customer requirements and specifications. Market segmentation is used to better define customer requirements, and diverse market segments often require separate and more focused operations. In all cases, market segments and operations focus need to be defined toward a specific niche. Whether a firm is manufacturing driven (as was Lincoln Electric) or marketing driven, the marketing strategy and operations strategy must complement each other.

The specification of the product/service design and process technology must be pursued in several steps and often in numerous product/process modifications. Finally, after customer requirements have been stated and the product/service design has been defined, the product must be produced/service delivered in conformance with that design. Techniques to define and measure quality depend upon the stage of the life cycle. Specific process control methods are used for various product attributes and variable situations. Integrating quality and customer service management is an extremely important yet potentially very complex area.

Quality strategy topics must include customer input and manufacturing processes. Thus, TQM programs must include not only the customer integration and product/service and process evaluations, but also perceptual considerations. Integrating these components

**TABLE 11-5 Principles of Quality and Customer Service Management**

1. A quality and customer service management program is essential to both manufacturing and service businesses. It is a productivity weapon through definition of customer needs, design to those needs, and production in conformance with the design. Quality and customer service management focus all activities of a company.
2. Quality and customer service management efforts must become increasingly effective because of the greater impacts of defects and broader application of product/service liability.
3. Quality must be controlled at the source (*poka-yoke* or inspection), or where the value-adding transformation occurs. Quality must be designed into the process or product; it cannot be inspected in.
4. Quality and customer service management must be visible, and continuous improvement must be encouraged.
5. Selection of the appropriate quality measurement technique is based on the product life cycle. Design of experiments should be followed by statistical process control. Lot acceptance sampling is used in distribution channels. Accurate process control requires the appropriate statistical method.
    - **a.** For attribute control, percent, unit, and count charts are computed from samples.
    - **b.** For variable control, the range ($R$) must be checked before computing the central value ($\bar{x}$).
    - **c.** For lot sampling, specification of risks ($\alpha$, $\beta$) and AQL and LTPD define the appropriate OC curve.
6. Quality is a discipline and a philosophy. It integrates all contributing factors from technology and human inputs to the distributed finished good. Such an approach requires total support from top management. Given this broadly integrative approach, quality is everyone's job.

into an effective quality program may well be the most challenging strategic task of the operations manager in the next decade.

## *Discussion Questions*

1. Briefly describe the three components of quality.
2. From your experience, compare a manufacturing system with a service system, using the characteristics of each.
3. What is the critical strategic difference between manufacturing and service operations? Give a few "real-world" examples.
4. Identify the costs of customer satisfaction. Describe an example of those costs and the effects on total customer satisfaction.
5. Identify several functional bases for market segmentation. Give an example of each.
6. Briefly describe the quality aspects of the seven product/service-process technology stages. Give an example of each.
7. Identify the two specific quality concerns considered in product and process evaluation.
8. List and describe two analyses used to address the concerns identified in question 7.
9. Define the "Taguchi loss function." How does it evaluate costs?
10. Briefly describe the difference between *poka-yoke* and source inspection. Give an example of each.
11. List and describe the two possible types of sampling error in lot acceptance sampling.
12. What is quality function deployment? What variables would be considered and how would QFD be used?
13. Why are the concepts of quality and customer service management inseparable?

## *Strategic Decision Situations*

1. Select a product or service. Prepare a quality function deployment analysis, using assessments of functional characteristics, customer demands, customer satisfaction, benchmarks, and market information. The analysis should be detailed, to the point that the recommendation is quantitatively supported.
2. The Desk-Mate Copier Company has developed a new technology to use plain paper in a small, portable, desk-top copying machine. In developing the prototype and designing the production system, however, problems have developed with the paper-carrying system. Paper jams at random but annoying intervals. Several types of paired comparison analyses and multivariate analysis have been completed, but nothing seems to explain the jams. A test copying job is equal to 1000 sheets of paper, or roughly a ten-minute run. The testing procedure involves noting the number of times a jam occurred in the 1000-sheet run. Evaluate the following factors and make a recommendation to the director of quality control.

| Job | Defects | Temperature | Humidity | Job | Defects | Temperature | Humidity |
|---|---|---|---|---|---|---|---|
| 1 | 9 | 95 | 73 | 11 | 2 | 94 | 64 |
| 2 | 3 | 86 | 68 | 12 | 5 | 92 | 78 |
| 3 | 1 | 102 | 66 | 13 | 14 | 85 | 79 |
| 4 | 9 | 88 | 76 | 14 | 6 | 88 | 68 |
| 5 | 3 | 97 | 62 | 15 | 2 | 95 | 67 |
| 6 | 8 | 96 | 75 | 16 | 6 | 96 | 74 |
| 7 | 3 | 91 | 63 | 17 | 12 | 89 | 72 |
| 8 | 10 | 89 | 71 | 18 | 8 | 98 | 73 |
| 9 | 0 | 93 | 67 | 19 | 4 | 83 | 63 |
| 10 | 5 | 87 | 69 | 20 | 16 | 84 | 77 |

**3.** The Long Grove Candy Company is concerned that its "Large Bar" comply with its label, which reads "Net Weight 5 Oz." Variation in product weight is particularly problematic in the Large Bar because of the relatively higher proportion of peanuts which, as a natural product, varies randomly. Thus, shipments of shelled peanuts are very carefully inspected for weight.

In one sampling process, lots of 100 peanuts are drawn from each shipment and defects (peanuts weighing less than 0.05 oz) are identified. The following data are provided.

| Lot | Number of Defects | Lot | Number of Defects | Lot | Number of Defects | Lot | Number of Defects |
|---|---|---|---|---|---|---|---|
| 1 | 6 | 6 | 3 | 11 | 3 | 16 | 1 |
| 2 | 2 | 7 | 8 | 12 | 4 | 17 | 5 |
| 3 | 5 | 8 | 6 | 13 | 3 | 18 | 2 |
| 4 | 1 | 9 | 4 | 14 | 2 | 19 | 2 |
| 5 | 4 | 10 | 2 | 15 | 5 | 20 | 5 |

In a second sampling process, a quality control employee suggested the following data:

| | Observation (1/100 oz) | | | | |
|---|---|---|---|---|---|
| Lot | 1 | 2 | 3 | 4 | 5 |
| 1 | 8 | 9 | 6 | 8 | 9 |
| 2 | 10 | 8 | 7 | 5 | 6 |
| 3 | 8 | 9 | 8 | 6 | 10 |
| 4 | 9 | 7 | 12 | 13 | 10 |
| 5 | 7 | 8 | 6 | 6 | 7 |
| 6 | 6 | 9 | 7 | 8 | 10 |
| 7 | 12 | 7 | 6 | 9 | 10 |
| 8 | 9 | 13 | 8 | 7 | 5 |
| 9 | 8 | 7 | 4 | 9 | 11 |
| 10 | 11 | 9 | 10 | 9 | 8 |

**a.** Advise the QC manager on the theoretical and practical acceptability of each approach.
**b.** Calculate the appropriate quality control measures and make a recommendation.

**4.** Prepare a fishbone analysis of a product that you are familiar with. The analysis should include a fishbone diagram and a verbal description of each of the major bones and secondary bones. It may be helpful to structure your report using an outline format, but with several sentences of elaboration for each outlined point.

**5.** The Seven Brothers Winery bottles and stores 1000 cases per day of red, blush, and white wines. Since they do not use chemical stabilizers or other toxins to control the fermentation process, they must watch the alcohol and sugar content of their batches. They have heard of precontrol as a quality control technique, and have evaluated its use on their bottle-filling machines. In one filling application, the one-liter bottle (33.8 oz) is filled to a mean of 34.2 oz with a process standard deviation of 0.15 oz. This process has been validated.

**a.** Evaluate the following pairs of observations and make recommendations.

| | | | | | | | | |
|---|---|---|---|---|---|---|---|---|
| 1. | 33.95 | 34.45 | 8. | 34.25 | 33.87 | 15. | 34.38 | 34.05 |
| 2. | 34.35 | 34.26 | 9. | 34.41 | 34.25 | 16. | 34.67 | 34.38 |
| 3. | 34.08 | 34.25 | 10. | 34.15 | 34.07 | 17. | 33.79 | 33.94 |
| 4. | 34.48 | 34.56 | 11. | 34.21 | 33.99 | 18. | 34.12 | 34.71 |
| 5. | 33.92 | 34.21 | 12. | 33.86 | 33.98 | 19. | 34.28 | 34.15 |
| 6. | 33.65 | 33.90 | 13. | 34.26 | 34.31 | 20. | 34.18 | 34.42 |
| 7. | 34.37 | 34.19 | 14. | 33.85 | 33.91 | 21. | 34.16 | 34.48 |

**b.** Is the precontrol method applicable to fermentation control? How? Why? Why not?

## *References*


Andrew, Charles G. "Focusing Manufacturing for Competitive Advantage." *1989 Conference Proceedings,* American Production and Inventory Control Society.

Berry, William L., Terry Hill, Jay E. Klompmaker, and Curtis P. McLaughlin. "Linking Strategy Formulation in Marketing and Operations: Empirical Research." *Journal of Operations Management.* August 1991, pp. 294–301.

Chase, Richard B. "Where Does the Customer Fit in a Service Operation?" *Harvard Business Review.* November–December 1978, p. 137.

Chase, Richard B., and David A. Garvin. "The Service Factory," *Harvard Business Review.* July–August 1989, pp. 61–69.

Corbett, J. "Design for Economic Manufacture," *Annals of C.I.R.P.* Vol. 35, No. 1, 1986, p. 93.

Cox, James F., John H. Blackstone, Jr., and Michael S. Spencer. *American Production and Inventory Control Society Dictionary.* Falls Church, Va.: APICS, 1992.

Crosby, Philip B. *Quality Is Free.* New York: McGraw-Hill, 1979.

Dean, James W., Jr., and Gerald I. Susman. "Organizing for Manufacturable Design," *Harvard Business Review.* January–February 1989, pp. 28–37.

Deming, W. Edwards. "Improvement of Quality and Productivity through Action by Management," *National Productivity Review.* Winter 1981/1982, pp. 12–22.

Deming, W. Edwards. *Out of the Crisis.* Cambridge, Mass.: Massachusetts Institute of Technology, 1986.

Fogarty, Donald W., Thomas R. Hoffmann, and Peter W. Stonebraker. *Production and Operations Management.* Cincinnati, Ohio: South-Western Publishing Co., 1989.

Fogarty, Donald W., John H. Blackstone, Jr., and Thomas R. Hoffmann. *Production & Inventory Management.* Cincinnati, Ohio: South-Western Publishing Co., 1991.

Frank, Susan, and Stan Halle. "Is Your Total Quality Effort Doomed to Fail?" *APICS: The Performance Advantage.* February 1992, p. 16.

Garvin, David A. "What Does Product Quality Really Mean?" *Sloan Management Review.* Fall 1984.

Garvin, David A. "Competing on the Eight Dimensions of Quality," *Harvard Business Review.* November–December 1987, pp. 101–109.

Greene, Alice H. "ISO 9000: Globalizing Quality Standards," *Production and Inventory Management.* September 1991, pp. 12–15.

Hagerty, Michael R. "Model Testing Techniques and Price–Quality Tradeoffs," *Journal of Consumer Research.* December 1978, pp. 194–205.

Hill, Robert C., and Sara M. Freedman. "Managing the Quality Process: Lessons from a Baldrige Award Winner," *The Academy of Management Executive.* Vol. 6, No. 1, 1992, pp. 76–88.

*ISO 9000: Handbook of Quality Standards and Compliance.* Needham Heights, Mass.: Allyn and Bacon, 1992.

Juran, J. M., and Frank M. Gryna, Jr. *Quality Planning and Analysis: From Product Development through Use,* 2nd ed. New York: McGraw-Hill, 1980.

Kachar, R. N. "Taguchi's Quality Control, Parameter Design, and the Taguchi Method," *Journal of Quality Technology.* October 1985, pp. 176–188.

Kotha, Suresh, and Daniel Orne. "Generic Manufacturing Strategies: A Conceptual Synthesis," *Strategic Management Journal.* Vol. 10, No. 3, 1989, pp. 211–231.

Kuhn, Ralph R., Jr. "How to Meet Europe's ISO 9000 Series Standards by 1992," *APICS 1991 Total Manufacturing Performance Seminar,* 1991, pp. 16–18.

Kuhn, Ralph R., Jr. "Integrating Customer Service with Manufacturing Planning," *APICS Just-in-Time Seminar Proceedings,* 1990, pp. 154–158.

Leonard, Frank, and W. Earl Sasser. "The Incline of Quality," *Harvard Business Review.* September–October 1982, pp. 163–171.

Levin, Irwin P., and Richard D. Johnson. "Estimating Price–Quality Tradeoffs Using Comparative Judgments," *Journal of Consumer Research.* June 1984, pp. 593–600.

Maddux, Gary A., Richard W. Amos, and Alan R. Wyskida. "Organizations Can Apply Quality Function Deployment as Strategic Planning Tool," *Industrial Engineering.* September 1991, pp. 33–37.

Martin, Richard. "The Watchdog. Gillette's Giovacchini Rules on the Quality, Safety of 850 Products," *Wall Street Journal,* eastern ed. December 12, 1975, p. 1.

Modic, Stanley J. "Fine-tuning a Classic; Don Hastings Helps Lincoln Electric Shed Its Shroud of Conservatism," *Industry Week.* March 6, 1989, pp. 15–18.

Montgomery, Douglas C. *Introduction to Statistical Quality Control.* New York: John Wiley and Sons, 1985.

Moran, William T. "Segments Are Made Not Born," in *Marketing Strategies: A Symposium,* Earl L. Bailey, ed. New York: The Conference Board, 1974, pp. 15–20.

Mundel, Marvin E. "Now Is the Time to Speak out in Defense of Time Standards," *Industrial Engineering.* September 1992, pp. 50–51.

Murdick, Robert G., Barry Render, and Roberta S. Russell. *Service Operations Management.* Boston, Mass.: Allyn and Bacon, 1990.

Paine, Frank T., and Carl R. Anderson. *Strategic Management.* Chicago, Ill.: The Dryden Press, 1983.

Phillips, Lynn W., Dae R. Chang, and Robert D. Buzzell. "Product Quality, Cost Position and Business Performance: A Test of Some Key Hypotheses," *Journal of Marketing.* Spring 1983, pp. 26–43.

Porter, Michael E. *Competitive Strategy: Techniques for Analyzing Industries and Competitors.* New York: Free Press, 1980.

Power, Christopher. "Sears Catches the Value Bug," *Business Week.* November 11, 1991, p. 140.

Power, Christopher, Walecia Konrad, Alice Z. Cuneo, and James B. Treece. "Value Marketing," *Business Week.* November 11, 1991, pp. 132–140.

Prizinsky, David. "Lincoln Hitches Star to GM in Bid to Sell Robots," *Crain's Cleveland Business.* August 7, 1989, p. 1.

Reddy, Jack. "Incorporating Quality in Competitive Strategies," *Sloan Management Review.* Spring 1980, pp. 53–60.

Schnaars, Steven P. *Marketing Strategy: A Customer-Driven Approach.* New York: Free Press, 1991.

Shapiro, Benson P. "Can Marketing and Manufacturing Coexist?" *Harvard Business Review.* September–October 1977.

Sharman, Graham. "When Quality Control Gets in the Way of Quality," *Wall Street Journal.* February 24, 1992.

Sheridan, John H. "America's Best Plants," *Industry Week.* October 15, 1990, pp. 27–64.

Stocker, Gregg. "Quality Function Deployment: Listening to the Voice of the Customer," *APICS: The Performance Advantage.* September 1991, pp. 44–48.

Taguchi, Genichi, and Don Clausing. "Robust Quality," *Harvard Business Review.* January–February 1990, pp. 65–75.

Templeman, John. "Grill to Grill with Japan," *Business Week.* October 25, 1991, p. 39.

Thomas, Dan R. E. "Strategy Is Different in Service Businesses," *Harvard Business Review.* July–August 1978, pp. 158–165.

Welles, Chris. "What Led Beech-Nut Down the Road to Disgrace," *Business Week.* February 22, 1988, pp. 124–128.

Whitney, Daniel E. "Manufacturing By Design," *Harvard Business Review.* July–August 1988, pp. 83–91.

Zeithaml, Valarie A, Leonard L. Berry, and A. Parasuraman. "Communication and Control Processes in the Delivery of Service Quality," *Journal of Marketing.* April 1988, pp. 35–48.

# Chapter 12

# Productivity and Work Force Management

*People are the catalysts that stimulate new productivity.*
—William B. Werther, William A. Ruch, and Lynne McClure, p. 31.

*You lead, follow, or get out of the way.* —Lee Iacocca

## Objectives

After completing this chapter you should be able to:

- Define productivity and state several measures of productivity.
- Identify the contribution of people to productivity.
- State why management styles have recently moved toward increased employee empowerment.
- Describe the activities of workers, supervisors, and management in an empowered organization.
- Define and describe job design strategies and identify the advantages and disadvantages of those strategies.
- Identify factors that contribute to productivity and show how they are interrelated.

## Outline

***Introductory Case: Innovative Work Force Management at McDonnell Douglas***

***Productivity as a System***

## *Introductory Case: Innovative Work Force Management at McDonnell Douglas*

In late 1991, John F. McDonnell, CEO of McDonnell Douglas Corporation,* was overwhelmed by the more than $36 billion of aircraft orders for its subsidiary, the Douglas Aircraft Company. While most CEOs would be pleased with such a situation, conditions at McDonnell Douglas were bleak. With defense orders down, the parent company had relied on the commercial business of its subsidiary for profits. But, the $36 billion in orders could not be filled on schedule, a common occurrence at the Douglas Aircraft Company.

Since 1975, Douglas had not reported profits due to inefficient manufacturing methods and poor management. Tired of such lackluster performance, in 1989 John McDonnell announced an innovative work force management system called the total quality manage-

*Materials drawn from David Lynch, "Turbulence Dogs Douglas Overhaul," *Chicago Tribune,* September 9, 1991, Section 4, p. 1, and from James E. Ellis and Bruce Einhorn, "Gone Is My Co-Pilot?" *Business Week,* July 6, 1992, pp. 71–72.

ment system (TQMS) program. More than 5200 vice presidents, general managers, and supervisors were stripped of their titles, though most remained with the company. Four levels of management were erased. Traditionally centralized departments, such as engineering, manufacturing, and customer relations, were decentralized. Though the company had created a new management structure, production methods were not changed. Those methods were based on a sort of "tribal knowledge." Because workers repeated the same tasks for each aircraft, they knew every operation from memory. They rarely consulted assembly instructions, even when the design changed. Thus, further down the line small mistakes required off-line correction, causing inefficiencies and risking other damage. Costs were increased and deliveries delayed.

By 1992, Douglas was expected to contribute 50% of the parent company's revenue and TQMS, an important component of the turnaround effort, was relied upon to change more than 20 years of abysmal financial performance. However, mass confusion resulted, which was perpetuated by the "Douglas salute" (crossed arms and index fingers pointing in opposite directions). Production workers did not know who was in charge, and the company's experienced, yet demoralized managers could not be consulted, since they were taking personality tests and doing role-playing exercises.

Ignoring years of employee experience, reassignments were based on handwritten essays, peer and subordinate evaluations, and behavioral tests. Employee average experience dropped from ten years to two. With more orders than it could handle, Douglas could not adequately train new workers; consequently, morale plummeted further and so did production. First-half losses in 1989 were $224 million. Though fourth-quarter profits were $25 million, the bottom fell out when first-quarter 1990 losses of $84 million were reported.

Seventeen months after the initial commitment, much of what had been taken apart began to be put back together. Because profitability had not been restored, the parent company opted for massive work force cuts during 1990 and 1991. Customer relations was recentralized after the company received complaints from customers who had to speak to a different Douglas executive for each Douglas aircraft they owned. Only the outlines of the program are now present at Douglas; however, its full collapse will likely not occur because, as John McDonnell said in a video mailed to employees in March, 1991, "I will not let TQMS collapse. . . . It is not just another initiative. It is here to stay because I want it to stay."

## *Productivity as a System*

Productivity, broadly defined, is a way to measure the effectiveness of resource utilization for individuals, facilities, companies, and societies. Each of these must periodically find new sources of productivity. Those that do not, fail. For individuals, this means retraining or retiring; for facilities, this means redesigning or closing; for companies, this means restructuring or going out of business; for societies, this means social and political reorganization. Among the numerous examples of this process of loss and regeneration are individuals whose jobs (in the printing and metal-working industries, for example) have been automated, the many plants and companies in the electronics and automobile industries, and the social turbulence and rebirth in Eastern Europe and the former Soviet Union.

In addition to these several levels of evaluation, productivity results from the synergetic contribution of numerous factors. The operations function is to integrate these factors or resources efficiently and thus add value to the output in manufacturing, distribution, and service businesses. Productivity does not result from the management of only one resource or one factor; it is management's job to weave the components into an efficient transformation process. Thus, productivity is achieved through the management of a system, which functions at several levels and with numerous contributing factors.

This chapter initially defines productivity and the relationship of people to productivity, and then notes evolving labor–management practices. Individual aspects of productivity, such as work measurement and learning curves, are discussed in detail, followed by other more broadly defined contributors to productivity, including job design and work force structure. Finally, productivity management is described as a process of continuous improvement.

## *Productivity and People*

Productivity is a people issue. Though productivity may be enhanced by technology and other tangible resources, it is the work force who are trained to use technology, it is the work force who must recognize and reduce wasted resources, such as materials, equipment, and capacity, and it is the work force as a synergy of labor and management that makes the operations system function. Labor has historically been suspicious of productivity improvement, expecting that productivity improvement would require more effort. Management counters that productivity improvement means working smarter, not harder—with benefits for all.

Numerous studies (Heizer and Render, 1991) suggest that of the roughly 2.5% average annual productivity increase in the United States over the past 100 years, 1.6% has resulted from management methods, 0.5% from labor improvements, and 0.4% from capital investments. Thus, people (labor and management) are responsible for 80% of the productivity gains during the past 100 years. Knowledge, a key component of management methods, is a major part of the people contribution, but training is also important, because labor must understand and apply the new methods, processes, and technologies. In fact, labor often understands the knowledge foundation of the production process better than does management. In either case, as highlighted by the introductory quote, "People are the catalysts that stimulate new productivity."

All companies have a labor-management style, supported by numerous explicit and implicit labor relations and human resource management policies. If the styles are not explicit (and often they are not), they are implicit in the standards and informal expectancies of both labor and management. These behaviors are likely conditioned by years of practice and tradition, and, in many cases, become corporate culture, but generally are not considered to be strategic in nature. Unfortunately, management styles directly affect worker expectancies, contributions, and demands, and labor responses affect management styles, all of which directly impact productivity. Because the human resource is so critical to productivity, operations strategy must include work force management as the central commitment and concern.

## *Productivity Defined*

Productivity is generally defined as "an overall measure of production/service delivery effectiveness." It can be applied to individuals, work groups, plants, companies, and nations. More specifically, productivity is measured as a ratio of production or service outcomes and resources consumed to achieve those outcomes, or

$$\text{Productivity} = \frac{\text{output}}{\text{input}} = \frac{\text{production/service outcome}}{\text{input resources consumed}}$$

The difference between the output and the input of an operations activity is the value added, which, recalling Chapter 1, occurs in the operations transformation. Because productivity is a measure of the amount of value added in the transformation process, it is a general indicator of the long-run viability of the company. Without productivity improvements in a competitive environment, operations of any sort are, or quickly become, irrelevant, as suggested by the quote of Lee Iacocca on the first page of this chapter.

## *Contribution of People*

Wickham Skinner (1971) is among the first to identify the infrastructure contribution in American factories. He defines infrastructure as "organizational level wage systems, supervisory practices, production control and scheduling approaches, and job design and methods," or all of the "software" of the facility. Each of these work force-management contributors to the infrastructure directly affects the productivity of workers. The term "work force management" is defined here as "all activities that improve the match between individuals and the job." Though most organizations have a human resources staff function to administer specialized programs toward this end, work force management, in the generic sense used here, applies to the management practices such as work methods and performance measurement, job design and compensation, and creation of work environments.

Knowledge, both labor's and management's, is a key input in most businesses to the productivity equation. Management information systems provide many types of information to various users, but information, unless used, is wasted. To paraphrase Drucker (1989, p. 209), knowledge is data that are endowed with relevance; individuals give data relevance. To be a resource, knowledge must be applied toward the productivity goals of the firm. Thus, people with relevant data are the common element of productivity; or, stated in terms of the productivity formula, people with knowledge are the common denominator of all productivity measures.

In most organizations, as Drucker (1992) points out, the basis for the informal structure and labor productivity is the team. However, there are several different types of team. Some teams, such as baseball teams, have fixed positions staffed by specialist players. Though there is some synchrony, most of the teamwork is in a series of sequential actions, as in an assembly line. A second type of team, the football team, also uses fixed positions, but there is a simultaneousness of effort. The team, like an orchestra or a hospital emergency room team, operates in parallel. Finally, there is the tennis doubles team, like the work relationships of the GM Saturn plant, or the team of senior executives who form the office of the president of a firm. Though each team member has a fixed position, the positions are highly interactive—that is, they can cover for one another. Though each type of team has various characteristics and capabilities, as Drucker notes, team definition develops as an informal process. Management is beginning to learn more about how these decisions are made.

Several studies of top management teams have shown that the team composition is related to the firm's strategy. The demographic traits of teams were found to be significantly related to corporate strategy, while demographic diversity was not found to be related. Notably, firms involved in dynamic strategic change are more often managed by top management teams who have a lower average age, shorter organization tenure, higher team tenure, higher education levels, heterogeneous education specialties, and academic training in the sciences (Wiersema and Bantel, 1992). Other research (Michel and Hambrick, 1992) found significant relationships between the team attributes, such as tenure, functional homogeneity, and core function expertise, of the top management team and the diversification strategy of the firm. These studies suggest that, at least among top management teams, team composition is an important and related factor to strategy.

## *Changing Face of Labor Relations*

Some managers view changes in workplace conditions with skepticism or contempt. To use Skinner's (1971) term, this is "anachronistic." The rate of change in most businesses is increasing. International competition, environmental concerns, openness of operations processes, and equity in work force management practices are driving and sometimes overtaking current change efforts. Equating these underlying factors to a short-lived economic downturn and suggesting that "this too will pass" is indeed short-sighted and risky. Further, rapidly developing technology (Chapter 13) requires changes in work force management styles. This section describes the emerging currents in work force management.

### *Emergence of Work Force Management*

Management, as Drucker (1989) notes, is a rather recent phenomenon, dating in most business areas to the beginning of the twentieth century. Prior to that time, the smaller, more entrepreneurial and less differentiated production processes and service operations did not require extensive and formalized management, particularly as we understand the term today. Notable exceptions are early military, insurance, and church organizations and construction or transportation companies, such as railroads and shipping firms.

In the early twentieth century, however, ownership of a business became separated from the operation of that business. A bureaucracy was subsequently created to support the operation of the business. Through the 1960s and 1970s, management structures became increasingly differentiated as organizations sought to define responsibility and capabilities for different functions or to comply with different externally generated requirements, such as government regulation. More recently, availability and ease of use of the computer have made it possible to distribute knowledge rapidly throughout the organization, which has effectively empowered the diverse contributors of knowledge in the organization.

As early corporations and management grew in power, labor was organized as a countervailing force. Buffa (1985) argues that labor was organized only to the degree that management misused and abused its prerogatives. The industrial-relations staff was created to work with the developing labor unions, and, in the process, absorbed many of the functions and powers previously exercised by the operations function. Human resource staff specialists, often isolated from an operations perspective, viewed labor relations as a process of appeasing and mitigating. Matters of infrastructure and such key contributors to productivity as job design, work rules, wage rates, and organization structure were bargained and compromised. In the long run, according to Buffa, productivity was undermined.

As the unions became more powerful in the mid-twentieth century, their primary strategy was to organize most of the competitors in a market, then, through pattern bargaining, enforce a relatively uniform wage contract. This effectively eliminated labor costs from the competitive bargaining environment by establishing an industrywide standard wage. However, by the 1960s and 1970s, international competition and deregulation diminished the ability of businesses to pass through to customers the high costs of standardized union wages. Customers and businesses sought the lower-cost nonunion and foreign goods and services, effectively undercutting the power of the unions and companies with organized labor (Cappelli, 1986).

## *Future Directions of Work Force Management*

The traditional model of labor relations, based on adversarial conflict and competition for resources, was necessary and effective in its time, but as the work force management environment has changed, that model has become increasingly counterproductive. Currently, in many industries, organizations must identify and emplace methods, structures, and management styles that encourage human resources toward continuously improving operations goals. These directions of work force management are apparent in the emerging information organization.

The information organization has subtly, yet explosively replaced the industrial organization. An early herald of the information-based organization was Bell (1969), followed by Toffler (1971), Naisbitt (1982), and Drucker (1989). Though each reflects a different perspective in defining the information-based organization, there are some striking similarities. The characteristics of the emerging information organization, compared with the traditional materials-based organization, are suggested in Table 12-1.

**TABLE 12-1 The Emerging Information-based Organization**

| Characteristic | Traditional Materials-based Organization | Emerging Information-based Organization |
|---|---|---|
| Strategic resource | Capital or labor | Information |
| Locus of power | Management and, as delegated, staff | Technical specialists |
| Decision logic | Judgmental | Computational |
| Decisions based on | Experience, opinion | Diagnosis |
| Distribution of power | To a few | To many |
| Operations | Sequential, segmented | Synchronous, integrated |
| Strategy | Peripheral showpiece | Integrating overview |
| Organization design | Tall | Flat |
| Knowledge location | Support staffs | Line operations |

The displacement of capital and labor by information as the key strategic resource permits numerous efficiencies. Notably, because information is easily duplicatable, it can be distributed to many people and different activities simultaneously. Capital and labor (the key resources in earlier eras) usually are not directly or cheaply reproducible; thus their management and use as a resource was limited to a few individuals. But now, the reproducibility of information permits greater distribution and synchronous interaction of specialists. In the emerging information organization, decision making is based on more elaborate sharing and diagnosis of functional-area information, rather than individual opinions or experience. In the industrial organization, decision making is based on management judgment; strategy contributes only as a peripheral showpiece. Computational processes and diagnostic values aid decision making, and strategy provides an integrating overview in the information organization.

The knowledge of an organization today resides with diverse technical specialists; these individuals are primarily in operations activities and are more closely in touch with the value-adding transformation of the business. Specialists do not require layers of management to serve as information relays, which would likely only create communication problems. Instead, the few generalist managers facilitate an environment of trust and internalization of organization goals. The shift toward an information-based organization suggests a significant flattening of the organization design with fewer levels of hierarchy, with less direct supervision, and with a greater span of control for each supervisor. Drucker (1988) offers examples of a hospital or a symphony orchestra. In such organizations, specialists contribute their knowledge in clearly identified frameworks of organization structure. Communications among specialists are often lateral, developing a synergy that would be lost if interrupted by a supervisor's review.

Such organizations, according to Drucker, have four special management problems:

1. To reward specialists and identify career paths for them.
2. To ensure the training and preparation of top management.
3. To establish a unified vision of the organization.
4. To devise the structure to manage the organization.

Each of these four management problems is exacerbated by the nature of the information organization. Because management is not fully aware of the specialist's knowledge contribution, rewarding and projecting career paths is difficult. Correspondingly, traditional ways of providing for promotion to and preparation of top management through staff positions are less available. Management must function with increased visibility to ensure understanding of both formal and informal needs of the organization and internalization of those needs by diverse specialists.

Drucker's assessment is contested by Elliot Jaques (1990), who presents a strong case in support of the continued need for hierarchy. Though acknowledging that hierarchies involve potential problems and misuses, Jaques insists that the use of the hierarchy is the only way to define discrete categories of job complexity (vertical levels) and to differentiate types of mental activity (horizontal levels). Hierarchies emerged with the beginnings of social organization and have persisted in business organizations because they are uniquely able to provide these functions. A distinct difference in perspective is required by each level and each function of the organization, with a discontinuity of perspective from one level to the next and from one function to the next. Typically, for example, at the lowest level, the decision-making time limits of technicians and operators is one or two days, that of first-line management is three months, and so forth to the CEO, who may have a five to ten year perspective. The hierarchy, whether relatively tall or relatively flat, is thus inherent in social and business organizations. It is required because incumbents cannot rapidly shift their range of horizontal or vertical involvement. Management's function within the hierarchy is

1. To add value to subordinates' work.
2. To sustain a team of subordinates capable of doing the required work.
3. To set the direction and get subordinates to follow willingly.

Given that many organizations have upwards of 15 layers of vertical structure, both Drucker and Jaques concur on the need for downsizing. The flow of information must be enhanced through structures and infrastructures, requiring greater emphasis on understanding and trust. The management style of such organizations inevitably changes.

McGregor (1960) first differentiated the elements of theory X and theory Y management styles; he suggested that organizations were moving toward greater acceptance of theory Y. However, the coming information organization makes subordinate-centered theory Y processes absolutely necessary. Figure 12-1 elaborates the management style from boss-centered direction (generally theory X) to subordinate-centered involvement (generally theory Y). The downward movement on this continuum toward greater employee freedom and employee-centered involvement is likely to continue for the foreseeable future for most types of organization. The positioning of management style on this continuum is a key management decision, one which directly affects productivity and which, as initially suggested by Figure 2-7, must be consistent with the internal and external factors of the environment.

When the formal and informal mechanisms of organization environment and values, communication, and individual responsibilities are changed, it is extremely important that both the old and new methods, and the reasons for change are understood. A method of

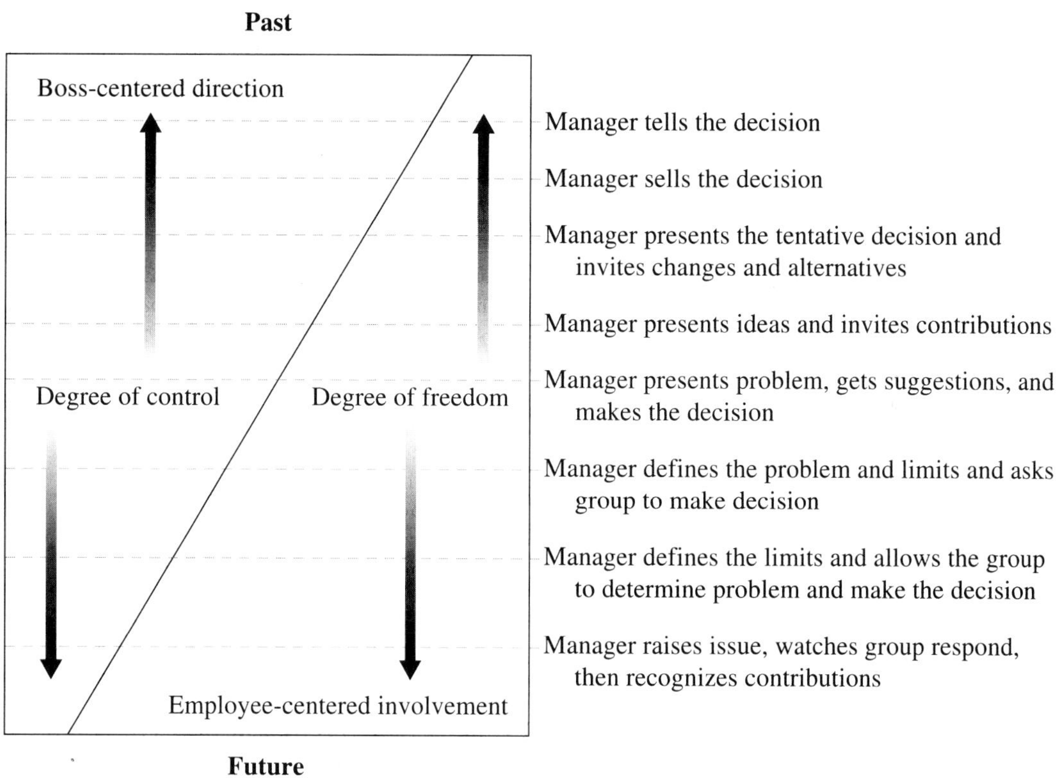
Past
Boss-centered direction
Degree of control
Degree of freedom
Employee-centered involvement
Future
Manager tells the decision
Manager sells the decision
Manager presents the tentative decision and invites changes and alternatives
Manager presents ideas and invites contributions
Manager presents problem, gets suggestions, and makes the decision
Manager defines the problem and limits and asks group to make decision
Manager defines the limits and allows the group to determine problem and make the decision
Manager raises issue, watches group respond, then recognizes contributions

**FIGURE 12-1 Emerging Management Styles**

visualizing the effects of the simultaneous pressures for change and resistance to change was expressed as field force theory by Lewin (1951). Change may be accomplished by either increasing the forces of change or by decreasing the forces of resistance to change. Schein (1984) suggests that the process of unfreezing, changing, and refreezing may be helpful in facilitating the change and minimizing discontinuities. An example of a management style change at Xerox Corporation is described in Application Box 12-1.

## *Employee Empowerment*

The upshot of greater employee-centered management styles is employee empowerment. Empowerment is a natural extension of the long understood and practiced idea of delegating authority commensurate with responsibility. But empowerment is also multidimensional, resulting from increased integration of persons with diverse and specialized perspectives. Such individuals are likely, either as individuals or teams, to develop and implement varied and multidimensional responses to specific situations. Additionally, empowerment means "define and solve the problem," a much broader charter than offered

## APPLICATION BOX 12-1 Changing Management Styles at Xerox

With the introduction of its first copying machine in 1960, the Xerox Corporation experienced growth and profits due to a near monopoly situation. Domestic competition did challenge Xerox during part of the 20 years following the product breakthrough, but only on service and reliability. It was not until Japanese companies entered the market in the mid-1970s with lower-priced equipment of comparable quality that Xerox was forced to compete on price and product innovation. Cost suddenly became paramount at Xerox; a companywide cultural change was mandated.

At the core of Xerox's reorganization was the altering of management styles. This meant adjusting from a highly technical management approach to a more employee-oriented style. Many changes had to be implemented; yet it was crucial to retain the commitment of Xerox's technology-oriented employees. The change process selected was the management style change strategy (Schein, 1984), consisting of three steps: unfreezing, changing, and refreezing. During "unfreezing," targeted areas are emphasized to unlock the "traditional ways of doing things." Next, managers are informed of the desired behaviors. Thus, "changing" of style occurs through identification and internalization of the modeled values, attitudes, and behaviors. Increased emphasis is placed on innovation and risk taking. An environment is developed to encourage employee participation. The final step is the "refreezing" of the newly defined management values, attitudes, and behaviors as the expected norm. Support mechanisms are put in place to reinforce the required changes, and organization rewards are implemented to further shape the behaviors of management.

Additionally, the company wanted an organizational climate conducive to motivation and change. The climate in which the employees operate directly affects the plausible methods of motivation. Lewin's field force theory views people performing in a field of restraining and driving forces. Typical examples of these two forces and their effects on the amount of productive effort are shown over time in the following diagram. These forces either limit or augment productivity. When the restraining forces are reduced or the driving forces are increased, the amount of productive effort is increased. The strength of the counteracting forces dictates overall actual behavior.

By dedicating itself to creating an employee-oriented work force, Xerox has been able to elevate some of the driving forces behind employee motivation. Such an overwhelming organizational transformation has allowed the copier giant to remain successful in a highly competitive market.

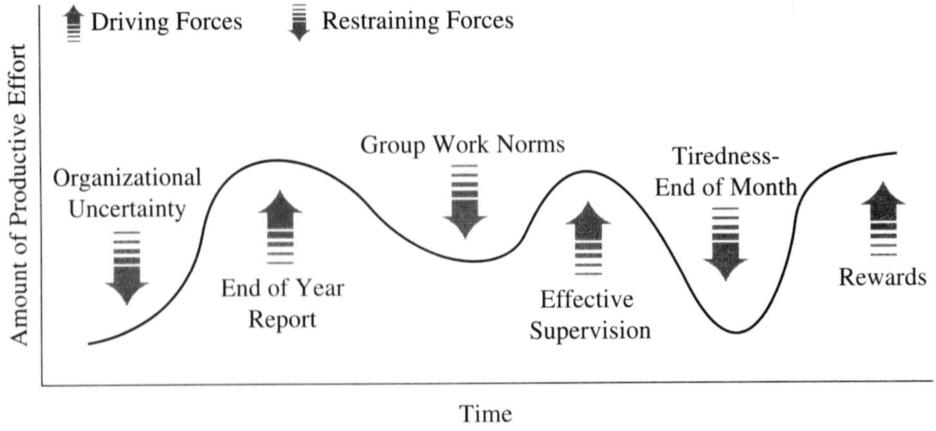


Materials drawn from Norman Deets and Richard Morano, "Xerox's Strategy for Changing Management Styles," *Management Review*, March 1986, pp. 31–35; Kurt Lewin, *Field Theory in Social Science*, New York: Harper and Brothers, 1951; and Edgar H. Schein, *Organizational Psychology*, Englewood Cliffs, N.J.: Prentice Hall, 1980.

by most delegation of authority. Employee empowerment is one of the most efficient ways to stimulate new productivity. This suggests a horizontal corporation of self-managing teams (Byrne, 1993).

Employee empowerment may have developed as a way to incorporate Japanese management styles in American practices. Empowerment, for example, engenders the collective decision-making and holistic values that long have typified Japanese management styles. Though the further techniques of lifetime employment and long-term evaluation processes are not included in empowerment, they are implicit, because empowerment recognizes the value of the employee and thus the need to hire the right employee, and then retain and develop that individual (Bowen, 1991).

Little is understood about the characteristics of the empowered organization or about the activities and characteristics of the individuals at various levels in the empowered organization. Some vestiges of the traditional organization design are likely to remain. Indeed, as Jaques (1990) contends, they are inherent in organizations, though they will likely be less formal or apparent. At the highest level of the hierarchy, top management defines the culture and creates the vision. At the lowest level of the hierarchy, specialists are integrated with the organization communication system to achieve the necessary synchrony. The several layers of management or supervisory employees are primarily involved with process cost, quality, flexibility, and delivery, which reduce lead times and waste. These dimensions of the empowered organization are shown in Figure 12-2.

The new organization design, or strategic architecture, is more focused toward organization processes and the internal development of the firm, rather than toward external factors. This refocusing of the strategic architecture of the firm emphasizes organization learning, motivation, empowerment, and other internal growth activities (Kiernan, 1993).

Hall (1991) reports that plants with the best labor productivity gains are involved in a combination of quality improvement, lead time reduction, and employee involvement. These are formalized in programs to cut costs and improve quality, process flexibility, and delivery times. Despite this refocusing of the firm, measuring productivity improvement remains an important yet difficult function.

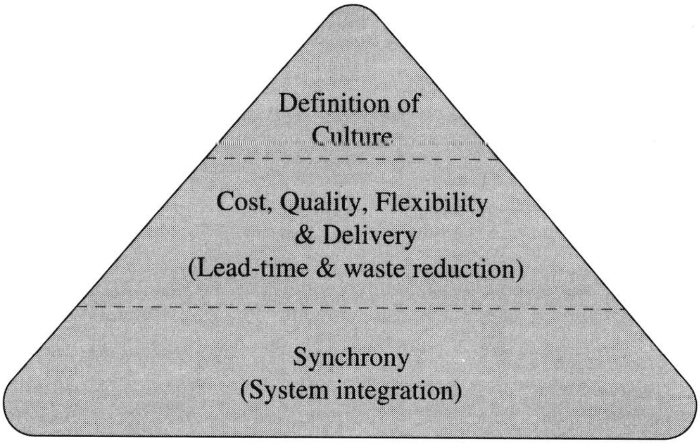


**FIGURE 12-2 The Structure of an Empowered Organization**

## Measuring Productivity

Despite far-reaching efforts and high levels of management support, productivity improvement has proven an elusive goal for many organizations, including McDonnell Douglas. Most productivity improvement efforts, as Skinner (1986) points out, have been directed toward labor efficiency, which is, in most manufacturing and many service situations, less than 20% of the total resource input. Without a coherent strategy, many innovations result in improvements in one area, but simultaneously incur problems and costs in other areas, resulting in limited, if any, gains. One difficulty is that businesses have long been guided by criteria of cost and efficiency, and managers draw conclusions based on these unidimensional measures and reject innovations that cannot satisfy cost or efficiency standards in the short run.

### Productivity Evaluation

Often productivity measures, though computed with the best of intentions, exacerbate the situation. Few measures are constant, and few are unperturbed by external factors. For example, the automobile of the 1950s and 1960s is strikingly different from that of the 1990s. Emission control, gasoline mileage, available materials, and manufacturing technologies have all changed significantly. Consequently, the output measure of "one automobile" has changed from year to year—reducing its accuracy as a measure of yearly productivity. Further, a measured unit for one product may not be the same as for another product. A carburetor for an economy car is not the same as that for a performance sports car. Such difficulties prompted Vaughn Beals, president and CEO of Harley Davidson, to comment: "Measuring productivity is a total frustration. Any numbers I could quote, the accounting department might choke on. We have just looked at gross measures; we count all the motorcycles that go out the door, then count all the people working in the plants . . . " (Willis, 1986).

#### *Measures of Productivity*

Despite these difficulties, productivity is measured in a variety of ways at national and regional levels, at company and plant levels, and at work group and individual levels. The United States Department of Labor, Bureau of Labor Statistics measures and publishes the gross national product. Most companies compute a variety of productivity indexes (see Table 12-2), which are often used with an appreciation of their limitations. Vora (1992) finds that the productivity measures in use by a sampling of manufacturing and service firms varies widely; physical output, sales revenue, and profits are measured as outputs, while labor, capital, materials, energy, and space or land all are used as input measures. Top management primarily uses measures based on profit and sales per unit of capital input, and first-level management typically uses measures of physical output per unit of labor or material. Additionally, individual and group productivity measures were used for a variety of purposes, including compensation and performance appraisal. The accuracy and relevance of those measures is only as good, however, as the input and output

**TABLE 12-2 Productivity Measures in Manufacturing and Service Activities**

| | | |
|---|---|---|
| Total factor productivity | = | $\dfrac{\text{output}}{\text{management} + \text{labor} + \text{capital} + \text{materials}}$ |
| Productivity index | = | $\dfrac{\text{productivity for a specified period}}{\text{productivity for base period}}$ |
| Labor efficiency | = | $\dfrac{\text{total units produced}}{\text{total labor hours}}$ |
| Quality yield | = | $\dfrac{\text{total units produced} - \text{rejected units}}{\text{total units produced}}$ |
| Safety—lost time | = | $\dfrac{\text{productive time lost due to accidents}}{\text{total productive time}}$ |
| Delivery—shipments | = | $\dfrac{\text{shipments on schedule}}{\text{total shipments}}$ |
| Inventory turns | = | $\dfrac{\text{cost of sales/period}}{\text{average inventory investment/period}}$ |
| Service application processing | = | $\dfrac{\text{number of applications processed correctly}}{\text{staff hours}}$ |
| Service response efficiency | = | $\dfrac{\text{responses within specified time}}{\text{total number of responses}}$ |
| Facility utilization | = | $\dfrac{\text{total hours of facility used}}{\text{total hours of facility available}}$ |
| Facility occupancy | = | $\dfrac{\text{average seats occupied/period}}{\text{total available seats}}$ |

Reprinted by permission from *Production and Operations Management* by Donald W. Fogarty, Thomas R. Hoffmann, and Peter W. Stonebraker. Cincinnati, Ohio: South-Western Publishing Co., 1989, Figure 1-9, p. 26.

information. As Beals suggests (Willis, 1986), they can be used as general measures to compare like activities or to evaluate performance of an activity over time.

Any measure of outputs over inputs may be used as a productivity measure or, if the output measure is compared to a base period, a productivity index. Improving productivity can be achieved by increasing outputs or decreasing inputs. The most common way to improve productivity is to increase inputs, in the hope that the outputs will increase at a greater rate. This is the rationale for economies of scale and scope, where an investment is made in technology in the expectancy that the increased productivity will be sufficient to permit higher volumes (scale) or greater variety (scope) and lower costs. Alternatively, a decrease in inputs that is greater than that of outputs also improves productivity. This approach is used during periods of recession, when layoffs and plant closings are used to reduce inputs (resources) faster than outputs (sales) and thus improve productivity.

### *Multifactor Models*

Though individual measures of productivity may be accurate, productivity is more useful when evaluated as a system of multiple factors. One example of a multifactor productivity model is the input–output model of the firm, developed by Ruch and Hershauer (1974). As shown in Figure 12-3, total productivity is a function of six general inputs: ownership, capital, management, labor, suppliers, and others, including government and utilities. However, those inputs are also constrained by the productivity of the firm, because the output is recycled as an input. This figure emphasizes why transformation must be a value-adding process. Productivity improvement is a dynamic and cyclic process, synergetically dependent upon the effects of numerous variables.

The input–output model of the firm can be related to the input–transformation–output cycle (Figure 1-2) and to the logo-motif of this book. Productive resources are input from various sources, and transformed into products or services for customers. This generates revenue, which is then fed back into the system as an input. Of course, each resource is closely monitored for changes in cost, availability, and quality in each iteration.

The input–output model views productivity as an integrated, synchronous system. Few, if any, products in today's marketplace can be built with inputs from only one resource. Most products require the integration of several different contributors and, in fact, often benefit from the synergy of many different contributors. For this reason, measures of individual resource contributions, such as labor efficiency, may not be as relevant over time as an integrated multiresource measure, such as the total factor productivity measure (see Table 12-2). The individual factors do not reflect the synergy of input resource combinations. The individual labor measure would not, for example, reflect the failure or unavailability of other resource inputs, which would affect output. It is for this reason that many individual measures of productivity, such as the labor cost per unit, are flawed.

The significance of the input–output model of the firm is that it identifies the contributions and cost of each input resource, and the price of the transformed output, permitting the measurement of productivity at the facility or firm level. Productivity may be improved if less resource per unit is required from any of the contributors, or if the resource cost is reduced. For example, if labor is able to produce a greater number of units per hour or if compensation is reduced, productivity is improved. Similarly, if equipment costs less or if the interest rate paid on loans for that equipment decreases, the firm has made a productivity gain. Productivity is also improved if the price is increased. Again, however, the use of such individual measures to project expected productivity outcomes may be flawed. In this example, if compensation is reduced, productivity is improved only if labor stays on the job and continues to produce at the previous standard. From a broader perspective, the use of individual productivity measures to identify and eliminate cost-ineffective functions may be problematic because of the interactivity of the productive system (Skinner, 1986).

Of course, the real world is rarely so simple. Many such changes are occurring simultaneously and when a productivity gain is realized, it may be difficult to isolate the cause or causes. Even more fundamentally, it may not be possible to realize from week to week that productivity is changing. Additionally, because labor contributes a small and decreasing proportion of total productivity, cuts in labor (often the easiest factor to reduce)

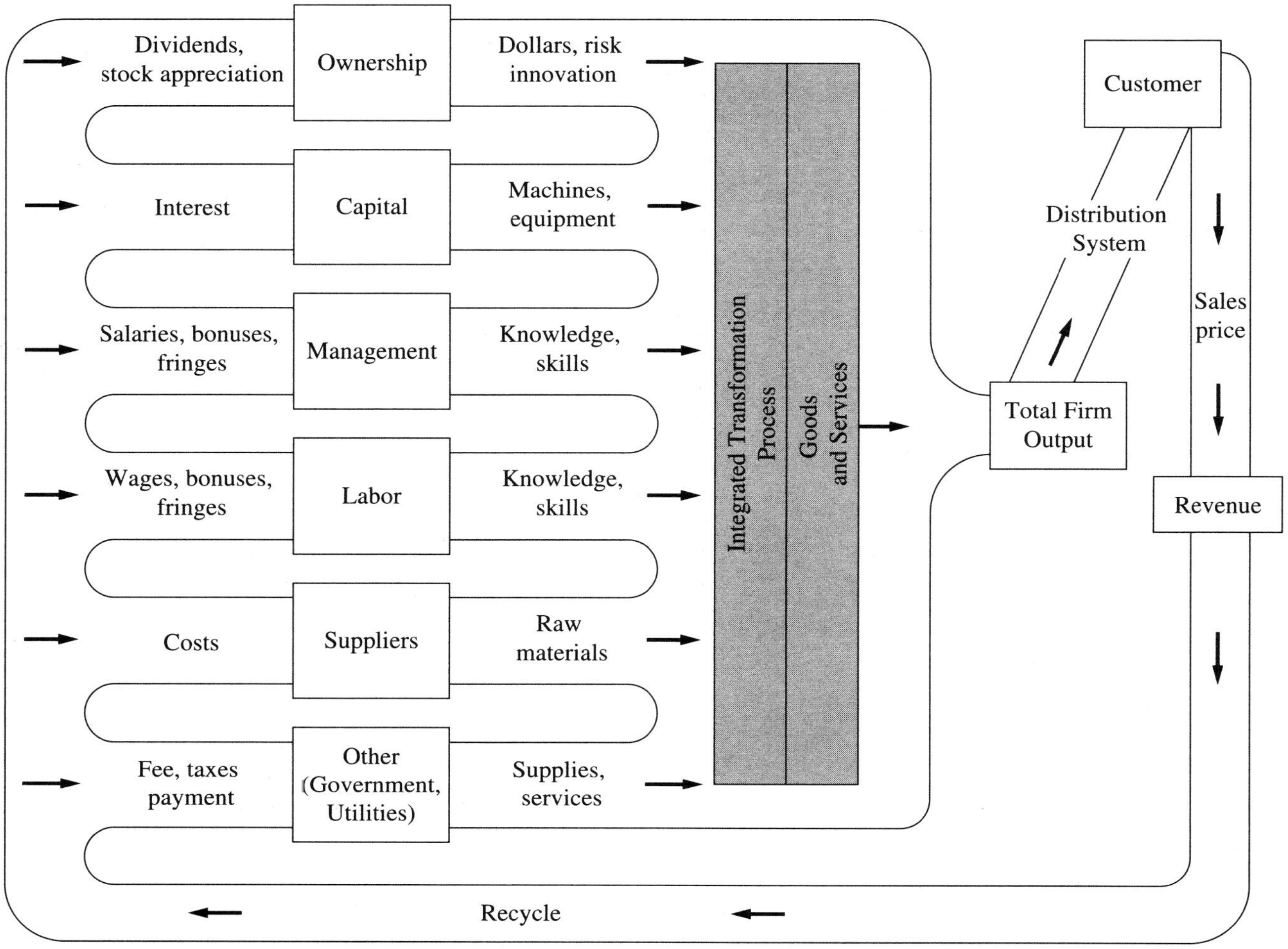


**FIGURE 12-3 An Input–Output Model of the Firm**

Adapted with permission from William A. Ruch and James C. Hershauer, *Factors Affecting Worker Productivity.* Tempe, Arizona: Arizona State University,

give little real benefit. Productivity measures thus are encumbered by numerous limitations. Though individual resource measures are easier to quantify, they may be less meaningful because of the synergy of multiple resources. Additionally, many resource contributors, particularly the more knowledge-intense contributors, defy accurate measurement because they frequently change or are inherently different, or because the activity itself (for example, thinking) does not lend itself to precise measurement. Productivity measurement must be used carefully to minimize these effects. Often it is used in conjunction with other evaluations or to provide a baseline.

### *Activity-Based Costing*

The development of an activity-based costing (ABC) system assists in allocating overhead to specific cost bases, often defined as products or services. The conventional or traditional cost systems use direct material and labor consumed as the basis to factor overhead; they worked well as long as overhead activities were a small proportion of direct labor. However, because labor has been reduced by automation, overhead may now be several times the cost of direct labor. Thus, the use of direct labor as the primary apportioning mechanism can cause significant cost distortions and poor strategic decisions. ABC resolves this issue by identifying many more cost-allocation bases, including all operations resources. As such, the ABC approach is highly dependent upon accurate bills of material, routings, and work center data. The individual resource contributions are measured and aggregated in homogeneous cost pools, which are meaningful resource measures for management (Rhodes, 1992; Dhavale, 1992).

## *Methods of Work Measurement*

With these reservations, work measurement is widely and successfully used to manage production systems and to identify areas of productivity improvements. Since the time of Frederick W. Taylor, industrial engineers have used methods, time, and measurement (MTM) studies to evaluate and categorize every type of work activity. Initially they studied the methods, time, and motions of industrial operations to determine the best way to do the job and define time standards. More recently, MTM has been used to evaluate service delivery options, such as telephone service inquiries, fast-food and full-service restaurant responsiveness, bank teller transactions, and retail checkout counter operations.

Work measurement techniques initially evaluate worker motions and collect time data to determine the best way to do a job. Numerous rules have been developed to govern efficiency of motion. These rules are helpful in placing the tools, parts bins, and other items in a work area. The work area should be designed to minimize human motion and to reduce the amount of effort required. Table 12-3 gives ten commonly used principles of motion economy.

After positioning the items in the work station, several work iterations should be practiced to ensure that the worker is familiar with the motions and setup. A particular task is usually broken down into several sequential subactivities, called *work elements.* Further adjustment and practice may be necessary before a specified work element becomes accepted. The importance of fitting the work environment to the human and to the task is

**TABLE 12-3 Principles of Motion Economy**

1. The two hands should begin and complete their motions at the same time.
2. The two hands should not be idle at the same time except during rest periods.
3. Hand and lower arm movements are preferred to upper arm and shoulder movements.
4. Arm motions should be simultaneous and made in opposite or symmetric directions.
5. The hand should be relieved of work that can be done by a jig, fixture, or foot-operated device.
6. Smooth, continuous motions are preferable to zigzag or irregular motions.
7. Rhythm is essential to smooth, automatic performance.
8. Tools, materials, and controls should be located close to and directly in front of the operator.
9. Gravity feed bins and containers should be used to deliver materials to the point of use.
10. Materials and tools should be located to permit the best sequence of motions.

Reprinted by permission from *Production and Operations Management* by Fogarty, Hoffman and Stonebraker, 1989, Figure 10-3, p. 346.

directly related to performance, as the rapidly growing field of ergometrics suggests (Kroemer, 1993).

A time study measures the amount of time that each work element takes. For accuracy and convenience, the stop watches used in time studies often represent hundredths of a minute, rather than seconds. The continuous observation of several cycles of the task permits recording the continuous time for each work element. Subsequently, the individual times of each work element are obtained by a series of subtractions. The continuous method has been traditionally preferred because it minimizes the measurement inaccuracies due to resetting a mechanical watch. However, more recently produced electronic watches and computers overcome this difficulty.

Time studies require completion of several steps. The average time is first computed for each work element, then adjusted through normalizing and standardizing. Adjustment to normalize the time is required, because a particular operator may be better or worse than "normal." Though controversial, experienced MTM evaluators have developed and published, through video tapes, normal performance rates for many work activities. Further, the normalized time must be adjusted for allowances, such as fatigue, personal needs, and unavoidable delay—for example, due to unavailability of materials. Adjustment of the normal time for allowances, usually by between 10% and 20%, gives the "standard time." An example of work measurement is shown in Decision Model Box 12-1.

In addition to the assumption of performance rates and allowances, which are often negotiated with union or labor groups, the key to work measurement accuracy is that the method has "stabilized" with low task and work element variance. Of course, changes in the employee motions, work place design, or in the technology of the job all affect the work performance. Such changes, if they result in productivity improvement, should be encouraged; however, the cost of a failed innovative method is likely a drop in productivity. Management may have to encourage innovation through explicit incentives or guarantees against loss if the innovation does not succeed.

## DECISION MODEL BOX 12-1 Work Measurement at the Mid-Continental Bank

The Mid-Continental Bank wants to evaluate the times of several teller transactions. One task, the crediting of cash to an account, has been studied and a description of standard motions and five work elements has been developed. The bank's security camera film was used as a source of time data, because it is less intrusive or disruptive than a work measurement engineer with a stop watch. Continuous time data are observed for 10 complete cycles of work. The continuous data are adjusted to unit times through a series of subtractions. For example, the work element unit time of cycle 1, element 2 is 0.156 minute, computed as 0.408 – 0.252 = 0.156.

| Cycle Number | Work Element Continuous Times (min) | | | | | Cycle Number | Work Element Unit Times (min) | | | | |
|---|---|---|---|---|---|---|---|---|---|---|---|
| | 1 | 2 | 3 | 4 | 5 | | 1 | 2 | 3 | 4 | 5 |
| 1 | 0.252 | 0.408 | 0.591 | 0.690 | 0.808 | 1 | 0.252 | 0.156 | 0.183 | 0.099 | 0.118 |
| 2 | 1.049 | 1.214 | 1.386 | 1.488 | 1.601 | 2 | 0.241 | 0.165 | 0.172 | 0.102 | 0.113 |
| 3 | 1.854 | 2.016 | 2.191 | 2.296 | 2.415 | 3 | 0.253 | 0.162 | 0.175 | 0.105 | 0.119 |
| 4 | 2.655 | 2.813 | 2.990 | 3.090 | 3.204 | 4 | 0.240 | 0.158 | 0.177 | 0.100 | 0.114 |
| 5 | 3.449 | 3.610 | 3.788 | 3.889 | 4.006 | 5 | 0.245 | 0.161 | 0.178 | 0.101 | 0.117 |
| 6 | 4.253 | 4.412 | 4.594 | 4.694 | 4.809 | 6 | 0.247 | 0.159 | 0.182 | 0.100 | 0.115 |
| 7 | 5.060 | 5.217 | 5.394 | 5.498 | 5.614 | 7 | 0.251 | 0.157 | 0.177 | 0.104 | 0.116 |
| 8 | 5.860 | 6.018 | 6.197 | 6.299 | 6.416 | 8 | 0.246 | 0.158 | 0.179 | 0.102 | 0.117 |
| 9 | 6.660 | 6.819 | 7.000 | 7.103 | 7.216 | 9 | 0.244 | 0.159 | 0.181 | 0.103 | 0.113 |
| 10 | 7.466 | 7.626 | 7.806 | 7.906 | 8.021 | 10 | 0.250 | 0.160 | 0.180 | 0.100 | 0.115 |
| | | | | | | Avg. | 0.2469 | 0.1595 | 0.1784 | 0.1016 | 0.1157 |

The data then are adjusted for performance ratings and total allowances by using the formulas:

Normal time = average time × performance rate (a measured or bargained value)
Standard time = normal time × percent allowances (18% is assumed here)

The standard time is computed for both work elements and tasks. Because there may be some variances and possibly error in the measurement of each work element, the number of required cycles to observe for confidence in the stability of the data is computed. That evaluation uses the formula:

$$n = \frac{Z^2 S_x^2}{e^2}$$

where $Z$ = the standard score of the confidence interval (for example, 2 for 95%, 3 for 99%)
$S_x$ = the sample standard deviation for a small sample, the formula for which is

$$S_x = \sqrt{\frac{\Sigma(x_i - \bar{x})^2}{(n-1)}}$$

$e$ = the acceptable measurement error

*Continued*

**DECISION MODEL BOX 12-1** *Continued*

If the acceptable error in measuring task times is 0.003 minute (which is 0.18 second or about one-fifth of a second error for activities that average from 6 to 15 seconds) and the confidence interval is 99%, the necessary cycles to measure for this data are shown.

| Work Element | Average Time | Performance Rating | Normal Time | Standard Time | Standard Deviation | Necessary Cycles |
|---|---|---|---|---|---|---|
| 1 | 0.2469 | 0.95 | 0.2346 | 0.2768 | 0.0043 | 18.5 ≈ 19 |
| 2 | 0.1595 | 1.10 | 0.1755 | 0.2071 | 0.0025 | 6.3 ≈ 7 |
| 3 | 0.1784 | 1.00 | 0.1784 | 0.2105 | 0.0032 | 10.3 ≈ 11 |
| 4 | 0.1016 | 0.90 | 0.0914 | 0.1079 | 0.0019 | 3.6 ≈ 4 |
| 5 | 0.1157 | 1.05 | 0.1215 | 0.1434 | 0.0020 | 4.0 ≈ 4 |
| | | | | 0.9457 min = 63.445 tasks/hour | | |

The analyst would conclude that the task standard time is just less than one minute, or about 63 tasks per hour. Based on the 99% confidence level and the range of acceptable error of 0.003 minute, the work elements would require between 4 and 19 cycles of observations, as indicated. Because in this case the standard deviation of the work element unit times is small, other measures can be relatively tight ($Z = 3$; $e = 0.003$) and the necessary cycles to measure remains quite small. In fact, all elements except 1 and 3 would require less than the ten cycles already measured.

## *Relevance of the Learning Curve*

The learning curve measures the improvement in performance or productivity occurring over time. It may be used for evaluations of individual or group productivity improvement. If group performance is considered, cost measures are usually used, but if individual learning is considered, time measures are more common. The curve is based on the assumption that each time an operation is performed, the required time or cost decreases at a stable rate. When the number of units is doubled, the time or cost to produce one unit is reduced by 100 minus the learning rate. Experience or learning curves can be computed in many manufacturing or service environments for both individual or cumulative units produced. The curve is calculated by the following formula:

$$T_n = T_1 n^x$$

where

$T_n$ = the time required to produce the $n$th unit

$T_1$ = the time for the first unit

$n$ = the number of units produced

$$x = \frac{\text{natural log } L}{\text{natural log } 2}$$

$L$ = the learning rate (in decimal)

Tables (see Appendix on page 598) or computer programs may be used to get individual or cumulative unit times or resource costs. The learning rate ($L$) is initially calculated for the first several units. The measurement may be stated as the amount of time per unit or the number of units per period of time. For example, if the first unit time was 20 minutes and the time to produce the second unit was 18 minutes, the learning rate would be 18/20, or 90%. Alternatively, the improvement in units produced per day or week may be used. For example, the first-week (40 hours) production of 40 units and the fourth-week production of 62.5 units would be converted to per-unit-times, respectively, of 1 hour and 0.64 hour, which is an 80% ($1 \times 0.8 \times 0.8$) learning curve.

Commonly encountered learning rates are 75%, 80%, 85%, and 90%, where 75% means that when the number of units is doubled, the processing time of the later unit is 75% of that of the earlier unit. This, of course, is a faster learning rate than, for example, is 90%.

The learning curve is useful (1) to estimate production costs of custom jobs, (2) to assess the duration of the start-up stage for a new process, (3) to determine how long it will take to train or certify a new employee on a piece of equipment, and (4) to evaluate individual or organization productivity improvement over the long run. Improvements may be due to any of several factors, including the use of better methods, increased familiarity with work motions, more labor effort, and changes in the technology, such as the use of a mechanical assist. Motivational effects, such as might result from the presence of a study team, cannot be evaluated by using the learning curve method. Early studies cited by Hirschmann (1964) show stable improvement in learning rates in a variety of applications, including petroleum refining production, repetitive maintenance operations, construction of new units of heavy equipment, and in steel and electricity output. These studies consistently showed roughly the same rates over as much as 55 years. An example of the use of the learning curve is shown in Decision Model Box 12-2.

However, there are limitations of the learning curve. The most apparent limit is that the learning rate may change, either by leveling off or by toeing down, as a result of a change in the technology, work methods, incentives, or other resource inputs. Additionally, projecting the curve too far into the future may be very risky. If such future projections are necessary, conservative improvement rates might be selected, and regular reevaluation of the learning rates should be considered.

There is, however, another more subtle problem with the learning curve. Technology and innovation do not typically change at a constant rate. Rather, rates of change are often quite stable for long periods of time, then irregularly punctuated by significant technological developments. Additionally, if workers do not do a task for a period of time, they may forget and would be slower when they return to the task. Further, the learning curve may encourage a short-term perspective by rewarding ways to achieve minor improvements that ensure the accomplishment of limited improvement goals, but avoid the potentially risky and costly transitions to major new technologies. This perspective, elaborated by Abernathy and Wayne (1974) and Bell and Burnham (1989), can result in missing the chance to implement the periodic major improvements or technological innovations. The outcome is a likely decline in the technological innovation and long-term productivity and competitiveness.

Work measurement evaluates the fit of the individual with the physical activities of the task or, if the tasks are sequential and repetitive enough, a job. Work measurement

## DECISION MODEL BOX 12-2 The Learning Curve—Product and Process Costing at The Wadsworth Garage

The Wadsworth Garage has been asked to bid on a required farm implement modification. It is estimated that 100 units will be modified in the first year. Experience with similar jobs indicates that Wadsworth mechanics have a roughly 80% learning rate for the first 50 units; but for estimation purposes, the company assumes no further improvement. Engineers estimate that the first unit will take 30 hours. The bid should be based on labor costs of $24/hour, parts costs of $15 per unit, overhead of $10/unit, and a 10% profit margin.

The learning curve table (Appendix A) suggests that, with an 80% learning rate, the first 50 units will take 30 × 20.122 (the first unit time multiplied by the cumulative learning rate factor, a table value) or 604 hours, and that subsequent units will take 30 × 0.284 (the first unit time multiplied by the per-unit learning rate factor, a table value) or 8.520 hours each. Note that any learning rate may be evaluated by dividing the hours per unit for a designated period by the hours per unit for the first period and finding the table value for that designated period which most closely corresponds to the calculated value. Costing for the first 50 units is:

| Labor | | Materials | | Overhead | | Total | |
|---|---|---|---|---|---|---|---|
| 30 × 20.122 × $24 | | $15 × 50 | | $10 × 50 | | | |
| $14,487.84 | + | $750 | + | $500 | = | $15,737.84 | |
| | | | | | × 0.10 | 1,573.78 | margin |
| | | | | | | 17,311.62 | |

For each subsequent unit:

| Labor | | Materials | | Overhead | | Total | |
|---|---|---|---|---|---|---|---|
| 8.520 × $24 | | | | | | | |
| $204.48 | + | $15 | + | $10 | = | $229.48 | |
| | | | | | × 0.10 | 22.93 | margin |
| | | | | | | 252.41 | |

The unit and cumulative learning curves are given below.

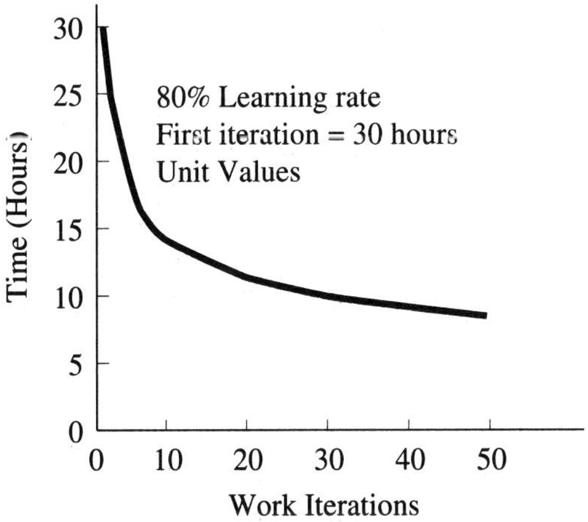


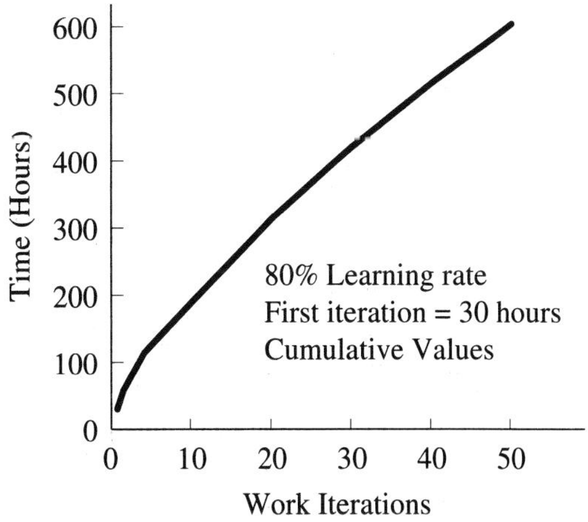


*Continued*

**DECISION MODEL BOX 12-2** *Continued*

Thus, the first year bid would be \$17,311.62 plus 50 times \$252.41 (which equals \$12,620.50), or \$29,932.12, which might be rounded to \$30,000.00. This bid may be rather risky because the labor, materials, and overhead costs may change, and also because the learning rate of this task may be slower than for previous tasks. There is little room for error, particularly considering that the bid for 100 units with an 85% learning curve would be \$38,796.30. You may want to check these computations yourself. (Table values for 85% per-unit and cumulative computations are 0.400 and 25.513, respectively.) Unless the environment is stable, projection of learning curve data more than several units or months into the future may be risky.

techniques are difficult to use with knowledge contributions and are best used after the task has stabilized—that is, after learning improvements have ceased, or have become relatively small. Learning curves measure the amount of improvement in job performance. Though some of these improvements may be caused by working harder or faster, most improvements, particularly over the long run, result from improved methods, technological assists, and knowledge contributions. This was also suggested by the 100-year productivity improvement data cited at the beginning of the chapter. These techniques are generally most accurate when used to evaluate individual or possibly small group productivity, though they can be used with care in applications with larger work teams, shifts, plants, and companies. Work measurement and learning curve analysis provide the initial baseline measures for productivity studies.

## *Job Design*

Job design efforts define and integrate the activities of an individual worker with those of other team members and with the rest of the organization. Though job design does focus on one job, or on a class of jobs, it is also concerned with identifying the source of all inputs to the job and the use of all outputs from the job. This information about the inputs and outputs of a job permits specification of the interactions required by the job with other jobs and functions.

### *Job Design Process*

Job design is a multistep process of assessing the work environment and the job, and then enumerating the specific knowledge, skills, abilities, effort, and working conditions required of the job. Subsequently, the hiring activities design a "rite of passage" to reinforce the person–organization fit. This process reaffirms the employment decision (Bowen et al., 1991). Concisely, job design is a consciously planned structuring of the work effort to define what task is accomplished, how it is accomplished, and with what standards, within the fabric of the organization. Though there are several ways to organize the job-design process, the following three sequential steps are often used:

*Assess the work environment*—the systematic collection, evaluation, and organization of information about the work environment and activities of a job. This job analysis process uses questionnaires, interviews, and standardized information formats to gather and initially structure work environment and job data.

*Infer the type of employee required*—the concise definition of the responsibilities, duties, and working conditions of a job. This job description document is often the formal part of the employment contract; it defines the individual performances and interactions that are required and may be used for recruitment, performance appraisal, and, if necessary, disciplinary actions.

*Specify the individual job*—the further specification of the demands of a job, in terms of knowledge, skills, abilities, effort, working conditions, and other factors. Job specifications may be used to supplement job descriptions for very specialized jobs or for training or reinforcement purposes.

Some organizations ask newly hired employees to write or rewrite their own job descriptions, a technique which ensures that the employee is familiar with the job requirements and facilitates internalization of those requirements, but gives an employee the opportunity to suggest innovative ways to perform the job. Historically, over much of the past 200 years, jobs have become increasingly specialized; however, several recent developments suggest a reversal of that direction. The historical growth of specialization in job design is shown by Figure 12-4.

Early production was very generalized. That is, a worker did all or most of the tasks required to produce a finished good. That same worker also performed the distribution and retailing functions. Adam Smith may have been the first to formally identify the benefits

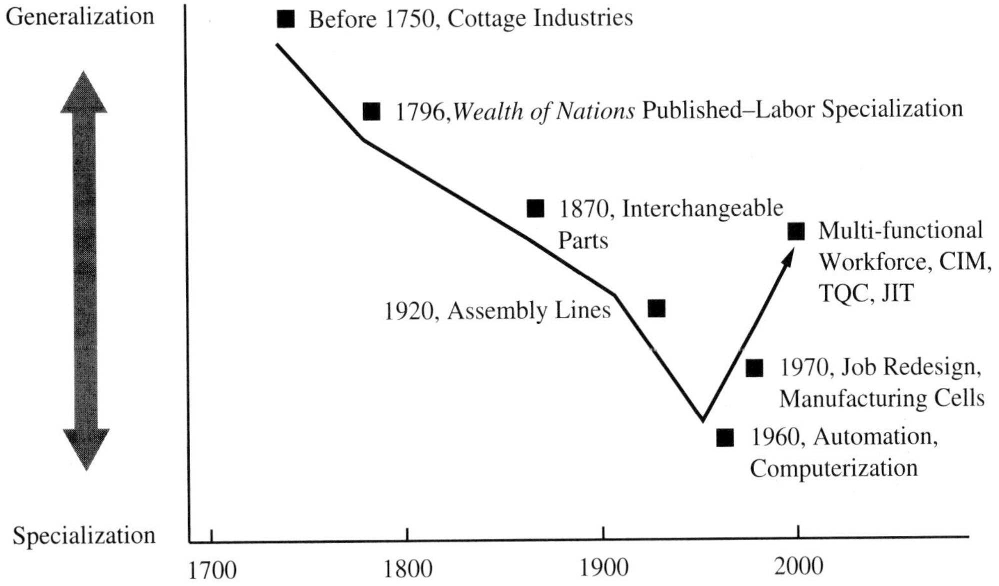


**FIGURE 12-4 A Historical Perspective of Job Specialization**

of labor specialization in the *Wealth of Nations.* Work became increasingly specialized as the efficiencies of standardized parts and standardized assembly processes became apparent. With job redefinition, the work contribution of an individual to the total product became smaller and more specialized. Mechanized and power assists to production, work automation, and early computerization furthered this trend toward specialization; however, automation and computerization also permit redesigning jobs toward more generalized skills. Computer-integrated manufacturing systems and distributed information systems define a greater range of individual tasks required for a job and more generalized labor contribution. The emergence of JIT, CIM, TQC, and the multifunctional work force suggests that this trend will continue, if not increase.

### Generalization Versus Specialization

There are likely limits to the amount of specialization that labor can tolerate. Job redesign was suggested in the late 1950s as a way to enrich the breadth and depth of the content of the job, thus increasing the scope of a specialist's activities. It was seen as a way of countering the increasing boredom and more serious symptoms of labor resistance to faster job cycles and increasingly specialized, repetitive jobs. Application Box 12-2 describes job redesign efforts at Volvo.

There are advantages of both specialization and generalization. Advantages of specialization include increased productivity due to repetition, lower skill requirements and thus lower wage costs, and simpler management processes due to routinization. Labor issues in such an environment would be likely to be simpler to define. However, the disadvantages of greater specialization include employee dissatisfaction, the boredom of repetitive work cycles, and the corresponding higher levels of absenteeism, tardyism, and turnover. Higher grievance rates and low-quality work due to lower employee incentives, motivation, and accountability, and less operations flexibility due to more narrowly defined jobs would likely also result. These disadvantages of specialization correspond to the advantages of more generalized jobs.

These pure job-design strategies identify a range of job-redesign options, but the actual strategy would likely be some combination of specialization and generalization. One approach is to design the job to fit the needs of the work force, as Volvo has attempted at Uddevalla and Kalmar. The alternative strategy is to reassert the engineering and scientific management goals of fitting people to the job. Redesigning the job to fit employee needs tends toward the employee-centered involvement style noted in Figure 12-1; fitting the people to the job more closely corresponds to the boss-centered direction style in that figure. Many compromise alternatives have been developed, including the Saturn plant work teams. In each environment, in each job and task, and with each employee, the management function is to get the best fit of job requirements, employee needs, and management style. This fit is the basis for an ongoing discourse between management and labor.

## Job Redesign for Quality of Work Life

Quality of work life (QWL) programs were developed in the 1970s as a systems approach to job redesign. QWL was expected to integrate various individual, structural, environ-

## APPLICATION BOX 12-2 Work Teams at Volvo: An Experiment That Failed

In August 1988, Volvo began manufacturing cars with a humanistic approach at its plant in Uddevalla, Sweden. This was Volvo's second redesigned manufacturing plant. The Kalmar plant was redesigned in the late 1970s to build trucks and some sedan models. Volvo was the first large-scale manufacturer to abolish the assembly line from its production process and to shape its factory jobs to be more generalized and team-oriented. At Uddevalla the team of workers spent an average of two to three hours building a car. This is drastically different from the traditional assembly-line environment, where specialization of jobs drives each worker to repeat the same task throughout an eight-hour shift and spend between thirty seconds and three minutes on each passing car.

Plagued by the highest turnover and absenteeism rates of the developed nations, Volvo executives envisioned that by encouraging Swedish workers to increase their range of skills and thus giving them more control over their jobs, working in a car manufacturing factory would become less monotonous and more personally rewarding. This generalization of jobs would result in increased productivity due to satisfaction and less absenteeism, tardiness, and turnover. The team approach necessitated the elimination of many of the middle management and supervisor jobs, plus the installation of revolutionary materials-handling methods.

The Uddevalla facility consists of two complexes with three small assembly plants, which are connected by an L-shaped building. Painted car bodies and parts are carried on an electric transporter through the L-shaped structure, where the larger components, such as exhaust systems, fuel tanks, and axles are assembled. The 650 to 700 required car parts are transported to the assembly teams by other electric carriers. In the middle of each complex, a shared area exists for the three small assembly plants to test assembled cars. The last stop before distribution is the L-shaped building, where the paint receives a final inspection, and rust protection and grease are added.

A total of eight teams, consisting of eight to ten highly skilled workers, work in each of the six assembly areas. With three or less people working on a car, each team builds four cars at one time. The 48 teams were expected to manufacture 40,000 cars per year. However, because the factory has used only 35 assembly teams and those teams took longer than expected to develop their individual production pattern, the 1990 production total was a mere 16,100 cars.

Volvo's executives have claimed that the quality of work life at Uddevalla has been augmented and the plant's 900 workers seem more content. Unfortunately, dismal productivity levels have caused top management to periodically reevaluate the team approach. For the first time in a decade, in 1990, Volvo's car division posted a loss; further losses occurred in 1991 and for 1992. In late 1992, Volvo president Sören Gyll announced that the company will close the Kalmar and Uddevalla plants. Even though some advantages of generalized job tasks have been evident, the company cannot be successful in the long term with factories that are not competitive. Unfortunately, the Kalmar and Uddevalla plants may be regarded by management historians as interesting but unprofitable social experiments. It appears that there are limits to the amount that a production process can be adjusted.

It is interesting to note that the General Motors Spring Hill Saturn Plant has retained the moving assembly line, but has incorporated a variety of team and group tasks. Clearly, the interaction of teams in monotonous task situations reduces boredom and improves productivity. The production process, however, also must be economic. Companies are expected to continue to search for the combination of human resources and technology that best facilitate profitable labor.

Materials drawn from Steven Prokesch, "Kinder, Gentler Plant a Failure," *Chicago Tribune,* July 14, 1991, p. 5, and from Richard A. Melcher, "Volvo and Renault: Marriage May Be the Only Answer," *Business Week,* November 23, 1992, p. 50–52.

mental, and technology factors in the job-redesign process. These programs go by a variety of names, including employee involvement, participative management, and team building. QWL can be more concisely defined as "processes by which an organization attempts to unlock the creative potential of its people by involving them in discussions affecting their work lives" (Guest, 1979).

## *Components of Quality of Work Life Programs*

This very general definition reflects the highly individualized nature of QWL programs; each of the thousands of successful programs have been situationally defined. Though there is no set formula for a QWL program, the following characteristics are commonly encountered.

**Job Redesign and Participative Management.** Job-redesign initiatives often define jobs toward more general tasks and greater participation in the decision-making processes of the job. Job redesign enhances the perceived job freedom and potentially increases involvement and internalization of job functions and tasks by employees. Decisions about how to do the job are done by those who, because they are closest to the situation, are best able to make the decision. This can be a positive motivator and, with appropriate work force training, can reduce one or several layers of management. Greater participation in the decision-making processes, however, ensures greater inherent employee training and commitment.

**Innovative Rewards and Compensation Structures.** Innovative rewards and compensation structures may be designed to more directly measure productivity and identify and reward contributions to productivity and overall firm performance. Individual and group incentive plans quickly emerged after work activities were shown to be measurable in the 1920s and 1930s. Initial methods tied productivity to pay through sometimes complex mechanical formulations. More recent plans have included cafeteria benefits programs and flexible work schedules. Lincoln Electric, an excellent example of the productivity effects of gain-sharing methods, incorporates peer evaluation to define the proportion of the annual bonus received by each employee. Lincoln Electric has survived for more than 60 years, partly because of the effectiveness of its gains-sharing plan, which pays more in annual productivity bonuses than in annual salaries (Hillinger, 1983).

**Enhancing a Climate of Workplace Democracy.** The mechanisms of workplace democracy include employee ownership, employee stock ownership plans, worker self-management, and participative or empowered work environments. Stock ownership plans have been quite successful, with participation ranging from 15% to 35% of the outstanding stock ("Labor's Voice . . . ," 1984). However, worker self-management efforts have been resisted due to the feeling that employee groups are not able to manage themselves. Participative theory Z (Ouchi, 1981) work environments, because they facilitate trust and consensual, participative decision-making, have been widely sponsored, though they may give more aura of participation than substance. Certainly, QWL programs, however defined, have the potential to be major contributors to productivity improvement efforts, but such efforts must be carefully planned to achieve consistency and fit of the worker with the job, and by extension, with the environment.

### *Developing a Productivity Improvement Program*

Clearly, productivity improvement is a multifaceted, difficult-to-measure, and continuous management task. Most managers would concur with Vaughn Beals' statement, quoted earlier, that productivity measurement "is a total frustration." Because of the vagueness and difficulty of measurement, the dynamics of the variables involved, and the continuous and cyclic nature of the process, most managers regard models of productivity with well-deserved skepticism. Yet, simultaneously, the skeptics are not able to offer reasonable alternatives, and at the end of the month, quarter, or year, management must be able to show measured improvement relative to prior performance or relative to the competition. Thus, productivity measurement is accepted for corporations or plants because performance must be measured, if only to avoid surprises and to permit early planning of necessary corrective actions. Additionally, performance measures must be tied to strategic objectives. Perhaps the best approach is to develop the most inclusive, interactive, and accurate measure possible, and then to recognize and understand its limits. The productivity paradigm, shown in Figure 12-5, reflects these limitations of productivity models. The paradigm shows a general model of the interaction of some of the more recognized contributing variables to productivity in a continuous improvement cycle.

Six general factors are depicted, each with several subfactors. The diagram moves from smaller-scale individual factors at the top to broader-scale corporate and external factors at the bottom. Though an effort has been made toward succinctness and to avoid elaboration and duplication, certainly other factors and subfactors could be included, particularly in specific applications. Productivity results from the synergy of all factors and most, if not all, subfactors. That is, each factor simultaneously makes a contribution which, when grouped with the others, achieves its effect. Correspondingly, the failure of any factor, such as the reward or material use, will very quickly, though often subtly, result in a decline of overall productivity. The productivity paradigm is related to the productivity formula and the input–transformation–output motif, because each of the factors is an input to the transformation process. This representation emphasizes both the central contribution of people to productivity and the simultaneous contribution of other factors. Productivity management necessitates regular vigilance over all input resources. As Davis (1991) notes, the main reasons for productivity improvement failure ultimately can be ascribed to ineffective integration of people and knowledge.

## *Summary*

Productivity is about transforming inputs into outputs; in the process, value is added to those outputs. Productivity may be evaluated by any of several measures of output divided by inputs, though such measures must be used carefully. Because people are direct contributors through labor to productivity, and indirect contributors to capital, materials,

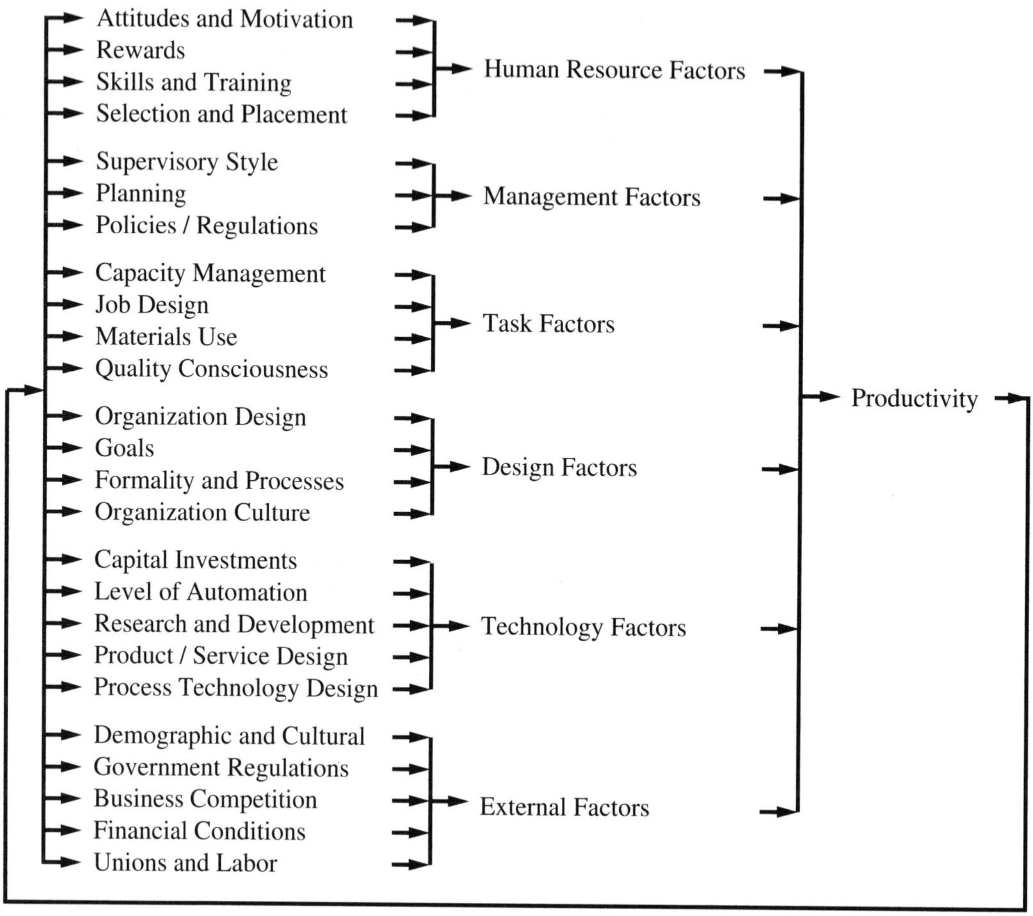


**FIGURE 12-5 The Productivity Paradigm**

knowledge, and other resources, people are the most important contributors to productivity and to new sources of added value. As labor has become increasingly specialized over the past 200 or more years, management has increasingly moved toward a style of empowerment, a technique that encourages innovation.

Productivity ultimately must be viewed as a system; the manipulation of one variable will likely have little effect, unless accompanied by corresponding changes in other variables. This is the productivity paradox (Skinner, 1986). Because of the synergistic nature of operations processes and productivity improvement, management efforts should not be directed toward squeezing more work out of labor, but rather toward total system improvement and fit. Work measurement and productivity improvement due to worker and team experience are described, and the limitations of these methods are noted. Job design and redesign methods can make a contribution to productivity, but even those techniques are probably best used as part of a QWL program.

The productivity paradigm summarizes the dilemma by representing some of the variables that can be incorporated in a specific productivity improvement program, the interactivity and synergy of those variables, and the iterativeness of productivity efforts. Though technology, capital, and external factors all contribute to productivity, ultimately, as noted in the introductory quote, "People are the catalysts that stimulate new productivity."

## Discussion Questions

1. From your work experiences, give examples of management, labor, and/or capital methods used to increase productivity.
2. Productivity equals production outcome divided by resources consumed. Give several examples of each component.
3. Briefly describe how the information organization has replaced the industrial organization by relating this transformation to a business familiar to you.
4. Identify and describe an organization that consists primarily of diverse specialists. Then give the four management problems which, according to Drucker, are inherent in such organizations and apply those ideas to the organization that you have selected.
5. How does productivity fit into the rationale for economies of scale and scope?
6. Explain why the transformation stage of the input–output model must be a value-added process.
7. What is the significance of the input–output model of the firm?
8. From your work experiences, briefly describe a job that applies some or all of the principles of motion economy.
9. What can the learning curve accomplish in service management organizations?
10. Why is it risky to project the learning curve more than several units or months into the future?
11. List and define the three sequential steps of the job-design process.
12. Identify the advantages of specialization versus generalization.
13. From your own experiences or readings, describe a quality of work life program.
14. List and briefly describe the six general factors included in the productivity paradigm. Describe a specific work situation and relate the six factors to productivity in that situation.

## Strategic Decision Situations

1. The Riverside Campus of Central State University has been required to reorganize due to budget cuts. The dean of the College of Arts and Sciences must manage the reduction of the

number of departments from 13 to eight. Several departments are very small; thus, the consolidation would reduce overhead (department chair positions). But the dean expects resistance from the faculty, many of whom are tenured. The dean also desires to use the normal events in the university calendar as driving forces to implement the change. Identify the restraining and driving forces and relate those forces to the university calendar.

2. The Global Health Care Corporation manufactures surgical instruments and packages them in kits that are designed for specific types of operations. For disease prevention and sterilization reasons, the kits are disposable, even though some components could be sterilized and reused. The Deerfield Surgical Instrument Manufacturing Facility produces most of the nonplastic components (primarily some form of blade or scissor) for such kits. To improve efficiency, a major portion of the facility will be redesigned from a line process to a U-shaped work center design. Previous work measurement of the line found that for 60 work elements (one for each employee on the line), the production time was 0.52 minute per instrument, with minor variations in time due to different instrument configurations. The facility was able to produce roughly 500 instruments per day. In prototype demonstrations, the production manager showed the following times for five consolidated work elements of the U-shaped facility. The plant manager is considering the use of either three or four such five-person U-shaped production centers. If 18% total allowances are used, and the performance rating for all activities is 1.05, and the acceptable error is 0.005 minute (0.3 second), with a 95% confidence interval, evaluate the U-shaped design in the following ways:

**a.** Advise the production manager on the number of U-shaped cells that should be designed.

| Cycle Number | Work Element—Continuous Times (min) | | | | |
|---|---|---|---|---|---|
| | 1 | 2 | 3 | 4 | 5 |
| 1 | 1.235 | 1.681 | 2.406 | 2.639 | 3.454 |
| 2 | 4.723 | 4.953 | 5.501 | 5.855 | 6.210 |
| 3 | 7.589 | 8.255 | 8.862 | 8.964 | 9.672 |
| 4 | 10.649 | 11.382 | 11.978 | 12.151 | 12.802 |
| 5 | 14.004 | 14.692 | 15.462 | 15.562 | 15.881 |
| 6 | 17.458 | 17.742 | 18.473 | 18.543 | 19.205 |
| 7 | 20.273 | 21.098 | 21.704 | 22.156 | 22.563 |
| 8 | 23.635 | 24.258 | 24.872 | 25.225 | 25.987 |
| 9 | 27.469 | 27.586 | 28.394 | 28.909 | 29.200 |
| 10 | 30.505 | 30.873 | 31.713 | 32.382 | 33.303 |

**b.** The corporate vice president of operations, a rather traditionally oriented manufacturing type, has expressed concern over the potential ramifications of this redesign. Provide comments that will place this action in perspective.

3. The Triquest Development Corporation plans to build a meat processing plant in the Tver Valley of the Russian Republic (roughly 100 miles northwest of Moscow). Local stock will be improved by the import of chickens, pigs, and heifers from the American heartland, and three separate slaughterhouse operations will be designed in one factory based on American models. Plans call for the plant to be built in the spring of 1995 and for operations to begin in August. Technology will be improved and training upgraded regularly, and distribution will be accomplished through privatized stores and Russian Orthodox Church charities. The following average daily production per week is expected during initial start-up.

| Stock | Number of Employees | Week 1 | 2 | 3 | 4 |
|---|---|---|---|---|---|
| Chickens | 10 | 500 | 650 | 750 | 800 |
| Pigs | 10 | 100 | 130 | 150 | 200 |
| Heifers | 10 | 50 | 70 | 80 | 90 |

*Hint:* the data are most useful for learning curve analysis if they are converted to hours per unit of production per employee, and learning is considered from work to work.

**a.** Calculate the learning rates for chickens, pigs, and heifers.

**b.** Use learning curve analysis to project the daily production of the plant per week (assume 40 hours per week) in each commodity for the eighth week (end of November), sixteenth week (mid-January), and thirty-second week (early May).

**c.** Discuss some of the limitations of this analysis.

## *References*


Abernathy, William J., and Kenneth Wayne. "Limits of the Learning Curve," *Harvard Business Review.* September–October 1974.

Albin, Peter S. "Job Design, Control Technology, and Technical Change," *Journal of Economic Issues.* September 1985, pp. 703–730.

Andrew, Charles G. "Motivation in Manufacturing," *Production and Inventory Management.* April–June 1986, pp. 133–142.

Bell, Daniel. *Toward the Year 2000, Work in Progress.* Boston, Mass.: Beacon Press, 1969.

Bell, Robert R., and John M. Burnham. "The Paradox of Manufacturing Productivity and Innovation," *Business Horizons.* September–October 1989, pp. 58–64.

Bowen, David E., Gerald E. Ledford, Jr., and Barry R. Nathan. "Hiring for the Organization, Not the Job," *The Executive.* Vol. 5, No. 4, 1991, pp. 35–51.

Buffa, Elwood S. "Meeting the Competitive Challenge with Manufacturing Strategy," *National Productivity Review.* Spring 1985, pp. 155–169.

Byrne, John A. "The Horizontal Corporation," *Business Week.* December 20, 1993, pp. 76–81.

Cappelli, Peter. "The Changing Face of Labor–Management Relations," *Management Review.* March 1986, pp. 28–30.

Chakravarthy, Balaji S. "Measuring Strategic Performance," *Strategic Management Journal.* Vol. 7, No. 5, 1986, pp. 437–458.

Davis, Tim R. V. "Information Technology and White Collar Productivity," *The Executive.* Vol. 5, No. 1, 1991, pp. 55–68.

Deets, Norman, and Richard Morano. "Xerox's Strategy for Changing Management Styles," *Management Review.* March 1986, pp. 31–35.

Dhavale, Dileep. "Activity-Based Costing in Cellular Manufacturing Systems," *Industrial Engineering.* February 1992, pp. 44–46.

Drucker, Peter F. "The Coming of the New Organization," *Harvard Business Review.* January–February 1988, p. 45.

Drucker, Peter F. *The New Realities: In Government and Politics/in Economics and Business/in Society and World View.* New York: Harper and Row, Publishers, 1989.

Drucker, Peter F. "There's More Than One Kind of Team," *Wall Street Journal.* February 11, 1992.

Ellis, James E., and Bruce Einhorn. "Gone Is My Co-Pilot?" *Business Week.* July 6, 1992, pp. 71–72.

Fogarty, Donald W., Thomas R. Hoffmann, and Peter W. Stonebraker. *Production and Operations Management.* Cincinnati, Ohio: South-Western Publishing Co., 1989.

Guest, Robert H. "Quality of Work Life—Learning from Tarrytown," *Harvard Business Review.* July–August 1979, pp. 76–77.

Hall, Robert W. "Empowerment: The 1990s Manufacturing Enterprise," *APICS—The Performance Advantage.* July 1991, p. 26.

Hayes, Robert H., and Steven C. Wheelwright. *Restoring Our Competitive Edge: Competing Through Manufacturing.* New York: John Wiley and Sons, 1984.

Heizer, Jay, and Barry Render. *Production and Operations Management.* Boston, Mass.: Allyn and Bacon, 1991.

Hillinger, Charles. "Big Bonuses at Lincoln Electric Get Big Results," *Professional Trainer.* Winter 1983, p. 1.

Jaques, Elliot. "In Praise of Hierarchy," *Harvard Business Review.* January–February 1990, pp. 127–133.

Kiernan, Matthew J. "The New Strategic Architecture: Learning to Compete in the Twenty-first Century," *Academy of Management Executive.* Vol. 7, No. 1, 1993, pp. 7–21.

Kroemer, K. E. H. "Fitting the Workplace to the Human and Not Vice Versa," *Industrial Engineering.* Vol. 25, No. 3, March 1993, pp. 56–62.

"Labor's Voice on Corporate Boards: Good or Bad?" *Business Week.* May 7, 1984, pp. 151–153.

Lewin, Kurt. *Field Theory in Social Science: Selected Theoretical Papers.* New York: Harper and Brothers, 1951.

Lynch, David J. "Turbulence Dogs Douglas Overhaul," *Chicago Tribune.* September 9, 1991, Section 4, p. 1.

McGregor, Douglas. *The Human Side of Enterprise.* New York: McGraw-Hill, 1960.

Melcher, Richard A. "Volvo and Renault: Marriage May Be the Only Answer," *Business Week.* November 23, 1992, pp. 50–52.

Michel, John G., and Donald C. Hambrick. "Diversification Posture and Top Management Team Characteristics," *The Academy of Management Journal.* Vol. 35, No. 1, 1992, pp. 9–37.

Naisbitt, John. *Megatrends.* New York: Warner Books, 1982.

Ouchi, William. *Theory Z: How American Business Can Meet the Japanese Challenge.* Reading, Mass.: Addison-Wesley, 1981.

Prokesch, Steven. "Kinder, Gentler Plant a Failure," *Chicago Tribune.* July 14, 1991, p. 5.

Rhodes, Philip. "Activity-Based Costing," *APICS—The Performance Advantage.* August 1992, pp. 29–31.

Ruch, William A., and James C. Hershauer. *Factors Affecting Worker Productivity.* Tempe, Arizona: Bureau of Business and Economic Research, Arizona State University, 1974.

Schein, Edgar H. *Organizational Psychology,* 3rd ed. Englewood Cliffs, N.J.: Prentice Hall, 1980.

Skinner, Wickham. "The Anachronistic Factory," *Harvard Business Review.* January–February 1971, pp. 61–70.

Skinner, Wickham. "The Productivity Paradox," *Management Review.* September 1986.

Stonebraker, Peter W. *Exercises and Problems in Human Resource Management: Using the Microcomputer.* New York: McGraw-Hill, 1989.

Toffler, Alvin. *Future Shock.* New York: Bantam, 1971.

Vora, Jay A. "Productivity and Performance Measures: Who Uses Them?" *Production and Inventory Management Journal.* January–March 1992, pp. 46–49.

Werther, William B., William A. Ruch, and Lynne McClure. *Productivity Through People.* St. Paul, Minn.: West Publishing Co., 1986.

Wiersema, Margarethe F., and Karen A. Bantel. "Top Management Team Demography and Corporate Strategic Change," *The Academy of Management Journal.* Vol. 35, No. 1, 1992, pp. 91–121.

Willis, Rod. "Harley Davidson Comes Roaring Back," *Management Review.* March 1986, p. 20.

# Case 5

# Motorola—In Pursuit of Six Sigma[1] Quality

## *Introduction*

Motorola,* the mammoth electronics manufacturer based in Schaumburg, Illinois, was founded in 1928 with an investment of $500 to make battery eliminators for household radios. Originally named the Galvin Manufacturing Corporation, after founder Paul Galvin, the company stumbled upon a new name when it began to produce car radios. The term "motor" was followed by "-ola" which is a "formative of no precise significance found in a variety of commercial coinages." When Mr. Galvin died in 1959, his son Robert stepped into the senior leadership position as CEO of the company. By this time, Motorola had transformed itself from a car radio manufacturer to a television manufacturer and to a prominent position in military and commercial communications. Motorola was also successfully operating its first production facility for semiconductors.

As part of his long-term strategy for Motorola, Robert Galvin directed the company away from consumer electronics in the 1960s and toward high-technology and international markets. It was also during this decade that he learned the importance of anticipating future markets. Motorola's competition, Texas Instruments, committed heavily to the development of the transistor in the 1960s, while Motorola merely thought about transistors. The results were catastrophic, and Robert Galvin vowed never to forget the lesson. He has developed registries at Motorola for "anticipations and commitments."

As a result of such lessons, Motorola was in serious trouble by the early 1980s. Foreign competition, primarily Japan's Toshiba and NEC, had knocked Motorola out of the global markets in color televisions and car radios. Additionally, Motorola was losing sales in its pager and cellular phone markets. Such disappointing results were mainly

[1]Six sigma is a measure of excellent quality.

*This case is prepared as a basis for class discussion, rather than to illustrate either effective or ineffective management of an operational situation.

attributed to Motorola's decreasing level of customer satisfaction and poor product quality. The direct link between satisfaction and quality did not take long to surface. Finally, at a corporate officers meeting in 1981, the manager of the best performing division at Motorola—two-way radios—exclaimed to the rest, "Our quality levels really stink!" That was the point of no return.

Several Motorola executives visited numerous factories worldwide. They found that the Japanese had plants with quality performance 500 to 1000 times better than Motorola, only one to two defective parts per million. Robert Galvin then decided it was time for Motorola to commit itself to being more responsive to customers and to improving the quality of its products and services. But that was not all. Galvin directed that all functional areas at Motorola achieve six sigma quality by 1992, effectively eliminating defects.

## *Six Sigma Quality*

The six sigma idea began in 1981, when Robert Galvin challenged the Schaumburg Communications Sector to attempt a tenfold improvement in quality within five years. The response was so positive that in 1986 Galvin set an even more ambitious goal—a tenfold improvement in all functional areas at Motorola by 1989, at least a 100-fold improvement by 1991, and the six sigma capability by 1992. Although the communications sector achieved the tenfold improvement during the period 1981–1986, expanding the quality program to encompass the entire company and thus tens of thousands of people posed many new challenges. What did Motorola do? Basically, they saturated the company through what Richard Buetow, vice president–director of quality, characterized as "a brilliantly orchestrated campaign of brainwashing and arm-twisting." In 1987, the company spent $25 million on a companywide crusade that included video tapes, Six Sigma posters visible throughout every building, and an "Understanding Six Sigma" training course customized for each Motorola division. With training costs included, total program costs approached $44 million.

Upper management pumped up the pressure in 1988 for employees to eat, sleep, and breathe Six Sigma. A "quality day" was held at all Motorola locations around the world (a total of 54) and memorandums on quality were disseminated from the CEO's office almost every week. Further, new employees were forced to meet stringent quality standards within a 90-day probation period or their jobs were placed in jeopardy. All of this was part of Motorola's "top-down commitment" which was required to maintain the level of intensity and leadership necessary to convince employees to not accept errors as a way of life.

The word *sigma* is a statistical term meaning standard deviation; it describes how far the output of a process varies from its average value in both a positive and negative direction. Thus, it is a statistical measure of variability around an average. In a normal distribution, represented by the bell-shaped curve, the values falling within one standard deviation (that is, one sigma) of the mean, or average value, include 68.26% of the total. When you move out to three sigma on either side, about 99.73% of the total values is included, and four sigma represents approximately 99.9937%.

The relationship between sigma and the quality of a manufacturing process is that standard deviation can be used to express the number of defects expected in work produced by a process. A one-sigma process would produce 32% defects and a three-sigma process would produce 0.27% defects, or 2 defects per thousand. Since six sigma encompasses 99.9999998% of the total, a six-sigma process would produce only 0.0000002% defects, or two defects in a billion.

However, the output of the manufacturing process generally varies around the process mean. The mean itself may shift as much as ±1.5 standard deviations. In the case of a four-sigma process, the normal variation around the process mean plus a +1.5 sigma shift in the process mean would result in the manufacturing process producing 6210 defects per million operations. A five-sigma process with such a shift would result in 233 defects per million. However, a six-sigma process with a ±1.5 sigma shift in the process mean would result in only 3.4 defects per million operations, or virtually defect free. This is why Motorola chose six sigma as its quality measurement goal.

These values are based on quality levels of single components. When a finished product contains more than one component, the joint probabilities of defects must be considered. That is commonly called the "rolled-throughout" yield, or the probability that all components and processes involved in manufacturing are defect free. With a six-sigma process, the probability of building products without requiring repairs during manufacturing, based on the number of parts in the product, is as follows:

1 part – 99.99966%
10 parts – 99.9976%
100 parts – 99.966%
1000 parts – 99.661%
3000 parts – 98.985%

An interesting comparison exists between six sigma and five sigma for products with 1000 and 3000 parts. As previously shown, a six-sigma process would yield a defect-free percentage of 99.661% and 98.985% at the 1000- and 3000-part levels, respectively. However, a five-sigma process with the same number of parts would produce only 79.24% and 50.15% defect-free products. When a company in such highly technical businesses as semiconductors for missile guidance systems, cellular telephones, and pagers strives for "total customer satisfaction," if it settled for five-sigma quality there would be many dissatisfied customers.

Six sigma cannot be achieved without efforts outside of the production area. Five additional specific initiatives are being pursued at Motorola in support of the six-sigma program.

- An effort to be an international leader in cycle time management, starting with product design and going through to customer delivery
- Manufacturing and technological leadership in all product sectors
- Participatory management within all its groups around the world
- Cooperative management across departmental and divisional lines
- Profit improvement, which Motorola expects as a result of all of the above

## The Baldrige Award

The Malcolm Baldrige National Quality Award was created by Congress in 1987 in order to recognize outstanding quality achievements by U.S. companies in manufacturing, service, and small business categories. Up to two awards may be given annually in each of the three categories. The awards are administered by the Department of Commerce, the American Society for Quality Control, and the American Productivity and Quality Center. The award is named for Malcolm Baldrige, who was Secretary of Commerce in 1987, when he died after a rodeo accident. Applicants for the award are evaluated by a board of experts from industry, professional and trade organizations, and universities. Site visits are conducted for finalists, and recommendations are made to a panel of judges for a final decision.

Criteria for the awards are as follows:

1. *Leadership.* Senior executive involvement in quality and their role in instilling quality, managing quality, and carrying out public responsibility.
2. *Information and analysis.* The scope, analysis, and management of quality data and the ability to effectively use competitive comparisons and benchmarks.
3. *Strategic quality planning.* Managing the strategic quality planning process, including the establishment of quality goals and plans.
4. *Human resource utilization.* Managing human resources toward quality goals, including employee involvement, training, recognition, performance measurement, and morale.
5. *Quality assurance of products and services.* Designing and managing a continuous improvement program for assuring high quality levels in materials, processes, and support functions.
6. *Quality results.* The actual results of quality performance in products, processes, support services, and suppliers.
7. *Customer satisfaction.* Ensuring high customer satisfaction through determining customer requirements, setting customer service standards, verifying customer satisfaction results, and displaying a true commitment to the customer.

Considering the firms that have won the award, Motorola is a member of a rather select group. The winners in 1988, the first year that the award was given, were Globe Metallurgical, Inc.; Westinghouse Electric Corporation's Commercial Nuclear Fuel Division; and Motorola, Inc. In 1989, Xerox Corporation's Business Products and Systems and Milliken Company won the coveted award. Four winners were named in 1990: the Cadillac Division of General Motors; IBM; Federal Express; and Wallace Company, Inc. The 1991 Baldrige Award winners were Solectron Corporation, Zytec Corporation, and Marlow Industries Inc. The six-sigma program contributed significantly to Motorola's distinction as the first-year winner in the manufacturing sector.

One of the axioms of quality, "It is learned best by example," is stringently followed at Motorola as top management sends powerful messages throughout the company by teaching the principles, answering questions, and demonstrating the desired behaviors. One such message is sent from the managers' carrying printed business-size cards in their pockets with the company's ultimate objective: "Total Customer Satisfaction." In addition, top management and business managers wear pagers to ensure that they are constantly available when a customer calls. Plus, customers are visited regularly so that the pros and cons of Motorola's overall performance can be evaluated. Further, the company's ex-chairman and current chairman of the executive committee, Robert Galvin, has been providing leadership by making quality the number one item on board meeting agendas and thus prioritizing it even above the company's financial matters. Robert Galvin is Motorola's missionary for quality, creating an aura similar to that of a crusade.

Managing change is rarely an easy task, and Motorola is no exception to this rule. Of particular importance is handling the problem of complacency. Richard Buetow, previously an engineer in the company's communications sector and appointed vice president–director of quality, inherited the responsibility of prioritizing the company's quest for excellence. Mr. Buetow has directed a three-part training program for Motorola employees. The emphases—top management commitment, training in quality, and measuring quality through audits—have become bywords of the corporation.

By counseling management on how to develop the company concept of being virtually perfect, they are better capable of leading by knowing where to create initiatives and emphasis for employees.

The teaching component is completed at Motorola University, where every employee undergoes at least 40 hours of training annually. This step is essential to the process of managing change, because it makes certain that everyone receives the same message.

The established policies and goals are analyzed during the auditing function; it must be ascertained that commitment exists from the top and is filtered down throughout the organization. At Motorola, such commitment to the company's goal of virtual perfection is highly prevalent, and senior managers from each plant meet eight times a year to review the quest for six sigma.

Motorola has proved that quality begets profit, and it will continue to improve upon this critical aspect. When the company realized that achieving six sigma was impossible without quality components from its suppliers, Motorola wrote to all of its vendors, even those in the nonmanufacturing areas like banks and insurance companies, asking them to make plans to enter the Baldrige competition. Why? Because the company believes that if they are being supplied by vendors who are competing for such a quality award, the suppliers have made a commitment to selling high-quality products, which brings fewer defective parts into Motorola.

## *Quality Pays*

Motorola has found that quality does pay. Prior to improved quality levels, Motorola was spending at least 5% and sometimes even as much as 20% of its sales dollars on poor quality. Such rates were equivalent to wasted dollars in the range of $800 to $900 million per year (almost $1 billion!). Such dollar amounts arise from scrapping parts and products, and reworking them because the job was not done right the first time.

In 1986, Motorola incurred about 6000 to 10,000 defects per million for component parts, equivalent to 1% defects in an average manufacturing product. As of August 1991, most of its operations were down to about 100 to 500 parts per million in defects, an approximate 5.3-sigma level of quality. The improved quality has simultaneously saved Motorola between $400 million and $700 million per year. The results are obvious: if quality improves, costs go down. Higher quality is really a form of cost containment.

Motorola has found that it costs less to do something right the first time. The company has not increased the prices of its "new and improved" products; rather, it is offering high-quality products at competitive prices. This follows the company's philosophy that competition would be invited to do a better job if price umbrellas were established. Further, Motorola does not believe in a point of diminishing returns with regards to the quality-improvement process. As a company, it has established a fundamental objective of total customer satisfaction and does not envision itself ever totally reaching that ideal. Because customer expectations are continually increasing, Motorola is chasing a moving target.

## *Total Customer Satisfaction*

Motorola is raising the old saying, "The customer is number one," to an art form with its commitment to accomplishing "Total Customer Satisfaction." In Motorola's quest for total customer satisfaction and its goal of virtual perfection by 1992, company officials and managers are constantly questioning customers' needs and desires. The information gathered is further supplemented by customer surveys, complaint hotlines, and field audits. Acting on these data is critical to the company's plan of anticipating customer desires and having the solution by the time the client is aware that there is a need for one. The Motorola workers seem to have accepted the company's perfect-quality credo. As one Motorola employee put it: "There's someone out there who *will* do it if I don't."

Improving Motorola's customer satisfaction has resulted from its participatory-management process. Employee involvement at all levels is emphasized and is credited with being a key factor in reducing product cycle times. A prime example was Motorola's "Operation Bandit" at its Boynton Beach, Florida, pager plant, so named because rather than designing products from scratch, good ideas were "borrowed" from wherever they could be found. Motorola studied American Express as the benchmark for billing operations; L. L. Bean was the example of product distribution; McDonalds' restaurants were evaluated for on-time delivery of buns to its restaurants, and numerous Japanese companies were evaluated for excellent product-quality levels. What resulted is Motorola's ability to build pagers based on orders in customized lots as small as one. Also, the company has reduced the order-to-ship cycle time from over a month to under three hours. And, because the reduced cycle times lessen confusion and focus toward quality, the pagers are four times more reliable. Motorola has developed a process that eliminates all the nonvalue-adding steps in the production process.

Another key example at Motorola is its 10.7-ounce MicroTac pocket-size cellular phone, introduced in April, 1989. By integrating 3-D design software into the computer-aided design and manufacturing (CAD/CAM) process, Motorola was able to decrease the usual number of design steps by one-half, thereby beating the competition to the market by nearly two years and banking over $1 billion in MicroTac phone sales. As might be expected, the statistical life of the phone, at roughly 150 years, is some three to five times that of the person carrying it. Because Motorola's legal department also participated in the six-sigma process, they were able to cut the time for filing patents from six months, or a year or more in some cases, to a few weeks.

Motorola has been benchmarking the best performers in the world in service support areas as well. To do this, it has generalized a process for dealing in service support areas and calls it Six Steps to Six Sigma. The steps are as follows:

1. What is your product/service?
2. Who is the customer?
3. Who are the suppliers you need to help you?
4. Map out the process you use to fulfill your mission.
5. Look at that process and eliminate the nonvalue-adding steps or the sources of error.
6. Establish some metric and measure yourself, and then drive for continuous improvement.

An example of one nonmanufacturing area that Motorola has benchmarked is its accounting department. Before this area was analyzed, the company's financial statements took 14 days to close. By 1991, the process was down to four days and the goal is to close the books in just two days. There are competitive advantages to shortening such a process, one being that the company gains more days to devote to other important aspects of running the business rather than adding up numbers. It also makes the company financial data visible in the market ahead of the competition, which gives Motorola an advantage in acquiring new investment dollars.

The dramatic cut in closing time was accomplished by a series of nondramatic changes. The solution did not involve implementation of a new computer system; rather, each department in the accounting area met to discuss ways to transact information faster. The single biggest delay in the information relay occurred during the manual entry of data into a keypunch system by an outside contractor. Today, Motorola uses its own accountants to input the data into computers that automatically detect errors. The costs of using the higher-paid accountants over the lower-paid keypunch operators are minimal compared to the higher quality and efficiency results. The cycle time in this process has also been cut, which minimizes chances for errors. In fact, errors have decreased from 10,000 per 750,000 error opportunities in March 1988, to 1000 out of over 1.9 million such opportunities in June 1991.

## *And Now . . .*

Although Motorola has experienced increased sales and profits and has received recognition for its excellent quality with the receipt of the coveted Malcolm Baldrige Award, the company is not content with its position. Quality improvement is regarded as the single greatest opportunity the company has for further growth and increased profitability. And, since customer satisfaction is a moving target, there is no point of diminishing returns, so Motorola does not plan to become static. The leadership of the company firmly believes that they must be excellent "anticipators and committors" and that management must be dynamic.

Further, Motorola is automating the repetitive precision of the highly mechanistic processes. This allows people to use their minds in other ways. It is a company goal to have a "self-directed" work force, with maximum flexibility because of extensive cross-training. A company that builds equipment in batch operations, as Motorola does, benefits tremendously from such worker flexibility. At Motorola, management lays out goals but allows the workers to manage their own planning, scheduling, maintenance, and testing. If necessary, workers can even shut down and fix the line.

The strategy is paying off, measured in terms of two key cycle times that are important as competitive discriminators. One is the time from the customer order to the time it is delivered, and the second is the time it takes for a new product idea to be put into production. The effects of new product introduction and new niche creation are that Motorola has been doubling in size about every five years. Special pride is taken in the fact that Motorola's U.S.-made electronic pager has outsold its Japanese competitors, even in Japan.

## Discussion Questions

1. How is Motorola's quest for "Total Customer Satisfaction" applicable to your business or industry or to a company with which you are familiar?
2. How is Motorola's crusade similar to that of the American automotive industry's?
3. From your own experiences, how does achieving quality improve profits?
4. Can you think of a way that a particular cycle time can be reduced in your area of work?
5. From your own experiences, describe how leadership toward quality improvement has been portrayed by top management.
6. List some methods suggested by the Motorola case that could be implemented in your business or industry which could augment customer satisfaction.
7. How could a nonmanufacturing area at your place of work improve quality and reduce a process cycle time?
8. Describe the notion of six sigma; include the concept of "rolled throughout" and the variation of the mean of a process.

## Primary References

Brian M. Cook, "In Search of Six Sigma: 99.9997% Defect Free," *Industry Week.* October 1, 1990, pp. 60–65.

Mark Stuart Gill, "Stalking Six Sigma," *Business Month.* January 1990, pp. 42–46.

# Case 6

# Operations, Inventory, and Quality Planning at Elco Manufacturing

## Introduction

This would be the first Friday afternoon in several weeks that he had not had to react to a problem, Bob Anderson (Vice President of Operations of Elko Manufacturing)* mused, as he pushed back from lunch. Since that first business planning meeting almost a year ago, when he and Susan Clarke had started the business strategy planning process, operations had gotten some credibility. Forecast errors were being reduced and operations planning was improving. Yes, things were looking up.

Linda Chavez, the assistant operations manager, put her tray on the table. "May I join you?" she asked.

"Of course," responded Bob, noting that he would have to look for a new assistant operations manager, as Linda would be taking over the facilities evaluation committee, which would likely lead to her reassignment as the plant manager of the startup facility. "I've finished lunch, but I've got several minutes before the meeting with of Finance."

"That's what I wanted to talk about," noted Linda. "I heard from Donald Kimes that the vice president of Finance is concerned about the inventory costs and rework."

"So that's why Ginny Thompson was so cordial when she invited me to attend the quarterly budget review. She just said that she wanted me to meet some of her people and to share some of the process they were developing. Thanks, now at least I can go to the meeting knowing that I am going to get beaten up." He grinned wryly at Linda. "Oh, while I'm gone, would you get that exercycle operations planning data together? And, remember, we are going to have to increase production in those last three quarters by 50%."

*To protect proprietary information, the company described in this case (a major U.S. industrial corporation) has requested that its name and other identifying information be changed. However, the basic relationships have been retained. This case has been prepared as a basis for class discussion, rather than to illustrate either effective or ineffective management of an operational situation.

## *Inventory Planning and Analysis*

Several minutes later Bob was introduced around the table to the four principal members of the finance staff by Virginia Thompson, the VP of Finance. Thompson had joined Elco several months prior to Bob. She had been brought in to upgrade the financial reporting and cost accounting systems. The meeting proceeded with an agenda that noted several administrative items, defined a required tax reporting change, then moved to an analysis of monthly costs.

Thompson introduced Arthur Kimbrough, the senior cost accountant, and commented that he had spent a great deal of time getting together some initial data to evaluate product costs. "This approach is being continually refined, and we hope that it will provide a model that can be extended to other product lines," she concluded.

Kimbrough's analysis captured annual demand and per-unit costs, and then estimated the stockout penalty based on the unit cost multiplied by the number of competitive products in the market. Kimbrough expressed the rationale that if the Elco product were stocked out, then the more competitors in the market, the more likely that a customer would purchase another product. As shown in Table C6-1, Kimbrough had sequenced the items by unit cost, suggesting that more costly items be more carefully managed.

Bob noted that Kimbrough's high-priority items corresponded closely to his own analysis. Arthur Kimbrough then defined various costs, including carrying costs, order costs, lead times, and standard deviations of demand. This information, as well as the economic order quantity, based on 20% annual carrying costs, is shown in Table C6-2.

After describing the computations is some detail, Kimbrough concluded: "The economic order quantity may vary, but shop orders should be close to these amounts."

**TABLE C6-1 Cost Analysis—Bench Apparatus Equipment**

| Stock Number | Name | Units/Year | Cost/Unit | Number of Competitors | Stockout Penalty |
|---|---|---|---|---|---|
| ES4 | Elco System IV | 600 | $671.32 | 1 | $ 671.32 |
| ES3 | Elco System III | 2,100 | 540.82 | 2 | 1,081.64 |
| ES2 | Elco System II | 1,475 | 356.87 | 2 | 713.74 |
| GM2 | Dual stack gym | 1,700 | 321.65 | 5 | 1,608.25 |
| GM1 | Flex bar gym | 1,350 | 225.42 | 2 | 450.84 |
| ES1 | Elco System I | 2,250 | 211.43 | 3 | 634.29 |
| BN4 | Olympic bench | 1,900 | 168.92 | 1 | 168.92 |
| BN3 | Flex bar and bench | 1,100 | 97.12 | 2 | 194.24 |
| BN2 | Butterfly bench | 2,450 | 84.29 | 1 | 84.29 |
| BN1 | Power bench | 1,250 | 66.94 | 3 | 200.82 |
| BR2 | Heavy-duty bar | 3,600 | 56.82 | 1 | 56.82 |
| BR1 | Arm blaster bar | 1,800 | 38.21 | 3 | 114.63 |
| BD2 | 5-position slant board | 3,100 | 31.28 | 2 | 62.56 |
| BD1 | Slant board | 750 | 18.95 | 2 | 37.90 |

**TABLE C6-2 Cost Analysis—Bench Apparatus Equipment**

| Stock Number | Name | Units/Year | Cost/Unit | Cost/Order | Lead Time | Standard Deviations of Demand | EOQ |
|---|---|---|---|---|---|---|---|
| ES4 | Elco System IV | 600 | $671.32 | $679 | 8 | 40 | 77.90 |
| ES3 | Elco System III | 2,100 | 540.82 | 462 | 7 | 50 | 133.94 |
| ES2 | Elco System II | 1,475 | 356.87 | 396 | 5 | 40 | 127.93 |
| GM2 | Dual stack gym | 1,700 | 321.65 | 428 | 2 | 30 | 150.40 |
| GM1 | Flex bar gym | 1,350 | 225.42 | 285 | 2 | 15 | 130.65 |
| ES1 | Elco System I | 2,250 | 211.43 | 484 | 4 | 30 | 226.95 |
| BN4 | Olympic bench | 1,900 | 168.92 | 524 | 4 | 20 | 242.77 |
| BN3 | Flex bar and bench | 1,100 | 97.12 | 124 | 7 | 50 | 118.51 |
| BN2 | Butterfly bench | 2,450 | 84.29 | 243 | 6 | 100 | 265.77 |
| BN1 | Power bench | 1,250 | 66.94 | 324 | 2 | 20 | 245.97 |
| BR2 | Heavy-duty bar | 3,600 | 56.82 | 34 | 3 | 30 | 146.77 |
| BR1 | Arm blaster bar | 1,800 | 38.21 | 21 | 2 | 10 | 99.46 |
| BD2 | 5-position slant board | 3,100 | 31.28 | 120 | 4 | 50 | 344.86 |
| BD1 | Slant board | 750 | 18.95 | 20 | 3 | 10 | 88.97 |

## *Quality Analysis*

The next part of Kimbrough's comments dealt with defect rates in several key areas of manufacturing and the cost of inspecting for quality. The exercycle computer unit, a purchased component, was particularly subject to defects, possibly because of damage during shipment. Kimbrough had gathered computer unit defect data from 20 different shipments, based on a standard shipment size of 50 units. His results appear in Table C6-3. He suggested that the solution might be better packaging. Coordination with the vendor and a quality acceptance program were recommended.

Kimbrough then evaluated the exercycle flywheel thickness. The flywheel was a critical component, because even minor variations in thickness would cause the flywheel to wobble, resulting in an obvious lack of riding smoothness. Flywheel thickness is presented in Table C6-4.

## *Work Measurement*

The final part of Arthur Kimbrough's briefing was a work measurement analysis of a quality control station that inspected the assembled Elco System units. At this station, work activities evaluated various quality control criteria, and then released the product for shipment. Kimbrough noted that his analysis was incomplete, as he had just received the data. However, he did show the average time for ten cycles of five work elements each. That analysis is shown in Table C6-5.

**TABLE C6-3 Quality Control—Exercycle Computer Unit**

| Sample Number | Number of Defects | Sample Number | Number of Defects | Sample Number | Number of Defects | Sample Number | Number of Defects |
|---|---|---|---|---|---|---|---|
| 1 | 3 | 6 | 1 | 11 | 4 | 16 | 6 |
| 2 | 4 | 7 | 3 | 12 | 2 | 17 | 2 |
| 3 | 2 | 8 | 4 | 13 | 5 | 18 | 3 |
| 4 | 9 | 9 | 2 | 14 | 6 | 19 | 5 |
| 5 | 4 | 10 | 3 | 15 | 3 | 20 | 1 |

**TABLE C6-4 Quality Control—Exercycle Flywheel Thickness (in Tens of Microns)**

| | Observation Number | | | | |
|---|---|---|---|---|---|
| Lot Number | 1 | 2 | 3 | 4 | 5 |
| 1 | 431 | 423 | 428 | 435 | 429 |
| 2 | 436 | 431 | 428 | 429 | 432 |
| 3 | 425 | 428 | 432 | 427 | 426 |
| 4 | 440 | 436 | 437 | 431 | 434 |
| 5 | 436 | 432 | 429 | 426 | 430 |
| 6 | 423 | 433 | 429 | 431 | 428 |
| 7 | 430 | 345 | 429 | 439 | 436 |
| 8 | 432 | 429 | 427 | 430 | 435 |
| 9 | 428 | 429 | 436 | 431 | 430 |
| 10 | 441 | 436 | 429 | 437 | 431 |

**TABLE C6-5 Work Measurement of the Quality Control Station (Elco System)**

| | Work Element—Continuous Times (min) | | | | | |
|---|---|---|---|---|---|---|
| Cycle Number | 1 | 2 | 3 | 4 | 5 | Time/ Cycle |
| 1 | 0.402 | 0.445 | 0.739 | 1.626 | 1.801 | 1.801 |
| 2 | 2.331 | 2.354 | 2.624 | 3.612 | 3.899 | 2.098 |
| 3 | 4.634 | 4.661 | 4.975 | 5.907 | 6.020 | 2.203 |
| 4 | 6.821 | 6.884 | 7.115 | 8.004 | 8.251 | 2.149 |
| 5 | 9.007 | 9.035 | 9.395 | 10.335 | 10.603 | 2.352 |
| 6 | 11.206 | 11.239 | 11.547 | 12.427 | 12.617 | 2.014 |
| 7 | 13.282 | 13.311 | 13.616 | 14.680 | 14.890 | 2.273 |
| 8 | 15.423 | 15.451 | 15.715 | 16.612 | 16.834 | 1.944 |
| 9 | 17.494 | 17.524 | 17.884 | 19.011 | 19.402 | 2.568 |
| 10 | 20.005 | 20.038 | 20.326 | 21.225 | 21.465 | 2.063 |
| | | | | | Average time | 2.147 |

"Your people told me that they use a 19% allowance and respectively 1.125, 1.050, 1.150, 1.100, and 1.000 as the performance ratings for these five work elements, but I have not had a chance to do the full analysis. I am not convinced that this will make much difference. On the basis of this data, the average inspection time of 2.147 minutes per unit indicates that we can inspect roughly 223 units per day. At a standardized labor cost of $25.00 per hour, that would be slightly less than $1 per unit in final quality inspection costs."

"To summarize, Bob," said Ginny Thompson, "Arthur may have found something here, and I wanted to make you aware of our approach. Certainly these are not final results and will not be briefed outside this group until your people have had a chance to review our results." Ginny paused and looked around the table until she had received an affirmative nod from each participant. "However, we are going to have to address this question in one way or another. I am concerned with the costs of our distribution system and of defects which we either catch or which we have to fix through component replacement at the customer site."

"The points are well made," Bob responded, glancing cordially at the stone-faced accountant. "I appreciate the opportunity to be a part of your initial presentation of these data. I would like to share the data with several of my staff, and then perhaps we can schedule a brief-back in several weeks. Do you think that I could get a copy of these charts?"

"Great idea," said Ginny. Kimbrough squirmed momentarily. "Arthur will make the copies."

After the briefing, Bob exchanged several minutes of pleasantries with Virginia and her staff. He then hustled back to his office. He wanted to catch Linda Chavez and Bill Grauf, the inventory planner, before they left for the weekend.

"How did it go?" Linda asked cheerfully, trying to put a positive spin on what she knew from Bob's dour look had been an unpleasant session.

"We'll survive," countered Bob tersely. "Can you and Bill join me in a couple of minutes? And you might bring in one of the quality people, possibly Pat. Also, since inventory is driven by the schedule and quality may be affected, perhaps we should provide a review of our work on the operations planning problem. Ed Thomas (the master scheduler) should be part of this."

"I expected as much. They are standing by; Joan will give them a call."

## *Operations Planning*

"Ok, folks," Bob commenced, after the quickly assembled group had had several minutes to review the data. "Virginia Thompson is right. Though I expect that Kimbrough's data can be easily challenged, they are correct in that we still have too much finished goods inventory, and we don't have tight enough control on our suppliers or on our production quality. Virginia was courteous enough to invite me to this preliminary showing of their data, so I think that we should not stonewall them or fight the problem. I want to cooperate, yet I want to do the analysis right. That means that we start by showing them our current operations planning methods and proposals, followed by a simple ABC analysis to identify the critical inventory items, and then some initial evaluation of our economic order quantities and economic lot sizes."

"Here is that operations planning data with assumptions (Table C6-6)," affirmed Chavez. "Additionally, we'll have to figure in overtime wages. I've tried to identify some rough numbers for the variables, but we may want to fine-tune them a bit."

"Perhaps," Bob started, "the best way to approach this is to identify the per-unit costs based on our present level strategy. Then we could figure a new level strategy for Susan Clarke's 50% increase in quarters 2, 3, and 4. Following that, we may look at the costs of chasing demand. I expect that the staff will not accept a full chase strategy because of the employee turbulence, but I would like to look at the level and chase strategy as a base-line cost to show the improvement of possible compromise alternatives. Then we might look at several seasonal and self-designed compromise alternatives. We need to compare unit costs using each operations planning. Let's define some constraints to limit this problem."

"First, we cannot change production by more than 3000 units in any month."

"Second, if we do use overtime, all employees will desire to participate, but for reasons of quality and safety, a limit of ten hours per week of overtime will be set. Thus, overtime will cost $2537 per month per employee for ten hours per week for all employees. With 40 hours of overtime per month, production per employee per month would likely be about 31 units."

"Third, a maximum of 35% temporary hires or new employees may be used. Currently, there are 118 labor-grade employees; let's say that we cannot have more than 160 full-time employees. And let's use a 24% annual carrying costs."

**TABLE C6-6 Elco Products—Exercycles**

Operations Planning Variables

| | | | |
|---|---|---|---|
| Monthly carrying cost | 0.02 | Hire/fire cost | $400.00 |
| Materials cost/unit | $400.00 | Capacity change cost | 20.00 |
| Average monthly wage and benefits | $2320.00 | Units/worker/month | 25 |

| Month | Requirements | Production | Inventory | Labor |
|---|---|---|---|---|
| 0 | | 2,950 | 525 | |
| 1 | 1,650 | 2,950 | 1,825 | 118 |
| 2 | 1,350 | 2,950 | 3,425 | 118 |
| 3 | 1,500 | 2,950 | 4,875 | 118 |
| 4 | 675 | 2,950 | 7,150 | 118 |
| 5 | 800 | 2,950 | 9,300 | 118 |
| 6 | 1,100 | 2,950 | 11,150 | 118 |
| 7 | 1,400 | 2,950 | 12,700 | 118 |
| 8 | 1,725 | 2,950 | 13,925 | 118 |
| 9 | 4,300 | 2,950 | 12,575 | 118 |
| 10 | 5,650 | 2,950 | 9,875 | 118 |
| 11 | 8,600 | 2,950 | 4,225 | 118 |
| 12 | 6,650 | 2,950 | 525 | 118 |

"Ed, these are my guesses. We might want to present the solution in a format like this." Bob roughed out a draft overhead like that shown in Table C6-7. "Would you start to run up these numbers?"

Bob paused, noting the quizzical look on Bill's face. "Yes, I know, Bill, this is not the MRP system that we talked about, but I think it might be a good idea to get some initial base-line numbers. And clearly, it will give us a chance to find out how accurate our data are, which of course is preliminary to MRP implementation."

Bill did not appear to be fully convinced.

"You know, Bill," Bob continued, "I expect that we could develop a manual DRP system to manage orders for the regions up to the central warehouse, and in that way demonstrate the potential of a full MRP system."

Bill broke into a broadening smile. "I knew you would think of something."

**TABLE C6-7 Operations Planning Alternatives**

Level Strategy

| | Base | Inventory | Labor | Hire/Fire | Δ Cap | Total Cost |
|---|---|---|---|---|---|---|
| Units | ________ | ________ | ________ | ________ | ________ | ________ |
| Cost | ________ | ________ | ________ | ________ | ________ | ________ |

Comments—advantages:

disadvantages:

Chase Strategy

| | Base | Inventory | Labor | Hire/Fire | Δ Cap | Total Cost |
|---|---|---|---|---|---|---|
| Units | ________ | ________ | ________ | ________ | ________ | ________ |
| Cost | ________ | ________ | ________ | ________ | ________ | ________ |

Comments—advantages:

disadvantages:

Compromise Solution—Definition

| | Base | Inventory | Labor | Hire/Fire | Δ Cap | Total Cost |
|---|---|---|---|---|---|---|
| Units | ________ | ________ | ________ | ________ | ________ | ________ |
| Cost | ________ | ________ | ________ | ________ | ________ | ________ |

Comments—advantages:

disadvantages:

"Pat," Bob continued. "We are going to have to develop some $p$- or $\bar{x}$-charts to look at some of these items. Perhaps check the computers when they come in to see if the problem is faulty components or shipping or customer assembly. Also, look at the time and cost of defect identification and corrections. We may want to consider some TQC approaches."

"I will get over to Human Resources and the other staff and get them up to speed on some of the impacts of these projections. What we really need is a detailed briefing for next Thursday. Linda, can you coordinate this?"

Bob paused again, noting Linda's concern. "Oh, don't worry; this one is a piece of cake. I will go over the models with you, and we have some software that might be helpful."

Over the next several days, Bob worked individually with the staff to develop the data for production planning, ABC analysis, lot-sizing computations, DRP, quality control, and work measurement. He also had several brief conversations with Ginny Thompson, describing the progress that they were making and generally identifying where Arthur Kimbrough's data were supported or not. This permitted a growing rapport with the VP of Finance, giving Bob a comfort level of team action and effectiveness. He was able to plant several seeds with Thompson about the likely costs and benefits of the computer-driven inventory and quality control systems that his staff needed.

Things were looking up.

## *Discussion Questions*

1. Suggest several additional constraints, in addition to those noted by Bob Anderson, which might be used to limit an operations plan.
2. In addition to the variables suggested by the operations planning analysis (see the top of Table C6-6), what other variables might you expect to encounter?
3. What are the advantages/disadvantages of the level, chase, and compromise alternatives?
4. Operations planning analysis usually is used to define an approximate operations plan for one or more years into the future. But by the time the particular planning month arrives, invariably changes must be made. If those changes must be made, what good is the operations plan?
5. In what way(s) would ABC analysis be an improvement over the cost-per-unit method of evaluating the most important finished goods inventory items?
6. What criteria should be used to differentiate the A from the B and the C items in ABC analysis?
7. What is the relationship between the economic order quantity and material requirements planning?
8. Elco Manufacturing currently inspects for quality only after final assembly. Is this a problem? Why? Why not? What alternatives are there?
9. Why do the exercycle computer unit and the flywheel require different methods of quality evaluation?

**10.** Why should a quality control evaluation using an $\bar{x}$-chart first evaluate the range (*R*-chart) for control than evaluate the mean ($\bar{x}$-chart) for control?

**11.** The extrapolation of continuous time work measurement information presented in Table C6-5 suggests a limited analysis format. In what ways should this model be enhanced?

**12.** Work evaluation permits a concise review of extremely detailed work methods. Suppose that work measurement efforts result in an unreasonably high number of work cycles required for measurement; what actions could the operations manager take to address the problem?

**13.** Though Bob Anderson appears to be responding well to a very demanding job within the context of traditional operations management methods, suggest some contemporary manufacturing methods and operations strategies that he and his group might look at.

## *Computer Assignments*

**1.** *Costs of level, chase, compromise, and self-designed plans.* Define the costs of level, chase, and self-designed compromise plans, using the data proposed by marketing with a 50% increment in the last three quarters. Note the differences. Recommend an operations plan; discuss disadvantages and advantages.

**2.** *Prioritization of inventory evaluation.* Which units of finished goods inventory should be of concern for inventory costing? Support your rationale.

**3.** *Order priorities.* Using EOQ and safety stock models, recommend appropriate order quantities for the items of concern.

**4.** *MRP and DRP.* Present the rationale for MRP and DRP. Show a concise example of how MRP can reduce inventory management costs.

**5.** *Quality control.* Show how you would measure quality for the computer and for the flywheel. Suggest control limits and offer guidance for line workers.

**6.** *Work measurement and quality costing.* Recommend alternative approaches to work measurement and costing of the quality control station.

# *Part* IV

# *Implementing Operations Strategy*

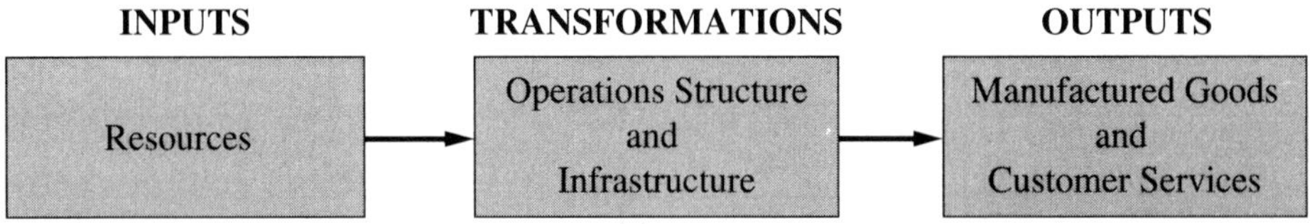
INPUTS
TRANSFORMATIONS
OUTPUTS
Resources
Operations Structure
and
Infrastructure
Manufactured Goods
and
Customer Services

# *Chapter 13*

# *The Management of Technology*

*Technology is today's great democratizing force, allowing ideas to travel great distances and worm their way past barriers to free thought and free commerce.* —Karen Pennar, 1992

## *Objectives*

After completing this chapter you should be able to:

- Identify the characteristics and levels of research and development projects.
- Define the incentives and impediments to technological change.
- List the decision variables in technology management.
- Describe several techniques of managing technology transfer.
- Differentiate methods of project management in terms of when they should be used.

## *Outline*

## *Introductory Case: How General Electric Bobbled the Factory of the Future*

During the early 1980s, manufacturing technology changed radically due to factory automation. Robots made their manufacturing debut, and many, including General Electric,* believed that factory automation was the production industry of the future. Founded by Thomas Edison and heralded as a cornerstone of American industry, GE was so confident that factory automation would be a "megamarket" that in 1980 it established the $500-million factory automation division. The company hoped to have 20% of the factory automation market by 1990.

General Electric's vision included automated systems to augment productivity and quality. Since automation requires many high-tech devices, such as controllers to turn on and program machines, cameras and sensors to regulate work, computers and software for applications, and communication networks to connect the technology, GE would establish itself as "America's factory-of-the-future supermarket." Because it did not produce all the necessary products, GE pursued acquisitions and licensing agreements. The first purchase, for $150 million, was a producer of computer-aided design (CAD) equipment, followed by licensing agreements with a total of 11 Japanese, German, and Italian robotics companies. What resulted, however, was a catastrophe, because the separate units did not work well together.

*Materials drawn from R. Mitchell and J. Dobrzynski, "Jack Welch: How Good a Manager?" *Business Week,* December 14, 1987 and from Peter Petre, "How GE Bobbled the Factory of the Future," *Fortune,* November 11, 1985.

GE had conservatively forecast that sales would reach $1 billion. However, by the end of 1982 customer interest in GE's factory-of-the-future was waning and the company had landed only nine projects, almost half of them within GE. Although it had hoped for 20% of this market, GE was forced to all but halt its robotics division in 1983. The products required extensive customizing to prevent the improperly designed system from paralyzing production. Also, robots were difficult and laborious to install. These and other obstacles resulted in low sales figures industrywide and about $10 million per year in losses at GE. Additionally, GE lost its position as the largest seller of numerical controls in the U.S. This business unit produced highly specialized computers that assist and guide large machine tools in cutting, drilling, and shaping parts. Annual sales of numerical controls declined from $86 million to $60 million, with losses equaling about $10 million. The CAD equipment division was also in disarray due to key personnel losses in the areas of sales and engineering. Further, the company neglected to focus the business on its primary product lines, resulting in inaccurate planning and development of new products. By 1984, the division was suffering losses of roughly $40 million per year.

In 1985, GE switched its strategy from becoming a predominant innovator in the factory-of-the-future megamarket to existing as a player in a smaller niche. Programming controls, an outgrowth of a GE laboratory project, became a $100-million-per-year business. Moreover, by fitting its own sensors to Japanese-manufactured robots, GE was the first to introduce a successful line of robots capable of welding dirty or rusty parts. By 1987, the company seemed to have recovered from its huge losses and lackluster profit margins, with operating profits of $5 billion up from $3.1 billion in 1982. When GE allowed its emphasis on innovative research to surpass its ability to develop and market products, its market dominance was shattered. By allowing desire for innovation to surpass its ability to develop products and process technologies, GE clearly bobbled the factory of the future.

## *The Technology Edge*

Because of the growing importance of knowledge and technology, this entire book, in a broad sense, is about the management of structure and infrastructure knowledg and technology. This chapter, however, focuses on the technology variable by considering Pennar's comment that technology is not just about production processes and tools, such as inventory, capacity, or the other chapter topics, but rather it is a "great democratizing force." It deals with how humans work, live, and think (Drucker, 1989). The management of technology, in this sense, includes the processes through which new knowledge is discovered and nurtured into a viable product or service or a competitive process.

Further, these management-of-technology topics gain greater relevance because an increasing number of products and services are customized. With greater amounts of customized units, speed in meeting customer needs, which results from flexibility of process technology, is likely to be a key to successful competition in the 1990s. New product/service development is thus doubly important (Civerolo, 1992). Although research and development (R&D) activities are often associated with manufacturing, many service system applications can be noted, including noninvasive surgery, most information and entertainment products, and new retailing formats (see Application Box 6-1).

The research and development (R&D) process to find and implement new technology is one of the most challenging and enigmatic, yet rewarding and logical of operations activities. It is also one of the single most important activities for long-range organization survival, if for no other reason than the pervasiveness and dynamics of technology in manufacturing and service delivery operations. In a recent year, 900 major U.S. corporations spent \$70 billion in R&D; the top two firms, General Motors and IBM, spent more than \$10 billion on R&D (Buderi, 1991). Additionally, the management of technology is necessary to long-term business survival because few organizations use the same tools, the same work methods, and the same processes that they did a decade or a generation ago. If organizations do not build new tools and learn new ways to work, they will not remain competitive and will not survive; or, following Drucker (1989), they will not be in the forefront in shaping the ways in which tomorrow's human works and lives.

There are, however, limits to the pursuit of the technology edge. As the experience of General Electric, noted in the introductory case, showed, it is difficult and risky to achieve quantum leaps of new technology. For example, acquisitions have been used as a surrogate for innovation, though recent evidence (Hitt et al., 1991) suggests that acquisition is not a substitute for innovative activities and that acquisition should be integrated with ongoing innovation through a carefully developed strategic plan. For this reason, the management of the discovery and implementation of new technology is one of the most difficult and demanding parts of operations strategy.

This chapter introduces and defines the concepts of technology, R&D, innovation, and the relevant management processes. Then the motivation and impediments to create and fund R&D programs are described. Several categories of R&D are defined and examined, and R&D is presented as an ongoing transfer process from the laboratory to the shop. Measurement techniques are suggested to evaluate the timing and control the implementation of R&D programs. Ultimately, the success of technology management rests with the process of efficiently integrating sources of knowledge and functional activities.

## *Function of Technology*

Though vitally critical to growing organizations or those in dynamic environments, the full implications and potential opportunities of technology are often resisted. The reasons are numerous, but they can often be reduced to an aversion to technology, a narrowness of perspective, or a fear of change. But research, by its very nature, is directed toward the discovery of new and abstract knowledge, whereas development is directed toward the practical application of that knowledge. Thus, both research and development inherently involve technology, broadness of perspective, and change, the very components that are often resisted.

Technology can be defined as the tools, including equipment, materials, and information, through which the physical and mental reach of labor may be extended. R&D efforts are directed toward the discovery and application of new knowledge, product/service technology, or process technology. Innovation, a related term, is defined as the proactive and systematic development and practical application of new technology through R&D activities. Innovation through R&D leads to new technologies.

Research and development efforts can be defined in five general categories: process technology, materials technology, product/service technology, information systems, and management systems. In some situations, materials technology is subsumed by product technology, and information systems are subsumed by process technology. Examples of the outcomes of technology improvement are shown in Application Box 13-1.

Despite the significant and wide-ranging impact of R&D activities, it is difficult to create and manage a R&D program. Though technology can easily be bought and installed in a factory, technology implementation requires an extensive human retooling as well. As Hayes and Wheelwright (1984) point out, simply increasing the R&D budget or conducting more research does not necessarily enhance the innovative posture of the firm. There must be a coordinated effort to create an effective platform from which to proactively project technology initiatives and break down barriers to innovation.

Werther et al. (1986) note several clear barriers to the development of innovation in a business. The financial incentives and reward structures of the organization typically compensate or encourage short-range performance at the expense of longer-range innovation. Or employees may be overwhelmed by the implications of change—avoiding change because of an unfounded fear of their own inadequacy. Due to the uncertainty, long time frames, and complexity often associated with innovation, it is tough to protect R&D funding at quarterly financial meetings, particularly during an economic downturn.

Among management, risk-taking must also be rewarded and encouraged. Without such encouragement and protection, few managers would pursue risky projects. In addition, by rewarding limited risk-taking, the company would reap the intangible benefits of spin-off technologies and of being the leading-edge firm in the field. Without incentives, both institutional and individual, such innovation is easily stifled. The organization should define and establish an appropriate amount of bias toward innovation.

## *Contribution of Research and Development*

Research and development activities are usually managed as projects because of their complexity, uniqueness, and the length of time that they require. This section will consider the effects of changing technology in the workplace, the characteristics and levels of a project, and key project management steps. The implementation of R&D projects involves extensive changes in both the infrastructure (software) as well as the structure (hardware) of the organization.

### *Effects of Changing Technology*

Changes in process technology, materials technology, product/service technology, information systems, and management systems of an operation significantly affect the policies and procedures governing the work and the labor skills required for the operation.

### APPLICATION BOX 13-1 The Outcomes of Technology Improvement

*Process Technology.* The General Motors Saturn plant has pioneered the lost-foam process for casting automobile engines. Foam molds in the shape of engine blocks are placed in a box containing sand for support, and then molten aluminum is poured into the mold. As it cools, the molten aluminum dissolves the foam, but the foam provides sufficient rigidity to define the shape of the engine until the aluminum hardens. This technology is much less costly than previously used metal molds, because the foam molds are cheaper and easier to produce and modify.

*Materials Technology.* The increasing use of aluminum and other alloys to reduce the weight of bicycle frames is no less notable than the replacement of these compounds in higher-grade models by graphite and plastic. Though there has also been some change in the geometry or structure of the racing bike, the use of space-age materials permits a lighter-weight, yet stronger, less flexible, and more durable bicycle frame. Other bicycle components, particularly the wheels and hubs, have also been redesigned with lightweight, yet strong materials.

*Product/Service Technology.* The electronics and computer chip industries are among several areas with rapid and pervasive product innovation. Disk cameras, for example, don't use film; laser printers don't use keys, elements or print wheels; many watches use battery power and quartz regulators, rather than springs and wheels; and music media use "no touch" laser reading of digital information, rather than tape heads or record player needles. In the services, automobile maintenance is facilitated by diagnostic tools, dashboard lights, and periodic maintenance requirements.

*Information Systems.* Material requirements planning (MRP) systems, integrated with computer-assisted design/computer-assisted manufacturing (CAD/CAM) and other information systems now manage the computation and repetitive administrative activities of production, freeing labor for other, more creative activities, such as programming the computers. Some factories are able to run third shifts without a substantial labor presence on the manufacturing floor, because the production process is managed by a fully developed computer-integrated manufacturing system.

*Management Systems.* The ethical, egalitarian, and judgmental dimensions of management are constantly evolving as the demands by society on productive organizations change. Pollution, industrial safety, and work-force equality are three examples of management concerns that have intensified in the past several years. Further, management decisions are more visible to the media and are reviewed as never before, for compliance with legal, egalitarian, due process, necessity, and appropriateness criteria.

Additionally, "ripple-down" effects are apparent in the work environment and quality of work life, and in the retraining requirements of the firm.

As Skinner (1985, p. 155) points out, technology is the primary driver of the work environment for two reasons. First, new technology requires different labor skills and, second, new technology has a pervasive effect on the entire operating system, including process management, policies, and procedures. The different labor skills imply labor retraining and often result in revised corporate training policies. Many nations and numerous companies have struggled with the question of defining a balance between subsidizing existing, though inefficient, technologies and encouraging the introduction of more knowledge-based technologies (Drucker, 1986). However, the different labor skills, combined with process management policies and procedures, also have effects on the work environment and quality of work life. Thus, the change of technology has the potential to affect a number of workplace structure and infrastructure variables and can have significant effects on the entire workplace environment.

For example, the development of word processing systems as a replacement for the typewriter dramatically changed the work environment of clerical employees. Until the late 1970s most clerical work was done with "memoryless" typewriters by decentralized secretaries who worked for one or several supervisors. One of the first impacts of early word processing systems was to aggregate clerical workers into word processing sections, permitting training on the high-cost, bulky, and centralized equipment. Training in software skills was required, and the technology made available a keystroke counting capability, which could be used for performance evaluation. The work function of those clerical employees was changed from a variety of direct and personal support activities within departments to the agency-level support of many departments. Though efficiency may have improved, the quality of work life was reduced. However, by the mid-1980s, the development of easy-to-learn, low-cost software packages and flexible hardware, such as simplified word-processing software and PCs, permitted the reassignment of clerical employees back to the individual sections, again requiring retraining and a change of work policies. Corresponding changes have occurred in factories as robotic equipment has replaced human labor on assembly lines, and humans have been retrained to program the robots or to manage the automated systems.

## *Characteristics and Levels of Research and Development*

Research and development activities are distinguished from other operations activities in several regards. Initially, the complexity, scope (in time, cost, and breadth of impact), and uniqueness of each activity set R&D apart from the relatively simplified, focused, and often repetitive activities of other manufacturing or service delivery operations. R&D projects thus have several distinct characteristics and can function at several distinct levels. The following characteristics are generally defined for most R&D projects:

R&D projects are a *one-at-a-time activity.* However, they often integrate other operations activities in the dimensions of time, space, and perception. Consider concurrent engineering, cycle-time-reducing projects, and others.

R&D projects have a *defined beginning and ending point.* Designing an assembly line or service delivery process to produce the first product/service constitutes a project; running that same line or process at a specified capacity is not a project—it is a repetitive activity.

R&D projects *can be subdivided into tasks,* each of which has a beginning and an end; many tasks may be further divided into subtasks.

The tasks of a R&D project have a *sequential relationship.* That is, each task either precedes, succeeds, or is independent of each other task.

The *duration of the tasks* may be estimated by a variety of methods, the most common of which are the deterministic method (each activity is measured as an exact, specified time) and the beta-distributed probabilistic method (each activity has an optimistic, most likely, and pessimistic time).

Management of R&D projects requires the allocation or reallocation of resources on several levels to achieve goals stated in terms of cost, time, or quality, some of which may rely heavily on engineering. Shorter-range, less extensive development efforts may involve only a minor change in the application. Manufacturing processes require changeovers for a new model or to accommodate a new technology or materials, or to change the flow or process. Similarly, service activities might change equipment to facilitate a broader line of service. Such short-range changeovers typically take less than three months. Though the materials or technology may have previously been proven through an extensive research process, the implementation itself is application driven. Thus, at the simplest level, project management involves the application of a generally proven technology.

At a second, higher level, implementations could involve the development and testing of a new material, product, or process. For example, the approval of a new drug or medicine may take as much as ten years and involve the efforts of as many as 300 or more employees. At this second level, R&D efforts involve the discovery and implementation of one or several new areas of technology; however, existing facilities, research teams, and equipment are normally used, though these may be reconfigured or redesigned.

At yet a third and higher level, a more extensive R&D project involves a combination of new products, materials, new processes, information systems, and management systems. The development of a new technology to build a product or deliver a service is also a longer-term effort, for example, the 15- to 20-year effort by Bell Laboratories and IBM to develop the silicon purifying technologies necessary for computer chip manufacture or the communications protocols for the proposed American "Information Highway." Such extensive efforts almost always require the construction of a new facility and the creation of a new organization. The Saturn project of General Motors is an example of such an extensive implementation of new technology ("Why . . . Tennessee," 1985).

## *Key Steps in Management of an R&D Project*

There are four essential steps in the management of a R&D project: planning, scheduling, monitoring, and adjustment. Those steps apply to all levels of projects and to all types of technology. As shown in Figure 13-1, the steps must be performed in sequence. The size of the boxes gives some indication of the relative amount of time that should be committed for each step. However, if time is not spent in the early planning and scheduling activities, more time will likely be spent monitoring and adjusting the project to correct the problems that should have been anticipated had the planning and scheduling process been managed more thoroughly.

**Planning.** Planning consists of defining project goals, tasks, and subactivities and developing a project management team or liaison with other activities. Project goals must be clearly stated and must receive the unequivocal support of top management. Additionally, the definition of tasks and subtasks and their timing and sequence will likely go through several iterations before an acceptable project structure can be defined. The planning effort will likely integrate budgeting, engineering, research, and human re-

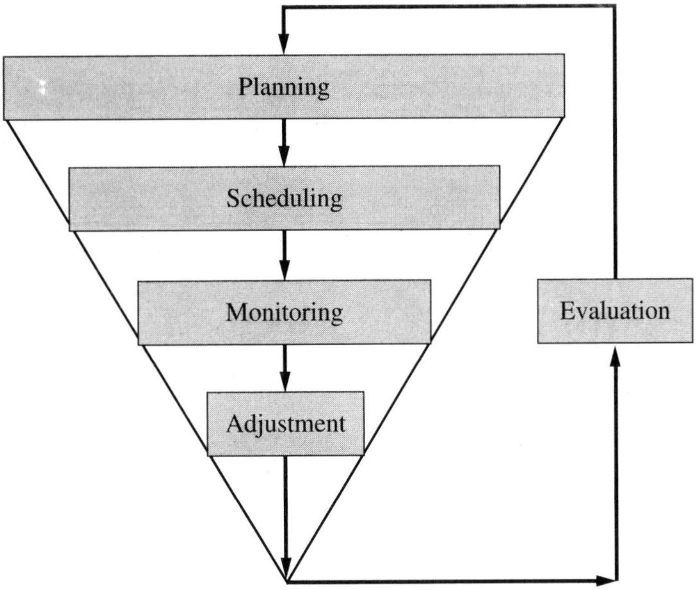


**FIGURE 13-1 Project Management Steps**

sources, as well as several activities in the manufacturing area. Consequently, planning often involves the team players from many different functions. Concurrent engineering is widely used to integrate various activities; however, particularly if the project is large, or involves extensive commitment of resources, the use of a project team or technology platform may be the best way to integrate and give voice to various activities of the organization.

**Scheduling.** Project scheduling follows, but is highly interactive with, planning. Scheduling defines the project plan in terms of available resources by tying units of resource (capacity, materials, people, finances) to a specified task. The schedule starts with an extremely vague projection of which resources will be used to accomplish which tasks. After several iterations, a revised schedule gradually solidifies, and is sufficiently "firm" that resource commitments can be made with confidence. Ultimately, a workable, acceptable resource-integrated schedule is defined; this schedule is sometimes called a *fully resourced plan.*

**Monitoring.** Project monitoring is used to evaluate the progress of the project and to shift resources as appropriate to meet time, cost, or product definition constraints. Often a trend or cost line (costs to date against expected costs) will be used to evaluate the proportion of the project completed against the proportion that should be completed. Among the typical reports used to monitor project performance are a listing of the time or cost budgets by activity and the delayed or slack activities, with revised expected completion times and actual contributions of resources or departments.

**Adjustment.** As deficiencies or variances become apparent to the project management team, the adjustment of resources can be made, often through negotiations, to ensure project completion or to minimize the delay. This adjustment may involve a rescheduling of assets and likely will require extensive coordination among the project participants. Though the R&D project is usually a one-time activity, it can be very beneficial for all contributors to participate in an after-action evaluation effort. A review of project successes and failures and consideration of the causes of difficulties is always helpful, because, even though a particular project may not be done again, the team may undertake another similar project.

If the planning and scheduling steps are done properly, the amount of monitoring and adjustment required will be reduced. The team or project manager can implement the schedule with full confidence in the plan and with the expectancy that monitoring and adjustment will be required only for unanticipated external-to-the-firm situations. Alternatively, if the planning and scheduling have been poorly or hastily accomplished, then extensive time and effort must be committed to the monitoring and adjustment steps. The process of implementing and managing technology and of planning and controlling a production process is demonstrated in Application Box 13-2.

The Allen–Bradley automation project is one of many such projects that major global manufacturing companies are implementing today. The technologies of such efforts involve shop floor planning and control, hardware and software, and a notable reduction in the direct labor contribution to production. These are all aspects of the factory of the future, which is considered in Chapter 15.

This section has defined R&D projects in terms of the breadth and nature of effects that technology changes have contributed to the workplace. Subsequently, the characteristics and levels of R&D projects were described and four steps of project management, planning, scheduling, monitoring, and adjusting, were noted. Because R&D projects require extensive work, the decision to commit to technological change should not be taken lightly.

## *The Motivation to Change Technology*

The time, resources, and impacts of a technology change effort necessitate a strong institutional commitment to that change. The probabilities and consequences of the failure of the project are sufficiently high that it makes little sense to compound those outcomes by insufficient organization commitment. Thus, each organization and each project manager must evaluate the motivations that drive and impede technology change. In such specific situations, some motivations are clear and objectively measurable, whereas others are less defined.

A number of trade-offs govern the decision to change technologies. The strategist may select, within feasible alternatives, to operate in the short or the long term. As pointed out by Banks and Wheelwright (1979), the pressures for short-term profitability can seriously impede the accomplishment of long-term goals. Similarly, Schoonhoven et al. (1990) documented the intuitive conclusion that, among new semiconductor ventures, substantial technology innovation reduces the speed with which the first product reaches

## APPLICATION BOX 13-2 Common Sense Technology Implementation at Allen–Bradley

Allen–Bradley is a manufacturer of industrial automation controls and information systems. These little black boxes, or contactors, are used to control a wide range of industrial equipment and machinery. In the early 1980s, foreign equipment was increasingly imported to the United States with contactors manufactured to specifications promulgated by International Electro-Technical Commission (IEC). The foreign contactors were smaller and easier to build, and Allen–Bradley quickly realized that they would have to design and build contactors to the IEC specifications or get out of the contactor business.

Engineers evaluated the IEC contactors and found that, on materials alone, they cost one-third the amount of those produced to U.S. specifications. Considering that U.S. labor costs were well above those of foreign competition, the prospects for Allen–Bradley appeared grim. Then the Allen–Bradley research and development team evaluated the situation further and realized that if they could produce contactors in a paperless, peopleless, and inventoryless environment, they could develop a competitive model. This planning effort was pursued as management realized that decision measures such as return on investment (ROI) and internal rate of return were not relevant, because those measures did not consider the strategic opportunities and threats of a technological advance. Prior models were based on labor's absorption of overhead, but they did not aid strategic thinking and did not address the technologies necessary for competitive global manufacturing. The costs of computer-integrated manufacturing may not be justified by traditional ROI analysis, but may be necessitated by the quality and flexibility requirements to compete in a world-class manufacturing or service environment. This strategic planning process took more than a year.

Scheduling, monitoring, and adjustment of the production process were all done by a complex information management system. The managing software of the technology, that is, the software to integrate the information system (which tells the machines what to build) and the control system (which tells the machines how to build the part and which tracks quality) required major redesign to reduce the computer time. The key risk of the project was in integrating the information system with the control system, but Allen–Bradley engineers used project scheduling methods. They were able to resolve the difficulties and monitor and adjust the project toward completion.

Along the way, Allen–Bradley faced numerous training and personnel problems. They had to find a project leader, and they had to address the needs of a union and professional staff, and to selectively integrate their suppliers. Few managers volunteered to lead the project because of the very substantial and risky hurdles it entailed, but the right person was finally identified. Similarly, the union leadership agreed to support the project by avoiding disparaging remarks about automation and by permitting employee selection based on aptitude, not seniority. Four workers were selected for the plant. Additionally, several groups of professional staff had to be brought together. Finally, the integration of suppliers played a key part in several process development efforts. Priorities and resources were readjusted, schedules were modified and integrated, and controls were tightened. Careful management was necessary to get the different divisions and groups to work together.

The effort at Allen–Bradley showed the necessity that senior decision makers, including CEOs, get directly involved with the technical level of the decision. Though top management does not have to know all the technical details, they must know enough about the problem to make an intelligent decision. In the words of CEO Tracy O'Rourke, "If you can't understand the fundamentals of a decision, you're a figurehead. You're not the CEO." Because of careful planning, scheduling,

Continued

**APPLICATION BOX 13-2** *Continued*

monitoring, and adjustment, the project went on line in three years, and it has exceeded profitability expectations.

Materials drawn from Bernard Avishai, "A CEO's Common Sense of CIM: An Interview with J. Tracy O'Rourke," *Harvard Business Review,* January–February 1989, pp. 110–117, and from Kim Blass, "World-Class Strategies Help Create a World-Class CIM Facility," *Industrial Engineering,* November 1992, pp. 26–29.

the marketplace. Further, they found that companies whose organization design included both marketing and manufacturing tended to ship their first products more rapidly than those that did not.

## *Incentives and Impediments to Change Technology*

The factors that impel or impede technology change could be elaborated extensively. The purpose here is to merely establish several basic dimensions of those motives, and then to evaluate the dynamics of the motives. Table 13-1 offers a general overview of the corporate and individual financial, marketplace, market position, and perception/reputation issues stated as incentives and impediments to change technology. Of course, management's orientation toward risk will also be a key factor in technology change, one which will ultimately emplace the various incentives or impediment structures stated here.

**TABLE 13-1 Incentives and Impediments to Technology Change**

| Issue | Incentives | Impediments |
|---|---|---|
| Quantifiable measures | | |
| Profitability of the firm | Profit contributions | Cost of equipment, materials, information systems, human resources |
| Individual compensation | Rewards and tangible recognition for substantive research and development contributions | Little tangible organization support for research and development contributions, thus higher costs |
| Qualitative measures | | |
| Market | Open, dynamic competitive markets | Stultifying, protected, or monopolistic markets |
| Goals | Prestige of being identified with high technology | Commitment to other goals, such as low-cost implementation of high-volume products |
| Perceived difficulty of change | Comparatively easy, given corporate experience | Comparatively difficult; corporate experience not as good as competition |

Considering the quantitative or objective measures, the potential profit contribution and costs of equipment, materials, and management information systems impose a financial reality on market decisions. Similarly, individuals are either encouraged or discouraged by the reward and recognition structure to make individual efforts toward technology change. Considering the qualitative or more subjective measures, the conditions of the market may be open, dynamic, and competitive, or stultifying, protected, and monopolistic. Additionally, firms or individuals may desire the prestige of a technology edge or may define a niche elsewhere. Further, the assessed technical, administrative, and organizational difficulty of the change may also constrain implementation efforts. Firms that have a competitive advantage in a particular technology or individuals with greater skills are expected to have greater incentive to pursue that niche. Those for whom the technology implementation is more difficult may have a greater incentive to find other potential product/service, or customer-related competitive advantages.

The positioning and prestige of the company as a technology leader and employee pride in that status offer a very strong individual, group, and corporate incentive. Alternatively, the company may choose to be a technology follower and pursue other goals, which would impede the implementation of technology change. These incentives and impediments are inextricably related in that impediments constrain or preclude incentives, and vice versa. The strategy, starting at the corporate level and projecting through the operations area, must interweave a mosaic of formal policy and informal culture that clearly describes the R&D strategy of the firm.

## *"Noise Versus Benefits" Evaluation*

The overall motivation toward risk by the firm may be viewed as the interaction of these quantitative financial and compensation factors with more qualitative factors. Certainly, other quantitative and qualitative factors could be elaborated, particularly as they apply to specific industries or firms. Following Baranson's (1977) term, the qualitative factors are called, in the aggregate, "noise," meaning perturbances or inconsistencies of various sorts. For example, bureaucratic review processes, both inside and outside the firm, constitute an impediment to technological progress, or noise, because the review subjects the technology to overview or scrutiny. The higher the noise level, the greater the impediment to technological change.

Each manager of a technology change can measure the risks and trade-offs of the situation on a curve, defined by the costs or profits and noise of the change. The curve represents the locus of all technology alternatives measured by profits and noise. In addition to the curve, each manager or organization defines a noise tolerance level, the limit of noise that is tolerable, to individuals, to a group, or to a corporation. A dynamic risk–trade-off curve situation and the noise tolerance level are shown in Figure 13-2.

The initial risk–trade-off curve of the firm is represented by curve *ab;* the firm may select from various technology innovation alternatives along curve *ab*. At the *a* end of the curve, there is a relatively high profit potential, but large amounts of noise; while at the *b* end, the options have a lower potential profit, but involve less noise. This concept is

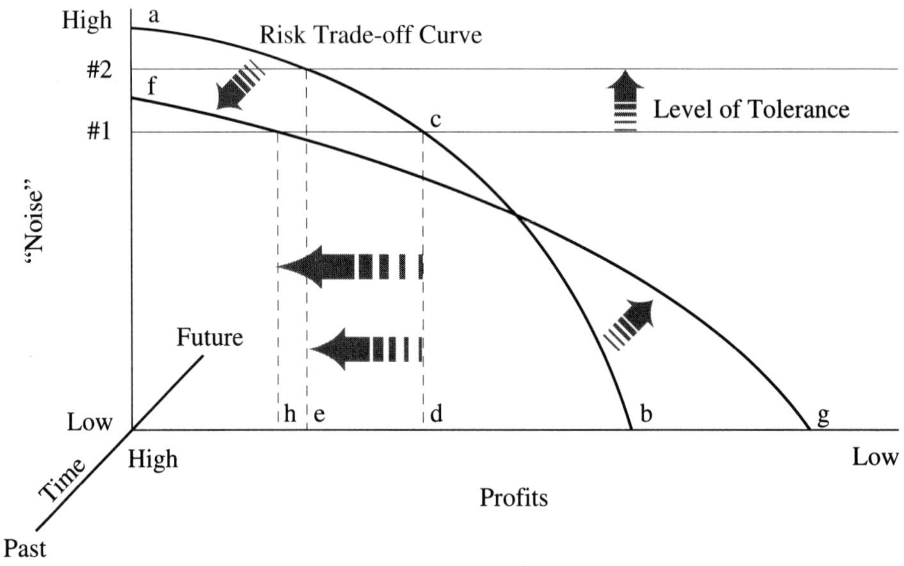


**FIGURE 13-2 The "Noise" Versus Profits of Innovation**

Reprinted from *The Engineering Economist,* Vol. 22, No. 1, copyright 1977, Institute of Industrial Engineers, 25 Technology Park, Atlanta, Ga. 30092.

presented as a continuous arc of alternatives; however, practically, there may be only a small number of discrete technology or capacity alternatives at several locations along or near the arc (see Chapter 5 for a discussion of "lumpy" capacity changes). Additionally, it is entirely possible that some of these innovative alternatives may be precluded by the defined level of tolerance of the individual, group, or organization; that is, options above a particular noise level may not be acceptable to the decision maker. If level of tolerance 1 is assumed to be the initial level, this unacceptable range of alternatives is depicted by the range *ac,* while alternatives in the *bc* range are acceptable.

If the risk taker were motivated to commit the organization to level of tolerance 1, then the risk taker would select the technology option as close to the level of tolerance as possible, resulting in profits at or close to *d.* If the level of tolerance were raised from 1 to 2, however, profitability would shift from *d* to *e.* Calm, stable management styles, in response to turbulence, can reduce the effects of outside factors and raise the level of tolerance.

An alternative management strategy would be to rotate the risk–trade-off curve by reducing the subjective impediments to technology ("noise") or by reducing the profit expectancies (that is, increasing the cost estimates). For example, management could work for reduction of protected markets, could change the niche of the company by enhancing the prestige and reputation of high technology, or could hire people with appropriate levels of experience to make tasks more easily achievable. If the flatter risk–trade-off curve (*fg*) were achieved and the level of tolerance remained unchanged at 1, a higher profit level at *h* could be realized.

Management's function is to use motivational techniques, rewards, and other tools to push up the level of tolerance to noise (develop capabilities to handle noise). Additionally, management establishes policy buffers to reduce the effects of noise, thus rotating the risk–trade-off curve in a counterclockwise direction. The opposite outcomes, which might result from poor management effort, would be that the level of tolerance drops and the risk–trade-off curve rotates clockwise, resulting in increased noise or decreased profitability.

Profitability may be improved in a technology change situation by careful analysis of the risk–trade-off curve and the incentives and impediments to motivation. Of course, levels of tolerance and the slope of the risk–trade-off curve cannot be rapidly shifted. Management of the risk trade-off over time, the third dimension of Figure 13-2, is not only possible, but necessary; yet it requires a proactive forward-directed vision of the corporation and its environment—and courage. Though the conceptual groundwork for this type of analysis is established by Baranson (1977), further research is necessary.

## Decision Variables in Technology Management

The operations manager must make technology implementation decisions within this general framework. These decisions range from high to low levels of innovation and from long to short range. Additionally, the technology decision may be defined in terms of commitment increments, reversibility, and redundancy of effort. Technology decisions that involve smaller incremental commitments, that are reversible at low costs, and that involve parallel and redundant thrusts are usually more acceptable than their opposites, because the risks are reduced and the likelihood of success is enhanced. Unfortunately, most process technology implementation efforts are lumpy (see Chapter 5), are not easily reversible, and are not disposed toward low-cost duplication.

Additionally, there are numerous ways to achieve innovation without incurring excessive noise, such as backward or forward integration, outsourcing for high technology component items, and moving operations to low-labor-cost areas. However, as Werther et al. (1986) point out, these approaches may be profitable in the short run, but they would likely hasten the demise of the company in the long run, causing it to become a technology-dependent marketing and service arm of the production company. From a global perspective, a nation can also become a technology-dependent service arm of a producing nation. Beyond these basics, however, the operations manager must make three strategic decisions with regard to technology implementation.

1. Technology leadership versus followership
2. Product/service technology versus process technology innovation (materials technology and information systems are subsumed in this discussion)
3. Dedicated versus flexible systems (information systems are subsumed in this discussion)

## *Technology Leadership*

The technology leader is distinguished from the technology follower in that the technology leader actively searches for, evaluates, and develops technology alternatives to the point that they can be either proved or rejected through testing or market mechanisms. The costs of a technology leadership strategy are high because of the irreversibility, lumpiness, and required redundancy of the effort. Alternatively, the technology follower actively waits and monitors the developments in the field until the leader shows some level of product\service, process, material, information system, or management system viability, and then enters the market by either modeling or acquiring existing innovations. The follower generally incurs lower costs due to adapting to, rather than creating, the change; but the technology follower is exposed to the risks associated with late entry into the market. Clearly, in some industries, there are significant advantages for the first entrant, and the technology follower must be prepared to produce at a lower cost and quickly close the product/service-differentiation gap that results from being the second or later entrant. Alternatively, the technology leader is likely to have a greater research orientation and must bear the risks and costs of technology failure, compared with a more development-oriented follower (see Chapter 2 for a discussion of market entrance strategy). A further elaboration of the trade-offs between the attributes of the technology leader and follower is given in Table 13-2.

The technology follower has the very difficult task of evaluating activities of competitors for inclusion in their own strategic analysis. This field, called *competitor analysis* (CA) is actively pursued by numerous Fortune 500 firms, one-third of which spend more

**TABLE 13-2 Technology Leadership**

| Factor | Leader ◄ | ► Follower |
|---|---|---|
| Market demand | Potentially large, but unpredictable market demands | Better defined and more predictable market demands |
| Market response | Potentially slow market response requires innovative marketing effort | Rapid product/service recognition and acceptance requires less innovative marketing effort |
| Market structure | Definition of market, sales, and distribution policies important and costly | Easy adaption of existing market, sales, and distribution policies |
| Integration of segments | Demand may disruptively cross existing market and product/service segments | Demand fits existing market and product/service segments |
| Risks and costs | Risks and costs of technology failure are high | Risks and costs of technology failure are lower because technology is better defined |
| R&D orientation | Greater research orientation | Greater development orientation |

than one million dollars per year on CA. In addition to strategic planning and management decision making, CA may be used to sensitize top management to a situation, to benchmark the costs, capabilities, or design of a competitor's product/service, and to focus problem resolution through legitimation (using competitor's problem-solving methods) and inspiration (showing that a problem is solvable). CA is a key method to increase the learning rate and reduce learning times, though CA raises concerns with the potential misuse of proprietary information or patented products or processes (Ghoshal and Westney, 1991).

Ali et al. (1993) define the "pioneering" and "incremental development" strategies, which pursue, respectively, highly innovative and less innovative projects. They examine how a firm's characteristics, such as the efficiency of completing projects, the ability to switch or adjust from a pioneering to an incremental strategy, and the first "mover" (first in the market), affect product development strategies. Additionally, as might be expected, the average completion time and variance of the completion time of prospective projects both affect project selection among firms with different strategies.

Technology leadership also applies to nations. Japan may have been unfairly stereotyped as a copier of technology developed by the United States and other nations. It would be likely more accurate to say that Japan has made a commitment not to develop technology that they can acquire more cheaply in other ways. Japanese firms identify strategic markets and the critical resources and components of these markets, and then build those industries. Numerous examples are found in polymers, composites, metals, and inorganic compounds. Specifically, the manufacturing processes for gallium arsenide wafers (used to make computer chips) were first pioneered by General Electric in the 1960s, but GE and other U.S. firms have gotten out of that business. Similarly, the hydrogen-storing alloys used in batteries were discovered by the Brookhaven National Laboratory in 1964, but were developed for production by Japanese firms, including Matsushita, Sanyo, Hitachi, and Toshiba (Gross and Black, 1991). VCRs, color televisions, and numerous electronics items are other examples in which the basic research was done in the United States but the development occurred in Japan.

## *Product/Service Versus Process Technology Innovation*

The operations strategist must decide upon the relative importance of product/service and process technology innovation. In this discussion, product/service innovation includes not only the product and service design, but also the innovation of materials and component parts, and process design includes the associated information and management systems. Typically, this issue is very closely related to the stage of product/service–process technology life cycle. Products or services in the growth state experience high levels of technology development, which subsequently decreases with the stable state and decline and renewal stages. Process innovation increases through the stable state stage, and then declines as follow-on products receive greater resource emphasis. The importance of product/service and process technology innovation and the product/service–process technology life cycle is shown in Figure 13-3.

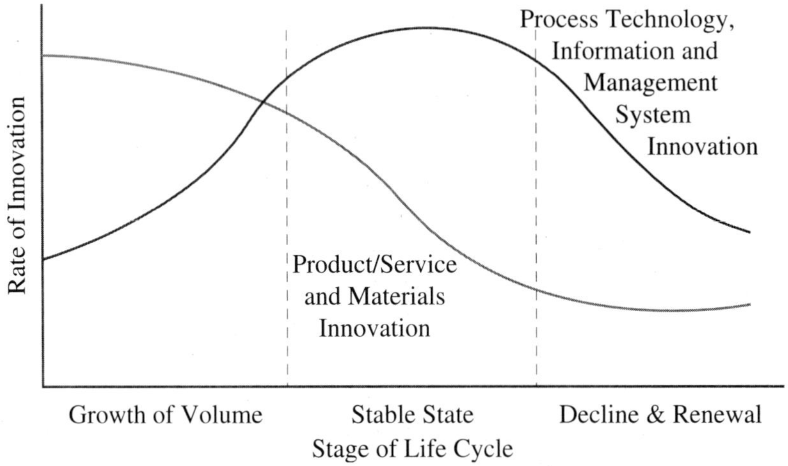


**FIGURE 13-3 Technology Innovation and the Product/Service–Process Technology Life Cycle**

Adapted from William J. Abernathy and James Utterbach, "Dynamic Model of Process and Product Innovation." *Omega,* Vol. 3, No. 6, 1975, pp. 639–657.

## *Dedicated Versus Flexible Systems*

The selection of a process technology implicitly involves the decision to use a dedicated or a flexible system. Dedicated systems fully commit resources to the specific process and product/service, while flexible systems commit to a more general process and broader product/service line. Flexible manufacturing systems involve greater use of rapid setup equipment and information systems, thereby achieving flexibility of process. There is a strong temptation to hedge the risks of purchasing dedicated equipment by incorporating the greater flexibility of equipment and information systems. However, the costs of flexibility must be included in total system costs and prorated as a fixed cost of the decision (Hill, 1989). Too often these extensive systems costs are ignored when total costs are computed, leading to an understatement of actual product or service costs. The optimal solution in a stable environment is to carefully plan the purchase and utilization of dedicated equipment for high volume operations, which, with minor supplemental costs, can be upgraded as the need occurs. However, if markets are dynamic, greater flexibility is necessary.

Thus, firms can be categorized as to whether they choose to develop new technology themselves or to model or acquire existing technologies; whether they choose to innovate products/services, process technology, or both; and whether they commit to dedicated or flexible systems. A study by Capon et al. (1992) found that four different strategies (product and process investors, process investors, noninnovators, and acquirers) may be used to focus innovation in different ways and with different results. For example, return on capital was highest for product and process investors and acquirers, but lower for noninnovators and poor for process innovators. Clearly, the selection of the R&D strategy is related to amount of effort as well as to the outcome.

## Managing Technology Transfer

Management of the technology transfer process through the product/service/process technology life cycle from the birth of the product/service through stable state to decline and renewal is supported by a number of evaluative approaches. Empirical studies (Roberts, 1992) have shown that the success of high-technology companies is closely related to careful management in transferring the product/service and process technology from early "incubator" stages to later growth stages. A clear focus on product/service and process development, visible marketing organizations, and a clear focus on customer needs were found to be important during the transition. Project management methods reduce the time required to make product/service or process technology design changes, and they permit the project to be evaluated simultaneously by several different activities. Application Box 13-3 describes the use of product design methods at Motorola.

Product mapping also can be used to dimensionalize and visualize the new product development process and needs. Mapping permits representation of the evolution of a company's product/service line over time and the needs for various types of "leveraged" products/services, such as enhanced, customized, cost-reduced, or hybrid units (Wheelwright and Sasser, 1989). The product map shows the dimensions of time and functionality or price, thus graphically depicting where the product line is and where it is not, which permits decision makers to visualize new product needs and competitive niches. Product maps are effective when used with product line mixes or modules, because they offer a graphical depiction of the product domain. Maps could also be used to depict competitor products and niches as well, permitting visualization of the market as a whole. These examples represent several of the many different ways to define and use product maps. Application Box 13-4 depicts a product line mapping situation.

Management of these methods, or other similar alternatives, requires a concerted effort. Often the organization chooses to build a "technology platform," which can be used for multiple R&D applications. The platform consists of several integrated teams, each with different focuses, various facilities, capacities, and knowledge, and the corporate background of experience in product/service and process technology development. In its simplest form, the technology platform might involve a project implementation team, consisting of market analysis, design, manufacturing, sales and distribution, and service system resources, each contributing simultaneously toward the project goal from their functional perspective. The combined effort, if carefully managed, contributes to the synergy of the group, because the output is greater than the sum of the inputs. Figure 13-4 describes the minimum components for the synchrony of a project implementation team.

Project implementation teams can be variously configured, depending upon the type of research or development project. Research scientists would form a team to consider a materials composition issue, and computer specialists would work together to identify a bug in a material requirements planning program. Project teams can also be used to define products and services or to address process issues. Synchrony is the simultaneous involve-

### APPLICATION BOX 13-3 Product Design at Motorola

Every product begins as an idea, but few ideas become products. This is true for various reasons. The idea may not be feasible or more importantly, the idea may be eliminated because someone else has the same idea or a similar or better idea. The success of one product over another in a competitive market is very dependent upon which product penetrates the market first. In the world of innovation, the process management methods that can cut the "gestation period" of a new product while simultaneously increasing manufacturing efficiency and quality have long been sought.

Motorola Inc. found such a phenomenon in the 3-D design software developed by a Toronto-based software company. What resulted, in April 1989, was Motorola's introduction of its 10.7-ounce MicroTac pocket-size cellular phone. By integrating 3-D design software into the computer-aided design and manufacturing (CAD/CAM) process, Motorola was able to decrease the usual number of product design steps by one-half, thereby beating the competition to the market by nearly two years and banking over $1 billion in MicroTac phone sales.

Before the 3-D computer software was available, product design was done manually and traditionally required four steps: (1) sketching, (2) rendering, (3) modeling, and (4) engineering/manufacturing. The 3-D software, however, requires only two steps. In the first, the sketching, rendering, and modeling processes are integrated. Using a work station, the design engineer can generate a realistic 3-D model of an idea, and the software automatically builds a mathematical data base of the product dimensions. With the versatility of being able to make revisions and try new designs without having to commit to costly tooling processes, more creative power is released by the designers. Problems can be detected early in the process, permitting reduced development time and increased product quality. After all of the revisions have been made, the data describing the designed 3-D model are transferred directly to the CAD/CAM system and the second step of the process, engineering/manufacturing, is completed. The CAD/CAM system then interprets the design parameters to machine instructions and builds prototype parts.

By integrating the 3-D software packages with their existing CAD/CAM programs, Motorola was able to electronically link every step of the design process from initial sketching to building molds. Moreover, the time to move the MicroTac from the work station to the market was cut in half. However, this speed of design did not result in the loss of quality. The MicroTac received not just one but two of Japan's top product quality control awards.

Materials drawn from William C. Symonds, "Pushing Design to Dizzying Speed," *Business Week,* October 21, 1991.

ment of appropriate levels and types of technical specialists to consider a specified technology issue. The term *technosynchrony* describes the further situation, where several different technologies are integrated. This integration provides a technological platform of innovation and often results in more rapid product/service, process technology, or system delivery. Technosynchrony is the basis for platforms of technical resources that, with minor reconfiguration, can be repetitively used for different projects.

The management of functionally integrated teams toward organization goals, however, is often very difficult. Kezsbom (1992) found that project goals, priorities, and personalities were consistently the most important reasons for conflict in implementation teams. This research emphasizes the need for regular status review sessions and team interaction, as well as active team-building efforts.

## APPLICATION BOX 13-4 Product Mapping at Acme Sound

Laura Eckersley, president of Acme Sound Systems, had just learned of the technique of product mapping from a visiting academic consultant. She was excited about the process because it could graphically depict the development of Acme's market and identify the specific market niche to which Acme produced.

Though the exact definition of a product map is based on user needs, it is usually defined on two dimensions. The horizontal dimension generally is used to depict time, and the vertical dimension depicts added product value, functionality, or price. Boxes are used to represent the company product line, indicating the market niche of the company. This depiction over time permits the strategist to graphically see the position of the company's product line within the domain and the market. Numerous variations may be used to show the positioning of the company's product versus that of one or all competitors, the percent market share, the types of products, and so forth. The dimensions of the product map must be specifically defined by the user.

The model with which Eckersley was working, shown on page 500, categorized product offerings as "core" and "leveraged" products. Leveraged products were further identified as "enhanced," "customized," "cost-reduced," and "hybrid" products. The core model is introduced first and often serves as a benchmark for evaluation of the rest of the product line. Enhanced products are developed from the core prototype; they possess additional features and are an initial attempt to define product differentiating features and to target more upscale markets. Customized models are built with specialized features for designated distribution channels or customers. A cost-reduced model, sold under another brand name, is designed to fulfill the demand for a low-end product. The cost-reduced model possesses much of the same technology as the enhanced model, except that it has less "frills" and is usually made with cheaper parts and has lower factory costs. Lastly, the hybrid model results from merging two core products or technologies.

The product map's configuration provides tremendous insight into the operations strategy of an organization. Each product point on the map indicates management's assumptions regarding corporate strengths and weaknesses and the existing market forces (threats and opportunities) shaping each product's evolution, such as distribution channels, product technology, manufacturing approaches, and market entry and exit barriers. When each functional area in an organization is looking at the same product development map, staff members and directors can understand new market opportunities and technological challenges facing the company. The process forces a team approach, because each area can identify complementary approaches and strategies for effective product development.

A quick review of the map suggested to Eckersley that Acme did not currently produce a home model of the cost-reduced compact disk (CD) player. Additionally, she noted that the company had put most of its recent research effort into the different models of multiple-disk compact disk player. But in the expected economic downturn, the cost-reduced, single-disk player with some basic quality features, such as a dolby noise reduction system and several memory function capabilities, might be better received. Eckersley quickly wrote a memo to her director of research and development, transmitting the consultant's materials, and suggesting that the process be considered for adoption as a standard research and development slide at the monthly president's strategic program review committee meeting.

Concept adapted from Steven C. Wheelwright and W. Earl Sasser, Jr., "The New Product Development Map," *Harvard Business Review.* May–June 1989, pp. 112–125.

*Continued*

**APPLICATION BOX 13-4** *Continued*

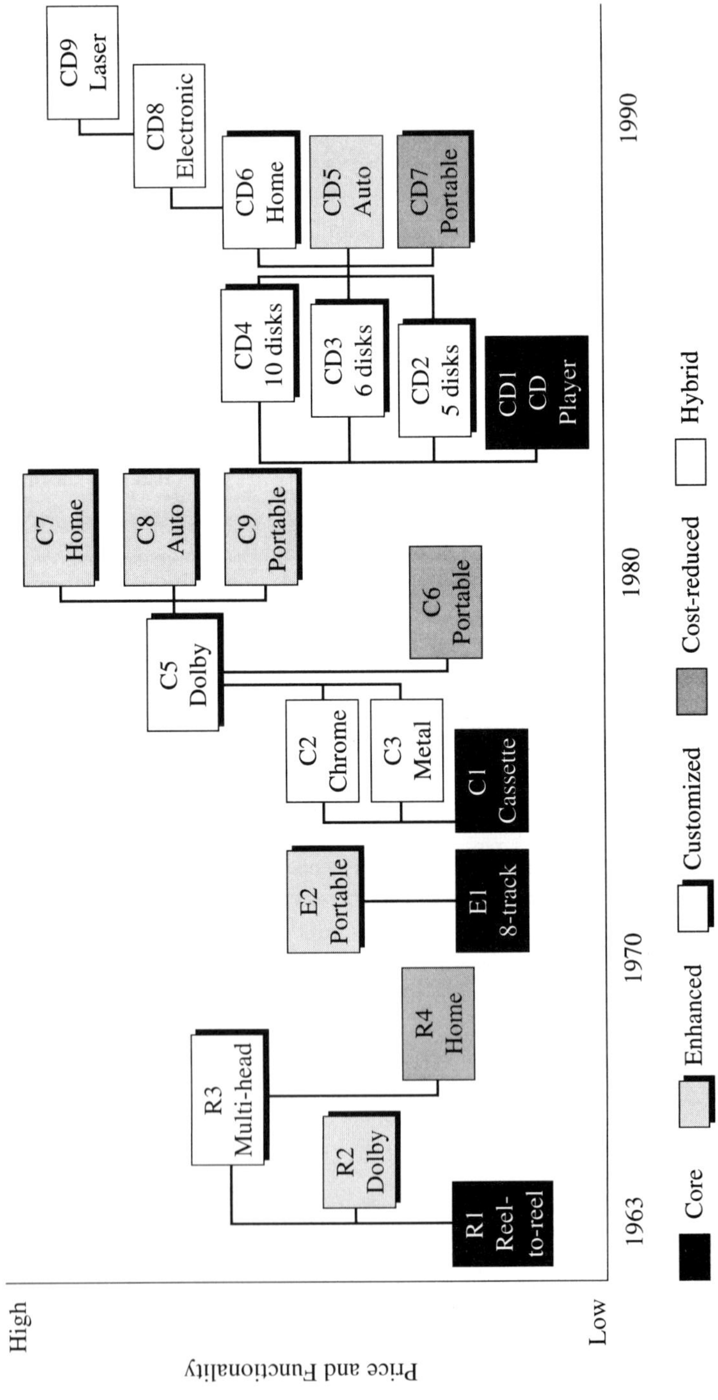


**The Product Map of Acme Sound**

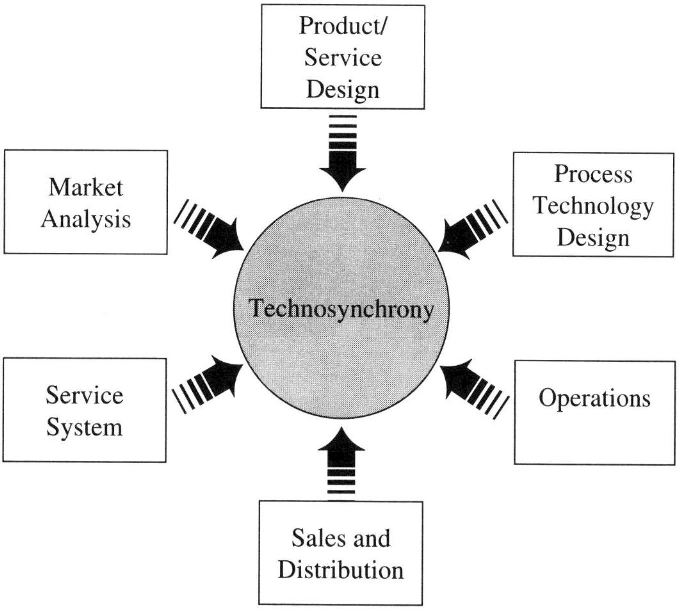


**FIGURE 13-4 The Synchrony of a Project Implementation Team**

## *Managing Product/Service Line Growth*

The management of a new model or the development of a product/service line over time requires a process by which to manage the project implementation team or technology platform. This process is often managed by "S curve" analysis, where several S curves represent sequential products/services or process technologies. The shape of the S curve results from an initial pattern of slow growth and market uncertainty, followed by a period of more rapid growth, and finally by another period of slowing growth as the limits of the technology or market are reached. Typically, a product or service line will be characterized by a progression of several models or technology variations, as suggested by the product map.

A key strategic decision for the operations manager or the R&D staff is when and how to abandon the current technology and transfer investment and effort to the emerging technology. Technology forecasts, the forecasting of technology developments, generally involve qualitative methods, such as the Delphi method; however, these types of methods are judgmental and very dependent on subjective inputs (Burgelman and Maidique, 1988). Though S curve analysis is usually applied to products or services, the same logic can be applied to process or materials technologies and to information systems. Figure 13-5 represents the S curve of one product, followed by that of an improved product. Several "cutover" options are suggested.

Given the S curve of a particular product and an improved product, the operations strategist must decide when to transfer investment emphasis from product 1 to product 2. Graphically, three alternatives are represented. The first cutover starts at $C_1$ as soon as

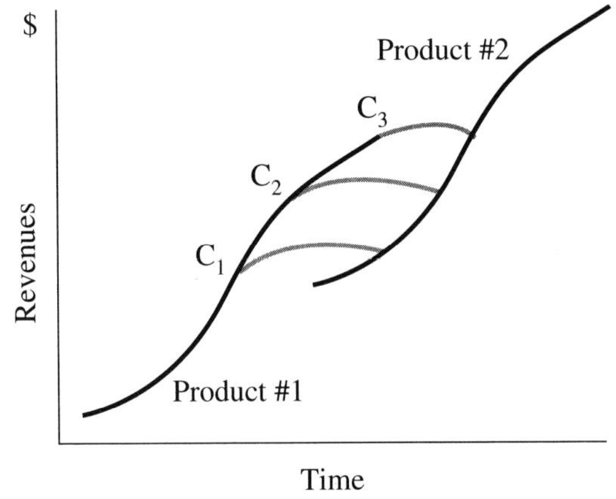


**FIGURE 13-5 The "S-Curve" of Product Growth**

product 2 is shown to be viable. At the other extreme, product 1 is permitted to achieve its natural stable state volume with a cutover at point $C_3$. An intermediate strategy shows a cutover at point $C_2$. Each alternative incurs risks. Immediate transfer at point $C_1$ abandons product 1 at its highest growth rate for an as-yet unproved follow-on product. Late transfer at point $C_3$ continues the existing technology until it has reached its highest volume, but does not capture part of the rapid growth phase of product 2. This may reduce the changeover costs and risks, but the liability is that the competition may enter the market ahead of product 2 with its own second-generation product. The middle option is a combination of these risks.

A method suggested by Swamidass (1987) is helpful to more specifically evaluate the costs and risks of technology changeover. Swamidass proposes three "deterioration of technology" indexes to measure the ratio of the currently installed technology to the state of the art technology. As adapted from Swamidass, the indexes would be represented as:

$$\text{Deterioration of technology} = \frac{\text{average } (X) \text{ for installed technology} \times 100\%}{\text{average } (X) \text{ for state of the art technology}}$$

where $(X)$ may be a cost, quality, or flexibility measure, or some combination of measures. Among the possible cost, quality, and flexibility measures noted by Swamidass are

| | |
|---|---|
| Cost | Average unit cost |
| Quality | Reject rate |
| | Rework rate |
| | Total quality control cost |
| Flexibility | Setup time |
| | Turnaround time |
| | Minimum lot size |

The periodic (perhaps quarterly) computation of an index would permit the use of an intuitively or experimentally derived modernization point to trigger planning action. Perhaps a modernization band, based on an index value of between 150 and 175, could be defined for a particular situation. The use of deterioration of technology indexes and modernization points is a very new and untested approach; it must be defined for specific industries and businesses, and judgmental evaluations of such indicator data will have to be made. However, this process does provide a computational base line for further periodic quantitative and judgmental evaluations.

## *Technology Portfolio Management*

The R&D manager is responsible for a variety of product/service, process technology, materials, and information technologies, each in various states of development. Some technologies may be current products/services and process technologies; others may be developing through the early stages of the life cycle, while still others may be only knowledge-building efforts. Each individual project should be evaluated on the basis of two criteria: technological potential and manufacturing potential. Technological potential is a research concept. That is, can the technology be proved in the laboratory or in some other related application, or has the technology been shown to be sound or derived from other known facts? Alternately, manufacturing potential is a development idea. That is, is the researched approach amenable to production methods, and are the production methods required by necessary volumes feasible, safe, nonpolluting, and so forth? Those technologies with a greater combined technology and manufacturing potential should be identified for heavier emphasis of the R&D program and for greater levels of funding.

However, R&D resources should also be managed with clear emphasis toward market assessment of future profitability. The pure R&D perspective must be tempered by market needs and viability, as evaluated by sales forecasts and measures such as break-even points, five-year return-on-investment rates, and the like. Though the R&D staff may cringe at the prospect of having their products evaluated by measures of market relevance, ultimately the R&D program must produce marketable goods and services at prices, quality, and availability that are acceptable to the market. Figure 13-6 shows a method of depicting and managing the portfolio of R&D alternatives.

The manufacturing/technology matrix on the left side of the diagram is used as a general and subjective screening mechanism for all projects. The two key criteria, technological potential and manufacturing potential, are used to evaluate projects as low, average, or high potential. Project alternatives A through F are positioned on that matrix. Further evaluation of the market potential of the projects would be used to estimate profit contribution, defined by one or a combination of several measures. Those projects that were expected to generate the greatest anticipated profits would get the greatest share of R&D resources. Corporate R&D policies are then used to define the categories of heavy, moderate, and light emphasis and the respective proportions of anticipated profits and share of R&D resources associated with those categories. The portfolio of R&D alterna-

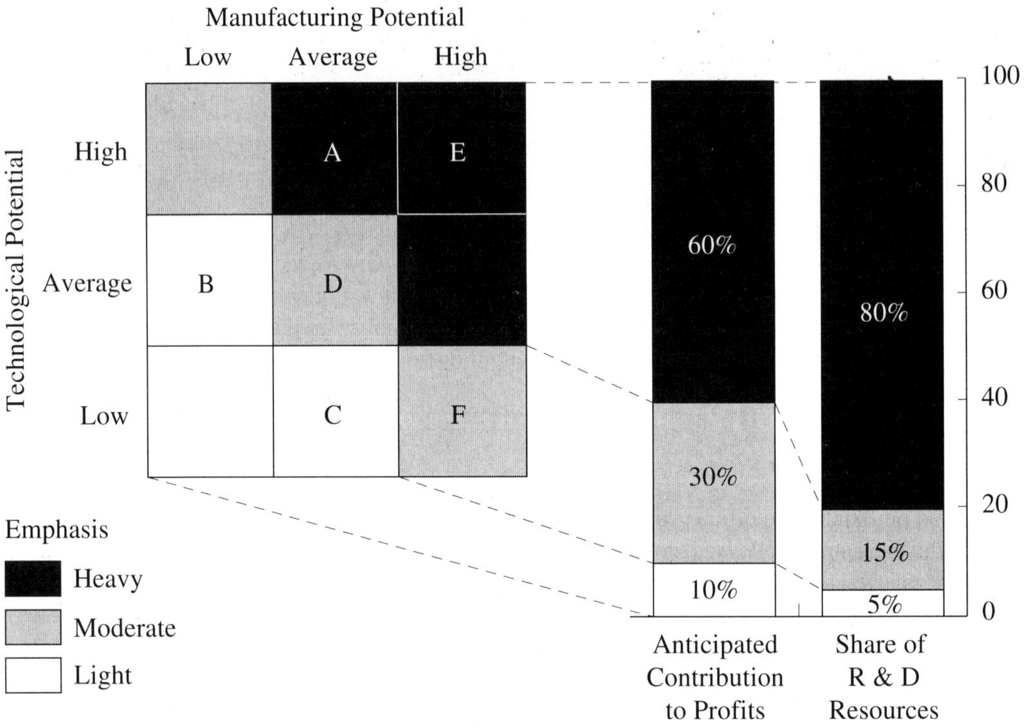


**FIGURE 13-6 A Portfolio of R&D Alternatives**

tives is an extremely effective method of managing the evaluation and funding of diverse projects. Wheelwright and Clark (1992) propose a very similar model, except that they categorize potential projects as derivative, platform, and breakthrough based on the amount of innovation required.

## *Managing Project Implementation*

Project management techniques integrate scheduling, materials, and cost information for businesses whose volume is counted in hundreds, rather than millions of products. Inefficiencies in scheduling and materials management can be extremely costly, and cost management of a project permits accurate bidding and clear performance expectations for each project. An example of how a project control method can be continually improved and refined is shown in Application Box 13-5.

Technical methods of managing project implementation permit accurate estimates of project flexibility, project cost, and the acceptability of project completion dates. The historically most used techniques are Gantt charts, program evaluation and review techniques (PERT), and critical path method (CPM).

## APPLICATION BOX 13-5 Refining the Process of Project Control at M. W. Kellogg Company

M. W. Kellogg Company, based in Houston, Texas, has an international reputation for the innovative engineering and construction management of petroleum and petrochemical process facilities. A subsidiary of Dresser Industries, Inc., M. W. Kellogg is one of the largest contractors in the world with construction activities in a variety of process markets, including ethylene, ammonia, liquified natural gas, oil, and synthetic fuel, as well as several specialized manufacturing processes.

Managing these numerous and widely ranging projects, however, requires expertise in project management and the innovative development of project management systems. Until the mid-1980s, Kellogg used a canned project management software program. However, the company requirements for the system quickly outgrew the system capabilities, and Kellogg management realized that they would have to work with a vendor to develop a hybrid system of their own.

The program would have to integrate time analysis, scheduling, aggregation, networking, and charting methods for project schedules, materials, and costs. The system also would have to independently manage and integrate the activities of roughly 20 different projects at a time. At Kellogg, a typical project would involve 1500 engineering activities, 1100 requisitions and purchase orders for materials, forecasts for 4000 cost account lines, and management of 150 project notices. Additionally, the system had to generate performance reports and progress curves. What resulted was a project control system called the integrated project control system, or IPCS.

Today, as new jobs are received by the company, a master schedule is developed. After approval by management, this schedule becomes the contract with the client and the basis for detailed schedules. Next, detailed engineering management and procurement schedules are established, reviewed and finalized. Budgets are defined and approved, then broken into cost accounts, which are integrated with the schedule. Project performance is tracked every two weeks by measuring the actual hours expended against planned base lines. Schedules are updated at least once per month. The process permits management to separately review the status of each project, and to schedule and evaluate the performance of teams. Additionally, the IPCS system is integrated with materials purchases. All bulk materials and equipment purchases or leases are tracked through a materials tracking system. This ensures that materials required for a job are ordered using lead-time offset and the status of the order is tracked to ensure performance.

The benefits of the system have been manifold. The most apparent initial benefit was that the prior system took as much as 24 hours for an updating run, while the IPCS can run a report or an update and provide the results in a matter of minutes. Both the convenience and reduced costs of labor interface with the system, and the reduced costs of system operation have been significant. Additionally, the system has managed the resources of the firm in ways that have saved significant amounts of money. Management can detect and correct potentially adverse scheduling or cost trends, and can adjust material requirements, either in due dates or in specifications to respond to customer-required or other changes. The system has permitted the company to develop an extensive historical data base, which improves the accuracy of cost projections and bidding.

The integrated project control system (IPCS) has been able to make the project management system at Kellogg more efficient than the competition and has reduced the labor time of system management activities. In the current very dynamic, highly visible, and safety-conscious environment of large-scale engineering projects, the IPCS is able to reduce risks, control projects, and give management more exact and flexible information than previously. Clearly, IPCS is a necessary and effective tool for project management businesses.

Materials drawn from Anita M. Hickman, "Refining the Process of Project Control," *Production and Inventory Management*, February 1992, pp. 26–27.

## *Gantt Charts*

The Gantt chart was developed in the early 1900s and named after Henry L. Gantt, a contemporary of Frederick W. Taylor. Gantt charts represent the project activities and the time line. This array permits a planner to identify the current period, the planned completion and variance of each activity, and progress toward completion, as shown by the time line. Today, the Gantt chart is used primarily for top-management briefings or as an initial step to organize the different activities and subactivities of the project. PERT and CPM methods provide more detailed and usable information for the project manager but may be unnecessarily complex for presentation to top management. Figure 13-7 gives an example of a Gantt chart.

The Gantt chart shows the project activities starting with the earliest at the top, sequenced through the latest. At the current time, shown by the time line at period 9, activities 1–2 and 2–3 have been completed, activities 2–4, 2–5, and 3–5 have been partially completed, and activities 4–6 and 5–6 have yet not been started. The chart shows that activities 2–4 and 2–5 were planned to have been completed by now and activity 4–6 should have been started; however, though the project is not late, it *appears* that effort should be committed to activities 2–4, 2–5, and 4–6 so that the project can be completed on schedule by the fifteenth week.

This visual analysis indicates a key limitation of the Gantt chart, that it does not show the sequence of each activity. This is emphasized by activity 4–6, which has not yet been

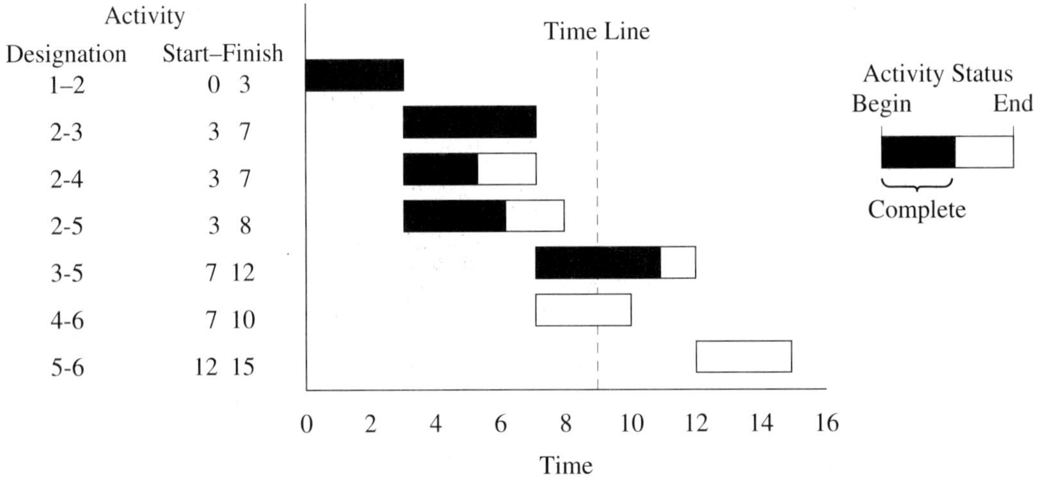


*Note*: The activity designation showing start and finish nodes and the start–finish times of activities are shown in this manner for comparison with the PERT method, which is subsequently described. Normally, however, in the Gantt format, activities are identified only by name or a designated abbreviation, and start and finish times are represented only by the activity status boxes.

**FIGURE 13-7 The Gantt Chart**

started, and which, from the chart, would appear to be late. In fact, as will be shown by the subsequent PERT analysis, activity 4–6 has some slack and does not have to be started until period 12. Thus, the Gantt chart does not clearly represent the actual earliness or lateness of activities.

## *Program Evaluation and Review Technique*

Though discovered independently, the program evaluation and review technique (PERT) and the critical path method (CPM) are very similar in concept, and over the years they have evolved together. The early CPM approach was generally deterministic (for example, no task time variances), whereas early PERT was generally statistical (task time variances permitted). Current CPM models, if defined as deterministic models, may be used for crashing trade-offs.

The PERT model computes the earliest and latest times to finish (or start) each task and the total project. The difference between the latest and the earliest finish times (start times may be similarly used) gives the slack (or unused time) for each activity. If the slack is zero, the activity is on the critical path. The critical path, the path that takes the longest time to complete, should be managed intensively, because any delay must be expedited or it will affect the project completion. Of course, near-critical paths must also be watched, because they can potentially become critical.

The program evaluation and review technique also permits the estimation of the probability that the project will be completed by a specified time. This is done by computing the variance of individual tasks using the beta distribution, which is appropriate for a one-time project. The variance may also be used to define a probability range around the expected completion time of the entire project. Usually, the standard normal distribution is used for the entire project, because of the larger number of observations. Thus, the PERT method improves upon the Gantt method in three ways. First, it gives a clear identification of the earliest and latest start and finish times of each task, which may be used to monitor task completion performance. Second, by specifying the critical path, PERT identifies the series of activities which, if not carefully managed, can cause delays in project completion. Finally, PERT permits an estimation of probabilities that a project would be completed early or late. These capabilities of the PERT model are demonstrated in Decision Model Box 13-1, using the same data as the Gantt example.

## *Critical Path Method with Crashing*

A further and valuable capability of the deterministic project evaluation method is its ability to assess crashing (or project time-reducing) opportunities. For example, if a project has a fixed per-period overhead cost, which may be stated as several different possible completion time and cost alternatives, the manager is able to trade off the costs of completing the project on schedule versus several alternative reductions in time. These alternatives would involve reduced project fixed costs but increased variable costs. For example, if one or several activities could be completed in a shorter time at a supplemental

## DECISION MODEL BOX 13-1 Program Evaluation and Review Technique—Driver and Passenger Protection Device

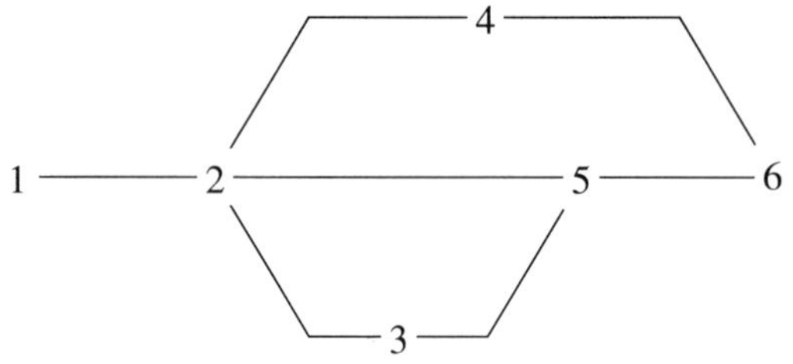


An auto manufacturer has decided to install driver and passenger protection devices (air bags) in all models as soon as possible. The VP of Manufacturing wants to make the change in 17 weeks, the deadline for next year's models. Development Engineering defines the flow chart and uses PERT to estimate the probability that the project will be completed on time. The following *general* tasks are defined, with optimistic, most likely, and pessimistic times. Task succession is shown both by the task designation and by the immediate predecessors.

| | | Times (weeks) | | | |
|---|---|---|---|---|---|
| Activity | Designation | Optimistic | Most Likely | Pessimistic | Immediate Predecessors |
| **1.** Redesign | 1–2 | 2 | 3 | 4 | – |
| **2.** Build prototype | 2–3 | 1 | 4 | 7 | 1–2 |
| **3.** Evaluate tooling | 2–4 | 3 | 4 | 5 | 1–2 |
| **4.** Write design report | 2–5 | 4 | 5 | 6 | 1–2 |
| **5.** Test prototype | 3–5 | 3 | 5 | 7 | 2–3 |
| **6.** Write tooling report | 4–6 | 1 | 3 | 5 | 2–4 |
| **7.** Prepare assembly line | 5–6 | 2 | 3 | 4 | 2–5, 3–5 |

Expected times and variances for each task are calculated by using the beta distribution with the formulas:

$$T_e = (T_O + 4_{ML} + T_P)/6 \qquad s^2 = ((T_P - T_O)/6)^2$$

| | | Completion Times (weeks) | | | |
|---|---|---|---|---|---|
| Activity | $T_e$ | Earliest | Latest | Slack | Variance |
| *1–2 | (2 + 12 + 4)/6 = 3 | 3 | 3 | 0 | 0.11 |
| *2–3 | (1 + 16 + 7)/6 = 4 | 7 | 7 | 0 | 1.0 |
| 2–4 | (3 + 16 + 5)/6 = 4 | 7 | 12 | 5 | 0.11 |
| 2–5 | (4 + 20 + 6)/6 = 5 | 8 | 12 | 4 | 0.11 |
| *3–5 | (3 + 20 + 7)/6 = 5 | 12 | 12 | 0 | 0.44 |
| 4–6 | (1 + 12 + 5)/6 = 3 | 10 | 15 | 5 | 0.44 |
| *5–6 | (2 + 12 + 4)/6 = 3 | 15 | 15 | 0 | 0.11 |

*Continued*

**DECISION MODEL BOX 13-1** *Continued*

The earliest completion time for each task is forward-calculated based on expected times of its own and preceding tasks. For example, the earliest completion time of task 3–5 is 12 (3 + 4 + 5), since it is preceded by tasks 1–2 and 2–3. Once the project expected time is computed (15), the latest times can be backward-calculated in the same way. The latest time of task 2–3 (followed by tasks 5–6 and 3–5) is 7 (or 15 – 3 – 5).

If branches or mergings of tasks are encountered, for earliest time computation, use the latest task completion time, and for the latest time, use the earliest task completion time. For example, the latest time for activity 1–2 backward computed by path 6–4–2–1 is 8 (15 – 3 – 4) but, if computed by path 6–5–3–2–1, it is 3 (15 – 3 – 5 – 4). Thus the latest time of activity 1–2 is 3, not 8. The critical path (noted by *) is where slack (latest time – earliest time) = 0.

The variance and standard deviation of critical path tasks are

$$\text{Var}_{cp} = 0.11 + 1.0 + 0.44 + 0.11 = 1.66 \qquad \text{SD}_{cp} = \text{square root of variance} = 1.29$$

Thus, the probability of completing the project by the desired time ($D^*$) of 17 weeks is

$$Z = (D^* - T_e)/\text{SD}_{cp} = \frac{17 - 15}{1.29} = \frac{2}{1.29} = 1.550$$

From the normal distribution table:

| | |
|---|---|
| Probability from 0 to 15 | = 0.5000 |
| Probability for $Z$ = 1.550 | = 0.4394 |
| Probability of 17 weeks completion | = 0.9394 ≈ 94% |

(for example, overtime) cost, the operations manager could reduce the number of periods for which overhead on the entire project was paid. A crashing extension of the same problem is shown in Decision Model Box 13-2.

The crashing process defines the crash cost per period, often called the crash slope, for each activity on the critical path. If the lowest available crash cost is less than the fixed cost per period, then crash; if not, the low-cost solution has been reached. The process is iterative, in that after each crashing decision, the critical path must be recomputed to assure that it has not changed. The crashing concept can also be applied to variables other than time. Badiru (1992) demonstrates an application to manage critical resources.

## *Importance of Project Management*

The importance of these project management techniques is highlighted by the fact that many markets are increasingly driven toward time-based competition. Though the effects of time-based competition can be seen in other areas, such as just-in-time scheduling, they are even more critical in new product development. Sony Corporation, for example, has

## DECISION MODEL BOX 13-2 Crashing—Driver and Passenger Protection Devices

The VP of Marketing reported that a competitor's new product market-entry date was moved up and asked if the project could be expedited, and, if so, at what cost. The use of crashing seemed appropriate to the VP of Manufacturing, because it permitted a trade-off of the extra costs of reducing task times (for example, by committing overtime) versus the fixed costs per period of being on the project.

The logic of the crashing method is to first solve the PERT problem, and then to determine project duration and the critical path. Next, possible crash opportunities (times and costs) are determined, often by engineering studies or judgment. Finally, the critical path tasks are evaluated to find the task with the lowest crash cost per period. When there are ≥2 critical paths, the tasks with the lowest combined crash costs/period are found. If the total crash cost per period is less than the fixed cost, the task should be crashed. If not, stop. In an iterative process, allocate the crash costs, recompute critical path(s) and reevaluate crashing alternatives.

Production engineers have reviewed the protection device project. They found that task times are absolutely accurate (that is, no variance), and they have advised that the following crash times and costs are possible and that the firm will spend $5000 in fixed costs for each of the 15 weeks on the project.

| Activity *i–j* | Expected Time (weeks) | Minimum Crash Time (weeks) | Maximum Possible Weeks to Crash | Crash Cost per Week ($) | | |
|---|---|---|---|---|---|---|
| | | | | 1st | 2nd | 3rd |
| *1–2 | 3 | 1 | 2 | 2100 | 3400 | |
| *2–3 | 4 | 1 | 3 | 900 | 4200 | 4400 |
| 2–4 | 4 | 2 | 2 | 300 | 400 | |
| 2–5 | 5 | 2 | 3 | 200 | 2100 | 4800 |
| *3–5 | 5 | 2 | 3 | 2700 | 4300 | 6300 |
| 4–6 | 3 | 2 | 1 | 3800 | | |
| *5–6 | 3 | 1 | 2 | 4100 | 4100 | |

Sequentially crash the critical path activities, starting with the lowest crash cost. Single-period crashings are accomplished, and then the model is reviewed to determine if the critical path has changed. Then the next critical path activity with the lowest crash cost is considered. In this problem, the decision is sequentially made to crash activities 2–3, 1–2, 3–5, 1–2, 5–6, 5–6, and 2–3. Each of these crash decisions permits reduction of one period; thus the project is reduced by 7 periods from 15 to 8 weeks. However, when the project has been crashed to 8 weeks, two paths are critical. It is possible, for $4600, to reduce the project by one week from 8 to 7 weeks by simultaneously crashing tasks 2–4 and 3–5. Additionally, one final week (from 7 to 6 weeks) may be crashed for $5000 ($4400, $400, and $200) by simultaneously crashing activities 2–3, 2–4, and 2–5. All other possible crashes would cost more than $5000; thus crashing would stop.

*Continued*

**DECISION MODEL BOX 13-2** *Continued*

| Crash Number | Task Number | Duration | | $ Cost | Overhead | Savings |
|---|---|---|---|---|---|---|
| | | Task | Project | | | |
| 1 | 2–3 | 4 to 3 | 14 | 900 | $5000 | $4100 |
| 2 | 1–2 | 3 to 2 | 13 | 2100 | 5000 | 2900 |
| 3 | 3–5 | 5 to 4 | 12 | 2700 | 5000 | 2300 |
| 4 | 1–2 | 2 to 1 | 11 | 3400 | 5000 | 1600 |
| 5 | 5–6 | 3 to 2 | 10 | 4100 | 5000 | 900 |
| 6 | 5–6 | 2 to 1 | 9 | 4100 | 5000 | 900 |
| 7 | 2–3 | 3 to 2 | 8 | 4200 | 5000 | 800 |
| 8 | 3–5, 2–4 | 4 to 3, 4 to 3 | 7 | 4300, 300 | 5000 | 400 |
| 9 | 2–3, 2–4, 2–5 | 2 to 1, 3 to 2, 5 to 4 | 6 | 4400, 400, 200 | 5000 | 0 |
| | | | | | | $139,000 |

An interesting alternative method is to crash the early tasks first, particularly if there is little cost difference. This enhances the decision-making flexibility because management may initially keep a project tightly crashed in case unforeseen situations develop, and then relax the crashing schedule if funding is short, or if the due date is extended.

typically brought new products, including VCRs and CD players, to the market first, but often competitors would evaluate and improve upon Sony's products, thus taking market share. Sony then adjusted their strategy to simultaneously market and evaluate several models, and then select the best received model for greater promotion—all within several weeks. Considering a more customizable product, Motorola produces pagers within 90 minutes of receipt of a new order. With overnight shipping, they can give next-day delivery to a customer.

Time-based competition is thus a strategy for shorter response to customer requirements (Bodinson, 1991). Practically, accelerating the product development processes can be easily achieved through "concurrent engineering" or cross-functional development teams. This linkage of the key product/service design, process design, and operations functions has the effect of significantly reducing the introduction phases of the traditional product/service life cycle. Three organizational premises are initially required to accelerate products to market: an innovation-supportive environment, integrative technologies, and management commitment (Vesey, 1992). In the experience of Intel Corporation, which is bringing new computer chip families to market every two years, speed to market is critical to their efforts to fend off clone-makers (Hof, 1992). However, speed to market can be a serious mistake if the technology is novel, if the venture is outside of the company's core business, or if the product is new (Utterback et al., 1992).

## *Designing Innovative Systems*

The development of management systems to overview the R&D process is an extremely complex and intuitive process. It is complex because the technologies of process, products/services, materials, and information systems are complex. Simultaneously, it is intuitive because there are few, if any, precedents. Despite the variety of analytic and computational techniques noted in this chapter, ultimately the numbers must be judgmentally evaluated and interpreted. The management, or "orgware," of technology involves these intuitive and evaluative skills. The use of a project team or technology platform is a good way to focus several key concerns of managing innovative systems.

Perhaps the most important concern of innovation management is that the R&D effort must be linked to business strategy. This linkage should be founded in the business plan and further elaborated in various subordinate plans and policies. Technology decisions should be based on the long-range objectives and strategy of the firm, because the technology changes are, for the most part, long range in impact.

A second concern is that the R&D effort must be linked to key management and stakeholder interests. One method of achieving this linkage is to incorporate key executives (division staff level) at periodic (often quarterly) R&D program review meetings. This body would serve as a steering committee for the R&D project team or technology platform. Such a review could define and update the costs of specific projects and use various techniques described in this chapter to link technology, operations, and marketing. Case 8, New Product Development at Elco Manufacturing, describes such a program review meeting.

Third, a carefully defined balance of organization design and controls versus freedom and self-discipline must also be established to manage the project. Research and development activities are highly innovative activities and thus require a looseness of control over individual inquiry and opportunities for broad ranging interaction of those involved. Without discounting the requirement to carefully document R&D, the genius of R&D must be afforded some latitude for unstructured inquiry. Unfortunately, R&D budgets are among the most visible and vulnerable budget lines, particularly in periods of economic downturn. Additionally, the results of R&D must be reviewed and understood (in general, at least) by various levels of management. The institutionalization of R&D is a necessary, albeit cumbersome constraint on a process that is by nature intuitive. Management of this dichotomy of freedom of inquiry versus structure of reporting and accountability is a difficult and very sensitive process.

Finally, the management of career paths for research professionals must be defined in policy. Whether research professionals are intrapreneurs, staff, technicians, or project managers, careful attention must be given to define career paths for them. Traditionally, employees in R&D positions have had little opportunity for advancement outside their function. This may be, in part, because R&D professionals are often not well understood by the rest of the organization and may have little opportunity to integrate and develop relationships with the rest of the organization. For this reason, R&D has traditionally been viewed as a career "dead end."

To avoid this problem, the R&D manager should use a variety of career-tracking methods to permit career diversification. For example, parallel career tracks would permit the research professional to switch between technical and management career paths. Alternatively, the program could define a R&D proponent for each major division, thus establishing an informal basis for personal linkages. Larger organizations may be able to transfer the research professional from one activity to another unrelated research program, thereby providing the necessary career broadening. Such efforts permit researchers and technicians to avoid professional niche-building activities and career dead ends.

## Summary

The management of technology effort is such a different process from that of other areas of operations, and the technology component of the operation is so central to competitive strategy that this separate chapter is warranted. In many organizations, the R&D component is one of the more underutilized, misused, and misunderstood resources of the organization. The R&D of technology is directed toward the vital process technology, materials technology, product/service technology, information system, and management system necessary to a dynamic and global organization.

The effects of short-sightedness in the management of technology can be cataclysmic, more so in dynamic product/service or process environments. Technological innovation is often shunned or guardedly accepted because of the uncertain impacts on the organization. Proactive decision makers must evaluate the risks associated with incentives and impediments to technological change, and then define strategies of the technology leader or follower, product/service or process technology innovation, and dedicated or flexible systems. These decisions are facilitated by product growth analysis and technology portfolio analysis and project implementation and management techniques. Ultimately, however, the risk taker must conceptually design a unique innovation management system. By way of summarizing this area, Table 13-3 defines several rules for technology innovation and R&D project management.

**TABLE 13-3 Rules for Research and Development Project Management**

- The technology management strategy must be defined in terms of incentives and impediments, and must consider the benefits and noise levels of alternative projects.
- The key strategic alternatives in technology management are the degree of leadership, process technology versus product/service changes and dedicated versus flexible process changes. Risks and rewards are associated with each alternative.
- Top management commitment to the objectives and resources of the project is essential.
- Projects must be clearly and simply defined; they should be realistic and should not reflect an overstatement of capability.
- One person should be ultimately responsible for research and development activities and for project management of those activities, though specialized teams can be very effective in accomplishing delegated responsibilities.
- Redundancy should be eliminated as an unnecessary cost, except where the redundancy contributes to project definition.
- Research and development organization policies must reflect the dynamic and nebulous nature of the environment, balanced by the requirement for reporting and accountability.
- Projects must be sequentially planned, scheduled, monitored and adjusted. Effort committed in the earlier activities reduces the effort necessary in the later stages.
- Project performance must be monitored and adjusted when appropriate but only with full concordance of the participants.

## Discussion Questions

1. From your personal experiences, briefly describe five different types of outcomes of technology improvement: process technology, materials technology, product/service technology, information systems, and management systems.
2. List several barriers to the development of innovative processes in a business.
3. Describe how technology is the primary driver of the work environment.
4. Provide examples, different from those in this chapter, of R&D project management at the simplest and higher levels.
5. List the four essential steps in the management of a R&D project and indicate the sequence and relative amounts of time required for each step.
6. Each manager of technology change has a risk–trade-off curve. What is the risk–trade-off curve defined by? Describe an example of a risk–trade-off situation and diagram that situation.
7. List the three decisions with regard to technology implementation strategy that the risk taker must make.
8. Briefly describe the characteristics of the technology leader and technology follower. Give an example of each.
9. Define technosynchrony and identify some of its benefits.
10. What is a key strategic decision for the operations or R&D manager regarding the changeover of technologies?
11. Describe the difference between the technical and manufacturing potential of a project.
12. Identify the benefits of using technical methods of managing project implementation.
13. List some of the career tracking methods available that can help avoid the professional niche building and career dead ends associated with researchers and technicians.

## Strategic Decision Situations

1. Define a product that you are familiar with and prepare a product map to represent the development of that product over time. Some product or model differentiation should be defined to distinguish product categories. Possible example projects might include the personal computer, a software product, telephones or answering systems, automobiles, soft drinks and other beverages, television and related electronic apparatus, furniture, and others. Initially prepare a one-page list and description of the models and categorize the primary model capabilities before preparing the product map.
2. Maureen Cabrero, the director of resource planning for the Mid-Continental Cellular Connection, an operator of fixed cellular connections and satellite communication systems, put down

the phone slowly. The geo-synchronous satellite had failed to turn on; possibly it had been damaged during launching. Though technicians would try to start it, and possibly a "rescue–repair" mission would be launched, it would be months, probably years, before the satellite would be repaired or replaced. Meanwhile, she had to implement "plan B," the establishment of a ground site. Though the plan B site would not have the coverage of a satellite, it would relieve present volumes on current sites.

The plan B cover said it all. "If necessary, be prepared to expedite at all possible costs." The reputation of the company was on the line, not to mention her job. The following activities were required.

| Activity | Predecessor | Description | Times (days) Optimistic | Most Likely | Pessimistic | Crashing Time (min) | Cost/ week |
|---|---|---|---|---|---|---|---|
| A | – | Purchase option/site | 2 | 3 | 5 | | |
| B | – | Survey site | 1 | 2 | 3 | 1 | 1200 |
| C | – | Purchase option/equipment | 2 | 5 | 6 | 3 | 1500 |
| D | A, C | Relocate and train workers | 4 | 6 | 9 | 3 | 5000 |
| E | B | Site hardening | 4 | 5 | 6 | 3 | 3500 |
| F | B | Bring utilities to site | 4 | 7 | 8 | 5 | 2000 |
| G | E | Construct facility | 8 | 9 | 10 | 6 | 4000 |
| H | D, G | Install equipment | 3 | 5 | 6 | 3 | 1000 |
| I | D, G | FCA site approval | 4 | 6 | 9 | 5 | 4000 |
| J | F, H | Test site | 1 | 2 | 4 | 1 | 1000 |
| K | I, J | Switch over system | 1 | 1 | 2 | — | |

Evaluate the current expected time. Then assume that the most likely times are exact and that the company is willing to commit unlimited resources to assure minimized project time; crash the activities to find the best possible schedule and the cost of that schedule.

3. Walter Edwards of Costello Laboratories was frustrated. Every new drug—and the company was marketing some 50 to 85 new drugs per year—had to be managed through a rather difficult, though standardized, process of product specification, product testing, patent application, Food and Drug Administration approval, and process development. About the only difference in the process from one product to the next was the amount that the firm was willing to expedite various phases of the process. Edwards had been assigned the task, by his boss, the director of new product research and development, to prepare a generic process to manage the activities. He had chosen an example new product, and had developed a standardized pattern of research and development activities. Edwards has turned to you, a project manager, for strategic advice. The following table shows the activities and the new drug, an immune system reinforcer. In this case, top management wants to market the drug in nine months.

| Activity | Predecessor | Description | Times (weeks) Optimistic | Most Likely | Pessimistic | Crash Time (min) | Cost/ Week |
|---|---|---|---|---|---|---|---|
| A | – | Product identification | 5 | 8 | 9 | 6 | 1200 |
| B | A | Preliminary research | 6 | 9 | 14 | 6 | 1000 |
| C | A | Market evaluation | 4 | 7 | 8 | 6 | 500 |
| D | B | Product specification | 4 | 7 | 9 | 2 | 2000 |
| E | B | Patent research | 2 | 3 | 5 | 2 | 900 |
| F | C | Product costing | 1 | 2 | 4 | 1 | 500 |
| G | C | Tissue testing | 7 | 10 | 12 | 2 | 4000 |
| H | E, G | Patent application | 5 | 7 | 8 | 5 | 1000 |
| I | C | Laboratory report | 2 | 4 | 6 | 3 | 1500 |
| J | F, D | Market report | 2 | 6 | 7 | 3 | 2500 |
| K | I | Process setup | 5 | 9 | 10 | 4 | 2400 |
| L | H, J, K | FDA application | 6 | 9 | 11 | — | |

The difficulty that Edwards encountered was in specifying a measure of fixed costs. "We can put a value on our facilities and find out what the monthly costs of these assets are," he said. "That does not consider, however, the costs of *not* getting to market. I would like to say that we crash the problem as far as possible (assume that the most likely time is a fixed time). However, how do I support that strategy in a cost-conscious environment? I just don't know how to handle this one." Use PERT to initially evaluate the problem and then consider crashing the alternatives. Address Walter Edwards' dilemma.

## References


Ali, Abdul, Manohar U. Kalwani, and Dan Kovenock. "Selecting Product Development Projects: Pioneering Versus Incremental Innovation Strategies," *Management Science,* March 1993, pp. 255–274.

Avishai, Bernard. "A CEO's Common Sense of CIM: An Interview with J. Tracy O'Rourke," *Harvard Business Review.* January–February 1989, pp. 110–117.

Badiru, Adedeji B. "Critical Resources Diagram: A New Tool for Resource Management," *Industrial Engineering.* October 1992, pp. 58–59.

Banks, Robert L., and Steven C. Wheelwright. "Operations vs Strategy: Trading Tomorrow for Today," *Harvard Business Review.* May–June 1979.

Baranson, Jack. "Risk Perception of Technology Decisions in Public Enterprises: A Framework for Further Research," *The Engineering Economist.* Vol. 22, No. 1, 1977, pp. 31–39.

Blass, Kim. "World-Class Strategies Help Create a World-Class CIM Facility," *Industrial Engineering.* November 1992, pp. 26–29.

Bodinson, Glenn. "Time-Based Competition Is the Competitive Advantage of the 1990s." *APICS:*

*The Performance Advantage.* December 1991, pp. 27–31.

Buderi, Robert, Joseph Weber, Charles Hoots, and Robert Neff. "A Tighter Focus for R&D," *Business Week.* October 25, 1991, pp. 170–172.

Burgelman, Robert A., and Modesto A. Maidique. *Strategic Management of Technology and Innovation.* Homewood, Ill.: Irwin, 1988.

Capon, Noel, John U. Farley, Donald R. Lehmann, and James M. Hulbert. "Profiles of Product Innovators among Large U.S. Manufacturers," *Management Science.* February 1992, pp. 157–169.

Civerolo, John J. "On-Time New Product Development—Fact or Fiction?" *APICS: The Performance Advantage.* January 1992, pp. 50–52.

Drucker, Peter F. "The Changed World Economy," *Foreign Affairs.* Spring 1986, p. 768.

Drucker, Peter F. *The New Realities: In Government and Politics/in Economics and Business/in Society and World View.* New York: Harper and Row, Publishers, 1989.

Fogarty, Donald W., Thomas R. Hoffmann, and Peter W. Stonebraker. *Production and Operations Management,* Cincinnati, Ohio: South-Western Publishing Co., 1989.

Ghoshal, Sumantra, and D. Eleanor Westney. "Organizing Competitor Analysis Systems," *Strategic Management Journal.* Special Issue, Summer 1991, p. 17–31.

Gross, Neil, and Pam Black. "Building New Materials from What's Lying Around," *Business Week.* November 11, 1991, p. 168.

Hayes, Robert H., and Steven C. Wheelwright. *Restoring Our Competitive Edge: Competing through Manufacturing.* New York: John Wiley and Sons, 1984.

Hickman, Anita M. "Refining the Process of Project Control," *Production & Inventory Management,* February 1992, pp. 26–27.

Hill, Terry. *Manufacturing Strategy, Text and Cases.* Homewood, Ill.: Irwin, 1989.

Hitt, Michael A., Robert E. Hoskisson, R. Duane Ireland, and Jeffrey S. Harrison. "Are Acquisitions a Poison Pill for Innovation?" *The Academy of Management Executive.* Vol. 5, No. 4, 1991, pp. 22–33.

Hof, Robert. "Inside Intel," *Business Week.* June 1, 1992, pp. 86–90.

Kezsbom, Deborah S. "Reopening Pandora's Box: Sources of Project Conflict in the '90s," *Industrial Engineering.* May 1992, pp. 54–59.

Lee, Hak-Chung. "Lordstown Plant of General Motors," School of Business, State University of New York at Albany, 1974.

Mitchell, R., and J. Dobrzynski. "Jack Welch: How Good a Manager?" *Business Week.* December 14, 1987.

Moody, Patricia E. *Strategic Manufacturing: Dynamic New Directions for the 1990s.* Homewood, Ill.: Dow Jones-Irwin, 1990.

Murdick, Robert G., Barry Render, and Roberta S. Russell. *Service Operations Management.* Boston, Mass.: Allyn and Bacon, 1990.

Pennar, Karen. "Reinventing America," *Business Week.* Special edition, 1992.

Petre, Peter. "How GE Bobbled the Factory of the Future," *Fortune.* November 11, 1985.

Porter, Michael E. *Competitive Strategy: Techniques for Analyzing Industries and Competitors.* New York: Free Press, 1980.

Roberts, Edward B. "The Success of High-Technology Firms: Early Technological and Marketing Influences," *Interfaces.* July–August 1992, pp. 3–12.

Schoonhoven, Claudia B., Kathleen M. Eisenhardt, and Katherine Lyman. "Speeding Products to Market: Waiting Time to First Product Introduction in New Firms," *Administrative Science Quarterly.* Vol. 35, No. 1, 1990, pp. 177–207.

Skinner, Wickham. *Manufacturing: The Formidable Competitive Weapon.* New York: John Wiley, 1985.

Swamidass, Paul M. "Planning for Manufacturing Technology," *Long Range Planning.* Vol. 20, No. 5, 1987, pp. 125–133.

Symonds, William C. "Pushing Design to Dizzying Speed," *Business Week.* October 21, 1991.

Umble, M. Michael, and M. L. Srikanth. *Synchronous Manufacturing.* Cincinnati, Ohio: South-Western Publishing Co., 1990.

Utterback, James, Mark Meyer, Timothy Tuff, and Lisa Richardson. "When Speeding Concepts to a Market Can Be a Mistake," *Interfaces.* July–August 1992, pp. 24–37.

Vesey, Joseph T. "The New Competitors: They Think in Terms of 'Speed to Market,' " *Production and*

*Inventory Management Journal.* Vol. 33, No. 1, 1992, pp. 71–78.

Werther, William B., William A. Ruch, and Lynne McClure. *Productivity Through People.* St. Paul, Minn.: West Publishing Co., 1986.

Wheelwright, Steven C., and Kim B. Clark. "Creating Project Plans to Focus Product Development," *Harvard Business Review.* March–April 1992, pp. 71–82.

Wheelwright, Steven C., and W. Earl Sasser, Jr. "The New Product Development Map," *Harvard Business Review.* May–June 1989, pp. 112–125.

"Why a Little Detroit Could Rise in Tennessee," *Business Week.* August 12, 1985, p. 21.

# Chapter 14

# Policy: The Guide to Implementation

*Strategy . . . is easier said than done.* —Wickham Skinner, 1988

*There is nothing more difficult to take in hand, more perilous to conduct, or more uncertain of success than to take a lead in the introduction of a new order of things, because the innovation has for enemies all those who have done well under the old conditions and lukewarm defenders in those who may do well under the new.* —Machiavelli, *The Prince*

## Objectives

After completing this chapter you should be able to:

- Define policy and discuss several dimensions of policy implementation.
- Describe the policy development process and identify and apply the four steps of the policy development process.
- State and integrate the activities of policy implementation.
- Identify the dimensions of fitting a policy to strategy and to the organization.
- Describe the characteristics of four implementation modes and the range of appropriate leadership styles.
- Explain why chaos is helpful to the operations manager in implementing policy.

## Outline

***Introductory Case: Implementing Strategic Change at IBM***

***Policy—The Rest of the Job***

## *Introductory Case: Implementing Strategic Change at IBM*

Since its founding by Thomas Watson, Sr., IBM* has dominated the computer industry. Its monopoly profits, technical preeminence, and incredible growth exemplify a classic American business saga. With $67 billion of annual revenues, the corporation houses manufacturing, software development, and systems integration units which are by themselves leaders in their industries. For example, the software development organization, with $10 billion in revenues, is five times the size of Microsoft Corporation, and the storage products division (also $10 billion in revenues) dwarfs industry leaders such as Seagate Corp.

*Materials drawn from John W. Verity, Thane Peterson, Diedre Depke, and Evan I. Schwartz, "The New IBM," *Business Week,* December 16, 1991, p. 112; John W. Verity, "Out of One Big Blue, Many Little Blues," *Business Week,* December 9, 1991, p. 33; and Judith W. Dobrzynski, "Rethinking IBM," *Business Week,* October 4, 1993, pp. 86–97.

Yet the recent profitability of this giant has been weak and declining. Profits in 1991 were a disappointing $2 billion. IBM has also lagged by other measures. In the 1980s, its share of the world computer market dropped from 36% to 23%, and its share of the PC market dropped from 27% to 16.5%. Much of the difficulty reportedly resulted from the slowness and heavy-handedness of IBM's bureaucracy. Though IBM research is considered excellent (it has merited several Nobel prizes), it has developed "techy" products that were introduced behind schedule, appeared overpriced, and did not meet market expectations. In some cases, these limits resulted from the positioning of products to be consistent with the mainframe-dominated product line, but in other cases, IBM has not been able to translate its technical excellence into market presence.

As rivals chipped away at IBM's markets, profits sank and IBM responded by eliminating jobs through attrition and the well-known voluntary departure and early retirement programs. Those programs have cut some 54,000 jobs (one-eighth of the work force), but have not stayed marketplace criticism that IBM should do more. In November 1991, IBM chairman John Akers launched a further and more extensive effort to get the company back on track. The major component of this redirection was the delineation of a set of wholly owned, but autonomous, companies directed toward individual goals and market segments. IBM would refocus the reporting of its senior management from emphasis on technical excellence and research toward return on assets. Autonomy would be permitted for those managers who improved the bottom line of their companies.

However, this redefinition of the company carries serious risks. IBM has built its corporate reputation on the strength of its ability to draw together for a customer the diverse components of a new and comprehensive information system. Though the individual components may not have been regarded as the best on the market, many customers were willing to sacrifice features or performance to get IBM's assurance of integratability or to have IBM to handle the complexity. The risk of the new strategy is that diversification will result in the loss of this central focus of the company and that the autonomous entities will not be able to define new and separate identities in their markets.

The question of an autonomous versus an integrated company took a new twist in early 1993, with the replacement of Akers by Lou Gerstner, previously CEO of RJR Nabisco. Akers had been a career IBM employee, but he may also have been a victim of the all too rigid and hierarchical IBM structure and mindset. Early indications suggest that Gerstner will attempt to reverse the disintegration of IBM and retain the core hardware, software, and service businesses that customers have grown to depend upon. It remains for Gerstner, a nontechnical outsider, to find the strategies and implement the policies and procedures to guide the company toward this end.

## *Policy—The Rest of the Job*

The definition of an operations strategy, as discussed in the previous 13 chapters, is only the beginning of the operations management job. As Machiavelli noted in the introductory quotation, the introduction of a new strategic direction is the single most difficult part of the strategy–policy process. Just because an acceptable strategy has been formulated, the implementation of that strategy does not automatically follow. In fact, because there are many potential sources of resistance and numerous pitfalls for the new strategy, the operations manager should have a plan to direct or guide the introduction and implementation effort. Strategy formulation is often best achieved through a process of successively asking the right questions, whereas the implementation effort is the very different process of successively answering those questions and achieving recognition and acceptance of the answers. Thus, implementation of a strategy through the associated policy is inseparable from the process of creating the strategy itself.

Though the consequences of an insufficient policy or no policy can potentially be disastrous, it is surprising how many companies have little or no formal business policies in place. Certainly, it does take time and effort away from other activities to prepare a policy document. Even in relatively stable environments, the policy should be reviewed and updated regularly. Additionally, policy creation is not a one-person activity; it requires a periodic and substantial time commitment by key executives.

However, the failure to define, carefully administer, and adhere to set policies can also be costly. This is even more true in larger and more regulated businesses, such as Waste Management Incorporated (WMI—see Case 1). The Chicago Incinerator, operated by WMI's Chemical Waste Management Inc. (CWM) subsidiary, may have violated its own and EPA policies. CWM has agreed to pay $3.5 million to settle, without admitting wrongdoing, EPA charges in connection with a serious incinerator explosion. Additionally, there were allegations of wrongful dismissal of an employee who reported crimes at the plant, of disconnecting pollution monitoring equipment, and of skimping on safety equipment, such as gloves and respirators. These situations and others have reduced CWM's profits—in fact, the Chicago facility did not operate profitably for much of 1991 and 1992. However, in addition to short-run losses, several states are considering invoking "good character requirements" which would force CWM to list all civil and administrative complaints in any new bid for business. This could be a nettlesome issue for CWM. The costs of either not having a policy or not following that policy may be very high—even disastrous—for many firms in the long run (Flynn, 1992).

Most academicians and practitioners would argue, as do Skinner (1985) and O'Rourke (Avishai, 1989) that manufacturing has not been effectively used as a "weapon." Rather, in recent years the key competitive edge has been achieved through marketing or finance. Thus, operations strategy, instead of being proactive in nature, has been relegated to a reactive "black pit," where people "throw things onto a truck" (Avishai, 1989, p. 117). Today, as operations strategy is being elevated in importance, a corresponding shift must occur for operations policy. Strategy without policy is an idea without relevance; operations strategy without operations policy is like a car without wheels.

This chapter introduces and defines policy as an implementation guide for strategy. A process of policy development is described, and several alternative implementation modes are considered. Subsequently, the effectiveness of policy implementation is discussed as the fit of the policy with the original strategy and with the organization. The implementation of strategy ultimately results in a paradox, that the tightly structured continuity necessary for implementation effectiveness is inconsistent with the innovative and chaotic environments that facilitate implementation. Thus, the operations manager with a truly strategic perspective is regularly confronted with the dilemma of encouraging either continuity or chaos. In fact, the best implementation strategy may be to give the appearance of some ambivalence toward either continuity or chaos. An example of these conditions is described in Application Box 14-1.

## The Nature of Policy

This section defines policy and elaborates several key parts of that definition. Policy issues are then presented as a hierarchy of possible activities, roughly corresponding to the organization design. At higher levels of the organization, policy tends to be more formal and more general than at lower levels of the organization. Policy is then further elaborated in three dimensions: scope, formality, and explicitness.

### Policy Defined

Policy is generally defined, as suggested by the chapter title, as a "guide to implementation." More specifically,

> *Policy is a* guide for the execution and control *of operations strategy that* suggests the values, rationale, or limits, *thus aiding the decision maker to* establish a balance between defined processes *(to ensure cohesion, consistency, and continuous improvement—the 3Cs)* and flexibility *(to permit involvement, individuality, and innovation—the 3Is).*

Considering several aspects of the definition, a policy is based on strategy. An effective policy is drawn from and grows out of the strategy that it implements (Ansoff, 1988). The strategy development process should ensure that sufficient direction is given to formulate appropriate and necessary policies. Policy, however, is more detailed than strategy and provides guidance for execution and for management control of the execution process. The strategy/policy interaction may be viewed as a Socratic process of sequentially asking the right questions, followed by the process of answering those questions and implementing the response. Of course, each implementation leads to the next question. Thus, the strategy–policy relationship is an integrative process, which is often projected down the organization hierarchy, with successive questions asked at a higher level, and answers and implementation defined at lower levels.

However, the process of strategy formulation deals with the long-term direction of the company and may not include statements of specific value, rationale, or limits. One reason for not including these values, rationale, or limits in the strategy is that, whereas major stakeholders of an organization can agree on the strategic direction, the details of policy implementation are best left to the company. Thus policy is often used as a separate, subsidiary, and supplemental process to flesh out the details and implementation timing of a strategy after stakeholders have agreed to the long-term strategy statement. Though every effort should be made to ensure that policies are consistent with the strategies that they support, the reality of stakeholder politics may preclude complete consistency. Ultimately, it is the function of policy to identify and elaborate ways to ensure the three

## APPLICATION BOX 14-1 The Scope of Operations Policy at Warner-Lambert

Few industries would appear to be more impervious to the vagaries of the economy than the pharmaceutical and consumer products industries. Products of those industries are directly related to personal health and hygiene, and thus experience relatively level demands regardless of the economic conditions. Example products of these industries include anti-bacterial lozenges, mouthwashes, and shaving products, as well as medicines and drugs. Yet, in the early 1990s, even the pharmaceutical and consumer products industries began to feel the effects of recession and widespread discounting. The long-term strength of Warner-Lambert, given its then current strategy, appeared to be in doubt.

Warner-Lambert, one of the major pharmaceutical and consumer products companies, had a solid record of financial and productivity performance through the 1980s. However, though earnings growth advanced at a 15% to 20% clip through the late 1980s, the projections turned gloomy in the early 1990s. The patent of a highly popular cholesterol-reducing drug would soon expire, the Food and Drug Administration had delayed approval of an innovative drug to treat Alzheimer's disease, and worldwide annual sales of consumer products slowed by 5%. These and other developments prompted Warner-Lambert CEO Melvin Goodes to undertake a downsizing of some 8% of the work force and a reorganization of Warner-Lambert's worldwide management. The organization was restructured into two core groups, pharmaceuticals and consumer products, with marketing efforts and reporting refocused geographically to more directly represent key markets in North America, Europe, and Japan.

Without this strategic repositioning, Warner-Lambert was expected to have continued its healthy earnings performance growth with a handsome 15% gain in 1991, which was a very bad year for many industries. But the repositioning resulted in a dramatic reduction of 1991 net income to $34 million on $5.06 billion in sales, or less than 1% profits. Setting aside the foregone 1991 profits, such a strategic decision is fraught with risks and potential complications, not the least of which is that the implementation likely will take longer and be more difficult than management had initially envisioned. Yet, simultaneously, the decision to restructure established the foundation to save the firm $1 billion over five years and reposition the firm to compete more nimbly against Merck & Company and others in the pharmaceuticals and consumer goods markets through the year 2000 and beyond. Reported 1992 results show that net profits had recovered to 11.5% of net sales, suggesting that the implementation had proceeded as planned.

The amount of time necessary to complete a restructuring and to return the organization to greater profitability is one of the more difficult parts of policy implementation to estimate. The restructuring of Warner-Lambert will result in a significant readjustment of both the functional and systemic concerns of the organization and will involve various modes of policy implementation and styles of management. For example, the restructuring involved doing away with the previous completely geographic-based hierarchy and establishment of a product-line-based reporting structure. All programs, as well as the subsidiary budgeting and reporting procedures of the organization, were redefined. In the first few months of reorganization, the environment of the organization shifted from stable continuity toward chaotic innovation and adaption. Modes of leadership were shifted, different leadership styles were developed, and redefinition of formal and informal policies, programs, and budgets were accomplished.

The definition of a strategic direction at Warner-Lambert has proved to be the easy part; the implementation and execution of policies toward that end are much more difficult. However, Warner-Lambert, like other organizations reconfiguring for the 1990s and beyond, has taken the difficult steps to identify and implement necessary changes before the organization gets really sick.

Materials drawn from Joseph Weber, "Curing Warner-Lambert—Before It Gets Sick," *Business Week*, December 9, 1991, p. 91.

Cs of the definition—cohesion, consistency, and continuous improvement—and sufficient flexibility to permit the three Is of the definition—involvement, individuality, and innovation.

## *The Policy Hierarchy*

Policy operates on several levels. As initially noted in Chapter 2, strategy and policy are directed toward the corporate philosophy and goals. However, numerous programs, budgets, procedures, and rules supplement and elaborate policy. These diverse components of the implementation hierarchy must be reasonably consistent with each other. That is, a lower-level component must be tightly integrated with the higher-level component. Any mismatch will decrease the efficiency of the hierarchy. Figure 14-1 shows the implementation hierarchy.

Initially, the components of the hierarchy are divided into an ends-oriented group (corporate philosophy, business strategy, and operations strategy) and a means-oriented group (policy, programs and budgets, and procedures and rules). The topics of this chapter generally deal with the bottom three levels in the figure, the means-oriented components.

One of the more significant attributes of the implementation hierarchy is that lower levels of the hierarchy have greater specificity and less individual discretion. Philosophy, goals, and strategy are relatively general and permit a wide latitude of individual evaluation. However, policy, programs and budgets, and procedures and rules become increasingly binding and permit less individual discretion.

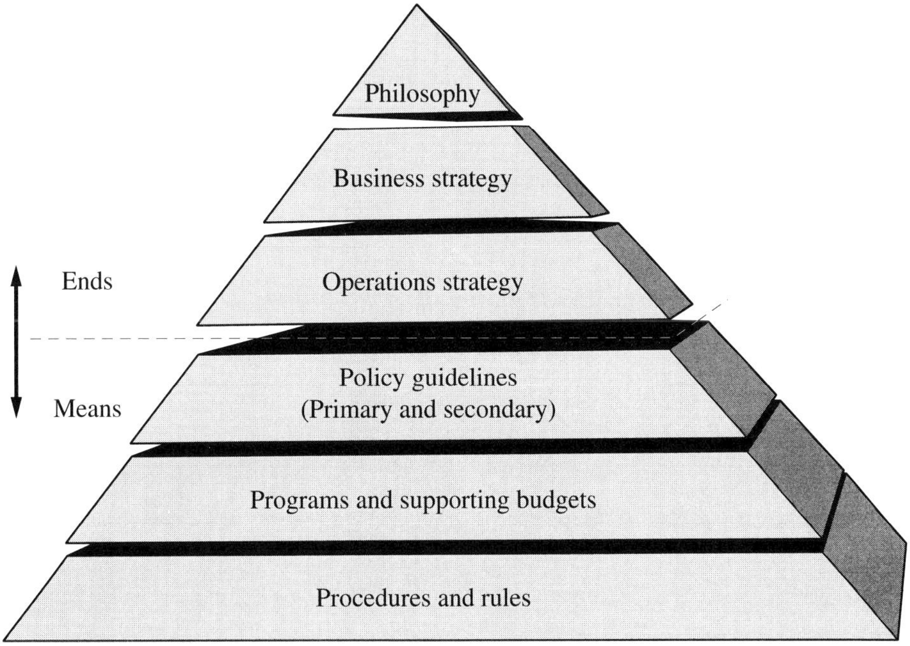


**FIGURE 14-1 The Implementation Hierarchy**

The distinction between primary and secondary policies may not be very clear except in an applied context. Primary policies originate at higher levels of the organization, are broad in scope, and are long-range in impact. For example, IBM's policy of employee job security was established at the highest level, applied throughout the company, and was in effect for some 40 years. Alternatively, secondary policies would be used for short-range, lower-level, and less important matters. For example, secondary policies might be used to clarify section or plant work schedules over a holiday period or to define how employee benefit payments would be handled in a period of transition from one benefits carrier to another.

A program is defined as a statement of activities or steps to accomplish a particular plan or to convert the plan into an implementable action. For example, programs might be defined by product lines or used to convert a production line from one process to another. A budget is a statement of programs defined in dollar terms. Programs and budgets are often reviewed on a quarterly, semi-annual, or annual basis for compliance with and movement toward the achievement of the goals elaborated by strategy and policy. Programs, with the associated budgeted resources, can be broken into a variety of action plans which, though like a program, focus in much greater detail on more specific actions.

Policies, programs, action plans, and budgets may be further elaborated by procedures and rules. While a policy is directed toward logical thinking or processes, procedures are specific, step-by-step methods that guide actions. Policy is often structured functionally or in terms of impacts, but procedures are usually chronological in sequence. Rules are the simplest type of policy; they define specific requirements for action and allow little or no individual discretion. For this reason, rules should not be used for contingent situations. The key difference between procedures and rules is that rules allow little or no discretion, while procedures require a sequence, but permit some discretion within the activities of that sequence. A procedure might have multiple logical loops or variations, which, if taken separately, would be rules. For example, a procedure such as "if condition X, then do action A; if not condition X, then do action B" could be broken down into the individual statements (for example, if condition X, then do action A) which, taken separately, are rules.

## *Dimensions of Policy*

A well-constructed policy, like the strategy upon which it is based, must incorporate the above definitional characteristics. In addition, it must:

1. Be a guide for the execution and control of strategy.
2. Suggest values, rationale, and limits.
3. Establish a degree of flexibility.

Further, policy must suggest or facilitate the formulation of a variety of programs and budgets, as well as procedures and rules. The design of a policy should consider three specific dimensions: scope, formality, and explicitness (Fogarty et al., 1989). These dimensions focus the policy toward its intended use and ensure that the policy is appropriate for the specific situation. The three dimensions of policy are covered in the following sections.

### *Scope*

The scope or area of usefulness of operations policy will vary both in breadth of functional application and in level of application. In some cases, policies are dictated by higher-level considerations beyond the immediate control of the operations manager; in other cases, policy is explicitly defined in one of the operations management subareas, though it may also affect areas outside the direct operations purview. Several representative examples of variations in breadth as well as in level of application are shown in Figure 14-2.

Typically, at the corporate level, finance and accounting policies predominate; there are few, if any, operations management policies. Policies pertaining to job skills testing would likely be defined by human resources at either corporate or division level to ensure compliance with equal employment opportunity or other requirements, though operations might further elaborate the policy by specific directives. At the division level, operations

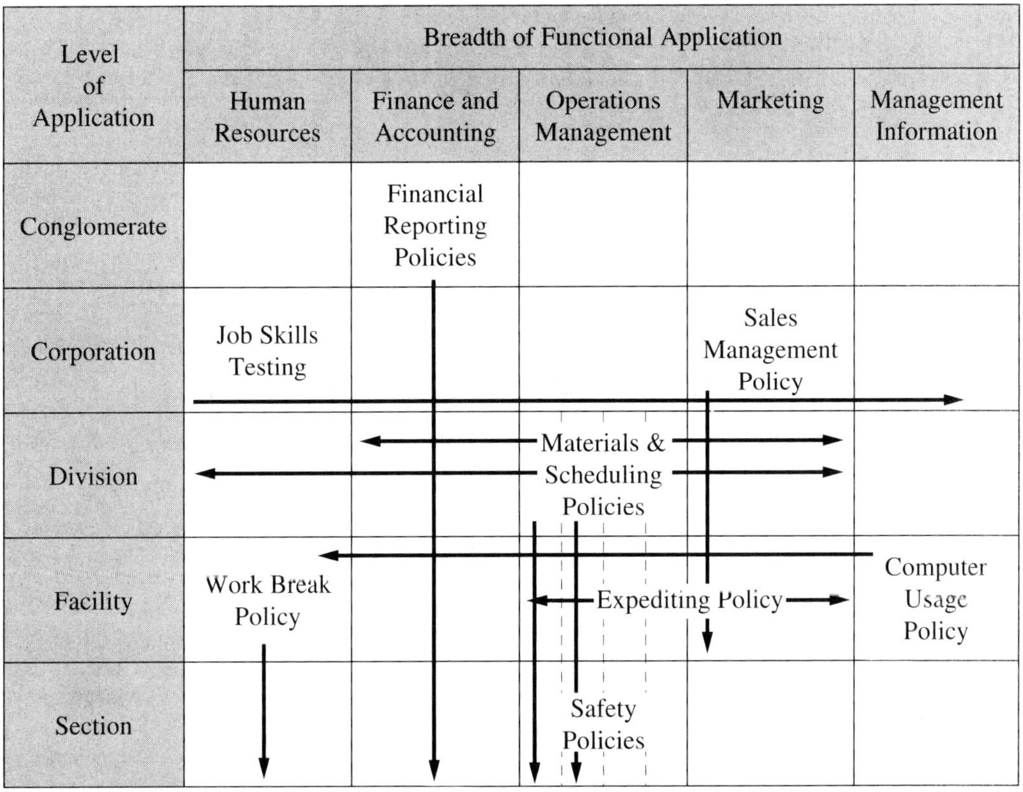


**FIGURE 14-2 Scope of Operations Policy**

Adapted with permission from *Production and Operations Management,* by Donald W. Fogarty, Thomas R. Hoffmann, and Peter W. Stonebraker. Cincinnati: South-Western Publishing Co., 1989, p. 662.

management subactivities are shown with policies in the scheduling and materials areas. These policies, though primarily effective in the operations area, likely will have impacts in other areas also. Materials policies will affect both finance and accounting and marketing, and scheduling will affect human resources and marketing.

Similarly, work-break and computer-usage policies would likely be specified by the facility or section. Expediting policies would likely be established by either formal or informal agreement between operations and marketing. Safety policies might be defined within each section and would have little impact outside the particular section to which they apply. As these examples indicate, policies may be very broad in application, or they may be quite narrow. They may be generally defined at a higher level and implemented at lower levels, or they may be defined and implemented at lower levels, and subsequently communicated for information to higher levels. The scope of operations policy must be adjusted by breadth of functional application and by level of application to fit the particular need. Additionally, operations policy must be interwoven within the subtle and rich textures of existing organization policies.

### *Formality*

The formality of the operations policy will vary depending upon the functional level and consequences of policy violation or variation. Policy tends to be more formally stated at higher levels, if for no other reason than that it must be clearly communicated across a broader range of organization functions and disciplines. Additionally, at higher levels, policy tends to be longer-range and more general. At lower levels, policy tends to be shorter in range, more specific, and often informal. Further, if the consequences of a breach of policy are serious, the policy would likely be more formal and prepared, or at least reviewed, at a higher level.

The amount of formality of policy instruments varies widely, depending upon the situation. Some types of policy are associated with more formality than other types of policy. For example, the master production schedule, the budget, and no-smoking rules are usually quite formal. Alternatively, policy direction, verbal guidance, and some instructions are less formal. Additionally, the formality of some policy instruments varies widely. In some uses, procedural guides are very formal, requiring a two- or three-person collaborative checklist (for example, aircraft takeoff and landing procedures or nuclear plant startup and shutdown checklists), but, in other cases, procedural guides may be very informal, for example, the procedures to decorate a store or employee cafeteria for the holidays.

The amount of formality is important for the operations manager, because it defines the level of concern of the operations function. The amount of formality also suggests the amount of variation in policy that is possible and the level of approval required for a necessary variation. The formality of policy definition is also a key part of the delegation process whereby the operations manager is in control of decision-making processes that affect operations.

### *Explicitness*

Finally, operations policy may be either explicitly defined or vaguely defined. Explicitly defined policies state exactly what actions are required under specific conditions; they give little freedom of individual discretion to those to whom the policy applies. But insufficient definition also inhibits individual discretion because, without some guidance, employees may be hesitant to take the initiative, particularly in controversial matters or where there is substantial political risk. In the conventional model, decision-makers or employees would desire some assurance that their actions would be supported by policy. However, empowerment suggests that employees should not be concerned with or constrained by overly strict policies. To ensure that individuals have the maximum amount of perceived freedom of action, a policy must avoid either excessive definition or excessive vagueness. These dimensions are shown in Figure 14-3.

The arc shows the general relationship between explicitness of policy definition and perceived freedom of action. For example, a no-smoking policy, due to safety, health, or other reasons, gives little perceived freedom of action. Similarly, a ten-year long-range strategic plan is often based on a quarterly or annual planning conference that the CEO and major directorate staff attend. Policy outcomes of such high-level groups are usually tough to change except, with difficulty, by the group itself. Operations managers would, for very good reason, have little freedom of individual action outside the parameters established by such a decision-making group. Alternatively, the work schedule, both as formally and informally defined, is often neither vaguely or explicitly defined. It is usually sufficiently flexible to accommodate individual needs (for example, child care or other personal responsibilities) by permitting employees to substitute for each other. The only constraint on work schedule definition would be that group work activities not be disrupted and that a fairness of individual contribution be considered. The scope, formality, and explicitness dimensions of policy definition are very important contributors to the policy development process. These dimensions are further exemplified in Application Box 14-2.

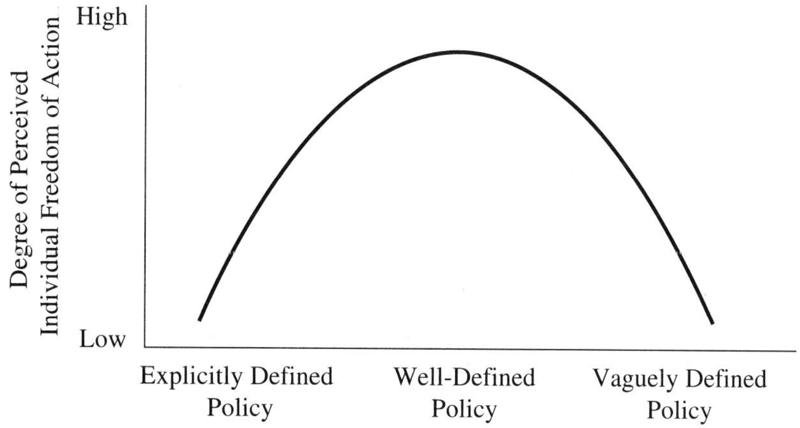


**FIGURE 14-3 The Explicitness of Operations Policy**

Adapted with permission from *Production and Operations Management,* by Fogarty, Hoffmann, and Stonebraker, 1989, p. 664.

## APPLICATION BOX 14-2 Operations Policy at Johnson & Johnson

*I almost never get distracted by J&J management.*

—Marvin L. Woodall, President
J&J International Systems Co.

Though most top managers would not like to be dismissed as a mere distraction, Johnson & Johnson encourages independence among the presidents of its 166 separate companies. These CEOs of the tiny startup J&J-chartered companies prepare budgets and marketing plans, oversee their own research and development plans, and make numerous operating and planning decisions. Though they are ultimately responsible to corporate executives, they are encouraged to operate independently—to the point that many do not see their headquarters bosses more than four times per year.

As early as the 1930s, then Chairman Robert Woods Johnson realized that smaller self-governing units were more manageable, more accountable, and more responsive to market pressures. The J&J method gives a "sense of ownership and responsibility for a business that you simply can not get any other way" according to current J&J chief executive Ralph S. Larson. The policy model that J&J uses is a combination of integration balanced against autonomy, one which constantly requires adjusting and fine-tuning. Despite the apparent ease of policy implementation, the success at J&J has not come without risks. "Entrepreneurial anarchy" is a real danger, where decentralized operating companies make embarrassing mistakes that could have been avoided by more home office guidance. The centralization–decentralization model at J&J is serving as an example for other major businesses, including IBM, DuPont, and Procter and Gamble.

As is often the case, the independence of the separate units at J&J has resulted in a rather significant overhead, compared with competitors, Merck & Co. and Bristol-Myer's Squibb Co. Even though such functions as accounting, computer services, purchasing, and distribution are centralized, J&J carries an overhead of 41% of sales, compared to less than 30% for its more centralized rivals.

However, this strategy puts people and products closer to the marketplace and aids in the development of new products. This is important because products introduced within the prior five years account for 25% of sales, or $4 billion of sales in 1991. New product development has brought a new stream of products on line with numerous variations of product items, as well as packaging. Such market responsiveness would be more difficult if corporate policies were more centralized.

Like their companies, J&J people have common standards but unique perspectives. Some policies are defined by J&J at the corporate level, while policies in other areas are left for the chartered operating companies to specify. In some situations policies are very explicit and focused, while in other situations, policies are vague and more divergent; some policy prescriptions are more formal, while others permit individual discretion; and policy effectiveness varies from situation to situation. J&J's Ortho Pharmaceutical narrowly focuses on one product and operates like a mature business. Alternatively, Janssen Pharmaceutical is a younger business and has a broader product range. As such, Janssen uses policy to encourage a more risk-oriented entrepreneurial spirit.

Career pathing at J&J is difficult, however. Though the company promotes and rewards smallness and agility, there is no safety net for failure. If a product fails or if a chartered firm loses money, a shake-up is likely. As Bernard Walsh, President of Vistakon, notes: "A company presidency is probably the best job in the corporation. You are left alone to run your own business." Of course, you have to keep beating the competition.

Materials drawn from Joseph Weber, "Johnson & Johnson: A Big Company that Works," *Business Week*, May 4, 1992, pp. 124–132.

## *Policy Development*

This section elaborates a process to develop policy, which is based on the definition and dimensions. Initially, the policy development process is discussed in a contextual overview, and then an iterative four-step process of policy development is elaborated. Subsequent sections offer a process of directing policy implementation and fitting or fine-tuning the policy to the strategy and the organization.

### *Context of Policy Development*

The development of a policy derives from the business strategy and the operations strategy, which are based on an assessment of tangible and intangible resources and an evaluation of the environment. Those inputs are combined in the conception and formulation of the business and operations strategy alternatives, which are evaluated according to criteria of cost, quality, delivery, and flexibility. This process should generate a single, internally consistent strategic direction based upon one (or possibly a combination of several) competitive criterion. Policies are then defined to direct the energies of operations toward the accomplishment of that strategy. The policy, once implemented, must be measured for effectiveness and periodically reassessed against the competitive criteria through a feedback and continuous improvement loop. This means that policies should be reviewed and updated regularly to ensure that they remain applicable and that the operations function is continuing to improve its performance against established goals. This contextual overview of policy development is shown in Figure 14-4.

Five general areas (capacity, facilities, technology, integration, and planning and control) are suggested here for policy definition, though several others (including research and development, work force management, and quality) could also be elaborated. Within each of these areas, numerous subareas are suggested for programs, action plans, or other elements of the implementation hierarchy. Explicit measures of policy effectiveness should be defined in each area; these would be the basis for measurement of effectiveness and for feedback and continuous improvement. A case in point is a recent strategic change at Procter and Gamble. In pursuit of a global business strategy, CEO Edwin Artzt has defined policies that would rapidly move new products to market. He has specifically enhanced the integration of suppliers and customers by refocusing product teams and recognizing individual team leaders. Artzt demands results, and measures them in each product area and each functional area of the business. "We are going to make a quantum leap in the quality and speed of execution." Through policy execution, Procter and Gamble has globalized, streamlined, and invested heavily in individual training and innovation (Schiller, 1992). In other situations, emphasis on other policy areas would be more appropriate. These policy development efforts follow a four-step process.

### *Four Steps of Policy Development*

This section identifies the four sequential steps used to develop operations policy. These steps, taken in sequence, generally offer operations managers a methodology to develop policy, though some situations may warrant additional steps or variations of these four steps.

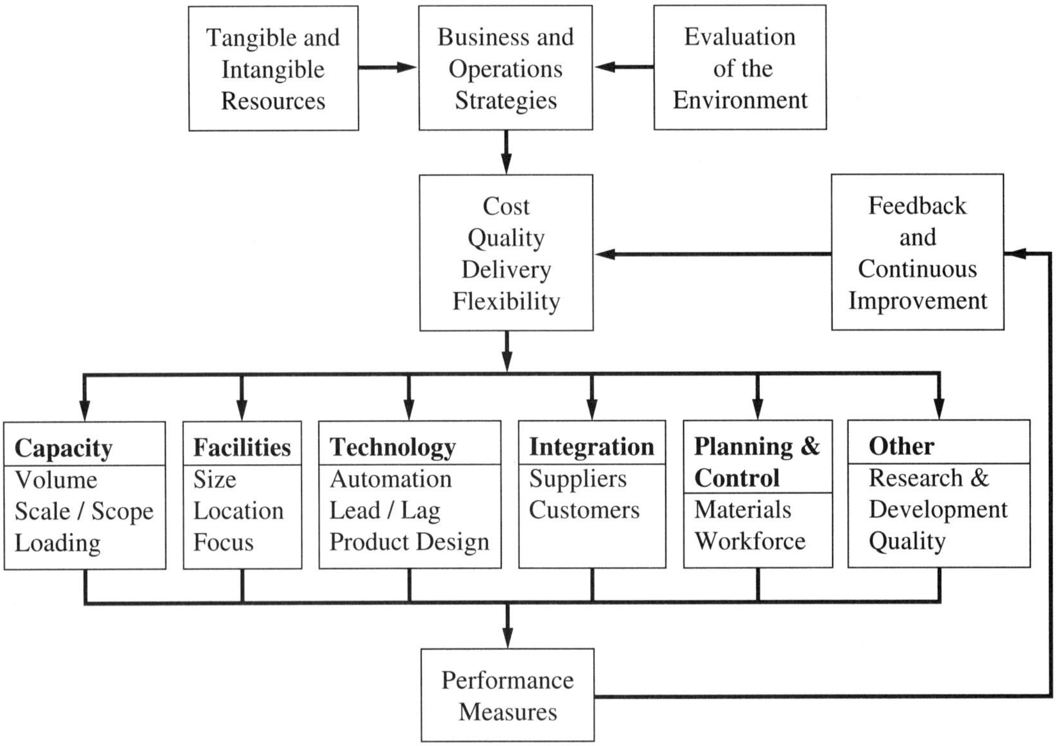


**FIGURE 14-4 Contextual Overview of Policy Development**

***Step 1. Define the Area of the Required Policy.***
The area in which there is functional or topical uncertainty or lack of policy clarity must be identified. This process includes the specification of the functional area and the level where the proposed policy is appropriate. A review of current policies is necessary to ensure that no other conflicting policies exist. The use of a diagram, such as Figure 14-2, on which relevant policies have been overlaid, may be helpful to identify policy voids and overlaps. Additionally, there must be initial general and informal agreement among management that the new policy is necessary.

***Step 2. Identify Policy Alternatives and Likely Impacts.***
This step involves consideration of all possible alternatives and evaluation of their potential outcomes. The interaction among several stakeholders tends to focus the policy alternatives, because such discussions invariably suggest the values, rationale, or limits of each alternative, which would either be supported or rejected by the stakeholders. A key management ability is that of identifying ways to differentiate one policy alternative from another. Policy alternatives must be stated in terms that are understandable to all parties and that would coalesce the group toward a particular goal. Quantitative approaches, such as simulation or other gaming models, can be used to measure the decision alternatives,

or to establish a base-line approximation. More subjective evaluations of the alternatives also might be required to ensure that the policy alternative accommodates various judgmental criteria. At this stage, the advantages and disadvantages of each alternative should be concisely defined and the potential outcomes and risks identified.

***Step 3. Make a General Policy Decision.***

The third step is to make a general policy decision. The initial policy decision may not fully elaborate all ramifications and implications of the policy. More often, an initial policy decision is quite general, designed so that the details can subsequently be filled in as more information or experience becomes available. This initial foundation or general policy decision is defined from among the various alternatives and must be sufficiently structured for discussion and must provide tentative directions for further evaluation.

***Step 4. Determine the Level, Formality, and Explicitness Required, and Assign Responsibility for Policy Preparation.***

A very significant part of the policy development process is ensuring "ownership" of the policy. The operations manager may ask a supervisor whose function is primarily involved with the area to draft the policy and provide a copy for review and subsequent dissemination. Policy must be prepared at the appropriate level, must be communicated with an appropriate amount of formality and explicitness to the necessary people and functions, and must be consistent with other requirements of the organization. This final step reflects the reality that policy is often initiated with varying amounts of direction from higher levels, but the actual policy is implemented at lower levels, often as a program.

A program has been defined as a statement of activities or steps to accomplish a particular plan or to convert that plan into an implementable action. A program is often directed toward one goal, but it may support several goals or plans, and it should be consistent with all plans. For example, a manufacturing policy may require a 10% cost reduction for a particular product line. The following programs might be developed in support of that policy:

1. A purchasing and vendor management program to reduce the number of vendors by 15% and to increase the use of common parts among the different products by 20%.
2. A quality and scrap control program to identify and reduce defects. Areas with a defect rate greater than 1 part per 1000 would receive the greatest emphasis.
3. A product redesign program to standardize components of the line and to enhance product options.
4. A marketing program to telephonically receive customer orders and directly enter them into a computer data base. This system would replace the current salesperson contact method of receiving orders for 15% of the business within two years.
5. A training program to explain the modular products to employees, covering both the production of product modules and telephonic representation of modules to customers.

Once such programs and action plans are developed, the budget process is initiated. The budget, as a statement of corporate programs in dollar terms, implicitly defines the relative values, priorities, and limits of several programs. The corporate budget is often delineated into several different programs with proponents (sometimes called program managers) and stakeholders in each functional area. This approach results in the once commonly used method of carrying forward the past year's budget each year, with each program adjusted, as a percentage increment or decrement. This past-based budget avoided an intense and often painful review of all expenditures, but often wasted resources. On the other hand, zero-based budgeting requires that each major expenditure within a program or action plan be reviewed and continued or rejected based on current needs. However accomplished, the budget process allocates available resources among programs and is a link between policy development and implementation.

## Policy Implementation

Policy implementation follows policy development. Management of policy implementation involves the management of programs and action plans, budgets, procedures, and rules focused toward the goals specified in the policy. Much of the daily interaction of managers is organized around defining, refining, and updating these types of policy. Skinner's comment, "Strategy . . . is easier said than done" might be restated by many operations managers as "Strategy is 80% implementation."

The best policies are irrelevant unless they are monitored and deviations are corrected, and then formally reviewed in a periodic process. The results of performance monitoring and variance adjustment must be compared to the program goals through a budget review and decision process. Deficiencies are rectified by adjusting either the program goals or performance criteria, or both. Those changes must be reflected in adjustments to the policy. A general perspective of the policy implementation process is shown in Figure 14-5.

The five implementation activities are shown on the left side of the figure with an example application on the right side. Note that the activities are sequenced and that the feedback loop permits review and reconsideration as needed. Though these activities are numbered and the sequence generally reflects that of initial implementation, the loops suggest that adjustment can occur in any sequence or with several steps simultaneously. Thus, except for the initial implementation, which is likely sequential, the ongoing implementation of policy probably will not be a sequential process; rather, it will be a simultaneous interaction of several activities, driven by the focus of operations concerns.

### Definition of Program Goals

Depending upon the level of the policy, the program may be as general as a business unit's annual or multiyear income goal or as specific as the implementation of a tool or machine changeover. These programs or requirements are likely derived from business and operations strategies, plans, or policies, developed as previously described. Programs may be further elaborated as action plans or stated as a variety of procedures and rules, including requirements, schedules, processes, and directives, all of which may operate at both the formal and informal levels to define how the programs will be achieved.

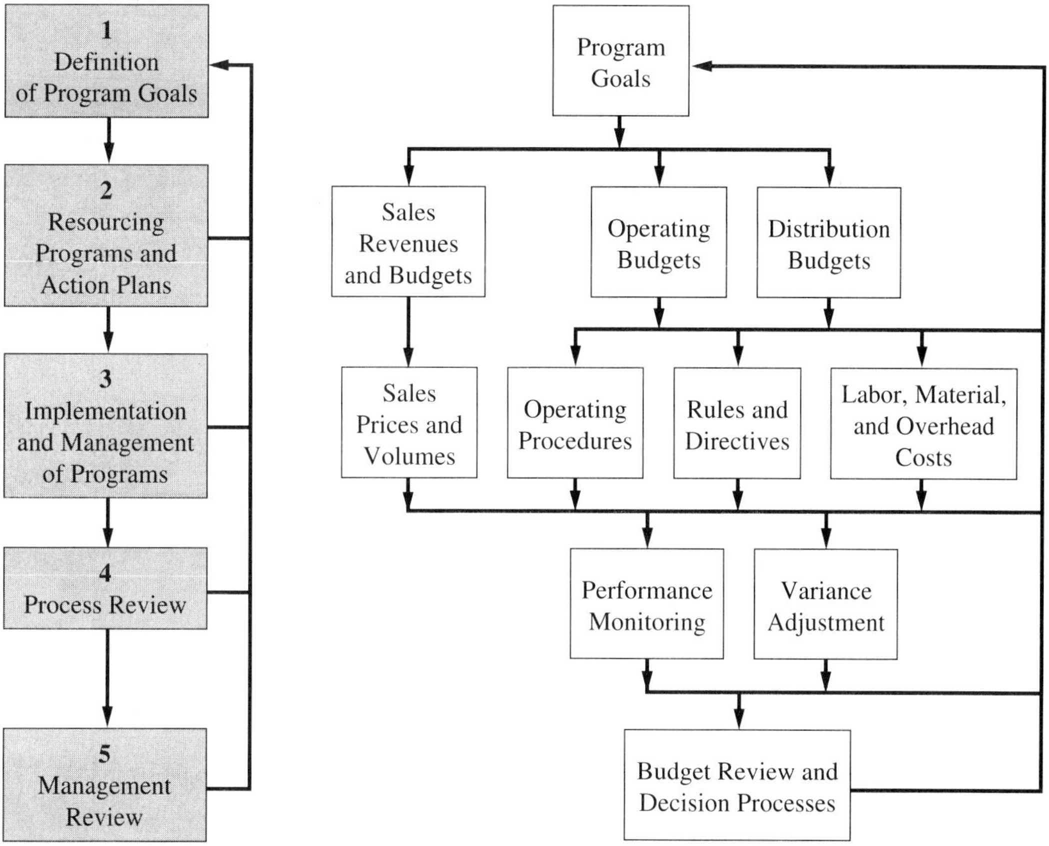


**FIGURE 14-5 The Policy Implementation Process**

## *Resourcing Programs and Action Plans*

The budgetary process is the primary means to make available materials, equipment and labor time, operating overhead, capital, or other resources for programs and action plans. Though the budget process may specifically consider only financial assets, other resources, particularly critical resources such as scarce materials, bottlenecked equipment, or skilled labor, should also be managed through this process. A quarterly budget review meeting, hosted by the finance staff and attended by almost all function staff, as well as the chief operating officer, the chief executive officer, or their representatives, is often used to manage resource allocations and the financial performance of particular programs.

## *Implementation and Management of Programs*

The proponent must now implement the defined program or action plan and manage it within the specified constraints. The implementation is often visible to a variety of other managers through reports or information system notices. For example, schedule changes would be visible to inventory managers and purchasing agents, and often to higher levels of management as well. This visibility assures that the activity performance is continually evaluated by management.

## *Process Review*

Formal process reviews are conducted at weekly or monthly intervals within the proponent activity. These reviews would likely identify shortfalls in program performance and correct those shortfalls with available assets. Such reviews may also result in requests for further policy clarification or for supplemental resources or may be the basis for an informal program status report to higher management.

## *Management Review*

The final step of the policy implementation process involves an even more formalized evaluation of each program to assess progress toward specific budgetary and performance goals. The primary functional areas of the organization, as well as some key staff members and top management, are usually represented in the management review step. Schedules and time lines, return on investments, and other performance measures are used to demonstrate performance toward goals. Such goals must be time-based, clearly measurable, and fully understood by all participants. Thus, formal application of management review methods permits a monthly or quarterly interaction of all activities involved or affected by the program. An example of the policy implementation process between Ford and Mazda is discussed in Application Box 14-3.

The partnership between Ford and Mazda exemplifies policy implementation at the highest level. It was built on trust and respect for each other's culture. Motorola used a similar approach in building its $400 million Silicon Harbor Complex in Hong Kong. After the building was completed, Motorola hired an 87-year-old diviner to check the building's "feng shui" (wind and water) for good luck. Motorola went to great lengths to accommodate local traditions by honoring the diviner's recommendations for a major renovation of the executive suite, thus ensuring good luck (Engardio et al., 1991). This example supports a broader, policy implementation perspective of facility layout considerations, as introduced in Chapter 6.

However, in other situations companies may achieve success by challenging the traditional rules and practices of the market. Toys "Я" Us entered the European market with unprecedented selection, low prices, an American-style year-round advertising campaign, and a "no quibble" return policy. In each respect, this strategy was contrary to the established practices in European toy markets. But the strategy was well received by customers and has changed the way several European toymakers and sellers do business (Oster and Reichlin, 1992). Similar approaches have been successfully used with Asian markets.

The sequence of the five activities may be more apparent in the first iteration of policy implementation; thereafter, it usually breaks down, and management must be cognizant of and interactive with all parts of the process simultaneously. This integration of the process and identification of the impediments to implementation should result in an internalized

## APPLICATION BOX 14-3 The Strategic Alliance of Ford and Mazda

The partnership between Ford and Mazda offers a striking example of how to implement strategic alliances. Though the activities of that international alliance are not as specific as domestic business policy implementation, the elements of the five-step implementation process are clearly present. The relationship between Ford Motor Company and Mazda Motors Corporation is one of the few successful international partnerships in the automobile business. It is the exception in a list of numerous failures, including GM–Isuzu, GM–Daewoo, Chrysler–Mitsubishi, Chrysler–Maserati, and Fiat–Nissan. Though failures have been numerous, the benefits of success are also high. Because the cost of developing a new model automobile can easily exceed $2 billion, the benefits of exchanging technologies are high, as is access to new markets.

***Definition of Program Goals.*** Goals of market access and technology exchange are established by top management. Top management must be regularly involved and must set the tone of the relationship. In global partnerships, sensitivity to cultural differences is a must, as is a recognition that at least one-third of the communication will be lost in translation. This means that you have to keep the relationship simple and basic, and that you have to work extra hard at ensuring that communication is complete. Social meetings are used to build trust among counterparts. Both partners understand that "Trust can't be built solely around a boardroom table."

***Resourcing Programs and Action Plans.*** Resources must be identified and committed. This requires cooperation on the development of new vehicles and the exchange of expertise. Ford's contribution is in international marketing and finance; Mazda's expertise is in manufacturing and product development. Ford and Mazda have jointly produced ten current models. Ford received help from Mazda on the Escort, Tracer, Festiva, Probe, Capri, and the Explorer. Ford gave Mazda help on the MX-6, 323, Protege, and Navajo. One in every four Fords sold in the United States benefited from this exchange, as did two in every five Mazdas sold in Japan.

***Implementation and Management of Programs.*** Program management has been the key to success. Though the partnership thrives on the quality of contribution of both partners, that quality of contribution explicitly results from the ability of each partner to concentrate on the characteristics that caused them to be worthy partners in the first place. The foundation of the relationship is partner independence, but simultaneously both partners recognize that the benefits of cooperation outweigh the costs of operating independently. However, as with all partnerships, there is a history of dispute. Mazda did not want to share an engine design; Ford did not want to offer a window design. Sometimes they just have to agree to disagree.

***Process Review.*** Regular review by top management and by an outside organization as a mediator have often been necessary. In some cases, there has been no resolution. Ford is a mass marketer, Mazda is a niche marketer; each wisely kept some parts of the business to itself. Those areas were off-limits to the partnership. Every eight months, senior executives of both firms hold a senior management strategy group (SMSG) meeting to review the partnership. Though the first two days are all business, the third is dedicated to social interaction.

***Management Review.*** The SMSG group provides a focus for subsequent meetings by the chairmen of the two companies to meet and discuss economic trends and the automobile business in the broadest strategic terms. These meetings are interwoven with counterpart meetings of various functional heads at several levels. These interactions generate volumes of suggestions for possible

*Continued*

**APPLICATION BOX 14-3** *Continued*

development of the partnership. Of some thousand items that are considered annually, only a half dozen or so survive. Yet, the important outcome is the current level of cooperation and that there is a process to manage an intercultural implementation plan. International partnerships are one of the most turbulent and tenuous of business relationships. The five-step implementation process, albeit generalized, ensures the effective policy implementation of both organizations.

Drawn from James B. Treece, Karen Lowry Miller, and Richard A. Melcher. "The Partners," *Business Week*. February 10, 1992, p. 102.

and spontaneous response by management to enhance the fit of policy to the strategy and to the organizational situation. Realistically, in a global market, this means extensive language training and cultural immersion (Titone, 1992).

The policy implementation process applies not only to the proactive management of policy but to the restraint of those processes as well. Most companies and most business schools can point to specific ethics programs to assure visibility and appreciation of ethical concerns. Dow Corning, for example, defined its program in the early 1970s; it included audits, management committees, and reviews by the board of directors. Yet this extensive (by comparison with other such businesses) effort failed to identify the problems of silicone implants. Somehow, the concerns were muted and the various audits, committees, and review processes did not permit the problems of silicone implants to surface. It is not enough to implement a policy; the management of the policy must be dedicated, alert, and involved (Byrne, 1992).

## *Fitting Policy*

Ultimately, the operations manager must design and manage policy implementation to be consistent with the intent of the strategy and appropriate for the organization. This section considers the more conceptual and theoretical questions raised by the fit of the policy with the strategy and with the organization. These considerations of fit lead to several apparent contradictions, which are discussed in the subsequent section.

### *Dimensions of Fit*

Policy implementation must be based upon the amount of functional integration needed and upon the intensity of the need for change. Horizontally, the integration of several functional areas, such as the different operations activities or different functional staffs of the firm, necessitates that the policy be adjusted to fit the different entities. For example, a particular company in a make-to-order business defines operations and marketing goals in terms of customized technologies and clearly stated service delivery lead times. But if top management feels that a shift toward a greater make-to-stock process would better position the company's product or result in higher profits, then a simultaneous repositioning of both the operations and marketing implementation policies would be required.

Otherwise, operations would miss the shorter lead times promised by marketing, or marketing would fail to exploit the less costly standardized product and process capabilities of operations. In either case, the outcome of such a functional policy mismatch is a deterioration of the competitive position of the firm. Thus, the amount of horizontal differentiation and concerns of the manager with integrating those various elements will delimit the implementation mode selected by the operations manager.

Similarly, vertical management processes and systems must also be evaluated to determine the amount of concern with systemic integration. A greater systemic integration would assure synergy among the various levels or internal components of the organization. In the most generic terms, there are at least five major vertical organizational systems and processes that should be considered.

1. Organization culture
2. Organization design
3. Employee development systems
4. Information systems
5. Management control systems

Each of these systems and subsets of these systems requires careful attention to ensure fit with other systems. For example, a corporation with several autonomous divisions would expect differences in policy implementation approaches between a high-volume, standardized process and a low-volume, customized process. Each of these five systems would be expected to function differently in the divisions. Those differences would be designed to reduce internal friction and inconsistencies within each division and thus enhance productivity and efficiency.

## *Implementation Modes*

The implementation mode, or approach, for a particular policy effort should be selected to correspond to the amount of concern for functional integration and concern for systemic integration. The situational conditions (function and systemic) significantly constrain the selection of the implementation mode. The four implementation modes, administrative, political, hands-on, and entrepreneurial, are shown in Figure 14-6.

The *administrative* mode is concerned more with systemic integration than with functional integration. The five organization systems (culture, design, employee development, information, and management control) and their processes and subcomponents will likely be managed in a very open and interactive manner, with emphasis on the quality of the process. Typically, this mode relies upon the loyalty and dedication of key subordinates, often to the exclusion of other individuals or groups, and engenders a high level of organizational commitment, particularly among immediate subordinates. However, this approach is very time consuming and, because it is not cross-functional, often serves to reinforce the internal systems and processes of one organizational unit to the exclusion of others. The administrative mode is found in most bureaucracies.

The *political* mode is heavily involved with both systemic and functional integration, concentrating on both the internal processes and external outcomes. This would require,

| CONCERN WITH SYSTEMIC INTEGRATION | CONCERN WITH FUNCTIONAL INTEGRATION: Low | CONCERN WITH FUNCTIONAL INTEGRATION: High |
|---|---|---|
| High | Administrative | Political |
| Low | Hands-on | Entrepreneurial |

**FIGURE 14-6 Policy Implementation Modes**

for example, spending the time and effort to integrate the policy both within and across functions, then reducing the negative side effects of a policy change. This approach generally takes more time, but causes less turbulence and ensures the continued support of all key proponents. Though the political mode will ensure that policy is smoothly implemented, time may not be available to create the extensive facilitative mechanisms required by the political mode. For this reason, the political mode is often most effective in organizations that have stable environments.

The *hands-on* motivator has little concern for either systemic or functional interaction. Instead, this implementation mode uses highly visible and charismatic activities to directly appeal to line employees. For example, this mode of implementation would use regular walk-throughs as well as spontaneous forms of communications. Organization staffs are managed through a combination of edict and loyalty. The process tends to respond to the needs of line employees and is particularly appropriate under circumstances of intense organization pressure, as encountered in environments of high dynamism.

Finally, the *entrepreneurial* mode is concerned with cross-functional integration, but pays little attention to systemic integration. Typically an entrepreneur will work across functional boundaries, achieving success through integrative efforts. This implementation mode has the strength of being able to rapidly achieve outcomes, though the lack of attention to detail may ultimately undermine the integration effort, because a foundation of systemic support for the policy or effort has not been established.

The selection of the appropriate leadership mode will depend upon the implementation requirements. The greater the diversity of the functional activities (in terms of breadth and variety) and of the systemic conditions (complexity of organization systems and processes) to be integrated, the more appropriate the implementation modes with high concerns in those areas. Alternatively, if the diversity of these dimensions is not as great, concerns directed toward those ends would be a waste of time, and low-concern implementation modes would be more appropriate. Thus, the situation, defined in systemic and functional terms, significantly constrains the implementation mode used by the manager. For example, the use of administrative techniques in an environment of high functional integration and low systemic integration needs would not only be inappropriate, it would be a waste of time and likely not successful.

In addition, the exact definition of an implementation effort in this matrix is also a matter of personal and individual leadership style. The art of leadership is to understand the situational limits imposed on the implementation mode, and to apply a leadership style that is appropriate toward those ends.

## *Individual Leadership Styles*

Policy is often used by operations managers to define their personal leadership style. This differentiates them or their section from other leaders or sections and recognizes the uniqueness of their activities. The leadership style variable permits operations managers to imprint their personal, ethical, or professional code or standard upon an activity. Such applications may involve decisions that have limited consequences or which are discretionary, for example, correspondence formats, meeting agendas, and the like. Toward those ends, four leadership styles are defined here: leadership by fiat, by intervention, by rational persuasion, and by facilitating participative groups.

These styles are differentiated primarily by the degree of assertiveness with which the leader chooses to impose outcomes. But they also suggest the amount of leadership interactivity and involvement with the decision-making process. At the one extreme, leadership by fiat imposes the manager's decision, while at the other extreme, leadership by facilitating participative groups permits the group-defined outcomes. Table 14-1 describes these four major individual leadership styles and indicates the circumstances where their use would be most appropriate.

Nutt (1987) evaluated these four styles in 68 strategy implementation situations. Rational persuasion was used in about one-half (48%) of the situations evaluated, followed by intervention (21%), fiat (16%), and participative group norms (15%). Intervention was found to be the superior leadership style, in terms of percent adoption of the new policy and rating of the quality of the new policy by those involved. Management by fiat, as might be expected, was the least successful method, both in terms of the outcome of a successful adoption and in terms of the user evaluation of the new policy. Rational persuasion and facilitating participative groups were both moderately successful as implementation methods, the principal difference between the two being that the source of the expertise in rational persuasion was external (for example, consultants or "experts"), and in participatory groups it was internal. The question of which leadership style should be used under which circumstance currently remains largely a matter of individual style, though research should ultimately be able to offer expected probabilities of success contingent upon several situational variables. Increasingly, however, companies are relying upon methods with high functional and systemic integration and greater employee

**TABLE 14-1 Individual Leadership Styles**

| Type | Description | When Used |
|---|---|---|
| Leadership by fiat | Manager uses position power to implement policy | Serious threat to organization, high cost, or high visibility of situation. Generally lower levels of functional and systemic integration |
| Leadership by intervention | Group offers advice, manager controls implementation | To minimize turbulence in implementing change in a dynamic or highly competitive organization |
| Leadership by rational persuasion | Manager demonstrates values and group recognizes and accepts approach | Highly technical, expert-oriented areas, often in dynamic environment |
| Leadership by facilitating participative groups | Group specifies outcomes based on group norms, sometimes within predefined management constraints | Strategic redirection requiring input from and representation of various, often technical areas. Generally higher levels of functional and systemic integration |

involvement. Both implementation mode and leadership style issues allude, however, to the paradox of implementation.

## *The Paradox of Implementation*

The paradox of policy implementation generally suggests that greater involvement by a policy implementer may be counterproductive. The more direct the presence of the leader in the implementation process, the more such efforts may potentially impede the implementation. Increased efforts to facilitate greater functional cohesion and systemic consistency may not yield the desired results. This is because they may constrain or delimit alternatives or reduce the opportunities for involvement by participants in the implementation project, thus constraining the implementation. Greater apparent involvement may impede effective implementation. This is the paradox of policy implementation.

### *Continuity versus Chaos*

Efforts directed toward consistency, cohesion, and continuous improvement (continuity) of an implemented policy, or any other component of the policy hierarchy imply increasing tightness of control with the process by management. Such greater control would seem to lead to better performance because it directs attention toward inefficient misfits in the organization, process, or product/service. Yet better performance also results from employee involvement, individuality, and innovation (chaos), which are promoted, at least in part, by a dynamic, chaotic, adaptive, and resilient organization and environment of the sort described by Drucker (1980, 1989). Though not completely mutually exclusive, these elements of continuity and chaos contribute somewhat dichotomously to policy implementation. In this sense, the more clearly articulated the implementation effort, the more inflexible and vulnerable it may become. Table 14-2 suggests these dichotomies of policy implementation.

Under some circumstances, the operations manager may desire to appear ambivalent between continuity and chaos. Continuity yields structure and discipline, almost mandatory to the accomplishment of policy goals, yet an element of chaos permits the adaptive involvement, innovation, and flexibility necessary to do a difficult job well. Continuity fosters a tighter, more integrated understanding of the business, while chaos encourages exploitative and divergent thinking. Carefully considered and documented decisions, followed by cautious implementation, characterize continuity, while bold strategic leaps and resourceful implementation are promoted by an aura of chaos. As the increasingly integrated and dynamic conditions of international business have greater impacts on business situations, the operations manager must move from policies that protect continuity toward those that engender some amount of chaos.

Too much of either continuity or chaos will be problematic in most environments. The continuity–chaos dimension of individual policy implementation is analogous to the explicitness dimension of policy. Leadership behavior may attempt to structure too much continuity, which, like the explicitly defined policy, would stifle initiative. Similarly, a leadership-inspired chaotic condition corresponds to the vaguely defined policy. Just as formulated policy must be neither too explicit nor too vague, the implementation of that policy should not be too structured. Excessive tightness of control can be stultifying, but insufficient structure can be equally counterproductive because of the lack of apparent order. A balance must be achieved which permits, yet restrains; which activates, yet impedes; which delimits, yet empowers; and which communicates those limits, both formally and informally, on a continuous basis. In cases where there is no clear-cut need for either continuity or chaos, apparent ambivalence on the part of the operations manager may be the best approach.

The operations manager must balance the need for continuity with an appreciation of the benefits of chaos. Studies of corporate downsizing by Cameron et al. (1991) suggest that the most effective efforts involved just such a duality. Ineffective firms, alternatively, attempt to maintain consistency, harmony, and fit—only one side of the duality. This paradox of implementation requires that the operations manager weigh the benefits of apparent ambivalence and, as clear-cut situations present themselves, adjust leadership

**TABLE 14-2 Dichotomies of Policy Implementation**

| Continuity | Chaos |
|---|---|
| Consistency | Variability |
| Organization cohesion | Entrepreneurial diversity |
| Risk focus | Dynamic adaptability |
| Commitment to order | Commitment to change |
| Careful decisions—cautious implementation | Bold strategies—Resourceful implementation |
| More definition | Less clarity |

behaviors. The use of inconsistent management behaviors, however, has limits. Though inconsistency encourages a multidimensional environment, as situations and decisions become more focused, inconsistencies should be resolved.

## *Resolving Inconsistencies of Policy*

The inconsistencies, both of the policy requirements in a particular situation and of the implementation modes and leadership styles selected by the operations manager, potentially can be extremely ambiguous. Inconsistencies (conflicts) often arise because goals are not sufficiently clarified. Because of the rather high incidence of such situations, particularly in global companies (see Application Box 14-3), it is necessary to have a mechanism to resolve inconsistencies of policy.

The theory of constraints offers an approach that helps resolve such ambiguities by identifying the specific resources required and the goals and criteria of conflicting policies (Fogarty et al., 1991, p. 619). The policy requirements, resource availability, and goals and competitive priorities of the policy are examined to ensure that there is a clear relationship and consistent linkage among them. If any of the linkages does not withstand examination, then the dichotomy must be resolved or reformulated. If these linkages are upheld, then the goal must be reviewed for a possible compromise. This process is demonstrated in Figure 14-7 and exemplified in the following discussion.

For example, such a dichotomy might result from a policy which, to placate labor groups, encouraged the use of overtime. The resources required to implement such a policy would be available labor and overtime payments. Alternatively, a second policy requirement directed toward global competitiveness might specify that operations select the low-cost resource. In many environments, the low-cost labor resource would likely be temporary labor, possibly with some additional supervision to ensure that quality and delivery requirements were met. Thus, the use of overtime (policy requirement 1) would

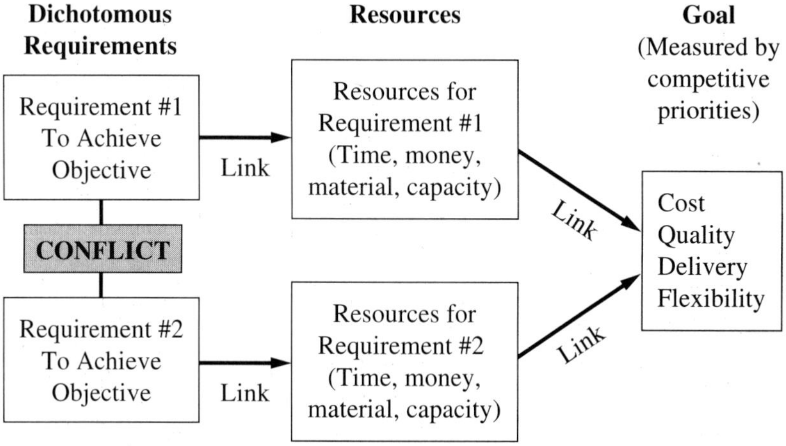


**FIGURE 14-7 Resolving Inconsistencies of Policy**

incur higher costs and excessive overtime would likely result in lower quality and poorer delivery performance. Alternatively, reliance on temporary labor sources (policy requirement 2) might result in lower costs and greater flexibility, but potentially lower quality and poorer delivery rates, unless the temporary labor were trained and supervised.

These policies are in conflict. The resources for each requirement are identified and achievement of the operations goal could be evaluated by using the competitive priorities. If an inconsistency among the requirements, resources, and goals were found (such as that temporary hires were not the best option), then the problem could be resolved or reformulated. However, if there were no inconsistency of the linkages, a compromise must be found.

This conflict might also be resolved by the incremental implementation of policy requirement 1 (overtime) up to a certain number of hours per month. Then the overtime employees could be supplemented by additional temporary hires, and the function of the overtime employees might shift toward training and supervision. This rather simplistic example illustrates conflicting policy requirements and a process of identifying associated resources and goals. The resolution of the conflict may be completely achieved through policy requirement 1 or through policy requirement 2. Alternatively, a compromise solution with some components of policy requirement 1 and of policy requirement 2 may be the least costly. In fact, operations managers may not initially have very good information on the cost of compromise options. Ambivalence, in this latter case, can be a very effective way to deal with incomplete information, until the resource costs and goals are clarified.

To add a third dimension to this situation, marketing might be concerned with the product quality and delivery effectiveness. A further policy must be formulated which satisfies and integrates each of the three dichotomous requirements. However, when the risks or costs, often stated in terms of time, money, materials, capacity, or other measured values, of each policy alternative or compromise solution are evaluated, a best approach will likely become apparent. This type of evaluation of apparently dichotomous requirements is often valuable in identifying conflicting policies and resolving inconsistencies of the fit of policy to the strategy or to the organization. Thus, the theory of constraints is a thinking process that permits a person to focus on the core problem and then to seek a resolution by challenging the assumptions (links) which are the basis of the conflict (Goldratt, 1993).

## *Summary—Continuity or Chaos*

The implementation process is one of dynamically balancing forces of continuity and chaos to project a defined policy toward the achievement of a strategic goal. Excessive continuity (consistency, cohesion, or continuous improvement) or excessive chaos (innovation, individuality, or involvement) will likely impede policy implementation. Management must create and control the structural process to realize strategic goals; yet simultaneously management must tolerate the blending of discordant and often chaotic elements to ensure sufficient involvement, incongruity, and innovation of the process. Defining this balance is suggested by Goold and Campbell (1987) as the toughest part of the process.

To this end, the promotion of a variety of demonstration projects, sponsorships, product, service, or project champions, or other specific techniques may be used. The operations manager must demonstrate strategic perception and appreciation of the near-chaotic elements of the organization and its environment, in addition to an administrative and structuring process. A much-repeated adage reflects:

> *When you are up to your neck in an alligator-infested swamp, it's hard to remember that the goal was to drain the swamp.*

## *Discussion Questions*

1. Policy is defined as a guide to implementation. In what ways does policy serve as a guide to implementation? Describe an example from a company with which you are familiar.
2. The hierarchy of implementation activities contains elements as general as philosophies, and as precise as procedures and rules. What key characteristic of each of these activities ensures the integration of the hierarchy?
3. Identify the three dimensions of organization policy. Give an example from your own experience of how these dimensions may be used by the operations manager to ensure that the policy is appropriate for the particular situation.
4. Why is it important that the scope of the operations policy be appropriately defined? Give an example, with regard to scope, of a flawed and a well-defined policy.
5. Describe and give an example from your own experiences of differing amounts of formality of policy.
6. What is the impact of a policy that is defined with an incorrect degree of explicitness? Give an example, with regard to explicitness, of a correctly defined and an incorrectly defined policy.
7. Describe a policy implementation situation from your own experience or from the business media; then concisely identify the five steps of the policy determination process and relate those steps to the implementation situation that you have selected.
8. Is policy implementation a simultaneous process? Under what circumstances? Briefly describe an example.
9. In what ways should policy implementation modes be fit to the situation? Describe an example of each of the four implementation modes.
10. From your own experience or from the business media, describe a policy implementation situation, and then identify the type of leadership style that you believe would be most appropriate for that situation.
11. From your experience, describe an example of one major organizational system or process. Identify, for that situation, five major vertical systems and tell whether the appropriate concern of the manager for systemic integration should be high or low.

12. "Policy implementation is tough enough; we certainly don't need some junior manager coming in here and creating chaos." State whether you agree with this assessment by a senior operations manager; then present the arguments in support of your opinion.

13. How does the theory of constraints assist in resolving dichotomous requirements, and how is leadership ambivalence related?

14. Describe a business situation when you have been "up to your neck in an alligator-infested swamp," and how you were able to resolve the issues and get the swamp drained.

## *Strategic Decision Situations*

1. From your personal experience or readings in business publications, define the current strategic situation in a business or in an operation. Then clearly define a strategy change that, in your estimation, must occur in the business or the operation within the next two to five years. You may want to specifically describe the situation, using the concepts noted in the structure or infrastructure chapters of this book or in Figure 14-4. Having provided the descriptive foundations, describe the policy implementation modes and individual leadership styles that are appropriate for the situation.

2. From your personal experiences or readings in business publications, describe a conflict situation in operations management. Use the terms and logic of the theory of constraints to show how the conflict should be resolved. Compare the TOC resolution with what actually occurred.

## *References*

Ansoff, H. Igor. *The New Corporate Strategy.* New York: Wiley, 1988.

Avishai, Bernard. "A CEO's Common Sense of CIM: An Interview with J. Tracy O'Rourke," *Harvard Business Review.* January–February 1989, pp. 110–117.

Byrne, John A. "The Best Laid Ethics Programs . . . ," *Business Week.* March 9, 1992, pp. 67–68.

Cameron, Kim S., Sarah J. Freeman, and Aneil K. Mishra. "Best Practices in White Collar Downsizing: Managing Contradictions," *The Academy of Management Executive.* Vol. 5, No. 3, 1991, pp. 57–73.

Dobrzynski, Judith H. "Rethinking IBM," *Business Week.* October 4, 1993, pp. 86–97.

Drucker, Peter F. *Managing in Turbulent Times.* New York: Harper and Row, Publishers, 1980.

Drucker, Peter F. *The New Realities: In Government and Politics/in Economics and Business/in Society and World View.* New York: Harper and Row, Publishers, 1989.

Engardio, Pete, Lois Therrien, Neil Gross, and Larry Armstrong. "How Motorola Took Asia by the Tail," *Business Week.* November 11, 1991, p. 68.

Flynn, Julia. "The Ugly Mess at Waste Management," *Business Week.* April 13, 1992, pp. 76–77.

Fogarty, Donald W., Thomas R. Hoffmann, and Peter W. Stonebraker. *Production and Operations Management.* Cincinnati, Ohio: South-Western Publishing Co., 1989.

Fogarty, Donald W., John H. Blackstone, and Thomas R. Hoffmann. *Production and Inventory Management.* Cincinnati, Ohio: South-Western Publishing Co., 1991.

Goldratt, Eliyahu M. "What Is the Theory of Constraints?" *APICS—The Performance Advantage.* June 1993, pp. 18–23.

Goold, Michael, and Andrew Campbell. "Many Best Ways to Make Strategy," *Harvard Business Review.* November–December 1987, p. 70.

Hayes, Robert H., and Steven C. Wheelwright. *Restoring Our Competitive Edge: Competing through Manufacturing.* New York: John Wiley and Sons, 1984.

Nutt, Paul C. "Identifying and Appraising How Managers Install Strategy," *Strategic Management Journal.* Vol. 8, No. 1, 1987, pp. 1–14.

Oster, Patrick, and Igor Reichlin. "Breaking into European Markets by Breaking the Rules," *Business Week.* January 20, 1992, pp. 88–89.

Paine, Frank T., and Carl R. Anderson. *Strategic Management.* Chicago, Ill.: Dryden Press, 1983.

Schiller, Zachary. "No More Mr. Nice Guy at P&G—Not by a Long Shot," *Business Week.* February 3, 1992, pp. 54–56.

Skinner, Wickham. "What Matters to Manufacturing," *Harvard Business Review.* January–February 1988, p. 16.

Steiner, George A., and John B. Miner. *Management Policy and Strategy.* New York: Macmillan Publishing Co., 1977.

Stobaugh, Robert, and Piero Telesio. "Match Manufacturing Policies and Product Strategy," *Harvard Business Review.* March–April 1983, pp. 113–120.

Titone, Richard C. "Going Multinational," *APICS—The Performance Advantage.* August 1992, pp. 40–42.

Treece, James B., Karen Lowry Miller, and Richard A. Melcher. "The Partners," *Business Week.* February 10, 1992, pp. 102–107.

Verity, John W. "Out of One Big Blue, Many Little Blues," *Business Week.* December 9, 1991, p. 33.

Verity, John W., Thane Peterson, Diedre Depke, and Evan I. Schwartz. "The New IBM," *Business Week.* December 16, 1991, p. 112.

Weber, Joseph. "Curing Warner-Lambert—Before It Gets Sick," *Business Week.* December 9, 1991, p. 91.

Weber, Joseph. "A Big Company That Works," *Business Week.* May 4, 1992, pp. 124–132.

Wheelwright, Steven C. "Reflecting Corporate Strategy in Manufacturing Decisions," *Business Horizons,* February 1978, pp. 57–66.

# Chapter 15

## Operations Strategy 2000: Toward the Millennium

*Information is a virus that transmits freedom.*
—Pundit Unknown

*Factories of the future require mindsets of the future.*
—F. Roy Piciacchia and Lockwood Greene, 1989

### *Objectives*

After completing this chapter you should be able to:

- State the conditions that have created an environment of hostility toward manufacturing.
- Describe three types of social structures, and show how such organizations make business decisions.
- Define the role of government in facilitating growth of business.
- Describe several specific transformations toward which competitive firms of the year 2000 must move.
- Identify the key resources of the operations environment of the year 2000 and suggest how leaders will integrate those resources.
- Describe several ways in which the mindset of an operations manager is expected to change by the year 2000.

### *Outline*

***Introductory Case: The Fable of Winston Marsaillis***

***The Forecast Is Always Wrong***

## *Introductory Case: The Fable of Winston Marsaillis*

The sun shone brightly as young Winston Marsaillis strode toward the golden arches, oblivious of the people exiting the monorail. As he passed under the arches and through the airway, the pressure hissed gently, but even that did not bother him today. He glanced past the modular displays and mockups and proceeded directly to the reception counter and entered his number.

Winston hummed to himself. At the screen's prompting, he placed his thumb in the identification panel and waited for the screen to recognize him. He was glad that he had come early, because he would avoid the crowds. He turned toward the fitting area and reflected over the past several weeks. The color selection panels seemed to be more bland today and the ergonometric modules somehow less attractive. Several salespeople were waiting for expected business. A whirring noise announced that the processors were starting up.

When the screen recognized him, Winston asserted, "I'd like a 191, color 46, options 33, 36, and 42." He recited the details from memory.

"Certainly," the screen responded automatically, confirming that the audio had correctly read the order. "That will be a 191–46, with 33, 36, and 42. Would you like a 48 with that? It would give you greater range at night."

Winston shook his head. "Fine," responded the screen. "Your thumb scan is good and we have your ergonometrics. That should be about ten minutes. Please go to the waiting room."

Winston wandered idly among the displays for several minutes. He did not like waiting rooms—the video materials there were distracting. The customer service area was as bright as ever. The customer questionnaires and sampling equipment permitted gathering customer information about life style, job, personal information, and psychological and motor responses. He watched as Sara, his customer rep, helped another customer fit the bubble protection system. He was not surprised that the customer winced with the envelopment of the form-fitting accident shell. He wandered nonchalantly past the audio testing chamber, still not able to understand how the audio equaiizer could neutralize outside noise except for the "danger" frequencies. The presses and extruders now moaned behind the walls, possibly extruding and assembling his order. Why could they not apply the same audio equalizing technology to the customer sales area that they did for the product? It would be such a convenience, thought Winston.

"Winston, your order is ready. Please return to the roll-out room," intoned the computer over the speaker system, interrupting the Muzak. Winston almost ran. He turned the corner and—there it was. Emerging from the washer behind the airway. His very own—Oh, it was beautiful.

As Winston proudly strode up, a technician appeared. "Let me hook up the magneto link, and then you can run a check. Your account is confirmed with Central Power and the Ministry of Density. Use it for a week or so, and then we will make any adjustments that you want."

Winston beamed as he stepped into his new 191, rolled back the sun panel, and turned his eyes right toward the magneto strip on the pavement. The optical scanner followed his impulses and he levitated his 191 personal transportation vehicle into traffic.

## *The Forecast Is Always Wrong*

This chapter has the formidable objective of identifying the conditions of operations strategy to the millennium and beyond. The millennium, the year 2000, may seem to be well into the future, but it is now well within the long-range planning horizons of most businesses—or should be. Though such a forecast may be wrong, no better alternative is available. Any projection may be disputed either as to the forecasted conditions or as to the evaluation of their impact. For example, Daniel Bell projected in 1967 that the United States would move into a fourth stage of economic development, the service economy. The resulting shifting of manufacturing businesses to international competition would be an acceptable part of this process, and Bell did not feel that this was of major concern. This forecast was widely heralded as extremely insightful at the time. Though Bell was correct in his projection, he may have erred concerning the impacts.

The projections of this chapter may be viewed not only as a summarization, but also as an opportunity to let the imagination wander. Similarly, we would ask the reader to accept the introductory case for what it is—a fable. These comments, then, are offered in the vein of numerous such projections, including:

*Towards the Year 2000, Work in Process* by Bell (1967)

*Future Shock* (1971), *The Third Wave* (1980), and *Powershift* (1990) by Toffler

*Managing in Turbulent Times* (1980) and *The New Realities* (1989) by Drucker

*Theory Z* (1981) and *The M-Form Society* (1984) by Ouchi

*In Search of Excellence* by Peters and Waterman (1982)

*Megatrends* by Naisbitt (1982)

*Restoring Our Competitive Edge: Competing through Manufacturing* by Hayes and Wheelwright (1984)

*Manufacturing: The Formidable Competitive Weapon* by Skinner (1985)

*Manufacturing for Competitive Advantage* by Gunn (1987)

*Thriving on Chaos* by Peters (1987)

*Dynamic Manufacturing* by Hayes, Wheelwright, and Clark (1988)

*Megatrends 2000* by Naisbitt and Aburdene (1990)

*Workplace 2000* by Boyett and Conn (1991)

*Reengineering the Corporation* by Hammer and Champy (1993)

As a result of such works, most managers recognize a need for a vision of the future, though there is still little agreement as to the substance of the vision. For example, Hammer and Champy (1993, p. 2) suggest that reengineering means "putting aside much of the received wisdom of 200 years of industrial management." Other authors suggest a similarly revolutionary transition to the future. Perhaps, then, that should be the purpose of this chapter: to focus discussion of operations strategy toward the millenium and generate discussion points, if not the specific positions of that discussion.

## *Mobilization of Operations*

Skinner (1985, p. 280) identifies five periods in the evolution of manufacturing management. Those periods are

| | |
|---|---|
| 1780–1850 | Manufacturing leader as technological capitalists |
| 1850–1890 | Manufacturing leader as architects of mass production |
| 1890–1920 | Manufacturing management moves down in the organization |
| 1920–1960 | Manufacturing management refines its skills in controlling and stabilizing |
| 1960–1980 | Shaking the foundations of industrial management |

Though Skinner's discussion is defined in manufacturing terms, such a categorization may also apply in different time periods to extraction, distribution, and service organizations. Additionally, Skinner's categories are historical, not projective, though the conditions of the fifth period, which have shaken the foundations of industrial management, presently show only tentative signs of abating in many industries. The period of 1980 to 2000 and probably several decades into the twenty-first century will likely be considered in retrospect to be an era of the mobilization of industry and significant international economic and operations conflicts and opportunities. These conditions are expected to result from such factors as explosive technology changes, empowered demanders, global economic competition, intensified regulatory pressures on business investing, and the "decoupling of operations."

In essence, the operations function in many U.S. corporations has the daunting task of rebuilding itself to be the credible and formidable competitive weapon that it was from 1780 to 1960. This rebuilding will require entirely different skills from those previously used, because the conditions and environment of operations have changed. Nowhere is this more apparent than in the potentially life-threatening damage done by operations practices to the Earth's ozone layer. For this and other reasons, today, as never before, operations activities are confronted with hostility.

## *Foundations of Hostility*

### *Explosive Technological Change*

During the second half of the twentieth century, the rapid changes in technology first affected products and services, then production processes, and finally management information systems. Though such changes have been a fact of history, the rate of these changes is new. Consider, for example, the computer. Early systems that would multiply or divide five-digit numbers were demonstrated in the late 1930s. By the 1960s, massive (500 ft × 500 ft × 8 ft and larger) arrays of racks of computer tubes were used to manage continental air defense systems. In the 1960s, the diode replaced the tube and, by the late 1970s, the diode was itself replaced by the chip. In each subsequent year, redesign of the chip permitted increased capacity and additional capabilities. Today, chips are required to build chips. The new technology was initially applied to the product, and then to the production process. Finally, with the emergence of modeling methods, decision-making technologies, and artificial intelligence, the computer has become a part of the information system and decision-making processes ("A New Age . . . ," 1983, and Baraiko, 1982).

Other examples of this revolution are found in digital instrumentation, sensors and switches, music and art, telephone systems, in the processes to build each of those products, and in the management systems used to operate those processes. Simply, the previously used mechanical knowledge is not sufficient for the new technology, just as a wrench is not useful to tune a computer or other recently designed products. For example, the engines of many current automobiles are diagnosed and managed by computers. This technology transformation is so complete that most of the tools of the industrial age are not relevant in the information age—and this has all transpired in approximately two generations.

### *Empowered Demanders*

During much of the past two centuries, economic conditions favored the supplier, which in turn favored operations. Transportation was costly and crude, thus limiting the distribution of supplies and encouraging de facto local and regional monopolies and collusion in many industries. However, development of the interstate highway system, global air package services, and global communications has created alternative sources of supply, which empowered demanders. Customers could select from international sources on the basis of various product or process criteria. For example, the demand for goods produced in highly industrialized nations has been challenged by roughly equivalent or better goods produced in emerging nations with significantly lower labor costs (Drucker, 1986).

### *Globalization and Regionalization*

Global pressures on manufacturing and distribution systems intensified in the 1980s. In all but a few industries, components are purchased on a worldwide market, and finished goods are sold in that same global market. Consider the automobile, electronic, photographic, clothing, and computer industries. Additionally, large amounts of food items, lumber, printing, investment services, fertilizer and pesticides, glass and pottery, and telecommunications services are sold on international markets. World trade in goods and services has been estimated at three trillion dollars per year and growing.

With the emergence of the European Community, the North American Free Trade Area, and the Pacific Rim trading zones, global trading patterns seem to be focusing toward regional blocs. Though national tariff barriers may be dropping, global trade is being restructured to create powerful regional economic zones, each with different regulations, processes, and objectives. Application Box 15-1 describes the emergence of these regional trading blocs.

### *Regulation and Media Visibility*

The visibility of operations decision making and ethical processes is increased by both greater regulatory effort and by greater media involvement. Though the unfortunate release of toxic chemicals by a Union Carbide plant occurred in the remote village of Bhopal, India, the communications media made both the incident and the settlement process globally visible. It is becoming increasingly difficult for firms or nations to export the hazardous or polluting portions of their production to less developed nations or to import hazardous products without incurring potential pressures of governments and world opinion. Similarly, international trade agreements, such as the North American Free Trade Agreement, contain sections that refer to pollution and to the environment.

### *Decoupling of Operations Variables*

Drucker (1986) suggests that changes in the world economy have decoupled operations in three critical ways. The production of finished goods has been decoupled (1) from raw materials, (2) from labor, and (3) from world trade. Even though the prices of finished goods have increased many-fold, the prices of raw materials (with the exception of oil, as Drucker notes) have been essentially stable on the world market for the past 50 years, and labor has made a decreasing contribution to those finished goods. Similarly, annual trade

## APPLICATION BOX 15-1 The Regional Economic Blocs

The traditional American approach to foreign competition is to view the competition as individual nations and their products, Japanese automobiles and electronics, British entertainment, French or Italian design, German glass, and so on. However, this system of bilateral trading relationships is past. The later decades of the twentieth century have seen the gradual emergence of three very powerful regional economic blocs: the European Community (EC), the Pacific Rim, and the North American Free Trade Agreement (NAFTA).

The EC, though envisioned as early as the Congress of Vienna in 1815, was formally structured by the 1958 Treaty of Rome. Though the integration process has been and will continue to be difficult, the EC has moved toward the economic union of 12 major European states. With the fall of the Berlin Wall, membership could be 20 or more states, and the EC could become a very powerful customs zone. This market of 350 million (potentially close to one-half billion) customers is encumbered by linguistic differences, but has a 200-year history of efforts toward commonality, and now has the foundations of an administrative process to manage that commonality. Note that among the 12 (or potentially 20) EC states, there is no significantly "dominant" state, and that the community is developing toward a confederation of states pursuing mutuality of interests. The productivity of the natural and human resources and the tremendous potential of the former Soviet Union provide an unprecedented growth opportunity. With the continuing development of communication and distribution systems, the EC is expected to continue to grow toward unity.

The second region, the Pacific Rim, consists of four segments: Japan, North Korea and South Korea; Taiwan, Hong Kong, and adjacent coastal China; Vietnam, Laos, and Cambodia; and Singapore, Thailand, the Philippines, Malaysia, and Indonesia. This area has a population of some 340 million persons, with potential growth into the tremendous population markets of mainland China. This trading bloc is currently the least developed, yet it has the greatest potential for growth. In the immediate future the bloc may take on the form of several subregions, each of which operates independently, as it gradually moves toward greater interdependence. Though presently hampered by the lack of contiguous land areas and limited transportation, the emerging air transport systems should mitigate these limitations.

The North American Free Trade Area, consisting of Canada, Mexico, and the United States, has a roughly equal population (340 million) and, if the other Central American and Caribbean nations are included, some 400 million. The variety of languages is much less of a problem than for either the EC or the Pacific Rim, and the area is more resource intense and less population intense than either of the other regions. Politically, the region has a history of cooperation, though that is sometimes tainted by "Yankee imperialism" or governed by a "Monroe Doctrine" mentality. While American foreign policy in recent years has not been particularly imperialistic toward its neighbors, its sheer economic might suggests that the bloc may be initially dominated by the American market and American business. Like the other regional blocs, NAFTA has experienced much turbulence in its steps toward integration.

These blocs are all in the northern hemisphere; yet both South America and Africa also have the potential to become very large and powerful economic blocs. Unless disrupted by major international conflicts, it is expected that these three, and possibly five, blocs will grow internally in the next several decades. Organization as trading blocs makes sense, because it provides stability of economic relationships in a period when national political structures (specifically those in the former Soviet Union, Canada, and Europe) appear to be weakening. However, the potential for alignment of any two of these powers against the third, or other blocs could be politically and economically disastrous (Albin, 1992).

*Continued*

**APPLICATION BOX 15-1** *Continued*

The effects of these blocs are already visible in the automobile, electronics, and electric appliance industries and will likely intensify as computer chips and computers, high-density television, and communications markets become more competitive. A specific example of this interbloc competition is the serious challenge by Airbus Industrie, a consortium of four European nations, to the American aircraft giants, McDonnell Douglas and Boeing. The development and distribution of products and services that are designed for the regional bloc and global markets are important considerations in formulating operations strategy.

of finished goods in the world market ($3 trillion), even though increasing, has been decoupled from international capital transactions ($76 trillion). According to Drucker, these decouplings are a clear break from the traditional economic theory that a good was valued as the sum of its parts, plus some profit for the value added. If conventional economic theory held, raw materials prices would be much more tightly bound to those of finished goods, as would be the volume of world trade and capital movements. These effects are sufficient for Drucker to call for a new economic theory.

However, these decouplings of production transformations may be due to the increased contribution of services and other intangibles to both components and finished goods. Such service contributions to production as customization, information, design and appeal, education, and employee assistance, and to world trade such as media, communications, entertainment, distribution, financial services, and others may have contributed to or caused this apparent decoupling. The decoupling of operations, particularly of manufacturing operations, from the inputs and outputs of the transformation process is shown in Figure 15-1.

Given that these changes in demand, technology, global markets, regulation, and visibility and in the chain of transformations itself are identifiable and measurable, one must accept Drucker's contention that the change is irreversible. Until operations can regain control of these contributors to production processes, the chain of transformations will continue to be "decoupled." These factors, both individually and in combinations, will make the future of the operations environment, and particularly manufacturing, rather hostile.

## *Defining New Linkages*

Even as operations management is constrained by those forces and the environment, described as early as 1980 by Hall as a situation of mature markets, is more difficult, if not actually hostile, it is possible to survive and succeed. As Hall notes, in mature markets some strategies are more appropriate than others. Simply, in the current and projected conditions, firms must achieve the lowest product/service cost or a meaningfully differentiated market position, or both.

The low-cost position is characterized by gaining an acceptable quality of a stable product/service design. This keeps operating costs down and permits pricing flexibility toward the objective of increasing volume. Alternatively, the differentiated product/

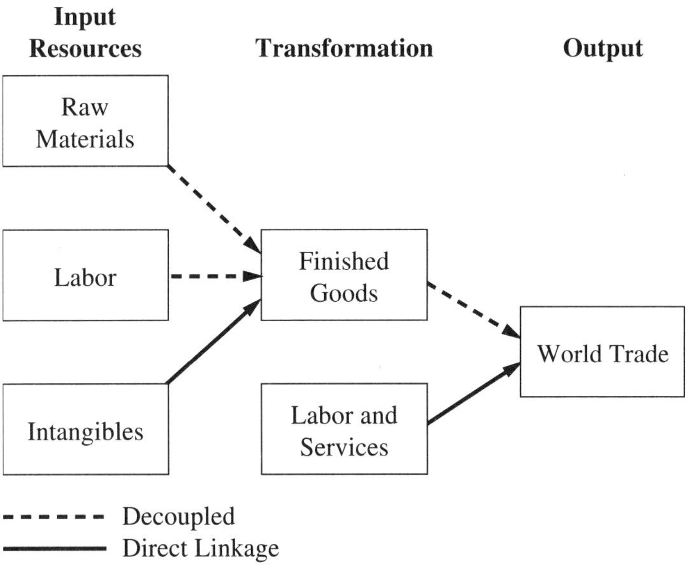


**FIGURE 15-1 The Decoupling of Operations**

service strategy grows faster than the low-cost position and has higher unit prices and margins. Research, advertising, and other service-differentiating costs are more easily recovered. Inventories are typically lower, with a higher proportion of the units sold based on either special order or back order. Such policies permit higher inventory turnover.

These conclusions are particularly appropriate, because they describe the conditions for success in hostile and global environments. Hall's study (1980) of 64 large U.S. manufacturing companies in major product industries (auto, steel, and the like) found that successful (measured by profitability and growth) operations are not necessarily the low-cost producers. High product/service differentiation, achieved through product/service or process focus and competitive costs, was found to be the key contributor to success in mature markets.

Such careful definition of the product/service-process technology niche is a necessary, but not sufficient, step. In addition, a firm must consider four further factors: national culture (or infrastructure), the national market (and government policies which regulate that market), business strategy, and the use of resources. These four factors must be carefully fitted together in appropriate and synergetic combinations, or recoupled, to create the conditions for successful global operations. These variables are the basis for the structure of the rest of the chapter.

## *Cultural Imperative*

Culture (or national infrastructure), according to Ouchi (1981, p. 35), is "a set of symbols, rituals, ceremonies, and myths that communicate the underlying beliefs" to various recipients, including citizens, neighbors, or employees. Cultural processes enhance the otherwise stark outlines of abstract philosophies and jargonistic laws, covenants, and missions. Culture communicates in terms that, like the fable of Winston Marsaillis, are simplistic and exaggerated, yet easily understood and internalized. Additionally, culture incorporates an array of common experiences, emotions, and backgrounds. This commonality of educational experiences, rites of passage, symbolic events, and their anniversaries, as well as value systems and standards, dramatically reduces the time necessary to develop a bond among people or employees. In most cases, the influence of culture, as it is translated through the mechanisms of social organization, amounts to a lifelong process of socialization. All of which means, as noted by Littal (1983), that culture is relatively stable and, even in periods of turbulence, does not rapidly change. Because culture is a stabilizing and defining influence, intercultural partnerships are difficult (see Application Box 14-3.)

## *Models of Social Organization*

Drawing from Durkheim, Argyris, Kanter, and others, Ouchi (1981) differentiates three predominant types of social organization or mechanisms through which culture is translated. Those models of social organization are the market, the hierarchy, and the clan; they are important because they define the context within which culture is passed or translated from one person to another or from one generation to another. The pure forms of the market, hierarchy, and clan are summarized in Table 15-1.

### *Market Model*

In the market model, social interaction operates in an open forum of demand through price and ideas. The focus of this forum may be a political election, a commodity exchange, or

**TABLE 15-1 Characteristics of Social Organizations**

| Characteristic | Market | Hierarchy | Clan |
|---|---|---|---|
| Format of interaction | Open forum of demand with price and ideas | Bureaucratic planning | Teamwork |
| Value criterion | Competitively bid value | Hierarchically defined objectives | Subtly defined and regularly reconsidered norms and goals |
| Measurement system | The market legitimizes value | Equitability of rewards | Group interaction makes individual contribution difficult to measure |
| Functioning | Acceptance | Surveillance | Internalization |
| Individual motivation | Self-interest | Faith in hierarchy | Acquiescence to group |
| Duration of relationship | Daily renewal | Based on power and faith | Long-term acculturation and commitment |

a job interview. The market mechanism enhances and clarifies the quality of the exchange, despite recurrent doubts as to its viability. Defining the value or demand for an item or an idea merely requires that it be entered into the marketplace, for example by floating a "trial balloon" of a political candidate, by directing a pilot market research project, by conducting a job interview, or by any other competitive bidding activity. Though the market can not ensure that the best product/service is selected, it can ensure reasonable openness of the process. Evaluation of the market is based on the acceptance by the population of the legitimacy and effectiveness of the process. The market functions through acceptance by self-interest-motivated individuals and requires regular, if not daily, renewal.

### *Hierarchy Model*

The hierarchy is differentiated from the market model in that it imposes a bureaucratic or planning interaction to define organization objectives. The hierarchy retains the faith of the people through the equitability of rewards or ensures compliance with these objectives through surveillance or pressure. Hierarchies can operate with varying degrees of benevolence or self-interest, and with varying levels of magnanimity or repression/surveillance. Most military organizations and numerous paramilitary and paraprofessional organizations, including police departments, fire departments, rescue and emergency medical care centers, are hierarchies.

### *Clan Model*

The clan is differentiated from both the market and the hierarchy because it is based on teamwork and acquiescence by the individual to group norms and goals. This homogeneity is achieved through a lifetime process of acculturation and internalization. These outcomes are tough to measure and thus require regular and subtle interaction of participants.

Each model has the same goal, the translation of values; however, in the extreme, each mechanism would be intolerable. Conducting political elections in a market culture on a daily, or even a quarterly or yearly, basis would be rather tiring, as would be the overly meticulous definition of hierarchical objectives and the constant intrigues of individual and team interactions in a clan. In each type of society, there are limits to the amount of time that can be spent on the maintenance of these cultural processes. As increased energies are committed to process maintenance, less time is available to achieve the goals toward which the organization is directed. Ultimately, any organization must move from process maintenance to production of goods or services. This involves a trade-off between process maintenance and operations outcomes, the focus of which is a leadership function.

The three alternative social processes, in pure form, are mutually exclusive. The behaviors and values are not, per se, intermixable; but these cultural extremes are also moved toward some accommodation of each other, at least to the degree that products and services are globally interchanged. "Boom box" radio cassette players and television sets are understood internationally, particularly in music and sports formats; however, it is more difficult to integrate manufacturing or service systems across cultures. Young (1992) identifies various additional difficulties in implementing Japanese manufacturing practices by American firms and Japanese firms operating in the United States and proposes a framework of conditions for the successful adoption of Japanese manufacturing practices in the United States. This integration of the pure cultural alternatives toward more homogeneous global product and service markets is also irreversible and has resulted in increasing social pluralism. These processes are shown in Figure 15-2.

## *Managing Pluralism*

The management of pluralism is at the foundation of the market social structure. The very survival of the marketplace depends upon its ability to enable and empower contributions on the basis of their value. An environment that is tolerant of pluralism ensures that multiple contributions can enter the market with relative freedom. However, the market mechanism only provides entrance; the evaluations of products/services are often based on some less than fully equitable value system. Though the judgments of market participants may be less than perfect, the mechanism itself is often biased to ensure reasonably free entrance and interchange. This dynamic acceptance of pluralism is extremely important to the market structure. Table 15-2 identifies the dimensions of pluralism.

Most Americans accept the notion of pluralism based on religious, ethnic, racial, and gender considerations. These dimensions refer to not only specific individual classifications, but also to variation in the strength of conviction and the intensity, absorption, or clarity of values, which may exist in each dimension. For example, an individual's religious, ethnic, racial, or gender-based values may be very strongly or vaguely defined. Additionally, a range of educational, technical, linguistic, dependency, and physiological characteristics may also be defined as dimensions of pluralism. Again, the variation in these dimensions encompasses a broad range. The methods of managing pluralism may run the gamut from establishment of role models, to group and individual sensitivity training, to updating employee education and skills, and to providing language training. The costs of such programs are high—conflict, job training and education, architectural redesign for physically challenged employees, electronic accommodations for employees

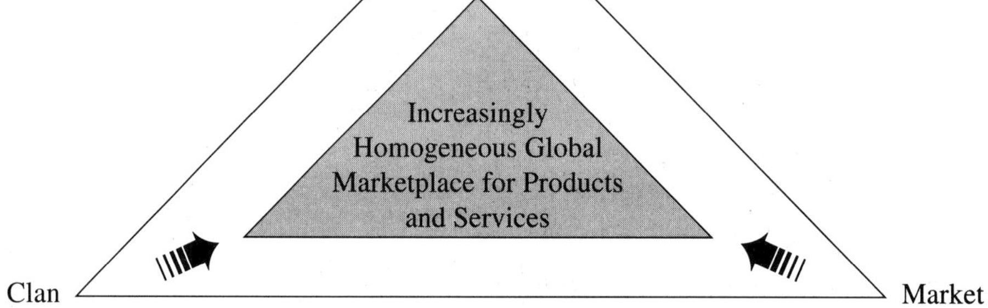


**FIGURE 15-2 Alternative Social Organizations in the Global Environment**

**TABLE 15-2 The Dimensions of Pluralism**

| Type | Variables |
|---|---|
| Religious | Nature and strength of conviction |
| Ethnic | Cultural heritage and level of absorption |
| Racial | Racial group and strength of racial representation |
| Gender | Proportion and positioning of gender mix and the clarity of gender-based values |
| Educational | Academic concepts versus technical skills and amount of retraining effort |
| Linguistic | Number of languages spoken and quality of usage |
| Dependency | Drug, alcohol, tobacco, or other dependencies, including psychological dependencies |
| Physiological | Physiological limits and capabilities |

with impairments, or other modifications. Yet these costs are small compared to the cost of lost contributions to the market. Operations managers must capitalize on the benefits of multiculturalism, yet control the costs of such diversity (Cox, 1991).

Immigration has had the dual effect of enhancing pluralism, yet simultaneously focusing the drive toward global product homogeneity. Most immigrant groups are absorbed into national societies within several generations by a process that encourages an open market exchange of products/services, values, and cultures. Mixed marriages, friendships, or professional associations ensue which result in an appreciation, if not outright acceptance, of another value system and culture. The globalization of industries has had a similar effect.

For example, in 1981, Arvin Industries produced a variety of consumer products, including portable heaters, electronics, and automobile parts, chiefly mufflers and catalytic converters. But the industry executives started talking about the "world car," and James K. Baker, CEO of Arvin, realized that his company had to change. He tackled the South American markets first, because they were closer to home; then he entered the European market during a consolidation. In entering the Japanese market, Baker responded to the comment of a Japanese friend: "American business executives are first interested in legal questions, second in financial questions, and third in personal relationships. The Japanese reverse that order." Thus, to encourage personal relationships and understanding, Baker held a quarterly meeting of his board of directors in Japan, where they visited numerous auto parts manufacturing operations. The globalization of Arvin Industries required it to adapt to various cultures (Nulty, 1992).

## *Role of Government*

Recent political events would suggest that some national governments are moving from a federal structure to a confederated union, and that the decentralization of power and increased local participation in the political process have reduced the need for national governments. On the contrary, the national government has an extensive role in facilitating the national position in the emerging regional and global markets. However, as national governments approach the millennium, their role must shift from that of a policing power to that of a champion, and a carefully designed industrial policy must be developed.

Though the term *federal industrial policy* may cause uneasiness and concerns in an entrepreneurial and capitalist society, there is a strong historical precedent (Phillips, 1992). The U.S. government was instrumental in building the transcontinental railroad, the land grant university system, the interstate highway network, and parts of the air transportation and telephone and telecommunications systems. Though this infrastructure has extensively facilitated industrial growth, there must be carefully elaborated controls so that the industrial policy does not perpetuate the inefficiencies of state-controlled monopolies.

## *Government as a Police Power*

Gilbert (1990) argues that the U.S. government continues in its traditional role of a police power and thus functions as a powerful restraint to trade and innovation. The moral imperative that resulted from World War II, and, one could argue, more recently the Gulf War, has been purportedly used to attempt to legislate an American standard of business and legal practices on an international scale. For example, the Foreign Corrupt Practices Act (1977) might be construed as an attempt to apply the standards of the Sherman Anti-Trust Law (1890) to American businesses worldwide. The role of government as a police power takes three forms: defender of the national well-being, legislative protections, and marketplace proponent.

The U.S. government has been perceived as the diplomatic and military police of the world. Though there are some exceptions, the activities of state and defense within both the executive and legislative branches have been historically the most visible and have wielded the most clout among government agencies. While the high technology of a cruise missile captures the excitement of the moment, that moment would never be possible without a massive communications infrastructure and an extensive distribution and logistics network. Modern warfare and diplomacy must be conducted from a position of strength of infrastructure (including economic, technological, and cultural attributes of the nation). However, in a global environment, the balance of military/diplomatic versus economic, technological, and cultural strength must continue to shift toward the latter, though not to the exclusion of the former.

The second role of government has been to define a legal structure to protect the people from various types of excess and irresponsibility. While that role will continue to be necessary, particularly with regard to such illegal products as drugs and some firearms, there are limits to the degree to which the government can project its legislative power. For example, cigarettes and alcohol are sold in most international markets without the stringent warning labels required for domestic sales. In dealing internationally, a government must clearly define its roles as a mediator of business practice and consumer needs, with often subtle and indirect enforcement.

A third traditional role of government, and particularly the U.S. government, is its almost habitual process of defining issues in adversarial and confrontational terms. The cold war and the associated armaments and military support businesses are very obvious examples of the use of confrontational government in support of industrial policy. This adversarial posture may result from our bicameral and bipartisan representative processes, as opposed to the multicameral and multiparty systems institutionalized in some other parts of the world. The advantage of bicameralism is that it forces an ultimate choice, avoiding endless political bickering and instability; yet the bipartite structure does not permit a choice from among directly contested multiple points of view. Few businesses could operate successfully through such adversarial techniques. To the degree that governments shed their adversarial role and adopt a facilitative and convergent posture, they will be more effective champions of national, regional, and world economic development.

## *Government as a Champion*

The era of such mandarin intrigues and machiavellian bickering is drawing to a close. Global communications ensure the increasing visibility of such practices. An unregulated industry in one country can have deleterious effects around the globe. Soot and pollutants from midwestern U.S. mills may have produced the acid rain that has denuded major portions of the German Schwartzwald. Freon and other similar chemicals released from one country may have depleted the ozone layer throughout the world, resulting in potential global warming and human illness. There clearly is a significant role for national or regional governmental bodies in such matters. Among the more significant issues for government to address are the following.

### *Promote Resource Creation*

Most nations are limited to several distinct resources. Some have abundant raw materials, but limited ability to use those resources; others, because of the lack of those materials, have developed a strong work ethic and labor skills; still others have found ways to manage and accommodate materials scarcity. Governments should facilitate the development of competitive resources and investment in resource creation. In the terms used in Chapter 2, the government should pursue a strategy of protection of its domain and its resources. Resources are most efficiently used in a fully competitive market, one in which innovation and ingenuity prosper. Examples of these activities are the high temperature superconductor research and Sematech, a consortium of U.S. computer manufacturers, which was established to research the next generation of computer chip.

One obvious contribution of government in an increasingly technology-dominated environment is education. Governments have critical responsibilities in the maintenance of knowledge and culture transmission facilities, including education systems, the national knowledge infrastructure (libraries, for example), and both pure and applied research. It is the function of government to be cognizant of shortages of technology and to rectify them through grants or other support. Additionally, other functions of government should be directed toward the protection of knowledge through patents, copyrights, and license agreements. Investment and national effort toward these ends must be encouraged by the government, because there are few other entities that can achieve such ends.

### *Limit Regulation of Resource Markets*

Though there may be exceptions, such as nuclear materials, some utilities, or a limited few key war materials stockpiles, the general regulation of national material resources is an inappropriate activity for government. Government should be involved in the creation of a resource or industry. However, as soon as the resource or industry becomes viable or self-sustaining, government should convert the business to the private sector, though perhaps with legislative controls. Many businesses could be assisted by "precompetitive" developments (such as computer architectures and electronics packaging), generic technologies (including measurement and control tools), and industrial extensions (such as interfaces with CAD/CAM systems).

### *Enforce Anticollusion*

Collusion is an additional way in which the efficient interaction of market forces may be preempted. These efforts may take the form of cooperation or consortia among competitors to achieve necessary economies of scale or to reduce waste and duplication, or to achieve horizontal integration through market agreements or restraints. Though such practices may be initially required for the start-up of an industry, ultimately all such practices guarantee inefficiency. Like government regulation of resources, collusion may be tolerated for short periods and toward specific strategic purposes, but it should be highly visible and as short-lived as possible.

### *Promote Product/Service, Safety, and Environment Standards*

Human welfare has traditionally been regarded as a domestic issue; however, there is an increasing basis for governmental activity in international policy. Drug and armaments trafficking, contaminated and unsafe products, and global environmental concerns are among the more important issues. Additionally, the protection of intellectual property rights through copyrights, patents, and licenses is becoming increasingly important as knowledge emerges as the dominant competitive resource. In this regard, issues of international protection are particularly critical, yet also sensitive. The regulatory process should be responsive and effective, not dogmatic and bureaucratic; even more importantly, it must be defined in the open market.

The government has a very real function as the guarantor of the marketplace. With some exceptions, if given half a chance, the marketplace will operate effectively and efficiently. Unfortunately, government, in its role as a guarantor, may create an overly structured, unresponsive, and political bureaucracy. This "cure" may be worse than the illness. In most cases, though the costs of producing a safe product by a safe process in a regulated market may be higher than with less safe methods in a less regulated environment, the benefits to humanity of such regulation and enforcement are clear.

### Necessity of an Industrial Policy

There are a number of practical ways to achieve these ends, including judicious use of research and development and technical assistance resources. Historically, the government has made extensive contributions to start-up industries, such as the railroads in the mid-1800s, agriculture in the late 1800s and through much of the 1900s, and more recently the computer, nuclear, biotech, and space industries. The resources of federal laboratories, research, and other grant and developmental assistance should be regularly reviewed to ensure focus toward specific national objectives, avoiding redundancy and excessive costs. The potential success that can result from an integrated industrial policy is amply demonstrated by the post-World War II Japanese experience under the Ministry of International Trade and Industry (MITI), although that model would probably not be directly transferable to the American situation.

Additionally, a strong infrastructure must be supported by the government. Traditionally, the infrastructure involved the transportation system (railroads, highways, waterways, and air routes), support systems (employment, retirement, and health care systems), and economic incentives (financial and tax laws). More recently, however, education and knowledge exchange systems (libraries, data transmission systems, and communication) have become more important. The term *government industrial policy* may suggest an extensive and difficult-to-reverse grant of power to the government. However, historically, the government has used specific programs to support fledgling and necessary components of the infrastructure. The management and focus of such programs is and continues to be a key contributor to national policy (Farrell et al., 1992). An example of the effects of government as a champion of business is shown in Application Box 15-2.

Though the concept of a national industrial policy has historically met with criticisms of "government intrusion," the United States has had an "undeclared" industrial policy for years, and there is clearly a need for government facilitation of business ventures (Greenhouse, 1992). Simply, there are some areas, such as space exploration and the establishment of foundation knowledge in emerging fields, and social objectives, including racial integration and compensation equity, where the scope of activity is larger than one company or a consortium. Government involvement is necessary to reduce the risks and facilitate interaction. Perhaps the most critical contribution of the government can be as a facilitator of industry groups toward greater communication and definition of strategic directions of major industries (Branscomb, 1992).

## Rebuilding the Firm

Business strategies were initially presented in Chapter 2 as a rather descriptive, structured, and hierarchic process of defining product/service, process technology, and markets, and then identifying the amount of focus, vertical and horizontal integration, and diversification of the operations system. That approach to business strategy is a necessary but not sufficient step for success in future markets. Many firms have concluded that a complete transformation of the organization is required, amounting to a different perspective or

## APPLICATION BOX 15-2 Small Business Has a Friend in Pennsylvania—and Many Other States

Industrial policy may be most visible when the federal government steps in, as, for example, through tariff support for Harley Davidson (see Chapter 2) or in the financial support for Chrysler Automotive in the early 1980s. However, industrial policy may be most impactful at the state level. For example, many states have seen manufacturing jobs decline—largely from steel, automotive, and other heavy industry closings—and have tried to replace those lost jobs through support to service firms and encouragement of manufacturing by foreign firms. In fact, these efforts were not particularly effective for a variety of reasons. In the words of Andrew Greenberg, Pennsylvania Commerce Secretary, "The lion's share of economic activity and job creation is going to depend on smaller entrepreneurs."

The Scheirer Machine Company is a Pittsburgh job shop that employs 65 workers and makes replacement parts for the steel and mining industries. The company recognized in 1988 that it was gradually losing its competitiveness, and applied to the state-funded Industrial Resource Center in Duquesne, near Pittsburgh, for productivity assistance. A team of experts helped Scheirer recognize its production flow and raise productivity by 15%. They then lent Scheirer $150,000 at a low interest rate to buy a computerized lathe. Scheirer expects to continue to work with the Industrial Resource Center to further continuous improvement efforts.

This model of state support to assist floundering or startup businesses costs Pennsylvania taxpayers roughly $9 million per year, or some 75 cents per resident per year. This money goes toward staffing eight regional centers and supporting low-cost loans and technical support for businesses. But the program is not without critics. Because of the initial funding, the program tends to work only with stable businesses and those that are most credit-worthy. It avoids assisting those manufacturing firms that are really struggling—those who need the most help. "We are not a turnaround operation," rebuts Barry G. Marciak, managing director of the Southwestern Pennsylvania Industrial Resource Center. Georgia, Maryland, Ohio, and other states have also developed such programs.

The contribution of these state-level models is that they support the state industrial infrastructure. Large companies can be competitive only if they have an established network of suppliers of high-quality goods at reasonable prices. Thus, state programs like the ones in Pennsylvania not only contribute directly to jobs and a stronger economic base, but they also indirectly contribute to the survival of industry giants that are dependent upon a network of smaller suppliers.

Though national industrial policies may most effectively be directed toward funding and applying cutting-edge technologies, facilitating educational programs, and encouraging free trade, the effects of those very important programs can be amplified many times by state-level programs. Those state programs encourage investment in new technology by small firms and diffuse that technology throughout the business structure. Additionally, it is quickly becoming apparent that infrastructure means more than roads, bridges, and harbors. Equally important components of the infrastructure include the job-shop manufacturers, which build components in a variety of metals and plastics and weave, print, or form those components to the specification of industry. Whenever possible, the government should, as Michael Porter comments, "press and prod industry to move to a higher plane." Done badly, it would waste precious resources; done well, it would recharge the knowledge base that is the foundation of our advanced industrial society.

Materials drawn from "Industrial Policy," *Business Week*. April 6, 1992, pp. 70–76.

value system. This shift is perhaps best represented in the changing from traditional operations value systems to world-class values, as shown by Table 15-3.

The traditional values of managing processes, products/services, and systems involved controlling employees through hierarchies that coordinate stable, rationalized mass production and service delivery processes. The products/services are simplified and standardized toward the goals of maximum volumes or minimized costs. Typically, traditional systems seek a competitive edge, are national in focus, and function monolithically in pursuit of short-term plans. Alternatively, a world-class system empowers employees by reducing organization form, by destroying barriers, and by directing itself toward intuitive, adaptive, and integrated processes to produce complex and customized products or services designed toward customer needs. World-class systems are collaborative, global, and pluralistic in pursuit of long-term objectives (McCann, 1991). Application Box 15-3 describes the makeover of an organization toward world-class values.

The traditional value system of operations management, which is analogous to a mechanical and fixed process, just doesn't work well as a model for operations of the millennium and beyond. The emerging world-class value system is much more comparable to a biological and protoplasmic process (Drucker, 1989, p. 256).

**TABLE 15-3 From Traditional to World-Class Values**

| Traditional Values | | World-Class Values |
|---|---|---|
| Process characteristics | | |
| Organize in hierarchies | → | Destroy form and barriers |
| Control employees | → | Empower employees |
| Use fixed technologies | → | Use flexible technologies |
| Rationalize processes | → | Intuit processes |
| Coordinate processes | → | Integrate processes |
| Stabilize production processes | → | Adapt production processes |
| Product/service characteristics | | |
| Maximize volume/minimize cost | → | Optimize response to customer |
| Standardize products/services | → | Customize products/services |
| Understand/accept complexity | → | Simplify design |
| System characteristics | | |
| Encourage individualism | → | Encourage teamwork |
| Define a national focus | → | Define a global focus |
| Pursue short-term plans | → | Pursue long-term plans |
| Function monolithically | → | Interact pluralistically |

## APPLICATION BOX 15-3 Building World-Class Values at AT&T

In 1982, when the American Telephone and Telegraph Company, AT&T, settled its antitrust suit and agreed to spin off some 77% of its assets, it recognized the need to transform itself. Since the 1950s, and perhaps earlier, "Ma Bell" was a tightly controlled hierarchy, directed toward one business, the manufacture of communications equipment and the delivery of voice communications services. Standardized processes were used to manufacture several of the highest-quality and most structurally integrated systems of equipment in the world. Similarly, the Bell operators and service personnel provided an emergency communications lifeline throughout rural America, as well as a tool for organizing and socializing. With the advent of global business, the model had to change.

In response to the impending Justice Department actions, a task force headed by Bob Allen, then a vice president, now Chairman and CEO, was convened to define the corporate strategy. The new direction—preserve the combinations of communications services and manufacturing—was defined for the "postbreak-up" organization. As the company stripped away its internal barriers and spun off the "Baby Bells," it created a vision of synergy directed toward putting together three services: a worldwide voice and data network, the equipment to run it, and the devices to hook up to it. AT&T expects to become the communications link for global business.

Toward that end, AT&T committed billions of dollars to develop its computer business. This culminated in the purchase of NCR Corporation in 1990. That acquisition makes AT&T the fifth largest computer manufacturer in the United States; yet the cost of $7 billion was nearly double NCR's market value, and the business recession of 1991 and 1992 has slowed NCR's growth, calling into question the appropriateness of such a heavy investment.

However, in other areas of business, the introduction of customized discount calling services for a wide range of users, the creation of the toll-free 800 numbers, and the definition of Easy-Link services, the nation's largest electronic mail carrier, have built the Communications Services Division into a profitable powerhouse. The gradual erosion of market share to other carriers has been stopped, but not at the cost of profitability. Communications Services reports net profit margins of roughly 14%. Because each penny reduced in the average rate for a telephone call costs the company over $1 billion in annual revenues, the company has avoided across-the-board cuts. Rather, it has met the competition with carefully planned surgical cuts and an attractive array of services.

Similarly, the Customer Products unit of AT&T had developed an extensive range of voice and data equipment, and has marketed that equipment to a variety of corporate and retail customers. Manufacturing operations were moved overseas to cut costs; even so, the manufacturing units overall are barely profitable. That may change, however, as the credit card verification and airline reservation services markets expand. AT&T estimates that those markets will quadruple to $200 billion by 1995. Product development is exemplified by the "Smart Phone," which uses a touch-sensitive screen that can be programmed for a variety of functions, including electronic funds transfers or various connections to a host computer.

Chairman Bob Allen has been responsible for the "rewiring" of AT&T management. A 30-plus-year career in the rule-based AT&T hierarchy is hardly the best preparation to lead the company through the pitfalls of deregulation and into the global markets of the next decade. Allen, however, has consciously pushed authority downward by decentralizing operations into some 20 profit centers. For example, the five-person operations committee is responsible for day-to-day decisions, but Bob Allen is not on it. This conscious attempt to put more ambiguity in the process has made some managers uncomfortable, but others have appreciated the "destructuring" of the organization. As AT&T moves to supply the communications system for global competitors, world-class values must be firmly in place.

Materials adapted from John W. Verity and Peter Coy. "Twin Engines: Can Bob Allen Blend Computers and Telecommunications at AT&T?" *Business Week*. January 20, 1992, p. 56.

## *Transforming Protoplasm*

Protoplasm is defined in biology as:

> *a typically translucent, colorless, semi-fluid, complex substance regarded as the physical basis of life, having the ability to sense and conduct stimuli and to metabolize.*

Protoplasm, the foundational element of life, offers a fine analogy to the processes of organization management required in future organizations. In previous eras, management used mechanical processes of interaction, which were appropriate because the technologies were mechanical. Like the gears of a factory, the process is stabilized, coordinated, and rationalized through hierarchical control to achieve mass production systems. The previous critical resources (land, capital, labor) responded predictably to those perspectives and values. Information (or knowledge) does not. Information is not stable, and its processes are often not rational. Information requires an organization that can, like protoplasm, sense and project stimuli and metabolize as a result of those stimuli. Management must transform itself so that it sees the organization as a protoplasmic organism, with the inherent ability to interact and self-energize. The management process becomes one of finding the best people, pointing them in a general direction, and turning them loose. This is a significant change from the current perspective of management functions and responsibilities.

This difference between the current and future management values is captured in the terms *manager* and *leader.* Managers pursue several specific activities, including planning, fitting, directing, and controlling. Leaders also pursue these activities, but more. As Boyett and Conn (1991, pp. 146–147) note:

> *Managers and leaders think in different ways. Managers are analytical and convergent. Leaders are intuitive and divergent. Managers make decisions and solve problems for their employees. Leaders set a direction and then empower and enable followers to make their own decisions and solve their own problems. Managers emphasize the rational and tangible. Leaders emphasize intangibles such as vision, values, motivation. Managers think and act for the short term. Leaders think and act for the long term. Managers accept organizational structure, policies, procedures, and methodology as they exist. Leaders constantly seek to find a better way.*

## *Creating a Successful Organization*

There are six considerations in transforming an organization from a mechanical to a protoplasmic perspective. The first, and most important, consideration is to examine the leadership processes. Management must view employees as inherently competent and self-motivating. If management does not enable employees with skills and knowledge and then empower them through responsibility and authority to use those skills and that knowledge, management must change.

The second consideration is that the organization must define itself as a leader in the global marketplace. Though there may still be areas of business where international competition is limited, such as beverages, gravel, and soap powder, most businesses operate in markets where a significant portion of the business is in interaction with foreign producers or customers. The trend toward a global marketplace will increase. To that end, the perspective of the corporation must include leadership in the global environment.

Third, the customer is number one. Companies must determine customer requirements, identify the attributes of those requirements that add value, and then determine how operations can build to those specifications. Customers may, in fact, define the specifications to which manufacturing produces. With certified suppliers, the customer defines quality and assumes that the product/service is produced and delivered to specification. This is a significant change from the previous process, in which operations produced to internally defined specifications. An effective link must be defined among product and process design functions, operations, purchasing, and customers. Vertically integrated businesses or other linkages along the chain of transformations must be well established and focused toward a carefully defined niche.

Fourth, competitive niches must be stated in the familiar terms of cost and product/service, or market differentiation. In future years, cost differentiation will increasingly mean process efficiency. This is because many variables that contribute to operations costs (labor, capital, and distribution) are being reduced, but at the same time, being leveled internationally. For example, hourly compensation for the United States, Japan, Canada, western Europe, and the 24 OECD nations had dramatically converged to about $14.00 per hour (Gilbert, 1990). Reduced transportation and communication costs mean that any global competitor with capital may be a bidder. As the global costs of manufacturing or services converge, responsiveness to customers and a reputation for quality will secure business, and efficiency of process technology will define the key competitive niche in terms of cost or product/service differentiation.

Additionally, facilities should be designed in self-contained modules and for economies of scope. Rather than building one large facility, competitive firms will enhance flexibility by housing processes in smaller, modular components. Production modules, like product modules, will permit standardization and interchangeability, enhancing flexibility of usage. Though there will be overall control of the process, each module will have its own leadership, permitting specialization and flexibility. Interchangeability within the corporation as well as internal flexibility of the module or facilities will be enhanced.

Finally, in the traditional model, time has been treated as a series of flow chart deadlines through which the product/service was sequentially developed. In the future model, time involves synchronous activities of teams and groups with one deadline for project completion, permitting faster time from concept to market, or time-based competition (Stalk, 1988). In the aggregate, these adjustments require no less than a change in the entire corporate value system, a change of mindset from that of setting up and managing a system of stable gears to that of transforming protoplasm. Or, as Drucker (1992) notes, managers must regularly integrate new knowledge, and new knowledge resources, into the organization.

## *Resource Management*

The key resource in workplace 2000 will be, as it is today, the human resource. However, the human contribution to future production or service delivery system processes will differ. In days past, operations involved knowledge, relatively unassisted by computer outputs, power assists, and mechanical controls; in days future, the knowledge worker will self-manage the integration of his or her contribution. The primary labor contribution will be analytic. That is, the knowledge worker will be responsible for process monitoring, system evaluation, and continuous improvement of processing resources. The leadership of such activities takes on three separate, yet closely related, emphases: the education and retraining of the work force (or the enabling of the resource), the delegation of authority (empowerment), and the creation of processes to integrate those resources.

## *Educational Crisis—Enabling Human Resources*

Ironically, as the knowledge worker has become increasingly important to operations, the creation of a minimal level of basic verbal and math skills has proved increasingly difficult for the education system, at least in the United States. By many measures over the past 20 to 30 years, the knowledge and applied skills of American graduates and entrant workers has declined, both in absolute terms and when compared to other nations. Various sources, among them Bloom (1987) and Silber (1989), have posited different definitions of the problem. Other studies have identified the implications for business in practical terms of entrant-level employee skills (Giffi et al., 1991, p. 269). Though opinions vary on the extent of the crisis and how to fix it, there are few indications that the resolution is at hand.

Clearly, the problem has numerous facets, the solution to which will not come easily. Yet, for the operations manager, there are two very real impacts: the skill and motivation of the available work force and the preparation and ethics of junior management. Though there may be other related and subordinate issues to these, these two problems are at the root of most operations concerns.

Business today is faced with sales clerks who have difficulty making change unless the cash register tells them the amount, with route drivers who cannot use a map and are able to find addresses only because they are familiar with the area, and with secretaries who cannot spell without a computer spell checker. These mathematics, logic, and writing skills are limited because of a lack of foundational education development. Such changes in entrant level qualifications suggest that business must modify the recruiting and selection process to target potential employee groups and carefully screen those applicants to verify the required skills. Additionally, business may have to conduct remedial entry-level training and periodic retraining to ensure the initial and continued relevance of employee skills. A variety of approaches, involving educational institutions, independent educators and consultants, and individual employee self-study, all have been used effectively. The educational technologies likely will remain the same, but the emphasis on quality and cost has and will continue to increase.

The required skills for management also have shifted dramatically. As Drucker points out (1989, p. 223), the emergence of knowledge as the critical resource has been paralleled by the growth of the business management field and its various subdisciplines. Because managers deal with science and technology, with people and their values, and with abstract philosophies (such as human nature, ethics, and creation) and with the application of knowledge, management is inherently a liberal art (Drucker, 1989). More generally, business disciplines originate from and are applications of the liberal arts and sciences; business courses were conceived to provide a "finishing" academic program for business practitioners with a liberal arts or science background and some experience. Today, in many schools, the business program offers both graduate and undergraduate degrees and is as large as the liberal arts and sciences program. Unfortunately, management trainees, in the rush to develop personal business skills, may have bypassed or cut short the foundational thinking skills inherent in the arts and sciences.

A more disconcerting issue is that of intergenerational differences in ethical attitudes. Longnecker et al. (1989) show that younger age groups are significantly more permissive in their assessment of 16 situational vignettes dealing with such questions as expense account padding, tax fraud, and illegal securities trading. This parallel between the rise of the business school and the decline of ethical perspectives is perplexing. Certainly it would be unfair to suggest a causal link between the two (decreasing ethics and growth of the business program), because there are other variables; yet concerns remain. Because it is an applied (as opposed to a "pure" art or science) education, the business program may appeal to materialism and lower acceptance of scholarship or pedagogic foundations. Business schools have responded by emphasizing ethics more strongly in their programs and as a requirement for accreditation. While this is only one step, such reemphasis of the liberal-art-and-science foundations of business knowledge may resolve some of these issues.

Ethical practices are also a corporate responsibility, which increases the importance of corporate efforts to define codes of ethics, to create training programs, and to provide mechanisms for reporting problems. Though numerous companies have codes of ethics (as many as 75% of respondents in some surveys), as few as 30% of respondents have ethics training, and even fewer provide positive mechanisms to resolve problems (Harrington, 1991). However, even with extensive training programs and corporate codes of conduct, in the absence of an active corporate social structure supporting peer reporting, work group members operate under severe pressures that constrain reporting of illegal or improper actions (Trevino and Victor, 1992).

## *Empowering Human Resources*

Empowerment, the involvement of employees in management decision making, is one of the more recent terms for the rather long-accepted notion of encouraging employees to commit to the outcomes of productivity. Empowerment is a natural continuation of the group incentive and gain-sharing structures that emerged in the early 1900s. Through the 1950s, more and more complex formulae were used to compute performance dividends. Gradually, the motivators shifted toward intangibles, including job security, medical coverages, insurance against catastrophe, free time, perks, and so on. Between 1950 and 1980, benefits programs grew to more than 30% of total compensation packages in most industries, and in the early 1980s, cafeteria programs were developed to permit individually tailored benefits programs. Employee empowerment extends these programs by permitting greater employee control over the job itself—an almost necessary step, given the reduction in middle-level management and generally flatter organizations.

Employee empowerment is defined as a systematic approach to enable employees to participate in decisions that affect them and their relationship with the organization. Various techniques of empowerment include employee specification of the time of work (such as flexible work hours, compressed work weeks, extended leaves, and contract work), the amount of individual contribution (including job sharing, part time, overtime, and vacation/holiday buy-back), and where the work is performed (work at home or at mini-offices located conveniently close to home). As automation is increasingly used in operations and as communication links become more available, work can increasingly be done in amounts, at times, and at locations that are convenient to the employee.

This revolution has caused some new and different problems for the fewer remaining leaders, among them: supervisory interaction, evaluating performance, and management decision making. Face-to-face contact must be replaced by other methods of communication, such as through telephones or recorded messages, and supervisors must be increasingly sensitive to indicators of problems. However, decreased supervision has the positive outcome that there is less interruption of work activities. Less direct supervision does, however, signal a very different approach to the supervisory processes.

Additionally, the mechanisms of individual development have been reduced. Because of decentralization and the wider form of the organization, there are fewer paths for advancement and less opportunity to prepare and test candidates for top management. Job requirements are much less clear and more directed toward integrative team skills, suggesting that greater lateral mobility or job hopping is desirable (McInturf, 1991).

## *Integrating Knowledge*

Management of knowledge, the critical resource of the next decades, requires the integration and evaluation of numerous sources of raw data and the elaboration of evaluated information as usable reports, video formats, and decision tools. Computer integrated manufacturing (CIM) is directed toward that end. CIM systems are often necessary to operate successfully in the emerging manufacturing environment. Flatter structures put managers closer to manufacturing and distribution activities and permit greater control over those activities in the high-volume, long-lead-time global environments. Linking manufacturing and distribution systems with MRP/DRP systems is costly, yet required for transnational operations. The information system is so important that it is usually set up before the warehouse, marketing efforts, or transportation contracts (Stratman, 1991). A prototype CIM system is depicted in Figure 15-3.

Due to space limits the diagram is only representative of a full computer information system. Though it defines many of the primary elements of a CIM system, it is hardly inclusive. Functional files are created at separated individual work stations for business planning, product/service design, process design, materials management, and facilities maintenance activities, among others. These files, though separately developed, are electronically linked. CIM permits independence of function, but synchrony of effort. Once a plan is agreed upon, the operations management staff monitors and controls the execution of that plan. Supervisory control activities project downward through the system, and operations monitoring information is regularly transmitted upward. Figure 15-3 represents

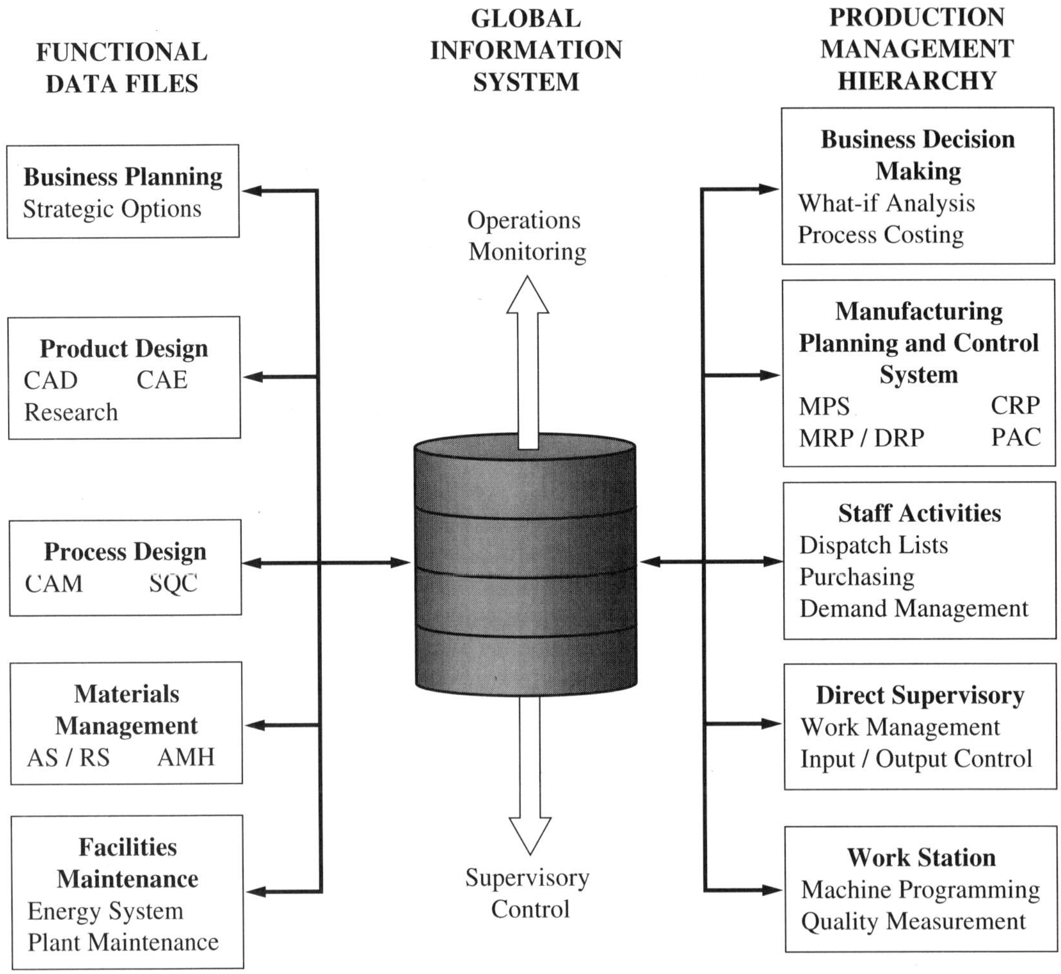


Note: The acronyms used in Figure 15.3 are:

CAD – Computer Assisted Design
CAE – Computer Assisted Engineering
CAM – Computer Assisted Manufacturing
SQC – Statistical Quality Control
AS/RS – Automated Storage/Retrieval System
AMH – Automated Material Handling

MPS – Master Production Schedule
MRP/DRP – Material Requirements Planning / Distribution Requirements Planning
CRP – Capacity Requirements Planning
PAC – Production Activity Control

**FIGURE 15-3 Computer Integrated Manufacturing**

CIM applied to one stage of the production process. Of course, true CIM must also link forward and backward along the chain of transformations.

The advent of CIM was hailed as a major breakthrough on the shop floor. Stories abounded of workerless factories or a zero-work environment, where work more closely resembled play (Black, 1991). More to the point, CIM is an integrative tool that reduces the more onerous work activities; it facilitates, but does not perform, the judgmental and human interactive elements of decision making. It is a tool to define base-level decisions, which then must be judgmentally applied by human technicians. Reports from CIM users confirm that, as CIM systems are increasingly developed, an untrained and unskilled work force becomes a hindrance. The CIM system implementation will be successful only if the company invests heavily in the talent, education, training, and motivation of the human resource (Ozan, 1992).

## *Operations Strategy 2000—The New Mindset*

The pace of change is accelerating; employees and managers can expect to change jobs numerous times in a career, and to change careers several times in their life. Education or skills training programs have shorter relevance, just as products, services, and processes have shorter life cycles. Taken from an overview perspective, these changes in the operations management environment are revolutionary in nature, though they may not appear so, particularly to employees in stable situations. They represent a complete shift in the mindset of management. As Paul Allaire, chairman and CEO of Xerox, comments: "We want a company that can change as the business changes" (Howard, 1992, p. 109).

### *Realities of the Millennium*

Production methods and service delivery systems of the next millennium will simultaneously experience the apparently contradictory phenomena of explosion and implosion. Markets, products/services, and production processes will explode at a fantastic pace; yet simultaneously, the available technologies will implode the detail of management information available. Managers must evaluate macro as well as micro environments and issues. New perspectives and different tools, and the ability to use them, are required to integrate appropriate parts of these environments.

The conditions of industrial competition in the next millennium have been likened to the performance of a dance musical, seen from overhead. Dancers glide together on the stage, then disband and regroup to form another design. Some vestiges of the traditional hierarchy will remain, but "spinning around these straight lines will be a vertiginous pattern of constantly changing teams, task forces, partnerships, and other informal structures" (Dumaine, 1991, p. 36) of the adaptive organization.

Operations strategy 2000 must be both telescopic and kaleidoscopic; it must be telescopic to focus exploding and imploding information and kaleidoscopic to capture the pattern and intensity of changing patterns. Identifying the dimensions and perspectives of key competitive variables will be difficult, and, if captured, they will quickly be supplanted by a revised image. Figure 15-4 identifies some of the telescopic and kaleidoscopic effects of contributors to successful global operations. The dimensions of structure versus infrastructure and corporate versus country or region level define four areas of concern for operations managers. Those four areas have been the major topics of this chapter. The level of detail suggests a process of investigation that might be pursued by the operations manager. For example, in the macro structure box (Figure 15-4, quadrant 2), there are numerous contributors to marketplace conditions, such as fiscal and tax policies or monetary policies, which could be further elaborated and individually considered.

Hayes and Wheelwright (1984, pp. 394–395) argue that the operations function should concentrate on the infrastructure of the company (quadrant 3), because these are the most controllable areas for the operations manager and will yield the greatest potential competitive success. Though that point is appreciated, however, the infrastructure of the company must reinforce the structure (quadrant 4), and the micro-level considerations must be consistent with the corresponding macro-level infrastructure and structure (quadrants 1 and 2). In fact, though company environments and situations may differ in emphasis, an operations manager must consider each quadrant in developing the operations

| | **INFRASTRUCTURE ("SOFTWARE")** | **STRUCTURE ("HARDWARE")** |
|---|---|---|
| **MACRO (COUNTRY- OR REGION-LEVEL)** | **1 Cultural Identity**<br>National Conscience and Traditions<br>Religious Influence<br>Family and Community<br>Social Behaviors<br>Education / Reeducation System<br>Individual Value Structures | **2 Environment Conditions**<br>Fiscal / Tax Policies<br>Monetary Policies<br>Trade Policies<br>Industrial Policies<br>Capital Markets<br>Organized Labor<br>Political Structure<br>Legal Processes |
| **MICRO (COMPANY-LEVEL)** | **3 Systems Management**<br>Management Selection and Development Policies<br>Supplier and Customer Relationships<br>Organization Design<br>Capital Budgeting and Allocation Decisions<br>Measurement and Control Systems<br>Workforce Policies | **4 Resource Management**<br>Business Market Selection<br>Plant and Equipment Decisions<br>Capacity and Facilities<br>Location and Specialization<br>Process Technology<br>Market Area Selection<br>Vertical Integration<br>Decision-making Technologies |

**FIGURE 15-4 Contributors to Successful Global Operations—Telescopic and Kaleidoscopic Effects**

strategy. Because the quadrants are closely interrelated, even though one may be easier to act upon than the others in a particular situation, none can be disregarded.

Simply stated, events in the macro structure and infrastructure are sufficiently dynamic and turbulent in most businesses that, though operations managers can do relatively little to affect them, they must be aware of and responsive to such events. Given the environment and structure of the firm, the task of the operations manager is to adjust the operations systems and resource management practices to these factors. Thus, *leaders* should spend a greater portion of their time understanding and, when appropriate, acting on these factors. Certainly the leadership vision must include and emphasize all quadrants.

Understanding the macro variables is important for another reason. Wholesale copying of successful Japanese methods in lagging American industries, or, more generally, the transmission of production methods across cultures, would be a mistake. The Japanese discipline and team methods structures are culturally unique phenomena which have taken hundreds of years to develop. The key to American success in international competition, and more generally, to any cross-cultural adaptation, is to capture the essence of the national cultural values in the operations strategy. As Paul Allaire, the CEO of Xerox, comments:

> *We're never going to out-discipline the Japanese on quality. To win we need to find ways to capture the creative and innovative spirit of the American worker. That's the real organizational challenge (Dumaine, 1991, p. 38).*

## *Globalization of Operations*

As the costs of communication and transportation continue to decrease, at least relative to other resources, the global market will become a reality in nearly all product/service groups. This globalization will require greater technical and management skills. Areas of technical consideration will involve such issues as facility location, transportation lead times, quality, and pollution and environmental considerations, among others. Similarly, management skills will involve operating with work forces across cultural boundaries and in varying forms of social organization. The just-in-time operating environment will become increasingly critical, both because it is a necessary way to manage inventories, but also because it focuses responsibility for operations matters such as training, scheduling, process organization, and quality down the organization to workers who are closer to the situation. These topics have been noted at various points throughout this book.

The dual emphases that have been projected throughout all chapters of this book have been the galloping globalization of operations and the need to review and, in many cases, change old rules (Hammer and Champy, 1993). Though financial and marketing strategies are important, the contribution of operations must invariably be considered, if not given a key role in the decision process. Simply, organizations must be redesigned toward the opportunities and threats in the global environment. The consequences of ignoring the operations contribution or paying too much attention to return on investment or other short-term financial variables may be disastrous. This objective requires the synergetic actions of government, corporations, labor, and other groups, and individual knowledge workers, each moving in kaleidoscopic and telescopic patterns in a seemingly vertiginous array. Yet the pattern has both purpose and direction to those who understand it. The pattern both recognizes and rewards those who can understand its dimensions and the subtleties of its dynamics.

## *Focus toward the Future*

The process to achieve a world-class operation is a series of steps, as shown in Figure 15-5. Some steps are very high or large, and others are rather simple; some steps are irregular, and others are very patterned. Those steps will likely involve components of organization design, human resources, technology, and performance measurement.

At another, more general level, the components of operations strategy, operations capabilities, and management direction must be defined. The focus of these efforts is to provide quality, but the more general goal is customer service and the continuous improvement of product or service quality. Continuous improvement must be a daily agenda of every employee of the firm. Because of these dynamics of the market economy, at the macro level:

> *This is the only country in the world that renews itself every day.*
>
> —Walter B. Wriston (1990, p. 78)

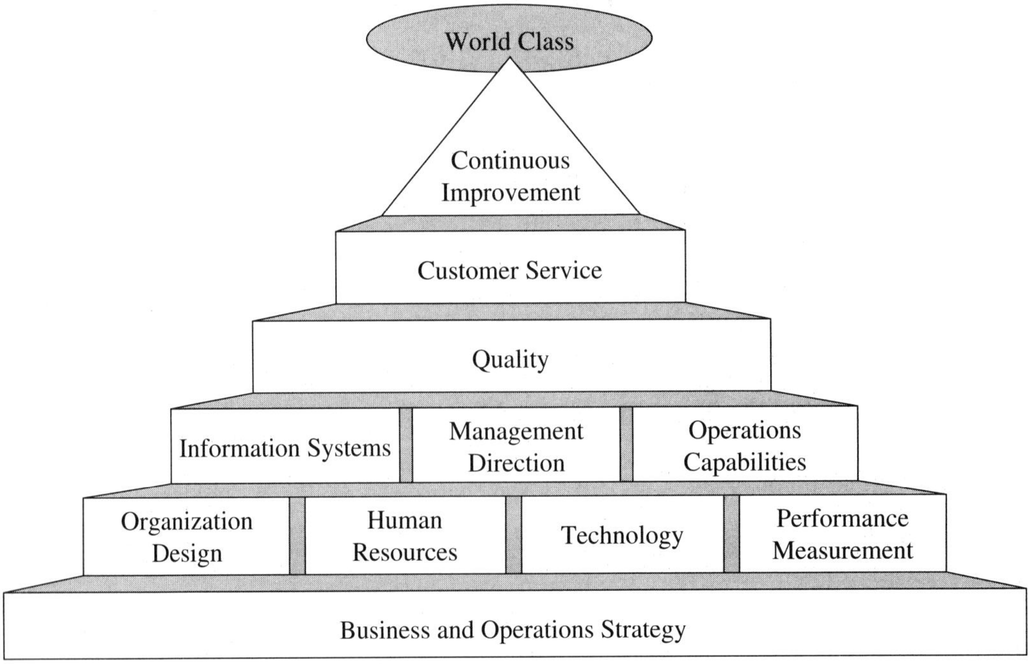


**FIGURE 15-5 The Thrust Toward World-Class Operations**

## Summary

The next millennium is closer than we think. In some businesses, the year 2000 is here today. In other businesses it imposes a serious threat to organization stability, to profits, and even to viability. Operations managers must take steps today to move their organizations toward success in the next millennium.

In response to the millennium, the United States must recognize the reality that we are a mature nation, both industrially and emotionally. Awareness of our strengths and weaknesses as a producer of goods and services and pursuit of our culturally and administratively endowed niche are the keys to our survival, as specific firms, as industries, and as a nation. The management of operations in this impending period of mobilization and conflict promises tremendously exciting and challenging threats and opportunities. As Hall so eloquently stated:

> *The laws of the jungle change as maturity comes and hostility intensifies. In such a jungle, the range of strategic options narrows, requiring both an early warning of the coming hostility and an early strategic repositioning for a company to survive and prosper.*
>
> —William Hall (1980, p. 85)

## Discussion Questions

1. Identify the conditions that have created an environment of hostility toward manufacturing.
2. List the alternative strategies recommended for survival and success in the hostile environment.
3. What are the contributors to successful global operations?
4. Describe and differentiate the three predominant types of social organizations or mechanisms through which culture is translated.
5. How is pluralism linked to the market social structure?
6. Define the role of government in facilitating the growth of business and identify the more significant issues that currently require addressing.
7. Describe some of the process characteristics that are necessary to change from a traditional operations value system to world-class manufacturing values.
8. Identify the elements of successful organizational competition.
9. List the key resource of the production environment in the year 2000 and suggest how leaders will integrate this resource.
10. Identify from your perspective several additional characteristics of work force 2000 not mentioned in Chapter 15.
11. Describe an organization that you are familiar with, and then define several specific actions which that organization may take to move toward world-class operations.

12. Define a product/service with which you are familiar, and then describe how the product/service is marketed in a global environment.

13. What are the effects of pluralism on operations?

14. Define a product/service with which you are familiar, and then describe the degree to which the product is integrated along the chain of transformations.

15. Identify one specific action/policy/law which you think the government should implement or eliminate toward improving the U.S. marketplace.

## *Strategic Decision Situations*

1. Identify a product or service in the international market and then describe, from your experience, knowledge, or research, the effects of international competition. Evaluate the company's response to global competition (suggested paper length: 5–15 pages).

2. What indications do you find that operations is, to follow Skinner's words, "The formidable competitive weapon"? Is operations more important or less important than other principal organizational activities (finance, human resources, marketing, and the like)? Should it be? Under what circumstances? Why? Why not? Use specific examples from your reading and experience (suggested paper length: 5–15 pages).

## *References*

"A New Age Dawns," *Time.* January 3, 1983, p. 4.

Albin, John T. "Competing in a Global Market," *APICS: The Performance Advantage.* January, 1992, pp. 29–32.

"Asia, The Next Era of Growth," *Business Week.* November 11, 1991, pp. 56–68.

Banks, Robert L., and Steven C. Wheelwright. "Operations vs Strategy: Trading Tomorrow for Today," *Harvard Business Review.* May–June 1979.

Baraiko, Allen A. "The Chip," *National Geographic Magazine.* October 1982.

Bell, Daniel, ed. *Towards the Year 2000, Work in Process.* Boston, Mass.: The Beacon Press, 1967.

Black, Bob. "All Play and No Work," *Workplace of the Future, Wall Street Journal Reports.* June 4, 1990, p. R17.

Bloom, Alan. *The Closing of the American Mind.* New York: Simon & Schuster, 1987.

Boyett, Joseph H., and Henry B. Conn. *Workplace 2000: The Revolution Reshaping American Business.* New York: Dutton, Penguin Group, 1991.

Branscomb, Lewis M. "Does America Need a Technology Policy?" *Harvard Business Review.* March–April 1992, pp. 24–31.

Cox, Taylor, Jr. "The Multicultural Organization," *The Academy of Management Executive.* Vol. 5, No. 2, 1991, pp. 34–47.

Drucker, Peter F. *Managing in Turbulent Times.* New York: Harper and Row, Publishers, 1980.

Drucker, Peter F. "The Changed World Economy," *Foreign Affairs.* Spring 1986, p. 768.

Drucker, Peter F. "The Coming of the New Organization," *Harvard Business Review.* January–February 1988, pp. 45–53.

Drucker, Peter F. *The New Realities: In Government and Politics/in Economics and Business/in Society and World View.* New York: Harper and Row, Publishers, 1989.

Drucker, Peter F. "The Emerging Theory of Manufacturing," *Harvard Business Review.* May–June 1990, pp. 94–102.

Drucker, Peter F. "The New Society of Organizations," *Harvard Business Review.* September–October 1992, pp. 95–104.

Dumaine, Brian. "The Bureaucracy Busters," *Fortune.* June 17, 1991, p. 36.

Farrell, Christopher, and Michael J. Mandel, with various others. "Industrial Policy," *Business Week.* April 6, 1992, p. 70.

Fogarty, Donald W., Thomas R. Hoffmann, and Peter W. Stonebraker. *Production and Operations Management.* Cincinnati, Ohio: South-Western Publishing Co., 1989.

Giffi, Craig, Aleda V. Roth, and Gregory M. Seal. *Competing in World-Class Manufacturing.* Homewood, Ill.: Business One Irwin, 1990.

Gilbert, Nathaniel. "Uncle Sam: Secret Enemy of U. S. Competitiveness," *Management Review.* January 1990, pp. 12–19.

Greenhouse, Steven. "The Calls for an Industrial Policy Grow Louder," *New York Times.* July 19, 1992, p. F5.

Gunn, Thomas G. *Manufacturing for Competitive Advantage: Becoming a World Class Manufacturer.* Cambridge, Mass.: Ballinger, 1987.

Hall, William K. "Survival Strategies in a Hostile Environment," *Harvard Business Review.* September–October 1980, pp. 75–85.

Hammer, Michael, and James Champy. *Reengineering the Corporation: A Manifesto for Business Revolution.* New York: HarperCollins, 1993.

Harrington, Susan J. "What Corporate America Is Teaching about Ethics," *The Academy of Management Executive.* Vol. 5, No. 1, 1991, pp. 21–30.

Hayes, Robert H., and Steven C. Wheelwright. *Restoring Our Competitive Edge: Competing through Manufacturing.* New York: John Wiley and Sons, 1984.

Hill, Terry. *Manufacturing Strategy, Text and Cases.* Homewood, Ill.: Irwin, 1989.

Howard, Robert. "The CEO as an Organizational Architect," *Harvard Business Review.* September–October 1992, pp. 107–121.

"Industry Policy," *Business Week.* April 6, 1992, pp. 70–76.

Littal, B. "The Corporate Culture Vultures," *Fortune.* October 17, 1983. pp. 66–72.

Longnecker, Justin G., Joseph A. McKinney, and Carlos W. Moore. "The Generation Gap in Business Ethics," *Business Horizons,* September–October 1989. pp. 9–14.

McCann, Joseph E. "Design Principles for an Innovating Company," *The Academy of Management Executive.* Vol. 5, No. 2, 1991, pp. 76–93.

McInturf, Robert. "Career Growth in the 1990s Will Require Changes in Skills, Attitudes," *APICS, The Performance Advantage.* November 1991, p. 18.

Moody, Patricia E. *Strategic Manufacturing: Dynamic New Directions for the 1990s.* Homewood, Ill.: Dow Jones-Irwin, 1990.

Naisbitt, John. *Megatrends.* New York: Warner, 1982.

Naisbitt, John, and Patricia Aburdene. *Megatrends 2000.* New York: Morrow, 1990.

"The New America," *Business Week.* September 25, 1989. Supplementary 60th Anniversary Issue.

Nulty, Peter. "Arvin Industries: A Quick Course in Going Global," *Fortune.* January 13, 1992.

Ouchi, William G. *Theory Z: How American Business Can Meet the Japanese Challenge.* Reading, Mass.: Addison-Wesley, 1981.

Ouchi, William G. *The M-Form Society: How American Teamwork Can Recapture the Competitive Edge.* Reading, Mass.: Addison-Wesley, 1984.

Ozan, Terrence R. "CIM and the Bottom Line," *Production and Inventory Management.* February 1992, pp. 21–22.

Peters, Thomas J. *Thriving on Chaos.* New York: Knopf, 1987.

Peters, Thomas J., and Waterman, Robert H., Jr. *In Search of Excellence.* New York: Harper and Row, 1982.

Phillips, Kevin P. "U.S. Industrial Policy: Inevitable and Ineffective," *Harvard Business Review.* July–August 1992, pp. 104–112.

Piciacchia, F. Roy, and Lockwood Greene. "Strategic Manufacturing Planning: A New Era for the 1990s," *APICS 1989 International Conference Proceedings,* pp. 307–311.

Porter, Michael E. "The Competitive Advantage of Nations," *Harvard Business Review.* March–April 1990. pp. 73–93.

Porter, Michael E. *The Competitive Advantage of Nations.* New York: Free Press, 1990.

Seal, Gregory M. "1990's—Years of Promise, Years of Peril for U.S. Manufacturers," *Industrial Engineering.* January 1990. pp. 18–21.

Silber, John. *Shooting Straight: What's Wrong with America and How to Fix It.* New York: Harper and Row, 1989.

Skinner, Wickham. *Manufacturing: The Formidable Competitive Weapon.* New York: John Wiley, 1985.

Stalk, George, Jr. "Time—The Next Source of Competitive Advantage," *Harvard Business Review.* July–August 1988, pp. 41–51.

Stratman, Arthur T. "Today's Information Technology Is the Key to Tomorrow's Success in Transitional Business," *APICS, The Performance Advantage.* November 1992, pp. 24–26.

Swamidass, Paul M. "Empirical Science: New Frontier in Operations Management Research," *Academy of Management Review.* October 1991, pp. 793–814.

Toffler, Alvin. *Future Shock.* New York: Bantam, 1971.

Toffler, Alvin. *The Third Wave.* New York: Morrow, 1980.

Toffler, Alvin. *Powershift.* New York: Bantam, 1990.

Trevino, Linda Klebe, and Bart Victor. "Peer Reporting of Unethical Behavior: A Social Context Perspective," *Academy of Management Journal.* Vol. 35, No. 1, 1992, pp. 38–64.

"Value Marketing," *Business Week.* November 11, 1991, p. 132.

Wriston, Walter B. "The State of American Management," *Harvard Business Review.* January–February 1990, pp. 78–83.

Young, S. Mark. "A Framework for Successful Adoption and Performance of Japanese Manufacturing Practices in the United States," *Academy of Management Review.* October 1992, pp. 677–700.

# Case 7

# General Motors—As GM Goes, So Goes the Nation[1]

*Sometimes I am almost forced to the conclusion that GM is so large and its inertia so great that it is impossible for us to be leaders.* —Alfred Sloan

## The Sloan Legacy

Alfred Sloan, GM Chairman in the 1930s, has been credited with much of the early definition of General Motors strategy and policy. In 1963, for example, when GM's profits were greater than any company had previously earned, Sloan was given credit for institutionalizing the fundamental management approaches that contributed to the firm's success. The management system that Sloan defined called for an organization plan giving unqualified responsibility to the operating executives of GM and equally unqualified authority to the central management group. What resulted was a company that could flexibly adjust between the extremes of pure centralization and pure decentralization, a contrived balance that became an important asset when diverse forces threatened the company.

One of the key elements of change that Sloan initiated was to place a high priority on how decisions were made rather than where they were made. He also attached great importance to the anatomy of problem solving, the dissection of decision making, and the attitudes by which people with different interests are moved to act in concert. Sloan created the "factual approach" of business analysis, though he later admitted that, while the company was a fact-finding organization, it did not always get the facts as completely as it should. This brand of management considered constant change as a way of life and allowed no place for decisions founded on how things were done in the past.

[1]This case is prepared as a basis for class discussion, rather than to illustrate either effective or ineffective management of an operational situation.

General Motors was so successful that it was hailed not only as a leader in auto making but as a model for other American and international companies to follow. It was such an influential part of the U.S. economy that one of GM's past presidents stated, "What was good for the country was good for General Motors, and vice versa," which was popularized as: "As GM goes, so goes the nation." By the early 1990s, GM employed 429,000 hourly and salaried workers in North America, the approximate population of Fort Worth, Texas, the thirtieth largest city in the United States. General Motors has 30,000 suppliers and 10,000 dealers which, in total, provide jobs for enough people to populate another large U.S. city. Further, the automaker is the country's largest consumer of steel, rubber, glass, plastic, and carpeting, and GM's gross revenues are equivalent to the GNP of several mid-sized countries.

## *Cracks in the Corporate Structure*

Though GM led American manufacturing through much of the 1950s, 1960s, and 1970s, by the 1980s, if not earlier, it was apparent that GM had lost its edge. Peter F. Drucker wrote in *Management: Tasks, Responsibilities, Practices:*

> *Stability is not rigidity. On the contrary, organization structure requires a high degree of adaptability. A totally rigid structure is not stable; it is brittle. Only if the structure can adapt itself to new situations, new demands, new conditions—and also to new faces and personalities—will it be able to survive.*

That lesson has not been lost on a GM executive vice president, who recently stated that the company's past culture was based on two assumptions: first, that the company was operating in a stable and predictable world, and, second, that the company's overwhelming competitive advantage rested in its ability to achieve large economies of scale. The executive concluded that the world today is neither stable nor predictable and that, in the current fragmented and competitive marketplace, it is impossible for GM to achieve economies of scale.

As problems began to surface, GM was criticized for not knowing its customer or understanding its competition. When American consumers began buying foreign cars, GM questioned their loyalty. There was a great reluctance to accept the fact that foreign cars might be of better quality. Then, during the 1960s, an attitude developed that the number crunchers (that is, finance and accounting types) could run the company better than manufacturing or marketing people. The power of the finance staff led to an overdependence on how numbers look. A prime example occurred in 1986 and 1987, when the struggling GM decided to cut the staff. Many of the engineers who received lucrative early-retirement or buyout packages were hired by engineer consulting firms that were then contracted by GM. The wages those engineers received as consultants were usually higher than their salaries at GM. A GM audit identified one individual situation in which the aggregate annual penalty was $21,000. This was no problem to the finance people, however, because the expenses showed up in a different account.

Toward the end of the 1950s a young ambitious law school graduate named Ralph Nader began to nag the company about its lack of commitment to vehicle safety; Nader particularly attacked the Corvair. He alleged that the car was unstable in turns, that the cooling system leaked deadly carbon monoxide into the car, and that in a front-end crash, a driver could be lanced by the steering column. Nader's book, *Unsafe at Any Speed,* vilified the Corvair for its safety defects. In July 1965, U.S. Senate hearings were opened on auto safety to consider the cars that the federal government should purchase. Subsequently, the National Traffic and Motor Vehicle Safety Act was passed and, by the end of 1967, one in three GM cars were recalled for safety defects.

The oil embargo of late 1973 also dealt the American auto industry a critical blow. GM was affected because its traditionally loyal customers demanded compact, fuel-efficient cars in lieu of the company's large, gas-guzzling vehicles. The phrase, "miles per gallon" was in, but the executives at GM believed the new wants of its customer base would be short-lived. Within five months of the start of the energy crisis, car sales plunged more than 35%. At this point, GM committed two serious mistakes: (1) They made small-car development a low priority because the Japanese had set a pricing standard at which GM could not operate profitably, and (2) they declined to make the small cars look too good, thus ensuring that big-car buyers would not be lured to buy those smaller cars.

Following the problems with the Corvair, and other difficulties with the Vega, the X-car, and the Cadillac Cimarron, the company continued to lose ground in the small-car sector through the early 1980s. They needed a success story. The S-car was scheduled to be launched in 1985. However, after CEO Roger Smith questioned whether GM could realistically make money on it, he commissioned a comparative study to find out how much it would cost Isuzu to build a comparable car. GM had owned a large stake in the Japanese company since 1971 but had never before investigated the foreign company's costs. The resulting six-week study convinced Smith that the S-car could not be built at a profit by GM in North America. The total cost of the S-car came to $5731, compared to the Isuzu model at $2857, a difference of $2874.

## The Road Back

By 1974, the company recognized that it needed to do a large-scale rethinking of their business. A group, called the Corporate Directions Group, was formed to develop a master plan for GM's future. The initial three-prong goal that resulted was (1) identify and eliminate the businesses where GM didn't belong; (2) get the domestic car divisions to think globally; and (3) identify new businesses in which GM should get involved.

When Roger Smith became CEO of GM in 1981, he immediately began to rebuild the company from the inside out and from the bottom up. He established the three Ss (structure, systems, and style) that he felt needed changing. Considering structure, he wiped out whole divisions and moved many people to different jobs. As for the new systems GM needed, Electronic Data Systems (EDS) and Hughes Aircraft were the company's biggest acquisitions. A joint venture was also formed with Japan's Fujitsu/Fanuc, which made GMF Robotics the largest robotics company in the United States.

GM also has formed a strategic partnership with two CAD/CAM vendors, McDonnell Douglas Manufacturing and Engineering Systems Company and Cadam Incorporated, to develop standards-based applications for automotive design. General Motors also purchased a 50% stake in Sweden's Saab-Scania. However, the last S, management style, proved to be the most difficult to implement. By 1981, the company had become extremely autocratic, and Smith wanted a more participative management style.

General Motors has moved away from multiple sourcing, annual contracts, and intense competition among suppliers toward fewer suppliers who are more heavily involved in future product plans. General Motors' larger, more sophisticated suppliers will eventually be responsible for supplying whole subsystems. Suppliers capable of doing this will preassemble these subsystems in their own plants and deliver them to GM's assembly lines, ready to be inserted in the modular car or truck. Examples of such subsystems are seats, instrument panels, door interior trim panels, and suspension components. The suppliers benefit from longer-term relations with GM. Instead of annual contracts, first-tier suppliers can expect to have three- to five-year contracts.

General Motors managers have learned that technology transfer requires innovative management, not just management of innovation. Furthermore, good technology is not sufficient by itself. A carefully constructed operations strategy is necessary for successful technology transfer. Toward that end, GM has identified the following ten specific steps:

1. Inform prospective users of the impact of the technology.
2. Encourage users to participate in developing the technology.
3. Apply a new technology yourself before attempting to transfer it.
4. Package the technology so that it is accessible to users.
5. Provide formal user training in the use of the new technology.
6. Determine the effectiveness of the transfer process through follow-up.
7. Provide users with opportunities to meet collectively and share their experiences with the technology.
8. Don't rely solely on written reports to sell technology.
9. Be willing to provide resources (people, time, and money) to sell the technology.
10. Consider transferring people along with the technology.

NUMMI (an acronym for New United Motor Manufacturing, Inc.) was the joint venture "experiment" between GM and Toyota that was expected to demonstrate that Japanese management techniques would work in the traditional American labor environment. The basic premise of the Japanese style was: Treat both white- and blue-collar workers with respect, encourage them to think independently, allow them to make decisions, and make them feel connected to an important effort. At NUMMI, workers were responsible for quality. A major difference between American and Japanese methods of quality management is that the Americans focused on the use of inspectors to find defects after the fact, whereas the Japanese managed quality as part of the production process. At GM, the way the company demonstrated its concern for quality was to add more inspectors to check for defects. The Japanese, however, eliminated defects at all stages, from raw materials, to components, to assembly. Thus, the workers, not the inspectors, had the primary responsibility for the quality of their work. In addition, the workers were given the tools to help them do a good job.

The secret of NUMMI's success was threefold: First, they were given a well-designed product, the Chevy Nova, to build. The Nova was a version of the Toyota Corolla, which Toyota was already making and selling in Japan. Second, NUMMI understood that the level of technology in a plant was not the primary factor in determining the quality or cost effectiveness of a product. Instead, good product design and an effective production system were the keys. Third, they realized that car-making was a people business, and high productivity had to do with the way people were organized and managed. NUMMI employed management techniques that were based on the assumption that workers instinctively wanted to do a good job. The Toyota production system was implemented at NUMMI. Its operating philosophy included seven points:

1. Kaizen, the never-ending search for perfection or continuous improvement
2. Kanban, or scheduling signals to reduce costs, through a just-in-time system
3. Full development of human potential
4. Building mutual trust among all employees
5. Developing team performance
6. Treating every employee as manager
7. Providing a stable livelihood for all employees

New materials were also developed to give GM more flexibility of design. For example, plastics and polymer composites provide greater flexibility in product design and manufacturing than does steel. Further, GM can make aerodynamic and aesthetic shapes with plastics that cannot be done with steel. Tooling and retooling for plastics are also simpler and less expensive. Plastics are not only lighter but are a lot more resistant to dents than more traditional materials. Furthermore, they don't rust.

General Motors has also redesigned many of its facilities in an attempt to improve its overall performance. For example, the Buick City plant in Flint, Michigan, builds the LeSabre, which is arguably the highest-quality car built in North America. But improvements have come slowly. The factory occupies only two-thirds the area of a typical GM factory and has implemented a just-in-time inventory system for nearly 600 suppliers. However, when delivery shortages or defects occurred, the one-hour supply of parts on hand caused the line to shut down. Additionally, the manufacturing process initially had several technology problems, the most obvious of which was that the robots designed to install windshields could not "see" black cars. These robots skipped the black cars as they progressed down the line. However, quality generally improved because the plant implemented a Japanese practice using *andon,* which allows assembly workers to halt production when a warning light comes on by pulling cords at their work stations. Implementation of these changes came slowly and was difficult to achieve.

General Motors committed to the Saturn project after it became apparent that they could not build a profitable small car within the existing manufacturing structure. A new division was created and $3.5 billion was allocated for the implementation of this revolutionary concept. The last time that GM had added a car-making division was in 1918, when it acquired Chevrolet. The development of Saturn required changes in manufacturing technology, labor, advertising, distribution, and supplier relations. At Saturn, GM has attempted to limit its suppliers to single companies in various commodity areas, so that both GM and the supplier can work together to drive costs down. The supplier/customer partnership is intended for the long term. This permits suppliers to focus their efforts on service and improving quality rather than rounding up sales contracts. The cooperative supplier partnerships with Saturn allow such efficiencies. One supplier has adapted to the new approach by replacing the old sales incentive plan with a new system based on the number of problems solved. Further, distributors have been challenged to become full partners in Saturn's attempt to gain market share from Japanese manufacturers. These, coupled with an extremely sensitive, almost finicky concern for quality and for the customer perceptions of the car, have done much to restore credibility.

## *The World-Class Company and Car for a World Market*

General Motors has recognized that it is no longer a "Midwest Car Company," but instead, a huge player in a very dynamic global market. In the past few years, foreign sales have increased dramatically. GM is currently one of the largest vehicle manufacturers in Europe. In addition, favorable international exchange rates have given American-made vehicles a competitive cost advantage. In addition, quality, design, and styling of all GM automobiles have been improved.

In 1990, GM was part of the major transformation in East Germany's car and truck industries, when it signed an agreement with Volkswagen AG and Mercedes Benz AG to join East German manufacturers in a venture to build cars for Eastern Europe and the former Soviet Union. The Asia/Pacific region is also seen to hold major potential for GM, especially China. GM's position in Taiwan has increased dramatically from virtually zero vehicles in 1985 to 10,000 vehicles in 1988, and it continues to grow. Lower import tariffs and taxes, along with improved quality and currency exchange rates, have aided in GM's growth in the international market. However, much remains to be done if GM is to emerge as a world-class company by the millennium.

The culture at GM must continue to move toward the customer, by responding to demands for vehicle quality. However, the movement to high quality and customer satisfaction has not been and will not be easy. When Roger Smith was trying to change GM's structure, few were informed of the vision he had for the company. For this reason, many did not understand why he was consolidating divisions and moving hundreds of people. Inevitably, resentment and feelings of betrayal resulted. When plants were closed, even though productivity had risen, the feeling was that management had not kept its promises.

General Motors' ambitious move toward participatory management, with its 800,000-plus employees worldwide, has been deemed the greatest such effort in history. Its NUMMI plant in Fremont, California, has activated the core values of participatory management (that is, honesty, fairness, cooperation, respect for individual differences, and participation in problem solving and decision making) with self-managing teams planning, scheduling, and working on the production line. As a result, absenteeism dropped from 20% under the previous autocratic management style to about 4%. Also, new cars are produced in approximately 20 labor hours, down from the previously required 35 hours.

General Motors has learned several valuable lessons from their continuous improvement effort, the most important of which are

Don't expect anyone to change if you can't change yourself.

Confront and conquer outdated and authoritarian corporate culture.

Create a climate of continuous improvement by designing and promoting mission, vision, and management philosophy.

Set the core values and vision—and then let go.

General Motors had net losses of $2 billion in 1990 and $3.8 billion in 1991. The problems that have plagued GM since the late 1950s are still tormenting the company in some key areas. For example, GM is 40% less productive than Ford in the number of labor hours it takes to assemble a car. In 1991, GM lost, on average, $1500 on every one of the more than 3.5 million cars and trucks it made in North America. Further, it ended the year with just over 35% of the U.S. market share. As the company has seen its own market share plummet, it has been forced to swallow Japan's swelling market. The biggest scare of all, however, is that analysts predict that Japan's combined U.S. sales may exceed GM's by the mid- or late 1990s.

However, there are positive signs as well. New models have been introduced in 1993. Additionally, GM is hoping that low U.S. interest rates will spark total auto sales. The Saturn plant is beginning to receive high accolades for its design and labor–management relationship. Cadillac's receipt of the 1990 Malcolm Baldrige National Quality Award has also boosted GM's image.

Recrafting the operations of a large corporation like GM takes patience. The strategy was defined in the early and mid-1980s, and the structure and system have been dramatically changed over the past 10 or more years. The changes in corporate style, which have proved most difficult, are also progressing, but more slowly. General Motors, like many American businesses, is learning and relearning the lessons of operations strategy, the processes of which are universal.

## *Discussion Questions*

1. According to Wickham Skinner, technology is the primary driver of the work environment. Use the GM case to defend or reject this view.
2. Is it reasonable to expect that the turnaround of a company like General Motors might take ten years? Suggest some considerations that would facilitate change, and other considerations that would likely retard change.
3. Describe several techniques that would be appropriate for GM to use in technology management and in management of the technology transfer process.
4. Suggest several specific applications of project implementation techniques used at GM.
5. The change programs initiated by Roger Smith, the GM CEO during much of the 1980s, have been maligned and misunderstood in many ways. Describe several aspects of the policy

implementation process which would suggest that this will likely be the case when extensive changes occur.

6. In what ways does the change mission of GM suggest the final quote of Chapter 14, that is, "When you are up to your neck in an alligator-infested swamp, it's hard to remember that the goal was to drain the swamp"?

7. Do you think that GM has taken sufficient action to emerge as a world-class company and produce world-class cars? Consider current materials pertaining to GM or to automobile design, manufacturing, and distribution.

8. Describe the changes in GM with reference to the characteristics of social organizations. In your opinion, how much change has occurred to date, and how much more change should occur?

9. What proportion of verbal and behavioral skills should be combined with what amounts of technical, structured, and mechanical skills to successfully manage a change effort? Cite specific situations in the GM case.

## References


Keller, Maryann. *Rude Awakening.* New York: Morrow and Company, 1989.

Kerwin, Kathleen, with James B. Treece and David Woodruff. "Can Jack Smith Fix GM?" *Business Week,* November 1, 1993, pp. 126–131.

Simmons, John. "Participatory Management: Lessons from the Leaders," *Management Review.* December 1990, pp. 54–58.

Smith, Roger, Wilton Woods, and Colin Leinster. "The US Must Do as GM Has Done," *Fortune.* February 13, 1989, pp. 70–74.

Taylor, Alex III. "Can GM Remodel Itself?" *Fortune.* January 13, 1992, pp. 26–34.

## Case 8

# New Product Development at Elco Manufacturing[1]

Jerry Green started the copier and stood back, wondering what would come up at this morning's meeting. Fifteen copies of the nine-page "Quarterly New Product Development (QMPD) Meeting" packet started moving through the machine. Jerry had been hired several years ago by the Columbus Plant of Elco Manufacturing as an inventory planner, and, when Linda Chavez had taken over the new Rocky Mountain facility, he had been promoted by Bob Anderson, the vice president of operations, to corporate assistant operations manager. It was Bob who had suggested that Jerry attend the QNPD meeting. "It would be a good opportunity to gain a better understanding of the way corporate headquarters operates and to meet some people"—or something like that. Jerry chuckled.

In the past few years, the company had grown rapidly. The exercycle and bench apparatus units had been consolidated into the Indoor Entertainment Division and the basketball equipment unit was now part of the much-expanded Outdoor Recreation Division. Additionally, the company had acquired a small electronics firm and an electric motor fabricator, which were now defined as separate corporate divisions.

The corporate staff had grown as well, despite attempts by Roderick Elvington, the CEO, to limit proliferation of the staff. In response to the very dynamic business environment of the early 1990s, the technical development staff was expanded to seek high-tech applications in the recreation and mechanical products area. Strategically, the company sought to define its leadership in high-tech recreation equipment. The QNPD process and meeting were developed as a spin-off of the more general Business Planning Group meeting.

[1]To protect proprietary information, the company described in this case (a major U.S. industrial corporation) has requested that its name and other identifying information be changed. However, the basic relationships have been retained. This case has been prepared as a basis for class discussion, rather than to illustrate either effective or ineffective management of an operational situation.

The copier had stopped. Jerry picked up the packets from the machine and walked slowly to the office to print the name and position of each attendee at the top right corner of the packet.

| | |
|---|---|
| Michael Murdock | Vice President for Technical Development |
| Dr. Rohit Patel | Director, New Product Development Group |
| Aubrey Edwards | Director, Product and Process Technology Group |
| Dabney Winters | Director, Technical Services Group |
| Tracy Lowe | General Manager, Indoor Entertainment Division |
| Chris Austin | General Manager, Outdoor Recreation Division |
| Jean Corey | General Manager, Tools and Equipment Division |
| Connie Johnson | General Manager, Electronic Products Division |
| Pat Yardley | Representative, Corporate Financial Services |
| Francis Leahy | Representative, Corporate Marketing |

It was after that first QNPD meeting that Bob Anderson had asked Jerry to be responsible for the manufacturing interfaces with the new product development process and to assist Michael Murdock with QNPD meetings. Anderson had hinted that Jerry, with a mechanical engineering degree and an expected MBA in operations management, would be a clear asset to the group. The Assistant Operations Manager and Director of Manufacturing Planning, Jerry's new title, was responsible for administering the new product development process and for hosting, though not running, the QNPD meeting. Michael Murdock, sometimes called "Mad Mike," ran the QNPD.

**TABLE C8-1 New Product Development Process**

Elco QNPD __________

Product name ______________ Release date to manufacturer ____________________

| | Year | | | | | |
|---|---|---|---|---|---|---|
| | 1 | 2 | 3 | 4 | 5 | Total |
| Financial | | | | | | |
| Costs | | | | | | |
| Capital and development—fixed | | | | | | |
| Labor, mat'l and overh'd—variable | | | | | | |
| Annual units produced | | | | | | |
| Cost/unit | | | | | | |
| Revenues/unit | | | | | | |
| Payoff | | | | | | |
| Product and process technology group | | | | | | |
| Feasibility and specification issues | | | | | | |
| Hours | | | | | | |
| Technical support | | | | | | |
| Product design and appeal issues | | | | | | |
| Hours | | | | | | |

Michael Murdock gaveled the meeting to order promptly at 9:30 A.M. and cast a disparaging glance at several latecomers as they scurried for their seats. Murdock reminded the attendees of the date for the next meeting and noted several points from recent executive board and business planning group meetings. Profits were up, but the organization was moving toward a period of belt-tightening and smart management. Murdock then signaled for the "process slide," shown as Table C8-1, noting several points by flashing a light pencil to highlight areas of the slide.

"Every new product goes through the QNPD process for financial implications, product and process feasibility and specification, and for implementation services. Activities and costs for research and product development through product prototype are managed by the product and process technology group. The manufacturing process is then designed and certified by the tech services group. Product redesign and market appeal issues are addressed at this time. Ultimately, each product is evaluated in terms of payoff, technical feasibility, and market appeal . . . " Murdock stopped the litany, sensing some amusement in the group.

"Oh, you all know this anyway. Let's see what the quarterly project status is." The New Product Project Status chart, Table C8-2, was projected for the group. "Moving right along, this chart shows currently ranked projects and two new projects. For each project, the rank, break-even point, and five-year annual return on investment (ROI), stated in current dollars, are given. Additionally, the hundreds of hours and delivery month are given for the P&PT and TS groups. . . ."

"Ah . . . Before you get started," broke in Aubrey Edwards, director of the product and process technology group. "I'd like to point out the extensive commitment by P&PT

**TABLE C8-2 New Product Project Status**

ELCO QNPD ______________

| | | | Financial | | P&PT Grp | | TS Grp | |
|---|---|---|---|---|---|---|---|---|
| Rank | Code and Name | | Break-Even (yr) | ROI (%) | Hours (00) | Delivery (+mo) | Hours (00) | Delivery (+mo) |
| 1 | XRT | Project | 8 | 4 | 180 | + ? | 130 | + ? |
| 2 | IE-21 | Air hockey table | 2 | 19 | 40 | + 4 | 8 | + 12 |
| 3 | TE-42 | Cordless multitool | 1.5 | 24 | 25 | + 2 | 15 | + 8 |
| 4 | EP-18 | Acu-site laser rangefinder | 4 | 28 | 150 | + 15 | 50 | + 24 |
| 5 | IE-96 | Magnet glide skier/rower | 5 | 4 | 180 | + 16 | 90 | + 36 |
| 6 | OR-38 | Boron graphlex golf club | 1 | 35 | 10 | + 3 | 12 | + 6 |
| 7 | IE-51 | High stepper stair climber | 2 | 21 | 5 | + 8 | 9 | + 16 |
| 8 | TE-68 | Orbital waxer/buffer | 1 | 27 | 3 | + 1 | 6 | + 8 |
| *9 | OR-24 | Six-level basketball backboard | 1 | 14 | 2 | + 3 | 6 | + 7 |
| *10 | EP-19 | Bottom stalker fishfinder | 5 | 17 | 15 | + 24 | 10 | + 42 |
| | | | | | 610 | | 331 | |

*New product

to new-product development. As you can all see from the chart, given the commitment of 61,000 hours and the budgeted 2500 hours per month, our total available hours have been committed for close to two years. I would also note that the XRT Project. . . ."

Before Michael could pick up the gavel, Jean Corey, general manager of the tools and equipment division, asserted, "You know, I never have really understood this process. The TE-68 Orbital Waxer/Buffer for automobiles has high potential, a quick payoff, and one of the highest payoff ratios, yet it has not received the commitment from Technical Development that the XRT has. Whatever . . . "

"I agree," interrupted Tracy Lowe, general manager of the indoor entertainment division. "We really don't know what the XRT project is. I'd like to have a full briefing."

"As you have been informed," Dr. Rohit Patel, director of the new product development group, calmly asserted, "the XRT Project is a contract among a consortium of businesses and the federal government. The project is very sensitive, but I can tell you that it deals with uses of our exercise technology in outer space. Because this is a multiparticipant project, we don't have the prerogative to change its rank.

"Ladies and gentlemen," Murdock interjected, finding the gavel and hammering the table. "Enough. Let's get down to business."

"But," interjected Chris Austin, general manager of the outdoor recreation division, "we really need to evaluate these projects in terms of expected payoff and resource utilization. For example, the Boron Graphlex golf club takes only 2200 hours of total resource time, is deliverable in six months, is profitable in the first year, and has a 35% payoff. If extra resources are available, we should commit them to the six-level basketball backboard, a top money winner."

"I think it is important," said Tracy Lowe, "to provide a solid product line that employs the latest technology. That's why the IE-96 Magnet-Glide and the IE-51 High Stepper must be brought on line together."

"Amen," intoned Francis Leahy, representative, corporate marketing.

Dabney Winters, director of the technical services group, rocked forward, extending both arms toward the group. "Simply, the driver product of this company is the EP-18 Acu-Site rangefinder. We have only 500 hours available per month, and this time must be optimally used. This low-cost electronics and optics system can be used for numerous hunting, sports, and game applications. If we don't get this product to the market first, we can expect, in the long run, to have our market share reduced by 15% to 20%, and also lose the opportunity to expand the applications into outdoor, indoor, and tool and equipment markets. The EP-18 has to be developed so that we can compete internationally . . ." Michael Murdock surveyed the group impassively as Winters droned on, slowly scanning each member of the group, looking for someone to break the monologue. A pencil clattered to the table and Pat Yardley's head snapped back, jolting both eyes wide open. All heads turned toward Yardley.

"Well," said Murdock, gaveling down the laughter, "moving right along, perhaps a discussion of new products might *awaken* our interest at this time. The agenda, published in the meeting notice, calls for a review of the OR-24 six-level basketball backboard and the EP-19 bottom stalker fishfinder. These topics should be easy to conclude, and then we can move on to the XRT/EP-18 issue. Tracy, do you have the OR-24 presentation?"

Lowe nodded. "I think Toni Herrera has that data." Jerry sympathized as Herrera moved through what was obviously a very meticulously prepared and practiced presentation. Supervisors, Jerry had learned quickly, never gave their presenters any idea of the questions that could come up at the QNPD meeting or of the motivation of the questioners. In Jerry's opinion, Herrera did a good job, concluding that the product had a relatively quick payoff and requesting small amounts of funding and hourly support from the P&PT and TS groups.

"I thought I stated . . ." said Aubrey Edwards. He was interrupted by the sharp rap of Murdock's gavel, and by an icier glare. "If there are no questions on the financials, I would like to move on to the EP-19 bottom stalker fishfinder project. We will deal with P&PT hours as a part of the XRT discussion. Who has the fishfinder presentation?"

"I'm Kimberly Novak. Connie Johnson of the electronic products division asked me to attend the meeting and to brief the EP-19."

"That's irregular," Murdock scowled. "General managers were told in the meeting notice to respond directly to me if they were not able to attend the meeting."

"Apparently, something came up; Johnson couldn't make it," Novak returned.

"All right, let's hear your pitch . . . and tell Johnson to give me a call," retorted Murdock.

Kimberly Novak provided the participants with an excellent technical description of the new generation of sonar scanning technology, represented by the EP-19. Conventional sonar devices had been replaced by an ultrasound emitter and sensor/reader system, which, because of its shorter wavelength, was less likely to scatter and was able to operate effectively under a wide range of light, temperature, and water conditions. Furthermore, manufacturing costs would be reduced. Kimberly spoke with the fervor and dedication of a practiced scientist, concluding with the numbers, which showed that the product involved slow volume growth, but a moderate profitability and payoff. "This project," Kimberly concluded, "should be managed as a mid-range opportunity, with assurances that a three-and-one-half year total of 1500 hours of P&PT time and 1000 hours of TS group time are available. The project currently is scheduled for release to manufacturing in three-and-one-half years."

"Really sounds good to me," commented Dabney Winters. "The technology looks good and the numbers are competitive." Several members nodded in concurrence.

"It is an interesting project," noted Jean Corey. "But it seems to me that this is an example of a technology that has no application beyond its immediate use with fishfinders. There is little use for it in the tool and equipment area, and I would not expect to find much application in the indoor and outdoor areas."

"I'm not presently aware of any other possible applications of this technology that have been developed; however, the possibilities extend from tool and instrument controls, games, and a variety of distance measurement applications. To be competitive, we have to be able to reduce manufacturing costs and enhance product capabilities and quality. The EP-19 does that very well," responded Kimberly.

Murdock edged forward. "Perhaps, since this is a mid-to-long-term project, we could take another look at it in three months. That would give Connie Johnson a chance to go back and recheck the numbers and review the applications a bit more carefully and present the results in person." Murdock's pronouncement was greeted by some knowing winks among several members of the group. Murdock did not like GMs to cut the QNPD. "Meanwhile, let's take a look at this XRT business. Patel, how about giving us as much as you can about it, without, of course, violating classification requirements."

"Well, that may be a problem," Dr. Rohit Patel started in measured words. "But I will try to give you everything that I can. Essentially, the XRT project involves the use of our exercise technologies with several space applications."

"Yeah," Tracy Lowe commented irreverently, "they're going to use our exercycles to generate electricity and power space platforms."

"That's rather off the mark," Patel laughed tightly; but Lowe noted that the rest of the group enjoyed the interlude.

"The difficulty with the 'hush-hush' nature of this project," offered Pat Yardley, financial services representative, "is that we just don't have the opportunity to know what's coming down the pike. We would like to be able to support the hours and dollars that we commit to your group, but we need some numbers."

"The project just can't be coordinated in the normal way," Patel retorted. "The nature of what we are doing is just too sensitive to discuss. We have received assurances from the government that the overall numbers are good and that we will have the testing and evaluation work as soon as it can be released from the Defense Systems Agency. We must be patient."

"But, I've got to know what the commitments are for the P&PT group," shot back Aubrey Edwards in exasperation.

"Even more important," inserted Dabney Winters, "TS group needs to plan for the detailed technologies, facilities, and installations that we are going to use. It is just not possible to conduct either a P&PT or tech services evaluation or implementation overnight."

"OK, let's cut the bull," Murdock injected. "The real problem is that we've got to come up with a realistic set of priorities for P&PT and TS, and we've got to plan for the EP-18 Acu-Site rangefinder. That project is a money winner. If we don't start it shortly, someone else will do the job for us."

"Amen," intoned Francis Leahy.

"You know," Chris Austin hesitated. "I don't know why we rank these projects in terms of so-called importance. Who knows what that is, anyway? Why don't we sequence the projects on the chart in terms of the deadline when they must be completed by P&PT and TS and what capacity those organizations have. I was reading over the weekend . . . "

Jerry watched, bemused, as the squabbling persisted. First, Tracy Lowe wanted the IE-21 air hockey table; then Dr. Patel wanted the XRT project; then Edwards and Winters wanted to know what the requirements were. Now and then others injected a small slice of self-interest. Jerry noted that Michael Murdock seemed oblivious to it all, watching, rocking in the chair, and doodling—then watching, rocking, and doodling some more.

"And you have to appreciate the importance of government contracts . . . ," Patel was saying. Murdock noisily jolted forward and stood up. "All right, I won't listen to another minute of this. I'm going outside this door, and not one of you is going to leave this room until you can agree upon a ranking of these projects for P&PT and tech services. I don't care if you have to stay here 'til next week."

"But," Chris Austin injected, "as you know, I have to be at the club luncheon presentation at 12:30 tomorrow. I do need to take care of some of the final details."

"I'm sure you do, but you will take care of this first." Murdock walked to the door. "And if you can't finish before the luncheon, you'll probably save yourself a case of indigestion." Murdock walked out of the room, closing the door slowly, but firmly. The smirks quickly faded.

Jerry watched the drawn faces in the very quiet room, waiting to see who would speak first. It was Edwards. "Well, if all of you hadn't been so assertive, we wouldn't be in this mess."

"Oh, get off it," several members said at once. The bickering continued until someone suggested that Jerry check to see whether Murdock had left. Jerry opened the door and was met by Murdock, who had found a chair and was comfortably reading a business magazine. Murdock looked up and grinned: "Hi, Jerry, how's it going in there?" Jerry closed the door behind him. "Let them stew for several minutes," Murdock advised quietly. "They'll sort it out."

Jerry got some fresh beverages, and while he was returning to the conference room, Kimberly Novak looked out. "Can a person go to the restroom?"

Murdock nodded. Passing Jerry in the corridor, Kimberly paused and whispered: "You ought to see what's going on in there. Those guys are actually talking with one another. I've never seen anything like it; general managers and directors actually talking with one another. I mean, they are even talking about some sort of priority structure to show the new product status based on time priorities."

Jerry chuckled and winked. "I think that we are going to have a meaningful quarterly priority from this meeting. I'd even bet that they find room for your EP-19."

Michael Murdock coldly glanced toward them and they each went about their business.

## *Questions*

1. What is unique about the new product development process that results in meetings such as the one at Elco Manufacturing?
2. What techniques did "Mad Mike" use to manage the new product development process?
3. Why should the new product development process be so quantitative?
4. In what ways should the new product development process be judgmental?
5. What criteria are appropriate to evaluate the importance of research and development projects? How would those criteria be developed and used?
6. How are the time and delivery month data presented in Table C8-2 developed?

## *Computer Assignment*

Develop and support a ranking process that resequences the ten projects in order of priority for the P&PT group and the TS group. Then show how your sequence may be integrated to achieve all requirements within the given constraints.

# *Appendix*

# *Learning Curve Values*

| Unit Learning Curve Table | | | | | | Cumulative Learning Curve Table | | | | | |
|---|---|---|---|---|---|---|---|---|---|---|---|
| Units | 70% | 75% | 80% | 85% | 90% | Units | 70% | 75% | 80% | 85% | 90% |
| 1 | 1.000 | 1.000 | 1.000 | 1.000 | 1.000 | 1 | 1.000 | 1.000 | 1.000 | 1.000 | 1.000 |
| 2 | .700 | .750 | .800 | .850 | .900 | 2 | 1.700 | 1.750 | 1.800 | 1.850 | 1.900 |
| 3 | .568 | .634 | .702 | .773 | .846 | 3 | 2.268 | 2.384 | 2.502 | 2.623 | 2.746 |
| 4 | .490 | .562 | .640 | .723 | .810 | 4 | 2.758 | 2.946 | 3.412 | 3.345 | 3.556 |
| 5 | .437 | .513 | .596 | .686 | .783 | 5 | 3.195 | 3.459 | 3.738 | 4.031 | 4.339 |
| 6 | .398 | .475 | .562 | .657 | .762 | 6 | 3.593 | 3.934 | 4.299 | 4.688 | 5.101 |
| 7 | .367 | .446 | .534 | .634 | .744 | 7 | 3.960 | 4.380 | 4.834 | 5.322 | 5.845 |
| 8 | .343 | .422 | .512 | .614 | .729 | 8 | 4.303 | 4.802 | 5.346 | 5.936 | 6.574 |
| 9 | .323 | .402 | .493 | .597 | .716 | 9 | 4.626 | 5.204 | 5.839 | 6.533 | 7.290 |
| 10 | .306 | .385 | .477 | .583 | .705 | 10 | 4.932 | 5.589 | 6.315 | 7.116 | 7.994 |
| 12 | .278 | .357 | .449 | .558 | .685 | 12 | 5.501 | 6.315 | 7.227 | 8.244 | 9.374 |
| 14 | .257 | .334 | .428 | .539 | .670 | 14 | 6.026 | 6.994 | 8.092 | 9.331 | 10.721 |
| 16 | .240 | .316 | .410 | .522 | .656 | 16 | 6.514 | 7.635 | 8.920 | 10.383 | 12.040 |
| 18 | .226 | .301 | .394 | .508 | .644 | 18 | 6.973 | 8.245 | 9.716 | 11.405 | 13.334 |
| 20 | .214 | .288 | .381 | .495 | .634 | 20 | 7.407 | 8.828 | 10.485 | 12.402 | 14.608 |
| 22 | .204 | .277 | .370 | .484 | .625 | 22 | 7.819 | 9.388 | 11.230 | 13.376 | 15.862 |
| 24 | .195 | .267 | .359 | .475 | .617 | 24 | 8.213 | 9.928 | 11.954 | 14.331 | 17.100 |
| 26 | .187 | .259 | .350 | .466 | .609 | 26 | 8.519 | 10.449 | 12.659 | 15.267 | 18.323 |
| 28 | .180 | .251 | .342 | .458 | .603 | 28 | 8.954 | 10.995 | 13.347 | 16.186 | 19.531 |
| 30 | .174 | .244 | .335 | .450 | .596 | 30 | 9.305 | 11.446 | 14.020 | 17.091 | 20.727 |
| 32 | .168 | .237 | .328 | .444 | .590 | 32 | 9.644 | 11.924 | 14.679 | 17.981 | 21.911 |
| 34 | .163 | .231 | .321 | .437 | .585 | 34 | 9.972 | 12.389 | 15.324 | 18.859 | 23.084 |
| 36 | .158 | .226 | .315 | .432 | .580 | 36 | 10.291 | 12.844 | 15.958 | 19.725 | 24.246 |
| 38 | .154 | .221 | .310 | .426 | .575 | 38 | 10.601 | 13.288 | 16.581 | 20.580 | 25.399 |
| 40 | .150 | .216 | .305 | .421 | .571 | 40 | 10.902 | 13.723 | 17.193 | 21.425 | 26.543 |
| 45 | .141 | .206 | .294 | .410 | .561 | 45 | 11.625 | 14.773 | 18.684 | 23.500 | 29.366 |
| 50 | .134 | .197 | .284 | .400 | .552 | 50 | 12.307 | 15.776 | 20.122 | 25.513 | 32.142 |

# Name Index

# *Company Index*

# Subject Index